I WANT YOU TO KNOW

A Grandmother Book

By

Ardelle Brown Hopkins

Dedication Publications
10556 Combie Rd., Suite 106496
Auburn, California 95602-8935

Copyright © 1994 by Ardelle Brown Hopkins
First Printing 1994
Library of Congress Catalog Number 94-68713
ISBN Number 0-9643467-0-2
Photo Copyright © Release Olan Mills 1994

All rights reserved.
No portion of this book may be reproduced without
written permission by the Publisher.

Printed in the United States of America

For . . .

Krista • Jonathan
Raymond • Eric • Jeffrey
Kevin • Shannon
Claire • Myrha • Aneece
James • Amanda • Daniel
Christopher • Andrew • Stephan
Misty • Nicholas • Matthew • Jeremy • Jennifer • Brittany
John • Rebecca • David • Christina
Brian • Shaun • Caitie
India • Jared • Haily • Macy

Cover Photo:

(Left to Right)
Christopher, Misty and Nicholas
With Grandma Ardelle

Contents

CHAPTER		PAGE
	Acknowledgments	i
1	That Little Girl Was Me	1
2	This Is The Way We Survive	15
3	To Grandma's House We Go	27
4	The Little Homemaker	41
5	Times of Trauma	55
6	Dear Ole Golden Rule Days	76
7	Ah, Romance!	93
8	Transplanted	115
9	The New Life in Illinois	128
10	The Quest	147
11	Hearing God's Call	159
12	To Hawaii With Faith	174
13	Different Food and Different People	196
14	Real Life Experiences on the Mission Field	214
15	God Leads His Dear Children Along	234
16	Really Trusting	251
17	Hoen Home and Horizons Beyond	278
18	The Biggest Adjustment of All	316
19	Moving Events	357
20	A New Life at Lake of the Pines	381
21	Life with Grandpa Darrell	395
22	Life Goes On - In California	418
	Epilogue	428
	A Special Message: Beloved, It's Up To You	429

Acknowledgments

I deeply appreciate those whose thoughtfulness helped make this book possible: My daughter-in-law Bonnie Brown, for her persistent hints and the initial boost I needed. Mr. Duane Newcomb, my writing teacher, for his instruction, advice and encouragement; Glenda Barbre, whose contributions helped me recall more accurately the years I lived in the South; Peggy Buck, and my son Keith and his wife Fredene, for books and souvenir material shared from their vacations in Hawaii which enabled me to authenticate the facts I had written about when I lived there. It was reassuring to find that in every instance I had remembered accurately.

Without my faithful computer I'm not sure I would have been able to complete my book. I am indebted to my son Jerry Brown for his patient assistance as I ploughed into the "high tech" arena, and my friend Bob Gray, who was always standing by when I had to flash an SOS in sheer desperation. My son Michael Brown was my faithful studio technician and typewriter doctor in those early days. Later, my son Hal Brown was tremendously helpful, and still is, even on the phone. He should be a teacher in that field. I can never repay my grandson Kevin Brown for his enormous help and thoughtfulness. I must not forget my dear computer friend Bob Caris, the knowledgeable one in the computer group I started when I was writing my manuscript. He still is my standby with his expertise, when I need him.

I could never have finished such a taxing, time-consuming project without the patient understanding and support of my husband Darrell, who was willing to let me spend innumerable early morning hours writing, and to accept an "accommodative" schedule during the other hours of the day and night, without apparent resentment. He helped me more than he realized. I shall always be grateful for that. He also spent many hours helping "proof" the book.

When I finally completed my manuscript, I was urged to contact several publishers. One well-known Christian book publisher expressed considerable interest but later decided not to take a chance on autobiography. Recovering from my disappointment, I prayed for guidance. When Thomas Schroeder, a local high school teacher who was also teaching a

Acknowledgments

Bible study which I was involved in, offered to read my manuscript and make suggestions, I knew it was an answer to prayer. I know he did not realize what an enormous project he was getting into, but he faithfully stayed with it, grappling with wordiness, errant commas and over all poor punctuation and sentence structure. He also helped me shorten it. Without the patient labor of love exhibited by my precious friend Thomas, and his wife Jill, publication of my book would not be possible at this time. Words cannot express my gratitude to Doreen and Dean Wood for their patient, loving cooperation in making this book a dream come true. It was a pleasure working with them.

Most of all I am thankful for God's mercy, His guidance and help, and for the strength and wisdom He supplied during the five years it took me to write the book. I also want to thank all those who were praying for me.

Many have expressed their hope that this book would be published so that they could read it in their lifetime. For those with vision impairment or other health problems, as well as time limitations, and for my ninety-nine year old friend whose autobiography has been such a blessing to me, I plan to record an audio version of my book, the Lord willing, so that they can hear it in my own voice.

October   1994

CHAPTER 1

That Little Girl Was Me

"Hi, Grandma!" eight year old Candice called over her shoulder as she hurried to hang up her heavy, hand-knitted sweater in the guest room closet.

"Please don't forget," she reminded me as she came back into the living room, "you promised to tell me about when you were a little girl."

She was soon seated comfortably in front of the flickering fire, her soft brown hair bouncing lightly against the tiny rosebud print on the beige upholstery of her favorite chair—the trim, overstuffed one, across from my leather recliner.

"You said you would tell me where you lived, and what it was like, remember? I really want to know."

Come with me, back to the early 1900's. Woodrow Wilson is president of the United States. He is weary from the stress of World War I and its complications. In the year 1919 he suffered a complete collapse. In 1920, the year I was born, he was awarded the Nobel Prize for his efforts toward peace.

We are in the deep South, a part of the country for which President Wilson had great concern. That was about all we had on our side. He was deeply affected by the suffering of the people in our impoverished area, even while he was still in Johns Hopkins University in 1886.

When he ran for president in 1912, the southern vote was responsible for his election to office. Whether he was a good president or not, I couldn't say. Even though I was too young to understand such things at the time, I am convinced that he cared about our kind of people. And as I look back now, I realize that his being the son of a Presbyterian minister may have given President Wilson a deeper insight into the plight of us poor southern people.

As Far Back As I Can Remember

Try to imagine if you can, the little cottage I see so clearly in my memory. It's right down the road there, on the other side of that deep creek with the rickety bridge across it.

Well, that's where my parents lived when I was born. It's such a little house; only two small bedrooms, a tiny living room, and a cramped kitchen and dining area in the added "lean-to" at the back. The house is old, poorly built, and weather worn. While not much can be said for the quality of the house itself, you would have to agree—those handsome oak trees on the nearby hillside, and the ragged old cedar trees in the yard are pretty impressive.

The earliest thing I can remember is walking up that lane with my parents and some family friends one spring afternoon when I was just turning four. The warmth of the sun felt so good as I skipped happily along beside them. From time to time I would venture out to pick a tiny purple or orange wild flower, or to explore a little stream trickling along nearby, making its way to the creek running by our home. Suddenly, I stumbled and fell into the cold water.

"Watch out!" my daddy yelled as he grabbed me from the brook and handed me to my mother. Without hesitation, she scolded me—right in front of their sympathetic friends.

"Shame on you!" Mama taunted, with disgust. "You ought to be more careful." I knew she meant I should not have been so careless as to disappoint her in the estimation of these people who seemed to me to be more important to her than I was.

I still remember clearly, the cold water and the embarrassment of being stripped completely naked and forced to stand exposed and shivering while waiting for Daddy to bring dry clothes from our house. But the feeling of being rejected and misunderstood—and for something I had not done intentionally, but quite by accident, made an even deeper impression on me. From that day I feared the consequences of displeasing my parents.

Trying Life On For Size

I have to admit, there were times in the next few years when I seemed to have forgotten the lesson of my earliest memory. One time in particular. [I even hesitate to tell you about this.]

My brother Charles, who was a year younger than I was, and I were playing in the barn when we ran across a small can of axle grease. Although we were not old enough to read, we knew what it was. We had watched Daddy apply it to the axles and wheels of our wagon. Charles tried to open the lid the way he had seen Daddy do it. He was not quite able to make it, his hands were so small, but with a little assistance from older sister we were soon peering into the can's interesting contents. [I remember it so vividly, Candi.] We were intrigued by its brownish, greenish, blackish color, and its smooth consistency. Together, we had a bright idea. Charles put it into words.

"Let's rub some on our face and hands and pretend we're 'niggers'", he suggested. I hesitated momentarily, more at the thought of hearing my little brother refer to colored people as "niggers", I think. Even at my young age, I had noticed the attitude and expression of friends or relatives when they surprisingly referred to black people that way. There were no colored people in our community but we saw lots of them every time we went into town. There were whole sections relegated to them and labeled as "nigger town".

But there was something tempting and exciting about the color change idea. It sounded like fun. I soon realized however, that being a girl I was getting in deeper; I had to also color my legs to be "authentic".

As we looked at each other we could imagine how we looked ourselves.

[You should have seen us, Candi. We were in fact, reasonably good facsimiles of the real thing.]

Suddenly, Mama appeared on the scene and discovered our devious game. [I knew I shouldn't have told you, you're probably taking sides with her.]

You bet we deserved punishment, and you can be sure we got the punishment we deserved. Even worse than the licking we got from Mama was the one Daddy gave us. It was a rule at our house, that if Mama had to punish us, a second thrashing was forthcoming from Daddy. I don't know how we ever let that threat slip our minds for one moment. And I have to tell you, Daddy's indignation was doubled—it included his anger over his wasted axle grease.

Then there was the painful operation of scrubbing the "colored" effect from our bodies. Even more distressing for me was the utter disappointment in my mother's eyes, that we would be so inconsiderate as to displease her and let her down in this way. That incident taught me another great lesson in life.

I Really Did Walk Two Miles To School

You laugh when you hear someone say, "When I was your age I walked two (or four, or five) miles to school." You usually don't believe them. When my brother Charles and I were old enough to start to school we had to walk over two miles each way, each day, to and from school. And that was short-cutting it through the fields and woods. But there were rewards. In the springtime the meadows were beautiful, and we enjoyed the pretty wild flowers. In autumn, we watched the colorful red, yellow and orange leaves come tumbling down, and later we enjoyed tramping through the thick, leafy carpet on the ground as we walked through the woods and the tree-studded pasture lands.

The different kinds of trees interested us a lot, though at times they were threatening. Some of them were so huge, and we were so small.

We always got a thrill from watching the squirrels flit about from tree to tree. An occasional rabbit, or a pretty black and white skunk would excite or amaze us.

But there were times when real fear would strike our youthful hearts. For instance, a rattlesnake scare, a rumor that a "mad dog" had been seen in the area, or when Mr. Blackwood would allow his bull to run with his cattle in the pasture we had to cross to get to school.

And I remember one day we discovered some strange looking soft, brown balls, and carried them carefully home to show our folks only to be told they were "the devil's snuff boxes". We knew what snuff was because our Grandma Adams "dipped" snuff from a fancy box. She would unashamedly deposit the brown tobacco powder under her lower lip, right in front of us kids. We thought it was a filthy habit but as we observed the obvious satisfaction she seemed to realize as she relished its lasting flavor, we tried to understand. Grandma was addicted to the stuff. It was a personal pleasure which she enjoyed.

It really shook us to learn that we had disturbed something that belonged to the devil, and particularly something as intimate as his "snuff".

[I never did learn what those suspicious looking brown pods were even though we saw them quite often.]

These individual, and sometimes combined concerns often overshadowed the pleasure of enjoying nature along the way. Often the time-consuming inconvenience of the long walk to and from school each day would be totally eclipsed by our fears.

I Came By My Fears Naturally

We didn't have nearby neighbors when we lived in that little creekside home on our secluded farm. My mother feared staying alone at night in such a remote area. When Daddy was away and would be late getting home, I could sense her uneasiness, as young as I was. Her apprehension was understandable, and explainable, however.

On one occasion she had been badly frightened. It happened in late fall, before I was born in April of the next year. Daddy had taken a wagon load of fresh-picked cotton to the gin to have it baled. It was the busy season and he had to wait his turn. He got home very late. In the meantime, my mother had fought off a would-be intruder at the door, with more strength than she realized she had. It was no doubt someone who knew my dad was not home.

Mama was terribly upset when Daddy finally arrived home, hours after dark. I don't think she ever got over that terrifying experience. And I've always suspected that as the result of that incident, some of her fears were passed on to me.

[You older grandchildren all know how I resist staying home alone at night. Fortunately, your grandpa, as well as most other members of my family, have been patient with this weakness of mine. Maybe my fearful tendencies were a little extreme. They have, however, prompted me to take what I consider wise precautions. I'm firmly convinced; a certain amount of alertness was proper for me, and I'm quite sure it would be wise for you too, Candi, and for all my precious granddaughters—and my grandsons too, in this age of unbridled crime in which we live today.]

The Birthday Party Nobody Attended

Our nearest neighbors lived about a mile away, on the opposite side of a heavily wooded area adjoining our creek-bottom lands. They were a young couple who had recently moved there and they wanted to make friends and be neighborly.

Mary thought the occasion of her husband's birthday would be a good time to invite all the neighbors in for a friendly get-together, so she did. We were invited of course, but for some reason we were unable to go. The next day we learned that nobody had attended Larry's birthday party.

I still remember my childish impression of the pain and sadness that little woman, who was hurt so badly, must have felt. Undoubtedly, her husband too, felt great disappointment when she told him about the surprise party that had turned into the wrong kind of surprise.

Murder In The Meadow

Poor Mary suffered even more a few months later when her husband, Larry was murdered in cold blood in the field where he was working, the result of a crop dispute.

The whole community was in shock as news of the terrible tragedy spread near and far. I overheard my mother discussing the details with some friends in the village. Later I asked her how it could be that anyone could take the life of another person, for any reason. She could not find words to explain such a dastardly act to a child. I pondered the matter for a long time, but it was never completely resolved in my mind. My compassion for human beings who suffer such indignities, and my insight into their deep needs may well have been rooted in that incident.

The Very Foundations Tremble

The year I turned eight, our family moved from Loredo to the community of Pleasant Hill. It wasn't that many miles, but it seemed a lot farther to my brother Charles and me. Our baby brother, C.N., was too young to be affected the way we were.

Of course we were excited, but at the same time our familiar world disintegrated. Rooms of furniture that had been so secure around us were suddenly displaced. Everything in our house, everything we owned, was stacked together on our old rickety wagon, and the wagons of our neighbors who had come to help transport our belongings to the house Daddy and Mama had told us would be our new home.

While our table, beds and clothing were in transit, we both had a sickening feeling in our stomach upon seeing empty rooms in both houses. Mama had assigned me the responsibility of looking after our younger brother, and keeping him out of the way while the furniture was being loaded and unloaded. C.N. clung to me for safety, hardly realizing what was taking place. Charles and I held hands and watched the whole moving process with mixed emotions.

Despite our uneasiness, Charles and I were delighted in a way. Our parents explained that we would now be living close to the same school we had previously attended. The prospect of having only a short distance to walk to school gave us a warm and welcome feeling.

The Bottomless Gorge

The new arrangement seemed pretty wonderful to my brother and me at the time, but when we started to school in the fall we made a startling discovery that gave us a new cause for concern; a deep ravine, with a narrow, somewhat shaky bridge, over which we would have to walk every day, to and from school.

There were no railings on the bridge, and the gorge beneath it was said to be bottomless. Fear struck our hearts as we cautiously peered over the edge into the murky water below. Some of the planks on the bridge were loose and would flop ominously when a wagon or buggy, or even a horseback rider would cross over it. To make it worse, the planks slanted downward. At the lower side, the stream beneath was wider and even more threatening.

In the wintertime, when the temperatures dropped to the freezing point, the old bridge became a solid sheet of ice. [I hate to admit this, Candi, but I well remember feigning illness numerous times to keep from having to go to school when that bridge was slippery.]

The danger element of that crisis situation still looms large in my memory. Even after I grew up and moved away from the area, the horror of that inescapable passage continued to haunt me in my dreams. At the time, it seemed to me that my folks were uncaring. I realize now that parents do not always realize the fears their children have or detect concerns that seem insurmountable to them.

Life In The Big House With The Long Porch

The house we moved into in Pleasant Hill had once, long ago, been painted white. It was much bigger than the little cottage we had lived in before. In my childish estimation it seemed enormous.

The rooms were large, and a porch with many thin, fancy but time-worn posts graced the entire front of the house. At one end a large living room opened onto the front porch. At the other end, the front door was an exit from my room. I rated my own room because I was the only girl, and I was the oldest.

Our living room was strangely furnished with two iron-frame double beds, a large dresser with a swinging mirror, a couple of odd-shaped chests of drawers, a wardrobe for hanging clothes in, and a comfortable panel-back rocking chair. We didn't own a couch, just the rocker and several unmatched straight-back chairs.

During the winter time, the only heat we had in the front of the house, for many years, was a most ineffective fireplace along the outside wall of the living room. Later we added a potbelly wood stove which sat out in the room, in front of the fireplace. While it added to the already overcrowded effect, it did provide real warmth and made the long, cold months more tolerable.

We had a large wood-burning range in the kitchen, which we used year round for cooking. It provided heat in the winter, and unfortunately, unneeded heat in the summer also.

When it was cold, Mama often cooked food in a cast iron kettle hung in the fireplace, or in a heavy Dutch oven half buried in the hot coals near the hearth. An ever-present iron teakettle on the stove provided continuous hot water, plus moisture in the air.

Togetherness At The Table

Mealtimes at our house were family times and fun times. Our parents insisted we all eat at the same time, no coming and going cafeteria style. We had lots of good times around the table and some tense ones, too. Everyone tried hard to contribute to a happy experience while eating. Those times of togetherness generated many lifelong memories.

Daddy would say grace before each meal, while all of us sat up straight and reverent, with bowed heads and closed eyes—at least we tried. We didn't always hear the words he repeated but we knew what they were. He always recited them in exactly the same tones. Most of the time we tuned out the content as our thoughts were distracted by the aroma of the waiting food.

It was inevitable that once in a while one of us would accidentally spill something at the table. Daddy would try hard to react calmly, but it was hard for him to be patient with us. On occasion, he was known to actually be guilty of bumping a glass of milk himself, causing a strained atmosphere momentarily. We would bite our lips, fighting to hold back laughter (which was almost impossible) on seeing the look on Daddy's face when caught in the forbidden act himself. If we did laugh, in spite of ourselves, he would get upset. But we were glad that at times, even he would accidentally slip. We secretly hoped that it would help him understand our situation a little better, when we were on trial.

The Family Comedian

During the evening meal and after supper, especially in the winter time when we didn't have to hurry to bed, my brother C.N. would perform as the family comedian.

C.N. was born with an unusual sense of humor, which God knew he would need for survival. For reasons which none of us will ever fully understand, this brother, the third-born in our family, was named Cathy Nutt, for the maiden names of our grandmothers. For obvious reasons, his initials became his nickname.

C.N. was a cute little freckle-faced boy with curly, red hair and big brown eyes. His happy, jovial nature was evident at a young age. I suspect he may have taken his sense of humor after Grandpa Adams, who had a similar disposition—and his own obstacles to overcome.

I don't think being called C.N. by his parents and siblings was ever a problem for my brother in his early years, but when he started to school he was soon made aware that his name was different, and that classmates can be cruel and teachers insensitive.

Adjustments at school may have contributed to C.N.'s need for special attention at home. I'm sure we didn't think of it that way at the time.

We appreciated his antics because they were funny, and they were good. He had a whole bag full of tried and proven tricks. The favorite of the littlest members of our growing family was when C.N. appeared to take a smile off his face and put it in his pocket, then like magic pull it out and replace it. This one always pleased guests, too, I remember.

Our delightful brother earned the high respect of our family. We all appreciated his ability to help keep our spirits up. No matter how gloomy the weather, how bleak the national economy, or how dire the families' financial crisis, C.N. helped us through. His ever-ready, carefree entertainment was a life saver for our overburdened parents.

What's For Dinner?

While we were pitifully poor, I don't remember ever going hungry because there wasn't enough food. The choice was not always the greatest, but we had plenty of what we did have. When we would have company, Daddy used to laugh and tell our guests, "One day we have 'taters and beans, and the next day we have beans and 'taters." And that's just about the way it was.

My mother was a genius at making a lot out of a little, and serving the food attractive and tasty. She had that special touch—as did so many mothers and grandmothers in those days; the knack of being able to combine some of this, and a little of that, and turning out a beautiful cake or pie, or some other delectable dish. I don't ever recall seeing her use a cookbook.

Mama often created innovative fruit pies, or yummy chocolate or vanilla ones with fillings she whipped up herself. They were so-o-o-o good, I can still remember that special taste.

When Mama made pies, she always made a little extra dough, and also turned out a batch of "homemade crackers" for us kids. Oh, how we loved those. Daddy would sometimes bring home some store-bought crackers when he went to town, but we liked Mama's specialty best. And we could taste that extra ingredient of "love" which she put in them.

I remember well how my mother made the homemade crackers. [Let me tell you how she did it.] She would roll the extra pie crust dough quite thin, cut it into narrow strips with a sharp knife, then cut them again crosswise—into short pieces. Then she would walk a fork across the ready-to-bake crackers, to make tiny holes in them. She would then sprinkle salt over them and bake them in a moderate oven until they were a nice tan color.

[Doesn't that tickle your appetite, Candi? Well, you can bake some yourself, or you can ask your mother to make some the next time she bakes pies.]

Most of the time we had buttermilk biscuits for breakfast, except for an occasional pancake splurge. And for dinner (noon), and supper (evening), we usually had corn bread, made from white corn meal, grown on our farm and ground locally at the village grist mill. We never had meal that was ground from yellow corn. To this day I do not care for the yellow corn meal, generally available in supermarkets.

We had to buy processed flour at the neighborhood country store. Mama made homemade yeast breads sometimes, usually with "starter risers", passed along in small portions from someone's batter. These were often circulated, along with favorite recipes, among neighbors and relatives around the countryside. Those homemade varieties were a lot tastier than the store-bought "light bread", as we called it, available in town. It was terribly white, and the flavor seemed blah to us.

Our breakfast menu usually consisted of home-cured bacon, large, rich, brown eggs (from our Rhode Island hens), along with browned flour gravy—and of course fresh-made baking powder biscuits. Sometimes we had ham, and red-eyed gravy—made by simply adding a little water to the skillet where the ham was fried, and boiling it for a few minutes.

There was always homemade jam, preserves or jelly, and sorghum molasses on the table. Once in a while Mama would heat the molasses and add a speck of baking soda. We loved this warm, foamy syrup with hot biscuits, or over yummy buckwheat cakes, which we sometimes enjoyed on Sunday morning.

Daddy operated the village sorghum mill and was known for the high quality molasses he produced. We kids loved to watch the process as Daddy supervised the cooking of the sugar cane syrup in large vats, and the neat way the "helpers" skimmed the top as the finished product was channeled into waiting containers. The sorghum molasses Daddy turned out was nothing like the kind you can buy in the supermarket today. It was more like the refined table syrup we buy for our pancakes now, only it had a special unique flavor which is hard for me to describe.

Sometimes, when we were going to be working in the fields, the breakfast menu would include fried potatoes. "You need something that will stick to your backbone," Daddy would say. "We've got lots of work to do today."

We loved nicely browned fried potatoes for any meal; we even liked them cold. Mama would cut the potatoes into thin squared strips like French fries, sprinkle salt and a little flour over them, and fry them in melted lard in our big iron skillet. They came out deliciously crisp and golden brown.

If we were going to school, our lunch the next day might include left over fried potatoes, sandwiched in a cold biscuit. [Don't laugh. You may think that sounds "icky", but we thought it made for a pretty tasty school lunch.] Whatever the challenge of the day, we headed into it—braced with a hearty breakfast.

Most of the food we ate was produced right on our farm, including our milk, meat, poultry and eggs. Other than the oft acclaimed "southern fried chicken", which Mama prepared on Sunday when special company was coming or on a week day when the preacher stopped by for dinner, we ate pork most of the time. We hardly knew what beef steak, or even ground beef was.

Occasionally, in winter, we might have rabbit or squirrel meat. Sometimes Daddy and my brothers, and maybe a neighbor, would go 'possum, or 'coon hunting for some extra meat.

[You know, Candi, it wasn't until I studied about animals in school and couldn't find the words in the dictionary, that I learned that a 'possum was really an opossum, and a 'coon was a raccoon.]

Hog Killing Day

We always looked forward to the first cold weather in the fall, and "hog-killing" day. What a thrill for all of us. A neighbor or two usually came to help with the slaughtering.

Daddy would choose the heaviest and fattest hog to be killed. While the men-folks shot the animal, cut it open, and hung it up to remove the entrails, Mama would flutter about between the house and the side yard where the operation was in progress, providing kettles of hot water.

We kids shared the excitement while secretly feeling the painful shock of seeing one of our nice pigs that we had helped to slop and feed, killed and mutilated. We enjoyed eating the meat, but we had mixed emotions about the slaughtering process.

The huge liver from the hog was shared with helpful neighbors, with plenty reserved for our big family of course. However, the first dish we enjoyed at our house was cooked brains. [Don't wrinkle your nose. We loved that special dish. My mother would scramble them with the eggs, and take my word for it, they were delicious. Even the youngest children in our family considered them quite delectable.]

All of us looked forward to having fresh liver. [Oh, I know you don't like liver, but I think you would have enjoyed it the way my mother fixed it.]

First, with a sharp knife, Mama would slice it very thin—that was her secret, then she would lightly flour and season each piece, then fry the liver in our old cast iron skillet until it was nice and brown. Um-m-m-m good! And she never added onions to alter the taste; she didn't have to, to get us to eat it.

Maybe it was partly because we only had it at hog-killing time, but I remember all of us loved liver.

Soon after hog-killing day, Mama would make something she called head cheese from some of the parts you would have thought should have been thrown away, things like gristle and fatty pieces. She cooked the scraps, seasoned them with her own concoction of spices, then molded them into cheesecloth bags, and hung them up to allow the "cheese" to set. When the process was completed, the sliced headcheese was like a lunch meat, and delightfully delicious.

[Did you know that you can buy a modern-day version of headcheese in the supermarket? You ought to try it sometime. I have, but it isn't nearly as good, nor as rich tasting as what my mother used to make, of course.]

Mama also made mincemeat—with real meat, as the name implies. Most mincemeat I've bought from the store these days contains no meat. Our mincemeat contained raisins, fruit, nuts—and meat.

Some parts of the pig were ground into sausage and pleasantly seasoned with ground sage, white pepper, black pepper and even red pepper. Our freshly made and carefully seasoned sausage was really a treat. And Mama always canned some in Mason jars for later use. There is nothing else in the whole world that compares to the taste of the home-canned sausage of yesteryear.

My parents cured large slabs of bacon, and the jowls from the lower jaw of the hog. They also preserved salt pork, with no lean to speak of. It was terribly salty but I loved the unique flavor of fried salt pork, or boiled and used as seasoning in a pot of navy beans.

They also cured the hams from the hogs we butchered, and smoked them over hickory wood in the smokehouse. I remember watching them rub the meat with a special blend of salt, sugar and saltpeter. [I always thought they were saying salt peter. It was actually sodium nitrate.] What I remember most about those hams was the delicious taste, fried or baked.

In addition to all this, my mother made chitterlings. We called them "chitlin's", with a lazy southern accent. They were made from the large intestines of the hog. [I know it sounds awful, but you could hardly believe how many people actually loved them. They were popular in that part of the country then, and they still are. However, that's one native delicacy that I never acquired a taste for. Incidentally, you can also buy chitterlings in the local supermarkets today; yes, even here in California where we live.]

My mother rendered our lard by cooking the fat of the hog in large kettles. When the residue of the meat scraps were skimmed from the top, the lard was then poured into cans and buckets Mama had kept for that purpose. She always saved the containers from the shortening she had rendered the previous year. And the proprietor of the local country store would save large containers for us. After the lard cooled, it was white and about the consistency of butter.

The fat that was not suitable for making lard, or anything else edible, Mama combined with lye and made soap for doing the laundry.

Two things about that old-fashioned lye soap stand out in my memory— the potent odor (oh, how strong it smelled), and the devastating caustic effect it had on our hands.

I think you could truthfully say, we didn't waste any part of the hog that could be salvaged in any way. We used just about everything but the squeal.

The whole hog-killing process was repeated a couple or three times each season, so that there would be enough meat and lard to carry us through the winter—and hopefully, until hog-killing time the following year.

More Food On The Farm

We had several cows of different colors on our farm, and almost always two or three of them would be giving milk at the same time. One thing we had plenty of was rich, creamy milk. We made our own butter too, in a large crock-churn. The lid was a round piece of wood with a hole in the middle. The dasher was a round plunger with stationary paddles on the end, which we manually churned up and down what seemed to us like hundreds of times, during the process. Finally, the tiny flecks of soft, yellow butter would start forming on top.

It was a boring, seemingly endless project, and one that all of us kids hated. We did enjoy the rich, delicious butter which resulted, however, if we stayed with it. And Mama always saw to it that we did.

I remember, my mother would lift the lid and look inside. When the butter was formed sufficiently, she would spoon it into a special mold.

Since we had no electricity we also had no refrigerator; we were too many miles from any power source. For many years we didn't even have an ice box. Mama would cool the milk and butter, and keep them chilled by hanging them in pails with handles, tied on the end of a rope and let down into the water in our cistern.

[What is a cistern? Well, its a tank where water is stored. Ours was underground and beneath our enclosed back porch. We caught the rain water and channeled it into the cement storage tank.] Milk and butter kept very well this way. The secret was in keeping the utensils and containers scrupulously clean to prevent bacteria from growing.

In Cooperation With God

My mother, like her mother and her grandmother, had a natural green thumb. The gardens which she produced, in cooperation with God, were beautiful to behold, and life savers for our family.

In early spring, Daddy cultivated the soil in our garden plot and Mama would take it from there. She tediously planted each seed, and transplanted from pots she had seeded earlier. My mother was truly an artist in her field. We could hardly believe our eyes when the various vegetables and flowers began to appear in their orderly, artistic pattern. But Mama, I believe, visualized the design when planting the seeds in the soft soil, as any true artist would.

We grew a large variety of vegetables to enjoy in season, and to can for winter use. The plants grew in long, even rows and beds bordered by narrow strips of flowers blooming profusely, with variegated color, just like Grandma's wonderful gardens that I always enjoyed so much when I went to visit her.

Not only do I have picture "remembrances" of Mama's growing plot of art, framed in flowering color, but I also have numerous taste "plates" stored on my memory shelves—the first "mess" of English peas from our garden in the spring [oh, how delicious], the long, thin white radishes, and the tiny red round ones; leaf-lettuce "wilted" in bacon drippings, and white sweet corn on the cob, or tender sliced kernels—served with homemade butter. I can still taste them all.

Several rows of sweet corn grew in a good size patch, at the back of our large garden. Mama explained to me one year that a certain amount of corn had to be planted together in one area, in order for it to pollinate.

I remember vividly, the unique flavor of the peach cobblers my mother made with the fruit from the old Indian peach tree that grew by the back garden fence. The mottled orange-red-pink color of the meat of the peaches extended from the cling stone to the skin. I have never seen or tasted anything like them since.

And there were the golden brown field pumpkins which we grew in the edge of the nearest cornfield. Seasoned with sorghum from our molasses mill, the pumpkin meat turned a dark orange or a light brown. This delicious field-grown food had a unique taste all its own.

Making Sauerkraut

Every summer we made large quantities of sauerkraut from the cabbages we grew in our garden. Making "kraut" was a big operation during harvesting season. We all got in on the major job of shredding the cabbage heads on a wooden board with two sharp blades; one for fine shredding and one for coarse shredding.

The finely cut cabbage was then placed in large ceramic-like crock jars, and inundated with a saltwater brine for a prescribed length of time. At proper intervals, the contents of each jar was checked for progress in the preserving process, then covered again with a heavy plate, used to weight the mixture down so that the salty brine liquid completely covered the cabbage.

Part of the reward for helping make the sauerkraut was getting to eat the cabbage hearts. We loved them; so much in fact, we usually ended up with a tummy-ache from eating too many.

We also had the privilege of tasting the sauerkraut at the different stages, as it was checked for fermentation. When it was ready, the cabbage was transferred from the large crocks to Mason canning jars and sealed, where it was kept indefinitely. The sauerkraut was good to eat just as it came from the crock, or from the jar when canned. Sometimes we heated it with a little shortening or butter.

Mason Jars In A Row

Another busy preserving season occurred when our cucumbers were ready to harvest. My mother made several varieties of "county fair" quality cucumber pickles. I remember dill pickles, bread and butter pickles, alum pickles, sweet pickles, and a few other novelty ones now and then. We always had plenty to last all year, and we had pickles on the table every day.

Mama also canned green beans, shelled beans, corn, tomatoes and beets. She pickled most of our beets, however. We loved them best that way. I even remember the way she made beet pickles, and the ingredient proportions: equal parts of sugar, water and vinegar. She would heat them together, then place the pickles in the hot, scalded jars and seal them. [I wish I could find words to describe how good they tasted.]

We also canned fruit from the scraggly peach, apricot, pear, plum and apple trees, growing here and there near our house, vague reminders of orchards of better days.

Mama proudly exhibited the colorful jars of fruit and vegetables on a large table on the back porch until they could be transferred to the shelves Daddy built for that purpose, in our partially underground storm cellar.

She also put up lots of jams, jellies and preserves which she made from various fruits and berries. And she made wonderful light brown apple butter. [I can taste its spicy flavor now, and smell its incomparable aroma!]

On the front row in our cellar storage area, the pickled peaches were quite conspicuous, accented by a few jars on one side made from the Indian peaches Mama was able to save after all the cobblers we begged for. The dark pieces you could see here and there in the jars, were bits of cinnamon sticks, and other spices. These, along with vinegar, and sugar, were responsible for the sweet pickling effect.

*** *** ***

"Remembering all those good things to eat makes me hungry, Candice. How about you? Let's have a snack before we go to bed. There will be another time to talk about all the things I want you to know."

CHAPTER 2

This is The Way We Survive

"Grandma, did you have to do chores when you were my age?" Barry asked me while we were refilling the hummingbird feeders on the deck, and the wild-bird feeder in the yard.

We had been discussing the validity of some of the little chores his parents required him to do regularly at home. While visiting us he wanted to feel his grandma out on the subject, and to make sure he wasn't being "overworked". Barry had just turned ten and was beginning to question some of life's realities.

"Let's finish feeding the birds, and the other things Grandpa asked us to do for him while he's gone fishing, then I'll tell you about the chores I was required to do when I was about your age," I answered.

We were just getting settled in the porch swing when we saw Barry's uncle coming up the driveway with his daughters, Candice, who was nine, and her six-year old sister, Nadine.

"Oh," I told Barry, "I'm sure your cousins would like to hear about it too."

"Can we stay and play with Barry?" Candi called from the back seat. "Daddy can pick us up when he returns the tool he came to borrow."

"I'm not going to play," Barry spoke up, before I could answer Candi. "Grandma is going to tell me a story about when she was a little girl."

Can we listen with you?" Candice begged.

"We like Grandma's stories too," Nadine chimed in.

***   ***   ***

A Hard Row To Hoe

When we still lived in the community of Loredo my brothers and I were quite small, but there were things we had to do to help our parents. We had our own little chores to help Mama in the house, and there were many things we could help Daddy with around the barn and in the fields.

In our new location, after we moved to Pleasant Hill, we farmed much of the 80 acres (two "forties") that had been willed to us by my mother's parents, plus 160 adjoining acres which belonged to two of my mother's sisters.

On the larger cleared areas of our farm we grew many acres of corn, or maize, as it was sometimes called, about the same amount of cotton, and only a few acres of Spanish peanuts. We also grew fields of wheat and oats for hay and grain to feed our livestock.

Daddy's work crew consisted of my brothers and myself, all under the age of ten. Planting, cultivating and harvesting were all monumental tasks for us.

At just the right time, when the weather was good and the danger of frost was past, my brothers and I (then later my sister and younger brother, and still later two more sisters) would line up across the end of the freshly tilled and furrowed field, each of us taking a row. We carried a bucket filled with corn in our left hand, and with our right hand we would reach in and lift out a handful of grain. We carefully dropped a few kernels at regular intervals in the center of the top of the rows which Daddy had so meticulously laid out.

We repeated this monotonous procedure over and over again, regularly refilling our pails from large sacks of corn. Daddy would then come behind us with an improvised piece of equipment which he used to cover the freshly planted grain with just the right amount of soil. We all worked together. It was a pretty effective system.

When we had completed the planting process, we left the next steps up to our Heavenly Father—to send the rain and the sunshine in proper amounts and sequences.

Once the corn had sprouted and started to grow, Daddy would schedule the next operation. We lined up again, this time with our little hoes, just right for small hands, and following Daddy's specific instructions, we began the monstrous job of "thinning" the corn.

Every foot of every corn field had to be thinned out, leaving only a couple of plants growing together, with a space the width of a hoe in between. When large fields of corn are calculated in segments less than a foot in width, the job to be done looms mighty large in the minds of such youthful workers as we were, especially on a hot, humid day.

A few months later the corn was ready to harvest. All of us, along with Daddy, would follow along behind our old wagon, pulled by our faithful team of stubborn mules, gathering the ears of corn and throwing them into the wagon. When the wagon bed was full, we would change our pace, take the load to the barn and carefully transfer the ears to our large corn-storage bins.

But planting, thinning and "plucking" corn wasn't the most difficult job on our farm. We also grew large fields of cotton. Daddy had improvised a cotton planting device, so that was at least one chore we were spared. Like corn, cotton had to be thinned in the early stages so that it would grown better and could be more easily harvested but it was a backbreaking job which we did not look forward to.

Only those who have actually experienced chopping cotton in the hot, blazing sun, thinning out the excess plants and removing weeds and grass in between, can fully understand the drudgery. Likewise, only those who have picked enough soft, snowy, seedy, cotton fluffs from prickly bolls, from stalks growing too close to the ground, to fill a large canvas sack trailing behind them while their backs ached and their heads throbbed, can identify with those who have.

[You kids can't even imagine that kind of hard work. I hope you'll remember what I'm telling you next time you're asked to do your little chores around home.]

Today, wherever cotton is grown, even in California, it is picked with machines. Some smart inventor along the way came up with a clever idea—a machine that could actually pick the cotton from the bolls, making one of the most menial of all tasks only a memory. That ingenious innovator was someone who succeeded where we had failed. We yearned to come up with a "better" way, as we laboriously toiled in "them 'ole cotton fields back home".

[Your grandma was born too soon, I'm afraid. She will always remain a part of the history of cotton farming the hard way. I'm sure I speak for all who identify with me when I voice my estimation of the horrible chore of cotton chopping and cotton picking, more particularly cotton "picking" in the South in the 1920's and 1930's.

Little Working Hands

The only help Daddy had in planting, cultivating and harvesting his corn and cotton crops was his large family of children. We were each assigned our own hoe, and our own long canvas cotton-sack, with adjustable shoulder straps to accommodate our age and size.

Daddy usually worked along with us. We performed a lot better that way, and the work load seemed much lighter when Daddy was carrying the heaviest end. And we were not tempted to falter along the way if he was right with us. We knew better than to try to get away with any fiddling around then. He would not accept less than the highest performance. But we still preferred working with him to being left alone, on our own honor, as was sometimes necessary.

During the busiest seasons Daddy would rouse us early. While it was still dark, he would stalk through the house, calling, "Come on, get out of there. Let's get going!" We knew better than to stay in bed and relish the "comfort" for even a few extra minutes.

I'm sure today my dad would be accused of breaking child labor laws. But I suppose you could qualify his actions then by saying there simply was no other way. As I look back now, I do not resent the fact that we had to work hard. It was actually good for us, I'm sure, although our health may have been threatened at times. Chopping corn and picking cotton was not only hard work for us children, but it was also a difficult, heartbreaking way for my dad to make a living for his big family.

The success of our crops was subject to weather-related setbacks, the temperament of the government, and fluctuating market prospects—

and as the old country folk-song says, the threat of the boll weevil that might come sneaking through the area at any time, "just lookin' for a home".

At best we were fortunate if we were able to repay the loan required to purchase seeds to plant in the spring. All the farmers we knew went through the same process. Many of them also bought groceries and supplies on credit through the year, just to get by. Of course this too had to be repaid.

My parents however, refused to buy groceries we couldn't pay for. They managed to grow enough vegetables and fruit, which we canned and preserved, and we had our own cows for milk. We grew hogs and chickens for meat and eggs. We always got by, somehow. While it often seemed like the going was really rough, we had it a lot easier than many people we knew— people who had to rent the land they tended, for instance.

It was considered a good year if there was money enough left over after the loan was repaid to buy each of the children in our family a pair of shoes, and those of us who were older, a change of clothes for school. There were years, I well remember, when the rewards for all the hard work of our whole family were pitifully small. I was painfully aware of the disappointment and utter hopelessness my parents felt at such times.

I was the oldest of seven children, and from my vantage point I observed how skillfully my mother managed hand-me-downs, passing them from the older to the younger children. We were taught to take care of our clothes so that they could be worn by the next child.

Mama made most of our garments, including shirts for my dad and brothers. They were so well sewn however, they never minded. She sewed all her clothes, and those my sisters and I wore too. Although times were hard I don't recall any of us complaining about the quantity, or the quality of our clothing.

I do recall the time when a close girlfriend whose family had more money than we did, ordered a pretty rust colored dress that was featured on the cover of a mail order catalogue. I admired (maybe envied) her for being so fortunate. (Though I never let her know how I felt.) I hasten to add, that same girlfriend was often envious of the nice dresses my mother made for me; her mother didn't sew.

I sometimes saw myself as shabby in my homemade dresses, but not because they were poorly made. They were exceptionally well sewn; my mother was a seamstress, but she often had to use flimsy material, such as cotton flour sacks which our store-bought flour came packaged in, or feed bags that we bought seed or supplement feed for our animals in.

But don't think I didn't appreciate my mother's expertise, nor all the time and effort she put into sewing for me. I truly did, and I often told her so.

[Candi and Nadine, I hope you express your appreciation to your mother for all the pretty things she sews for you.]

Although, at the time (when I was your age), we could buy all kinds of beautiful fabrics, it hadn't been long since women in our part of the country carded their own fresh cotton, or wool, spun the skeins and wove them into cloth. I never saw it done first hand, but I had relatives who still had the spinning wheels they had used. In earlier days, making their own cloth was done on top of all the other time-consuming work pioneer women had to do. I used to wonder how they managed to get it all done. I still wonder. My Mama, your great grandmother, worked very hard but she was spared the spinning chore.

The Dirtiest Job

Corn and cotton were not the only crops grown on the Chappell farm. We grew rows and rows of Spanish peanuts, mainly as a food supplement for our livestock. Sometimes, if we had an excess, we would sell them to realize a little extra cash. And we ate what we wanted. Mama made delicious peanut butter, and we often had them oven-roasted.

[You've probably never seen peanuts growing in the field. Let me tell you about them.]

The peanuts grow underground. When ours were ready to be harvested, we pulled up the entire plant—tops, nuts and roots—by grasping the bush- like stalks, jerking them from the soil and shaking the dirt from the roots and nuts. Then we would stack them around poles in "shocks", as my daddy called them, with the peanuts next to the pole to protect them from the weather. Each shock was approximately six feet high, and about three and a half feet in diameter. We arranged the top in such a way that it would seal and prevent the rain from soaking the peanuts, causing them to mildew and rot.

As with cotton and corn, there are now peanut-picking machines. We harvested them the old fashioned way, an unpleasant, dirty job.

When the peanuts were dry, and "seasoned" sufficiently, Daddy, my brothers, my sisters and I would load them into our wagon and haul them into our "extra" barn, which was like an oversized garage. It was located between our regular barn and our house. Later, on rainy days when we couldn't work in the field, it was our job to pluck the peanuts from the vines while sitting atop the unfinished task, the shocks, in the dust-filled barn.

[You're smiling, because you're thinking about how we must have looked when we finished working in the peanut barn. You're right. We needed a bath and a shampoo. The dust buildup around our eyes looked like overdone eye makeup. Our eyelashes resembled dirty fringes around our clear eyes. That's about the only part of us that was clean.]

But, I'll tell you, those little pea-goobers "shore were good". It took more will power than we usually had to come through the process without getting a tummy-ache.

The Magic Forest

While we cultivated much of the land on our farm, we also had some heavily wooded acres of dense forest. How I loved that enchanted wonderland! [It's no wonder I enjoy trees so much today.]

My brothers and sisters and I would take long walks into the deep, dark recesses of the forest, where the sun was never able to penetrate. In many spots, the moisture never dried up. The tops of the trees were intertwined. It was scary in a way, but the adventure challenged us. We imagined frightening encounters with robbers-in-hiding, or with wild, exotic animals.

In autumn, the large white oaks and black oaks at the edge of the forest exhibited gorgeous colors ranging from deep red hues to soft yellow, contrasted against the green foliage of cedar and pine trees. If I close my eyes I can see the vivid color, even now. And I can still smell the woodsy aroma of the pine needles and the thick moss that formed on the side of the trees. Even the damp soil, in places where the fallen leaves were not so thick, smelled earthy.

The Grapevine Swing

Just at the edge of the dark, mysterious forested area was a marvelous grapevine swing attached to a large oak tree. How it stands out in my memory! What a thrill to swing dangerously high—up and out, towards the bright blue sky, while the big, fluffy white clouds went floating by. It gave us an exhilarating airborne sensation.

My brothers were braver than I was. They would swing so high it looked like they were going to make a complete loop, and come over backwards into the branches of the tree (if they didn't fall first). I would hold my breath, expecting the worst, then scream with relief when I could catch it again.

"I'm going to tell Daddy you're swinging too high!" I would threaten loudly. This would slow them up a little. Then they would start bargaining with me, so I wouldn't tell on them.

Itchy Vines

Near the grapevine swing were some colorful poison-ivy vines, clinging to the trees, climbing up the trunk and out onto the branches. One day our cousin Imogene, who was visiting from the city, wanted to take some of the brightly colored branches home to her mother to decorate with. She didn't suspect anything and it was mean of us not to warn her of the danger. Of course later she broke out with a horrible rash.

When Imogene came to visit us again she refused to get near the poison-ivy vines. I seemed to be immune. I would jump up and down on the broken vines, calling out to her, "See, they don't bother me!"

[I didn't realize it then, but the joke was on me. In later years, and to this very day, as all of you know, I'm extremely allergic to poison-oak plants and bushes, which is the form it takes here on the west coast.]

Unfulfilled Dreams

In another part of our beloved forest the trees grew more sparsely. My brothers begged Daddy to let them cut down some of the younger saplings that were growing to replace the larger trees we had cut down for firewood.

[I can hear them now.]

"Please, Daddy," they would plead. "Why can't we build an Abe Lincoln cabin?" They even drew up some crude plans to try and convince him. It was a dream my brothers were reluctant to let go of. But Daddy never gave in.

I realize now that most young men, at one time or another, dream of living in the wild, and maybe building a cabin in the woods. It is just a normal desire, I guess, for most of us—to want to get close to nature.

Persimmons, Blackberries and Muscadines

In the same area where my brothers dreamed and watched their dreams fade, there were a number of persimmon trees. We always anticipated the first heavy frost, which would mellow them and render them sweet enough to eat. [I can still taste that wild, juicy fruit! Oh, how we loved those luscious, ripe persimmons! The ones we can buy in the supermarket today don't begin to compare in taste but they do trigger a lot of memories for me.]

At the edge of the forest were also large patches of wild blackberry bushes. We harvested the fruit every year for seasonal pies, and for jams and jellies for the winter. And there were wild muscadine grapes growing here and there. They translated beautifully into jelly that had a distinct, unique "wild" flavor.

New-Ground Potatoes

My dad cleared another area at the edge of the forest and planted Irish potatoes. Soil that had never been cultivated before was referred to as "new-ground" soil. Mr. Chappell's new-ground potatoes were the talk of the countryside. He took great pride in them. The rich virgin soil produced an abundance of large, flavorful spuds. We children delighted in helping to harvest them, pulling them up by the tops, releasing them from their confinement in the dark, fertile soil, and shaking the dirt from them.

[You know, Barry—and Candice and Nadine, we thought potatoes were one of the grandest foods people could eat. We never knew that at one time in Europe, potatoes were thought to be poisonous.]

The Great Divide

The opposite side of the "forty" acres occupied by our wonderful forest, bordered on a winding ravine which separated our property from our neighbor's farm, to the east of us.

A year round stream moved ever so slowly in the direction of the dreaded "bottomless gorge" my brothers and sisters and I feared so much. Our neighbor, Mr. Chris, considered it a natural barrier, protecting his property from possible invasion by the Chappell children. Such partitions were not necessary however. We knew we were not allowed to trespass, even if we had been tempted to.

The stream at the bottom of the ravine turned sharply, just to the left of the bridge, and followed alongside the public access road across our property and Mr. Chris's.

We cultivated our land across the road from our house. On the other side of the road, next to the old rickety bridge, an old fence separated our property and the pasture where Mr. Chris grazed his cattle herd. The fence was sufficient to keep the cattle in, but it could have easily been crawled through, or climbed over, by the Chappell children. That never happened though. Daddy and Mama taught us to respect other people's property. Even if there had been no fence, we wouldn't have dared to wave a hand over the invisible line.

When confronted with the issue, Mr. Chris had to admit, "Mr. Chappell sure has a good bunch of kids."

We stood in awe of Mr. Chris, and his wife, Mrs. Bliss. The only time we set foot on their place was when we were invited, which was seldom. We admired their large herd of cows, and their fancy fenced corral, just like out West. But one thing really "bugged" us. When Mr. Chris's cows were calving, he would sometimes name the new babies after Mr. Chappell's children. We deeply resented that. [A cow named Ardelle? Well, it did rhyme with cowbell.]

I guess they just couldn't come up with enough names, so after scraping the bottom of the barrel, they fell back on us. I don't know who was the most honored—the calves, or us.

A Hard Nut To Crack

Before we leave the fields and grounds of our country plantation I would like to tell you about a huge black-walnut tree that grew in the meadow, surrounded by our cotton and corn fields.

When the walnuts fell to the ground, Daddy would insist that we children gather them into containers, clearing the clutter from the cultivated areas, and store the nuts to dry.

We hated this backbreaking chore, and the dark green, almost black, stain from the hulls on the nuts, which couldn't be washed off. It had to wear off and that took a long time.

The only enjoyable aspect of this operation was the tasty meats, which could be extracted only after the walnuts had been dried and husked. And they were difficult to crack. You really had to work hard to extract the meat. They had to taste good to be worth all the hard work required.

Those were fun times associated with our walnut gathering, however. I remember one afternoon when we were tired and bored with our messy job, my sister Sue took off suddenly across the meadow as fast as she could run. Then she stopped and hollered back over her shoulder from a distance, "I beat you, Dorothy!" Well, Dorothy, our youngest sister, didn't even know a race was on. We all had a good laugh, releasing some of the tension. In those days, such incidents helped us to retain our sanity.

Those old fashioned black walnuts made us appreciate the easily available meats of the English walnut variety. These came from trees that had another type of walnut grafted onto the black walnut tree.. They were scarce, and we seldom saw them in those days. When we did, they were usually so expensive we couldn't afford them. A few might appear at Christmas time. If we found two or three in our sock on Christmas morning, we were really thrilled.

Charting The Wheels Of Progress

While chopping cotton in that same meadow, near the big black-walnut tree, on a long hot afternoon, we would often halt on our hoe handle while watching an occasional passerby on the road nearby. It was usually a wagon, or someone riding a horse. Sometimes a buggy with a top that could be folded down, would slither by. Mr. Blackwood, our country doctor, had one of those. Sometimes he would be hurrying to visit a patient. Then we would wonder who was sick.

A few times we saw a very strange vehicle called an automobile, and heard the funny putt-putting noise it made, as it struggled along on the rough road. It would thrill us to the tip of our toes. It was always someone passing through; we didn't know anyone who owned a "car" as they were sometimes called.

The first one we saw go by on the road, so close to the field where we were laboriously toiling, frightened us terribly. Daddy was not working with us at the time. My brothers and I huddled together and fearfully wondered if we were being invaded by some strange mode of transportation from another planet. The next time we saw one, we were a little braver, and each time one of these strange contraptions went by we became less frightened, and more thrilled with the phenomenon.

How exciting, we finally decided. What scenes and dreams they generated! We would try to imagine where they came from and where they were going. Our vivid young imaginations came up with some pretty far-fetched possibilities.

"Someday, "we would tell ourselves, "someday, we too are going places.

And we're going to have better things to do than working in these old cotton fields."

But the possibility was very remote. It was as though we were hopelessly and helplessly locked into our circumstances. We hardly dared to dream, and in our lowly state, even dreams were hard to formulate.

By and by night would come and we would at least get to go to the house and eat supper, and sleep a few hours before it was time to arise and begin the same drudgery all over again. Usually we were so tired we would fall asleep immediately after eating supper and preparing for bed.

Grandpa's New Toy

Our fantasies about someday taking a ride in "one of them newfangled horseless carriages" suddenly came alive one afternoon in late autumn, more quickly than we had imagined.

We had just finished eating our noon meal when we heard the strangely familiar putt-putt sound in front of our house. We all rushed to peek out the front windows. Daddy went bravely out on the porch to confront the situation head-on. Each of us was watching, waiting cautiously, not knowing what might happen next. When we saw a big smile break across Daddy's face, we knew everything was okay. My brothers hurried out to help him investigate. I hesitated a bit, and stayed close to Mama for safety's sake.

Now, we could see—it was an automobile—with our Grandpa getting out of it, strutting like a millionaire.

I will never forget that day. I remembered that dreary morning when we had been picking cotton and pulling our sacks wearily along; exasperation overcame us. We eased the slack in the shoulder straps of our cotton sacks, and through wishing-weary eyes, we watched the nearby road, hoping for something to happen. Then we saw it! It was an automobile! We had captured a staggering—and a big frightening image of a real car that day.

Although you could buy a Ford touring car brand new for around $300 at that time, that was more than most people could afford. I don't know how my Grandpa Chappell managed it, but he was the first person in our area, and the first person we knew, to purchase the newly invented motor machine. And our own Grandpa had driven it to our home. There he was, standing right in front of the funny looking vehicle, with a radiant smile on his face. He wasn't scared of it at all.

Grandpa could hardly wait to bring his new toy to our house to show it off to his son Bill, and his wife Thelma, and their children. He was so proud he could hardly contain himself.

I remember, it was black, and it had a heavy cloth-like, flexible top that could be let down. As we looked in wonder, we thought how nice that a person could be protected from the sun in the summer, and the rain in winter. Or he could have the top down and enjoy all the fresh air he wanted to.

And this wonderful car had two seats inside— one for the driver, and a passenger beside him, and another immediately behind it for additional passengers. We could hardly believe what we were seeing.

It was a big improvement over riding in our wagon. Only three people at the most could ride in the one seat, called a "spring seat".

These unique features on this new invention really fascinated us.

To start the motor [Grandpa explained to us that was what pulled it along] he took a short, bent rod—which he called a "crank"— from its storage place, and inserted it into the center of the front of the car. Then he turned it around in quick jerks until the funny sounding motor started to sputter and choke. My brothers and I stood at a safe distance, staring in wonder. They were braver than I, but they too were cautious.

After Grandpa bragged about each amazing feature, pointing out and explaining them from every angle, he proposed a free ride for all. Daddy and the boys thought it was a great idea, but I was hesitant.

"Just a short ride," Grandpa encouraged, "over Bailey's Hill, and back."

"Bailey's Hill!" I gasped, and put my hand over my mouth to hide my astonishment. "Oh, no!

Bailey's Hill, named for the politician who had been instrumental in creating funds for construction of the road and its constant upkeep, was a steep incline, parallel to a cliff, or bluff area which we always referred to as our own Grand Canyon. I was afraid to even ride a horse-drawn wagon up THAT hill.

Getting into the back seat of this funny looking machine, and heading up that mountain road was more than I was about to do without at lease some resistance. Suppose it would stop on us before we could reach the top of the hill, I reasoned. Grandpa would have to get out and crank the thing up, while we all stayed inside the vehicle sitting in a precarious angle. What would keep us from rolling backwards down the hill, and into the deep ravine on the side of the road?

Daddy decided however, that this would be a real historical experience for us, so he gently assisted me up onto the running board, which was like a step running along the side, and into the back seat beside my brothers who were excitedly awaiting the great adventure. Mama had gone back into the house with the excuse that she had to wash the dishes. I've often wondered what was going on in her thoughts, as we took off with me screaming and begging not to go.

Somehow I managed to keep fairly calm, once we finally got underway, even when crossing a narrow bridge. But as we approached Bailey's Hill I began begging Daddy to have Grandpa let me out.

"Please," I pleaded, "tell Grandpa to stop. I want to get out of this thing. I don't want to go up that hill!"

Grandpa was smiling, and obviously enjoying the show at my expense.

Daddy was torn between his father's elation over his new automobile, and his young daughter's consternation at being forced to participate in a show-off tour. But Grandpa didn't stop. And not surprisingly, I lived to tell about the episode.

What Kind of Bird Is That

The following spring I experienced an equally historical event in our area. I will never forget the day. It was a Saturday afternoon. Quite a few people had gathered to watch a ball game in Mr. Cooper's pasture, near the sawmill. Mama and Daddy had allowed me to go with our neighbors. Their daughter and I played together and our families were good friends. My folks trusted them to look after me.

While we were waiting for the game to get underway, young Phil Senter came over and excitedly told everyone about a strange machine in the field on the other side of the mill.

It was an airplane! A small, single engine craft. Someone had landed it in a level area where there were no trees. It was so small we would hardly notice it today, but it was the first "flying machine" any of us had ever seen. It reminded us of a huge bird.

The atmosphere was charged with excitement. Community residents, and those who had come from surrounding areas to watch the game, all gawked in amazement at the strange object. Some people finally got up courage enough to venture close enough to touch it. But not fraidy-cat me. I was too scared to get anywhere near it. I had the idea that if I got too close to this weird looking thing, it might suck me up like a magnet and pull me right up into the sky, when it took off. [I always seemed to have a reservoir of vivid images and imagined fears to back up any given incident.]

It seems hilarious now, remembering those ridiculous fears, especially after having flown numerous flights in modern airplanes. But it was anything but funny then. It's amazing how far we've come in the field of transportation in my lifetime. Travel via unbelievably advanced automobiles and huge jet aircraft are as commonplace today as getting from place to place in our old wagon was when I was a child. And that really wasn't that many years ago.

* * *   * * *   * * *

"Barry, how would you liked to have lived in those days? I'm sure you would have enjoyed the adventures, but the chores and all the hard work— well, I don't think you, or Candi or Nadine would have liked that part of the good old days.

Yes, there was a lot of hard work for many children during those times, but we had a lot of fun too. Another time I'll tell you more. Here comes someone down the driveway now.

CHAPTER 3

To Grandma's House We Go

"Grandma, I like the birds and trees, and the deer, here where you live." Stanley told me as we walked down our long driveway to the mailbox.

"And I like the quail," his five year old brother, Alvin, said.

Their sister, Emmalene, confided that she liked the long walks, and the open "outdoors" feeling she always had when she came to visit. "I just love to come to see you, Grandma."

"Did you ever go and visit your grandma and grandpa when you were a little girl?" Emmalene wanted to know.

"Oh, yes, many times." I told them. "And I loved it too. It was always a lot of fun."

Their seven year old cousin, Judie, who had skipped ahead of us, stopped and called back, "Grandma, will you please tell us about it?"

"Yes, please do," Emmalene, Alvin and Stanley all said in unison.

"I'd love to, " I told them, as we got back up to the house. "Let me check the mail and get us something to drink. Shall we sit here on the porch?"

* * *   * * *   * * *

A Ride In The Goodness Wagon

Yes, we often went to see my grandma and grandpa. Their farm was on the edge of a good size town. Grandpa also owned a little ice-cream wagon. He peddled his wares from his small vehicle, pulled up and down the city streets by one of his mules. I thought it was a pretty important operation.

We grandchildren always loved being treated to a fancy cone, filled with beautiful, rich goodness, when we came to visit.

Grandpa's business trips originated at a small ice cream store that made the delicious stuff in big cans. He would then transfer the wonderful ice cream to the boxed-in bed on the back of his tiny wagon. He kept it tightly packed in a special kind of ice so it would be just the right consistency to dish up to the patrons along his daily route.

There was a rich chocolate flavor that was the favorite of many boys and girls. The strawberry ice cream contained real strawberries, fresh in season and added at just the right stage, as the delicious goodness was being frozen, in the old fashioned way. Ummm-mm good! But my favorite was plain vanilla—rich, smooth and creamy, and beautiful to behold.

On one particular visit, Grandpa got the idea of giving me a special treat. He suggested I ride along in his funny little wagon, while he delivered ice cream to the city children. He thought I would enjoy watching the boys and girls as they came running from their homes and yards when they heard the catchy tunes coming from his ice cream cart. How they loved that melodious music. And how they loved Mr. Adams' ice cream. In fact, they loved Mr. Adams too, just like he was their own grandpa. [I was almost jealous of their devotion to MY grandpa.]

Well, that hot, sunny morning I stood there watching my grandpa as he was getting ready to take off. I looked at that funny little animal hitched to his ice cream vehicle. It's legs looked so tiny and spindly, I didn't see how it could possibly pull anything. I wondered how it could even stand up.

A lot of questions were racing through my thoughts. I reasoned that Grandpa would have to dish out the ice cream from the back of his little wagon. That meant I might be left sitting there at the mercy of that funny little animal. What if he started to run? Or maybe he would just suddenly collapse.

I suddenly decided I didn't want to go. The threat of potential disaster outweighed the intended pleasure Grandpa had planned for me. I started to cry. Softly at first, then louder when I realized my grandpa wasn't getting the point. Finally, I let out a little girl scream as I insisted, "Grandpa, I don't want to go. I'm afraid of your donkey. Look at his little legs!"

But my dear grandpa was understanding. He picked me up and held me close in his arms.

"Why, you don't have to be afraid," he comforted. "You know I wouldn't let anything hurt you." Of course I knew that, but somehow I had just let my imagination get away from me.

"Come on," he whispered, as he set me on the little seat inside his ice cream wagon. "You can get out and help me serve the children." Then we were on our way, as Grandpa gently urged his donkey on.

Trembling, I sat beside my grandpa. I believed he would take care of me but I didn't exactly enjoy the special treat he had so thoughtfully planned for me.

Grandpa loved to tell about that little incident, especially at family gatherings, but I never thought it was funny.

Portrait Of My Grandma

As I grew older I was allowed to visit my grandparents by myself and sometimes stay a week at a time, as long as no field work was pressing. Those were precious times in my young life.

My Grandma Adams was a tall woman of German, English, Dutch and Norwegian decent. I know, because I remember hearing her repeat it many times, in that order.

Grandma "ruled the roost", as people back then would say. But my grandpa loved her so much he didn't seem to mind. I don't think he even noticed how critical or unfair she was, or how she would cut him down. Although I was young at the time—maybe seven or eight years old—it was quite evident to me. I learned much from observing my grandparent's relationship that I have never forgotten.

Grandpa was the most enduring, tolerant person I have ever known. And the love he expressed for his "Annie" was a living interpretation of 1 Corinthians, Chapter 13.

But my grandma was a wonderful person in many ways and I loved her. She had some outstanding qualities that I appreciated very much. One of the things I remember most about her was that she was an exceptionally good cook. Waiting for supper, when I was visiting them, was a mouth-watering experience.

Porch Swing Talks

While Grandma was preparing the evening meal, Grandpa and I would sit in the swing which hung from the rafters on their front porch, and talk. Grandpa loved those times, and so did I.

On one such memorable evening he related to me how he and Annie had met. They started to the same school together, at the same time.

He often told me about the wonderful times they had playing together at recess. And he loved to emphasize how they had acquired their education together. Maybe that was part of the reason why she acted as though she owned him, and had a right to control him.

Grandpa vividly remembered it all. With a gleam in his eye he told me, "When I first saw Annie, I knew I wanted her for my wife some day." That struck me as being rather unusual. They were both young children at the time.

When he told me that, he chuckled, then tightened his lips and added emphatically, "I never even looked at another girl." Knowing my grandpa as I did, I don't believe he did either.

Grandpa enjoyed telling me about early pioneer days, when that part of the country was dense forest and wilderness, and lots of wild animals roamed around the area.

He told me about the year their twins were born. Grandma was plagued with numerous physical problems, and the babies cried a lot. Sometimes a mountain lion would venture near their cabin and frighten them with bloodcurdling screams that sounded like a woman in distress. They believed the mountain lion was responding to their babies' crying.

They often saw bears. I loved to hear Grandpa tell about these sightings and how he and his daddy would trap them. Many times I've wished I had written down some of those scary, exciting accounts, but I was too young to realize then, how they would so easily be forgotten. Anyway, that might have spoiled the magic of those exciting story times.

Sometimes Grandpa's long talks would have hidden meanings, and a purpose not fully understood by me at the time. Once, I remember so well, he talked about life—leading to a statement I have never forgotten.

"Ardelle," he told me one day, "there's something I want you to always remember." I was listening intently. He went on. "The best thing in this world is a good woman". He had my complete attention. "And the worst thing," he said, looking me straight in the eye, "is a bad woman."

He was serious. I took it to heart. Grandpa's loving concern and wise advice was like a protective light, guiding me through adolescence and young womanhood. I'm sure he was praying to that effect that day, and I know his prayers for me continued as long as he lived.

Usually our porch swing talks would end with Grandma calling, "Supper's ready!" As much as we enjoyed those heart-to-heart talks, we sure looked forward to supper.

Grandpa thought his Annie was the best cook in the whole world. And I loved many of her specialties myself. Her pound cake, for instance, which she made from scratch, of course. By that I mean, she put all the ingredients together herself. There was no such thing as boxed mixes in those days.

I loved those delicious cakes when they were several days old. Often, when Grandma knew I was coming, she would bake my favorite dessert ahead of time, allowing it to "set", just to please me. I will never forget that special thoughtfulness. This was just one of the many delightful things I loved to eat at Grandma's house. She had her own time-proven methods of cooking, that made even plain, ordinary foods taste extraordinary.

A Living Masterpiece

Many of the good things Grandma served on their table were products of their garden and farm. As I recall, Grandpa farmed about one hundred sixty acres adjacent to the city limit. They lived in the country, but homes across the street were in town.

Grandpa grew cotton, corn, and grain—just as we did on our farm out in the country, 12 miles north of town.

I remember his lush fields of corn, growing next to the big trees along the winding stream that meandered across his rich, creek-bottom land. And his cotton fields reminded me so much of ours at home, it always hurt my back just to look at them.

Grandpa recruited townspeople who were eager to make a little extra money, to help him pick his cotton. I used to wonder what it would be like to have a variety of strangers come in to help with the harvest. Not only would it relieve the work load, I thought, but I imagined all the opportunities it would provide for meeting new people. It was something I would daydream about when we were working so hard in our fields at home.

I also remember how hard my dear grandpa worked in his fields. I can see him now, with the sweat rolling down his face, his eyes so irritated from the salty perspiration that he could hardly see. He was fair complexioned and it seemed like all the blood in his body would rush to his head. No doubt the work syndrome we both experienced, and understood, helped to cement the bond between my grandpa and me.

Immediately behind their house, my grandparents grew a wonderful garden. To me, it was a living masterpiece. There were straight rows of cultivated plants, bordered with color-planned flower beds.

There was a wide variety of garden vegetables. String beans grew on perfectly aligned frames which Grandpa had built to Grandma's specifications. They held the wandering vines up to bask in the sunshine and drink in the rain. The huge tomatoes seemed to smile in appreciation of their supportive lattice work.

[The produce from my grandparent's super garden would compare with the finest you would ever see in any supermarket today.]

There were neat rows of English sweet-peas, growing on their somewhat fragile vines. These fascinated me. And I loved the taste of those delightful peas which grew in roundish pods in early spring. They were one of my favorite things that grew in my mother's garden at home too.

I loved to help Grandma Adams pull round, red radishes—and long, slender, pale white ones—from her lovely garden. And tasty green onions, too. Later, the long, feathery, green-topped, golden carrots intrigued me. She would pluck them from the soil, often laughing at some of the grotesque shapes they had grown into. [I don't know if I remember correctly, but it seems to me those fancy carrots tasted better than carrots do today.] Carrots are still one of my favorite foods.

Grandma also grew some vegetables that we didn't have in our garden. I wasn't at all familiar with them. I enjoyed trying dishes she prepared using them, mainly because I loved to explore new things. And Grandma could make anything taste good.

Along the garden fence, climbing, clinging dipper-gourd vines always thrilled me. Sometimes Grandpa and Grandma would give me a couple fancy gourds to take home. I would show off the brightly colored, neatly designed-by-nature treasures to our neighbors. Sometimes I would take them to school to share with classmates. [An early version of show-and-tell, I guess you would say.] My friends at school would gasp with envy as they admired the charming specimens that had grown in my grandma's garden.

On the other side of Grandma and Grandpa's garden fence were asparagus beds. This unique flower-vegetable had green fernlike tops. In Season, the tender, pale green sprouts were delicious to eat.

Stretching from the asparagus beds to the opposite corner of the yard, were patches of phlox, morning glories, four-o'clocks and other varieties of beautiful flowers, all blooming during the different times of the year.

Lovely flowers filled not only my grandma's garden and yard but every area of her home, including the front and back porches.

In the living room, rows of flower pots sat on tier risers. They were situated by the windows toward the south and east, to catch the morning sun. And regularly, Grandma rotated each pot in turn, because—as she explained to me, "the plants keep growing toward the sun."

A Palace In My Estimation

Grandma and Grandpa's house seemed like a mansion to me. My three unmarried aunts still lived there. All of them had graduated from a nearby college, and were qualified to hold good-paying civil service jobs with the government. Sharing the expenses they bought many lovely things for their house—nice furniture, pretty rugs, curtains, bedspreads, bed linens, table cloths and pretty towels. We were so poor we couldn't afford any of these things.

There was one special room which they called the parlor. Nobody was allowed in it. "Parlors are just for the single lady and her 'beau", or her boyfriend," we children were told. They never used theirs because they never had a boyfriend. It seemed like such a waste to me.

I remember one of my aunts let me peek through the door once. Inside was an overstuffed piece of furniture called a davenport, and a big, fat matching chair. For days I dreamed about what it would be like to sit on a chair that was big enough for another person to sit beside you. And I tried to imagine what it would be like to sit on one end and have a soft place to rest your arms.

The floors were made of narrow hardwood planks. [I admired them so much.] In the middle of the room was a large, colorful-looking rug. It appeared to me to be lying there, just daring someone to step on it.

But the most beautiful item in that room was the organ, sitting cateangling across one corner. It was the most interesting piece of furniture I had ever seen. It stood high, and the mirror in the center of the top reflected a small round table with a crocheted covering on it, from across the room. Two small, half-round shelves, carved with intricate designs around the edge were on each side of the organ. My aunts kept a pretty lamp with a beautiful flower painted on it, on one side and some sort of a vase or figurine on the other. A small, round stool, cushioned with material that at least blended with the huge couch and chair, sat in front of the organ. Above the short keyboard on the organ were several round knobs. I was told these were to be used to affect the different sounds that came forth from the organ when you pumped hard with both feet on the pedals in the center of the bottom of the lovely instrument.

When I finally heard someone play the organ, it sounded like magic to me. The varied puffs of sound bouncing against my ears, intrigued and fascinated me. Oh, how I wished I could try to play it myself. But how would I know which keys to press to make the right sound come out? I wondered.

I would lie awake at night, trying to imagine what it would be like to actually play music on that big organ in Grandma's forbidden parlor.

Sometimes I would even wake up wondering how old, or how good, or important, or smart, or whatever you had to be to get into that room and play that majestic organ.

[I'll have to admit, kids, now I know—that old organ was not nearly as tremendous as it seemed to me at the time, in comparison to anything I had ever admired before.]

Magical Posts and Soft Sunbeams

Then there were the bedrooms at Grandma's house. How I admired the fancy wood bedsteads with dressers and chests to match. [They bought them that way, in sets.] We only had old iron bedsteads at home.

The bedroom set I liked most sat in one of my aunt's bedroom. The bed itself had high, round wooden posts on the headboard and at the foot.

"Someday," I would tell myself as I ran my hands over the beautifully finished wood, "someday, I'm going to have a bed with high wooden posts. And all of you know that Grandpa and I spent weeks looking for just the right bedroom furniture. I was determined to finally realize my dream.

I've wondered many times how my mother must have felt when she visited Grandpa and Grandma's house and saw all the pretty things my aunties had furnished their home with. But you know, I think Mama was richer and far better off. She had a husband and children who loved and appreciated her. I always imagined she felt sad not to had the opportunity to finish college like her younger sisters. She had only been able to attend a girl's school and only for one year.

I almost felt guilty enjoying the luxury of the smooth white sheets, pillow cases, and other linens that I admired so much at Grandma's house. We simply could not afford such things.

Mama usually made our sheets and pillow cases from a harsh, tightly woven tan colored material known as unbleached muslin. As hard as she tried to bleach them, they never looked white. Frequent launderings in "hard" water which we had to "break" with some sort of chemical compound didn't help.

And our sheets usually had a seam down the middle. Mama had to sew two widths of muslin together to make the sheets wide enough to use on a double bed, or even on a three-quarter bed. Those were pretty common in those days.

When company came, it was a common practice to put three or four cousins in one bed. I remember nobody wanted to sleep in the middle.

In addition to our regular size bed pillows, we had a couple of long ones which Mama called "bolsters". They were as wide as the bed and required special pillow cases. We had two, and so did Grandma.

I didn't have to be envious when it came to quilts, though. Nobody had prettier quilts than we had at our house. Making quilts was another of my mother's artistic abilities. Because we couldn't afford to buy chenille or satin coverlets like my aunts had for all the beds at Grandma's house, we had to use our lovely quilts for bedspreads.

One of the special things I remember about the bedrooms at Grandma's house, was the soft sunbeams shining through the open windows, and the pretty, dainty curtains blowing in the breeze.

I remember they also had nice cotton mattresses for their beds. When I was small, we had tightly packed straw mattresses, with a feather bed on top. A feather bed was like a huge pillow. It was tightly stuffed with feathers, and it was big enough to cover the whole bed. We made ours from goose feathers which we saved until we had collected enough. We would then stuff them into leakproof feather ticking, which was a heavy, strong, very closely woven cloth.

Mama would sew the seams several times until the ticking was practically air tight. When stuffed tightly with fluffy feathers it made a buoyant, comfortable bed to sleep on. I would almost compare it to sleeping on a water bed today. Of course we had to keep sunning and pounding the feather bed to keep the feathers from knotting down.

Grandma also had feather beds at her house. I usually slept on one when I went to stay overnight. It sort of made me feel at home. Hers were more comfortable though, because they were on top of firm cotton mattresses.

One year when I was maybe seven or eight years old, a man came through our area organizing classes for learning to make cotton mattresses. Most everyone participated, including us. If I remember right, we all got together at the school house. The man showed us how to sew the ticking, and how to put the layers of cotton together inside, and how to "tack" the mattress every so often with a large crooked needle. [The strange looking, curved needle made a big impression on those of us who were looking on and trying to help. But I remember most, the blissful comfort of laying on a real mattress when we got ours home. My parents slept on it, but we all got to try it out before Mama made the bed up.]

The Inside Out-House

Grandma and Grandpa had an outhouse, like we did, but theirs was a lot fancier. It was a complete building all by itself. Ours was just an addition on the back of, and a part of, our chicken house. Theirs had half- moons on the door, and it was snake-proof, and spider-proof. They even had lids, with hinges, on the two seats. Ours only had holes.

Grandpa would spread a white powder—I think it was lime, around the outside as well as inside, as a disinfectant. As I recall, it was required by a city regulation, since it was just across the street from town.

My dear aunts loved to remodel. They were always changing a wall or adding something, even if it was only new steps on the front, or the side porch. In an evident effort to keep up with their friends at church, they determined to really upgrade Grandpa and Grandma's house. This time

I Want You To Know   35

they undertook the biggest project of all. They decided to install an indoor toilet. People referred to these unusual rooms as "bath rooms".

The big undertaking required piping city water across the street, and a lot of work which had to be done by someone whom they had to hire to do the job.

When it was finished, the little room had a strange white seat, with a hinged two-piece cover attached. There was a matching white tank hanging over it on the wall. When you pulled the chain that hung from it, it measured a small amount of water that would wash out the "bowl", as it was called, with a gush, then more water would rush in to replace it. This struck me as being real sanitary.

The little room also contained a funny looking thing called a "bath tub". That's why it was referred to as a bath room I supposed.

I doubt if anyone appreciated the idea of taking a bath in a big tub that drained out one person's bath water, so that the next could have his own fresh, clean bath, more than me. The idea was really neat and exciting, and a relief for any germ-conscience person. It was such an improvement over the way we had to get by at home.

In a way, the funny looking tub was rather scary. It sat on four claw-like feet, almost giving the impression that it could just up and walk away if it was so minded.

The rim of the tub was rolled over and under, making it easy to clean. Taking a bath in that nice, big, long tub—in city water that had been preheated—was quite an experience. It really made you feel clean.

You would let the desired amount of water run into the tub, then after a luxurious bath you would simply pull the plug out by the chain that was attached to the tub, and let the dirty water run out.

As I stood on a soft mat and dried myself with one of my aunt's pretty towels, I wished and wished and wished, as hard as I could, that we could have a room like that in our house. But, for many reasons, there wasn't a chance. We had neither running water nor electricity.

That special bathroom also had a little built in basin, where you could wash your hands, then let the dirty water out through the drain.

Grandpa got a bright idea. He installed a small basin himself, outside by the watering trough, near the gate to the barnyard. He had allowed for a water faucet there when the water piping project was underway. Unless the weather was very cold, he would wash his hands out there before coming inside. The women of the household complained when he got the good towels dirty. [Poor Grandpa, he couldn't seem to win on any score with his women folks.]

The aunts also had the kitchen remodeled and a sink installed. Grandma sure liked that. It was so much easier to prepare meals, and to clean up afterwards. I would watch her enjoying such a luxury and wish ever so hard that Mama could have one of those newfangled kitchen sinks too.

[Of course I knew that too was impossible, but I could dream, and wish couldn't I?]

Honesty And The Corn Crib

I have to tell you about my grandpa and his corn crib.

Each year during harvesting season Grandpa's storage barns overflowed. At the same time, the bounteous supply would begin diminishing—far too fast to be accounted for as far as normal usage went. Grandpa's family, and his friends, tried to point this out to him, and suggested that a good lock on the door would no doubt remedy the problem. But Grandpa refused to believe that anyone would steal his corn.

"Nobody would do that," he insisted, even when little telltale trails of corn kernels, coming from the barn were pointed out to him. Grandpa truly believed that everyone was as honest and as trustworthy as he was.

[You know, if he were living today—in our sick society, where thefts and burglaries are so blatantly prevalent everywhere, I doubt if your great grandpa's faith in mankind would be shaken. I might add, no thieves were ever caught, and Grandpa never put a lock on his corn crib door.]

Country and City Cousins

Sometimes when I visited my grandparents, my cousin Moleva would also come and stay while I was there. Her family lived in town, not too far from where Grandma and Grandpa lived.

Moleva was less than a year older than me. She was born in September and I came into the world the following April. We were the two oldest grandchildren and Grandpa was pretty attached to us.

I remember how he loved to tell us stories about the "old days", and he got a big kick out of watching our eyes gleam with excitement.

Grandpa was a jovial type person, and full of jokes and humor. His young granddaughters loved that about him.

I vividly remember one day when we were visiting with them. Grandpa came home from taking care of some business in town, and told Grandma, very seriously, and in front of us, that a train had just run over him.

Of course Grandma was wise to his teasing. She knew he had just happened to be going under a railroad overpass, as a train was going over it. Moleva and I were starting to get scared, then Grandpa began to laugh and we knew he was joshing.

The next day we were sitting on their front porch when a man stopped and asked directions to some place on down the road. He asked Grandpa, "Where does this road go?" Grandpa got that funny look on his face that always tickled us pink. Then he told the man, "I've been living here for almost twenty years, and it hasn't gone any place."

Grandpa had a serious side too. His true concern for his favorite little girls was always evident. When Moleva and I, at an early age, exhibited an inclination toward good and decent things, he rejoiced inwardly, and his deep pleasure showed on his face. I think it was at those times, that Moleva and I secretly sensed the satisfaction of his appreciation for our sincere interest in the spiritual aspect of life.

Our grandpa was greatly concerned about world conditions in his day, and the prospects of the future, as he watched his grandchildren growing up. He often expressed those concerns when we had long talks, just the three of us. Only our Heavenly Father knows the true result of our grandfather's prayers and concerns for us. No doubt one of the greatest joys my dear grandfather knew in his lifetime, was watching Moleva and me grow up with a sincere personal love for the Lord, and a deep desire to know Him personally, and to serve Him completely. This fulfillment of his dreams and hopes brought him much comfort and pleasure.

Moleva and I thought our grandpa was the greatest man alive, except our own daddy, of course. His strong convictions, and his beliefs and opinions made a strong impression on our young lives. We especially admired his sense of and relativity and application regarding up to date affairs. He was "with it". Life to him had meaning. He didn't just live in a corner and let the world go by. Grandpa kept informed. He observed politics and trends. Moleva and I thought he was the smartest man in the whole world. He seemed to know so much about everything.

One of the reasons Grandpa came across that way to us was probably because he was alert and inquisitive. He always seemed to know the answer to our questions, or where to get the information. And he didn't talk down to us. He treated us like we were real people, not just little unimportant kids. That made us feel pretty special.

His Master's Voice

New inventions intrigued Grandpa. I remember when he bought a music box, called a gramophone, or phonograph. He could hardly wait for his young granddaughters to visit again so he could show off his new acquisition. Naturally, we were overwhelmed with the whole idea.

It was a square piece of furniture that stood up about the height that was easy for my grandparents to lift and lower the lid. They would wind the spring with a little handle, then turn the mechanism that made the disks, or "records" as they called them, revolve round and round.

A strange looking arm with a needle in the end of it, made contact with the black record, causing a scratchy musical sound to come through the cloth covering on the front of the strange piece of furniture.

The brand name, Victrola, was printed under the picture of a dog listening to a voice coming out of a large horn. A caption underneath read, "His Master's Voice".

The strange new instrument was produced by an American company, an affiliate of The Gramophone and Typewriter Company in Europe. It was, of course, one of Mr. Thomas Alva Edison's marvelous inventions.

One of the most beautiful sounds that echo back to me from the memories of those wonderful years, is the instrumental music of a tune called "Over the Waves". I remember the magical world that romantic tune would waft to me an imaginary world of ocean liners and exotic islands.

We had a lot of futuristic fun, listening to the few records that Grandpa and Grandma had for their phonograph. One I well remember, featured a female opera singer. This was a strange, unfamiliar sound to us. We preferred the snappy instrumentals, or the sentimental songs sung by male voices. Or those with a Country-Western flavor.

[I ought to tell you that the quality of the recorded music then was a far cry from what is available today, especially in stereo. The single recordings, as well as the long-play albums that contained several songs which came out later, were called "high fidelity". You would laugh at the sound if you heard it today.]

The Wonderful Invention

Just when everyone seemed to be enjoying the "modern" music machine, suddenly another new invention, also created by Mr. Edison, made its appearance. [He had in fact, invented it, and the electric typewriter in 1920, the year I was born.]

His newest was another music machine, and a talking box, only this one could accomplish even greater feats. I will never forget the tremendous excitement this "latest invention' generated across the country. It was the radio. Naturally our grandpa bought one. He and Grandma felt quite up to date actually owning one of these new gadgets, which everyone was just talking about.

Moleva and I were terribly excited when Grandpa demonstrated the new Zenith radio they had just acquired. Although we were just little girls, he shared its capabilities with us as happily and as eagerly as if we had been adults.

He explained to us what the funny box, with a piece of fancy cloth stretched over the front side, and the little knobs in the center, was supposed to do, the best he understood it. He said it was able to pick up the voice of a person, and carry it long distances through the air. And he explained that the sound would come into the room where we were, that we would be able to pick it up with our ears, just as it was being spoken at that moment. He told us that he himself had picked up a man's voice, right out of the air. In fact, he said, the man was telling people all across the United States, that is those who had one of the radio contraptions, what was happening in our country. Grandpa thought that was fantastic. He was so thrilled, he instilled the excitement of the "new" in us.

We could hardly sleep that night. Grandpa showed us how by turning one of the little knobs, you could choose what you wanted to listen to. That incredible control button really fascinated us. Not only could you choose between different voices as you dialed across the little indicators on the front, sometimes you could even bring in music like we heard when we played the records on Grandpa's phonograph.

I remember the first time Moleva and I stayed overnight with our grandparents after they bought their new radio. We spent hours getting acquainted with the new invention. To our surprise, they actually let us listen to it in the room where we slept.

Early in the evening we heard an exciting song entitled, "Wagon Wheels", on some far away station. It was a song about crossing the prairie in a covered wagon, heading out West. In those days about the most exciting thing anyone had done that they could write or tell about was traveling in this way to the new frontier. This song was about that experience. The melody was bouncy and bumpy, giving the impression of wagon wheels bouncing along.

My cousin Moleva and I thought that song was really "far out", as you would say today. Oh, how we longed to hear someone sing that song again. We kept trying for hours to find a station with some voice singing the same words again. Sure enough, about four a.m. the next morning we actually heard that wonderful song once more. It was an unbelievable thrill to us. By that time we were so excited and keyed up we couldn't get to sleep at all. We didn't sleep a wink that night.

We always looked forward to experimenting with that intriguing instrument when we went to visit our grandparents. And we really became quite proficient at playing the radio. Oh, how we two little girls loved that radio-box. Little did I dream that I myself would one day actually be very involved with this fascinating phenomenon.

A Traumatic Experience

[Yes, I often went to see my grandparents when I was your age, and I have many fond memories of those special times. I also recollect some experiences that were not so pleasant. One in particular, happened the summer I was eight, when my cousin Moleva and I were visiting them.]

We always enjoyed playing on the school grounds at Northside School, which was just across the street from Grandpa and Grandma's house.

During one visit we discovered several new pieces of playground equipment which had been installed since the previous time we were there.

It was exciting to explore some really modern innovations, such as the new, so-called "crooked slide".

Unlike the old slide which we could climb up and slide down with ease and safety, the new one was designed to take you around and around, as well as down. It was meant to provide a thrill and a sense of adventure.

My cousin Moleva, was much braver than I was. She quickly attacked the new high-flying swings, and of course the crooked slide.

"Come on Ardelle," she yelled as she ascended the steps to the top, "this ought to be a lot of fun."

It looked interesting as I watched my cousin, and some other children who were there along with us, as they came "chute-ing" down the odd-shaped slide, with their hair flying in the air. They always seemed to come down so gracefully, and land on their feet, in the hard "cinders" at the foot of the new slide.

I hated to be considered a "fraidy cat", and to be laughed at, but I simply could not get up enough nerve to try the new slide innovation.

Finally, when I could see that Moleva was becoming impatient with me, I decided to take a chance on it.

I slowly climbed up the and estimated the situation carefully, as I looked down that really crooked slide.

At last, when some children climbed up behind me and urged me on, mainly so I would get out of their way, I took the plunge.

To my surprise, I came down just like the other children did, landing upright on my feet. It wasn't so difficult after all. In fact I liked the exhilarating feeling. I decided to get in line and participate, along with Moleva and the other children who were having so much fun.

Each time I climbed up and slid down the popular slide I did so with less fear and more enjoyment.

Then suddenly, as I came breathlessly down once more, I failed to land on my feet. Instead, I fell in an awkward sprawling position. I was in so much pain I feared I had broken my back.

The other children all stood around looking terribly frightened. Moleva ran to find Grandpa and tell him I had been hurt. As fate would have it, just as she found him, my parents drove up.

Soon, all of them were bending over me, trying to determine how badly I had been injured. Daddy and Grandpa lifted me carefully into our wagon and took me to a doctor's office down the street. When the doctor realized he had an emergency on his hands he dropped everything and examined me.

Fortunately, it was determined that my back was not broken, but my injuries were such that I was in a great deal of pain as we drove the 12 mile trip home, riding in our old wagon with steel rim tires.

It was during that long, agonizing ride that Daddy came up with the idea of putting automobile wheels—with rubber tires, on our wagon so that riding would be easier for me, and more comfortable for the whole family.

It was several weeks before I was able to walk or do much around the house. I don't think I ever completely recovered from the effects of that back injury.

My dear cousin always felt bad that she had urged me to get on that crooked slide. I didn't blame anyone but myself however, for the accident that had a profound effect on my life from that time forward.

* * *   * * *   * * *

"You can see, I have some wonderful memories of visiting my grandparents. I think that's all the time we have for remembering today, but we can do it again if you'd like. There are many more things I would like for you to know about."

CHAPTER 4

The Little Homemaker

"I don't like to wash dishes, Grandma," Lynelle admitted, "but I'll help you anyway. You don't make me do them all the time like Mommy does at home."

"When you grow up and have your own home, you'll have to do dishes," I told her, "or hire someone to do them for you."

"Did you have to help your mother a lot when you were my age?" nine year old Lynelle wanted to know.

"Well," I said, as we finished scrubbing the pots and pans, "let me tell you about that."

"I'd love that Grandma," she responded with a smile. "Can we sit in the dining room and have some of your fresh squeezed lemonade while we talk, please?"

*** *** ***

Keeping Real House

It's almost unbelievable how much work an eight or nine year old girl can do in the fields on the farm, especially when she has already had several years of experience.

Almost as far back as I can remember I worked during the planting, cultivating and harvesting season—right along with my daddy, and my brothers, and my sisters when they were old enough to help. However, after I injured my back while playing on the crooked slide at Northside School while visiting my grandparents, I could no longer thin corn or chop cotton. And certainly not pick cotton. [That menial chore was hard enough for a child who was healthy and strong.]

It was at this point that my folks decided that I could at least look after the younger children who were too young to work, or to take into the fields, as Mama had sometimes been forced to do during the rush season. And I could do the cooking and seeing after the house, they thought. Perhaps the cleaning too.

Mothering the small ones was a natural for me. In time, the baby could not distinguish between her "second mother" and the real thing. I couldn't help noticing how this troubled Mama.

By the time I was eleven or twelve I must have changed upwards of a million diapers. You could say I was "experienced".

I accepted my grown-up assignments with adult responsibility. My parents trusted me implicitly, with the little ones, and with the house.

Early on, I had already exhibited grown up trustworthiness. They didn't have to "prove" me to determine if I could be depended upon. Mama often said she trusted the children with me as much as when she was looking after them herself. And more than once I overheard her tell a friend or a relative that I had a "mother hen" instinct.

As a "fill-in" mother, and keeper of the house, my hours were consumed with as many chores as a nine-year-old could possibly handle, especially one with a weak back.

There were the never-ending chores of changing diapers, doing dishes, and cooking. I really picked up on the homemaking art however, and quickly learned how to cook in quantity for a large, hard-working family.

It was with a great sense of relief that my overburdened mother could come in after a hard day of intense labor, and sit down with Daddy and my brothers and sisters to a completely prepared and efficiently served evening meal. And when Daddy would compliment me on my cooking or housekeeping, my spirit literally took wings. I felt like a princess. It was reward enough for all my work and tedious managing.

After supper, Daddy and my brothers would take care of the barnyard chores, except for milking the cows. Mama always did that, no matter how tired she was.

My little sisters got to gather the eggs that the hens had laid that day. They also carried arm-loads of wood from the woodpile outside, and stacked it in the box behind the kitchen range.

It was my job to wash the dinner dishes and clear the kitchen. This monumental task rested heavily on my shoulders.

[I know you think its pretty tough, Lynelle, helping with dishes for four at your house. But can you imagine what it was like for Grandma at your age? You have a sink, and a portable dishwasher. We didn't even have running water, much less a sink.]

We all had to work very hard at a young age. When it was bedtime we were tired and ready to fall asleep. Seldom did anyone beg to stay up a little longer.

Un-Modern Inconveniences

We were so back-woodsy and poor that we didn't have plumbing of any kind. In the kitchen, we had a makeshift shelf near the door to the back porch, where a large galvanized water bucket with a long-handled dipper that hooked over one side, sat beside a small wash pan. This was where we washed our hands through the day and where Daddy and the boys washed up before meals. (Women and girls usually had clean hands from helping in the kitchen.) We dried our hands on a towel, my mother had made from harsh, rough feed sacks.

Nearby, in front of a south window, was another shelf, a little wider, where two round aluminum dishpans sat. One was used for washing the dishes, and one for rinsing them. In between dishwashing chores, they were hung on nails on the wall nearby.

When we washed dishes, some water had to be heated to add to the cold water. When we used well water for doing the dishes, a little water softener was added to "break" the water.

We would wash the dishes in one pan, filled with hot sudsy water, and rinse them in the other pan which contained clean hot water—at least it was clean when we started. We had to dry the dishes right away because there was no sink or any place to drain them. [Can you imagine that?] Washing dishes in those days was a difficult chore.

A large cream separator sat in one corner of our kitchen. It was used only when we had more milk than we could use for drinking or making butter. At such times we would separate the cream from the whole milk, and exchange it for staples such as flour, sugar, salt, baking powder and baking soda, at the country store in the village. We bought vanilla flavoring and spices from the Raleigh man who came around regularly, like the Avon lady does today. We also had to buy handsoap, bluing and starch.

We hated to have to use the cream separator because it was hard to clean, and everything that had to do with milk had to be kept very clean, so that bacteria wouldn't grow and cause it to spoil.

Another chore that fell to me was the responsibility of seeing that the children were kept clean and bathed. Naturally, since we had no plumbing, we didn't have a bathroom. We didn't even have a regular outhouse. Our privy was actually an extension on the end of our chicken house. It WAS a "two-holer", but beyond that there wasn't anything positive you could say about it.

Our outhouse was situated a distance from the house, which was a necessity during the summer months. In the wintertime it seemed even farther away. At night we used a white porcelain "slop-jar", with a close fitting lid, and a handle for carrying it. It sat under the side of one of the beds. The following morning someone had to carry it to the outhouse and empty it.

There was an old joke that the expired Sears Roebuck catalogue ended up as toilet tissue. At our house it was a stark reality. That was just another one of those things about the "good old days" that was not so good.

[You know, Lynelle, if I were to make two lists, one of the good and one of the not-so-good, I would have to keep them far apart, so that the good wouldn't be swallowed up by the bad aspects of those days.

Now, you're wondering how we took a bath?]

As you've already guessed, we had no bathtub, so we used the largest galvanized laundry tub we had for bathing. In winter, it sat in the kitchen, and in the summer on our enclosed back porch. We had to heat water on the wood-burning kitchen range. This also insured a warmer atmosphere in winter.

Two or three children would be bathed in the same water, one right after the other. It seemed terribly unsanitary to me. [What do you think?] No wonder the Saturday night bath was considered enough in those days. This didn't satisfy my mother, however. I bathed the children in my care almost every day. And the field workers certainly had to have a bath more often than once a week.

Blue Monday

There was one heavy-duty job that I was simply not up to doing all by myself, following my back injury. Mama had to allow time out from working in the fields to help me with the laundry.

Washing clothes in those days was some operation. We had never heard of, or even dreamed about, a machine that could wash clothes. Even if we had, there was no running water or electricity to operate an appliance.

Monday was wash day at our house. It was not a day we looked forward to. I certainly can understand how the term "blue Monday" originated. No wonder my mother always washed on the same day, and only once a week. It would have been a crime to ruin more than one day with that horrible long drawn-out chore.

As you can imagine, the accumulation of soiled garments for a large family, including the dirty work clothes, bed linens, and towels, loomed high like a formidable mountain. You can understand, I'm sure, that this would have been too much for a nine-year-old to tackle alone. But I did as much of it as I could.

We always tried to begin washday chores as early as possible, when our strength was at its peak.

In the wintertime, we first had to draw water from a deep well, and then carry it in large buckets to fill the oblong boiler which we used to heat water on the kitchen range.

While the water was heating we would sort the dirty clothes by color and by degree of soil. Then we would set up three large laundry tubs on a low table, along one wall in the kitchen. We would then carry enough water to fill two tubs for rinsing, and enough to partially fill another tub for soaking and scrubbing the dirty laundry. Hot water from the boiler would be added to this tub.

When we had scrubbed each piece as clean as possible, it would be transferred to the boiler on the range, where the clothes would be allowed to "simmer" boil, while we were scrubbing the next batch.

From time to time we would stir the simmering load of laundry with a stick that looked bleached from stirring clothes in hot, soapy water through numerous launderings.

While one batch of laundry was slowly boiling, we would be scrubbing the next load on an old-fashioned scrub-board that sat on two legs, against the side of the initial soaking and scrubbing tub. Using one of these crude gadgets was really hard work.

I Want You To Know

Not only was washday hard on the back, it was terribly rough on your hands. We had to use a soft bar of homemade lye soap.

[You have never seen such caustic soap. Nor can you imagine the effect it had on your hands and the clothes you were washing. I think I appreciate good laundry soap more than most people today, Lynelle.]

After the items were boiled for the prescribed length of time, we would lift them from the boiler by twisting them around a bleached stick, and squeezing them against the side of the boiler to remove as much of the hot, soapy water as possible, to save it for the next batch of clothes. Then we would deposit the squeezed batch in the first rinse water.

Mama was very particular about getting the soap completely rinsed out so that the clothes wouldn't be dingy. And she didn't want our clothing to be uncomfortable or to cause skin irritation.

The last tub of water that we rinsed our clothes in contained a bluing element which was intended to help make the white clothes looks whiter and the colored ones brighter. I remember "bluing" balls—they were the size of marbles, which we had to dissolve. Mama would use bluing and a little bleach too, to insure a white wash.

It took a long time to do the weekly laundry. Each piece had to be scrubbed, wrung out with both hands, boiled for a time, then rinsed in clear water, followed by the last rinse which included the "bluing" process. [I always suspected this was another reason why Monday was labeled "blue".]

Finally, the pieces that needed to be starched were subjected to still another dunking and squeezing. We used to cook our starch, I remember. Later, a new and improved variety that you simply added to cold water came along. This saved a little time, and every little bit helped.

By the time we were able to get all the clothes hung on the heavy wire clothesline in the yard, Mama and I would be completely exhausted.

[I don't think you can identify with the terrible weariness we felt, Lynelle.]

Mama took great pride in the way the laundry was hung for anyone to see. She also got a certain thrill out of it herself. Even as a child I marveled at the beautiful laundry she was able to hang out, despite such adverse circumstances. As I look back now, I marvel even more.

She insisted, as she taught me, that all the sheets should be hung together, all the diapers hung in a row, matching socks together and so on, with all the laundry neatly grouped. Maybe they would have dried just as well hung haphazardly, but Mama would never have stood for that. To her, white and brightly colored clothes blowing in the breeze, catching and reflecting the full impact of the sun, were a picture of art, a picture which she (or we) had created. It was like a reward for hours of grueling work.

Even in rainy or cold weather, we had to hang clothes outside to dry. When the temperatures were quite cold, each piece would freeze while we were attempting to get it pinned to the clothesline. (We used square, wooden clothespins that resembled tiny wooden dolls with no arms.)

Sometimes while struggling to get the clothes fastened, our hands would stick to the wire clothesline. It was painful and often tore the flesh.

Because of Mama's meticulous laundry habits, our clothes not only looked better, but they lasted longer than most people's we knew. I think you could honestly say that they were "sparkling" clean.

Doing the laundry was one of those constant chores that was never done with. At times it seemed like the family actually enjoyed getting things dirty, with little concern for our continuous backbreaking effort.

Summer Laundry

In the summertime the laundry was something else again. We would heat the water for washing the clothes in a huge three-legged iron teepee with no covering.

Water still had to be drawn from our deep well, though it didn't have to be carried as far or up steps. If we had plenty of rain during the previous winter months, we would draw water from our cistern in our enclosed back porch. We loved that. The water was soft and did not have to be broken. And the wash looked cleaner and brighter.

[What is a cistern? Our's was a sunken cement reservoir. Rainwater was caught in pipes at the edge of the roof, and funnelled into the cistern where it was stored. Our cistern was round, and five or six feet across. Some people had water storage reservoirs the size of a small bedroom. We did well to catch enough water to fill our small one.]

We appreciated rain water for bathing and shampooing, and for cleaning, as well as the laundry. We were very grateful for the alternate water supply, but it was always far too inadequate.

We also drank the water from our cistern unless the supply was low. When it seemed like we were drinking dregs, we probably were. I'm not sure it was clean or healthy at any time—that was always a concern to me.

On a summer wash day, when we had filled the iron kettle we would start a wood fire underneath it to heat the water. Then we would fill the galvanized tubs just as we did in the wintertime, only now they were on a low table outside our house. The strong odor of lye from the homemade soap we had to use was more tolerable when we were able to do our laundry outside—it was overwhelming when we had to be confined to the kitchen.

For many years, Mama made all of our soap, once a year at hog-killing time, from the scraps left over after making chitterlings and lard. The soft bars were a grayish-tan color. She would cut the finished product into blocks, the right size to hold in our hand while scrubbing the laundry on the corrugated wash board, and some smaller blocks to use for doing the dishes. Later, a similar but firmer soap called Fels Naptha could be bought at the village store in our community. When I was a little girl, most of our laundry had to be ironed. Some people in those days would iron almost everything, except maybe socks. They would even iron underwear.

[In this age of "wash and wear", I know it's hard for you to visualize what it was like then.]

Some of us today seldom set up an ironing board. And some people don't even own one. We have learned to remove clothes from the electric dryer immediately. Personally, I don't feel any guilt at all about deserting my ironing board. I think I have paid enough tribute to it in my lifetime already. I consider it a great blessing to be able to use my time and strength in better ways.

Although I had to have help with Monday's laundry, the ironing chore was a different story. As bad as my back was, it was just not possible for Mama to take another day off from work in the field to help with the ironing, especially during the rush seasons. I can remember ironing for hours at a time while looking after little ones around my feet or just outside in the yard. And while watching dinner boiling away in a pot on the back side of the stove, where the irons were being heated.

While we ironed more of the wash than some people we knew, we didn't iron underwear. But Mama insisted the sheets had to be ironed. And the pillow cases had to starched and ironed. Of course the table cloths and dresser scarves had to be starched too, as well as most of the shirts and dresses. They were easier to iron that way, Mama said, and they soiled less easily, and lasted longer she insisted.

When the items to be starched were dry and taken down from the clothesline, they were immediately dampened by sprinkling them with water from a bottle with a perforated aluminum cap on a cork. Then, each piece was folded tightly into a laundry basket, and covered with a heavy towel so that the moisture would be evenly distributed.

Ironing for several hours at a time, with two or three "sad irons" (and I know why they were called that), was an extremely tiring chore, especially with the large amount of laundry that seven children and two parents produced.

When I was very young, we did our ironing with three heavy, solid irons, each with its own handle. In later years we acquired three or four sad irons, with one handle which we switched from iron to iron. These too, were heated on top of the kitchen range, or sometimes on the pot-belly stove in the living room, in the wintertime. In cold weather this was a good arrangement, but in the summertime ironing was a hot, difficult job. The whole operation was not only tiring but very time-consuming. Washing and ironing each required most of a hard day's work, and just about all the strength a person could muster.

[You can be thankful, Lynelle, that times have changed in that respect. And you should be grateful that today sad irons are mostly seen only in museums.]

You would think that under such difficult circumstances, we would have been satisfied to iron, and especially starch, fewer pieces. But, as I say, Mama was very particular about the laundry.

I learned early in life to appreciate the feel of clean, freshly ironed sheets, and starched, ironed and creased pillowcases. One of my most precious memories is of the sense of cleanliness my mother instilled in us. Despite the hardships involved in the laundry chores, she always saw to it that we slept between clean sheets, and wore clean and neatly ironed clothing. I do however, remember a few times when one or both of us would not be feeling well; she would take down the sheets from the line and put them right on the beds. As she would put it, by way of excuse, "with all of the sunshine locked in". And there were times when we didn't have enough sheets to change the bed and wait for them to be ironed. In the cold wintertime we sometimes resorted to using blanket sheets.

I well remember the year a new invention came to our rescue. At the time, it seemed to us a great step forward. I'm referring to a simple gadget called pants stretchers. Instead of hanging men's and boys trousers, we would insert these ingenious metal frames into the wet pants legs, stretch them tightly, and let them dry. When the gadget was released and removed, the pants were smooth enough to wear without ironing. At first my mother insisted the top part be "touched up" with an iron, but in time she got to the place where she was satisfied to let Daddy and my brothers wear their work clothes, at least, without ironing.

My Mother, the Seamstress

During the busy years of helping with all kinds of chores, when I held the reins of the household (age nine to nineteen), I learned many things about homemaking and caring for children. My training was good preparation for managing and maintaining my own home in later years.

I learned to cook, wash, iron, clean and to be responsible for small children. I also learned to sew. Mama was a seamstress, and an articulate one. As her family increased in number she had less and less time to sew for other people. During the "off" crop season, she did manage to sew a little for hire. This was a great help to us financially. Sometimes she was given material in exchange for her services.

At a young age I was anxious to sew like my mother. I watched carefully as she drafted her own patterns. I don't think she ever owned a store-bought pattern. I was intrigued as I watched her cut the fabric, then sew the seams on our old treadle sewing machine.

As soon as I could reach the pedal on the sewing machine, I learned to sew while standing up. I would stand on one foot and pedal with the other.

Mama let me learn to sew for myself and my sisters. That was a big thrill. I tried hard to do my best, to earn the praise of my mother.

Mama loved to crochet. She created many beautiful items, including bed spreads and tablecloths. I admired her skill and learned to crochet myself, but she discouraged me from becoming overly involved or "addicted" to it, as she often told me she felt she herself had done. She believed too much tedious, close work had affected her eyesight. She had worn glasses since she was nine years old and was convinced that she had not been careful enough about eyestrain.

My greatest pleasure was doing fancy work and embroidery. I learned to do it as a child, and as I grew older the handicraft that resulted from my hobby reflected my hopes and dreams. Numerous items went into my "hope chest". These were a great blessing to your grandpa and me, in our first home. Later, I combined my artistic talents with lace and ribbons. My little boy babies wore dresses much too pretty to be wished on a male child. (I had three boy babies before I had a girl.) I hasten to tell you, however, in those days all babies wore dresses; boys as well as girls.

I never learned to actually draft patterns the way Mama did, but I did inherit her ability to look at a picture in a catalogue or a garment in a store window, and turn out a reasonable facsimile.

Mama not only taught me to sew on the sewing machine and to crochet and do fancy embroidery, she also taught me how to make quilts.

Most of the covers we used on our beds were homemade quilts, or comforters, which we sometimes created from garments that couldn't be worn anymore. I can remember using such things as the lower leg part of old jeans, when the seat and knees were worn beyond repair. Sometimes we would use pieces of material left over from sewing. We kept all the scraps from all the garments we made. Or we would order a bundle of "remnants" out of the mail-order catalogue to use for making quilts and comforters.

Those scrap bundles we received from a mail order company were like magic to us—they were real surprise packages. We had a lot of fun opening them, wondering what they might contain. At times there would be remnants of cloth large enough to make a dress for my baby sister or a shirt for my youngest brother.

We would usually sew the blocks for our quilts or comforters on the sewing machine. After they were sewn together we attached the comforters to a back with a layer of cotton batting in between. Then we would "tack" them evenly with heavy colored thread, pulled through the front, filling, and backing, then tied and clipped on the top. Usually we would embroider a briar stitch over each seam to make it look nice and last longer too.

Sometimes, instead of using new cotton batting we would use an old worn quilt, freshly washed, especially if we were using a top made from the best parts of old garments.

Making new quilts was more tedious and time consuming. When we had pieced a new top and connected the blocks, we would combine the top and lining with new batting in between put them into quilting frames and quilt them.

Sewing through all the thicknesses was accomplished more easily by having the quilt-in-progress attached to wooden frames which Daddy had made for my mother when they were first married. In this way, the sides of the quilt could be rolled under, enabling us to sit comfortably in chairs on each side and reach under the quilt with one hand while sewing with the other. It was quite a trick.

While it was a challenge, and rather difficult for a nine year old to reach and sew through, I took great pride in learning how to do it like Mama and Grandma. It was almost a mark of growing up and becoming a woman, to actually assist in making quilts.

I remember how hard I tried to learn to make tiny stitches like Mama and Grandma did. At first the needle would prick my fingers and make them sore; sometimes they would bleed. That's when I learned to use a thimble. [I still use a thimble today for any kind of hand sewing. I think I'll always use one. I can't understand how some people sew without this protection.]

When we had finished a quilt or a bright colored comforter in the frames, we would fold the lining over the edge to finish it off. What a thrill and what a feeling of accomplishment when we had completed a lovely quilt. They were really beautiful, and oh, so warm and comfortable. And I can remember how nice they felt to the touch; I loved those wonderful creations.

We had heirloom quilt patterns that were kept in the family and some we shared with others. From time to time Mama would come up with her own ideas. She was truly an artist when it came to sewing.

A couple of the special patterns I remember were the double wedding ring, and the necktie, both of which truly resembles the real thing. One time I recall, I got carried away and designed my own version of a little Dutch boy and a little Dutch girl. I drew them and created my own applique design—the little boy with overalls and a hat, the little girl a dress and bonnet.

Quilt making was THE thing in those days. There were no electric blankets, at least not where we lived, and there was no electricity to operate them. The winters were cold, and we needed the quilts to keep us warm. You might say we made quilts out of necessity, but we really enjoyed making them. They were rich rewards for having created something beautiful.

Women in those days learned to make necessary chores pleasurable. Somehow, this helped them to retain their sanity.

[Lynelle, I wish you, and all of my granddaughters, could experience the thrills of artistic quilt making.]

The Friendship Quilt

I will never forget one special quilt I helped to make. It was called a friendship quilt. Actually, I helped make more than one over the years. But the most memorable was for one particular pastor's wife.

The Anderson family had lived among us for about three years. Reverend Anderson was the minister of our Pleasant Hill church. It was a policy of that particular denomination, at least in those days, to send a pastor to a church, and just about the time he got settled and seemed to be making some progress, to send him somewhere else. Those dear people moved around like the families of military personnel.

We grew to love the Anderson's. They were precious to us. Their children were about the same age as my brothers and sisters and me. We had many wonderful times together. They often came to visit us and we were invited to their home frequently. Then one day, Pastor Anderson announced that he was being sent to another circuit.

When they learned they had been "called" to another parish, they were sad to have to leave. They broke the news to us as gently as possible. A dark cloud-like shadow crept over both our families. We all loved each other. There were many tears. I clearly remember the pain. From the day we knew they were going to be taken from us, we cherished every moment that we got to spend together.

The ladies of the church decided to make a friendship quilt for Mrs. Anderson. Every woman who wanted to participate was given a square block of plain muslin, each the same size, and instructed to design her own sentiments. It was to be an expression of our love and our feelings on parting with dear friends—something special to remember us by.

Mama tearfully took a block and I wanted one too. I don't remember what design I came up with. I think it was a poem I wrote especially for her. I do remember that my contribution was tear-stained. I think they all were.

When everyone had finished their square, they all came to our house to finish the quilt. With sad hearts, we quietly sewed the sentimental blocks together with a colored strip in between each one to set them apart. Each block was a separate work of art. It was a beautiful quilt top. We then put the pretty top with its pastel colored lining and the batting in between in the frame and unitedly quilted it.

My mother could quilt more neatly than anyone I knew, but some of the other ladies ran her a close second. Everyone did their best work on this special quilt. I had never tried harder to make tiny stitches.

On a Sunday morning, in front of the whole church, the ladies presented the lovely quilt to Mrs. Anderson. Each block revealed the name of the one who had created it, the date, and a special message of love. I'll never forget that day. There wasn't a person who could hold back their tears. I'm sure Mrs. Anderson treasured that friendship quilt for many years.

The day we said good-bye to our friends was a sad day for all of us. We knew we would probably never see each other again. Parting is always so painful. We got little solace from the fact that a new minister, along with his family would be arriving soon. We were sure they would never take the place of the Anderson's in our hearts. I think subconsciously at least, we were all determined to never allow ourselves to become so attached to a pastor's family again.

Some Work - Some Play

Of course we had many other friends who weren't so mobile. Our nearest neighbors had a son and a daughter close to our ages with whom we spent many happy hours playing.

As hard as we all had to work, there were times of release. My brothers and sisters and I were allowed to get together with our friends and play. I think our parents realized the importance of being able to enjoy friendships, as well as having some time set aside for leisure. We worked together; we played together. This helped to give us a balanced perspective on life. And no doubt seeing things through the eyes of our peers made a difference.

I may have been beyond my years when it came to assuming responsibility, but I was still a child at heart. And its a proven fact—too much work and not enough play CAN make one dull, and I might add, unhappy.

Our neighbors on the other side of us had no children. They provided us with a different slant on life. Our association with them taught us about some realities—first hand. We often felt they resented having Mr. Chappell's big family as next door neighbors. I think they visualized us trespassing and perhaps damaging their prized property and possessions. However, they needn't have worried about that.

We lived twelve miles from the nearest town. Today, that isn't very far. The world has shrunk and distance is viewed differently now, with so many modern means of rapid transportation.

From time to time it was necessary for us to go into the city for supplies. The way we had to travel it was an all-day event. When there was no field work pressing, Daddy would suggest the whole family go and make it a day of diversion and rest. Of course we kids got all excited and thought that was a super idea. Mama would plan a special lunch to carry along. We always looked forward to her surprises.

We would get up early and rush through the chores. It was easy to get up early on those special days, and we didn't have to be called a second time.

Our only means of transportation was our rickety old wagon. Before my accident on the crooked slide, our wagon had wooden wheels, with outer steel rims. It was rough riding, even on the smoothest roads, especially for us kids. We usually had to sit on an old comforter on the floor of the wagon or on a wooden box turned upside down. And there were times when Daddy would be in a good mood and let us ride with the tailgate down, our feet dangling out the back of the wagon. It seemed daring to us but of course Daddy never went fast enough for it to be dangerous.

Mama and Daddy would ride in the "spring seat", which had a built-in back and springs underneath to help break the shock of the rough riding. If one of us could convince them that we were not feeling well we would get to ride in the middle between them. We considered that a real treat, worth being labeled "sort of sick". It certainly was a lot more comfortable. The springs were designed to absorb some of the jolt when we encountered rough places in the road. There were lots of those between our house and town.

After my accident, Daddy was concerned about the pain I suffered when riding in the wagon, even in the spring seat. Since we couldn't afford an automobile, Daddy decided to convert the wheels on our wagon so that instead of steel rims he could use rubber tires, like those on a car. It seemed rather ingenious to me, and I appreciated my daddy's thoughtful consideration.

The twelve-mile trip to the city took us up, over, and around the hills, down through the valley, and often detoured us around especially rough places, occasionally a washed out bridge. We took it all in stride.

There was the ever-present Bailey Hill, which I always dreaded, and was relieved when we got over. And there were places with deep ruts in the road and several narrow bridges.

Usually, we made one "pit stop", about half way to our destination, and another at the same place on our way home. We consequently labeled the wooded area where we made these routine stops, Pit Hill.

We enjoyed the sights and scenery along the way. It was exciting to see an occasional house and to observe how other people lived. We also noted how other farmers were progressing with planting, cultivating or harvesting their crops.

We all enjoyed those trips to the city. I can still see the restful smile on Daddy's face as he drove his happy, relaxing family along that country road. I'm sure that's why he seemed to love to take us all along. There were times however, when for one reason or another, we couldn't all go along on those necessary trips.

I remember when Daddy went alone, or maybe took one or two of us kids along, he liked to eat in a family-style restaurant he had discovered in town. As far as I know, that was one of the few personal extravagancies he ever indulged in. I remember very vividly, the times he took me with him to the restaurant. Being extremely germ-conscious, like my mother, I never felt sure the dishes and utensils were clean, nor that the food had been prepared under sanitary conditions. Daddy would become very aggravated with me. [I still feel the same way today about eating out.]

When Daddy couldn't take us all with him on those trips to town, he would always bring home a bag of candy corn, orange slices, or jelly beans. Naturally we would wait anxiously for his return. Of course we missed him when he was gone all day, but we also wanted to see what he had brought us from town that day. That always helped to relieve the disappointment that we didn't get to go.

I had to become a young woman very quickly, as far as responsibility was concerned, but I didn't outgrow the need to be a child. I'm thankful life afforded me those opportunities, as meager as they may have been.

* * *   * * *   * * *

"Lynelle, I think that gives you an idea of what I had to do to help out at home when I was your age. You have it pretty easy don't you? And you have so many more times of fun and recreation, too. I hope you appreciate them.

There are a lot of other things I want to tell you another time. Right now, we'd better get supper ready before Grandpa gets home."

CHAPTER 5

Times of Trauma

"Kathye, please don't cry," Marissa comforted. "It's going to be all right. The doctor says Tina will live, and you didn't even have to be admitted to the hospital."

Kathye and her friend Tina had been involved in a tragic automobile accident. Tina had been seriously injured. Kathye had escaped with a broken leg and some shoulder and back pain, but the trauma of the experience had caused her to relive the almost fatal incident over and over again. Every time she mentioned Tina, she would burst into tears.

"You have to be brave so you can help Tina get well again," Marissa told Kathye. "Isn't that right, Grandma?"

I agreed, she should try to be brave for Tina's sake. It was evident, she would try harder for her friend's sake, than for her own.

Kathye's cousin Barry was watching her intently. He was obviously trying to imagine what it would be like to have something terrible happen to himself. He turned to me and asked, "Grandma, were you ever really frightened?"

"Oh yes, many times." I told him.

"Would you tell us about some of them?" Kathye begged, expressing sincere interest. Wiping her eyes, she sat up, waiting expectantly.

* * *   * * *   * * *

Traumatic Times

You've heard me say before that I have always had an inborn fear which I attributed to an incident when my mother was terribly traumatized before I was born. It might seem to you that I had an unnatural fear or an overly sensitive reaction to things that went on around me.

Yes, you might say that such things as my fear of Bailey's Hill, of riding in an automobile for the first time, of eating in restaurants that might have germs, or seeing an airplane for the first time was ridiculous. But then, the world has changed a great deal. Airplanes and automobiles were always commonplace in the world you were born into. They were just there, like the things around you in your home—radios, televisions, and other modern appliances and gadgets.

The Country Bum

When I was your age, life was a bit frightening for me, and attempting to survive seemed a challenge. Ordinary daily living could be hazardous in those days. There were times of real concern. I remember so well the hidden fear I detected in my parents' eyes, when a "bum" who was passing through would knock on our back door and ask for something to eat and permission to sleep overnight in our barn. It was even scarier if Daddy was not home.

None of us ever slept too well when we knew a stranger who hadn't impressed us as being overly responsible was in our barn. We feared he might carelessly set the barn on fire or maybe attempt to rob us. Our greatest concern was for the welfare of family members.

Usually the suspicious character would already be gone when we got up the next morning. Daddy would always check to see if anything was missing. Occasionally, a saddle, a tool, or something of lesser value would be gone but most of the time everything would be intact.

It was always a scary experience. Even so, we never locked a door. Actually, I don't think any one of them even had locks.

[Do you think you would have been scared, Barry? I'm sure Kathye and Marissa would have been. And I think you would have reacted like my brothers did. They stayed mighty close to Daddy and Mama. We all did. I honestly believe God protected us in a special way in those days.]

The "Railroad Bum" In the City

While visiting my cousin Moleva in the city, I learned that there was such a thing as a city bum too. I thought they were even more frightening.

Aunt Bertha's family lived near the main network of railroad tracks in town. Real authentic tramps, bumming their way across the country on freight trains, frequently knocked at their back door. It would scare me terribly. My cousin Moleva and I would peek around Aunt Bertha's full gathered skirt to see what the poor creature looked like. He would always be filthy dirty, as if he had never taken a bath in his life. When Moleva asked her mother what was inside the man's dirty old bandana tied to a stick which he carried over his shoulder, Aunt Bertha would shake her head sadly and say, "Probably all the possessions the poor ole fella owns in this world."

Moleva and I had great sympathy for these poor old down-and-out men, but we wondered why they didn't work for their keep, like our daddy's did.

Aunt Bertha, with her big heart, never turned one of them away. She always managed to find some food to share with them. It didn't seem to scare her too much to have these bums come to the door. It happened so often she was used to being asked for a handout.

The Chicken Thief

Another scary incident comes to mind. It happened on a Sunday evening when I was nine years old. My mother was ill and couldn't go to church. Daddy took my two oldest brothers with him and left me home to be with Mama and to look after the younger children.

I was terribly afraid that night. No matter what happened, Mama would be too sick to get out of bed. I tried to be brave for her sake and she tried to convince me that everything was going to be all right. Suddenly we heard an awful ruckus in the chicken house. The chickens were usually quiet as they roosted at night. We knew something was disturbing them. It was some kind of animal—a fox, a weasel, or possibly, a person.

Frozen with fear, I blew out the lamp and tiptoed across the dark kitchen to peek out the window. A three-quarter moon was shining outside, making it light enough so that I could see a bent-over figure clutching some chickens as he passed by the window. It was a chicken thief! I was so scared I could hardly breathe.

Stealing chickens was a common practice in that part of the country. This time, it was happening to us. Someone who knew that Daddy was not home, and they probably knew that Mama was sick in bed. They would be sure the women folks would be too frightened to try to catch them. I knew they wouldn't fear being shot at, which is what most men did when something bothered their chickens.

It seemed like hours before Daddy finally got home. The little ones were asleep. I sat by Mama's bedside, too scared to even whisper. I could tell that she was pretty upset.

We later learned the culprit was a young man Daddy had hired as an extra hand, during haying season. When he had seen Daddy in church without Mama, he had seized the opportunity to raid our chicken house. There were other times when our chickens were stolen, usually when the whole family was gone at night.

The Devastating Plague

The plague of locusts was another unsettling experience. I remember it striking more than once. People would shake their heads as they reminded each other that the locusts could be expected at about the same time every seven years, for seven consecutive years. The inevitability always added to the concern, as the damage of each bout with the destructive insect was estimated.

The dreaded grasshopper-like creatures would swarm through the fields, yards and trees, leaving everything bare behind them. As the time of their arrival approached, everyone was noticeably nervous. After the first year they hit, those pesky locusts were as predictable as the swallows to San Juan Capistrano. Their appearance was catastrophic for parents, and upsetting for their children.

The Dust Storm

I also remember the time a dust storm enveloped our area. We had heard frightening accounts of the terrible clouds of powdery, grainy dust that rolled across the "plains" states. Then one day we found ourselves experiencing our own dust storm.

The first thing we noticed was the strange brown color of the sky. The sun, attempting to shine through the dirty atmosphere, cast a weird, rose-orange color on everything.

As always, when something unusual happened, there were those who would suggest that the world was coming to an end. [They even said that about the plague of locusts.] I'm not sure where they got the idea, unless it was from something someone read in the Bible. Anyway, the mere suggestion aroused fear in everyone's heart. And the concern of the adults was amplified as it was transmitted to and reflected by the young.

It certainly was overwhelming, I remember, to watch the approaching cloud of dust, whipped up by the wind as it crossed the sun-parched fields. The gritty debris in it's path was obviously being sucked into it's bulk.

We stood by helplessly as the threatening dust cloud enveloped our house. The thick brownish-red dirt penetrated everything, forcing its way through and around every poorly caulked window pane and each ill-fitted door. It was shockingly apparent in every room. There was dirt in the closets, the dresser drawers, and the kitchen cupboards. It was in our food, and quite visible in our drinking water. To our dismay, we discovered it was even in our beds, which had been made up before the dust storm hit.

Our neighbors, who were not home at the time, happened to have laundry on the clothesline. The sheets and diapers were so dingy from the dust they were never white again, even with several bleachings. Everything outside and inside our homes was affected. There had been no escaping it. We heard about some people with respiratory problems who had to fight for breath.

When we saw the terrible dust cloud headed our way, we tried to cover the windows to keep the stuff out but it was no use. The obnoxious dirt came in anyway, as we stood helplessly by. You could write your name in the thick layer of dust that settled on our dining table, and every other surface in our house. It seemed like we battled the dust for weeks.

The Great Northern Lights

I vividly remember the year we experienced another dramatic occurrence in our area. It happened so long ago I can't remember the time of year or the day of the week, but the incident itself I will never forget.

The spectacular display of folded streaks of varied colors, arched high across the sky, was the most unusual sight our family had ever seen. Authorities said it was very unusual for our location on the globe. I doubt if one person in our community had ever seen anything like what we saw that day.

While we practically held our breath from fear and excitement, my parents explained to us that it was a display of the Great Northern Lights, the Aurora Borealis that we had studied about in school. They were enthralled that we should be seeing it in the deep South. I could tell they were unnerved, but they tried to quiet our fears as they reminded us that the unusual display of color was believed to be the sun's reflection at an angle from the ice in the northern hemisphere.

Mama actually seemed to be more thrilled and excited than fearful. She reminded our family that because of her Norwegian ancestry, she was named after the heroine of a book entitled "Thelma", and subtitled "Land of the Midnight Sun". I couldn't wait to read the book, when she finally found it in an old trunk. It was a beautiful story about romance in a brilliant far-north setting. I learned more about the Aurora Borealis while reading that book than I ever did in school.

I'm sure I'll never know why that tremendous once-in-a-lifetime, heavenly show was splashed across our southern sky that day. I always felt it was a special performance to emphasize and call attention to someone I considered to be the most important person in the world—my mother, Thelma.

[Barry, Kathye and Marissa, if you ever have the good fortune of getting to see the Aurora Borealis, I hope you remember the tiny bit of Norwegian in you, and instead of being afraid, think of your great-grandmother, and her beautiful name, Thelma.]

When It Was Dark At Mid-Day

Another unnerving experience happened one day when I was at school. With loving concern, our teacher gathered us around her. She knew a total eclipse of the sun was expected and she tried to prepare us by explaining as best she could what was going to take place. But it was still frightening for all of us, including the teacher. As it grew darker and darker in the early afternoon, we all became more and more uneasy. Most of us probably wished we were at home with our parents. I know I did. I'm sure our folks were thinking about us too, and wishing the same thing. My mother knew how fearful I was about everything, and how I always clung to her when I was afraid.

I'm sure none of us students nor our teachers ever forgot that day. Every time I hear of an eclipse today it comes back to me so vividly.

The Graves and the Quake

The hill where our school building was situated was stark and foreboding, The view from the front entrance looked out over a deep canyon and beyond to an expanse of flat-lands, stretching out to a forest in the far distance.

In the opposite direction, looking from a back window, you could see our house. We didn't live very far, but because we had to go around fields and other people's property, it seemed further. To the left, all you could see was the forest on our property and adjoining forested areas.

Just across the road from the school, to the right of the canyon, was the community cemetery. The graveyard itself was scary to us children.

At the nearby church, they often sang songs about the resurrection and about graves being opened up. I remembered hearing ministers say the Bible predicted a great earthquake after which certain people would come forth out of their graves. I most certainly didn't have the picture in true context but I had bits and pieces of information which my wild imagination distorted.

One day we had a real earthquake, which was another unusual occurrence in our area. It was terribly upsetting and many were certain that this truly meant the end of the world.

[You know children, I've often wondered if God in His tender mercy, wasn't trying to speak to people, to warn them to turn from their wicked ways. Many people in that area were far from God and couldn't have cared less about the Bible and it's teachings.]

In our community were many people who had sold their livestock, farm equipment, household goods, sometimes even their property and migrated to California, only to return shortly, broke, disheartened, and full of tales of earthquakes on the West coast. These were usually over emphasized and used as an excuse for their return. These disgruntled families would spread their misgivings and frustrations among neighbors and relatives. It was not long until everyone had developed a horrible fear of earthquakes.

After all the talk about earthquakes in California, it was no wonder we were so shaken by the quake that hit our community that day. Years later, I actually moved to California, from an area in Hawaii where up to three or more quakes were felt almost every day. I wondered why people were so upset.

[Kathye, Marissa and Barry, you are not that scared of earthquakes because you were born in California and you have not yet experienced a severe quake.]

Electrical Spectaculars

While earthquakes were seldom felt in the South, one thing we did frequently experience, and with great severity, were electrical storms. I'm sure they would have scared some native Californians terribly if they had been suddenly caught in one for the first time.

When I was growing up, people were so used to electrical storms, I don't think they ever thought of them as being God's attempt to get their attention. Nor did they interpret the fiery display as heralding the end of the world, as they did most other frightening occurrences. Maybe it was because they had survived so many of them and knew they would be subjected to many more in their lifetime.

It's difficult to describe the fierce, potential power and danger of an electrical storm in the South to someone who has rarely even heard thunder.

When it thundered during an electrical storm, the earth trembled. And we trembled too. The flash lightning was constant, and as the storm progressed, the high-powered forked lightning would streak across the sky in quick, wild escapades, followed by loud claps of roaring thunder.

As children, we were told you could measure how near the lightning danger was by how close it was followed by loud thunder. We would try to judge the severity of the flashes, while attempting to hide in a safe place. We would bury our faces in Mama's skirt or if we were in bed pull the covers up over our head. One afternoon, while we were still in school, a wild spring storm struck with intense fury. We huddled around Miss Serena, our teacher. The storm may not have been any more severe than usual for that time of year, but that day we were not near our parents where we usually sought solace, so it seemed more threatening. Miss Serena was young and obviously frightened herself. I remember my concern for her and for my fellow class mates tempered my own feelings of fear.

On numerous occasions, while we were working with Daddy in the fields, heavy, dark clouds would erupt into a fearful electrical storm. It would give us a feeling of helplessness as we were caught between the earth and a boisterous sky. It was not uncommon to hear of a field worker being struck by lightning while chopping corn or cotton with a metal hoe. We had been told that metal would attract lightning. It was no wonder we were filled with fear when caught in the field during an electrical storm. When a lightning storm was imminent, we would beg Daddy to let us go to the house.

The Terrible Tornado

The electrical storms were worse in the springtime, and tornado warnings would go into effect. Everyone feared the terrible cyclones that ripped through various communities every year, leaving destruction and often death in their paths.

Many strange and frightening stories of killer tornadoes circulated among friends, neighbors and relatives.

"Did you hear about Lizzie Johnson's son and his family in Plainview?" a neighbor asked my dad as they sat on our front porch one evening.

"A tornado wiped them out. Yep," he said, "house, barn, everything. The only thing left standing was part of their fireplace chimney." He shook his head sadly, looking down at his shoes.

"Worst thing, though," he added, "his wife and two of his kids were killed. Another child and Johnson himself wuz hurt purty bad."

I was sitting nearby, taking in every word. That kind of story always tore me apart inside. I tried to imagine what it would be like to have such a terrible thing happen to your family. Those things can sure do a lot of damage, I thought to myself as I listened to Daddy and Mr. Ed talking.

We had been very fortunate—none had ever touched down in our immediate area.

Hearing that conversation that evening, started me thinking about storms. I laid awake that night, remembering some of the stories I had heard. I just couldn't get them out of my thoughts.

Then it happened. On April 10th, a few days before my eleventh birthday, one of the feared twisters hit our quiet community. It was an experience far beyond my wildest imaginations and previous fears.

My two brothers and I were bedridden with severe cases of measles. I can remember that day as clearly as if it had happened yesterday.

In the early afternoon, we noticed the distant sound of thunder. As the afternoon wore on, the thunder increased in frequency and volume. I could tell Mama was uneasy, even though she tried to hide her concern from us. She kept pacing back and forth to a kitchen window to check the storm's progress.

The sky was steadily growing darker. Finally, after I kept begging, Mama let me get out of bed and go into the kitchen and watch the approaching storm with her. I could see it was going to be bad. The funnel-shaped outline of the cloud, which was what Mama was worried about, grew more ominous by the hour.

By four o'clock, it was getting so dark outside it was like nighttime. The atmosphere was heavy. Lightning flashed continuously, more and more violently, followed closely by loud thunder which seemed to engulf us. We were relieved when Daddy finally came in from doing the chores which he had to do by himself since we were all sick.

By this time the lightning was flashing in the windows, uncomfortably close. For some reason, I don't remember why, Daddy started to shave. A couple of times the lightning's reflection skipped along the edge of his long-bladed straight razor, as he stood shaving. Mama begged him to put his razor dawn and get away from the window. The lightning was extremely close and there was a lot of static in the air. I could never understand how Daddy kept from being electrocuted that day.

Suddenly, the tornado hit! The wind was blowing terribly hard. We could hear the deafening sounds of destruction outside. I remember wondering why we weren't being tossed around more inside.

As sick as we were, we children scrambled together against the panes of the window near our bed, trying to see outside. Daddy and Mama were close by, peeking over our heads. Mama clutched our baby sister closely. When the torrential rain finally let up a little, we could see clearly outside. In the constant lightning, it was almost as light as day. We could see trees being uprooted and practically sucked and twisted from the ground. Our neighbor's barn and corral was being torn apart and we could see pieces flying through the air. We watched our milking shed across the road go over on its side then lay down flat.

Another neighbor's two-story home was being twisted and moved on its foundation. We saw two people twirling in the air along with farm machinery, a cow and a calf, some chickens, an old junked wagon, and a conglomeration of debris.

We learned later that it was the man's wife and their daughter that we had seen and amazingly, neither of the women were killed. The daughter, however, was affected mentally and was never the same again. Their house remained standing but it was badly damaged.

As we watched that awful scene from our window we could see the huge whirlwind as it moved quickly towards our large, old two-story school. It skirted around the nearby church, and as we watched in dismay it spun, full strength, right into our school. We practically held our breath as the building completely disintegrated. Not one wall was left standing.

It was sickening to see the school building we all loved being ripped and torn into small pieces by the big wind and scattered flatly across the hillside. We were grieved and frightened—it would have made us sick if we had been well.

The Pleasant Hill church, a well-built old structure, stood about five hundred yards from our school. We could see it being buffeted but it was still standing. We later found that the large building had been lifted up in the twirling wind, and set down again at a different angle. This large old country church still stands today, a monument to the miracle of survival, not only from that raging storm, but through many years of withstanding all kinds of weather.

The Loredo church, located about one and a half miles from the Pleasant Hill church, was also spared, although it too suffered considerable damage. We helplessly looked on in amazement as all the destruction was taking place—then it suddenly stopped. Everything became deathly quiet in the early night air. We were told later that all the devastation had happened in just a few minutes. It had seemed much longer.

Daddy opened the front door and we all looked out upon a ghastly scene. An almost visible hush seemed to whisper, "Quiet! Reverence, please!" We were acutely aware of the mercy of God on our behalf.

It was surprising to find that the worst damage to our house was on one side of the roof, where a large, partially uprooted cottonwood tree had fallen across it. A couple of windows were broken and some small limbs were laying on the floor of my bedroom which was at the opposite end of the house from where we were watching the storm. It was hard to believe that we had completely escaped the fury of the storm. We never doubted that we had been miraculously spared.

We learned the next morning that several people had been killed in the terrible tornado including one entire family. A short distance down the road where the twister had dipped, three members of another family had also died in the cyclone. There were no radios, televisions, or even telephones in our community, but the news spread rapidly.

As is always the case following a tornado, some strange things were reported after the twister passed through. My girl friend Evelyn's family happened to live in the path of the storm. Evelyn herself was not at home when the storm hit. The next morning her elderly parents were found crouched in the corner of the only two walls of their home that were left standing. They had certainly experienced the mercy of God.

When the roads were cleared of fallen trees and other debris and we puny kids were feeling better, Daddy loaded us into our wagon and we toured the damaged areas. We had already heard numerous stories about some of the freak effects of the tornado, such as chickens being plucked of all their feathers, cisterns being sucked dry and objects such as straws and two-by-fours being driven through posts or trees. Some areas, right in the middle of total destruction, were completely untouched. Viewing these strange things gave us a weird feeling.

In many places the roads were impassable for weeks after the storm, but people continued to come from miles around to view the massive destruction.

The Storm Cellar

The fierce tornado affected everyone in our community. A certain fear clutched people's hearts and most of them started at once to build storm cellars. We were among them.

Across the road, in front of our house, was an ideal spot just waiting to be converted into our very own safety retreat. A hill had been cut down when the road had been constructed several years before and Daddy simply dug into the side that was straight up and down, and cut out an area about the size of a small bedroom. He set some strong wood posts at the corners, put a door at the front, and a sturdy frame at the top of the interior so it wouldn't cave in on us.

Our new "safety cellar" resembled the shape of a half-buried football, partially visible above ground. The door lifted to open, and steps descended down into the earth-room. Daddy filled in the side of the hill with the dirt he had removed so there would be no places to catch the wind during a storm.

[In driving through the state of Idaho today, you will find potato storage rooms that look a lot like our old storm cellar in the South. Grandpa and I saw them there a few years ago.]

Daddy cut a shelflike bench around the walls of our new storm-proof room so that we would have a place to sit when we had to flee to its safety. Later he built shelves on the walls too. This was where Mama stored our canned fruit and vegetables. They kept well for long periods of time in the dark cellar.

The damp earth was smelly, I remember. I dreaded going down into the underground room, for fear of all the creepy, crawling creatures that made their home there. They were almost more threatening to me than a raging storm outside. I even hated to be sent to the cellar to get a jar of canned fruit or vegetables.

We only went into the cellar when a storm was really bad, sometimes in the daytime, but usually in the middle of the night. I can still hear Daddy's anxious words, when he would awaken us to the sound of thunder and the flashing of lightning.

"Wake up," he would whisper softly, as if he didn't want the storm to be aware of where we were, or where we were going to be. "We're going to the storm cellar. It looks like this is going to be a bad one."

We were instantly awake and ready to evacuate. My parents insisted we take every precaution possible. But as far as I know, there has never been another killer tornado that followed along the same path.

The Spirit Of Conviction

The trauma of that terrible tornado had lasting effects on my life.

Throughout the spring and summer of that year, the gnawing fear that another bad storm might hit us, haunted me day and night. I tried to tell myself that it was highly unlikely that another cyclone would strike in the same place, especially that soon. The more I dwelt on that possibility, or imagined some other catastrophe that might become a reality, the more miserable I became. I got to the place where I would beg my folks to take us to the storm cellar, a place that, in spite of the worms and bugs, represented at least a degree of safety, even when a storm was not really that threatening.

All the turmoil inside me caused me to do some serious thinking. I was struggling constantly, trying to resolve the internal conflicts. I knew without a doubt that God had spared our family during that awful storm. But the haunting thought kept pounding away in the deep recesses of my mind—if He spared us, and took others, He must have had a purpose. Maybe God was trying to say something to my family or to me. If that was true, what would the consequences be if we failed to listen? Many similar questions kept bombarding me.

I was becoming increasingly aware of the uncertainly of life at its best. On the other hand, I was trying to reassure myself and calm my fears by believing that all was well, that there was nothing to be concerned about. But the more I tried to put the whole thing out of my mind, the more uneasy I became. The more I tried not to think about it, the more I could think of nothing else.

In my desperation, my thoughts continued to turn more and more to God. All that I knew about Him, all that I had ever heard or learned about him, crowded to the forefront of my mind and demanded a rehearing and a reviewing.

I became increasingly aware of my unresolved spiritual relationship with God. The Holy Spirit was definitely seeking my attention. I was only eleven at the time. Because of the lack of spiritual training, I was not aware of what was happening to me.

One thing I was sure of—if I had been killed in that awful tornado, or if Jesus should come again as I had been told He was going to do, I was not prepared to meet Him face to face. This thought was extremely unsettling. The reality of my lost condition enveloped me. I could find no peace. Hell was very real and frightening to me.

Bible verses that my godly school teacher had taught me kept coming to mind. Verses like, ". . . except ye repent, ye shall all likewise perish." Luke 13:3.

That verse shot painful darts of fear through my heart. I knew it included me. When I read the reference again I noticed that this warning of Jesus was repeated again in verse 5 of the same chapter. But repent? I wasn't exactly sure what that meant but I knew it had to do with my attitude toward my lost condition, and my response to God's divine provision for my redemption.

Miss Elsie, my teacher who had true spiritual concern for her students, had read to us in class at school, a verse from the book of Romans that says, "There is none righteous, no, not one." Romans 3:10, and another, verse 23 of the same chapter: "For all have sinned, and come short of the glory of God." I remembered this one so clearly—I certainly knew I was not good enough to please God.

In my troubled state of mind, I sought answers in my old, neglected Bible. The faded pages were ragged; it was cheaply bound, with an imitation leather cover. But I knew it contained the direction I so desperately needed.

As I cautiously held that old Bible as if afraid of what it might say, it fell open to the book of John. I flipped the pages to chapter 3, since I vaguely remembered Miss Elsie calling my attention to that portion of Scripture. Sure enough, some of the verses were underlined. John, in the New Testament.

["Barry, hand me my Bible from the table there. I want to make sure I remember the references correctly."]

I know Miss Elsie must have thought the third chapter of John was pretty important; she'd had me mark so many verses.

That afternoon I read the entire chapter, then went back and carefully examined each verse.

With a fearful heart I read in verse 3, *"Except a man be born again, he cannot see the kingdom of God."*

I wasn't sure what being "born again" meant, but I hoped the rest of the chapter would explain it.

I remembered that Miss Elsie had pointed out the last verse in the third chapter of John, which says, *"He that believeth on the Son hath everlasting life and he that believeth not on the Son shall not see life but the wrath of God abideth on him."*

With trembling hands I noticed that verse, as well as verse 18, divided everyone into two categories. The repeated emphasis was unsettling for me as a young girl searching for the truth from the Bible.

I was glad to have some time alone with no work pressing, so that I could study these verses on my own. I tried hard to pray but I didn't know how.

Then I was surprised to see right there in the third chapter of John, that a man named Nicodemus whom Jesus was speaking to, didn't seem to understand about being born again either. That encouraged me. Surely God would forgive my ignorance, especially since I was really trying to understand.

Taking heart I read the chapter again, trying to determine how Jesus would explain these things to Nicodemus.

In verse 16 I discovered hope. It read, *"For God so loved the world, that he gave his only begotten Son, that whosoever believeth in him should not perish, but have everlasting life."*

Now I saw it! God had provided a way through the gift of His Son, so that I wouldn't have to perish because of my sinfulness. But how could I get across that awful gap—from one category to the other?

"If only Miss Elsie was here now," I kept saying to myself as I walked up and down in my room. "She could answer my questions."

So many concepts that she had tried to get across to me, now seemed important as I faced them in crisis. I was a sinner, lost and without hope. But God loved me and had provided a Savior.

As I continued to read the chapter, two words stood out. "Believe," and "receive". I knew I believed the Scriptures, and I wanted to receive Jesus, even if I didn't know how.

I wanted to discuss the matter with my parents but we never discussed religion at home and I didn't know how to bring the subject up. It was easy to talk about the weather, the neighbors, how many eggs the chickens were laying; we even talked about the preacher occasionally, but never about God.

That Sunday when I went to church I desperately hoped the minister would notice I was distressed and try to help me. Nothing he said gave me any more understanding and he didn't seem to even notice I was there. I went home with a heavier heart than ever.

This was a struggle I would just have to get through all by myself. I was so disturbed I lost my appetite and I couldn't sleep at night. My mother finally asked if I was sick. I admitted I was. When she wanted to know where I hurt, I told her I was "just sick, that's all." And I was, the worst kind of sick you can be.

Late in the afternoon the following day I took my Bible and went for a walk in the orchard. I was soon distracted by the spectacular display of cloud formations overhead. [If I close my eyes I can still see them vividly.] They resembled shocks of golden grain against a pale blue and soft pink sky above the old fruit trees nearby and the more distant cedars and oaks.

The heavenly scene reminded me of harvest time and a song we often sang at church entitled, "Bringing in the Sheaves".

As I stood there in awe, I felt like I was standing in the edge of heaven. I envisioned Jesus being just beyond those beautiful clouds. Surely He was showing me that He was harvesting souls. I wanted so much to get over, onto the other side where He was.

At that moment I became even more aware of my sinfulness. I had never committed a crime but I felt as guilty as if I had. I sat down under a tree and opened my Bible with a pleading gesture. It fell open to the book of Romans, chapter 10. My eyes looked down upon verse 13. As I read the words I felt sure God was directing them to me.

[Let me read them to you.] *"For whosoever shall call upon the name of the Lord shall be saved".*

That was it! I saw why Miss Elsie, had pointed out that verse to me years before when she had lived with us. She told me I could put my name in place of the word "whosoever" and read it that way.

I clutched my old Bible to my breast and hurried to the house because I knew Mama would be wondering where I was.

As she passed me on her way to milk the cows, she called back, "don't forget to watch the little ones."

They were playing in the yard so I hurried to my room, my heart throbbing with the sudden realization that I could call on God and ask Him to save me.

I fell on my knees beside my bed and talked to the Lord, just like I'm talking to you now. I told Him, "I don't understand the Bible that well, Lord, but I know I'm not prepared to die. If you should call me right now, I know I would be lost forever." I shuddered in His presence, at that thought.

I wept as I remembered afresh the terrible death Jesus had suffered in my place. Then I looked heavenward and pleaded, "Heavenly Father, will you please forgive me, because Jesus died for me?" No one was ever more sincere. God knew it. He accepted me, just as I was.

There are no words to adequately describe the relief I felt. Peace flooded my whole being at that moment. The terrible burden was lifted.

I was free. I felt so light I could have floated through the air. I didn't know what was happening to me at the time, but I know now—I was experiencing the new birth that Jesus told Nicodemus was absolutely necessary.

That night, for the first time in weeks, I slept peacefully, knowing all was well between me and God. I was a brand new person. The old "me" was just a bad memory.

The next morning I awoke in a new world. The sky was a heavenly blue. The air was pure and clean. The flowers seemed to be nodding in rhythm in the gentle breeze. And food never tasted so good.

A mockingbird in the huge old cedar tree in our front yard was singing a celestial melody. I suspected it was echoing the song they were singing in heaven, as they rejoiced over another sinner come home. [There is actually a verse in the Bible that tells about that: Luke 15:7. Look it up and read it for yourself.]

That was the first day of real life for your grandma. The experience was so real that I have never forgotten nor doubted it. That day was the beginning of my eternal life which will never end. When I leave this world, I expect to be with Jesus, my Savior, forever and ever in heaven. It will be worth all the difficulties leading up to that day.

All of you know that my greatest desire and prayer is that all of my children, my grandchildren and my great-grandchildren, will make that same decision, and join me there.

Death in the Family

I think I ought to tell you, becoming a Christian doesn't guarantee smooth sailing ahead. Any person who is attempting to follow Christ will agree. The Bible doesn't promise that. It does however, assure us that the Holy Spirit will be with us, to comfort, guide, teach and assist us.

And I believe the Bible teaches that God's grace is sufficient to see us through trying times. Such experiences are inevitable, but if we are living close to the Lord He will enable us to withstand the storms of life.

In my early years as a Christian, I was just a hard-working, yet naive child. I didn't even realize how important reading and studying the Bible is to spiritual growth. I was severely tossed about in my flimsy little boat, on the stormy sea of life, not fully aware of what was happening. There were times of intense testing—indeed, times when I despaired of life itself.

[You see, Kathye, I understand what it's like to go through trying times when you are a young person.]

I well remember, a few summers later, when my dear brother who was less than two years younger than me died. We were very close and I simply could not understand; one day he was there, the next day he was gone— forever. I will never forget that hot day in July, the tenth to be exact. Daddy and my brothers Charles, and C.N., left early to attend a church outing. It was the annual Sunday School picnic held at a popular river resort. I was ill at the time so Mama and I and the younger children stayed home.

I remember it seemed like a very long, tedious day with such a big part of our family away. When Daddy and my brothers hadn't returned by early evening as expected, we became uneasy.

It was almost dark when one of the men from the church came back to break the news to us. My brother Charles, who had just turned fifteen, had drowned in the cold river. The diver Daddy employed to find and recover my brother's body from the river told us that Charles, who was an excellent swimmer, probably had gotten cramps in the cold water, and was no doubt sucked into the swift undercurrent.

[Kathye, Marissa and Barry, I don't think you can imagine how traumatic that was for me.]

My only previous association with death had been when a neighbor's tiny baby had died. I was not prepared for such a painful experience. I certainly couldn't understand why God would let it happen.

Charles had been a handsome, intelligent, and likable boy. Everyone in the community knew and loved him. Daddy had high hopes for Charles. Some people even accused him of being partial to his eldest son. Whether that was true, I couldn't judge. I do know that Daddy was deeply saddened by the death of his beloved son.

I was so broken by the loss I sincerely prayed, "Lord, why Charles? Why didn't you take me instead?" I felt Charles had been cheated, having his life cut so short. At that point, I couldn't see that I had any future. I didn't know how to trust God, for myself or for anyone else. I now know that He doesn't make mistakes, even though at times it seems that way. I've since learned to trust His wisdom.

The next morning a hearse brought my brother's body to our home where, as was the custom, it was on display until the day of the funeral. The casket was set up in one corner of my bedroom because there was more room for it there than anywhere else in our crowded house.

When I saw how they had laid out my precious brother, and made him look like he was just asleep, I cried and cried until my sick body was ready to collapse. It just didn't seem possible that Charles was gone and we would never be able to talk to him again.

Family, friends and neighbors came and went. Someone was always there to sit with us, all day and each night, until my brother's body was moved to the Pleasant Hill church for the funeral.

The entire community and people from miles around came for the service. I had never seen so many people in the church. All the seats were taken and people were standing around the walls and in the doorways.

As was the custom at a southern funeral, the entire congregation sang songs which our family had chosen—songs about heaven, and the next life. They sang, "How beautiful heaven must be," and I thought about Charles being there, enjoying the beauty, making it even more beautiful by his presence. I never doubted he was there.

My thoughts went back to the time when my cousin Moleva would visit us. We would hold our own church services in an improvised arbor in the side yard by our house. We would sing songs and read the Bible and talk about what it meant to be a Christian. We wanted to make sure all of us knew the Lord personally. I was sure. Moleva said she was sure also. We carefully explained God's plan of salvation to Charles. When we were sure he understood what the Bible said and he had indicated that he wanted to know Jesus like we did, we all got down on our knees and prayed.

Charles asked God to forgive his sins for Jesus' sake and to save him. I distinctly remember how serious Charles was. There was little opportunity to accept Christ in the church services we attended. I believe this was God's way of giving my dear brother a chance to prepare for the day He knew was coming so soon, and His way of answering our prayers for him at that time.

When they sang, *"O, Think Of The Home Over There"*, *"The Sweet By And By"*, and *"Nearer My God To Thee"*, I believed every word of those songs.

The minister described Charles and talked about how good and how kind he was, and how much everybody loved him.

I Want You To Know

It was easy for me to think of him as being with the Lord, but only because I truly believed he had accepted Jesus as his personal Savior.

I knew my brother Charles was a good boy, and as I look back now, he seemed destined for heaven.

The Scriptures plainly state that a person gains eternal life only by having the right relationship with God, through accepting Jesus as their Savior. That transaction has to take place before death, and it is between that person and the Lord personally; no one can wish it for someone else, or do it for them. No matter how good a person may have been, or how well liked, those things will never save them.

With a soft, reverent voice, the minister reminded everyone present about the brevity of life and how no one can be sure of even the next breath, no matter what their age. He pointed out that there are short graves as well as long ones in every cemetery. He emphasized the need for each one present to prepare for that time when they too would be called to meet the Lord because, as he put it, "we will all go sometime, and we don't know who will be next."

Our hearts were torn with grief as we watched the box containing the casket that held our precious loved one, lowered into the grave, and dirt being poured in on top of it. The beautiful floral arrangements given by relatives and friends in their attempt to comfort us in our bereavement, helped us to know that others cared.

As they gently led us away from his grave, all we could think about was how much we were going to miss this absent member of our family. There was going to be a big, empty space. He had occupied such a special place in our hearts and home.

I think Daddy took it the hardest. He experienced a period of deep grief that lasted for weeks. He had been especially close to Charles. In this time of bereavement and soul-searching, Daddy's thoughts kept going back to certain incidents when God seemed to be trying to get his attention.

When Charles was a small boy he wanted to be with Daddy constantly. I remember one day a sudden snow storm left a couple of feet of snow on the ground. Daddy hugged Charles tightly and told him to wait on the porch while he hurried to do the chores. About halfway to the barn Daddy turned to wave at Charles and saw his little boy trying to follow him. He was attempting to walk in the big tracks Daddy had made in the snow. Daddy walked back, took Charles in his arms and wept openly. Daddy knew he was not worthy of such devotion and it touched him deeply. At that time he made a sincere effort to get back to the Lord, but as so many times before, his commitment didn't last.

Now, Daddy was trying to work through his grief. He was certain God was punishing him and that he was responsible for Charles death. In brokenness he bared his deep feeling to us.

"Since God couldn't get my attention any other way, he took that which was closest to my heart," he concluded, trying hard not to be resentful.

We were all concerned about Daddy, but in time he agreed that God was more qualified to know what was best for all of us, including Charles.

It was difficult for each of us to adjust to the loss of our precious family member. Mama and I would sometimes set a place at the table for him without thinking. She would find herself looking around for Charles, and wondering for a minute where he was. We inevitably allowed for his presence in things the family planned. For a long time it seemed he was just away and would soon be home.

[I'm glad neither of you have had to experience death in your family yet. Knowing what it's like could help you face such a crisis.]

The Big Deception

From the time I was a very young child I remember Christmas being a special time of the year. I have many precious memories of that season that will be remembered fondly as long as I live.

You wouldn't expect anything bad to happen at a time when everyone is supposed to be happy, but one of the most traumatic experiences of my life was also associated with Christmas.

One of the things I liked best about the Christmas season was the special foods we enjoyed. My mother would start baking the week before Christmas. She always made three or four large layered cakes, of different kinds. One of my favorites, and one we always knew we could look forward to, she called her "candy cake". She would bake three or four layers of her unusually good yellow cake from scratch and without a recipe. Then Mama would tie hard Christmas candies in a strong piece of muslin cloth and hammer them into a multicolored powder. This she added to her own special "seven minute" frosting.

She would spread the icing generously between the layers and lavishly finish off the top and sides. It was beautiful and almost too pretty to cut into, but we could hardly wait to sink our teeth into it, it was so delightfully delicious to eat.

And there was always a nice big layered white cake filled with thick coconut frosting. After finishing off the top and sides with the snowy frosting, she would sprinkle on as much of the remaining coconut shreds as would cling to it. It looked like a small mountain of snow, covered with coconut. Oh, how I loved those cakes!

Daddy loved her rich, dark, moist chocolate cake, so she always baked one of those too, as well as a spice cake and numerous kinds of pie.

I couldn't help noticing how much Mama loved to make desserts that pleased Daddy.

Mama would always bake a ham which we had cured ourselves earlier in the fall. And she would cook a large pot of navy or pinto beans, or maybe split pea lentils with ham hocks. Daddy would insist we eat something, as he put it, "to counteract all those excessive sweets".

At certain times during the week of our feasting from Christmas Eve through New Years's Day, Mama would bake sweet potatoes and yams.

She would bake them whole, scrubbed clean and brushed with butter because we all loved the skin when they were baked. Served hot from the oven, with still more rich, homemade butter on them, they were a treat indeed.

During the second week in December people in our area began thinking about Christmas trees. I always dreaded that part of the holiday season.

Daddy would take us kids and drive out into our forest and cut down one of our beautiful pine trees, bring it back to the house, trim the limbs off, put it on a stand, and then set it up in our crowded living room.

Even as a child, I disliked everything about this procedure. It was painful for me to watch a lovely, healthy tree, growing straight and stately in the forest, being cut down and dragged into an unnatural setting. [I guess that's where my concern for threatened trees began.]

I remember trying to discourage Daddy each time he asked, "Would this be a good choice?" I felt as if he was putting the blame on me for cutting the tree down. As far as I was concerned, none of them were right to be chopped down. My voice didn't seem to count though. In spite of my reluctance, we always dragged a choice specimen into our old wagon before heading back to the house.

Mama would insist that a shorter tree be chosen due to the lack of space and because she felt a bigger one was more of a fire hazard. As I grew older, I often suspected that she really felt somewhat as I did about the traditional Christmas tree practice.

Cutting down a beautiful living tree and bringing it inside our home was distasteful to me, but there was something I disliked even more. Every year a big community Christmas party was held in the Pleasant Hill church near us. Everyone always expected us to continue our generous tradition and contribute a large pine tree for the occasion. And each season they would expect a tree that was a little bigger than the one we had cut down the previous year.

I well remember the year they had to cut off the top of the tree because it wouldn't fit into the church. Those in charge decided it would be nice just to have it spread out more over the stage area, even though there was no room for the angel they always placed on top.

The oversized outdoor tree looked so out of place, right up in front where the minister stood when he preached to us from the Scriptures on Sunday morning.

The giant Christmas tree always commanded the interests and efforts of everyone in the community. As soon as it was brought in a couple weeks before Christmas, the attention of everyone was focused on it.

During the day, on Christmas Eve, people came from miles around to tie their gifts for family members and friends on the branches, or set them under the tree. Every effort was made to make it appear as if the fat man in the red suit had actually placed them there. I was young but I remember how repulsive that was to me.

When everyone had worked themselves into a frenzy, the long awaited get-together, which they went so far as to call a "service", finally came on Christmas Eve.

The Sunday School children would present a "program", around the fringe-edge of the giant tree. Nobody except the family of each performer noticed the child who was talking, or what he was saying, as much as they did the imposing tree and all the gifts it held on its branches. (My family kept thinking about the fact that we had sacrificed the tree from our forest.) I had my own thoughts too, bordering on disgust.

The children had a hard time concentrating on what they were supposed to be saying. They were torn with the emotion they were caught up in, and anxiety about what was waiting for them on the tree. And from anticipating "Santy Claus", the impostor, who posed as the one from whom the gifts came.

In my younger years I tried to identify with the boys and girls, but when I grew older and wiser, I realized why they had "Santa" sitting down, and only saying "Ho, ho" and making silly noises while someone else read the names of those the gifts were intended for, and still others delivering them to those who were holding up their hand indicating where the gift went. It was because the "impersonator" was so drunk he couldn't stand, or see to read the names himself. This was rather shocking to a young "believer" like myself.

Every year the whole scene became more disgusting to me. There was nothing sacred or Christ-honoring about anything that went on. In fact, I was scared to go to the church on Christmas Eve. It seemed like every man and boy over fifteen years of age, was drinking and carrying on disgracefully inside the church, or just outside. One or more fights could always be expected among those who had too much to drink. It was such a terrible way to celebrate the birth of Christ the Savior. I would often beg my folks not to go and participate. They felt however, that it was something everyone was supposed to do, so we always went.

At home, our family had a box of homemade ornaments, and a few that my "city" aunts had bought for us, which we used to decorate our tree.

There were years every so often, however, when there were very few gifts to put under it.

The leanest year I can remember was the Christmas when the only present we older children received was a fifteen-cent dictionary. Mine had an ugly orange-red cover and the words inside were printed on such cheap paper that it was brown and old looking even though the book was new. And I remember all too well the hurt, disappointed look in their eyes as my parents struggled to find words to explain why "Santy Claus" couldn't, or didn't bring us more. They were covering for the fabricated fat man, rather than apologizing for our meager circumstances.

That was the year I suffered what was perhaps the most traumatic experience of my entire life. From earliest childhood I learned to trust my mother and father in every way. No matter what happened anywhere, I didn't worry; I just trusted Daddy and Mama. I never had reason to doubt them. They had never violated my trust—until that time, that is.

When they tried to create a fantasy, like all the other parents they knew, I believed them. As I grew a bit older I did question the fallibility of the "fat man", and the reindeer story. I wondered about the supposedly all-knowing character who appeared to be everywhere at once and I marveled that he could so easily tell what I wanted for Christmas. But I still didn't question my parents. I figured if they said it was that way, that was the way it was.

Then, one terrible day, when I was much too old to still be believing in Santa Claus (and much older than I'm willing to admit), I woke up to the naked truth. I had been deceived, and by those I had trusted most—my parents. The horrible pain was accentuated by the realization that I had allowed myself to be duped by a deception that I should have known for myself was wrong.

If my folks had explained to me that the fifteen-cent dictionary was all they could manage that year because times were so hard, I could easily have handled it. But my trustworthy parents, trying to apologize for a nonexistent entity like Santa Claus? That was something I never quite got over.

I knew how poor we were. And I was very much aware of how much my parents struggled, and how they sacrificed for us. I never complained because of what we didn't have or felt sorry for myself for being so deprived. But I suffered immeasurably from the deception that dawned upon me that fateful Christmas so many years ago.

I'm sure my folks meant well. To them it probably seemed innocent, but to me it was a terrible blow, and inexcusable. Putting into words now, what I believe I felt then, I would have to say that giving credit for what parents do for their children, and for what God does for them—to a false pretender, is quite unacceptable.

I was only a child, but I thought it was more reasonable to accept our poverty and to thank God for what we had, even though it may not have seemed like much at the time.

*** *** ***

"Kathye, Marissa, and Barry, I have opened to you the innermost depths of my heart tonight. Now I think you will understand a little better how I feel about some things.

"There's much more that I want to tell you about. Some of it will surprise you. But that will have to wait. It's getting late now, and I think we'd better prepare for bed."

CHAPTER 6

Dear Ole Golden Rule Days

"Hi, Grandma," Carmelle called as she waved to her parents. They had just dropped her off to stay with me while they went shopping.

"Guess what I want for my birthday?"

I hesitated. "Well, let's see..., oh, I don't think I could ever guess. Can you tell me?"

"I want a bicycle, so I can ride to school with my friend, Nancy," she told me. "A blue one, with white stripes," she added, wrinkling her nose and tossing her curls.

"That's wonderful!" I agreed. "What else would you like?"

Carmelle was going to be six years old on Wednesday and I was hoping for a hint. She already had just about everything a little girl could want.

She thought for a moment and then said, "Oh, anything is O.K. Grandma, but I think I would really like a pretty tote bag to carry my books in."

"Are you looking forward to school?" I questioned further. "I mean real school."

"Oh, yes, I can hardly wait," she answered excitedly. "Last year, in kindergarten, we mostly played. I want to learn to read, all by myself." She paused. "Grandma, would you tell me about when you were my age—what was your school like?"

"You know that's just what your cousins Karl and Tania asked me last week. Then they had to leave because their daddy was waiting for them. I told them the next time they came to visit maybe we could talk about it.

Oh, here they come now." We could see them in the front seat of their daddy's pickup as he was driving up. "This would be a wonderful time to tell all of you about something I love to remember again and again."

Karl was nine, and Tania was going to be eleven in a few weeks.

"Hi, Carmelle!" Tania called, as they came up the walkway. "We didn't know you were going to be here."

Karl was running ahead of Tania. "Grandma, Daddy said I could ask you if we could stay a little while with you. He has to pick up some lumber."

"Sure, Karl," I replied, and waved to his dad to go ahead.

"Remember, you promised to tell us a story the next time we came?" he reminded me.

"Oh, please tell us more about when you were a little girl, and what it was like." Tania spoke up. "Let's sit around the picnic table here on your back deck, O.K.?"

"Grandma is going to tell us about school—a long time ago," Carmelle announced.

* * *   * * *   * * *

The First Day of School

I'll never forget the year I started to school. There were no kindergartens then, at least not where we lived. Children didn't go to school until they were six years old.

On the first day of school Daddy hitched the horses to the wagon and got ready to take me. We lived a long distance from the school house.

We had been discussing school for weeks and I had actually looked forward to going, as long as it was some day way out there—in the future. But when the day finally arrived, I begged my parents not to make me go.

Daddy sat in the spring-seat on the wagon, waiting for me to ride beside him. Mama stood in the doorway holding the baby, with my younger brother nearby.

Inside, I kept stalling. I had reluctantly put on one of my pretty new dresses, the pink one with bloomers, which Mama had especially made for me to wear the first day of school. I liked it more than any dress she had ever made for me. I had tried it on numerous times and admired myself in the mirror. I liked the smocked yoke and the ruffles around the collar. For a few minutes, as I was getting dressed, I almost forgot I was going to have to leave Mama.

About that time she called to tell me to hurry up. She wanted to have time to brush my hair and braid my pigtails.

"But, Mama," I hollered from the bedroom, "these bloomers are too tight. I can't wear them." Sure enough, when she came in to check them she realized the elastic was too tight and that I was not just using that for an excuse to keep from going to school.

"All right," she said, "put on the blue dress for today. I'm sure it will be fine."

Mama kept hurrying me along, knowing Daddy was getting impatient. At last I was ready. Mama handed me a little round, blue and white striped bucket with a wire handle on it. It contained the lunch she had prepared for me.

We had bought some strange-tasting jelly in a cute container with the idea of using it for my lunch pail. Daddy had scratched my name on it, so it could easily be identified.

I could hear the harness rattling on old Sam and Nell, and I knew Daddy was not very happy having to wait for me. My oldest brother Charles yelled from the yard, "Ardelle, Daddy said to hurry up or you'll be late."

I lingered inside the house, wishing as hard as I could that I didn't have to go to school. I could see Mama was dreading having to make me go. She knew I was going to hold out to the last minute. She also knew Daddy would make me go, even if she softened. The baby sensed the tension and started to cry.

In a last minute try, I grabbed hold of Mama's hand and clung to her. "Please," I begged, as big tears rolled slowly down my cheeks, and landed on my new blue dress, "please, Mama, don't make me go."

"Hurry up, Ardelle," Daddy called, loud and gruff. I trembled. Mama practically dragged me across the yard. She hugged me sympathetically, and helped me into the wagon. I was bawling loudly by that time. My whole world was falling apart. I didn't think I could stand to leave Mama. I didn't know the teacher and I was scared of the children, thinking I probably wouldn't know any of them either.

I waved a weak good-bye to Mama. She looked so sad. I know she went inside and cried after we left.

Daddy put his arm around me and tried to console me. "You're going to like school," he promised. He kept talking to me as we drove across our pasture, up past Mr. Wilcoxson's house, and out onto the main road. Having him talk to me like I was a big girl made me feel a lot better.

"Stop your crying now," he said, taking his handkerchief out of his pocket and handing it to me. "Wipe your eyes and blow your nose. You don't want your face to be all red when you get to school, do you?" I tried to laugh when I thought about that.

We had a lot of time to talk before we got to school. Daddy explained to me that there was a law that required parents to send their children to school. That sounded terrifying to me. It was almost like hearing someone say there's a law that says you have to go to jail. The thought made me nervous.

As we drove up to the schoolhouse, the boys and girls were running all around. Some of them were yelling and hollering as they threw a ball back and forth. Others were chasing each other. They seemed to be having a good time.

The teacher, who looked young enough to be one of the children's big sister, was standing in the door smiling.

"I'll bet Miss Laura's a nice teacher," Daddy said.

I wanted to stay in the wagon and go back home with Daddy so very badly. But I didn't want to break the law and maybe have to go to jail. I thought I'd rather go to school.

When Daddy started to leave I wanted to cry again, but he reminded me that I was a big girl now. He told me not to worry, he would be back to pick me up when school was out. I suspected it was going to be a long day.

[Tania, do you remember what it was like the first day you went to school? I'm sure you do, Karl.]

Before I got to Miss Laura she began ringing the bell, and all the children stopped playing and started to go inside.

"Good morning!" I heard the young teacher say. Looking around I realized she was speaking to me. She placed her hand on my head. "She likes me," I thought, "and I'm going to like her too," I resolved at that moment.

Everyone scrambled to get the seat of their choice. Some wanted to sit next to a pal. Others wanted up front and some in back. I didn't know where I wanted to sit.

At first I didn't see anyone I knew. About the time Miss Laura motioned for me to come up front and sit in one of the smaller desks, I spotted Coreen, Mr. Wilson's little girl. She waved to me and asked if she could sit next to me. We remembered each other from Sunday School.

I felt a lot better, knowing someone wanted to sit with me. School wasn't going to be so bad after all.

"That's a pretty dress," Coreen whispered as Miss Laura tried to get everyone's attention.

We soon discovered that Miss Laura had her own ideas about seating. She asked several of the older children to move. Everyone laughed when she separated Henry and John by several seats. She also instructed Alice and Carrie to sit on opposite sides of the room which they didn't like. Both of them groaned and after a few minutes Carrie reluctantly got up and moved.

When Miss Laura asked Jack to come up towards the front and sit in the end desk of the third row, everyone snickered. When I turned around and looked, I could see why. Being a little on the heavy side, he had to squeeze himself into the desk. Miss Laura knew from experience that Jack would have to be constantly under her watchful eye.

When she was finally satisfied with the seating arrangement, Miss Laura asked everyone to stand beside their desk and salute the American flag that was displayed at the end of the blackboard.

Though some of us didn't know all the words to say, we put our right hand over our chest like the others did and tried to follow along. Then she had us sing all the verses of "My Country 'Tis of Thee", which I did know.

"Before you sit down," she said, "I want you to bow your head and close your eyes while I pray."

Suddenly everything was very quiet. I don't remember the exact words Miss Laura prayed. I know she thanked God for each of us and asked Him to be with us through the day and protect us. I felt so much better when I found out that God was going to be there too. I hadn't expected that.

"Before we give out books," Miss Laura said with a smile, "we're going to get acquainted."

Starting with the bigger students sitting in the back rows, she asked each of us to stand and clearly give our name so that everyone could hear. I was glad I was almost the last one but I was still scared with everyone looking at me.

When I told them who I was Miss Laura said, "Ardelle, what a pretty name."

Then she called the roll from a list on her desk. She read the names slowly and waited for each one to reply.

She told us she hoped we would be able to come to school every day. In fact, she said, she would have a prize for each of us who didn't miss any days during that grading period. I thought that would be nice and I decided I didn't want to miss a single day all year.

Miss Laura then asked us to listen carefully as our names were called to come up front and get our books, tablets and pencils. She had already figured out what each of us needed. The older boys and girls got more than one book. Some of them were thick and I learned that they had to study different subjects.

By the time she got to Coreen and me we thought she had run out of books. But we each got one. Of course we couldn't read yet, but we soon learned that the word on the front said PRIMER. We looked inside the book, then at each other. We doubted if we would ever be able to read those big, difficult words.

She also gave each of us a tablet with lines and a brown wood "penny pencil" with no eraser. The lead in it was so light that you could hardly see the marks it made, especially on the dingy pages of the tablet. I figured that there was no eraser since the marks you made on that paper were too faint to erase anyway.

When all the books, pencils, and tablets were given out, Miss Laura looked at the clock on the wall behind her desk and told it was time for recess. I waited to see what that meant.

Suddenly all the children began hurrying toward the door, laughing and calling to each over a jumble of mixed voices. Coreen and I were not sure what to do, but Miss Laura seemed to understand our hesitancy.

"You can go outside and play until I ring the bell," she explained. So that was what recess was. Next time we would know.

At noon, she asked us to bow our heads while she said "grace". Then we ate our lunch at our desk, including Miss Laura.

One little boy had forgotten his lunch. He looked so sad and embarrassed, I wanted to share mine with him. The teacher said she had brought extra so she gave him some of her lunch. I felt relieved; he looked so hungry. [I found out later that his folks were very poor. Miss Laura and some of us children often shared with him.]

The rest of the day went pretty quickly. When school was dismissed, I slipped my book, our reader, into the satchel Mama had made for me to carry my things in, along with my tablet and pencil. When I put it over my shoulder, I couldn't help noticing it fit like a short cotton-picking sack. I went outside with Coreen and another little girl named Amy.

I looked all around but I didn't see Daddy anywhere. Just as I was beginning to get worried, he came around the corner of the school building looking for me. I was really glad to see him.

On the way home Daddy was all ears. Actually, he hardly had a chance to say a word, I had so much to tell him. He laughed when I told him about the boy who had to sit in a desk near the front because he didn't behave well.

When I told Daddy I wanted to share my lunch with a little boy who had forgotten his, he said he was proud of me. When I told him I didn't want to miss a single day of school, he was pleased and relieved. I don't think my parents were looking forward to having to drag me to school every day.

Mama was waiting anxiously for us to arrive home. I repeated all the important details to her as she beamed with pride.

That was a wonderful day, and a very important milestone in my life.

[You know, Carmelle, I feel quite sure you will enjoy your first day in school, too.]

Readin', Writin', and Real Concern

There was so much to learn at school. At first it seemed hopeless; everything was so unfamiliar.

The first two words I had to learn to read were the "in" and "out" signs on the door of the outhouse. It was difficult for me to reach high enough to touch them, but we had to learn to read them, then turn the sign so it said "in" when we were inside, and when we came out we had to turn it over so the next person who needed to use the privy would know it was unoccupied.

The more I looked at the new book which Miss Laura had issued me, the more I doubted that I could ever learn and understand those big words. But each day Miss Laura helped Coreen and me, and the other five children in the first grade learn how to print the letters of the alphabet, then put them together to make words—and later how to read the words after they were constructed into sentences.

I loved learning how to read and write. And I learned pretty quickly, because I really wanted to learn and I tried hard.

Miss Laura was a good teacher, and she was the only teacher for all eight grades, one through eight.

[Can you imagine that, Karl?]

Our versatile public school teacher also served as superintendent, sports director, music teacher, counselor, and health nurse. And she was our spiritual adviser, too. The men who hired our teachers made sure they exhibited sufficient evidence of being Christians as the first requirement.

Although some of them were quite young when they came to teach us, they were soon almost as efficient as an entire staff in a modern day school setting.

[You may think it would be impossible for one teacher, no matter how efficient, to handle eight grades at one time, and teach all the grades well. In those days, teachers were amazingly well organized. I suppose they had to be. Now I know that the secret of their source of ability and strength was their dependence on God.]

First thing in the morning, after roll-call, our teacher would read from the Bible and lead us in prayer. There were no restrictions to prevent us from beginning the day honoring God's Word and seeking His guidance.

There were no apologies. No one on the school board nor any of the parents wanted it any other way. You might say we had our own Christian school, without the tuition. Prayer and Bible reading was normal. This gave us a good foundation for learning the required academics.

The fruit of the high morals taught and the discipline administered, always with the teacher in complete control, the well mannered behavior and cooperation with the teacher, were all answers to prayer. They were also the rewarding results of her diligent efforts as a dedicated teacher.

I don't mean to say there were no problems. Of course there were. Wherever people attempt to work or learn together, and especially where there is a wide age span, there will be problems. But when there is dependency on God, there is strength to manage and persevere, and grace to work out difficulties.

Sometimes the school trustees would hire a very young teacher, usually from a fine Christian family. She would often be accused of coming to "learn on us." Most would stay at least two or three years, and by that time they would have become quite proficient.

I remember Miss Vena taught us, then her sister, Miss Ina. After that there was Miss Serena. I will never forget how soft-voiced and kind she was. We all loved her very much.

Then Mrs Calvert taught us for a few years. When her husband became very ill and she was needed more at home, their daughter Miss Elsie came to finish out her mother's term. Miss Elsie and her mother had both stayed in our home week nights, during the school term, and went home on weekends.

Miss Serena had taught us several Bible verses in school when she was our teacher. Mrs. Calvert had continued the memorization program. But I remember it was Miss Elsie who took a special interest in me. She often told me she was praying for me. One afternoon when I was helping her straighten up the classroom before we went home, she said to me, "Ardelle, I believe God has a special plan for your life."

That evening, while Mama washed the dishes, Miss Elsie graded papers and I did my homework. When we were finished she suggested we read some verses from the Bible. She pointed out certain references and urged me to read them for myself. As we read the third chapter of John, she stressed the "new birth."

She had witnessed to me, but if the Holy Spirit had tried to get my attention I had not realized it. I was young and carefree and spiritually unconcerned. The seeds were planted, however, and in time they would grow—and bear fruit.

We Loved Our School

School was a respected institution in those days, and appreciated by all. You never heard any student singing degrading little tunes about wishing the school would burn down, or that something terrible would happen to the teacher.

School was a welcome reprieve for those of us who had to work hard in the fields, and that included most of us.

It was inspiring to sit in the classroom, along with our friends, and learn about great men and women who had endured hardships and persevered. They were our heroes. Learning about them gave us incentive and initiative. Many hopes and dreams that grew to fruition were ignited in those old-fashioned country school classrooms.

As I grew older, history became my favorite subject. I learned to love and respect the great men who founded our country on Christian principles. They became almost as real to me as people I actually knew.

Although we had only one teacher for eight grades, our school building was not the proverbial one room "little red school house". In fact, it was a large two-story structure with four rooms upstairs and four downstairs. I often wondered about the early days when the school had been built. Perhaps our poor, impoverished area had at one time been more thriving and affluent.

While that building was still in use, we held classes in one of the larger downstairs rooms. It seemed strange to have so many unused rooms.

In the wintertime our classroom was heated with an old homemade, "pot belly" wood-burning stove. Somebody, usually the teacher, had to brave the early morning cold to start a fire so that the room would be warm when the students began to arrive. Sometimes one of the older boys would volunteer to come early and assist her. I remember one teacher actually assigned that chore to a different eighth grade boy for a week at a time.

When the teacher lived with us, my brothers and I would go early with her and help start the fire. How we dreaded that cold room! We would nearly freeze before a stubborn fire could be persuaded to take hold and the room would finally start to get warm. [I shiver when I think about it.]

We also helped the teacher sweep the room and straighten the desks after school. I don't think our sacrifice helped our grades, but our efforts were appreciated by the teacher—and they were required by Daddy. He wanted us to learn from the experience I am sure.

Since the school had no plumbing, a very old and dilapidated outhouse, had to suffice, no matter how cold or wet the weather or how deep the snow. [I don't think you can even imagine what it was like.]

We drank water from an old well that was rumored to be contaminated from the cemetery across the road from the school. That always concerned me. Each student carried their own collapsible cup in their satchel. It folded nearly flat and opened up to hold a full cup. At least these were more sanitary than having a community dipper, such as they did at the country store and other public places.

The School Ma'am Lived With Us

The school teacher was a very important person in our community. During the school term, we were in her care more of our waking hours than we were with our parents.

Parents were very particular about those who served on the school board and were responsible for hiring the teachers. They wanted the best available and affordable applicant that could be acquired.

Our teachers had a lot of influence on us and we naturally became attached to them. I remember the year our teacher died, along with three other members of her family, due to an influenza epidemic that hit our area. It was a sad time for us.

Another time, our teacher died suddenly and mysteriously in her late twenties. When I grew older I learned that her death had been the result of her attempt to end an unwanted pregnancy. She had not been married. In those days, people only talked about such things in utmost secrecy. I remember how shocked my parents were when we heard about her death.

Most of our teachers were outstanding and, incidentally almost all women. Instinctively they always looked after us like an old mother hen hovering over a flock of baby chickens. When a storm threatened us, she would try to quiet our fears as we huddled around her.

Fortunately, the terrible tornado that touched down one dark April day and totally demolished our big old school hit late in the afternoon when we were all at home.

That catastrophe came as a terrible blow to all of us. The school term was dismissed and work began immediately to construct a new two-room school building, so that it would be ready in time for the fall session. [Surely you can imagine how much we appreciated that new school house.]

When I was in the eighth grade, there was no high school available to attend. One was under construction, however, and was scheduled to open for classes a year later. Several communities had consolidated and plans were being made to bus us to the new school when it was ready.

After being together with such a close school-family and over such a long period of time, we dreaded that last day of school. It was sad and tearful. That year, for those of us who were finishing the eighth grade and didn't have the prospect of being together again in the fall, the day was especially heartbreaking.

I loved school. The thought of not being able to attend at all for a whole year, was almost unbearable. The inward pain I felt is still fresh in my memory, after all the years that have gone by. I suspect that is one reason my heart really hurts when I hear someone belittling school.

Miss Agnes, our teacher that year, sympathetically observed my reaction. Since I had helped her a lot with the younger students that year, she suddenly got a bright idea. She asked if I would enroll in the eighth grade again and just be there to assist her the following year. I couldn't wait to ask my parents. They agreed it would be a good experience for me.

The year I helped Miss Agnes in a special way, I learned a lot myself, I also acquired a taste for teaching children and enjoyed the satisfaction of assisting my teacher, and giving of myself to others.

School Relationships

One of the characteristics increasingly evident in my life may have had its roots in that special year of tutoring at school—that was my ability to understand and communicate with others. I was always quick to sense the difficulty another student might be experiencing.

I remember that one year—Nellie Ames sat across from me. She was always on the war path. Nobody liked her and she didn't like anybody. I suspected she was struggling with some hidden problem, so I gave her a lot of special attention. She soon warmed up to me.

One day when the teacher made her stay in at recess, I stayed to help her with an assignment. She was so touched with my kindness, she started to cry and began to reveal to me things she had never told a single person.

Nellie's home life was so unsettled I couldn't even imagine what it was like. Ours seemed to me to be so stable. But I tried to understand. From that day, Nellie had at least one friend who cared, one person she could turn to in time of need. Her grades improved and she was happier with school.

Then there was Jack. He had the reputation of being the school bully. He was good-looking and fairly smart, and he was bigger than any of the other boys. The teacher always interpreted his antics as intentional disruptions. He was often sent to the ante room to study in isolation. He was required to sit on a box underneath hanging coats, surrounded by lunch pails, boots and overshoes. He didn't seem to mind, however; he would smile smugly, as though he were receiving special treatment rather than punishment.

The rest of the class would snicker and Jack would consequently be punished again. There were times when it seemed to me he was being punished unfairly. Sometimes the teacher would make him stand in the corner for an entire period. A more severe punishment was to make him stand at the blackboard with his nose in a circle drawn with chalk. His face would be so close to the blackboard that he would have to keep his eyes closed.

For some reason I sort of liked Jack. Maybe it was because he often helped me with my arithmetic problems. And I think I sympathized with him when he was punished while the other students laughed at him.

Once in a while Jack would smile at me with a certain twinkle in his eye. It would warm my heart. I secretly wished I could help him want to behave better so he wouldn't be accused of being bad. We later became quite fond of each other.

It was always my nature to make friends easily. In school I developed numerous in-depth relationships. After more than fifty years, some of them are still intact. [You know how much I enjoy getting cards and letters from them at Christmas time. Do you have some really good friends at school, Tania and Karl? I'm sure you do. Carmelle, you'll make some lasting friends this year too, you'll see.]

I had several close girl friends in school. There was Virginia, Pearlie, Helen, Artie, and Evelyn, to name a few.

Evelyn and I had a lot of good times together. She was a little older than I, but that was not a problem. She did have one well established habit that contradicted my nature however. No matter where we went or what we did, she would always see to it that we were late. Late for school, late for church, late to a party. Always late. Being a prompt person this irritating quirk really bugged me. As much as I liked Evelyn, this hopeless trait of hers finally cooled our relationship. After a time we were only casual friends.

Pearlie was a precious friend. We were also neighbors, and would walk to school together. Sometimes we did our homework together. We even chopped or picked cotton together when our families combined forces during a peak period. Pearlie and her brother Lester (he was called Lec for short) would come to our house and play sometimes on rainy days.

One of the things I remember most about Pearlie was her ability to make the best pecan pie I ever ate. She also insisted on doing everything just like her mother did. Pearlie and her dear mother, and I'm sure her grandmother also, had one really strange habit. When drying dishes, they would dip a dry dish towel in very hot water, wring it out, and then proceed to dry the dishes with it. The steam, they explained, dried them.

And Artie? Well, Artie was a lot of fun to be with. She had a tremendous sense of humor. Everything was funny to Artie. She was what you might call a "giggler", and you know how giggling can beget giggling. Many times I was embarrassed to be known as Artie's close friend. She derived a great deal of pleasure from instigating laughter in others. The only time she could keep me from laughing was when I would get so disgusted with her that nothing was funny.

[As you know, I'm a fun-loving person, but I try not to laugh out of turn.]

There are times when laughing or giggling is totally inappropriate. Artie loved to try to make me laugh in class and get the teacher to scold us. I think that was mainly because I always wanted to please the teacher and she was jealous.

When we went to church together, she would insist on sitting in the back seat. Then she would try to get me snickering with her so that when the preacher paused in his message, and everything was quiet, everyone would look back and wonder whose children were acting up in church. Again, I think she wanted to embarrass me, but Mama put a stop to that —really fast.

Mama liked Artie and tried to help her overcome her silliness. She would just tell her right out why she wouldn't let me sit with her in church. She explained to Artie that it was irreverent to "show out", as she called it, in church.

Artie took Mama's counseling well and never seemed to resent it. But she never changed. She often visited us and if she was there at meal time, Mama would ask her to eat with us. She would always resist, saying,

"Oh, Mrs. Chappell, don't set a place for me. I'm not hungry." My dear mother would set a place for her anyway and insist that she at least sit at the table with us while we ate.

It may have been subconsciously, but soon Artie would reach for a piece of bread, then, some meat. Before long she would have taken a helping of potatoes, some vegetables, and then be ready for a second helping of bread. Mama would reach over and refill her glass with milk. Artie loved dessert and usually chose the largest piece of anything that was passed to her.

[I could never understand how Artie could put away so much food and still remain as skinny as a sapling.]

By the time we had finished eating, Artie would have consumed more food than anyone around the table. That always tickled Mama. After she had left Mama would say, "It's a good thing Artie wasn't hungry."

A Note-Worthy Friend

Then, later there was Helen. Dear Helen. She was pleasant and likable, and she had a big, sharing heart. She also played the piano well, and I admired her a lot.

My grandma Adams had promised to let us bring her organ to our house so that I could learn to play it. It was already at Aunt Bertha's (my mother's oldest sister), so her family could learn how to play. Aunt Bertha and my cousin Moleva had both learned to play and Grandma decided the organ should be moved to our house so that we could have our turn. By that time, the old organ had been pretty well abused.

Daddy and Uncle Hub wriggled the old organ sideways through the door and into my room. That was the only place in the house where there was room for it. I was really excited at the prospect of learning to play; I never once doubted I could learn.

When Helen found out I had an organ, she was thrilled too. She had also learned to play on an old-fashioned organ.

Helen rode the bus many miles to school, much further than I did. Sometimes she would stay overnight, or longer, with us. When she spent the weekend at our house, she would go to church with us on Sunday morning. Since the church didn't have a pianist, they would ask her to play. She always played for her church in the community where she lived too.

Watching Helen play made me want to learn even more and we really needed someone to play the piano at our church. My parents promised that if I would learn to play the old organ they would buy me a nice piano. That was enough incentive to spur me on.

Helen wanted so much to help me learn to play. She had learned all by herself with little outside help. She could see I had the same determination. She had taken a correspondence course and through it, she had learned to read music from "round" notes. I wanted to be able to read them too.

All the music I had ever seen was printed in notes that were various shapes. Each year a singing teacher would come to our church and teach us to read the strange looking notes and to sing from them.

The scale, as he taught it, read: do, re, mi, fa, sol, la, and te, and back to "do" again.

Do was shaped like a pyramid, re like a wash kettle, mi like a diamond, fa like a triangle, sol was an oval, la a rectangle, and te like an ice cream cone.

I can still see Mr. Beasley, our teacher, his hair tousled and unkempt. He would take out his tuner and Jew's harp and try to get just the right tone. He was so funny looking we could hardly keep from laughing.

Helen decided she wanted to learn to read round notes because her Aunt Genevieve, who lived in Chicago had told her they were better. Her aunt promised Helen's parents she would pay for music lessons for her, if they could find a teacher. When none could be found, Helen learned about a correspondence course and took it instead.

When Helen and I met again at the new high school, she already played the piano quite well. Since she never used the lessons anymore, she offered me the course. I cherished it like a treasure. I was determined to learn to play like Helen. I wanted so much to please my parents and to play at our church.

I lost no time in getting started. Every spare minute I pored over those complicated lesson sheets. From early in the morning, until late at night I pounded away, straining to get just the right sound. Sometimes I would sing or hum along, listening carefully for the correct tone. I would pick out the tune with one finger, then try the notes together. I was really surprised at how quickly I was able to play with both hands and make it sound good.

Two weeks from the day that Helen gave me her music course, I played the two songs I had learned, at church. They were, "Shall We Gather at the River", and "Just as I am". My folks were so proud of me, they couldn't hide it. The song leader too, praised me; he made me feel like I could do anything. [I will never forget that wonderful day.]

My parents decided it was time to go look for a piano. We excitedly drove into town and looked up the only music store. Daddy proudly explained to the salesperson how they had promised to buy me a piano if I proved I could learn to play. He was very gracious to us and seemed to understand.

Free piano lessons were included with the beautiful instrument we chose, but we lived so far from town that I was never able to take advantage of even one. Oh, how I longed to have professional help, but there was just no way it could be. I was terribly disappointed, but I became even more determined to learn to play, regardless of the circumstances.

In retrospect, I think it would have been wonderful to have had the opportunity of being a concert pianist. As it is, I am only mediocre. It has been my pleasure down through the years, however, to accompany church congregations and vocalists whenever needed. I love to play for my own enjoyment too, and I find playing the piano is also good therapy. When I am weary, if I sit down at the piano and play for fifteen minutes, all the tension and weariness works right out through my fingers.

Our home was a gathering place for musically inclined youth. My brother C.N., played guitar, mandolin, banjo, or any other stringed instrument he ever tried. Several of his friends also played one or two. Most of the time they had a band which functioned mainly for their own pleasure. They were invited to perform a few times on radio as guests of Jim Moe's Cotton Pickers. I personally thought they sounded better than Jim's regular group.

My folks felt it was a worthwhile sacrifice to buy a piano, to have me play at church, and to have the neighborhood youth congregate at our house. They always knew where we were, who we were with, and what we were doing.

Music was a good, wholesome pastime. We spent many happy hours singing and playing music. It kept us occupied and satisfied. I never once remember hearing my parents complain about the noise or about our friends always being there. They didn't even seem to mind if they were there at mealtime. Our friends had great respect for my parents.

I shall always be grateful for a musical friend like Helen, who, through her generous kindness and sharing, opened to me and to my family that extra dimension in living, and the fulfillment that music brings.

Virginia was one of my closest friends through elementary and high school. Her family was among the more well-to-do in our community. Her aunt was the local doctor's wife. All of them had a lot more than any of us poor farming families.

Virginia's folks liked me and appreciated having me spend lots of time with their daughter, in their home and ours. My folks liked Virginia a lot too. She was an exceptionally pleasant, sweet and lovable girl.

I also enjoyed Virginia's parents and her older sister. Their lovely home was large and they had nice furniture. In comparison to ours, it seemed like a palace. I also enjoyed eating with them; they could afford store items that we never had.

Virginia had pretty clothes. I remember one fall she ordered a rust-colored dress that was featured on the cover of a mail order catalogue. I was glad for her, but I'll admit, I was envious.

Mama made all my clothes. She sewed well, and I should have been more grateful. After Virginia's fancy store-bought garments had been worn a few times, they looked cheap and would start to rip. She told me one day she envied the well-made things my mother sewed for me. I felt a secret pride, and a slight pang of shame as well, that I had not been more appreciative of the dresses Mama had worked so hard to make for me.

Virginia was a true friend and I don't recall ever having a falling out with her. We have remained the best of friends through all the years since, and we still keep in touch. She still lives in the same general area where we enjoyed so many happy times together. When I receive a fat letter from Virginia, I can expect to hear all the news about people we have both known for over fifty years. I always know there will also be reports of those who have passed on since we last communicated. I also still correspond with Helen and Pearlie. Since I live so far away in California, their letters are a vital link to the past for me. They help me maintain an association with the area where I was born and raised.

The Bug Bites

History was my favorite subject in school, English was next. Writing essays and stories was thrilling, and I loved to write poetry.

In the spring of my seventh grade year, we studied about poetry. This resulted in an assignment to show what we had learned. I wrote a long poem entitled simply *"March"*. I remember how easily it came to me. I just wrote down the rhyming words as they seemed to flow onto paper. Next day, the teacher complimented me highly in front of the whole class.

"This poem has all the elements of good poetry," she said. "It's a perfect illustration of what we've been studying." Then she told the class, "because this poem is exactly what a good poem should be, I want each of you to memorize it."

I froze. What if the class would resent me for being singled out? Or maybe refuse to memorize it because I wrote it? I realized the poem was awfully long. I was scared to look around to get the reaction of the class. About that time they all started to clap their hands in approval.

I was overwhelmed. I couldn't hold back the tears. That was my first taste of the thrill of recognition for creative writing ability. The bug had bitten. I wrote many poems after that, enough in fact, to fill a large book.

High School Versus Health

The year the new high school was completed, we rode the bus many miles each day in order to attend. I had to leave home very early in the morning, walk a distance to catch the bus, then reverse the whole procedure in the afternoon. In the wintertime, it would be dark by the time I would wearily approach our house, carrying more books than I was physically up to with my bad back.

High school subjects required long hours of tedious homework and I felt compelled to maintain my usual good grades. I would often be up until midnight, studying by the poor light of a kerosene (we called it coal-oil) lamp. Then I would have to get up very early the next morning in order to catch the bus for the long ride to school.

My unceasing back pain may have been aggravated by having to wear cheap shoes that did not fit. They were so uncomfortable that I would have to stop and remove them at times and rub my aching feet and cool my blistered heels. I never had a pair of shoes that fit.

I inherited my Grandma Chappell's narrow feet. We were so poor we couldn't afford good shoes, so I wore cheap ones, often ordered haphazardly from a mail order catalogue. It's a wonder I can even walk on my feet today.

[I'm always pleased to see the well-made, good-fitting shoes that you children have to wear. Can you imagine having to wear shoes that are too wide, or not the right length?]

Despite health problems, I was thrilled with high school. In addition to basic subjects, we studied music, art and drama. I really enjoyed glee club, where we learned to read music and sing in harmony. We also participated in sports.

[You'll laugh, and it may be hard for you to believe, but your grandma was pretty good at girls' basketball, in spite of having to constantly fight back pain.]

I was popular in class, and often took the initiative in leadership. This led to numerous responsibilities. I was elected class president twice. When the teacher would have to leave the room for an extended time, I was usually the one left in charge. And I received extra credit for my speaking ability.

Not everything came easy in high school, however. I found algebra and geometry to be rather difficult. They seemed like senseless subjects to me. An especially nice boy in my math class tried to help me understand how to solve the complex problems. I sincerely appreciated his concern and patience. A few years later, I was shocked to hear that Emmett had been killed in action, in World War II.

I have many wonderful memories associated with my high school days. I vividly remember one occasion, however, that was tragic.

It was an exciting evening. We had all looked forward to the drama class performance. A huge crowd filled the auditorium to overflowing.

Shortly before the play was scheduled to begin, two shots were heard, followed by screams. I remember how frightening it all sounded. My girlfriend and I and some junior boys had been hurrying along, making our way through the crowd, when the shooting occurred, right in front of us. Security officers rushed past, pushing everyone back to let a doctor through. Law officers were quickly on the scene.

The next day's newspaper reported that the shots were fired by a young man who had been drinking. The accused murderer had stolen a vehicle that day and when he discovered a revolver under the seat, he had hidden it under his coat. Later that evening he began arguing with another boy who had also been drinking. In his anger, during the heated quarrel, he pulled out the revolver and aimed it at the other young man. The bullet missed him, however, and hit two innocent bystanders, a senior girl and her male escort. Both were killed almost instantly. Two other students nearby were seriously injured.

It was a terrible thing to have happen, right on the campus of our high school. The girl who died was a student at our school, her boyfriend was from another high school. That was the most drastic thing I can remember ever happening at school.

During my sophomore year my back problem intensified, forcing me to drop out of school. It was an extremely disappointing decision, but there was no alternative. The long bus ride became intolerable. My back could no longer endure the jolting that resulted from the bumpy ride over increasingly rougher roads.

Due to the lack of sleep, while studying late at night, my resistance against illness had weakened and I fell victim to frequent colds, often bordering on pneumonia.

That last year in school I battled a number of different allergies. For some reason, we were never able to determine their cause.

If we had lived closer to the high school I'm sure my chances of completing the courses and graduating would have been greater. As it was, I didn't even get to finish the tenth grade.

I have always regretted this unfortunate development in my life. I know that I have missed tremendous opportunities due to my limited education. Even though I have tried to make up for some of that loss, I know things could have been much different.

* * *   * * *   * * *

"I pray that each of you, Karl, Tania and Carmelle, will be able to complete high school, and go on to college—a good Christian college I hope. Well, look at that clock. It's time for your folks to come for you, Carmelle. One of these days we'll do this again."

CHAPTER 7

Ah, Romance!

"Hi, Grandma!" Joanna greeted me at the door. "Come on in. Mother and Dad aren't here. I'm not sure when they'll be home."

"Oh, that's okay," I told her as she removed her books from the chair I always sat on when I came to visit. "I can't stay long. I just happened to be in town, so I thought I'd stop by for a few minutes. I called earlier but no one was home."

"I'm glad you came by, Grandma," Joanna said soberly, "There's something I want to talk to you about." She sounded so serious it concerned me.

"I hope nothing's wrong," I said, trying to remember what it was like to be sixteen.

"Oh, don't worry, Grandma. I just wanted to tell you about Andy." I looked at her with surprise. Andy? We all thought she was so much in love with Phil. He was all any of the family had heard about for months. We had gotten the impression that Joanna thought Phil was simply wonderful. He was a soft-spoken, sincere young man, and nice looking too. And he obviously adored Joanna.

I was afraid to ask what had happened to Phil. Joanna could see I was at a loss for words.

"I just met the neatest guy!" she blurted out. "Oh, Grandma, just wait 'til you meet him. He's really handsome." She paused momentarily as if waiting for my reaction, then she said, "He's going to be a doctor. He has already decided which college he's going to." Suddenly she decided she was going too fast for me.

"You're wondering what happened to Phil, I guess." I didn't reply.

"Well," she said with hesitation, "I don't think he's the right one for me. He's too . . . I guess you'd say, he's not exciting enough . . . Oh Grandma, that's what I wanted to talk to you about. I just don't know what to do. I still like Phil an awful lot, but Andy is really neat."

"I'm glad you want to talk to me about it, Joanna." I told her, sincerely. "I can't really advise you, but I can sympathize at least. I remember when I felt the same way."

"You did?!" She was quick to catch the idea that I might be able to offer some suggestions.

"I've often wondered what it was like when you were my age. Would you tell me about your boyfriends? And I'd like to know how you met Grandpa, and how you knew when you were in love, for real. Can we talk about that Grandma?"

"It's a long story," I said. "but I'd like to tell you about it."

*** *** ***

Grandma Tells All

As I've already told you, I assumed great responsibilities at an early age and consequently grew up quickly. I matured early and was treated as if I was older than I was. By the time I was twelve I was torn between being a child and being an adult. The year I was twelve I received my last doll for Christmas. It was a "big girl" doll, imitating a popular skating personality. I thought it was beautiful, but somehow getting a doll for Christmas that year seemed inappropriate. I was mature enough to want to be like some of the older girls at school, including those who were interested in boys.

I was always friendly and understanding, and some of the older boys were attracted to me. My dad was very strict so I had to suppress my feelings toward the boys. I was close to Mama and I never wanted to do anything to hurt her. I knew she wouldn't want me to have anything to do with boys at my age.

I tried not to notice, but new feelings were being aroused in me. Whether I wanted to admit it or not, and even if my parents weren't ready for the change, I was beginning to turn into a young woman. I enjoyed having the boys like me.

I had not forgotten the way I felt when Jack, the school bully, looked at me the way he did. I could tell he liked me. As time went by, Jack would sit near me every chance he got. That really warmed my heart and stirred up those new feelings.

Jack had handsome, deep brown eyes. When he looked at me, I felt as if I could see right into his very heart and soul. No matter what the teacher or the other students in class thought, I saw Jack as being really quite nice. He didn't mean to be bad at all.

Jack's sister, Juanita, was pleasant but she would look at me as if trying to size me up. (I suspected that Jack had shared his feelings about me.) Juanita had smiling eyes, and a cute turned-up nose that seemed to be waving to you. I had no reason to react negatively to her scrutiny.

During those days when we were still in school, Jack and I became really close. I remember one day when we were in the eighth grade he whispered to me, "Ardelle, I like you." Even though I suspected it already, I was swept off my feet to hear him say it.

For days I walked around with my feet dangling out of the clouds, touching earth only now and then. At recess Jack stayed with me and seemed to enjoy my presence. He would sometimes lovingly brush my hand while pretending to be playing a game. I don't think our classmates suspected. Once, he got closer than usual, and while it appeared to those around us that he was talking about a baseball bat that he was holding in his hand, he was actually asking me if I thought Daddy would mind if he came over to our house to see me.

We discussed the idea several times in coming weeks before school was out, but both of us knew it would not work. Daddy would simply not allow it; we were both sure of that.

My girl friend Virginia asked me several times if I liked Jack. "I think he likes you," she confided.

One day a group of us were playing together at recess. All of a sudden Calvin began chanting, "Jack's in love with Ardelle, Jack's in love with Ardelle.."

We were both so embarrassed we could hardly look at each other. Fortunately, about that time, the bell started to ring and we all had to go inside. From then on everyone watched us closely. Someone must have discussed the matter with the teacher because she seemed to have her eyes on us as well.

The end of school that year was also the end of my childhood love affair with Jack, but I've never forgotten the impact of our special relationship during my early adolescent years.

During that summer, I often thought of Jack but never got to see him. His family lived several miles from ours and as hard as I hoped we would just happen to see each other at church, in town, at a community picnic, or any of the other places I daydreamed about, it never happened.

Larry, From Alaska

One afternoon in early summer, I was embroidering near a window in my bedroom, lost in my daydreams. Pausing momentarily to rest my eyes, I gazed casually out the window and across the field beyond our barn. I noticed as a slender figure emerged from our neighbor's barn and walked across the road toward the pasture where some cows were grazing. I could see it wasn't our neighbor Mr. Chris, or his wife, "Miss Bliss", as we called her.

I stood up and looked more carefully, squinting my eyes and shading them with my hands. I watched as the figure walked past some trees and out into an open field.

I laid my sewing project on the bed and went outside to get a better look. I could see from the way he walked that he was a boy or a young man. Who could that be, I wondered. Mr. Chris was known for being mean and he would never knowingly let anyone shortcut across his fields. I was certain of that.

Although I was curious, I didn't mention him to anyone. The next morning I kept my eyes focused in the direction of our neighbor's farm. Sure enough, just as I thought might happen, I saw the young main again, walking toward the hay storage shelter behind Mr. Chris's house.

I kept a close watch in that direction all that day. It was hard for me to concentrate on anything else.

At the supper table I wasn't hungry. All I could think about was the interesting young man I had spotted on our neighbor's farm. I decided I wouldn't mention it while we were eating. While I was trying to figure out how to bring it up, Daddy said, "I was talking to Chris this afternoon. He tells me he hired a hand from Alaska to help him for a few months." I was all ears.

"His name is Larry," Daddy went on, totally unaware of my interest. "Chris says he's a real good worker."

That night I couldn't sleep. My thoughts and imagination went wild. I remembered the tales Mr. Chris and Miss Bliss had told us about their visit to Alaska when they were younger. One of them had a cousin, far removed, who lived there.

They had told us about the wilderness country and how the sky seemed to be very high. The rugged, snow-capped mountains and glaciers had impressed them. Hunting and fishing was great. They had seen bears and caribou, and moose roamed the city streets. They told us of people who had gone there searching for gold. Some had gotten rich, they assured us. They both had a dream of some day living there themselves.

I imagined far-out stories about the young man who walked as gracefully as a young deer. I wondered how it was that he had come from that distant land to work for them. Perhaps he was the relative they had told us about, or the relative's son.

I was sure Mr. Chris had not mentioned to his newly hired hand that a young lady lived on the next farm. For one thing, Mr. Chris wouldn't think of me as a young woman. To him, I was probably just one of Mr. Chappell's bratty kids. Even if Mr. Chris had thought of me as someone Larry might like to meet, I'm sure he wouldn't have told him about me. He would want to make sure all of his hired hand's attention was on his duties on the farm.

I sincerely wanted to meet this young man. Being from Alaska seemed so romantic. He was so close, but the chance of me getting to meet him was slim. As the weeks slipped by, the possibility seemed less likely. Summer would soon be over. Wasn't there some way I could meet Larry? I knew if Daddy had his way, I would never meet him.

When we went by Mr. Chris's farm on the way to church or to the country store, I would strain to see if Larry was anywhere in sight. I always scanned the congregation on Sunday, but I never saw him in church. I hadn't really expected to, however. Mr. Chris didn't go to church; he probably wouldn't allow or encourage his hired hand to go.

I would sit in front of the mirror and arrange and rearrange my hair, trying to figure out how to wear it so that I would appear older than I was. Never having seen Larry, I had no idea how old he was. I only judged him from the way he walked. As I looked at my reflection in the mirror I realized I was much too young to fool anyone.

I was just about to give up on meeting Larry and hearing about Alaska.

I Want You To Know

Then, one morning Daddy came in from doing the chores and called to me,

"Ardelle, would you and Charles like to go with me to check the fences?"

When Daddy had a slack day, we always went around our farm and checked the fences and repaired them where needed. The old fence between our property and Mr. Chris's property was in bad shape. Occasionally, one or two of his cows would find their way through a weak spot and get into our cotton fields. That was bad if it happened to be when the cotton plants were young and growing.

That fence was never so interesting to me as it was that morning. Charles stayed close to Daddy as they worked their way in and out among the bushes, checking for holes in the fence. I lagged behind; my mind wasn't on the fence at all.

It wasn't long until Daddy found a large break in the old fence. One post was leaning badly and when he tried to stand it up, it broke completely off.

"Ardelle," he called to me, "I'm going to have to go back to the barn and find a post to replace this one."

Laying his tools in a pile, he said, "Can you stay here and see that none of Mr. Chris's cows get through while I'm gone?" I was startled. I imagined one of the cows trying to butt me with its horns.

Before Daddy got very far, Charles hollered to him, "Wait for me, Daddy. I'm coming too. I'll get my hammer and help you."

It was very quiet out there by the fence with no one else around. I could hear some of Mr. Chris's cattle on the other side of the trees but I couldn't see them. I was getting concerned about those cows. Then I heard footsteps. I had actually forgotten about Larry momentarily. I could imagine Mr. Chris coming upon the scene and accusing me of pushing the fence over. What would I say?

I quickly looked back across the field to see if Daddy was coming back but he and Charles had not yet arrived at the barn. They would still have to get a post, find Charles's hammer, and then walk all the way back across the field.

"Hello," I heard a strange voice behind me speaking. Turning my head cautiously, I saw a young man standing just across the fence.

"Hi, I'm Larry," he said, "I'm checking the fence for my boss." [I couldn't believe my ears, or my eyes, Joanna. I had wanted so much to meet Larry. Now, in an unexpected place, and in an unexpected way, I was meeting him, face to face. And he was alone. I didn't know what to say. Fear, more than anything else, gripped me. It was such a sudden surprise.]

When I was finally able to speak, I said, "Hello, I'm Ardelle. I'm helping my dad check the fences also. We just found this broken post. He went to the barn to get a replacement."

"That's good. I'll wait here and help him," he said with a warm smile.

"So, you're Mr. Chappell's daughter." He at least knew I existed.

I wanted to tell him how much I had longed to meet him, and I wanted to ask him about Alaska. Instead, I just stood there looking at him.

It was evident that Larry was at least twenty-five, maybe thirty, years old. I was sure he saw me as the child I actually was.

I didn't want to appear dumb so I asked, "How do you like our country, Larry? I understand you are from Alaska. It must be really nice there."

Obviously pleased with my interest in Alaska, he said, "Oh, I like it here, but I'm anxious to get back to my home and my family soon. I just came to spend the summer with my cousin and help him out a bit."

His family? Was he married, I wondered. I had never once thought of that. I had just supposed, since he was alone, that he was single. I had been chasing a farfetched fantasy all summer. How foolish I had been.

"Ardelle," he repeated my name. "That's a pretty name. My little girl's name is Janelle. Sort of rhymes with Ardelle, doesn't it? Here comes your dad now. Sure was nice meeting you, Ardelle. We would love to have you come visit us in Alaska, if you're ever up that way."

[Even if I had not been so taken aback from such an abrupt revelation, Joanna, I could never in my wildest dreams have imagined that one day I would in fact visit Alaska.]

While the broken fence was being repaired, I started walking slowly back across our cotton field, towards the barn, nursing a broken heart that needed mending. There was a huge crack where I had cultivated a fantasy romance that could never be.

"Oh, well," I told myself, shaking my head as I thought about how foolish I had been. "So much for Larry from Alaska."

I had learned an important lesson that summer. And I had managed to forget Jack for a time, too.

Lowell and the Mystery

The year I started high school was a year of change and adjustment for me. I made a lot of new friends and in spite of physical problems, long bus rides and unbelievable homework, I managed to have some wonderful times that school year.

Shortly after school began a nice boy named Lowell and I became good friends. We had a lot of fun together. We rode the same bus. He got on after I did, and got off first on the way home. He was soon carrying my books and helping me with my algebra. We became more and more inseparable. At first, my folks didn't catch on that we were anything more than just friends.

Mama and Daddy were always anxious about me since it was practically dark by the time the bus reached our stop and I walked up the tree-lined lane to our house.

One night I came home proudly wearing Lowell's wrist watch. I could see Daddy was really upset when he saw it, and Mama had a strange look on her face.

"Who's watch is that?" Daddy demanded. I couldn't understand why they were so upset. It hadn't occurred to me that my parents didn't realize how much Lowell and I cared about each other. I thought they would surely like him, he was such a nice boy.

"It's Lowell's," I proudly announced.

"Well, you give it back to him tomorrow." Daddy ordered sternly.

"Why?" I asked, wondering why Daddy would say that.

I noticed Mama kept wiping her eyes with the corner of her apron. I wondered why she was crying. Then she left the room. I thought maybe she couldn't stand to hear Daddy talk to me so gruffly.

"You do as I say. Give it back to him tomorrow." he repeated. Then he stalked out of the room also.

I was confused and hurt. I couldn't understand their behavior. I hadn't done anything to cause them undue concern. It seemed so unfair not to be told what the fuss was all about.

I could not keep my mind on my homework. When I finally got to bed at a very late hour, I was so disturbed I couldn't fall asleep. The next morning, it was with a heavy heart that I wearily trudged down the road to meet the school bus. I was not used to getting such cold shoulder treatment from my own family. I simply could not understand it.

As soon as Lowell got on the bus and made his way to the seat next to me, which I always saved for him, he saw something was wrong.

"What happened?" he wanted to know. I tried to explain that my folks were acting very strange and I didn't know why.

"Here's your watch," I whispered, fighting back the tears. Lowell placed his hand on mine, underneath an open book so that the bus driver and those around us wouldn't notice.

"Don't worry," he consoled me. "We'll talk about it some more this weekend." I thought I detected a look in his eye that meant, "I know something you don't." Funny, I thought to myself, I seem to be the only one in the dark.

When I got home from school that night Mama approached me with a little more composure. After supper she said she would like to talk to me for a few minutes before I got into my homework. I was relieved that at least there was going to be some communication.

First, she apologized for her closed-mouth reaction the previous evening.

"I just didn't know how to tell you," she said. "It isn't fair to not explain why we feel the way we do."

"Mama, what are you talking about?" I demanded. "Please tell me what you're getting at." I could see she was becoming tense again.

Finally, she began trying to explain. "We had no idea you and Lowell had developed a boyfriend-girlfriend relationship. We thought you were just good friends."

"But why isn't it all right for us to be more than friends?" I asked, pleadingly. "I thought you liked Lowell. He's a nice boy, Mama. What do you and Daddy have against him?"

"We don't have anything against Lowell. It isn't that . . . it's just, well . . . " She couldn't seem to say what she was trying to tell me.

"What is it then?" I asked again, bursting into tears.

"We didn't know how to tell you . . . ", she hesitated, ". . . but, well . . . Lowell is a distant cousin to you."

I almost stopped breathing. I couldn't understand why someone hadn't said anything before. My heart was broken. I really thought a lot of Lowell. Now I understood why he had looked at me the way he had, that day on the bus. He had probably known all along. I blamed him most of all. I was so crushed I refused to talk with him as he had suggested. I felt betrayed by everyone. It was painful to be hurt in this way once again.

Jack had been unreachable and unattainable. Maybe I was young, but I suffered immensely from the pain of parting and not getting to see him again. Larry was older and married. Realizing I had been a fool and admitting it to myself was not easy. I promised myself that would never happen again. I thought my lesson on disappointment would stay with me for a lifetime, but here it was once more.

This cousin bit is ridiculous, I told myself. It seemed as if we were related to almost everyone I knew. How would I ever know for sure who was not related to me? I literally had dozens of cousins, including some double cousins; these were related to me on both sides of the family.

Mama's Boy

Daddy finally gave in and willingly let me go out with a boy he and Mama thought was safe for me to date. Bill and his mother lived in another community, and even though my folks didn't know him very well, they liked him and they trusted him. He impressed them as being a decent, well mannered and respectful boy.

I met Bill at the annual Fourth of July picnic. He had dark hair and nice brown eyes. (I always seemed to be attracted to brown eyes.) The first thing he did after we were introduced was to take me over to where his mother was sitting on a blanket by their picnic basket. I wasn't sure if he was more anxious for me to meet her or for her to meet me. It was plain to see that he was devoted to his mother. At that point I couldn't see anything wrong with that.

I must have passed her approval because he asked if he could take me out. I felt honored. That date was the beginning of a relationship that lasted almost two years. My parents grew to appreciate Bill more and more. His mother at least pretended to think highly of me. Friends and family took it for granted that we would eventually get married.

Although we didn't face the issue for a long time, we both gradually began to realize that we were not for each other. I had been cautious from the beginning because I didn't want to get hurt again.

We finally began to discuss our relationship realistically, then one night we decided to go our separate ways. It was painful of course. We had been going together for such a long time. I think our folks almost took it harder than we did. I often wondered if Bill really cared that much. He was seven years older than I was, and still very much attached to his mother. I'm not sure if he would ever have been able to break away from her sufficiently to be a loyal husband. I never heard if Bill ever got married.

Beyond the Horizon, With Mel

Soon after Bill and I broke up, one of my girl friends introduced me to Mel. He was a tall, good-looking guy with wavy blonde hair. I thought he was really handsome. He too, was older than I was. (I was usually attracted to older boys.)

It was plain to see that Mel was a man about town. Daddy didn't trust him at all. Mama tried not to say anything but I could see she was uneasy when I was with him. To be honest, I never fully trusted him myself. He was good to me, however, and showed me great respect. He often told me he wished he was good like me. That made me nervous.

Despite my uneasiness, we continued going together for over five months. To my surprise and utter dismay, he convinced Daddy to let him take me across the state line to meet his folks.

I will never know what possessed Daddy to agree to that deal. I knew Mama was terribly frightened. I was too. I tried hard to back out but Mel was determined to take me on what he thought would be an exciting adventure for me. I had never been more than twenty-five miles from where I was born, which Mel thought was tragic. He had been around the country and traveled through many states.

That sunny autumn day Mel drove through areas I had never seen before. I saw things I didn't know existed. The river that divided our state and the adjoining state was wider than any river I had ever seen. I was all eyes and ears. Mel thoroughly enjoyed being my tour guide for a day.

It was nice meeting Mel's parents and his sister, but I saw right away that their lifestyle was much different from the way I had been raised.

I was so glad Mel had solemnly promised Daddy he would have me home by a certain time. I took solace in the fact that ever since I had known him he had never once failed to keep his word.

When Mel reminded me that we had come fifty miles from my home, I had mixed emotions. I was thrilled in one way, but I was also frightened. There was an element of mystery about Mel and I couldn't help feeling uneasy. I tried to enjoy the scenery as we retraced the route we had taken.

[You know Joanna, it makes me shiver even now, just remembering that experience. I don't recall ever feeling such fear and excitement at the same time. Like so many things in life, flying in an airplane for instance, we could enjoy them only if we knew for sure we were safe.]

Mel kept looking at his watch. I kept watching mine, but I knew mine was not right; no watch I had ever had kept accurate time. Not knowing what time it was made me feel very uncomfortable. I didn't dare let Mel know how concerned I was; I could always tell it irritated him when he felt I didn't trust him.

He wanted to stop at a nice restaurant and have dinner, but I insisted I wasn't hungry. The truth was, I wanted to get home.

When it started to get dark, I became even more tense. I knew Mel could turn off on an unknown road and I would be helpless. I felt relieved every time we passed something I remembered seeing before, or a state road marker, assuring me that we were still on the right road.

I remember how glad I was to get back on our side of the river. Oh, how I wished we were closer to home at that hour.

Mel was silent for a long time as we drove along at the speed limit. I could tell he was making an effort to get me home on time. Finally he broke the quiet.

"Did you enjoy the trip today?" he questioned.

"Oh, yes," I answered quickly. "It was a lot of fun. I didn't realize how much I was missing."

Do you think your folks are real worried?" he asked. I thought that was a foolish question. He knew, as well as I did, that they were terribly concerned.

"What do you think?" I asked him. He didn't answer.

I really did appreciate Mel's kindness in truly wanting to show me some new areas and helping to alleviate some of the "green country girl" stigma I must have exhibited. But I didn't like the idea that he felt sorry for me.

As we drove homeward that night, I decided not to go out with Mel again. I knew if he didn't get me home on time, Daddy would take care of any future plans anyway. Mel also knew that.

Almost like magic, we drove up in front of my house, one minute before the deadline. I was more relieved than anyone, I'm sure.

Daddy was sitting in a chair on the front porch where it was dark, when we drove up. I'll never forget the look on his face when he came out to meet us. I know he already had his speech formulated and ready to deliver if we had been even one minute late. He was too surprised to even speak. He just sort of smiled.

I saw Mama peeking out the window. I could imagine how glad she was to hear us drive up.

As always, Mel came around to open the door for me. I read the satisfaction on his face at being able to deliver me safe and sound and on time to my parents.

I didn't have the nerve to tell him that night that it was all over for us, but I think he knew it wouldn't be long.

Reflecting back on the months I dated Mel, I know God was looking after me. I don't recall being overly concerned with spiritual matters at the time, but I do recall praying earnestly though silently during our times together. Somehow, I never felt I really knew him. I was especially concerned, and praying the best I knew how, the day Mel took me across the state line. I know my parents were really praying too.

[Joanna, I sincerely believe there are times when God looks out for our safety and welfare, simply because we belong to Him, and not because we've asked him to specifically, or because we are consciously trusting Him at the moment. During my relationship with my friend Mel, I know God was in control.]

When rumors about Mel's character and reputation began circulating among the girls I knew, I was glad I was no longer associated with him. I was a lot more at ease when he left our area and went back to his home state. I never saw Mel again.

Golden School Days

After breaking up with Mel, it was wonderful to be free again to mingle with my classmates more and to enjoy some of the boys at school.

My friend Emmett, who had helped me so much with my algebra and geometry problems, began showing me more and more attention. All the girls were "struck on him". He was strong and athletic, and always active in school sports. And he was rather good looking, I thought. He seemed to ignore the other girls, showing preference to me. I was flattered, but Emmett never once asked me for a date. He, like me, lived many miles from school. We both rode the bus, but in opposite directions. We had a lot of fun at school but never had an opportunity to get better acquainted beyond the campus and classroom.

Emmett enjoyed teasing me. I remember he would sometimes look me straight in the eye, and when no one was close enough to hear, he would whisper, "I want to marry you some day." I would smile and whisper back, "Oh, you're just teasing me", and we would both laugh at our private joke.

Emmett was a special kind of young man. When we no longer saw each other, he was often in my thoughts. I secretly hoped he still liked me, and that he didn't have another girlfriend. If he ever had a girlfriend or ever dated anyone, I didn't know about it. I often longed to see or hear from him again but I never did.

I felt a great loss when Emmett died in action in World War II, but I was always grateful for our precious friendship. And I probably would have failed in geometry classes without his help.

I had more boy friends than girl friends in high school. One of my best pals was Norman. He was a down home, happy-go-lucky young fella. You couldn't help but like him.

Actually, I don't think Norman ever thought of us as being anything more than good pals. I often thought he looked after me like an older brother. I'm not sure I realized the real value of friends like Norman and Emmett until later.

Early in the second semester of my sophomore year, I was forced to drop out of school due to my health problems. It was heartbreaking not to be able to follow through and graduate with my classmates.

The disappointment was softened somewhat by the kind and understanding response of my friends at school, however. They included me in all their plans and activities. I was never left out of any party and I was always made to feel a part of school functions.

My faithful, loyal friends kept me up to date on what was going on. When my friend Helen came to stay overnight with me, she was always bubbling over with news.

"Carrie is our best player on the basketball team this year", she would say. "Eric is planning to attend college in Illinois. Can you imagine him going away to school?" We had a good laugh about that. Eric was such a "homebody". The other students loved to tease him about being tied to his mother's apron stings.

"Oh," Helen would say, after a short pause while deep in thought, trying to remember other tidbits of news, "did I tell you about Doris? She was in an automobile accident a couple weeks ago. I don't know if she'll be able to come back to school this year." I listened intently to everything she so faithfully relayed to me.

And so it went, through the coming months. I hoped so much to be able to get back to school in the fall, and maybe catch up and graduate after all, but it wasn't to be.

[I cried often, Joanna. It broke my heart to think of missing out on the graduation exercises, and not being able to get a certificate showing I had finished high school. I suffered a lot of pain because of that.

The New Boy From New Mexico

One weekend Helen invited me to visit her. As usual, she was full of exciting news about the kids at school. But she was careful and considerate about how she mentioned graduation plans. Only when I specifically asked, did she release any details. Then she would hasten to change the subject.

"Oh, Ardelle", Helen said, "we have a new boy at school. He just moved here from New Mexico. He's such a nice boy. He's in my math class." Then she got that faraway look in her eyes.

"He's sort of blond, not real tall, but not short either. And he's rather nice looking. His name is James." She seemed to be reminding herself, more than telling me. "Guess who made friends with James right away . . . Norman."

"That reminds me," she went on, "I don't think I told you, Norman volunteered for the armed forces. He's going in the Navy, right after graduation." She gave me a quick glance as if to get my reaction. I was really sorry to hear about that.

"We're planning a party for him," she said, hoping to cheer me up. "I'm inviting you now. You'll be hearing more about it."

She had given me a lot to think about. I couldn't get the news about Norman out of my thoughts. Why would he want to volunteer for the Navy? When I thought of his room, all cluttered with model boats, and the many pictures of ships at sea on the walls of their home, I could understand why. Norman had probably dreamed of being a sailor since he was a little boy.

Norman was an only child and his mother was very devoted to him. I could imagine how upset she would be at the prospect of having him go away to fight in the war.

Even before I received a formal invitation to Norman's going away party, I figured it would be at Samantha's house. She liked Norman a lot and wanted to be thought of as his girlfriend. Norman, however, was unresponsive and carefree. He evidently enjoyed girls but no one girl was any more special to him.

The night of the party, Samantha asked Norman to swing by and pick me up since I didn't have a boy friend at the time.

As Norman and I drove down the country road in his old stripped down truck, the strange looking radio he had installed in it was blasting so loud, people ran out of their houses to see what the commotion was all about. Some country-sounding male voice was singing loudly, "I picked her up in my pickup truck . . . " I was embarrassed, but Norman was having a great time.

The party that night was lively and everyone was enjoying themselves in spite of the prospect of loosing Norman from our midst.

On the way to the party, Norman had told me about the new boy at school. "I'll introduce you to him," he had promised. But Norman was soon caught up in the spirit of the party given in his honor. He wasn't thinking of me or the new boy at school.

I forgot the new boy myself, until I noticed a young man I had never seen before. He was standing near the piano with his hands in his pockets, watching the rest of the kids apparently having a wonderful time. I immediately felt concern because no one was paying any attention to him.

I looked around for Norman but he was not in sight. I knew if I wanted to meet this new guy I had better not wait for Norman to introduce us.

Despite my reputation for making friends easily, I struggled to work up the courage to approach this boy I had not met before. I tried to put myself in his place and imagine what it would be like to be a stranger in his situation. Finally, I just walked over to him and introduced myself.

"Hi, I'm Ardelle. What's your name?" He just stood there looking at me, so surprised to have someone notice him that he didn't respond at first. After a moment he said, "My name is James."

We were both soon at ease and engaged in pleasant conversation. I learned he had been transferred to the local high school at midterm, from Santa Rosa, New Mexico. And as I suspected, he had indeed been a real, live cowboy, on a large ranch which his grandfather had homesteaded in the early days of the old West.

We soon found we had a lot of things in common, and despite all that was going on around us, we enjoyed the evening tremendously. When it was time to go home, he graciously asked if he could escort me. I was overwhelmed.

Neither of us would ever forget that evening. I was wearing a new green rayon dress with tiny flowers, which I had made myself. The neck and sleeves were finished off with a cream colored piping, and the full skirt draped softly around my trim figure.

I was impressed that James had noticed and complimented my "pretty dress". He thought it was really neat that I had actually made it myself. (What other young man would pay attention to my dress?)

James later told me he thought I was beautiful that night. I'm sure what he saw was my kindness, and that I tried to make him feel welcome and accepted.

After that night we were together every weekend, and often in between. Most of the fellows I dated had some sort of car, but James did not own or have access to a vehicle of any kind. Neither that nor the fact that he lived several miles from me, prevented him from coming to see me often.

I was pleased that he cared enough to walk such a long distance to visit me, and even more that he gladly accompanied me to church. So were my parents. In their estimation, he was more responsible than any of my previous suitors. He was also courteous, respectful and well-mannered.

My folks liked him. He didn't strike them as a young man who would ever try to take advantage of me.

The Competition

Our romance quickly accelerated and continued in full swing until one fateful evening in July. Faye's boy friend was home on furlough and she decided to throw a party. She happened to live in the general direction of James' family. My friend Artie and her boyfriend offered to give me a ride to the party. I would meet James there and save him the long walk down. I planned to also ride home with Artie and her friend.

When we arrived at the party, I looked all around for James. He was nowhere to be seen. This seemed strange to me. He was never late when he came to see me; usually he was early.

I was beginning to get uneasy. Then I saw him. He was just coming through the door, at least a half hour late. And he wasn't alone. I could see he was glancing across the room to find me. I sat quietly observing what was happening.

As James started across the room to where I was, I noticed he kept stopping to introduce his guest. I rebelled inside. What was going on? There were no telephones so he couldn't have called me to explain why he was late. I was completely in the dark. Who could this person be that he kept introducing, I wondered.

No, it wasn't a pretty girl by his side; it was a tall, dark haired, good looking young man. In fact, the closer they got to me the more I could see how handsome this guy was. But why was he with James? And why were they so late getting to the party?

Then they stood right in front of me. "Ardelle," James said, "I'd like you to meet my cousin, Barney. He just arrived, late this afternoon from New Mexico. Barney, this is Ardelle."

The way Barney looked at me I was sure he had already been filled in on all the details about me. He was also sizing me up for himself.

Right away Barney began to flirt with me. I was simply swept off my feet by this handsome, imposing young man and the flattering attention he was giving me. I suddenly knew I had to get to know this guy better.

James was completely taken aback. He could see I was impressed with Barney. He was taller and darker than James. Despite being introduced as cousins, they didn't resemble each other at all. James had his good looking features, and he was pleasant and likable, but his handsome cousin was overpowering.

[For the rest of that evening, Barney hardly strayed a foot from me. He seemed to have forgotten that I was his cousin's girl friend, and I have to shamefully admit, Joanna, I at least acted like I had forgotten that I was anyone's special friend.]

Being so caught up in the overwhelming charisma of this dapper young man who had just arrived from New Mexico, I hardly paid any attention to James.

After a while Barney asked if he could drive me home. I didn't know what to say. Would James be along, I wondered. They had come together. I wondered what kind of car Barney had.

Barney smiled politely and whispered, loud enough to make sure James would hear, "I'll come back here and pick up my cousin."

Somehow, I couldn't seem to say no. I didn't want to. I was a little scared, but I was so caught up with this Barney, I just fell right into his trap. As we made our way through the happy crowd of young people, all talking at once, I didn't even look back to see how James was reacting.

It wasn't long after Barney left my house, after driving me home, that I came to myself. I hurried to my room after saying good night to Mama, who as always, was awake and waiting for me to get home. She didn't suspect that I hadn't come home with James.

As soon as I was alone and had a chance to think clearly, the whole picture began to come into focus. Two distinct personalities stood out in my mind, and demanded comparison.

There was Barney, imposing, tall, dark-haired, somewhat older than me, and, as I had just observed, without manners.

And there was James, not as tall, and definitely built smaller. His neatly groomed hair was brownish blonde, his eyes were the softest, kindest blue I had ever seen, and he was a true gentleman.

How could I ever, even for a few minutes, be dazzled by this young man who was probably getting more pleasure out of cutting in on his cousin than he was in spending an evening with me. He would soon be gone; he had told me he expected to be in St. Louis by the weekend.

I know Barney received a great deal of pleasure from showing his cousin he could steal his girlfriend with little effort.

[I was torn apart at that late hour, to think that I could ever have been so foolish, Joanna.]

There was no way for me to get in touch with James. I knew I would have to suffer this foolish mistake out. I couldn't blame him if he never wanted to see me again. I walked around my room wringing my hands. I cried, I clenched my fists. Finally, in desperation, I started to pray. I begged God to forgive me for my shortsighted actions and I prayed that He would help James to forgive me; I couldn't forgive myself.

As tired as I was I could not get to sleep. Long after midnight, as I tossed and turned, I remembered that James had previously arranged to take me to the pie-supper at the church, the following evening. I grabbed hold of a faint ray of hope. Maybe he would still come. He had never stood me up. He wasn't that type. Grasping at the faint possibility that he still might come, I was able to finally fall asleep.

The dawn of a new day challenged me. I knew it could be a day when my faith in God would be renewed. Or, alas, it might usher in the portals of gloom, and dump me into the realms of despair.

I cautiously proceeded to bake my "hopeful" pie, and to decorate the mystery box, designed to conceal my identity, with tiny flowerets of hope. I worked carefully at the project, knowing full well that that day might hold the greatest disappointment of my life.

Earlier than usual that evening, I put on my green dress with the tiny flowers. I gave special attention to my hair. Then my eyes charted a regular circuit, first to the clock, then towards the window facing the road, back and forth, again and again until my neck hurt.

My coconut cream pie sat like a pleading symbol on the kitchen table. Each time I passed by, the hope I had packed inside that decorated box tugged at my heart.

"Please, Lord," I prayed, "let him come. And let him understand, and forgive me."

"Ardelle," Mama called from the living room, unaware that her voice had suddenly summoned me back to reality. "I hope you're dressed and ready for tonight. Looks like your date is early."

"Thank you, Lord," I prayed, half aloud. "He did come. I knew he would."

I didn't know what to expect, but I knew a showdown was near and hoped the matter would at least be resolved, one way or another.

[Joanna, can you imagine how I felt as I opened the door to greet him? I assure you, it took all the courage I had been able to generate through prayer, and premeditated thought, to be able to face him.]

I was hardly able to look James in the eye, and I was at a complete loss for words.

"Hello," he greeted me, with a kind, understanding smile which I will never forget. He could see I was speechless and on the verge of tears. I motioned for him to come inside.

"I'm sorry . . . I was so foolish." I finally blurted out.

I wanted desperately to express all of my true feelings so that he would understand, without a doubt.

"I've asked God to forgive me, and I hope you will too."

"Don't feel bad," he comforted, as he drew me close and kissed me on the forehead. "I understand."

How could anyone be so kind after such a brush-off, I wondered.

"I know my cousin pretty well." he said, in a soft voice. "I don't blame you. He affects most girls that way, but it doesn't take long for them to see through him."

He stood back and looked at me as if trying to determine the true extent of my remorse.

"I don't know what ever came over me," I confessed honestly. "I can't believe I did that to you. I am sincerely sorry."

"I'll forgive you, sweetheart," he assured me. "I believe you, and you know something, I love you."

[That day, I saw James as he really was. And that day I knew I loved him, though I think I knew it all along, since the day I met him. Joanna, I will always remember that incident.]

We enjoyed a wonderful evening together at the pie social. When my decorated box was auctioned off, James had been tipped off with enough hints to insure he wouldn't miss it. He truly wanted to share the contents with me, and I wanted nothing more than to have his company.

We left early because we just wanted to be together and talk. We had stepped over the invisible line. I think at that point we sensed that the future held something special for us together.

Most of all that evening, we talked about the Lord and our individual relationship with Him. For the first time I told James about my conversion. He listened with great interest, then he told me how he had come to know the Lord in an intimate way.

He, like me, had undergone a period of deep conviction, and he had experienced the same spiritual thirst that I had.

James and his family lived on a large ranch in New Mexico, where houses were few and many miles separated them. There were no churches. Occasionally a traveling evangelist would come through the area and hold a few services in the little building which the scattered ranchers had built for use as a school.

Sometimes an attempt would be made to organize a Sunday School. Usually, after a few weeks, whether due to lack of interest among the poor ranchers or the difficulty in getting to the services, the missionary effort would fizzle out.

Most of what James knew about spiritual things he had learned at his mother's knee. She told him about Jesus, and showed him pictures in an old book, depicting Jesus dying on a terrible wooden cross. She had explained to him and his brother that Jesus had taken their place there, and that He had willingly died for their sins, and the sins of all who would believe in Him and accept His gift of love.

As James grew older, a growing concern about his carelessness in response to God's provision in his behalf made him increasingly miserable. One day while he was riding the range and herding the cattle, the burden became so intense that he got off his horse and down on his knees. There, alone, under a pastel late-afternoon sky, he poured out his heart to the Lord. He asked God to forgive him, and to save him for Jesus' sake. Right there on the prairie, he sincerely accepted Christ as his personal Savior, and received Him into his heart.

I understood perfectly when James tried to explain to me the overwhelming peace he had experienced that day.

Our hearts were closely bonded together as we revealed our innermost feelings about the things that mattered most to us, our spiritual relationship with the Lord.

He didn't propose to me that night, but we both knew that God had brought us together, and that He had a purpose for our lives. I don't think the possibility that we might spend our lives separately even crossed our minds at that time.

After that, I was never tempted to look at another guy out of the corner of my eye. Each relationship I had previously experienced paled in comparison. James brought a special and unique dimension into my life that I had never known with anyone else.

We spent more and more time together each week, and it wasn't long until we talked about spending the rest of our lives together.

Two Become One

We met in May; the following September we were united in marriage. It was a short courtship, and we were both young, but we felt confident that we were in God's perfect will and in the sphere of His timing.

My folks were too poor to even consider giving us a church wedding, so we planned a simple ceremony to be held on the lawn under the trees in our front yard.

It was a lovely Sunday afternoon. Our family and friends were there to witness our vows. The Pleasant Hill minister who married us had spent hours talking with us abut our proposed marriage. We wanted to be sure we were doing the right thing. Both of us did a lot of praying during the final weeks before the wedding.

We felt comfortable having Reverend Addington perform the ceremony. Beginning our married life with the approval of our minister, our parents and most of all the Lord, gave us a good start into the greatest adventure, perhaps, any couple can take,

In order to provide for his new family your grandpa had gotten his first job away from home. He was hired as a farm worker on a ranch, located between his folks' farm, and where my parents lived. A tiny house was provided and we were to receive milk, eggs, and some meat as part of his wages. Cash benefits consisted of a small percentage of the farmer's profits on certain crops previously agreed upon. There was really nothing we could count on for sure. You might say we started out living on love and our faith.

Like our parents, we set up a new household with the barest necessities. We had little earthly goods but we had each other and we were in love. That was enough. We were happy.

Our folks gave us some necessary items that we could at least get by with temporarily, such as a bed, table and two unmatched chairs. A small, four-burner, wood burning stove in the kitchen and dining area also provided adequate heat for both rooms of our home.

[We cleverly improvised and, believe it or not Joanna, we were comfortable. With some wooden shipping crates which we had access to, we arranged shelves along one kitchen wall for storage. Most houses did not have cabinets, certainly not those of the type that we moved into.

A few weeks before the wedding I had been honored with two different showers. The first was a bridal shower from the ladies of the Farmer's Home Demonstration Club, which I attended along with my mother as we worked on quilting and other home related projects.

They gave me beautiful towels and other linens, many of them handmade, as expressions of love and best wishes to a young bride with all her homemaking days ahead. Their willingness to share with me blessed my heart at the time, and our home for years to come.

Shortly before the wedding, the church ladies and my relatives and girl friends also planned a shower for me. They intended to surprise me, and they almost did. I usually caught on to such things easily, but this time I was not expecting another one. The night before the planned surprise, however, I dreamed about dishes with legs on them. In my dream I was really excited about some pretty glass bowls that stood on a base with little legs.

The dream was so real I couldn't get it out of my thoughts the following morning. When I noticed family members casting knowing glances at each other and whispering around corners, I suspected something was cooking that I wasn't supposed to know about.

Later, when Virginia lured me to her house for some silly reason, I went along without questioning her, though I certainly wondered about it. When she suddenly suggested that we go back to my house, I just smiled. By that time I knew something was going on behind my back but I tried not to let on.

When we turned the corner and our house came into view, I could see we had company. I saw that my aunts who lived in the city were there. That was unusual, but I didn't say a word. As we got closer I could see several people walking around inside, and once in a while someone would peek out of the window.

When Virginia and I entered the door everyone started shouting, "Surprise! Surprise!" I pretended it really was one, but the real surprise came when I had almost finished opening my gifts. There were so many pretty things I was quite overwhelmed. The thoughtfulness of each one in choosing what I needed, and things they thought I would like, was touching.

There were embroidered scarves and pillow cases, reflecting many hours of loving handwork, just for me. There were kitchen items that thrilled me so much I squealed with delight.

Then I opened a large, heavy box which contained a set of beautiful dishes. "Oh," I cried, as I took a closer look, "they are all alike. They're too pretty to be true."

My family had never owned a whole set of dishes that matched that I remembered, not even as many as four of any one thing, and certainly not cups, saucers and bowls.

I couldn't hold back the tears. Those lovely dishes were mine, for my own home, for me to share with my new husband. And they were just what I would have chosen, in design and color.

"Wait a minute," exclaimed one of my aunts who was in on the gift. "There's more. This box goes with it."

My heart was overflowing with excitement and gratitude. How could I be so blessed?

I tearfully tore away the ribbon and the pretty paper from the other gift. It too was heavy. Whatever could it be, I wondered. My heart was beating fast. How could I stand any more? I was bursting with gratitude.

I couldn't believe what I saw inside that box. Dishes, with legs! A large cut glass fruit bowl, with eight small bowls to match. And they had legs! They resembled little three-legged stools, with bowls sitting on them. The pink tinted glass had intricate cut designs on them. They were intended to complete my set of dishes. I thought I had never seen anything so pretty.

"They're lovely!" I cried. "And you know what, I dreamed about them last night. I dreamed about dishes with legs!" Everyone laughed when I told them about my dream, and some of them, I noticed, also dabbed tears from their eyes.

Those two thoughtful showers had not only provided the necessities, but many thoughtful "extras", to make our home comfortable and cheery.

Facing Life's Realities

The first year we were married and lived on that little farm, we planted a large garden. It was my first feeble attempt at an art that my mother and grandmother had excelled in. While mine did not compare with theirs, it turned out quite well. My weak back refused to let me do as much as I wanted. I had to enlist the assistance of James in planting and cultivating our living food supply.

That year I canned many jars of lovely vegetables from our first garden. I even came up with some creative ideas of my own. I combined a variety of vegetables, to be used in soups during the long winter months. I canned English peas, carrots, and green beans together. This proved to be an excellent idea. When combined with a diced potato, some home-canned tomato juice, and sometimes some bacon pieces, my soup specialty was quite tasty. Your grandpa was proud of me and he told me so.

During that first year our parents were supportive and helpful in every way possible. They were certainly aware of the economic pressures that faced us. We were both the oldest children in our families. Your grandpa had three brothers and a sister at home. I had two brothers and three sisters. His youngest brother and sister were twins.

Grandpa's mother, your great-grandmother Brown, had to work very hard. Twin babies were a heavy strain on her. She amazed me. I never understood how she could do so much under such adverse circumstances. Your grandpa, who was her oldest child, had been a big help to her. I felt guilty taking him away from her. She had taught him to cook and to do many things around the house. He was willing to help her, and she was most appreciative.

[I had always heard that a boy who was good to his mother would make a good husband. I know that is true, Joanna. Your grandpa was quite capable and always willing to help out around the house.]

On Being A Good Cook

Your great-grandmother, Lessie Brown, was a wonderful cook. I have never seen anyone who could make so much out of so little. I often marveled at her ability to turn out a gourmet dish from practically nothing.

The first year your grandpa and I were married I tried hard to compete with her cooking. My mother had taught me to cook and I had a lot of experience, but my dishes just didn't come out as tasty as those my mother-in-law prepared.

A few times, I remember, Grandpa James commented about the way his mother would have done it. As much as I admired her cooking, I couldn't help resenting the comparison. He didn't mean to hurt me. In fact, he did it without even thinking about it. When it was brought to his attention, he was quick to apologize. He promised not to ever let it happen again—it didn't. From then on, he was always especially careful to show his appreciation for my best efforts. And I did try hard. He would often say, "That's the best cake I ever ate." Or, "These potatoes are delicious; how did you do it?"

It was my pleasure to cook for the man I loved, and he was so grateful for all my effort. He knew that secretly I wished I could cook like his mother.

My mother-in-law was thankful for me I knew. She was close to her thoughtful son and she appreciated the fact that he had me to love and care for him. I was aware that she had prayed often that he would find a wife who would meet her desires, and most of all the wife whom God had provided.

The year after we were married, your grandpa's mother became very ill and was rushed to the hospital for emergency surgery. Following an appendectomy, she seemed to be recovering well. Then she developed complications and died. It was a shock to her family, and to the community, especially since her twins were still babies.

Your grandpa and I offered to take at least one of the babies and raise it, but my father-in-law insisted that he could manage and wanted to keep all the children together.

[I am thankful that I had an opportunity to know your great-grandmother Brown. I learned so much from her, and knowing she appreciated me was a bonus for loving her son. I hope I have at least given you an idea of what she was like, Joanna.]

* * *   * * *   * * *

"Thank you, Joanna, for the pleasure of sharing with you. Now you know more about many of my romantic experiences. I know you can easily identify with some of them. And I think I have given you a pretty good portrait of the two young persons who became your grandparents. I sincerely hope you will someday enjoy sharing your story with your grandchildren."

CHAPTER 8

Transplanted

"Grandma, please tell us another story," Andrea begged, as she skipped out of the kitchen and over to her favorite listening spot at the dining room table.

Whenever she came to visit, she was always happy to help with the kitchen duties so that we could get to our "remembering" sessions which she enjoyed so much. Her ten-year-old cousin Gregory, who lived nearby, came running from the other room to join us. He never wanted to miss a single word, nor the special treat which I always had for them.

"So you want to hear about some of the ways God has answered prayer for our family?" I smiled and silently thanked the Lord for their interest. I so much wanted them to know about their spiritual heritage.

"Well," I said "there are a lot of instances. I would love to share some of them with you."

* * *   * * *   * * *

The First Step Going Up

The second year after we were married, your grandpa and I moved from the country into town. We made the transition, hoping desperately for a miracle that would improve our standard of living and our outlook for the future.

It was as though we were standing at the foot of an invisible ladder. We visualized a way of life which far exceeded the long, drawn out days of drudgery we had both experienced, eking out a bare existence, a lifestyle we had both known since childhood. We had seen our parents work so hard, for so little reward. We hoped for and dreamed of something better.

I'm sure we both realized it wasn't going to be a sudden, miraculous change. We would have to move up the ladder slowly, step by step. And this we intended to do.

Our first home in our new location was provided as part of Grandpa's meager salary. It was a little white bungalow facing busy Gee Street at the edge of town and next to the pony ring we operated for a wealthy Jewish man. He considered it a business but it seemed more like a frivolous recreation to us.

Evenings and weekend days, parents would bring their children to ride the Shetland ponies. Sometimes doting grandparents, or an aunt or uncle, would show up mid-morning or afternoon during the week with two or three tots, anxious to experience the special treat they had been promised. And sometimes we would accommodate groups of children celebrating a special child's birthday.

Grandpa would provide gentle ponies, fulfilling eager children's dreams. Some children were brave and confident. Others were timid, and scared to get near the tiny animals. Grandpa would lead the pony with its rider around a circle, or walk alongside holding onto the very young ones, and the very frightened ones. Soon, repeat customers could hardly wait to choose a pony and take off on their own.

One little boy named Brett had his daddy trained to bring him out several times a week. He got so he thought he owned one of the horses.

"That's my pony," he would tell the other children, pointing to Dory, his favorite. Dory was the favorite of most of the children. She would patiently respond to their every whim, not showing any evidence of agitation no matter how rough the treatment. We never feared that she might buck one of the children, not even Brett, the rowdy one.

Dark haired and bright-eyed, Brett was quite a character. One year his birthday wish produced an elaborate cowboy outfit, complete with real western boots, a Jr. Stetson hat and, of course, a nifty "it looks real" gun. He was required to keep it in its holster, however. We didn't allow him to shoot it or make sudden noises around the ponies. But we had to enforce this regulation ourselves. Brett's parents never denied him anything he wanted or desired to do. He didn't know what "no", or "you may not" meant.

Brett's young cousin, Susan, often came with him. At first she was afraid to get near the ponies. She would stand at a distance, clenching her fists and squinting her eyes as she watched Brett performing his show-off antics. Eventually, however, Susan became almost as clever as Brett with her riding tricks. Holding tightly to the reins, her long, dark pigtails bouncing behind her, she would call over her shoulders, "Look Brett, see what I can do!"

Grandpa would spend a lot of time during the day grooming the ponies to keep them in show-horse condition. They were beautiful animals. He also kept the grounds neatly mowed.

Most of our clientele were well-to-do city folks, who, like Brett's parents, came on a regular basis. But almost every day, some child whose parents were too poor to afford the luxury of paying to ride a horse would count out the pennies and nickels they had saved with great effort and restraint, to pay for a limited number of rides around the ring.

[As you can imagine, Gregory and Andrea, it was easy for your grandpa and me to identify with them.]

Then there were those who in passing by would spot our sign, GEE STREET PONY RING, as they approached. This would catch their attention, then they would see the pretty ponies as they came closer. If there were children in the car they usually ended up stopping for a ride.

It was an easy, pleasant job. We enjoyed the children and the nice people who brought them. Our boss was likable and kind, but the amount of money he paid your grandpa was inadequate for a family.

In May of that first year when we were enjoying the ponies and the children who came to ride them, our own little son was born. The pleasure he brought into our lives was even greater than we had anticipated. It was as if he had been sent straight from heaven into our home. Our hearts overflowed with joy as we cared for him and watched him grow and change constantly. But along with our new-found happiness, we felt the added responsibility and prayed for better employment.

The Next Step

In time, Grandpa found a better job. We moves into a duplex in town. He went to work for a dry-cleaners. We recognized this new venture as step number two on the ladder we were attempting to ascend. Even though it wasn't much of an improvement, we considered it as God's provision and we were thankful.

Grandpa worked regular hours there, sometimes helping with the cleaning process, but usually delivering the freshly cleaned garments and picking up soiled ones. It was not very stimulating but he did enjoy meeting people, and the work was not as hard as doing farm labor.

This job produced your grandpa's first real salary, a certain amount of money for so many hours of work. He wasn't earning a whole lot more than he had on the pony ranch, but it WAS a small advancement and we were grateful for it.

Your grandpa worked faithfully to provide for his little family and I diligently strove to manage the household well. Our experience growing up in poverty stricken homes helped us to cope with financial limitations.

While we didn't have money to buy extras, and barely the necessities, we had each other and we learned to be happy in our simple way of life. In the back of our minds we dreamed of some day being able to provide more for our children than we had ever had.

Since moving to the city we had been terribly disappointed in our efforts to find a church that would meet our spiritual needs. At that point this was our greatest problem. We were searching and trusting God to help us, but the situation seemed hopeless. Each congregation we visited impressed us as being less spiritual than the previous one, certainly not the type we desired and that we were trusting God to lead us to. We were praying for an appropriate church to raise our children in. While we were discouraged, our faith was strong. We were confident that our prayers would be answered.

A Hovering Cloud

Another problem was lurking in the background and becoming more evident every day. World War II was escalating. Our uneasiness increased daily as we listened to the news on our old radio with its continuous static and poor reception.

One evening a newscaster announced that married men, including fathers, were soon going to be called into the armed forces. It was a terrible threat as it hung ominously over our young family. By this time we had two little boys.

Grandpa didn't fear going into the service for his country, nor was he unwilling to do his part. He certainly did not want to be identified with those who were looked down upon because they had purposely shirked their duty. [They were referred to as "draft dodgers", and there were quite a few of them around.] We knew of several able-bodied men in our area with no families to support, who had managed to keep from going into the service.

Grandpa was not that kind of person, but he WAS a family man. He knew, if he should have to leave us, being left alone with two babies would constitute a grave hardship for me. He did not deny his secret hopes for a better solution. Whether we were right or wrong, we reasoned that it was only fair that single men with no dependents should be drafted first. We even suggested to the Lord in prayer that your grandpa was needed more at home.

There was a lot of talk about defense jobs that would provide family men with an opportunity to serve their country on the home front. We discussed that alternative and prayed about it. And he decided to file an application with the local employment agency, just in case such a job should turn up.

When we got home from the employment office that day we held our two-year-old son and his two-month-old brother in our arms and laid our hearts open before the Lord in prayer. We truly wanted God's will, regardless of what it entailed, even if it meant being separated by government orders. We trusted God for a job that would enable Grandpa to serve his country, provide for our material needs, and hopefully allow him to remain with us. We did not doubt such employment existed, somewhere.

We were also concerned about finding a church where Christ was honored and the Bible taught as the Word of God. We were certain there was such a church and we were trusting the Lord to help us find it.

Our faith was strengthened as we claimed such Scripture references as:

Trust in the Lord with all thine heart; and lean not unto thine own understanding. In all thy ways acknowledge Him, and He shall direct thy paths. (Proverbs 3:5,6) and:

Commit thy way unto the Lord; trust also in Him; and He shall bring it to pass. (Psalm 37:5)

The Man From Chicago

One morning a few days later, when your grandpa was at work, I answered the door bell. A pleasant man—whom I judged to be in his late thirties introduced himself as Mr. Brady, from Chicago. He politely removed his hat and held it in his hand. With a noticeable accent he explained that he had just come from the employment agency where he was inquiring for a man to work on his dairy farm, north of Chicago.

"Your husband's application sounds like he might be just the man I'm looking for," he told me. I was speechless. When I could find the words I asked if he could come back when my husband was home. He made an appointment for that evening and went on his way.

[Andrea and Gregory, can you imagine the many thoughts that were racing through my head all afternoon?"]

I was so excited I couldn't concentrate on my work, so I just tried to think things through. We were waiting expectantly for answers to our prayers, but we also wanted to hear the right voice. We wanted God's choice when it came to a job AND a church. It had to be a complete package. But how would we know for sure?

Illinois was a long way from our home in the South. We had no money to pay for the expense of moving. Our families both lived near us. What would they say if we told them we were going to move to another state and take the grandchildren they adored so much so far away that they wouldn't see them again for a long time?

There were many questions. How could we know if we should trust this complete stranger? Were we brave enough to actually pick up and move to an unknown area over six hundred miles away?

We had just assumed that God would provide employment essential to aiding the war effort in our own state. The possibility of having to relocate, perhaps hundreds of miles away, had not occurred to us. The idea was new and somewhat frightening.

Finally, after what seemed like hours, your grandpa arrived home from work. I met him at the door as I always did. That did not surprise him. But he could see right away that I had something pretty important to tell him.

"Please hurry and get washed up for supper!" I urged. While he ate I recounted what had happened and told him that the man from Chicago was coming back to talk with both of us about a job in Illinois. Again we prayed earnestly, asking God to help us to know His will and to prevent us from making a serious mistake.

At the appointed time, Mr. Brady arrived, smiling as pleasantly as before. He explained that he owned property at the edge of our town and while he was down South, he was also looking for help on his dairy farm near Chicago.

"We have over one hundred Holstein dairy cows," he told us. "And we regularly milk ninety or more at a time, to supply a dairy there." He went on to say he was looking for someone who understood cattle and loved working with them.

"And," he added quickly, as if he could read our mind "I assure you, it is considered strategic work, and would qualify as civil defense employment."

Grandpa and I looked at each other in disbelief. Could this be the answer to our prayers?

Your grandpa certainly knew about cattle. He was born and raised in New Mexico, and was in fact an "authentic" Western cowboy. He did know a lot about cattle, and he loved working with them. This impressed Mr. Brady.

"There's just one thing," your grandpa said. "What are the churches like up there? That would be a major consideration for us."

Mr. Brady looked surprised. "What do you mean?" he asked cautiously. "What did you have in mind?"

We explained that we were hoping for something like a Bible church; one that wasn't emphatically denominational. A good, solid church where the Bible was preached, and where Jesus was lifted up as God's Son.

[I will never forget the expression on Mr. Brady's face, Andrea and Gregory.]

With a puzzled look and moist eyes, this unusually quiet, gentle man reached into his pocket and pulled out a folded brochure.

"There just happens to be a church . . . ,"

He hesitated for a moment, then went on, "the pastor's father gave this to me a few days ago and invited me to visit the church."

He handed us the folder. "I haven't been there yet," he admitted, "and I can't vouch for it's validity, but I know the church has a good reputation in the community. Read about it and see what you think."

We were practically overcome. How strange that he would just happen to have this information with him.

ROLLING HILLS BIBLE CHURCH, the brochure said, and underneath it was written "interdenominational". Mr. Brady said it was located about five miles from his dairy farm.

"It's a country church, with lots of charm," he added.

Could this be the assurance that God was answering our prayers? And, could this possibly be step number three on the ladder opening up to us? It sounded like a sure indication that the Lord was showing us this new opportunity, but we had to be positively certain.

A Big Decision

"We're certainly interested," your grandpa told Mr. Brady, "but we couldn't make a life-changing decision like this, right on the spot. We will have to pray about it."

"Yes," I agreed. "And, we will want to discuss it with our parents, too." Our visitor from Chicago agreed that both were in order and asked if he could come back to discuss the matter further the following day.

We tried to imagine what our folks would say when we told them about the surprising, even shocking, developments. We decided to put out a "fleece", like Gideon in the Bible. Both of us were sure my dad would not approve, so we decided to let his reaction be the determining factor. We knew, if it was God's will that we make the move, He could cause Daddy to agree that it was perhaps the right thing to do.

Early the next morning, as soon as your grandpa could get in touch with his boss to ask for the day off, we left with our two little boys and my sister Louise, who was living with us at the time. We planned to go first to Pleasant Hill then to Walcott, to talk to both our families. As we drove along we discussed the pros and cons of the whole thing. Louise contributed her opinion also.

I was really nervous and apprehensive as we drove up to our old home place. Daddy was standing on the front porch. He was surprised to see us at such an early hour.

For a moment I thought about how terrible it would be not to see Mama and Daddy for a long time, and I almost wished he would discourage us, as I felt sure he would anyway.

Once inside, we cautiously began to explain to my parents what had taken place the day before. All the time I was watching Daddy's face to get his reaction, since we had agreed to seek our answer there.

I could almost hear Daddy saying, "Oh, no, that would be too risky. What if . . . ? " He would never agree that we should risk going.

My dad just sat there, thinking quietly. He seemed to be weighing the matter very carefully before expressing his feelings.

Finally, Daddy looked up at us with a painful but determined look on his face. [I'll never forget his expression.] Finally, he spoke.

"You know," he said, "that might not be a bad idea. There isn't anything to look forward to in this part of the country."

I could not believe what I was hearing. This was not like my Daddy at all. While he was hesitating and debating how to answer, he was no doubt recalling the hard life all of us had known on the farm, as far back as we could remember. I think he reasoned that even though a move like this, on the spur of the moment, would indeed be taking a chance, it would probably be worth the risk in the long run.

The big catch was that Mr. Brady had indicated he needed someone immediately. He was leaving to go back to Illinois in a couple of days. If we were going to accept his offer, he wanted to take our furniture back with him in his truck. So our answer had to be yes or no—right away.

By this time my mother was weeping softly, saddened at the prospect of losing us and her precious grandchildren for an indefinite time, maybe for years.

"You know how much I hate to see you go," Mama said, wiping her eyes with the corner of her apron. Trying hard to be brave, she suggested, "This opportunity could be the answer to your prayers, and mine too, in fact." She was terribly concerned about me being left alone with the children if Grandpa should be drafted. "I don't want to be the one to hold you back," she added, her voice breaking,

My sister Louise, who had been working in a drugstore in town while living with us, spoke up at this point. Addressing Mama and Daddy, she asked, "Can I go to Illinois with them, please . . . ? "

As much as they didn't like the idea, they were more concerned about what might happen if they didn't let her go.

Louise stayed with Mama and Daddy to try to work things out for her, while your grandpa and I and our little boys went on to Walcott to talk to his loved ones about the proposed move.

Once we were alone the seriousness of the matter really hit us. We knew we must not miss God's will. Daddy's response seemed to be a clear indication but we had to be sure. Oh, how we prayed.

When we told our other family about the opportunity we had been offered, we were so excited they could see it was something we felt we were supposed to do. They didn't try to discourage us. By this time we were convinced we knew God's answer to our prayer for guidance.

After picking Louise up on our return trip, we headed home to meet with Mr. Brady again that evening. He came earlier than expected, anxious for our answer.

When we told him about the fleece and how we felt God had showed us His will, he confided in us that when we refused to make a hasty decision, without praying about it, and were insistent about the prospects of a good church, he knew he wanted us to work for him.

"Do you think you can get your furniture ready by tomorrow afternoon, so that I can take your belongings back with me to Chicago?" he wanted to know. He could see we didn't have that much that was worth moving so far. He said the house was partially furnished. As he got up to leave he said, "I'll get bus tickets for you to Chicago when you are ready to go. I'll give you directions to the dairy, then."

Is This For Real?

We could hardly believe that so much could happen in such a short time. Your grandpa and my sister Louise immediately contacted their employers to resign from their jobs. It was the end of the month and we hadn't paid our rent. The landlord didn't mind at all that we gave short notice that we were moving. Rentals were in demand and it would give him an opportunity to increase the rent. The timing was perfect. We could use the money to help make the adjustment.

So many things were happening in such rapid succession, as well as the usual taxing activity that goes with a normal move. Our heads were spinning. I think we may have subconsciously been wondering if we wouldn't suddenly wake up and find that we had been dreaming. But no, it was really happening. It was unbelievable that we could be transplanted over six hundred miles in three days time.

Early the next morning Mama and Daddy and my brother and younger sisters came to help us finish packing, take care of the items we couldn't move, help with the cleaning, and to see us off.

Just as we arrived at the bus station, your grandpa's dad and his sister and brothers drove up. We hadn't expected them.

Our excitement and joy at the prospects of a better life was mixed with the bitter pain of parting, as we bade a tearful farewell to our loved ones, not knowing how long it might be before we would see them again.

I had never been away from my family and I had never traveled before. I was twenty-two years old and had not been more than fifty miles from where I was born.

The trip was exciting for all of us, especially Louise and me. Your grandpa had moved from New Mexico to our area, so he had traveled across a few states.

Louise hadn't even been twenty-five miles from our home. She was very young and quite excited about the sudden move. She was obviously trusting us to look after her enroute, and in our new location.

All of us eagerly took in the ever-changing scenery as the Greyhound bus sped us on our way to our new home, and hopefully, a better way of life.

Country Kids In The Big City

Mr. Brady, who had asked us to please just call him "Brady", had bought our tickets to Chicago, and from there we were instructed to take the Chicago Northwestern train to Barrington, which he said was thirty five miles northwest of the big city. He promised to meet us at the depot.

We got to Chicago on the first day of April. It was a day I will never forget. We were wide-eyed and apprehensive. Although it was already spring, I remember it was snowing.

After riding the bus for what seemed like hours, we were still in Chicago. We could hardly believe any city could be that huge. Chicago was more than twenty miles square at that time.

The bus driver went slow and stopped often. His route took us through some of the seamy parts of the city, including the "stock yards" district, which we had heard about. I realized later, the softly falling snow was like a white curtain which God hung over the ugly parts of town as we drove through.

I remember being surprised to see as many black people as white, everywhere across the city. Until that time I had thought that all colored people in the United States lived in the South.

At last we reached the bus depot in downtown Chicago. It was large and complicated, with numerous departments and sections. What a contrast to the terminal where our journey had originated.

Soon we were fighting our way through the noisy throng of people, attempting to round up our luggage. It was extremely frustrating for us.

Most people appeared to know what they were doing, but we were utterly confused. Under great pressure, but bolstered by prayer for divine guidance, we worked together and somehow got through the ordeal.

We managed to locate all but one of our suitcases and were terribly concerned about the errant one. We felt we had lost a part of ourselves, but we were assured that our luggage would be waiting for us at the train depot when we arrived.

When we arrived? Wasn't it next door?

"Oh, no!" the receptionist explained, shaking her head as if to say, "What's wrong with you, don't you know anything?"

"It's a long way from here," the girl behind the counter said, trying to hide her amused smile. She quickly told us how to get to the depot.

Grandpa attempted to protect Louise and me from the frustration he felt, but he couldn't hide it. "We'll just try to do what they tell us," he comforted.

"Let's see, which way did she say to go?" he mumbled to himself, hoping we wouldn't hear him. But we did.

A taxi, I remembered she had said. I tried to remain calm for Louise's sake, but I was thinking, "I wonder how much they charge. Do we have enough money to cover all the extra costs we haven't counted on?"

We hailed a taxi and eventually found ourselves at the train depot. A funny little man in a dark colored uniform and wearing a red cap offered to help us but we were concerned about how much we would have to pay him, so we tried to work things out ourselves.

For a brief time we weren't sure if we were going to make the scheduled train to Barrington. All three of us "green" country kids realized that day just how back-woodsy we really were.

"What do we do now?" I nervously asked your grandpa. Louise looked scared. "I wish I had stayed home with Mama and Daddy," she admitted.

"Oh, we'll figure it out, somehow." Grandpa consoled us, trying to manage all of our luggage, including the lost suitcase that had mysteriously turned up.

Louise carried our two year old and I held the baby, who was starting to get cross. Each of us had a couple of small bags to deal with, in addition to our purses.

"I'll be glad if we ever get out of this place," my sister Louise announced. We all felt the same way. "We'll have to try and find the right train," Grandpa said firmly.

Finally, as if by some miracle, which it probably was, we made it through the elaborate maze and eventually ended up on what turned out to be the last train to Barrington that night.

Although I had seen lots of trains in our home town, I had never ridden on one before. I remembered visiting my cousin Moleva, who lived in the city, and how the rattling, banging trains that constantly passed near her home had kept me awake all night. Their family was so used to the noise they didn't even hear them.

Now a train was taking me and my loved ones to a new life in Illinois. Was this an indication of the complexity we faced in our new life, we wondered.

As we chugged along on that old passenger train, each of us was getting more and more excited by the moment. What would our new home be like? Would Brady continue to be as nice as he had appeared to be? Would our new job work out as promised? These questions and more battered our weary minds as we headed into the chilly April evening aboard the Chicago Northwestern train we had somehow managed to catch, and just in time, we gratefully realized. When we arrived at the depot in Barrington, we found it closed. It was dark and cold; and no one was stirring about. Mr. Brady was not there as he had promised. Fear gripped our hearts.

We were so weary by that time, it was easy to imagine the worst. Looking around, we spotted a telephone booth. But when we looked in the directory, there was no listing for Mr. Kenneth Brady. We didn't think to look under Bellwood Dairy Farm. In desperation I frantically began looking through my purse for the phone number he had given us.

"Dear Lord," I prayed. "Please help us. We've trusted this man so much." Then your grandpa suddenly remembered—Brady had asked us to call him from Chicago so that he could be at the depot to meet us. We had been so involved in trying to find our way around, we had forgotten until that moment. Grandpa also remembered that he had the phone number in his billfold.

When Brady answered the phone, he sounded as relieved as we were. He couldn't imagine what had happened to us. [We were embarrassed to have to tell him about all the confusion we had experienced.]

"I'll be down in a few minutes to get you," Brady told your grandpa over the phone. And he was. By that time we were all three utterly exhausted. The little boys were restlessly sleeping in our arms.

Getting Acquainted With Our New Home

When we arrived at Bellwood Farms, the place that would be our new home, we learned that Brady's previous dairy herdsman and his wife and children were still there. This was disconcerting to me. Was there some mistake? He had not mentioned them to us. We had expected only Brady to be there.

We were at a loss for words. What was going on? Were these people supposed to be there, to help train grandpa for the job? It was evident that they were not ready to move out.

We soon understood that it was as difficult for this family to have us come barging in, anxious to occupy our new home, as it was for us to find them still there.

Although they knew they were going to be moving sometime soon, they evidently didn't realize Brady was bringing new employees back with him from the South. It was easy for me to detect the irritation they felt. How could Brady be so inconsiderate as to bring us in on them without any warning? We all found it hard to understand why he had allowed such a strange situation to develop.

It wasn't long before we learned that the herdsman and his wife were also Christians. I don't like to think about what it would have been like if we had not been tolerant and understanding of each other.

We were indeed a full house until they were able to get moved out, but we learned from each other. I'm sure God was looking after their family and ours in a special way. It was a lesson of patience and understanding for all of us.

The Big House

The huge two-story house, along with all the beef, poultry, and eggs we could eat, was included in your grandpa's salary. We had never had so much. In taking the third step up the ladder, we had actually skipped some rungs, moving up into a completely new status category.

The house was fairly old but had been kept in good condition. It was built much better than homes we were used to in the South. Because the winters were so severe, we were told, the houses were very well insulated.

This house had some very modern features, or at least very modern to us. The laundry chutes, for instance, shuttled dirty clothes from the upstairs as well as the downstairs rooms, right down into the laundry area in the basement. There was an electric washing machine which I could use. I had been used to washing clothes by hand or taking them to a coin operated laundry center, which I disliked doing. I don't think anything pleased me more than having a washing machine available. But there was no dryer. Brady explained that there were two sets of clothes lines. During the summer months, we would use the neat, stationary ones in the side yard by the house. During the long, cold winter months we would use the lines that were set up in the large basement. [There was no way we could have imagined how cold it would get when winter came, Gregory and Andrea. You have never experienced such cold and stormy weather.]

Brady pointed out the huge coal-burning furnace which occupied a large area of the basement, and the coal storage bin which was the size of a small bedroom. Coal was something we would have to learn how to use.

When Brady told us about the terrible winters we could expect, we became tense. We remembered how much it cost to heat our small apartment when we lived in the South. Grandpa and I looked at each other uneasily.

"But," Brady hastened to assure us, probably because of the worried look on our faces, "all the utilities are included in your salary." We were instantly relieved.

It was hard for us to assimilate all that was taking place. Everything seemed to be taken care of. Each week, Brady told us, we would take the surplus eggs to a nearby rural market and exchange them for staple groceries such as flour, sugar, salt, and the sundry items we needed for the laundry and personal care. We had just about everything we could possibly want provided.

The small salary Grandpa received was ours to use as we chose. We had never had it so good. A lovely, comfortable home with all these good things included, all added up to blessings beyond our wildest imagination.

We were full of praise to God already, and we hadn't yet even had a chance to check out the church we were so much looking forward to.

*** *** ***

"That was just the beginning of a happy and blessed period of our lives. There's so much more to tell you, Andrea and Gregory, but that will have to wait until another time."

CHAPTER 9

The New Life In Illinois

"Grandma," Gregory called to me as he came into the living room, "don't forget you promised to tell us about your new home up north."

"Yeah," Andrea echoed, "I want to hear about the cold winters and the snow. And I can hardly wait to hear about what it was like to live on a big dairy farm in Illinois."

"Well, you sure have a big order there," I responded, "but I think I can manage it. You know something, I believe we have time for a story right now. The dishes can wait."

A cold rain was falling outside, a sure indication that it was snowing in the Sierra Nevada mountains not far above us.

They both scurried to get comfortably close to the woodstove where it was warm and cozy.

"Let's leave the police scanner on, Grandma. "Gregory suggested. "I want to hear about the snow in the mountains."

"The way it's raining here, I know it will be great for skiing up there tomorrow. I can hardly wait." Andrea spoke up, excitedly. "I'm glad we live in the foothills. I love the snow; skiing is my favorite sport."

"Oh, I don't know," Gregory questioned. "Skiing may be fun in the wintertime, but soccer is my favorite sport. It doesn't cost as much either."

He thought for a minute, then he added, "I also like to go fishing with Grandpa, on the lakes, and I enjoyed hunting deer with him this year."

"This is a wonderful place to live," I agreed with both of them. "The Lord is good. When we trust Him, He sees to it that we live where it's best for us. You know, I think that's one of the most wonderful things about the way God has worked in my life. Let me tell you more about it."

* * *   * * *   * * *

Beauty Abounds

We loved northern Illinois and enjoyed the beauty of nature there, the lakes, the rolling hills, the trees and the well groomed estates in the Barrington Hills countryside.

Actually, every place I've ever lived, I've thought it was the most wonderful place in the world. I believe I was born with a keen awareness of beauty, an enlarged capacity to enjoy its many faceted manifestations around me. I know the colorful world of my youth carved deep impressions into my sensitive memory.

In the South, where I grew up, we enjoyed four seasons, each distinct, producing its own variety of splendor.

In the springtime, the leaping hills and lush valleys bulged with exciting, colorful new life. While our summers were hot and humid, we usually received enough rain to maintain color and freshen the atmosphere, in spite of the torrid temperatures.

Autumn always splashed an overwhelming display of color across the countryside. Multicolored leaves on a variety of native trees showcased their artistic palette of earth tones, in a frame of intertwined evergreen trees.

Winters were full of beauty and wonder too. We cherished even the stark beauty of the bare oak and elm trees. They didn't fool us; we knew their secret. They were not dead, but were only sleeping and would awaken in the spring.

Even now, I can see the tall, graceful cedars and pines, waiting, along with us, in anticipation of the first snow. And when the waiting was over, the quiet, white beauty of the intricate, soft designs of God's icy, frozen creation would transform our world into a temporary magic wonderland.

[You know children, after almost fifty years, those vivid scenes are clearly etched in my memory. I want you to know, however, that we did not move to the north country in search of enhanced beauty. The spectacular revelations of mother nature's masterpieces were totally unexpected bonuses.]

We moved to northern Illinois in early April. So much was happening around us in our new home that we did not realize how nature was struggling in preparation for springtime's dramatic arrival. Not until after we had experienced our first difficult winter did we fully appreciate the significance of the return of spring in Illinois.

We witnessed the transformation in awe that first year. What seemed to us an infinite number of new and unfamiliar trees and flowers came to life and filled our scope of vision with contrast and surprise.

The heat and humidity of summer was even more uncomfortable than in the South. The native Northerners took it in stride.

"It's because we're so close to Lake Michigan," they explained, although this didn't make it any easier to cope with the heat.

We observed some of the tricks the local people had come up with to help them survive the sweltering temperatures. In the middle of the night when it was difficult to sleep, they would wrap themselves in large, Turkish-knit towels wrung out in water. We also noticed that everyone always seemed to have a tall glass of iced tea in hand.

"Don't worry," they would comfort us as they wiped the sweat from their foreheads, "summers here are very short." We felt fortunate to have lived through one.

After what seemed like one long, continuous heat wave, summer ended abruptly and it was fall. Autumn in Illinois was unbelievable and overwhelming to us. September and October were indescribable. It seemed as if God had delicately poured a cup full of living color over the landscape.

During the horrible heat of summer and the majestic autumn season, we had been warned to "watch out for winter".

"You haven't seen anything until you've experienced a winter here," our neighbors told us, with a mixture of reverence and warning in their voice. But it was hard for us to dread winter while anticipating the snow we had heard so much about.

An Authentic Blizzard

With winter approaching, the sky appeared bleaker and colder. One Tuesday afternoon in late November of our first year there, we watched as the sky took on a strange bluish-gray cast. Great snow-bearing layers of massive clouds soon began to hover ominously.

"A northerner is coming," Brady told us as he began to prepare for what he knew was inevitable. He had sent your grandpa to check out the strange fences on the nearby hillsides earlier. These fences didn't encompass anything, they were just short stretches of lightweight wood panels woven into wire, so that they could easily be rolled up. They were called "snow fences" and were placed where windblown snow usually drifted. When a sudden storm would hit they would have to be quickly rehung on existing posts.

Brady kept glancing up at the clouds as if trying to judge the time of the storm's arrival. Then suddenly, before they were finished hanging the last of the snow fences, huge flakes began to tumble down.

The snowflakes fell so densely and so quickly that we could only see a few feet ahead of us. I hurried inside.

I will never forget our reaction as that first big snow storm closed in around us. My sister Louise and I stood in front of the picture window in the living room and watched with awe and wonder. Nothing we had ever seen could compare to the overwhelming spectacle we had suddenly become caught up in.

Our admiration and appreciation for the snow, which God was sending from heaven, overflowed. We couldn't find words to express the exhilarating thrill.

My little son was caught up in the ecstasy. He jumped up and down, clapping his hands as if watching a good show. Louise and I laughed, and cried tears of joy. The majestic view out our front window grew more picturesque by the moment.

The tall pine trees that lined our yard became solid white Christmas trees. The fence turned into a phantom wall. Power lines swayed under the weight of the snow, at times threatening to fall. I tried to remember where I had seen some old fashioned lamps on a shelf, in case we lost power.

We could no longer see the barn or the milk house. I knew your grandpa and Brady had probably managed to get the cows into the fenced area next to the barn early, because Brady had recognized the approaching storm in time. We hoped they were both inside the barn now.

Glancing at the clock, I wondered how they were coming along with the chores. At the time we were milking about one hundred cows and I wondered how much later they would be because of the storm.

As the storm intensified, I became more and more concerned about how the men were going to get to the house. It was snowing so hard that they wouldn't be able to see two feet ahead of them. Just that short distance between our house and barn would be dangerous.

I had read about people being lost in snow storms and even dying from exposure, only a few feet from their destination. I couldn't help fearing that this might happen to them.

When darkness fell and we could no longer watch the raging storm outside, I turned my thoughts toward preparing a hot, nourishing meal.

Hours later, with great relief, we heard them at the door. There was a great deal of excitement when we sat down to eat. Brady could hardly believe our reaction to the snow storm.

"I have never seen anyone so excited about snow," he told us. While we ate our belated evening meal, Brady shared interesting details of snow storms from previous years, and their complications. He failed to suppress our enthusiasm, however. By bedtime we were so emotionally stimulated we found it hard to wind down and get to sleep.

We were not prepared for the sight when daylight dawned the following morning. Every building, tree, bush, fence, and even the mailbox stood like white statues, their outlines hardly distinguishable against the snow-covered hills behind them.

The fragile snow fences leaned wearily under the huge mounds of drifted snow. The power lines along the roadside were sagging under unbelievable amounts of snow, balanced on the wire, strung between the white posts that stood like ghastly pillars.

The roads were buried under several feet of snow. In some places, where it had drifted, it was piled as high as the side of our house. Roads were impassible, schools were closed, and even the mailman could not get through.

We had never seen so much snow nor a scene so beautiful. We couldn't understand how anyone could keep from admiring snow. Yet since we had moved there, we had heard many uncomplimentary remarks about the effects of snow. All we could see was a masterpiece of white art, too majestic to describe. It was so pure, so clean, so inspiring, so wonderful.

Early that morning, Brady and Grandpa had shoveled a fresh tunnel to the barn in order to feed and milk the cows. But there was no possible way to get the ten-gallon cans of milk up to the main road where the truck from the dairy processing plant always picked them up. And we knew that the milk truck could never make it.

Brady told us that the road near us would be among the first to be cleared by a huge snow plow, since Bellwood Farms was a licensed, accredited dairy farm, and depended upon by many people.

Later that afternoon, the snow plow reached our road, and with all the exerted effort of the county crew, one narrow lane was finally cleared. Now and then they would clear a pullout area to allow oncoming vehicles to pass.

In the days that followed we learned why the Northerners felt the way they did about snow. We soon realized that the beauty was only part of the picture.

The Ice Storms

In those years, living in Northern Illinois, we weathered many snow storms. We also discovered another treacherous aspect of winter; ice and sleet storms. We observed the first one in shocked unbelief. We felt trapped as we watched the roads turn into solid sheets of ice. Trees, shrubbery, and plants were frozen in grotesque shapes as they withstood the cold, wind-driven sleet.

But we adapted quickly. Soon we were as brave as the natives who were used to driving on the icy roads.

We didn't suffer from the cold in ordinary daily living. Our house was well-built, and adequately insulated. The windows and doors were weather-stripped on the inside. Storm doors and windows were installed in the fall, and taken down when winter was over. (We often wondered why they bothered to take them down, only to have to put them up again in such a short time.)

Most houses in our area were centrally heated with huge coal-burning furnaces located in the basement of the large old homes. We used a large especially made bucket to carry coal upstairs to the kitchen for the cookstove. It was messy and I had to get used to the fact that it made a hotter fire than wood.

We also had a kerosene range in the kitchen which we used in the summer so we wouldn't heat up the kitchen. It was considered dangerous and I always feared it.

The living room, dining room, and bedrooms were heated with iron registers which stood along the wall. Hot water, heated by the coal furnace in the basement, flowed through pipes in the registers. It was a damp heat and we constantly had to fight mold on the walls caused by excess moisture. It was also hard to keep the walls clean. Coal dust from the basement seemed to filter upstairs and made it difficult to keep the draperies and curtains clean.

Life On The Dairy Farm

Life on the dairy farm was complicated. The cows had to be milked twice daily, starting long before daylight. Grandpa and Brady got up at 4 a.m. every morning and slipped out to start on the chores. You can be sure the men were ready for a hearty breakfast as soon as they could possibly take a break from their morning routine.

After the herd of approximately one hundred cows was milked, the milk had to be pasteurized and cooled. It was then transported in large, ten-gallon cans to a specified location on the county line road where it was transferred to a large milk truck and taken to the processing and bottling plant near Chicago. Milk was sold in glass bottles in food stores.

Twice each day the milking machines had to be washed, sterilized and disinfected. This was to counteract bacteria, which could quickly spoil the milk.

Feeding the cows was a major chore. Your grandpa quickly learned each cow's name and her particular diet formula. He was a natural-born dairyman.

There was little time for rest, physically or mentally, for dairymen.

What could one do during the short break in the middle of the day, or after the afternoon chores and late dinner? By evening the men were so tired they couldn't get excited about going out. They required rest since they would again have to get up very early the next morning.

When we moved to Illinois, we got into the habit of going to see a western movie in town once a week. We especially enjoyed Gene Autrey, and I liked the ones featuring Dick Foran.

Later we became involved in church activities and we seldom went to the theater. In fact we became convicted about it, and convinced that attending movies was not something a Christian should participate in. The shows we saw in those days were nothing like those shown in theaters today.

We had a lot of fun around the farm. There were two nice lakes on Bellwood Farms where the men sometimes went boating and fishing. They also hunted pheasants. And we found things to do together as a family. [Those were wonderful days, Gregory and Andrea.]

There were other chores, in addition to milking the cows. In the summertime large fields of grain had to be sown and then harvested to produce food for the cows and other farm animals.

We all enjoyed the fun and the food on the farm. [I have to admit that those big meals, which included lots of rich Holstein milk and homemade butter, resulted in my first battle with a weight problem. I soon put on about forty pounds. I was really very thin when we moved there. Can you imagine your Grandma ever being real slim? Well, I was.]

Even though fattening, the milk, butter and ice cream were delicious. I learned to make cottage cheese (also fattening), with all the added cream. But our family was healthy and happy in those days.

Family Matters

We truly loved Illinois and our new standard of living that far exceeded what we had been used to in the South. But there was one big problem. Louise and I missed Mama and Daddy and our brother and sisters terribly. Brady tried to comfort us by suggesting that they get to a telephone so that we could talk to them occasionally. They would have to drive a distance to the nearest phone to make two-way contact.

When we talked to them we could tell that they really missed us. They kept lamenting the fact that the grandchildren were so far away, and growing and changing so quickly. This would tear our heart out. At both ends of the line, we always ended up in a big crying session.

Brady liked us and he loved your grandpa's herdsman abilities, so he came up with a brilliant idea. Why not ask our parents if they would like to move to Illinois also. He said he really needed another farm hand.

"Do you suppose your dad would be interested?" he asked. The tears in our eyes slowed, and stood still. After we thought about it though, we felt sure it was no use; Daddy would never make such a drastic change. But we decided it was worth a try anyway. After all, he had agreed that it might be a good idea for us to move north and try to improve our living conditions, hadn't he? There was at least a tiny ray of hope.

Grandpa and I prayed desperately. We all wanted very much to have them move up but we didn't want them to do something they would be sorry for. We tried hard to be unselfish about it. It certainly would be a big step for them and we didn't want them to blame us later if it didn't work out.

We arranged another telephone encounter and cautiously brought up the idea and presented the suggestion to them. We knew there was a good chance they would say no. To our delight they responded enthusiastically, however, and promised to give it some serious thought and get back to us. Louise and I were so excited we could hardly contain ourselves. Whenever the phone rang, we practically held our breath. Both of us would run to pick it up. We could hardly wait to hear our parent's answer.

We thought about what it would be like for them to uproot themselves and move that far at their age. It didn't seem likely, so we tried not to get our hopes up too high. Brady was busy excitedly working out a deal to present to them to help them make a final decision.

Later that wonderful afternoon when they called to discuss the matter further with Brady, and then tell us they had decided to come, still stands out in my memory.

Shortly, miracle of miracles, our parents, Bill and Thelma Chappell, our brother Kenneth, and our sisters, Sue and Dorothy, were with us in Illinois. The place we loved so much was now like heaven on earth. We truly believed our prayers had been answered. Our joy was indescribable. Louise and I couldn't have been happier.

Romantic Developments

Brady loved our family and in time he became one of us. It wasn't long after our family was reunited in Illinois, that it became clear that Brady and my sister Louise were enjoying each other a lot. When we went to the movies they would always sit together. Each day they seemed to find more and more things to do together. It was apparent to all—they were falling in love.

At first this blossoming romance troubled our parents, because Brady was quite a bit older than Louise. That didn't seem to matter to the lovebirds, however. We all loved Brady and nobody doubted that he would be good to Louise and take good care of her.

Brady was exceptionally kind and thoughtful. He was actually from the South but had adapted so well to the ways of the North that he fit in well there. He had even picked up the northern accent.

He had lived in Chicago and worked there before assuming the management of Bellwood Farms and Dairy. In the South, before that, he had been a hard working farmer so he easily identified with all of us.

Before long, Brady, in his gentlemanly manner, asked Daddy if he could marry Louise. Daddy consented and they were married. To no one's surprise, they were very happy together. A couple years later, God blessed them with a precious little son whom they named Michael.

Brady never ceased to be impressed by the way we trusted the Lord when making decisions. I'm sure he never regretted having met the Brown's, or the Chappell family. They certainly affected his life tremendously.

Dell, You Can Do It

When we moved to Illinois, I had never learned to drive a car. I had wanted to learn, and we had often discussed it. Finally, in our new location, I got up nerve enough to try it, with your grandpa as my brave and patient instructor.

My first efforts were pretty bad. I really didn't have confidence that I would ever be able to drive on my own, though I did manage to learn the basics. I wasn't brave, however, and I wasn't convinced that I could ever overcome my fear of public roads and busy highways. My tendency to fear things always surfaced when I got behind the wheel.

One day during the busy haying season, when all the men were rushing to finish harvesting a large field of grain, one of the combines broke down. Brady rushed to the house and called from the back door "Dell, we need a replacement part for the binder. You'll have to go into town and get it for us."

I froze. Oh, no! I couldn't! It wasn't possible. I had never driven the car alone. Elgin was at least ten miles away and I suddenly remembered the hills in that part of town where the parts store was located. Horror struck my heart.

"I couldn't possibly drive the car there," I told Brady with all the emphatic conviction I felt. "I don't have sufficient command of the car and I don't have a driver's license."

But Brady didn't pay any attention to what I was saying. He was thinking of the emergency in the field. He threw the cars keys at me and then handed me a piece of paper describing the equipment part that had to be replaced.

"Hurry as fast as you can . . . " he pleaded. "Tell them to charge it to my account, and . . . oh, when you get back, come directly to the field so we can get that machine working." Then he was gone, back to the field to keep the rest of the operation going until the broken equipment could be repaired.

I stood in the middle of the kitchen, trembling and wringing my hands. What in the world was I going to do?

I didn't believe that I could drive the car, nor that I should dare to try. What if . . . ? But Brady thought I could do it, and he definitely left the impression that I had to do it. In that terrible moment I couldn't even find words to pray.

About that time my sister Louise came downstairs and observed my utter consternation.

"What in the world is wrong?" she asked, expecting me to say something terrible had happened.

"Help me get the boys in the car," I told her. "I'll tell you on the way."

She wanted to ask more questions but turned instead and rushed out the door to round up the children from the side yard where they were playing.

Louise was more alarmed at my fear than at my inability to drive the car. "Oh, you can do it," she encouraged. "Let's go!"

Somehow I managed to get our old Dodge backed around the milk house and headed in the general direction of Elgin. As we came to the main road, I was beginning to get more and more tense.

"Oh, Lord," I prayed silently, "I don't think I can face that awful hill in Elgin." But we were on our way. The emergency, Brady's insistent, urgent instruction to hurry, and Louise's encouragement spurred me on.

As we approached Elgin, I was reminded again that I didn't know how to get to the equipment company address. Louise and I decided that we should turn onto a street that seemed vaguely familiar.

"We'll ask someone," I told her. But soon I noticed the name of the street Brady had mentioned. We turned onto it and lo, there was the feared hill up ahead. Then, I remembered we should turn at the top of the hill. Sure enough, we saw the sign directing us to the large equipment company. I had made the hill, and we had found the place.

With all my other concerns, it had not occurred to me that the part we had come for might not be available. I handed the man behind the counter the paper with the description of the part. He scratched his head and looked puzzled.

"I don't think we have it in stock," he said, "but let me look."

I could just picture Brady's face if I should drive up and break the news that they didn't have the replacement part. I wondered why he hadn't called first when he was at the house. I hadn't thought of that before.

"They really need that part—they just have to have it!" I told the clerk. Then I remembered I hadn't prayed about it.

"Dear Lord," I begged, half aloud, "please let them have it." Unusual faith overwhelmed me. I suddenly remembered how God had answered some specific prayers recently. And, hadn't He helped me drive the car there and find the place? I felt sure he wouldn't let me down now.

In a few minutes the man came from the back of the store with the part. "You know," he said, shaking his head, "I was just sure we sold the last one of those yesterday. I almost didn't go look, but you were so insistent, I thought I'd better at least pretend I had checked." He could see how relieved I was.

"It was lying underneath some other things. I almost didn't see it," he said with a warm smile. "I'm sure glad I can oblige you."

I thanked him very sincerely and on my way back to the car where Louise and my little boys were, I thanked the Lord too.

I got into the car with tears on my cheeks. How wonderful to know that the Lord was with me in every instance. The fear of going up or down that steep hill seemed to have lost it's threat. I simply put the car in gear and drove home like an old pro.

When we got to the field, the men were just finishing up all that could be done without the new part. Brady was so pleased with my accomplishment, he just beamed. He looked at me with an expression I will never forget. "Dell," he said, "I knew you could do it."

Your grandpa was proud of me too. He must have been really praying hard because he knew I had never driven alone before and that I didn't have confidence that I could drive.

No one ever teased me about driving the car after that. That experience gave me the kind of confidence I had never had before. It was a great victory for me; Brady had done me a greater favor than I had him.

[I shall always be grateful for that turning point in my life. You know, children, sometimes the things we think are impossible for us to do, turn out to be the greatest opportunities for God to show that He is in control and that He is working with us, and for us.]

A Dead Giveaway

We loved the way people talked in Illinois. The quick, fresh accent and perfect diction was so much more interesting to me than the lazy drawl we were used to in the South. I wanted to talk like them. I tried hard to fit in wherever I went and not let people have reason to suspect that I was from the South. On numerous occasions I had noticed how someone would poke fun at the way Southerners talked. I was always conscious of that and tried to avoid being laughed at.

One day Brady sent me to the general store to get a can of coal-oil for the kitchen range. I walked up to the storekeeper and asked, "Have you got any coal oil?"

The store clerk broke into an unabashed chuckle. I didn't know what he was laughing about.

"Where ya'all from, Georgia?" he asked, trying to imitate my southern drawl.

"What do you mean?" I replied, wondering why he suspected me. "What makes you think I'm from the South?"

"It wasn't your accent as much as the words you used."

I hurried out the door, trying to figure out what he meant.

When I told Brady what had happened he roared with laughter. He told me a native would have asked, "Do you have any kerosene?" rather than, "Have you got any coal oil?" [Well, as you can imagine, I never quite lived that one down. Brady often brought it up, and he never stopped laughing about it. After that experience I tried even harder, not to reveal that I was a country girl from the South. But occasionally, even now, a complete stranger will ask me where I'm from, or where I was born. "I detect an accent," they will say.]

Is It A Girl Or A Boy?

When we moved to Illinois, our oldest son was a little over two years old, and our baby was two months. They were healthy, active little boys, and they filled our lives with all the joys of parenting.

Late in the second year at our new location, a third baby came to bless our home. As we prepared for the coming of a new little one, family and friends wished us well. Many suggested that since we had two boys, surely this one would be a girl. By that time we had accumulated many friends and I was not surprised when they gave me a lovely shower. I was a bit taken aback, however, when some of them went so far as to pick girl type gifts. We weren't sure if this was predictive or presumptuous on their part.

Our baby was due near Thanksgiving. I fully expected to be in the hospital on that special family day. A month later, our baby still had not arrived. The doctor assured me I was going to have a "ten-month" baby. He said I would probably be in the hospital for Christmas. I wasn't. After what seemed like the longest month in my life, I ended up in the hospital two days before New Year's Day.

I'll always remember that week. A sudden snow storm had shut us in and we were concerned about how I would get to the hospital. The doctor had emphatically informed us that under no circumstances, weather included, would he come to our house to deliver the baby. Our church family joined with us in prayer as we faced a crisis situation.

The giant snow plow moved in on the road just in time to open up a one-way route, with pullouts for passing, and on December 30, we made our way through the tunnel-like road, through drifts of snow as high as a roof's edge, to get to the hospital in Elgin where I gave birth to a cute, cuddly, little redheaded son.

Our new little son didn't suspect that a very pink layette awaited him at home. We were considerate parents, however and fell back on the blue, yellow and aqua colors (of which there were plenty), especially when we took him to church or showed him off at home.

Uncle Sam Needs You More

We were tremendously happy with our little family in our home in Illinois. At that time we had moved to a nice house on Bellwood Farms known as the "point house" because it was near the point where three roads converged.

Your grandpa loved his herdsman job. My folks lived nearby and we had found the church which we believed God had provided in answer to prayer. Our hearts constantly overflowed with praise. Who could ask for more?

News reports described the war that was raging and we continuously heard of men being drafted. We were concerned for their families, but we felt secure. We were living on a large dairy farm, which we had been assured was considered to be necessary to civil defense, and which made your grandpa eligible for draft deferment.

We also had three children, which in itself was enough to prevent your grandpa from being called—we thought.

We were careful to notify the local draft board of our new baby's arrival. We had not forgotten for one moment that Grandpa was in the draft age bracket and that he had come close to being drafted earlier. But now, we were certain that everything was under control.

[Try to imagine, if you can, how I felt one morning when I opened our mailbox and found a notice for Grandpa to appear for induction. My legs almost gave away beneath me. My heavy heart sank as I slowly made my way back to the house where my precious little boys were waiting, oblivious to this new development. I hurried to sit down. It was a dark moment for me, Andrea and Gregory.]

The baby was sleeping, and the older boys were happily engaged in one of their little games. I started to cry. "What has happened?" I questioned. We felt sure Grandpa's draft status had been kept current at the local draft board, which he had been transferred to. Surely pertinent information got forwarded, I reasoned. I was shocked and falling apart inside.

[Fortunately, it was time for your grandpa to come for lunch. Oh, how I hated to show him that letter. He was even more shocked than I had been. He sat down heavily, hardly believing the indictment he held in his hand.]

"Maybe it isn't that kind of letter," I suggested, with a faint ray of hope. "Open it quick and see what it says."

But it WAS what we feared. The letter indicated a definite date, place, and time, for him to report for induction into a branch of the armed forces.

Your grandpa quickly contacted the draft board where we lived. They informed us that he had been chosen on the basis of his status, as shown on the records at the previous location, in the South, where he had registered. It was clear the local board had not relayed the necessary information to them as we had taken for granted they would.

There wasn't enough time for him to get things under control before the date he had to report. When he broke the news to Brady, he too was stunned. He didn't think he could get by without your grandpa.

Of course we shared our predicament with our church family. Everyone prayed, and prayed, and prayed some more. And we believed our prayers would be answered; we all expected a miracle.

Our pastor went to the draft board office and explained to them that your grandpa was doing required civil defense work, and that his absence would cause a great hardship to his family. It became evident, however, that nothing anyone could say or do would change matters. All we could do was accept the verdict.

Since your grandpa would no longer be working for Bellwood Dairy Farm, we knew we would also no longer be provided a house to live in and all the other good things we were used to. The replacement herdsman would need our house, so we would have to find another place quickly. That constituted one of our biggest problems—in that area there were no houses to rent.

Being as conscientious as he was, your grandpa felt he had to get his family comfortably settled before leaving.

After much prayer and a lot of looking, we were finally able to rent a small brick school building that was no longer being used for classes due to the consolidation of several schools into one district.

It was a well-built, attractive building, located in a remote forested setting, among oak and pine trees. But it was a public school facility, with many large windows across the front, far too many to attempt to drape. Fearful as I was, that presented a monstrous problem for me—I had always hated uncovered windows at night.

There were no smaller rooms to use as bedrooms and to stay in at night when we were alone. We had to divide the one large room into sections for cooking and eating, for sleeping, and for a living room area.

[As you can imagine, Andrea and Gregory, that was a rather unusual situation.]

There were two small restrooms, but of course no tub or shower. There were two small basins in the restrooms, but no sink or kitchen. A few shelves and a few small closets had been built to store school supplies in, but they were not in the proper place to be substituted for kitchen cabinets, or for clothes closets either, for that matter. [We had to do a lot of improvising, I assure you.]

Two things we were thankful for; the excellent furnace and heating system to keep us warm in winter and the numerous shade trees to help us endure the heat in summer.

It took a lot of ingenuity to create a cozy homelike atmosphere in such an academic setting. But believe me, the most difficult aspect was trying to stay alone at night with a baby and two other very young sons, in an abandoned public building, in the woods, miles from the nearest house. We were not even able to get a phone installed.

Those were unbelievably busy days, getting everything under control before the deadline. Grandpa hurriedly installed a kitchen sink, which someone had given us. He was able to rig up a makeshift shower. We were not able to find a solution for the multiple bare windows, however.

We had barely moved into our strange new home when it was time for your grandpa to report for duty. [I will never forget that day.] His little family, my folks, and Louise and Brady, and of course many of our friends from church were at the train station that sad day, to say goodbye to him.

Those of us who had prayed so hard could hardly believe that he had actually been required to go. We had held on in faith until the very end. I'm afraid some, including myself, were tempted to feel that God had let us down by not answering our prayers.

My heart was torn in shreds and I cried until I was sick. A part of me was being taken away on the train that day. It was almost too much to bear.

It wasn't long until we were notified that our loved one had been accepted into the Navy and assigned to the Great Lakes Naval Station, which was, as I remember, less than one hundred miles from where we lived. We couldn't help realizing that God had surely intervened in that respect. We had feared he might be sent to another state, perhaps clear across the United States.

I adapted quickly to living alone, with only my three little boys, and I did surprisingly well in the day time. I suffered agony every night, however, as I tried in vain to be brave in that lonely building.

Louise and Brady lived in the big house on Bellwood Farms and my parents lived near where they both worked. The children and I were on our own most of the time. I tried hard not to depend on my family. After all, I was a married woman, with my own family. But we got terribly lonely at times.

We were also stranded much of the time due to gasoline rationing. I was barely able to get into town for groceries and to visit my folks occasionally, to help me retain my sanity.

After Grandpa finished his basic training, we were allowed to visit him. I remember so well the excitement and anticipation as I loaded my three little boys into our old 1942 Dodge, and set out on an unknown route to see their daddy at the navel base.

It was a shocking surprise, seeing him for the first time, since the government had taken him. I expected him to be in uniform, but I guess I just hadn't thought about the way he would look with his hair cut shorter than I had ever seen it. He looked more like a boy in a sailor suit, than my husband the dairyman.

We had a tearful reunion and it was wonderful seeing where he was based.

It wasn't long until he was allowed to come home on occasional weekends. How thankful we were to be so close to where he was stationed. We enjoyed every minute we had an opportunity of being together as a family. Farewells were always difficult for all of us.

[I had a difficult time equating justice during those days. It seemed to me your grandpa was needed much more at home, especially since I was aware of several unattached single men roaming free in the area. Please believe me, I tried very hard not to harbor resentment. I prayed a great deal and the Lord helped me to realize more and more that He was in control of the total picture.]

Sometimes my folks would invite us to stay overnight with them. Feeling safe there, I would sleep soundly, something I was unable to do when we were alone in the old school house. It was a blessing to get a good night's sleep once in a while at least.

One morning at my parents home, I was awakened from sound sleep, early in the morning, by the radio playing loudly downstairs. Daddy always tried to be thoughtful about waking me up, especially when he knew I wasn't getting enough rest, but that morning he heard a song on the radio that he thought I would enjoy hearing, so he turned up the volume. Before I was awake enough to hardly realize where I was, I heard a male voice singing, "Bell-bottomed trousers, coat of navy blue; she loved a sailor, and he loved her too . . . "

I had not heard the song before, though I heard it many times after that. It made me cry, but my little boys missed their daddy too, so I always tried to be brave and strong for their sake. They often wanted to know why Daddy couldn't be home with us. That was hard to explain to children so young.

Little Bandaged Bundle

Assuming full responsibility for three small children, one of them under six months, was no small task for me, even when all of them were well and everything was going smoothly. When our baby became unusually cross and continued to cry almost constantly day and night, it was extremely difficult for me. My folks stopped by to see how we were doing and found me completely exhausted and the baby still crying. They insisted I bundle him up and that we go home with them, so they could help me care for him.

After trying our best to find out what could be causing my little son so much pain, we finally decided it must be an earache. My mother administered the same remedy she had used on all of us as babies, but when that was not successful we knew it was time to get him to a doctor.

The physician examined my uncomfortable little one and discovered a lump behind one of his ears, which he termed a mastoid infection. I had never even heard of a mastoid before, and I had no idea what it meant.

[I will never understand why neither my mother nor myself found the lump when we had examined him so thoroughly trying to discover the source of his pain, and especially since we suspected an ear problem. But we didn't.]

It's hard to describe the terrible frustration I felt as I sat there across from the doctor. Mama and I were both extremely weary from loss of sleep and from watching a baby suffer and not being able to do anything about it.

The doctor stopped his examination and looked at me as though I had committed a crime. In a sharp, condemning tone he asked, "Why didn't you bring this baby to me sooner? I don't know if we can save him now . . ."

[You can imagine how that struck me. My mother also felt the sting of his accusation.]

"We thought he had an earache," she tried to explain, when she saw I was unable to speak.

He looked straight at her and asked in a stern voice, "And what did you do for it?"

When we told him we had dropped some warm oil in his ear to try to ease the pain, he muttered, "That's the worst thing you could have done."

He turned to the nurse who was standing by helplessly. She looked as if she wished she could do or say something to express the pain we were feeling. The doctor gruffly ordered her to call the hospital and arrange for surgery for our baby—immediately.

Then he focused his attention on me again and asked about the baby's father. When I told him he was in the Navy and stationed at Great Lakes, he softened a bit. He picked up the phone and personally put a call through to the base. With his back to us, I heard him sternly order "See that that man gets to the hospital as quickly as possible. His baby is very ill."

Mama and I rushed to the hospital. I called Daddy, my sister Louise, and our pastor. Then we began the long, anxious vigil in the waiting room at the hospital where the doctor had directed us. Daddy and my brother and sisters arrived soon to be with us, and shortly afterwards Brady and Louise came, as well as our pastor. We knew your grandpa would get there as soon as it was humanly possible.

All we were sure of was that the operation was really serious and that the doctor had said he didn't know if they could save him. He didn't try to explain to us what a mastoid infection really was, nor why it was so serious.

[I was greatly relieved when your grandpa finally got to the hospital. He had received the news of the impending surgery, and the Navy had immediately arranged for him to get to the hospital so he knew our baby's life was in grave danger.]

After more than seven hours in surgery, the doctor finally came out to talk to us in the waiting room. All that time we had waited and prayed, anxious to hear how the operation went, but also fearing what might happen.

The doctor introduced himself to your grandpa saying, "I presume you are the baby's father . . ."

We were all practically holding our breaths. The doctor looked so weary, we knew it must have been a tedious process.

"Well, folks," he said very seriously, "we saved him, but we almost didn't. We had to work awfully close to his brain. You are fortunate indeed. He'll make it now, but it will take a while for him to recover, completely."

Then the doctor let us see him for a few minutes, in the recovery room. I was relieved to see that a nurse had been assigned to watch him closely every moment.

[We had to take their word that the little bandaged bundle in front of us was indeed our baby. His head was so wrapped up with bandaging that we could see only his eyes, mouth and the end of his nose. As you can imagine, it was painful for us to see him like that, but we were grateful he was alive.]

The doctor made arrangements for me to stay with our little patient, in the same room. I was nursing him for one thing and they thought it would be less traumatic for him to have me near.

With a kindness in his voice that we had not heard before, he told me, "He will need all the help we can all give him."

I have always been grateful to that hard-hearted doctor for his part in saving my baby's life. I know it was God who spared him and allowed him to live. It was clearly evident, however, that the doctor had worked especially hard at it. I often suspected he felt guilty for being so harsh with us in his office that first day.

In time, I was able to forgive him in my heart. My mother and I both knew we had done all we knew to do for our sick child, and there was no way we could have known that he was suffering from anything more than an ordinary earache.

Early in my role as a mother, I had been scolded by doctors more than once for rushing in with a cross baby, only to be told "it's nothing." That would always make me feel so foolish. I tried to diagnose my sick children's symptoms myself after that, but this time I had failed, and in a painful way.

I believe it was only with the help of the Lord and the strength He so graciously supplied, that I was able to make it through that crisis period.

[It was extremely difficult to manage, with my recuperating baby's daddy away from us, with gasoline rationing, and with no one to assist me in any way so much of the time. My parents were both working, and my sister too was busy with her own little son. I learned to lean heavily on the Lord, Andrea and Gregory. And He never let me down.]

Prayer At The Ironing Board

In the months following our baby's operation, I had to confront numerous crisis situations. One of them was managing to get by with the gasoline rationed to me, since we lived so far out in the country.

The doctor let us take our baby home earlier than he would otherwise have because I was nursing him. But I had to take him to the doctor's office, daily at first, then gradually less often, so that he could change the dressing.

Our old car needed more gas than I was rationed in order to make it. Others tried to help me as much as possible, but getting to the doctor often required much prayer, and many times it was nothing short of a miracle. I recognized it as such.

I became keenly aware of the distance one can travel on a gallon of gasoline. In those days the amount of gas available was more crucial than how much we had to pay for it. I also had to manage our budget very closely. I had plenty to keep me prayerfully humble before the Lord.

Maybe I was selfish, but I longed to have your grandpa home to help me, especially with caring for our recuperating baby. But I couldn't allow myself to become engulfed in self pity. With the Lord's help, I carried on from day to day. I prayed constantly for His grace, and for His will, rather than my own.

Early one afternoon, as the midday sun filtered through the many windows of our schoolhouse home, I stood behind the ironing board, praying as I had often done before while doing my ironing.. The older boys were playing nearby. Soft music from the radio produced a calming effect.

I was just finishing the last starched piece, when I heard a voice coming from the radio. "We interrupt this program to bring you this bulletin..." the man said.

I quickly rushed to turn the volume up, just in time to hear the announcer say, ". . . has just passed, allowing men in the service who have three or more children, to be honorably discharged at their own request."

He went on to say, "it is generally believed, that in many cases, the families of these men are suffering needless hardship. Each man will have the opportunity to choose whether or not he wishes to be discharged, and if so, his particular case will be evaluated."

I couldn't believe my own ears. The voice continued, ". . .this is a bulletin, I repeat . . ." I listened very closely again, to make sure it was true.

With trembling hands I unplugged the iron and put it safely on the stove to cool. I switched off the radio and fell on my knees weeping. I believed that announcement was a direct answer to my prayers.

I knew God was aware of our situation and that He was acting on my behalf, as well as all the other wives and mothers in equally trying circumstances. I knew many of them probably did not know the Lord or how to pray. I thanked God on behalf of all of us. Our men had been brave and obedient. We too, had tried to do the best we could, but we had found the going awfully rough at times. I knew that my loving Heavenly Father was fully aware of each specific sacrifice.

With a grateful heart and my young baby in my arms, I hustled my other two little boys into our old car and drove off to tell my parents the good news. They were skeptical at first until they heard it for themselves on the evening news. They were well aware of my faith in God and the confidence I had that He would answer my prayers.

Later that evening, your grandpa called my parents' home to inform us of the news. I happened to be there and he told me that he had already submitted his request to be discharged.

Brady was almost as pleased as we were at the prospect of having your grandpa back home. He had not been able to find a replacement for him. We all believed God had kept the spot open for him.

It was only a matter of weeks until your grandpa was again working at the job he enjoyed so much and which was considered essential to the wartime effort. And best of all, he was home with those who needed and wanted him most, his family.

* * *   * * *   * * *

"As is always the case when we trust the Lord, Gregory and Andrea, this real, live, true story had a good ending. As hard as it was for us to understand at the time, some good can actually come out of such painful experiences. And it did. But that's another story, for another time. Right now, we'd better check the fire. I think it's getting colder."

CHAPTER 10

The Quest

"Grandma, I want to hear about the church you found in Illinois, the one you prayed for. Could you tell us about that?" Andrea asked eagerly.

"Yeah," Gregory agreed, "me too."

"You know, that's something I'd like to tell you about. And I don't know of a better time than right now. Why don't we sit near the fire here, where it's nice and cozy," I said, as I motioned to a couple of inviting places to sit.

"We'd like that," They said in unison.

"Because both of you, Gregory and Andrea, have been brought up in good, solid evangelical churches, it may be hard for you to understand why we prayed so earnestly for the right church for us to be a part of and to raise our children in. But the long search for such a church was very real and an especially serious matter for your grandpa and me."

* * *   * * *   * * *

What Kind Of Church Is This?

Our parents began sending my brother and me to Sunday School about the time we started to attend the school at Pleasant Hill. They considered us old enough to be trusted to walk alone to church, just like we went to regular school.

We went there because it was closer to our home than the Loredo church, which was almost two miles away. The Pleasant Hill church was only about half of a mile away. Our schoolhouse was nearby.

As we grew older, our parents would sometimes take us and we would all attend the worship service following the Sunday School hour. Most of the time the two churches would alternate holding a Sunday evening service. That way, just about everyone who attended church at all would go, no matter where the service was held.

Everybody in the community knew everyone else and everything that was going on. Most people shared the good and the bad and got along pretty well. But any dissension, it seemed to me at my young age, was usually among people who called themselves Christians, sometimes between the two congregations, and strangely, I thought, often between members of the same church.

Sometimes the Loredo church members would become so divided the church would split. One faction would become so infuriated that they would follow the most vocal member and go off to start another church. Their efforts usually fizzled out after a short time. As I grew older I became more and more disenchanted and disappointed with churches as I had come to know them. [I realize now, I had never experienced a really spiritual church. I don't know why I felt the way I did. I'm sure I didn't know what I was missing. I just knew something was not right in those churches.]

At first, the Pleasant Hill church was on a circuit, which meant that a minister came only once a month. Later, they sent someone twice a month and in time a minister came to stay. When there was no preaching service at Pleasant Hill, we all simply went to the Loredo church. Special functions were always scheduled at one or the other of the churches, and the entire community could be counted on to attend. This arrangement was not unusual.

[In Sunday School I learned about Daniel in the lion's den, David and Goliath, and Jesus as a young boy just like you did. But unlike you, I was never told that Jesus was the Son of God, or that He came to be my Savior. They didn't tell me about God's plan of salvation, because the teachers hadn't been taught about it themselves. I remember one teacher stating very adamantly that she was NOT a Christian, and that she had no desire to become one. Yet she was teaching young, impressionable minds about God. Although I was young, I was able to discern the sham of that situation.]

Our teachers either read standard Bible stories to us from a book, or some of them even memorized them and then recited them to us word for word. Either way, they came across lifeless. I remember thinking that my reader at school was more interesting.

The same was true of the sermons we heard in church. There was no life in them either. They were merely cold exhortations. Most listeners went away disappointed, because the services had really offered nothing spiritual.

During the slow summer months, between cultivating and harvest, special revival meetings, sometimes referred to as "protracted" meetings, were held in the Pleasant Hill Church. We would have a visiting evangelist. These services were held every night for a week, sometimes two. We always looked forward to going to church every night. The meetings were interesting and offered a variety, although we did get very tired, not being used to such long days.

The evangelist usually had some life in his messages and sometimes people would actually be moved to consider their ways. And during those evangelistic meetings some guest minister would occasionally present Christ as the Savior of the world, and give the individuals of our congregation an opportunity to make a commitment to Him.

Sometimes, we had "arbor" meetings in the early evening before the regular 7:30 revival service. The men in the church would build a framework of limbs and branches in an attempt to imitate the arbors referred to in the Old Testament.

We sat on planks laid across lengths of logs, cut so they would be the right height when stood on end. Lanterns were hung on the framework rafters, casting a glow upon the faces of each one present.

During these preliminary meetings, previously selected leaders would share with us some portion of Scripture from the Bible and explain what it meant, as best they could.

Different people would spontaneously share what God had done for them. It bothered me that many of them were living lives that were in sharp contrast to their testimonies. The adults would try to answer questions posed by the older boys and girls who were allowed to attend. I can remember considering it an honor to be allowed to sit in on those outdoor meetings. There were times when I don't think they appreciated me being there, especially when I asked questions they couldn't answer. I wasn't trying to stump them; I was inquisitive because I truly wanted to know more about spiritual things.

There was always a great deal of anticipation when we gathered in the church for the evening service following the arbor meeting. At times, the evangelist would really seem to be anointed by the Holy Spirit, so that he would have something to say that would stir the hearts of young and old alike. Even the boys and girls would sense God speaking through the evangelist.

It was not always that way, however. In retrospect, and with the knowledge I have acquired in my study of the Scriptures, I am sure that many of the spiritual leaders who were sent to those denominational churches were not filled with the Holy Spirit but were rather attempting to lead in their futile human strength.

[You know, Gregory and Andrea, I truly believe God helped me to recognize the emptiness of those cold church systems, even as a young child growing up under their influence.]

From the time of my turning to Jesus, I hungered for and sought after truth and direction from the Scriptures. I seemed to have an inborn desire to grow in the things pertaining to the Lord and an insatiable longing to have my questions answered from the Bible.

Spiritual matters were considered a taboo subject at our house, except when my parents argued about doctrinal differences. Anything and everything else could be discussed freely, but it was almost as if talking about the Lord in a personal and intimate way was not a Christian thing to do. I could never understand why it was that way, except that my parents probably felt inadequate, due to the lack of spiritual training. They had both been brought up in those same cold, unspiritual churches; they had hardly been prepared to give us more than they had acquired themselves. The same was true of my grandparents.

I'm not sure why I was so sensitive about spiritual matters. It was no doubt mostly because God knew all along the details of His future plan for my life, and He was preparing and protecting me for that time.

Trying To Get Things Straight

As I grew older, I became more and more concerned about the church situation I was in. The fact that my mother belonged to the Pleasant Hill while Daddy belonged to the Loredo church didn't help matters. There was constant bickering between them as to which church was right and usually their arguments were in front of us kids.

There was tension in church and tension at home. This was a constant heartache to me. I hated to see my parents at odds with each other and especially over spiritual issues.

Mama held her ground. She insisted she couldn't join the Loredo church with Daddy, even for the sake of the children. The reason, she emphatically declared, was that there were so many different kinds of churches in the denomination he belonged to, how could she be sure of choosing the right one? It would be her luck, she said, to get into the wrong one.

Daddy too, stood firm, more on a vow he had made, I believe, than his convictions. He had promised his mother on her death bed, that he would always remain a member of that denomination.

In my childhood years I never understood why my Grandma Chappell was so insistent that her children remain in that denomination. But I understood when I became a mother and experienced a mother's concern for the spiritual welfare of her children. And also when I learned that particular denomination believed that once you were saved, you could never loose your salvation. Grandma simply wanted her children to be saved and to be with her in heaven. She didn't understand that being a member of a denomination and being a Christian are two different things.

[The doctrine of "once saved always saved" is very controversial, Gregory and Andrea. Some believe as my grandma did, and others believe that you can be saved one day and lost the next. I believe these are two extremes and that Satan uses such issues to distract people from the most important doctrine—that salvation is by grace, through the Lord Jesus Christ. I hope you will study the Bible for yourselves and let God help you see His truth. I personally, do not believe I have been "lost" at any time since I was found by my Lord and Savior and I sincerely believe we can have that perfect assurance.]

That was my background as a youngster. Your grandpa Brown's was similar. His parents too, were members of two different denominations. The group his father was involved in declared they were not a denomination. They were, however, sometimes accused of being a sect. Your great-grandpa was extremely adamant about his convictions and he insisted that his church was the only church teaching truth. He, like my grandma, wanted all of his children to believe as he did.

Your grandpa Brown's mother did not agree with your grandpa's point of view, however. The only group she had any contact with, before she met your great-grandpa, was still a different denomination. She wasn't too sure that some of their doctrines were Biblical either. Certainly they were different from what her husband believed. Yet they too, believed they were the only church with the "truth". [From experience and research, I have learned that any church which teaches that they are the only true one, may well be suspect. This is one of the marks of a cult. As you grow older, you will want to learn to be very cautious in this area. I urge you to base what YOU believe on the Bible itself, not what some individual says or some organization or denomination teaches.]

One In Unity

Before we were married, your grandpa and I determined one thing—when we had our own home, we would be unified on spiritual issues. Whatever we decided was truth, according to the Scriptures, we would agree upon. It was important to us to bring our children up in a different atmosphere from what we had both experienced.

Up until that time, we had not found the kind of church we were looking for, but the quest was constantly ongoing. We were praying and trusting God to answer.

When we moved into town, we made it a high priority to find the best church available. But once more, we were headed for disappointment. Right away we visited a church near our new home. The first Sunday, the congregation gave us a warm welcome. On our second visit they asked us to join their church. We were not yet ready to join any church. We explained to them that we were searching, and wanted to make sure we had found the right one before we joined.

At that point they gave us such a cold response, we didn't care to go there again. In fact, we believed the Lord was definitely showing us that this was not the right church for us.

Then we tried another church, this time one that was the same denomination I had been raised in. They too gave our family a warm welcome, partly because we were sort of a novelty. Their congregation was made up entirely of older people, while we were very young. They hardly knew how to act toward us.

It didn't take us long to realize, however, that they didn't have anything to offer us. It was no wonder they didn't have any young people or children.

Their pastor didn't preach from the Bible and their teachers used books about "great men" who had founded their denomination. They taught character studies of these men whom they had been taught to respect highly, but they never included any Scripture.

We decided to visit a few more times to see if maybe we could help them. One Sunday during the worship hour, they discussed a current best seller whose author didn't even claim to be a Christian. We never saw a Bible in that church, except for the one that we carried with us.

To my surprise, they asked me to speak at one of their ladies' meetings. In preparation, I asked the Lord to give me an appropriate message. When I shared with them from the Bible, the women all sat enthralled. They had never heard anything like it.

"That was wonderful!" a couple of them commented. But many of them were upset. When the women who had been thrilled at the Bible message saw how the others reacted, they joined in. They were corporately blind. Not one of them had enough backbone to stand on their own convictions. One of them told me, "All of our lives we have believed as this church teaches and we will continue to until we die." Poor things, they didn't realize that their church had died long ago, and that because of their attitude, they too had also died spiritually, if they had ever had real life.

God gave me great pity for those dear women, but they were completely beyond my reach. I went home with a sad heart. [When I shared my concern with your grandpa, he agreed with me, that that was not the church we were looking and praying for.]

Among our most pressing concerns at that time was the need to find a spiritual church. It seemed that our search had come to a hopeless standstill.

[I think you can understand, Gregory and Andrea, why Brady made such an impact on our lives. He was a definite answer to prayer at the time. We had no doubt that God would lead us to the kind of church we believed existed.]

We Found It - At Last

The first Sunday we were in Illinois we were not able to make it to church, having only recently arrived. The following Sunday, however, we had things under control and we couldn't wait to visit the church that offered us so much promise. We sincerely hoped it would be the answer to our prayers. We had driven by the location a couple of times, to make sure we knew where it was and just to relish the anticipation of attending this unique church which we had learned about in such a wonderful way.

I will never forget that first Sunday we visited Rolling Hills Bible Church. We approached the old but exceptionally well preserved structure with reverence and anticipation. There was no doubt in our minds that God had led us there. We didn't know what to expect, but we felt sure we wouldn't be disappointed.

The old church looked friendly and inviting as it stood with open doors, welcoming hungering hearts from near and far.

We were greeted by friendly folks getting out of their cars and entering the church and by a kind man at the entrance who handed us a colorful bulletin.

Inside, another usher greeted us with a pleasant smile and invited us to sit on the left side of the church, about half way back. Our children sat with us. There was no nursery.

From where we sat we had a good view of the pulpit and the front of the church, including a picture of Jesus knocking at the heart's door, which hung on the back wall.

"Look, Daddy, Jesus wants to come in," our oldest son whispered. We both smiled and nodded our heads in agreement.

Looking around, we quietly observed the congregation. Some were thumbing through a hymnal. Others had their heads bowed in silent prayer. A few turned to see the new young couple with their young family. We noticed there were very few other children present.

Soon the song leader called out the number of a beautiful old song that we were familiar with. We felt right at home. Then they sang some songs that we had never heard before. We knew we would soon learn them as well.

A couple we had met in the parking lot introduced us as a new family who had just moved into the community. The friendly smiles of those around us gave us a warm and welcome feeling.

When the pastor began to speak, we were delighted to hear a Christ-honoring message, right from the Bible. Not one word was mentioned about a denomination nor about joining the church. No great church leaders were referred to.

When the service was over, we were greeted by members of the congregation and by the friendly, inquisitive pastor, who was by then at the back of the church shaking hands with each one as they filed out of the church.

We were happy to answer any questions. We wanted to get acquainted with everyone. By this time, we were sure we had found the church we were looking for.

At last, after much fervent prayer and years of searching, we had been rewarded with an overwhelming answer to our search for the right church. We had found what we had so urgently and faithfully sought in our unrelenting quest.

In the weeks, months and years that followed, we grew spiritually. We were happy beyond our wildest expectations. God became very real to us.

We soon made many friends and enjoyed rich fellowship with other believers. We were blessed with some very close friends who shared our joys and our concerns.

I remember there were times when heaven seemed almost in reach. God constantly answered our prayers, and proved to us that He cared about every aspect of our lives. Our faith was constantly strengthened. It was no wonder that God was able to speak to us in such a special way.

A Beautiful Miracle

We had been attending that beloved church a few years when God blessed our home with a fourth baby, a precious little girl. When she was a few months old, she had a health problem that troubled us. A yellow matter collected in one eye and caused her lashes to mat together. The condition just wouldn't go away and we became quite concerned.

Our friends at church would look at her with pity. One dear lady who was always telling us how pretty our little girl was, would weep softly as we continued to ask for prayer on her behalf. She would shake her head and say, "Oh, the poor little thing". That really bothered me.

The doctor told us she would probably outgrow the condition, but he couldn't say for certain that she would. He said a canal from her nose to her eye was blocked. The fear that this awful condition might not ever go away, or at least for a long time, was a constant burden to us.

One morning when I bathed her and got her ready for her morning nap, I examined her eye again and sadly wondered once more how long she might have to live with the problem. I imagined what it would be like if she should have to start to school with it still that way.

As I prayed, the thought came to me—the One who gives life itself, certainly could repair a part of the body that was not functioning properly. I knew that God could do it, and that He could do it instantly. At that moment I believed that He WOULD heal my baby's eye.

As I held her close, I asked the Lord if He would please remove the condition that afflicted her. I remember saying, "and I will be sure to give You the glory."

I laid my sleeping baby in her crib and was soon busy with the chores at hand. As always, I hurried through my work, hoping to have some time to read and study my Bible.

The next Sunday at church, our attentive friend, Mrs. Ida Korintz, hurried over as usual to get a glimpse of "the pretty little Brown baby", as she called her. I saw her coming and was just waiting for her to say, "Oh, the poor little thing", when she cried out, "She's been healed!"

Sure enough, she had been. Her eye was completely well. I was overwhelmed. I will never know why I had not noticed it earlier. It may have just happened.

I remembered that I had promised to give God the glory for what I fully expected Him to do. At that moment I felt terrible. Surely the Lord knew I was not ungrateful. He had done a beautiful miracle in answer to my prayers, and I had not even acknowledged it!

I handed my baby girl to Mrs. Korintz, who was rejoicing as the tears rolled down her cheeks. Then I rushed down to the front of the church and knelt at the altar. With mixed emotions I wept and thanked God for healing my child and I begged Him to forgive me for not noticing the miracle and for not thanking Him sooner.

Then suddenly I realized—I had not failed God, I had really just trusted Him completely, so much so that I had put the matter out of my mind for the first time since the condition had become so apparent. I was then able to praise Him acceptably.

From that day on, our daughter's eye was never marred again by the blocked canal. It was indeed a beautiful miracle.

A Sacred Treasure

Soon after starting to attend the new church in Illinois, we decided to replace our old, ragged, cheap Bible. We reasoned that since we had both been raised in divided homes and had been adversely affected by varying concepts of what the Scriptures really taught, we really should read the Bible all the way through and make our own determination as to its interpretation.

We ordered a leather-bound, King James version Bible with large primer print from Moody Press. We had to do most of our reading and studying at night, Grandpa even more than I. By then we were usually pretty weary, so we thought a good sized print would be easier on our eyes.

Another reason we chose the particular Bible that we ordered was because it contained only the text of the Word of God. It didn't even have chapter headings or captions at the top of the pages. It contained only the book names, chapter numbers and verse divisions. It was the Bible we were hoping for because we wanted to learn what the bible itself said, without comments by any man that might influence us in any way.

I'll never forget the day that wonderful Bible arrived at our home in the mail. We anxiously opened the box and held up our treasure to admire it. It was the most beautiful book we had ever beheld. It was bound with genuine leather. The edges of the pages were gold. This seemed appropriate to us because at that moment we realized we were holding a priceless treasure. To us, it was more valuable than if it had been solid gold.

As we opened the pages, we realized we were looking upon the very Word of God. The gloriously large primer print almost spoke audibly to us. It was the same print we remembered form our first learning book when we started to school. Now we were anticipating learning what God Himself had said, and hoping that we could keep from being influenced by the various biased views of the Scriptures that we had been raised with.

As we sat there that day, being introduced to our new Bible, I can honestly say we were overwhelmed. It seemed fitting to fall on our knees and thank God for such a tremendous blessing—His holy Word, made available to us by the Holy Spirit.

We could hardly wait for a fresh new look at God's holy Word. We started reading it at the very beginning, in the first chapter of Genesis. We decided to read that new Bible all the way through, to the book of Revelation.

We read with an open mind, prayerfully searching for the meaning of each word and phrase. We spent every possible moment reading and studying that wonderful book. We were so starved for the truth we literally "hungered and thirsted" after it.

[Your grandpa worked long, hard hours on the dairy farm and I kept unceasingly busy at the job of being a good dairyman's wife and caring for our four children. But we saw to it that we made time each day to pursue our private study. Our quest was to find the truth in the Scriptures. Those were unforgettable days, Andrea and Gregory. There is nothing so fulfilling as studying the wonderful Word of God.]

I remember reading that precious Bible while my children played around my feet, never out of my peripheral vision. There were times when I was transported right into the very edge of heaven as the Scriptures came alive to me.

In those days I had a hard time balancing homemaking, mothering, and being a farmer's wife with the consuming desire to just sit at the feet of Jesus, reading His words, and letting Him speak to my heart.

I identified with both Mary and Martha in the Bible. I believe I know how Mary felt sitting at Jesus' feet and yet I also understood Martha's resentment toward Mary, as I went about doing the necessary chores.

We proudly carried our beloved Bible to every church service, and followed every reference in the pastor's sermons. We shared from it in group Bible study sessions. That precious Bible had cost so much, we had to share it because we could not afford to each have our own.

[I must tell you, Gregory and Andrea, we believed the Scriptures just as God revealed them to us during those days of intense searching and study. And in the years that followed we never considered ourselves "enlightened" by any person or group who tried to influence us doctrinally, no matter how hard they tried to convince us. Our personal quest in the Scriptures gave us a solid foundation in our own Christian life, and in our preparation for serving the Lord in the ministry He gave us later.]

I am sure it was during those months of intensive study in that special Bible that my appetite for the Scriptures was whetted, and I learned to reverence the Bible as I do. It pains me to even see something lying on top of a Bible.

[Oh, how I want each of you, my precious grandchildren, to realize the value of this great treasure which God has divinely protected, down through the centuries. He has seen to it that it was preserved in its purity, even to my lifetime and yours, indeed, to these very last days, I believe. I know, on the authority of God's Word itself, that the Bible will outlast everything else. Jesus said, *"Heaven and earth shall pass away: but my words shall not pass away."* "Mark 13:31)

Don't ever forget what I'm telling you today. The Bible is a unique Book. It is God's Word, and it is where you must go for truth and dependability.]

That Others May Know

The more your grandpa and I understood the Scriptures, the greater was our concern for others who were where we had been. When we found the truth which we had so earnestly longed for and sought after, we naturally wanted to share it with our family. We realized that they had not passed down to us these important truths because they did not know about them themselves.

It frightened us to realize that our parents had been satisfied to accept what their parents and grandparents has passed on to them concerning the Scriptures, without ever questioning the validity of their interpretations. They had accepted their ideas and traditions without bothering to check our their accuracy. How tragic, we thought.

It's also frightening to realize that we could also have been caught in the same trap. But because God in His mercy wanted us to help others, He created in us a desire to study the Bible for ourselves and discover the truths He wanted to reveal to us. He knew that because of our experience, we would be able to identify with many who needed to be awakened to spiritual reality the way we had been. And He knew He was going to use us to help others want to know the truth of the Scriptures.

God gave us great concern for those who were frustrated as we had been, as well as for those who were totally unconcerned about this aspect of their lives. We could understand because we had certainly been exposed to passivity, and we had also experienced a sincere quest for truth.

We were burdened to pray for our family nearby and for our family still in the South. We prayed for the people in our community who didn't know the Lord. As we came in contact with people in public, or observed men and women walking down the street, God gave us a heavy burden to pray for their spiritual welfare. We got to the place where we saw every human being as a soul for whom Christ died, and envisioned what it would be like if they should face death at that moment, unprepared to meet God.

The more we read and studied the Scriptures, the more we became aware of our responsibility to God. He was clearly showing us that we would also be judged for not warning others concerning their spiritual need.

Our church was quite missionary minded. We often had speakers representing various mission fields around the world come to our church and we began adding people in foreign lands to our prayer list.

We did not dream nor could we have imagined what God had in store for us. We only knew we were being saturated with a consuming passion to reach out to a lost and dying world with the message of God's love and His provision to save them.

[Oh, how I wish I could adequately describe to you the overwhelming burden that God placed on our hearts, the tremendous responsibility of attempting to find His perfect will for us at the time and following through on it. I can only say, I sincerely pray that you will not doubt my account. It was as real as our presence in this room here tonight. Our quest for a church, and for truth in the Scriptures was satisfied, and it led us far beyond what we had ever imagined or anticipated.]

* * *   * * *   * * *

"There's so much more that I want to tell you, Gregory and Andrea, but our time has run out for now. We'll watch for another chance to get on with our story."

CHAPTER 11

Hearing God's Call

"Hi, Grandma." Gregory called from the driveway. "I brought you some pretty flowers from our yard!"

"Oh, they're beautiful!" I replied, as I went to meet him. He loved to share a fresh picked bouquet with me. He always had, even as a little boy. He would often bring me wild flowers he had found in the woods when he was only three or four years old.

While we arranged his floral offering in a tall glass, I sensed he perhaps had a request.

"Are you really busy, Grandma?" he ventured, hesitantly. He knew I was always busy in my office-studio.

"Why do you ask?" I smiled, knowingly.

"Oh, Andrea and I, and Marissa and Barry have been talking about it. We want to hear about how you and Grandpa knew you were supposed to move to Hawaii. I know you had to have a real good reason. Could you tell us, please?"

I was busy and had deadlines to meet, but Gregory's sincerity and the urgency of his request would not allow me to excuse the opportunity.

"This is as good a time as any," I agreed. "Why don't you call Barry and Marissa right now, and see if they can come over. I'll make us a pitcher of lemonade."

* * *   * * *   * * *

Listening And Learning

During those busy days on the dairy farm, caring for my four young children and looking after Grandpa, I still managed to spend hours reading and studying our beloved Bible. And I also found time to read some other inspiring and helpful literature.

A small bookshelf library at our church provided a wide selection of small books published by Moody Press which we could check out and read. Since I had been accustomed to reading every good book I could get my hands on for as long as I could remember, I was naturally attracted to these short books which I could work into my schedule.

I read every one of them. Each one packed a powerful message which the Holy Spirit used to speak to my heart. Each one of them seemed to coincide with the thrust of the particular Scripture portion I happen to be studying at the time. [It was a precious experience, I assure you.]

Our church also had a large rack of tracts in the lobby. A young Christian man who attended the church kept it well supplied with excellent, colorful tracts and booklets. He urged everyone to take them and read them and then to distribute them as a means of witnessing to others.

Many were blessed and inspired by this outreach. Numerous thrilling reports proved the value of his unique ministry. No doubt there were many untold stories. Only God knows the true extent of the results of any method of getting the gospel message out.

I read every tract displayed on that rack and I found it easy to share the attractive little messengers with others. When one would particularly speak to my heart, I would lovingly place it in our Bible. Sometimes I would use it to mark where I had discovered some rich nugget of truth then I would forget I had placed it there. Later, the tract and the marked reference would once more speak to me.

His Special Call

One morning when I sat down to read and study for a few minutes, a little tract that I had placed in our Bible fell out. It was about a man who had refused to accept the Gospel message because he said it was a "butcher's religion". He declared it was too "bloody" and "messy" for him. He preferred, he said, the cleaner, bloodless philosophy of good works and "higher thought" which he had been taught. It seemed good and acceptable to him.

This concept was new to me. At this point in my life as an adult, I had never encountered such an idea and didn't realize that there were people who actually considered the cross Jesus died on repulsive and unnecessary. This shocked me.

As I read this disturbing tract again, the thought really troubled me. I wondered how many people believed the same way this man did. I was just beginning to realize there were churches that actually believed and taught that way.

Even the two churches that had disappointed me so had at least stressed the importance of Jesus' death on the cross during seasonal revivals. And we always sang such songs as, "The Old Rugged Cross", "At the Cross", and "Are You Washed In the Blood of the Lamb?". As I contemplated this rude awakening, I wondered how anyone could be so misled. Even before I had accepted Christ as my own personal Savior and realized clearly that His horrible death at Calvary was for me and necessary for MY sins, I believed that He died for the whole world.

It was easy for me to see that the terrible load of sin that sent Jesus to the cross could only be dealt with through the shed blood of the Son of God, as He is referred to in the Scriptures. This is the clear-cut message of both the Old and New Testaments.

It is difficult for those of us who read and study Scriptures to understand how anyone could get around that. I realize now, years later, that the problem arises mainly when a person does not check the Bible out for themselves.

[Oh, how dangerous, to accept the false interpretations so cleverly purported by those who do not have the truth themselves. I urge you, my precious grandchildren, to become thoroughly acquainted with the Bible and to always steer clear of any teaching that is not backed up by God's Word. Please don't ever forget what I'm telling you today.]

As I picked up that little green tract, laying there in my open Bible that day, these words of illustration and its Scriptural content seemed amazingly alive to me.

It was so long ago, I don't recall the exact words of the little pamphlet, but I distinctly remember that it brought out the fact that life can only be accomplished through death. That each seed that is planted must die before it can bring forth life, and that some animal had to die to provide meat to eat, or shoes to wear. Most of all, Jesus had to die to give us spiritual life with Him. This is the heart of the Gospel message. It is the truth that God wants every person to hear and to have the opportunity to accept.

That day God showed me that nothing in this world is more important than first of all, applying this truth to my own life, and then helping as many other people as possible hear that urgent message before it was too late for them.

The significance of that two-fold realization and conviction enveloped and overwhelmed me. I knew the Holy Spirit was making it so real to me so that I couldn't escape it. I found myself clutching that little tract in my hand as if to keep that revelation from ever getting away from me. In those moments, God gave me an all-encompassing burden for every person who had not yet heard, and for those who had refused or neglected to respond to the Gospel message.

How clearly I saw it; no person would ever be able to find his or her way to God apart from the way He provided—through His Son. No matter how strongly they believed in any other way they would simply be clutching at a false hope. The tragedy of this kind of deception gripped my heart. I wept with concern for the world's lost souls.

While weeping and frantically trying to get my bearing, I was made acutely aware that God was attempting to say something to me. I wanted to hear it, but I was afraid, and I didn't know what I was afraid of.

I began to pray desperately that God would help me understand what He was trying to tell me. An extremely heavy weight descended upon me. I tried to get free but I couldn't. All I could do was pray and read the Scriptures. I couldn't eat and I couldn't sleep. This very painful condition continued for days.

Then one morning God spoke to my heart, as plainly as if He had spoken it aloud. I heard Him clearly say, "I want you to give me your life completely. I have impressed you with the importance of the pure Gospel because I want you to share its truth and simplicity and its urgency, with whomsoever I direct you to."

Oh, no! It was a startling awakening. God was calling me, asking me to surrendered my life, my all to Him. I loved Him and I wanted to please Him, but if I totally surrendered myself to Him, what would He require of me? I was terribly scared.

In my thoughts I began to reason. Surely I must be imagining what I thought was happening. Maybe if I brushed it all aside, I could get back to normal, back to a peaceful though busy life with my family. Little did I realize at that moment that my life had been changed forever. I tried hard to pretend nothing had happened. I tried to hide my fears and convictions and all that I was feeling from my family. But when I could neither eat nor sleep, your grandpa became concerned. Even though I denied there was a problem, he could see that something certainly was bothering me.

[When your grandpa was at work I would pray and plead with my heavenly Father. "Lord," I cried out in agony, "you know I can't serve you now. I have my young children and a hard-working dairyman husband. You know I can't leave my family. They need me."]

I was so frustrated in those days that I searched and searched to see if there was any Scripture references that mentioned a wife and mother leaving her family to be a missionary or a full time Christian worker. I didn't believe there was anything like that in the Bible. I was sure hoping there wasn't.

In the 14th chapter of the book of Luke, verse 26, I read, *"If any man come to me, and hate not his father, and mother, and wife, and children, and brethren, and sisters, yea, and his own life also, he cannot be my disciple."*

That verse seemed to indicate that there might be a loophole that would allow a man to leave his wife and children (I didn't like that idea either), but it didn't say anything about the wife leaving her family, even to serve the Lord.

The whole issue had me terribly confused and upset. I wanted to obey the Lord, and I didn't want to do anything that wasn't according to His Word and His perfect will.

Just as I would seem to get a little relief, another overpowering burden, which I believed was from the Lord, would sweep over me.

"I know, Lord," I would pray, "when I was in elementary school, and again in high school, that I wrote essays saying I wanted to be a missionary. I meant it too, but Lord," I argued, "now I can't. I have a successful dairyman husband, and four children. You know, I can't do it now . . ."

I cried and begged the Lord to help me see what He was trying to get me to understand.

For almost two weeks I battled the conflict alone. Finally, your grandpa pinned me down and insisted that I tell him what the problem was. He felt he had a right to know. I wanted to tell him but I was afraid to. And

I didn't know how to tell him.

When at last I broke down and tried to explain, he was understanding and tried to console me.

"You just listen to God's voice," he comforted. "He won't tell you to do anything that isn't right. I'll help you pray."

I was greatly relieved to have your grandpa share my burden. Together, we continued to pray for a clear understanding of what God was attempting to show me.

Slowly I began to understand that what He really wanted was my full commitment, just for me to say "yes" to His call. That would mean that I would be willing to do anything He wanted me to do, and to leave the rest up to Him.

After days and weeks of agonizing, I knew I had to answer the Lord with a yes or a no. I simply could not continue as I was or put the matter off any longer.

For selfish reasons, I wanted to say no to God. How could I just yield and give up the rest of my life, to do whatever He wanted me to do? It might mean going to the mission field. I couldn't do that!

A yes would mean I was putting my complete trust in God. I would be at His utmost disposal. It was a terribly big step.

In anguish, I cried out, "Lord, I want to be willing to obey you. Please help me and accept me—with all my weaknesses." I knew I had to say yes. "Please give me strength," I earnestly prayed.

Suddenly, all the struggle was over. There was peace in my heart. I had sincerely surrendered. It was the same kind of peace I had experienced the day I was born into God's family.

[Your grandpa and I both knew it was the Lord's doing. We were humble in His presence. I truly believe, Gregory and Andrea—and Barry and Melissa, that if I had not yielded to God's will at that point, I would have withered, spiritually. At that point, I had no idea what the future would bring, but I felt confident that I could trust God with that.]

We kept my wonderful experience to ourselves. It was our secret. We continued to read and study the Bible and we spent a lot of time in prayer, seeking further guidance from the Lord.

During that taxing period in our lives, one puzzling question kept crossing our minds; why had God only spoken to me? At times this really frightened me. Could I have been misled? It was reassuring, though, to have your grandpa express confidence that it was the Lord's doing. I don't know what would have happened if he had reacted differently. How blessed I was to have a husband who was so understanding and so sensitive to God's leading.

Somewhere, There's A Young Man

A few weeks after my life-changing experience, another wonderful thing happened in our family one Sunday afternoon, as we were getting ready for church.

Worship services at Rolling Hills Bible Church were held in the afternoon because many people drove long distances to attend. We appreciated the schedule. It was easier for Grandpa to adjust his dairy farm duties, so that we could be in regular attendance.

That Sunday afternoon we were listening to Dr. Charles E. Fuller's "Old Fashioned Revival Hour" broadcast, as we always did while preparing for the service. Dr. Fuller stopped suddenly, right in the middle of his sermon.

"There's something I have to say right here, before I go on," he said, pausing. "Somewhere on a farm in the Midwest, there's a young man whom God has been speaking to. If that young man is listening right now," Dr. Fuller challenged, "let me urge you to let God have His way in your life."

He hesitated again, then went on, "You are happy where you are," he said with confidence, "but if you are willing to give yourself to the Lord, without reservation, He will bless and use you."

That certainly was not anything anyone would have expected this rather conservative radio minister to say, especially on an actual broadcast.

Your grandpa turned pale. He hurriedly ran to the boys' bedroom and closed the door behind him. I could hear him sobbing and praying and I began to pray also. I knew what was happening.

I continued in prayer, while Grandpa agonized for over an hour, alone in the back bedroom. The children were playing quietly in the living room. Not once did they try to disturb their daddy who was in their room; God was in control of the situation.

When your grandpa came out of the bedroom some time later, his face was beaming. He held me in his arms and told me how the Lord had been dealing with him for several days, while he was busy milking the cows and doing the chores.

He, like me, did not want to give in, because he was afraid of what God might ask him to do. Not only was your grandpa a highly respected and recognized dairyman, he also enjoyed it. But he also, like me, realized we had no right to be selfish and smug while enjoying the truths of the Scriptures that we were constantly being awakened to and the quality of worship and fellowship at the church we had discovered. We were both beginning to clearly realize, it was God's will that we share His Gospel with others from this point on.

It took me a while, but I finally saw clearly the reason God required a complete commitment from me, before He called your grandpa. I can be stubborn, at times. For instance [and I hate to admit this, children] I have to be fully convinced about something before I am willing to take action. In some ways, of course that can be a good thing.

I am not easily swayed by the convictions of others in my behalf. I have to be reasonably sure of the Lord's leading for myself. God knew that, so he broke my will first, then I was willing to fall in line with His direction for our combined ministry.

By this time I was truly thankful that I had been able to detect God's voice, and that I had been willing to trust Him to the point of full surrender. It was such a relief to be able to get an overall picture and to know for certain that I had not been just imagining things. God was indeed calling me into full time service. And now I could understand how it all fit in with scriptural teaching. I did not have doubts about that any more.

When your grandpa came out of the bedroom, following that encounter with the Lord, it was too late to get to church in time for the service. We knew everyone would be wondering what had happened, because we never missed church. We decided to go on over to the church and tell our pastor and the congregation what had happened. We know they would be dismissing the service about the time we would arrive.

When we got there, we learned they had all been praying for us. They were convinced something unusual must have happened. One of the ushers saw us drive up and came rushing out to inquire about our welfare.

As soon as everyone saw that we had been crying and yet our faces were shining radiantly, they urged us to come to the front of the church and explain.

It was a thrilling time as we stood there crying and talking at the same time. We told them about your grandpa's experience that afternoon and what had happened to me a few weeks earlier.

Almost everyone was weeping tears of joy with us and thanking the Lord for His answer to prayer and for what He was doing in our lives, and in the church.

A Missionary Bible Class

Our call by the Lord and our response to that call prompted some other young couples and some single young people in the church to make a decision to also fully dedicate their lives to the Lord. As it turned out, some of them were merely inspired to get into the limelight where the focus of attention was. Most did not follow through, but a few did. We were thrilled about that.

[Your grandpa and I knew we needed a much better knowledge of the Scriptures if we were going out to share it with others and we knew the others in our newly formed group did also.]

We urged our pastor to begin a missionary Bible class, and we invited them to come to our home for the study sessions. Since we were the only couple with children, we could put them to bed at their regular time and be free to study with the other young people.

There was a lot of interest and enthusiasm in the class. We decided to study one book of the Bible each week and combine some of the shorter books so that we could get through all sixty-six books in one year.

Each participant was encouraged to give themselves wholeheartedly to an intensified study of the Scriptures. [I assure you, children, it was a thorough, in-depth look at the Bible. We loved every minute of it.]

Every week, each of us bubbled over with more discoveries from our personal study than we had time to share. We were all determined to learn as much as we possibly could about God's Word, in order to be better equipped to serve Him, wherever He called us to serve.

Since your grandpa and I had a family and many associated responsibilities, it was not possible for us to attend a resident Bible school, as we would have so much loved to do. Instead, we prayerfully enrolled in the Moody Bible Correspondence School and took several of their personal courses by mail. We chose subjects we knew would help prepare us for the types of missionary work to which we felt we were being called.

Your grandpa also enrolled in Wheaton College, which was within commuting distance from our home. He took as many units as he was able to handle and still work on the dairy farm, which was necessary at the time. He would begin his work day by milking the cows at 4:30 a.m. Several hours later, he would shower and head for the college. In the afternoon, he would hurry home in time to milk the dairy herd again at 4:30 in the afternoon. Of course he would have to manage time for reading and study. On more than one occasion he fell asleep at the wheel, only to be awakened by the horn of an oncoming vehicle, just in time to avert an accident. [God protected your dear grandpa many times as he traveled to Wheaton College, far too weary to be on the road. How I thank the Lord for that.] Grandpa loved the concentrated Bible courses, the encouragement of the instructors, and the fellowship of other students. Those days at Wheaton College were a highlight in his life. He would have loved attending as a full-time student.

[I sincerely pray that each of you will have the desire and opportunity to attend a Christian college when that time comes.]

To Whom Shall We Go

It was a happy, although busy period in our life as we made every effort to prepare for fulltime Christian service. We did not know where God wanted us to go, but we spent our time studying the Scriptures and praying for the lost. We were sure that God had a special work for us to do and would show us where.

To that point there had been no indication as to when or where we might be called to go. It could be years or only a matter of weeks. We hoped it would be soon. We were young, ambitious, and anxious, and we felt up to the task.

[I have to tell you, anxious as we were, we were determined not to be influenced by suggestions from well-wishers, lest they deter us from the leading of the Lord. We wanted to be certain that we were in God's perfect will. You can be sure we were extremely cautious.]

Missionaries from various countries came to our church from time to time. We were challenged as each one presented the needs of their particular field. No one ever came to tell us about South America, but we were prayerfully interested in the various countries on that continent. We read, studied maps and tried to learn all we could about South America.

We thought we would be able to travel there overland, and Grandpa went so far as to draw up plans and to build a sturdy little house on wheels (an early version of today's travel trailer) which could be pulled with a four-wheel-drive vehicle. We anticipated getting there with it and perhaps living in it there also.

In those early days our thoughts were primarily focused in that direction. I'm still not sure why. We had had no contact with anyone in that country. We were just burdened for the people there.

Then our pastor went to Hawaii, which at that time was only a territory of the United States. While there, the needs of a specific couple who had been serving as missionaries in the Islands for a number of years, were discovered. Those needs were presented to our church, since we were "missionary minded" and a number of people were already preparing for missionary service.

This missionary couple were both in bad health. The wife was suffering from severe arthritis, and both were physically weary.

From our pastor's viewpoint, we were the most eligible candidates from our church. When the missionaries learned about our call, our desire to serve, and our continuing preparation, they indicated we certainly could be the couple they had been praying God would send to help them.

When we were approached privately and briefed on the details and the special need of that particular field, we promised to pray about it.

[Gregory and Andrea, Marissa and Barry, I'll have to admit to you that I rebelled inside at the very thought of going as missionaries to the Hawaiian Islands. You may find that hard to believe. Today, Hawaii is one of our United States, and everyone wants to go there.]

I knew in my heart that I wasn't going anywhere unless I was absolutely sure God was sending us. I kept telling myself that nobody was going to influence me to do what THEY thought was God's will for me. God would have to show me—definitely—that this was where He wanted me to be.

I think I had already settled the matter in my own mind; we were going to South America. Our thoughts, prayers, and preparations had all been in that direction.

Who Will Go?

During the weeks that followed, our pastor came often to visit in our home. Each time, the subject would be brought up and the specific needs of the elderly missionaries on the little island of Maui repeated. And each time we were respectfully referred to as the ideal couple for the situation there. I'm sorry to say, each time I would just change the subject. When pressed I would respond defensively, "If the Lord wants us to go there, He will call us there." and that was it.

[The idea of someone continually suggesting what seemed to me, perhaps more than to your grandpa, to be that person's judgement rather than God's, was repulsive to me.]

I felt certain if God wanted us to go to Maui, He would let us know in His own way, and very definitely. I kept hoping He wouldn't. The more I thought about it the more I disliked the idea. In fact, I imagined myself stepping onto that little forty-eight-mile-long island and sinking right into the ocean. The thought of living on that tiny speck of land in the middle of the largest ocean in the world, frightened me sick. I tried not to think about it. The continent of South America, I reasoned, would be much safer.

Our indifference, (especially mine), prompted our pastor to begin considering other possibilities. When the challenge was presented from the pulpit again, a single girl who had been attending our church for only a short time, decided she would like to go to Hawaii.

None of us knew Ellen very well. She was short and to compensate for her lack of height she wore high heels and very short dresses, believing that would make her appear taller. The short dresses troubled the pastor and church officials. When it was suggested that she be considered as a possibility for the needed ministry on Maui, the members also expressed concern. All were slow to accept her willingness to go, but promised to pray about it.

The mysterious young woman in our congregation began to plan to go to Maui, but nothing seemed to work out. Everyone was hesitant about her eligibility. The money for her supplies and passage did not come in.

The missionaries on Maui discouraged the idea of having a single girl sent to assist them. They insisted they needed a couple. Finally, the young lady gave up the idea and even stopped attending our church.

A couple who had recently moved into the area and started attending our church decided Hawaii would be an interesting mission field, so they offered to go. They were also new in our church, however, and of course not very well known, either. Even so, because of the urgent need on Maui, plans were set in motion to attempt to send the couple and their children.

Strangely, as with the single girl, all efforts to collect supplies and the money necessary for transportation to the islands, were thwarted at every turn. The situation was embarrassing. The couple finally gave up the idea as well and also left the church.

Our pastor was terribly disappointed because it looked like no one could be sent to Maui. It was especially troubling for our congregation since the missionaries had requested help from our church specifically. For awhile, Hawaii was no longer mentioned in church. Several continued to pray for Maui, however, including your Grandpa and me.

He Makes You Willing To Go

When God began to speak to us about Hawaii, we kept our thoughts and convictions to ourselves. We didn't mention the subject to our pastor or to anyone else. We knew God had called us to serve Him and we thought we were willing to do His will, but there was a wall of resistance in our hearts, especially mine. I was willing, but with certain reservations. Without realizing it, I actually wanted my own will. I was willing to do God's will so long as it was the same as my will.

[Deep down in my heart, I knew God was speaking to both your grandpa and me about going to Maui, but I still was not willing to go.]

One morning while I was doing my housework, I had a Christian radio station tuned in. The Palermo Brothers, a popular singing group at that time, came on singing an interesting song I had never heard before. The message of the song hit me really hard. I don't remember exactly how the words went, but I could never forget one line; "The Lord don't force you to go against your will, He just makes you willing to go."

I ran to the bedroom, fell across the bed, buried my face in a pillow and cried and cried, and then cried some more. "I don't want to go to that tiny little island!" I told the Lord. A tremendous struggle was going on within me. I just was not willing to give up my stubborn will.

Come Over and Help Us On Maui

Soon after that agonizing experience, I had a dream, or a vision, I'm not sure which. I only knew that I was terribly afraid because I had heard of such experiences and could not believe they were from the Lord.

In my dream, or whatever it was, I was on Maui. I saw the physical makeup of the island: the flowers in profusion, the volcanic soil, the bright blue sky, and the aqua blue ocean with white foam peaks dashing against the shore. I saw flowering trees, laden with colorful blossoms, hugging a winding roadside, and tall eucalyptus trees on the mountain slopes.

All of these things were hard for me to describe to others because I had never seen anything like them before.

More importantly, I saw the Island people—a conglomeration of many nationalities, just as they were when we saw them later. It was as real as if I had actually been there and come back.

In my dream-vision, I was very much aware that these people were my people, just like a part of my family. I didn't want to leave them and come out of my dream. As I pulled away, they were waving, as if to say "Come over and help us".

When I tried to explain the strange experience to your grandpa, he was surprised that I could describe the island so vividly. He knew I could not and would not have made up a story like that. It was evident to both of us—a remarkable thing had happened to me. We both agreed that God was speaking to us about going to Maui as missionaries.

How Shall We Tell Them

We were over one big hurdle, but we had a long way to go before actually beginning our missionary work on Maui. First of all, we were afraid to disclose our decision to the church congregation for fear they would not accept our turnabout. They could easily say, "You had your chance." The fate of the two previous missionary attempts were still fresh in everyone's thoughts. We stood a good chance of encountering the same kind of disappointment and we weren't sure we dared take that risk.

We didn't have the nerve to tell our pastor either. It was going to be difficult, we knew, because we had previously refused to discuss the subject. Now, our interest might not be welcomed.

After much prayer, we finally got up enough courage to call our pastor and make an appointment "to discuss something personal". We sensed a hesitancy at the other end of the line which was disconcerting to us. We later learned that we had frightened a nervous pastor by asking for a "personal" conference. Although we were not aware of it, there was a problem in the church at the time. A so-called minister, who had recently started attending the services, had been attempting to present himself to some as a more desirable pastor, trying to split our interdenominational church. When we learned more about the ugly situation, it was easy for us to see why our pastor might fear that we were going to announce our intentions to take sides with the "wolf" who was moving about in our church. That, of course, was the farthest thing from our minds at the moment.

When we sat down in our pastor's living room that evening, a lot of tension and apprehension was evident, on both sides. Neither of us knew what the other had on their mind.

We immediately blurted out what we had come to say. As we shared our unexpected story, we all three wept openly. We confessed our stubborn resistance, described my almost unbelievable "vision", our change of heart, and our willingness to go at last. We also expressed our concern that the church might not accept our change of heart.

I'm not sure if our pastor was more relieved that our call didn't have anything to do with the disruption in the congregation, or that we were finally ready to obey the Lord and go to Maui, as the entire church had been convinced all along we were supposed to do.

What rejoicing there was in our church the following Sunday as our grateful pastor announced, "At last, our missionaries are ready to serve on Maui."

We were still fearful that there would be those who would be reluctant to stand behind us, that the financial provision might not be forthcoming, and we would be embarrassed. We did a lot of praying while anxiously awaiting their reaction.

Parting With Possessions

We estimated the value of our possessions and figured out what it would cost us to get to the mission field. We talked about which things we should take with us and what we should sell.

We had recently purchased new dining room furniture that was beautiful. And my piano! [Oh, how I loved it!] It was like one of the family. How could I ever part with it and all the other things that meant so much to me?

As long as my thoughts lingered on earthly things, it was very hard to imagine giving them up to go over the ocean to a foreign mission field. But, when I remembered Jesus, and how much He gave up for me, I saw things differently.

He was willing to give up the glories of heaven to come to this sinful, dirty, and corrupt old planet to be my Savior. How could I even think of putting anything before Him?

When I remembered my call and my commitment, it was easier to think about giving up our few worldly possessions in the interest of lost humanity.

[Your grandpa also went through a difficult phase of adjustment. He loved the dairy, and he loved that beautiful area in Illinois, as I did. He loved the church we had found, after such a long search. There was so much to live for, and to look forward to, in our new location. But we both knew that since God had blessed us so abundantly in every way, especially spiritually, we could never be happy again unless we shared our faith with others.]

Our burden for the lost and our desire to serve the Lord was so great that we wished we could go not only to Hawaii but also to Venezuela and the southern United States. We were overflowing with a passion for souls and a desire to go and tell a lost world about a Savior who died for every person on this earth, no matter where they lived. We felt a great urgency to tell each and every one that they must believe that Jesus' blood is absolutely necessary for their salvation. We were thoroughly convinced of this after reading and studying the entire Bible.

We had finally reached the place where "things" faded into nothingness compared to the driving force of our missionary zeal.

Parting With Loved Ones

We soon realized that parting with things was the easiest part of carrying through on our dedication. The hardest part was telling our loved ones and preparing to say farewell to our own flesh and blood.

Nothing was more painful and difficult for me than trying to explain to my folks that God had called us to serve on a foreign mission field. I will never forget their reaction. They could not believe that we would actually take their four precious grandchildren away from them. Maybe they would never get to see them again, they said. They were crushed.

My parents were especially attached to our oldest because he had been their first grandchild. By that time, my sister and her husband also had a little boy. It would help having at least one grandchild near, but it was going to be terribly painful for them to watch the others leave, and especially to go so far away, out in the middle of the Pacific ocean.

Mama was more upset than Daddy was; at least she showed it more. And the more she thought about it, the more defiant she became. Finally, she was just plain angry. How could we do this to her? And how could we do it to our children? Could we be so inconsiderate as to take them to a heathen island and expose them to unsanitary conditions there? And, she wanted to know, how could we risk the possibility that there might not be schools for them to attend?

My dear mother would ask one question after another, then break down and sob. It tore my heart out. I didn't want to leave my parents, any more than they wanted to see us go. After all, they had followed us to Illinois. It did indeed seem cruel to leave them again. We all knew they couldn't follow us to Hawaii. But what could we do about it? Our first responsibility was to God. That was hard to explain to them, however. At the time they just couldn't understand our dedication.

That heart-breaking ordeal was the bottom line proof of our commitment to the Lord. It was extremely painful. There is no way that we could have made it through that phase of our preparation for missionary service without the sustaining help of the Holy Spirit.

[I assure you, children, when you become a missionary, there is a big price to pay, and it costs our loved ones as well.]

We also had to notify your grandpa's family. This too, was a difficult situation. The beliefs of their religious persuasion did not allow them to accept our devotion to the Lord.

Since we didn't embrace their doctrines, they didn't believe we were even Christians. Certainly they would never agree to the big step we knew we had to take. Your great-grandpa Brown was angry. It was a tense situation. All we could do was tell them what we were going to do. His dad refused to reason with us. When we moved to Illinois, he didn't disagree, but this was different. This was a spiritual matter.

As difficult as it was to resolve our family relationship problems, we had long since passed the point of no return.

While we were attempting to reconcile our family parting difficulties, the Lord was working on our behalf. We were told that most of the money needed for our supplies and transportation to the mission field had come in. This gave us the reassurance we needed that we were in the center of God's will. We had prayed that if it was His perfect will for us to go, there would be no problem with finances.

Word came from Maui that we were sorely needed and anxiously awaited. This too, spurred us on.

Things were moving fast. Plane reservations were made. Farewell showers and services were planned. Excitement was tremendous. However, the mixed emotions of pleasure to serve the Lord and the pain of leaving loved ones and church family behind kept our feet on the ground. Otherwise, we would have floated right out to our field of service on a cloud.

Prospective missionaries today scramble to get to serve in our wonderful Hawaii, which of course is now one of our fifty states. At that time, Hawaii was considered a foreign land.

Anyone going to the Islands to live today knows that it is much like living here in California, where we live now. But at that time it was quite different. I fully expected to have to wash clothes in the ocean, and to dry them on the rocks, the way I had heard they do in some countries. Once I was finally convinced that it was God's will for me to be there, I was willing to go, regardless of the conditions I might find there.

* * *   * * *   * * *

"Grandma, I can hardly wait to hear about what it was like in Hawaii. Can we have another story session soon?" Gregory begged.

"Please . . . tomorrow, or the next day?" Marissa pleaded.

"Just as soon as we can all get together again," I promised. "I'm looking forward to reliving those experiences myself and to sharing them with you."

CHAPTER 12

To Hawaii With Faith

"Hurry up, Gregory," Andrea called impatiently. "Grandma's going to tell us about Hawaii, like she promised."

Barry and Marissa were waiting anxiously in the living room.

I found myself almost as excited as my grandchildren were, at the prospect of adventuring in Hawaii.

When everyone was seated comfortably, Barry suggested, "Grandma, before you tell us about Hawaii, we'd like to know about your trip there."

"Were you afraid to get on an airplane and fly?" Andrea wanted to know. They all remembered that I had always been a "fraidy cat".

"Well, I'll have to tell you about that," I told them as they waited in anticipation.

* * *   * * *   * * *

Enroute To The Islands

Can you imagine what it was like getting ready to take our first plane trip, and amid the stress of moving ever so swiftly to a new home six thousand miles away? It would have been overwhelming for one person, or even a couple, but we were a family of six. Our young sons were seven, five and three years old, and our baby daughter was fourteen months.

There was so much to think about, and so many things to do. I remember shopping for traveling attire for each of the children. They ended up dressed cute enough to visit the queen of England. The boys wore darling little brown gabardine suits—all alike, trimmed with tan stitching on the collars, and topped off with little beige colored hats with brims. They looked something like stair-step triplets.

Our little girl was adorable in a sweet little pink coat with matching bonnet-hat, made of the same material as the boy's outfits. Underneath she wore a soft, frilly pink dress, chosen for her by her doting Grandma Chappell.

Special friends had driven us across the country, from Chicago to San Diego. That trip in itself was an adventure for our little family. By the time we reached the West Coast we all felt like world travelers. The children were excellent troopers, and fortunately we encountered no mechanical problems with the car.

As we waited for the plane that would take us from San Diego to Honolulu, we felt pretty brave. [Even your usually weak-kneed grandma managed to put on a convincing front. No doubt I was at least trying to think beyond the actual plane trip, to being on the mission field we had been called to.]

Our plane was scheduled to leave San Diego at a ridiculously late hour. When we were informed there would be a delay we urged our friends who had driven us from Chicago not to wait to see us off. They finally agreed to go to their hotel and get some rest so that they would be up to traveling the following day, as they headed back to Illinois.

Soon after they left we were told there would be still another delay in our takeoff. By that time we were becoming a bit apprehensive.

What could the problem be, we wondered. There was no explanation except that the plane we were scheduled to board was being "checked".

After what probably seemed longer than it actually was, we were finally ushered on board the huge craft. To say I was afraid at that point, would be an understatement. I was petrified with fear. However, I tried hard to hide my feelings for the sake of our children.

Even though the hour was late (actually, early a.m.), the boys were wide-eyed and alert, having slept while waiting in the terminal. Their little sister was sleeping soundly, against her daddy's shoulder.

When we were all settled in our seats and safely "seat-buckled" in, I found myself sitting next to a young military bride, enroute to Pearl Harbor to join her husband. Linda was traveling alone and this was also her first airplane flight. I have never seen anyone so scared.

I soon realized the Lord had put us together, and that He had given me a preview missionary assignment. It was no doubt intended to benefit both of us. My own concerns were overshadowed as I attempted to ease the mounting anxiety of the nervous young woman seated next to me. I was also trying to put on an act for the sake of my husband and small sons, who were sitting just across the aisle.

While we were getting seated and settled, and accustomed to our fears, the plane was taking off down the runway, and out over the ocean.

We had been airborne only about twenty minutes when I noticed, as I looked out the window alongside where Linda was sitting, something that resembled oil dripping intermittently from one of the engines. A terrible fear gripped me. It was plainly evident, we were in trouble.

About that time the copilot came on the intercom and announced that we were experiencing some difficulty, and that it would be necessary for us to return to the airport in San Diego.

"Please refasten your seat belts at once," he instructed, with grave seriousness. While he was speaking, the airlines stewardess was moving down the isle, making sure everyone was complying with his orders. She also had an opportunity to exercise her training to help quiet fearful passengers in the event of an emergency.

I remember the tense atmosphere, but I don't recall any actual panic.

However, that twenty minutes back to the airport, flying in the opposite direction of where we were supposed to be going, and over the ocean too, was extremely stressful for all on board. [It was the longest twenty minutes I have ever experienced—before, or since.]

While praying silently but earnestly, I clutched by baby daughter close to me, held the trembling hand of my new-found friend—Linda, and talked soothingly to my little boys across the aisle, who had been roused from sleep by the warning words over the intercom.

[Your grandpa had a surprised look on his face at my apparent calmness, but he knew I was praying fervently. He had learned to depend on me for that. He was also aware that I was helping ease the fears of others around me.]

With indescribable relief, and deep gratitude to God for answer to prayer, I audibly expressed what everyone felt, as we safely set down on the runway.

"Thank you Lord!" I said out loud, with deep appreciation. An almost unanimous "amen" echoed through the plane. Everyone was truly grateful for a safe landing, and glad to have someone voice their own gratitude aloud.

It was a trying experience for passengers of all ages as we waited wearily back in the terminal in San Diego, while our plane was being checked and repaired.

Older passengers tried to sleep as they hunched in various positions in their seats. Children found it somewhat easier to accomplish the trick of sleeping in "knotted" positions as they sat in their parent's arms, or leaned wearily against their shoulders. Ours all managed to sleep soundly, hardly affected by the problems that plagued their parents and their fellow travelers.

Airlines personnel and airport employees distributed pillows and offered food contributions in an attempt to relieve the obvious discomfort and inconvenience of the weary passengers.

At last, after several hours of waiting, we were on our way once again as we headed out across the great Pacific ocean, in the same plane which was now supposed to be repaired, and safe.

My new friend, Linda, stayed close to me. Her need for comfort and assurance contributed much to my own composure. She was so exhausted from the trauma of our initial trip that she finally fell asleep, leaning against my shoulder.

As we winged our way through the clouds, high above the ocean, I spent the hours that seemed so terribly long—praying. I cannot describe the resulting peace, and the assurance of safety I derived from knowing that God's everlasting arms were underneath us. I recalled consoling Scripture references, and I remembered stories I had heard about similar in-flight incidents. I even called to mind a joke I had heard about a lady who on her first flight expressed her fears to the pilot. When she apologized for being afraid he replied, "That's all right, I know how you feel. It's my first flight too". I chuckled to myself, as we quietly sped through the sky, high above the ocean.

[Let me tell you, on that flight, and numerous others since that day, I only trusted the pilot because I trusted God.]

Hello, Hawaii

We approached the Hawaiian chain of islands just as the day began to break. None of us had been consciously aware of the time zone we had passed through in the dark night space, high above the bottomless sea. Most of those on board had fallen asleep and had not realized how long we had been flying across the ocean. None, I was sure, had been aware that at least one person on board had been awake, and praying for their safety. I had not slept at all.

I don't think I have ever prayed more fervently than I did that night, and the sweet communion I enjoyed with the Lord, alternately praying and thanking God for numerous answers to prayer, was unforgettable.

Yes, I had plenty of time to pray about Maui, and our arrival there. I prayed about how we would be received, and that we would be able to detect and carry out God's perfect will. I prayed for health and strength and protection. I prayed about where we would live.

Suddenly, everyone was wide awake. The stewardess was pointing out what resembled a pattern of lily pads on a pond—far below us.

"Those are the Hawaiian Islands," she explained. We all strained to get a better look.

After praying—in the very presence of the Lord, as we flew over the ocean, I felt like I was coming down out of heaven, into Hawaii.

"We will be landing soon," the trim, attractive stewardess announced.

By that time the "lily pads" appeared much bigger as we peered down through a hole in the huge, soft, white-edged cloud we seemed to be riding on.

We could see some color now, and soon the foam-washed shoreline stood out like a floating frame around the colorful flowers and swaying palm trees. We had never seen such vivid color, even in our beloved and beautiful Illinois, nor in the picturesque Southland. The trees were the greenest green, and the sky the bluest blue. Gorgeous, bright colored flowers were blooming profusely, everywhere we looked.

"Oh, how lovely!" I exclaimed, hardly able to believe what I was seeing.

The stewardess pointed out the outline of hotels where many of the tourists would be staying. We were painfully aware that there were no reservations awaiting us, at any hotel. We had no idea where we would be sleeping that night. We were at the complete mercy of those who awaited our arrival on Maui.

So this was Hawaii! This was the place I didn't want to come to; the place where God had to make me willing to go and live and serve Him.

As we came to a halt on the runway, and slowly approached the airport terminal, we were physically and consciously brought back to earth. We were suddenly confronted with the question, what do we do now?

We still had to get from the island of Oahu to Maui, where the missionaries would be waiting for us—we hoped. We wondered if they had been made aware of our delay. Would they still be waiting, or would they have given up and gone home? Many questions plagued us. We hadn't expected anyone to meet us in Honolulu.

As we departed the plane, Linda kept as close to me as possible, all the while scanning the small crowd waiting to meet the flight, watching for her husband, Randy.

"Oh, Lord," I prayed. "Please let him be here."

We had also wondered if he had heard that the plane would be late.

Then, she saw him! She began waving her arms to get his attention. As their eyes met, I was moved to tears by the relief that came over Linda's face.

Randy pushed his way through the disembarking passengers and those who were there to meet them, and was soon by her side. It was a touching scene. They were in each other's arms, with tears running down their cheeks.

In spite of her obvious joy in being reunited with her husband, Linda remembered to introduce him to us. They both thanked me sincerely for befriending her on the disrupted flights. Then they were gone, and I never saw them again. God had sent Linda as an angel in disguise to help me, and I'm sure she always remembered me as an angel He had sent to be with her in her most trying hour.

You Are Here

Now, we were faced with the question of what to do next. As we had been instructed, we took a taxi to the terminal where we were scheduled to take the plane that would transport us across the channel to Maui.

With our three little boys, our baby girl, and our baggage, we pretty much packed out the dilapidated old taxi, driven by a smiling dark skinned man who looked somewhat like the colored taxi drivers around the Chicago area.

The strange looking vehicle jerked along in a reckless manner, while the jolly driver chatted away in the funny "pigeon" lingo that we would later come to know so well. He pointed out highlights of the area and explained some things he thought we might like to know about that part of the island of Oahu. It was his way of giving us a warm, friendly welcome, we concluded.

Maui Coming Up

As we boarded the Hawaiian airliner we were somewhat startled to learn that it was only a two-motor craft. The huge plane that had taken us across the ocean had four motors. Once more we had to assemble our courage and face another takeoff and landing.

As we took off across the channel and island mountains, heading for Maui, the little oriental-looking stewardess sensed our uneasiness and quickly explained that the airlines had never had an accident. (We later learned that the airlines and the local people took great pride and comfort in that fact. It seems almost unbelievable that I never heard of an accident involving a plane flying between the Islands, until about forty years later.) On my first flight I reasoned to myself that there always has to be a first time, and that it would probably be my luck to be on board when it happened. But the turbulence we encountered at times was normal, the attentive stewardess insisted.

The Welcome Party

As we came in for a landing at the Maui airport, we were practically overcome by the breathtaking beauty of the island that was going to be our home.

We were excited, but even more apprehensive, I think you would say, not knowing what to expect. So much was happening, so quickly. Our children clung to us. We felt the strain they were experiencing. I was holding on desperately to the unseen prayer line I had established with the One who was looking after us from above.

We peered anxiously through the window as the plane came to a smooth stop. Then, we saw them—our welcome party; a small group of young people, some who were older, and some small children.

The older missionaries were standing to one side. We easily recognized them, from the description we had been given. The man was heavy-set and white-haired. The woman was tall, with darker skin. She had white streaks through her hair. We noticed she held a walking cane.

The first one to greet us was a young Puerto Rican girl named Bobbie. Her soft, brown eyes and angelic smile impressed us. Surely she was an angel, sent by the Lord.

It was obvious that Bobbie was intrigued by the extremely white skin of our children. We arrived in May, following a severe Illinois winter. They were even "whiter" than they would have been in the summertime. We had not thought of it that way until we observed the contrast that eventful morning.

Everyone was much darker than we were. There was a Filipino man and his wife and son, and their two daughters; an older Chinese man; a Japanese couple with two small children, and a brown-skinned, round-faced, smiling woman, with a pleasant looking man with similar coloring by her side. We took him to be her husband. We later learned they were full-blooded Hawaiian. The man reminded us of the taxi driver on Oahu.

Bobbie introduced us to her sisters, June and Jackie, and pointed out her mother, who was standing over by the chain link security fence.

We felt the warmth of each one as they greeted us. We noticed the older missionaries were watching as if to observe how the natives would accept us. When we finally worked our way among the sweet, smiling faces and got to where they were standing, we got the feeling that their welcome was a bit guarded.

The Welcome Feast

We were ushered into a funny looking vehicle which they called a "san- pan", as they explained that they had prepared a welcome meal for us. We were taken to the home of a Hawaiian family, where the "welcome feast" awaited us.

What a lovely surprise it was. They had each prepared some of their specialty delicacies. We had never seen or tasted anything like any of them before.

There was steamed rice, which we were totally unfamiliar with. The dry, cooked grains fell apart. The meat dish was canned corn beef, seasoned in their own special way. These were served with something they called "soy sauce". We had never even heard of it. And the Hawaiian couple had prepared an authentic native dish which they called "poi". It looked really icky, we thought. It looked something like light purple wallpaper paste. To us, it tasted as awful as it looked.

The Japanese couple had made a dish they called "sushi", which was a delicately seasoned rice, wrapped in a dark green substance—which they told us was "sea weed".

The Filipino family brought a chicken dish. The meat had been cut up into small squares. [I never learned how they did it.] It was delicious. We decided it was the seasoning they used which gave it such a delightful taste.

There was also a cooked banana dish. [Yes, Barry, cooked bananas. You look as if you doubt that would be edible. I assure you, they were very good. Of course you should know, they were a different type of bananas than what you are used to.]

They had also brought several kinds of island fruits, and naturally, some sliced, ripe pineapple. It was a beautiful feast, even though there was not one food that we could identify with, except the pineapple. It certainly was an ideal way to initiate us into true Hawaiian life.

My stomach was not at all settled, after experiencing the frightening plane trip across the ocean from California, as well as a scary one between the Islands. The natives seemed to accept my feeble excuse of having an "upset stomach", and I managed to get around my first hurdle with strange food.

[Your grandpa, however, made one grand initial impression as the super missionary he later proved to be. He tried a little of everything the kind, generous natives had brought. As he commented about each one, showing his appreciation, you could see they had already accepted him as one of them.]

The children were so excited and unsettled they pleaded "not hungry". I really felt for them, not seeing any food they recognized. They hardly knew how to react to all the coaxing to try this and try that. They had been taught good manners, and didn't want to let us down.

[You can imagine what a predicament they were in. I prayed desperately that they, as well as their parents would be able to get through this test and not offend these precious people we had come to minister to. Of course the children were not as aware as we were that the natives—and the older missionaries, were critically scrutinizing us.]

From the first day our missionary children adapted themselves to the circumstances exceptionally well. They were always an asset to our ministry there.

International Cuisine

It wasn't surprising to find that each race of people took special pride in the food specialties they had learned in their homeland, before coming to Hawaii. I think we were surprised, however, to learn that each type of food—even though so very different from the American food we had been used to, was very tasty in its own way. Learning to eat widely varied types of cookery was an educational experience for all of us.

Later, when we enrolled our children in the public school, we learned they had an excellent cafeteria program. We were unable to afford the reasonable cost of the program, of course. Fortunately, an older "haole" couple, living on Maui and active in educational projects on the island, quickly offered to provide for our son so that he could enjoy hot lunches, along with the native children.

It was an exceptional hot lunch program. We had never heard of anything like it. At first we were afraid the children would find it difficult to fit in. (That fall both of the older boys participated.)

They served a different type of food each day of the week; Hawaiian, Chinese, Japanese, Filipino, and American. We prayed that the boys would adapt quickly. We wanted them to be able to take advantage of the program, so graciously provided by the Lord (we believed). And we wanted them to fit in with the different races so that we could help them spiritually.

Our prayers were answered beyond our faith. They soon learned to eat all kinds of foods. It was a good thing we had taught them to eat what they took on their plates. At the school they had to eat everything, if they wished to participate in the hot lunch program. Waste was not allowed. We thought this was rather unusual for a public school. We appreciated the requirement. I don't remember that any child complained. It was an expected procedure and they all accepted it.

The older couple who paid for our boy's lunches, also paid for other children as well. We always suspected that they were responsible for the "no waste" regulation. [You may not agree that it was a good principle for children to follow, but we did.]

I No Can

We arrived on the field in May. Our little white "haole" son had only a few weeks to get acquainted with a public school—in a foreign country, before it was time for school vacation.

In the fall, both of our older boys were in school. They were the only "white" children attending school, on the whole island. Even so, I don't think they were considered as being that different. The island children were used to associating with boys and girls of different nationalities.

The teachers, who had come from the mainland to teach in Hawaii, were delighted to have our—as they put it, "cute little American boys" in their classes. One of them said to me, "What beautiful, "perfect" diction they have! They will surely influence the island children."

The native students were very lax with their language, and the native teachers were not much better. They all spoke what was referred to as "pigeon" English, which was a broken, lazy mixture of different languages. Since we had lived in the South, we could understand how a person's accent could easily be affected by their carefree way of life.

I was beginning to get uneasy, and feared that our sons would lose their perfect diction—which was typical of Northern Illinois. Their teachers were hopeful they would be a good example to the island children.

[Guess what? In only a matter of weeks our boys had lost their beautiful accent. They were beginning to speak perfect pigeon. Just as I had feared, they had been overcome by the poor speech habits of the island children, rather than being a good influence. They mimicked specific words and quickly picked up strange phrases which we would all soon become familiar with.]

It was funny in a way, though at the time it seemed tragic. I remember so well the first day of school. Our six-year old came bursting in the door very excited about his new experience.

"Me, I came home some speed!" he announced.

When we asked what happened at school that day he said, "the teacher wanted me to read, but I no can read."

Soon both of the boys were filling our home with strange lingo and very broken English. [We were disappointed, as you can imagine.]

Their reaction to the bad speech habits they were exposed to; being affected by others rather than helping influence them for the better, is a frightening illustration of how most of us react to our evil environment. Instead of helping pull others up to our standards, we allow them to pull us down to their level.

Maui no ka oi - The Best of All

When we moved to the islands, in response to our "call" from the Lord to go and help fill a special need at a specific time, we hardly knew what to expect.

I Want You To Know

The older missionaries who had requested help from our church, specifically our missionary training class, had sent us a colorful map of the five major islands—with pictures depicting the topical layout, and special features of the Islands, for our perusal.

[I know you believe me when I tell you, we studied that map very carefully. And we read and studied everything we could find about Hawaii before we moved there. Long before we went there, we knew Maui was a tiny island. That was one of the things I had to conquer. As I already told you, I had to be made willing to go there. At first, I vowed to go anywhere the Lord sent us, then I decided—anywhere except that little speck of earth in the middle of the biggest ocean in the world. After I yielded to God's will, the island still seemed small, but it didn't matter to me then. I was not only willing, I was anxious to go.]

When we got to Maui, I found it was even smaller than I had imagined. The island is approximately 48 miles from the outside point of each end of the island, and only about 9 miles across the narrowest place, at that time—about fifty years ago.]

They told us the island was at one time actually two mountain peaks coming up out of the sea, and that Maui had been two very small islands.

They had been taught to believe that the whole land mass had continued to rise until the two islands were one. With expressions of sincerity they added, " . . . and the island is still rising, ever so slowly."

[You know, they may have been right. Just last week I read in the newspaper that scientists say the islands are actually rising, and that the volcanic activity we hear so much about is also helping to extend the shoreline of what is now our fiftieth state.]

The three principle sources of income in the Hawaiian Islands, at the time we were there, were the production of sugar cane and pineapple, and tourism. However, tourism then was nothing like it is now.

We were soon to learn much about how sugar cane was grown and harvested, because Maui was like one big sugar plantation.

We were intrigued with the picture-book layout of Maui. Thriving young stalks of sugar cane waved in the soft breeze, in surprisingly large fields for such a small island.

As time went by we were more and more enlightened regarding the production of sugar, which had always been an important element in our diet. Sugar cane was all around us and ever with us on Maui. We seemed to always be learning more and yet ever being surprised at its uniqueness.

That first year we were there we watched as they planted the young seedlings in long rows, then irrigated the fields during the growing process. This all seemed logical. However, when at just the right stage of maturity, they actually set the fields on fire to burn them over, we could hardly believe what we saw.

We were told that an accidental fire had revealed the advantages of having the unwanted stalks, etc. removed before being received at the mill. At the time when we were there it was an established process to burn the fields purposely at harvest time.

In the old days the charred cane had been loaded into old, dilapidated trucks and hauled to a point where the cargo was transferred to a funny little train and transported to the mills for processing into what was referred to as "raw sugar". It was then shipped by freighters to Crockett, California, where it was further refined into white sugar.

The Giant Tourneauhaulers

A few years before we moved to Maui, Mr. R.G. LeTourneau, of Stockton, California, had gone out to the islands and studied the needs of the industry. He then proceeded to build equipment designed especially for hauling sugar cane to the mills, and pineapple to the canneries.

These huge and amazing machines almost overwhelmed us. The tires stood at least seven feet high. The "tourneauhaulers", as they were called, were operated with levers and buttons. When a worker who did not appear to be too alert happened to be at the controls, they looked terribly frightening. However, we never heard of a single accident involving one of them.

As one would expect, these giant carriers were able to haul much bigger loads than the old trucks.

When the tourneauhaulers were brought to Maui, new and improved roads had to be built to accommodate them. The islands were already undergoing post war improvements as well, which included better roads for other transportation as well.

The little engine which had pulled the cars that hauled sugar cane and pineapple from the fields to the mills and canneries, in the early days, was already permanently installed in Baldwin Park, on one of the Maui's favorite beaches when we got there. Our children spent many happy hours playing on the old engine, along with the native boys and girls.

The Sweet Smelling Fruit

We also learned about pineapple production in Hawaii. There were several large fields of the interesting fruit growing on Maui. We had eaten pineapple, when it was available, back in the states. However, we had never tasted anything like the vine-ripened variety that we were served in the islands.

There was also a large pineapple cannery on Maui, which was owned by a well-known company. We were invited to tour the plant and were really impressed with the obvious cleanliness in the canning process. We had heard stories about the careless way peaches and tomatoes were canned in the states. We never learned if the rumors were true, but we were convinced that we need not question the quality of canned pineapple.

I don't have words to describe the fragrant aroma emitted by the large trucks, hauling the ripe fruit to the local cannery to be processed. During the peak canning season, a delicious fragrance permeated the air for miles around. [Ah! I can smell it still! Um-m-m-m]

While living in the islands we enjoyed all the field-ripened pineapples we could eat. Upon returning to the mainland we found it hard to eat the pulled-while-still-green variety, which is shipped to the states to be sold in supermarkets.

The Island Territory

At the time we lived on the island of Maui, Hawaii was not a state. It was a territory of the United States. It was generally thought of as being much farther away than we think if it today.

There was some tourism in those days, but nothing like today. Practically everyone now dreams of going to our beautiful fiftieth state. Many people who fear traveling abroad feel quite comfortable planning a vacation in Hawaii.

Hotels were quite limited when I lived in the Hawaiian Islands. They are certainly plentiful today. A large, modern hotel now stands on the spot where we lived for a period of time, on the beach at Kahului.

The airport has long since been relocated and enlarged to accommodate huge jet aircraft. Many tourists will tell you that with the easy accessibility, the excellent accommodations and the outstanding attractions, not to mention the preferred climate, Maui is indeed the most desirable island of all. It certainly is, in my estimation.

Often tourists will visit two or more islands on their first visit, then plan to spend their entire vacation on Maui when they go back again. I certainly can understand why it is the favorite vacation spot of so many. I truly believe it is Maui no ka oi, the best of all.

That's What They All Say

The day we arrived on Maui seemed like the longest day we had ever seen. We were exhausted from trying to cope with the new and unexpected, as well as the time variation. And with what I suppose is today referred to as "jet-lag". (This was before the jet age.)

[Your grandpa and I needed rest more than anything. We were utterly worn out. I can't remember ever being more weary.]

Finally, when we had spent the afternoon and evening with the kind natives who had come to welcome us and then fed us so graciously, they all went home, leaving us alone with the aged missionaries.

Observing that the children were very tired, they showed us where they had planned for us to sleep, so that we could get them settled. Oh, how we wished we could go to bed too, but the inquisitive missionaries wanted to talk to us. We couldn't help feeling they were insensitive, not to consider how terribly weary we were. Was it that they didn't see, or that they didn't care, we wondered. We soon realized they had a very selfish motive in mind. They didn't want to wait until the following day to find out what they wanted to know.

We wearily observed that our hosts were settling down for what they intended to be a nice long conversation. They asked many probing questions, which we realized were "loaded". In addition to being physically weary, we were extremely uncomfortable. We felt trapped. If we had been in a hotel room we could have at least prayed aloud. Both of us detected an "ulterior motive" undertone and knew they wanted to learn certain things right away. [We may have been young and inexperienced, but God had given each of us at least a degree of the gift of discernment. We saw right through their questioning.]

The mental strain, in addition to the physical weariness, was almost more than we could hold up under. We prayed silently, "Lord, please give us wisdom to answer these unfair questions at this awful hour, when we so much need to be resting."

Our hosts shifted their position, as they sat in familiar surroundings, so that they could be more comfortable. Not once did they ask if we would like to go to bed. They were intent on getting certain things settled before any of us retired.

During that time they told us, in long, drawn out detail—most of it with an undertone of disappointment and discouragement—about their experiences as young missionaries. We could tell they were leading up to something. We caught on early in the conversation and carefully worded our response. At last, when they could wait no longer, they asked how we expected to be supported in the field.

They knew from previous arrangements and correspondence with our pastor that our church had promised to send us as much as they possibly could each month. Even so, they pretended not to know, wanting to hear it from our own lips.

We wearily related how the Lord had led us and assured them that our home church was firmly behind us, both in prayer and financial support. There was a moment of terrible silence as they looked knowingly at each other. Then in unison, almost as rehearsed (certainly as premeditated) "That's what they all say."

With bitterness and deep disappointment they told of how their home church had likewise promised to support them, but after the first month they had never heard from them again. They were obviously very bitter and doubted whether it would be any different with us. They seemed to comfort themselves in reasoning that we could, and maybe should, experience the same disappointment they had known.

The first night on the mission field was a difficult one. We were sure then, and even more so later, that Satan himself was responsible for that very excruciating hour of intense discouragement. He had been working through two people we had put our trust in. It was a graphic reminder that we were not to trust man but God, who had called us.

When our missionary friends finally stood and suggested we all go to bed, they mumbled that we shouldn't expect to receive any support from the people there. With that they went to bed, leaving us to find our way around and get to bed on our own.

When at last we were in the tiny guest room with our little boys asleep on cots, and our baby daughter in the bed assigned to us, we held hands, reinforcing our convictions regarding our call.

There in that little room on Maui, with the oppression of the evil one so evident, we were never more aware of the comforting power of the Holy Spirit. We knew we had committed our lives to God and we knew He would not let us down, even on a tiny island in a faraway land. We also believed that our home church would never let us down, as these embittered missionaries had assured us they would. But if they did, we felt sure that God would provide in His own way.

In weary resignation, we soon fell into a deep, exhausted sleep.

The Meanest Man on Maui

A frantic search to find a place for us to live had apparently been underway for days before we arrived. After the painful strain of that first evening, we were more anxious than ever to find a house. We felt we could not endure another day imposing on the senior missionaries. We suspected they felt the same way about us, too.

The native people befriended us from the very first day. Our little friend, Bobbie, had taken us into her heart and was not only praying but was also looking for a home for us. She discussed our need with an older Puerto Rican man she knew.

Although Mr. Pellegrini had the reputation of being the "meanest man on Maui", he had recently become a Christian. Most people were still afraid of him, but not Bobbie; she considered him just another member of God's family. She even asked him to help her pray for a house for us.

The rough-looking exterior of this old fellow and the fact that he was rumored to have killed a man while in a drunken stupor—which he denied and which was never proven—didn't affect Bobbie's estimation of this elderly man nor her faith in him. She saw him as God saw him, a new creature in Christ.

When Bobbie showed Mr. Pellegrini real Christian kindness, he was overwhelmed. He felt like an important person; like a child of God, now that he had accepted Christ as his personal Savior. He was thrilled to have someone believe in him and took Bobbie's request to heart. After thinking about it, and after attempting to pray as best he knew how, he decided God might be speaking to him; that He might want him to help. He quickly found Bobbie and generously offered to let us live in part of his house.

When Bobbie came to tell us about his offer she didn't spare any details about the elderly man's terrible reputation. We could see that she was not at all concerned that it could not be a safe arrangement. She knew, however, we would want to pray about it.

[I'm sure you know that we certainly did pray about it. It was another big hurdle for us to get through.]

When Mr. Pellegrini met us he liked us. He told us his work took him away from home a lot, and that when he was home he only used one room of his three-bedroom house. He expressed a kindly welcome, in fact a real desire to share his home with us. At that point it was such a good feeling to be "wanted". We considered his offer and his attitude to be an answer to our desperate prayers.

The two bedrooms of the old sugar plantation home, that he offered us, were large and roomy. There was a nice big living room, and a kitchen that was large enough to also use for a dining area.

This kind man told us he would reserve the one bedroom with an outside entrance for himself. He ate his meals out, he said, so we could have all the rest of the house. It seemed like a good arrangement to us. It would certainly be something we could take advantage of until we could find a better place anyway.

Sensing that we really didn't want to impose on him, he quickly assured us that we should feel free to stay as long as we wanted to. His unconditional welcome was most reassuring, at that hour.

[I can see you are all thinking that your grandma would certainly be frightened in a situation like that. I'm sure I would have been even more scared if God had not helped us to see that here was an angel in the strangest attire ever. He looked to others like the man he was reported to be, but by this time he looked to us like the deliverer he was, sent by God Himself.]

This precious elderly man, who had so recently come to know Christ as his Savior—and friend, had made himself readily available to befriend us. His kindness and sincere willingness to help us all he could, soon completely overshadowed any fear we may have felt at first, on seeing his rough exterior, and hearing about "the bad man who carried a machete", a man who was feared throughout the island.

Actually, Mr. Pellegrini did carry a hatchet-like implement. He used it to cut coconuts down from the high tops of the tall coco palm trees. He also had the "honorable" reputation of being the only man on the island who could climb to the top of the coconut palm trees. He was much in demand for his services, we learned. That was why he was away from home so much.

The natives were amazed that we would agree to live under the same roof with Mr. Pellegrini. Everyone that is, except our little angel friend, Bobbie. [We recognized both Mr. Pellegrini and Bobbie as real "sent ones" from the Lord.]

We actually forgot our fears as we gratefully moved into the home of the kind man with the bad reputation. In fact, we hardly saw our new, very close neighbor. We sometimes wondered if he stayed away on purpose so that we would be more comfortable. He assured us, however, that he was quite busy as he traveled around the island gathering fresh coconuts.

The generosity and kindness of this elderly, time-beaten, mistrusted man—who had so recently become a Christian, was soon matched by other hearts and hands. Everyone seemed anxious to do something. Their efforts did not necessarily meet the approval of the senior missionaries, however. Nevertheless, we soon had beds, a table, and some chairs. Some brought dishes and pans to supplement the few items we had brought from the mainland.

In a couple days we were all set up and quite cozy and comfortable in our first home on our new mission field. It was clearly evident, the natives were thoroughly enjoying the privilege of helping provide our needs, in answer to prayer. We rejoiced in the beautiful way they responded, and in God's method of providing. We knew, without a doubt, that we were loved and respected by the natives from the very first day.

Those Old Plantation Homes

Mr. Pellegrini's home, which he so graciously shared with us, was one of a group of older homes—originally built in clusters, for workers on the sugar cane plantations. They all seemed to be cut from one pattern, very much like our lower priced tract homes, here in California. I remember, they were exactly alike—except that now and then a house would have the floor plan reversed, to sort of break the monotony. That was about where the similarity ended, however.

[They were much different from any California home you have seen, and certainly far from the quality of those we were used to in Illinois.]

The type of workmanship on those old houses came as a shock to us. We had never seen anything like them. Of necessity, the homes in Illinois, because of the severe winters, were well built and well insulated.

[I doubt if you can understand our surprise to see that the first homes we came in contact with in Hawaii were built with single walls. In fact, there were places where you could see daylight through the cracks.]

At first we could hardly believe people actually lived in those flimsy homes. Even the poorest quality, sorriest looking shack in the impoverished southland we had come from, was more weatherproofed.

It was a strange feeling to realize, not only did these natives live in them, we ourselves called one home. Many of the native Hawaiians had at one time lived in grass huts. A few still did. They, no doubt, thought these "wood" houses were pretty nice.

We decided the quality of the plantation homes probably depended on the perspective. They looked pretty sorry to us. Even so, our first home in Hawaii was one of them. It was provided by God, and in many ways it was like heaven on earth.

During the first months we were there we really suffered from the damp cold; at least it seemed cold to us. It may have been partly because we were in the process of being acclimated. It was hard for us to understand why we had not been advised before we came that we would need warm wraps and bedding. Because we had not brought them we were unprepared for the "chilling" effect we encountered.

We were so cold in fact, we wrote to our home church about it. Even though they couldn't understand why we would need them in Hawaii, thoughtful friends in a cold clime responded quickly with sweaters and blankets.

[No doubt we felt the change more than someone moving there from California would have. However, I assure you, if I were moving to Hawaii today—yes, even from California, I would take blankets and sweaters, and rain boots and an umbrella. Oh, how we wished for them. Of course the houses there are better today, and the roadways and walkways are surfaced in most places.]

Hibiscus and Red Mud

The old plantation homes in Upper Paia (Pi-e-ah), on Maui, had one redeeming quality. They were usually camouflaged with colorful native flowers, blooming around them and climbing over them. If a person had an eye for beauty, he saw only the flowers and hardly noticed the "shack" quality of the old house itself. On the other hand, if one had a critical eye, he might completely miss the "blooming beauty" and see only the inferior structure.

We had recently moved from the frigid Midwest, where all outside plants had been frozen by winter's cold blasts. Naturally, we observed with delight, the bright colored Hibiscus—Hawaii's state flower, and other equally brilliant and beautiful varieties, blooming profusely everywhere. Our new home on Maui, which happened to be one of the old plantation houses, was enveloped in so much of this gorgeous "growing color", we hardly noticed the actual structure.

We arrived in Hawaii in May. The next few months we mostly enjoyed the flowers, not thinking too much about other aspects of our new location. Then, the tropical rains arrived. The "Kona" storms, coming in with fierce winds, blowing from the opposite direction than usual, dumped torrents of tropical downpours on us, threatening to inundate our tiny island in the Pacific. The sky seemed to collide with the sea. In Illinois—where we came from, it rained "buckets", as they would say, during the heavy rains, but this was something like we imagined a hurricane would be.

At first, the wet fury of the Kona storms seemed frightening to us. However, when we saw there was no thunder and lightning in them, like we were used to in the Midwest and South, we weren't afraid anymore.

We no longer feared the tropical storms but we did have to adjust to the annoying results. We had never seen so much mud in our lives. And it was red mud; as red as a clay pot. The volcanic soil seemed even redder to us, since we were used to the rich, "black" soil of Northern Illinois. We had not thought too much about the color of the soil until the tropical rains arrived, and the awful mud became a serious problem.

Most roads and footpaths were just plain dirt, with no surfacing of any kind. The heavy Kona rains rendered the so-called "roads" almost impassable. The bottomless ruts were hopeless. The natives were used to it and took it all in stride. We were alarmed. They walked barefoot in the red mud, or wore rubber "thongs" and would simply wash the mud off of them, and their feet.

[We hadn't yet learned to wear the strange sandals—which fit between your toes, and we couldn't stand the murky red mud on our feet. It also seemed too cold to us, to go bare footed. But the biggest problem for us was that our meager shoe supply was threatened, then ruined in spite of anything we could do about it. And we couldn't afford to buy new shoes.]

It was a crisis time for our family; a matter which required a great deal of prayer. Fortunately, the rains came at Christmas time, and a package containing shoes for each member of our family was already enroute. It was a definite case of having our prayers answered even before we asked.

A Tropical Christmas

Here in America we have come to associate Christmas with evergreen trees and beautiful snow, along with the annual sentimental and commercial celebration of the special time of year.

[All of you, my precious grandchildren, know how I feel about the traditional connotations attached to something so sacred as an attempt to honor the coming of God's very own Son to this earth. But let me tell you, those flippant, commercial attempts never appeared more ridiculous, or more out of place than they did that first Christmas in Hawaii.

I don't think we anticipated Christmas trees, and certainly not that "Santa Claus" would appear in that tropical clime. I really don't know what we did expect.]

"Gaudy" was an inadequate word to describe the unusually inappropriate appearance of a decorated tree—in a missionary chapel, on a tiny little Polynesian island in the middle of God's wonderful ocean creation.

From our viewpoint, it was a sickening sight. At least one other person agreed with us. An older visiting missionary from the states; the father of a missionary who had just come to help us with the work there, had the same conviction about Christmas trees at we did. And he was as opposed to allowing a satanic nonentity to upstage the One whom Christians, of all people, should pay homage to when celebrating in honor of Christ's birth, as we were.

I will never forget that first Christmas, after we moved to the Islands. We were heartsick on seeing the extent of worldliness the native Christians had been allowed to believe was acceptable, especially when it came to celebrating the birth of Christ.

Before missionaries had ever come to these islands, the people were steeped in heathen traditions. They needed to be set free, not further entangled. We wanted so much to help them but our hands were tied. We had already learned in the months preceding the holiday season, that we were expected to fit into their already established patterns.

Long before Christmas arrived we saw that we were going to be in for a confrontation. There was no way we could even pretend to sanction or participate in their gaudy festivities.

We tried to ignore the scrawny little tree, even though the natives practically begged for compliments on their decorating skills. We didn't believe there was any semblance of true worship of Christ, the Savior of the world, in what was taking place. The emphasis was mostly focused on the mysterious "man in the red suit", expected to arrive at any moment.

During the hastily put together Christmas program, the children rather haphazardly recited their halfway memorized pieces, but their thoughts were toward the back of the church, in anticipation of the arrival of Santa Claus.

The adults did little better than the younger participants. We could tell it was all just a senseless repetition of previous years, but on this particular Christmas eve the procedure took a rather unexpected turn.

Sure enough, the usurper in a red suit arrived—and at the climactic moment of anticipation. To no one's expectation, however, the older missionary from the states, who was sitting on the platform, suddenly jumped up as if shocked at the appearance of a "Santa" in this setting. He ran over and quickly leaped right through an open window. (It was open because it was warm.) He landed on the porch that ran alongside the building.

We were amazed at the development. The "surprise" incident got the attention of all. There was a look of fright on everyone's face. A fearful sigh swept through the packed-out little church.

[I remember someone whispered out loud that the Holy Spirit had no doubt moved the elderly, retired minister to make such a "conviction provoked" move. I assure you, that annual Christmas program was a bit dampened by this unscheduled incident.

Your grandpa and I somehow made it through that first Christmas eve program, the year we moved to Hawaii. As soon as we could get out we took our little family, and with heavy hearts hurried to the solitude of our humble home.]

Instead of snow, as we had been used to at Christmas time in Illinois, a tropical rain was pouring down as we headed home. Our hearts were as heavy as the atmosphere around us. We felt disappointed and helpless to see these native Christians so caught up in the practices so prevalent back in the states, but which we had hoped had not been introduced on the tiny island.

[I've since learned that Santa, Singer, and Coke all preceded the Gospel in most far corners of the earth.]

Christmas is such a sentimental time. There's no doubt that as we hurried home that night, in the pounding downpour, and the aggravating red mud—following the shocking evening at the church, our hearts were suffering a certain degree of pain from being so far from our loved ones.

During the preceding week we had received packages from our parents, and from our church family in Illinois. Although we were far away and feeling lonely, their numerous, thoughtful gifts assured us they were thinking of us.

In the "we care" packages we had received, each member of our family had been remembered with loving consideration. We could "feel" the love of our family at home and almost see tear stains on each gift as we unwrapped them. I know we wept over each one as we opened it. It was clearly evident, they had tried to make our first Christmas "overseas" as painless as possible. They knew we would be missing our family even more than usual.

In the same way we sensed the love and thoughtfulness of the members of our home church; those we had known, and those who had come into the fellowship after we had left. It was plain to see that they had been inspired by the enthusiastic efforts of the others to provide for "our missionaries" in Hawaii.

Tucked in here and there were extra "bonus' blessings; a handmade tablecloth, for instance, to give our table a touch of formality reminiscent of Northern Illinois, something we missed very much. Or a kitchen gadget which helped to remind us of their faithful prayers every time we used it. There were a couple wall plaques. One said "GOD CARES", and the other "WHY WORRY WHEN YOU CAN PRAY".

One dear Christian friend had embroidered a beautiful pair of pillow cases. What a blessing, at the close of a long, stressful day, to lay our weary heads on these silent reminders of their faithfulness—and God's.

Of course there were items of clothing, with sizes carefully chosen, for each member of our family. We gratefully noted how well God knew our sizes, and how alert the dear ones had been to listen to His prompting when choosing for us.

As you would expect, there were toys and games for the children, as well as necessities and clothing such as shirts, pants, and underwear, for the boys, and dresses as well as all kinds of girls clothing for our little daughter. And of course there was shoes for the whole family. The packages from our families had not been planned to coordinate so that our specific needs would be met, but they came out that way.

Driving home from the Christmas program that evening, we were remembering our thoughtful gifts with sincere appreciation. We were also aware of the loving kindness shown us so often, and certainly at Christmas, by the natives. In fact, they had given us a cash offering that evening, along with several small packages that had been handed to us.

We were aware that the Island Christians had tried to show us extra love and attention because they knew we would be feeling the effect of the distance between us and our own families at this special time. They were unusually sensitive about such things. They never suspected, however, the pain we were experiencing because of the way they had been taught to celebrate Christmas.

The Biggest Surprise

With so much on our mind, we were totally unprepared for the surprise that awaited us when we returned home, after the Christmas program that night.

[When we opened the door we could hardly believe what we saw. Our living room was filled with so many wonderful things, it's hard for me to describe the scene to you.]

There were toys of every description for the children. It was evident that someone had spent hours shopping for each child specifically. More toys than we had dreamed they would ever have, sat right there in front of us, waiting to be enjoyed. Masculine toys, for three little stair-step boys suddenly brought them awake and alive. They were soon busily involved, investigating their exciting new world.

The thoughtful, almost unbelievable choice of just the right toys for our almost two-year old daughter had to wait until the next morning for inspection. Understandably, our blond-haired baby girl slept through the entire surprising discovery.

Our little MK's were so involved with their exciting toys they couldn't be distracted to rejoice with us when we discovered the new clothing for each of them, and their baby sister—and yes, for us too.

The new, appropriate garments were all the correct size, and the things we needed most. Whoever had done this amazing thing had been exceedingly insightful, and undoubtedly guided by God.

We were too momentarily overwhelmed by the heavenly shower to immediately discern who might be responsible. By the time we found the more than extravagant food items in the kitchen, so well planned and so complete, we decided whoever planned, coordinated, and carried out the whole affair, definitely had an in-depth insight into our family.

We wept with gratitude to the Lord—and to our unknown benefactors, as we knelt to thank God, and to ask Him to bless whomever was responsible, and so used by Him to supply our needs, and much more.

We finally insisted the boys put their new toys aside and go to bed. Then, we sat down ourselves and silently surveyed the whole scene.

Suddenly, we knew who had done it. The meticulous handmade items—which stood out, even above all the store-bought ones, could only have come from one place; our dear friends, the haole couple who had retired on Maui, and who had insisted on paying the boys' lunches at school. That's who it had to be.

We knew this couple operated a home for older men, located up the mountain side. Mr. Hanley had taught these men to do fancy woodwork as a pass-time project, and for therapy.

He and his wife had expressed great interest in our family from the first time we met them; the day we registered our oldest son at Paia school. We were certain he had instructed and supervised these elderly men to make the special toys for our children.

There was a child's wagon, so well made and attractive it would have taken the prize in any woodwork competition. The wheelbarrow too, was equally well crafted. It fascinated the boys. It was a clever toy. The youngest son latched onto the rocking horse, which was no doubt intended for him.

They had fashioned a small cradle, beautifully decorated with a pretty decal, for our little girl to rock her soft, new dolly in. The most intricate of all the custom-made toys was a miniature ironing board, made to scale. We marveled at its perfection. It looked exactly like the ironing board her mommy had had in Illinois. It folded to store, just like a real one. It was a bit beyond her age at the time but those responsible for the unique gift, were looking forward to when she would be older. For the moment she was completely occupied with her dolly's cradle which the crafters had made.

Mrs. Hanley had hand-crocheted a dress and bonnet for the doll she had chosen for our little girl. [It was only one of the three she received that Christmas. We had been terribly concerned she might not even have one. One was tucked away in the missionary box we received from our home church, and another was from her Grandma Chappell.]

We later learned that the men in the home had enjoyed making the really neat toys, almost as much as the children who received them enjoyed playing with them.

The first Christmas we were in Hawaii we were greatly blessed, not only with things we desperately needed, but also with bonus blessings far beyond anything we could have imagined or hoped for.

[Let me tell you, those were experiences we would never forget. We knew we could never thank everyone enough. We prayed that God would repay each one who had contributed so lovingly to our special needs. I believe that He did.

I hope I have been able to help you understand what it was like for our little family, as we moved through such an emotional period that first Christmas—so far from home. I think you can see how God blessed us abundantly and repaid us with extra blessings too; more than enough to make up for anything we may have given up for Him.]

* * *   * * *   * * *

"Oh, look what time it is! There's so much more I want to tell you about. Why don't we take a break while I fix us something to eat. You boys look hungry. I'm sure Grandpa will have to eat soon also. You want to go find him, while I get busy in the kitchen?

"Andrea, would you and Marissa like to set the table?"

CHAPTER 13

Different Food and Different People

"Thank you for making that good spaghetti, Grandma. You make it just the way I like it." Barry commented as we finished eating.

"I liked the apple pie," Gregory quickly voiced, patting his tummy. "It was good!"

"Could you tell us more about Hawaii when we finish in the kitchen?" Marissa wanted to know.

"Oh, please do." Andrea begged.

"I would like to know what kind of foods you ate in Hawaii." Gregory suggested.

"And I would like to hear more about the different kinds of people, and how they lived," Barry told me as he carried dirty plates to the sink.

"I would love to answer your questions if you're not too tired for another session before bedtime."

"Oh, we're not," they all assured me.

* * *   * * *   * * *

Food From Heaven - Hawaiian Style

We had barely moved into our new home, when the native Christians gave us an old-fashioned house warming. They came from every direction bringing gifts of love. We were very much aware that they were sharing generously of that which meant most to them.

We ended up with a large quantity of rice, something which we didn't even know how to cook at the time, much less eat. As a child I had eaten rice that my mother had cooked, but it tasted something like tapioca pudding. She had boiled the rice grains until they were soft, then added milk, eggs and sugar and called it rice pudding.

We looked at all the bags of rice and wondered how we would ever be able to use so much. But it was food and we were grateful that God had provided it. But rice wasn't the only thing they brought. Their contributions included many cans of top-brand corned beef. We soon learned that fresh meat was very scarce and very expensive, beyond the means of the natives and us.

We were overcome by their love. We knew these caring people had truly given unselfishly from their hearts. They knew that plain rice would not seem very good to us, at least until we learned how to cook it properly. They were sharing their canned meat to make a more tasty and complete meal for us.

Our new friends also brought a quantity of canned milk. It was what they all used and, again, they shared their best. We knew we might as well get used to that kind of milk because the meager supply of fresh milk on the island was not considered safe. This really concerned us, since our children were young, the youngest being only a baby.

The island people hardly knew what fresh milk was. The missionaries told us that some of them actually believed that canned Carnation brand milk came from carnation flowers. Most of them had never even a cow. Having moved from a large dairy farm in Illinois, learning to do without fresh milk was perhaps the biggest dietary adjustment we had to make.

It was easy for us to see that these people were sharing more than they could really afford. We saw true Christian love in action. It warmed our hearts and gave us added assurance that God would never let us down.

Some of the other items we received included bags of fresh fruit and nuts, coffee (grown on the "Big Island" of Hawaii), white and brown sugar (grown on Maui), and several items which we were unable to identify. One couple brought a large box full of avocados which they had gathered from their back yard. [Can you imagine that? I can tell by the look on your faces, you think that would be really great. I would think so too, now. But at that time we had never seen an avocado and certainly never tasted one. The kind folks who had brought them had to explain to us what they were and how to eat them. We never did learn if they were a fruit or a vegetable.]

When our thoughtful, caring friends had gone, we were so overcome with gratitude that we sat down right in the middle of God's incredible and indescribable provision and wept and praised Him for His goodness to us. Then we knelt by the rice and asked Him to help us learn to cook and to eat it. At that point it seemed like a mountainous task but we had lots of faith. We really believed God could do anything, if we asked Him and then trusted Him to do it.

We looked at those strange looking avocados and we thanked God for everything even though we still did not know what some of it was.

In the coming days I received many suggestions as to the "best" way to cook rice, so the grains would fall apart. Each cook took great pride in the way she did it and each thought their method was best. I experimented with various suggestions and tried hard to learn. Soon I was able to cook rice as well as those who had taught me.

The avocados? Well, a sympathetic haole (a newcomer, like us; one who was not native to Hawaii) told us that they had learned to eat them by putting catsup on them. It worked. [You know, I still like avocados with catsup on them, but I also like them plain and every other way too.

In fact, I love them. Unfortunately, I can't forget that the University of Hawaii discovered that avocados contain more calories than any other single food. You have never seen avocados like those our Hawaiian friends showered upon us that day. The best ones we get in the supermarket today are scrawny in comparison.]

Our eating habits were changing dramatically. Foods we loved were not only unavailable, but they would not have seemed to fit in a tropical climate. Instead of fresh meat, eggs, potatoes and baked foods, we found ourselves eating and enjoying foods like rice with corned beef and variety of fresh island fruits.

Greens and vegetables were not as available as we had expected them to be in a mild, tropical climate. Those who grew small gardens to produce their own fresh vegetables were aware that they were not as nutritious as they appeared to be. Volcanic soil, we were told, lacked most of the valuable nutrients required to produce healthy vegetables.

Fresh vegetables were shipped in and were available to the food markets only during certain seasons, and of course they were terribly expensive. They certainly were out of reach for us. [I have to admit, we often craved fresh mainland type vegetables and salad greens which we had been used to year round, even as far inland as the Chicago area where we lived.]

It didn't take us long to acquire a taste for locally grown fruits, which were always available in abundance, and which our island friends graciously shared with us. To my surprise, I was able to tolerate and enjoy bananas and pineapple, both of which I previously had difficulty with. That may have been because the fruits we got on the mainland had been pulled green and not allowed to ripen first, as they were in Hawaii.

Pineapples intrigued us. We had never seen such a plant. Thirty or forty stiff long leaves are spaced around a flowering center. In five to six months the fruit is ripe and weighs anywhere from three to five pounds when ready to harvest. We lived near a very large field of pineapple. It was estimated that the pineapple grown in Hawaii at that time represented approximately fifty-five percent of the world's production.

Pineapple was one of the two principle crops grown in Hawaii in the forties and fifties. Sugar cane was the other. We were surprised that so much of each of them could be grown on such a tiny island as Maui.

Soon after we moved to Maui, we were told that it was acceptable to stop by any pineapple field and pick ripe fruit, as long as you ate all of it. It was common practice and was not considered stealing. That was hard for us to do at first, but we were urged to enjoy the fruit that grew so abundantly on the island. We could hardly believe the difference in the taste of field-ripened pineapples and those we had been accustomed to.

All staple groceries were unbelievably expensive, so we began to eat less expensive items. One by one we gave up foods we thought we had to have. Dry cereals and fresh milk were the most difficult to give up. We lost our taste for potatoes soon after we learned to eat rice; that was an easy adjustment for us to make. Rice soon became one of our favorite foods. We wondered why people in the Midwest didn't eat more rice.

[When we came back to the states we continued to eat rice. We discovered that California residents also eat a lot of rice. Now I prefer rice to potatoes.]

One of the basic foods on the islands, especially among the native Hawaiians, was called poi. It was made from the roots of the taro plant, which is similar to a yam. The edible rootstocks were steamed, peeled, then pounded into a starchy pudding, which to us strangely resembled wallpaper paste.

In the early days of Hawaiian history poi was considered the "staff of life". When we were there it was still thought of as a very nourishing food and was especially regarded as good for the ill, the elderly and the young.

I found it difficult to even try poi. I think it was because I wasn't sure it was always prepared with cleanliness. But I came up with an idea. Since it was supposed to be such a nourishing food, and our family needed that, I decided to recook the prepared mixture that was available in the marketplace to make sure all the germs were killed, and to add seasoning to improve the bland flavor. Eventually we learned to enjoy this unusual food and to appreciate the fact that it was so good for all of us.

Meat On Maui

Fresh meat other than fish was difficult to find and it was certainly beyond our budget when it did appear occasionally in the local market.

There were two cattle ranches in Hawaii at the time, one of them on Maui. This one didn't provide any meat however; it was merely a dude ranch. What little beef appeared in the markets either came from the Parker Ranch, on the Big Island, or from the mainland.

The famous Parker Ranch on the Big Island consisted of more than 300,000 grazing acres. We often wondered why it couldn't provide all the islands with ample fresh beef. People in Hawaii didn't seem to care all that much for beef. Poultry was available occasionally in the markets but it too was too expensive. We really enjoyed the chicken dishes which the natives prepared. Sometimes they cooked chicken just because they knew we enjoyed it so much. It was typical of their gestures of appreciation for our ministry there.

When we first moved to Maui, someone told us that in the old days, the Hawaiian people actually killed their dogs and ate them. We did not believe this to be true then, but every time we saw one of their thin, scrawny dogs we thought about the rumor.

[I have to admit, we also thought about the dog story every time the Hawaiians served a dish in which we couldn't identify the meat.]

We knew for a fact that the Hawaiians did kill wild boar hogs on the slopes of Mt. Haleakala. They cooked them on hot rocks in an underground oven which they called an imu. This was usually done only when they celebrated some special occasion with one of their famous luaus. Most of the time they served regular pork. I'm not sure how they did it, but the meat turned out to be very moist, tender, and flavorful. [A Hawaiian luau is still a popular tourist attraction today, however the pork served is not wild boar meat from the mountains.]

Naturally, fish was the most available and economical meat. We also loved fish and I learned new ways to cook it. We could hardly believe it when we saw natives eating raw, completely uncooked fish. They tried to teach us the trick. [I'm afraid I never learned that one. Your grandpa, however, thrilled the islanders with his ability to comply with most of their strange customs, including eating raw fish. I always managed to find some graceful way to get around it.]

The native Hawaiians loved to eat the little opihi (o-pee-he), which were actually tiny raw shellfish. They enjoyed picking them from the oceanside rocks and munching them as they went along.

There were times when we got pretty hungry for meat that was not fish. The natives were used to doing without it but it was hard for us. In Illinois we had enjoyed an abundance of beef and poultry.

A Strange Source Of Delicious Meat

I remember so well an incident that convinced us that God was aware of and cared about our meat deficiency.

One morning some Hawaiian fishermen spotted a huge turtle on the edge of the beach behind the house where we lived. The discovery generated considerable excitement. We hurried out to see what the commotion was all about. As we approached the men who were talking excitedly we saw for ourselves the turtle they had found. We could hardly believe the size of it. We estimated that it would barely fit into the bed of a pickup truck. [Please believe me when I say, it was some show!]

We could not fully appreciate at the time what the natives were so thrilled about. Those huge aquatic animals were not spotted very often. The islanders were familiar with them, however, and knew they were edible and that they were excellent meat.

When the fishermen had killed and butchered the turtle, they naturally shared it with us in their usual big-hearted manner. While we stood by, curiously watching the operation, they explained to us that there were several types of meat in the turtle. Some resembled beef and some tasted a little like pork. One of them who had been to the mainland and tasted lamb, insisted some cuts reminded him of leg of lamb.

[I have to admit, at first I was not very excited about trying the meat they so graciously shared with us.Your grandpa insisted, however. To my surprise I found it tasted surprisingly good. We knew that God had provided it. And it was meat, wasn't it? That was one incident I will never forget.]

The Hawaiian Huki-lau

We have all enjoyed the New Testament account of Jesus and His disciples, fishing off the shores of Lake Galilee. I'm sure almost every true fisherman has thrilled at the account of the miraculous netfuls of fish caught by Peter and his fellow fishermen.

On one unforgettable day, we heard the same sounds of excitement we had heard the day the turtle was discovered. This commotion was louder, however, and it was evident that more men were involved. We knew something unusual was taking place.

We just happened to be home that morning. We hurried down to the beach and saw that from every direction a large crowd was gathering. All were carrying containers of various sizes, buckets, pans, bags, to receive their share of whatever it was that was so suddenly available. They seemed to know; we couldn't tell what was happening.

When we asked what the excitement was all about, a Hawaiian man explained that it was a "huki-lau" and that it rarely took place.

A large school of fish had been discovered off shore and a real Hawaiian fishing party had ensued. It was probably something like the miraculous catch of fish which Peter and the other fisherman experienced that day while Jesus was here on earth. One big rough-looking fisherman told us they were taking in so many fish their nets were breaking. He had not read the Biblical incident but we felt like we were standing on holy ground. [Your grandpa and I looked at each other knowingly, sharing the awe.] We stood in reverent silence, watching with great interest as the scantily clad fishermen pulled their bulging nets from the beautiful Pacific Ocean. It was a real, live illustration of that miraculous "huki-lau" on the shores of Galilee, so long ago.

[I've always believed God staged that one just for our benefit. Why not? He has done many other miraculous things in our lives.]

Once again, our Hawaiian friends shared graciously and liberally with us. What a fine fish-feast everyone had!

You know, I've always wondered what happened to all those fish that day at Lake Galilee. Perhaps they were distributed in the same way.

The Big Food Crisis

There were times when our family faced real food shortages. Our income of only one hundred dollars, sent faithfully to us every month from our home church, was gravely inadequate for a family the size of ours, even in the "good 'ole days". But there were times when the prospect of not having enough food was a problem not only for us, but for others on the island.

I remember one food crisis which affected the entire island chain. A longshoreman's strike, which lasted for weeks, cut off all food imports from both the mainland and the Orient. Soon existing food supplies began to dwindle and a gnawing uneasiness swept across the Islands.

When rice became increasingly scarce, some residents began to panic. Many of the older folk, particularly the Oriental people, actually thought they would die if they did not have rice to eat. They had been used to eating rice all their lives, three times a day. They would not be comforted by the fact that there was plenty of some other foods to keep them from starving. They were sure they could only survive on rice. They hardly considered other edibles real food.

I will never forget the fearful look on the faces of those dear elderly people as their rice supply began to dwindle away. They had always managed somehow to have plenty of rice. They were totally unprepared for this unexpected scarcity.

It was easy for us to get along without rice, even though by that time we did miss it. We could easily have fallen back on potatoes, but the small supply still available was selling for twenty-eight cents a pound. They were simply unaffordable for us.

The airlines were still in operation, but most food came to us via large ocean freighters. [I assure you, it was pretty frightening for all of us to be completely shut off from the outside world and the lifelines which supplied most of our foods.]

The extended longshoreman's strike posed a serious threat to the health and welfare of the entire island population. No one knew how long it would continue.

As a last resort, some of the wartime military food supplies stored on the island were tapped. These were leftover from when the enlisted men had been stationed on Maui, following the attack on Pearl Harbor. The so-called "Igloos", where the rations were stored, resembled the underground storm cellars we were familiar with in the South. My dad built one for us after the terrible tornado we experienced.

I well remember the uneasy atmosphere among the natives when the surplus rations were brought out. Fearful memories were aroused. We had moved there after the war, but we could imagine how frightening it must have been to be trapped on a tiny island with nowhere to escape to. [Later, when we lived in one of the camouflaged homes that had been occupied by officers during the war, we could visualize it even more. Heavy, dark green shades were still on the windows.]

We found the surplus K-Rations quite tasty, but eating food which had been stored underground in metal containers for a few years did seem a bit scary to me.

Another source of food we discovered during the great food crisis was the large company store operated by those who owned a majority of the land in Hawaii. They brought out foods that had been stored on their dusty shelves to help alleviate the emergency food crisis. I vividly remember a couple of items that we particularly enjoyed. One was a very tasty jam packaged in quart size jars. It, too, had been stored on their shelves for a long time but age had only enhanced the flavor. Another unforgettable food item we found in the store was quart size jars of peanut butter. It was indescribably delicious. And one of the things we especially appreciated was that they sold us each of the delectable and nourishing food items for only pennies a jar. [You know, I can still remember the special taste of that peanut butter and jam.]

The island people would not eat the peanut butter and jam. They didn't want it at any price. I don't think they would have accepted them if they had actually been starving. The proprietor was happy to let us have them for almost nothing just to get rid of the aged merchandise. We appreciated the fact that both the peanut butter and jam were packaged in glass. And there were other leftover food items which we took advantage of. We had a field day purchasing and enjoying affordable foods during the crisis period. We believed they were lifesaving provisions from the Lord.

God Provided - People Shared

Despite the subtle discouragement tactics of Satan, we immediately directed all our efforts into the work we had been called unto and sent to do. We didn't waste any time worrying about what we would eat or wear. I have to give full credit to the country church that commissioned us to go out. They faithfully stood behind us in prayer, and in sending one hundred dollars per month, as they had determined to do.

The discouraging forecast of the senior missionaries that our home church would surely let us down kept us even more aware that we were dependent on God, not man. We had learned to trust God for each day's needs.

The check we received regularly every month from our home church was a tremendous blessing to us. It was as if it came directly from the hand of the Lord. It was an indication that He was looking after us. But that small amount was far from adequate, since it was the only income we had for our family of six, in an area where everything was more expensive than in the mainland. We had to carefully manage every penny.

[Many times I fasted and prayed for enough food for our children and for your hard-working grandpa, who was willing to work all day and half the night, often without enough nourishment. But I never once heard him complain. I can honestly say, he was utterly dedicated.]

Answered prayer was so definite at times, we couldn't help but be assured of God's constant care. Our complete dependence on Him for our every need only brought us closer to Him and to each other.

The senior missionaries did not approve when the natives wanted to help us monetarily. They felt all monies given should go to them, no matter how much work we did. Their jealously due to the fact that our home church had not failed us as theirs had only added to their resentful attitude towards us.

The island people truly loved us and appreciated our ministry among them. They wanted to help us but were aware that all tithes and offerings given to the church went totally to the older missionaries. Instead of money, the native Christians insisted on giving us food and other items. Had they not done so, there were times when food scarcity would have been life threatening for us. Our provisions in those days came through heavenly channels, often in surprising and unusual ways not only from our new friends that we were ministering to, but also from various sources back in the states.

One family who had moved from our home church in northern Illinois to the eastern part of the United States sent us a check for fifty dollars occasionally. It always came when it was most desperately needed. It was almost as if it was dropped from heaven, in direct answer to prayer, usually when I had been fasting and praying. This family also subscribed to *Moody Monthly* for us, an outstanding Christian magazine. We knew it cost them more to send it overseas and we appreciated it very much. It came to our mailbox every month we were in Hawaii and was an encouragement and inspiration to us during many trying times.

[During those years we learned through experience what it means to live by faith. We proved that God will never let you down if you put your trust in Him rather than in people. Often God allowed us to be reminded of that. We always knew what He sent was from Him, no matter who He sent it through.]

Sometimes a visiting missionary or a tourist would give us an envelope containing money explaining, "God put it upon our hearts to do this." Again, it was always in answer to prayer regarding a specific and pressing need. [One of the most difficult adjustments your grandpa and I had to make before going to the field, and after we got there, was to be willing to let people help us. It was so humiliating at first. We had always been independent, though poor. And we vowed never to "poor mouth" our needs, as we had seen so many others do. We were always repulsed by that approach.]

The Lord had to constantly help us, as we tried to learn to be gracious receivers. It was never easy for us to do. We actually preferred to do without as much as possible, rather than risk having any person, even one, feel that we were imposing on them.

More and more we learned to trust God and to make our needs known only to Him. We were constantly amazed at the methods and channels He used to provide our basic needs and often to send a bonus blessing just when it would honor Him most.

We never felt forsaken. There were down periods and times when we were honestly concerned. But never once did we doubt that we were in God's will or that He had sent us there.

I will never forget one period of testing we experienced during those years on the field. For a few days, all we had to eat was two coconuts we had picked up along the roadside where they had fallen. And we had no prospects of getting any other food soon. As much as we loved coconuts, they tasted much different under those circumstances. They were heavenly manna, divinely provided for the moment.

Coconuts were not that plentiful on the island. We felt that these two had been literally dropped out of heaven, as God's provision for the hour. We had always appreciated His loving care, but even more so after that short crisis. Soon afterwards we received an unexpected check in the mail, as had happened so many times before.

Many will share with us any rewards we may receive for our labors on that field. I'm glad God keeps the books. He sees and knows all about the contributions each of us makes toward the spreading of His Gospel around the world.

Many who gave had little more than we did, but they had big hearts and wanted to share what they did have.

Songs In The Night

God often touched our hearts with His unexpected thoughtfulness. One family gave us an old Zenith radio which they were not using. It turned out to be a real bonus blessing from the Lord. It provided input from our new island home community, and put us in touch with the outside world.

Our heavenly Father knew it would help ease the terrible feelings of isolation which inevitably effects every missionary on a foreign mission field.

[I think only those who have found themselves living in a far away land, among people of another nationality--in our case several different ones--can identify with this awful unspoken loneliness.]

As the months dragged by, that old radio was an increasing source of blessing and release. One night we discovered that in the late night and early morning hours, when many "sunset" stations went off the air we could pick up stations from the distant mainland. One night we stayed up until 2 a.m. and finally heard a station in Cincinnati and a few from Chicago. It was so thrilling we could hardly bring ourselves to turn the radio off. We found a program called *"Songs in the Night"* but couldn't tell if it was being broadcast from Wheaton, Illinois or had just originated there. It didn't really matter to us which. It was so refreshing and comforting, we wept with gratitude for the blessing which seemed to us to have actually originated in heaven, and was being beamed right at us.

[I think that was one of the numerous experiences in my life that endeared my heart to radio, preparing me for my own broadcast ministry one day.]

There were many special blessings in those days, which we recognized as the loving thoughtfulness of God, assuring us of His love and continued care and protection.

A Startling Discovery

Soon after arriving on the field we were startled to learn that some of the clothes we had chosen for the tropical climate were considered to be inappropriate by the senior missionaries and some of the natives.

In Illinois, the summers were short, hot, and humid. During that brief season all winter clothing was stored away and everyone concentrated on trying to keep comfortable, and surviving the intense heat. We were used to wearing lightweight, summer clothing. Women wore dresses and blouses made of sheer fabrics, usually sleeveless. The main objective was to keep cool. The idea that such garments were immodest or sinful never occurred to us.

I was puzzled at the apparent shock on the faces of local Christians when I appeared one day in a dress with sleeves that barely covered my shoulders. I couldn't imagine what the problem was. What had I done wrong, I wondered. The women and girls looked at each other, shaking their heads, but nobody volunteered to tell me what their unusual reaction was all about.

Then the senior missionaries explained unabashedly that my clothing was inappropriate for a "Christian" and especially for a missionary from the mainland. I was shocked. They went on to explain that it would never be acceptable for me to wear sleeveless garments. They had taught the natives that Christians should never be seen with their arms bare, but they had neglected to tell us about this when we were preparing to go to the field. They had however, told us we wouldn't need sweaters or wraps, so I didn't even have a garment with sleeves that I could wear to cover my arms.

This was difficult for us and it seemed like a ridiculous requirement for a year-round tropical climate. We felt they had put the emphasis on the wrong aspect of Christian living.

Perhaps the biggest shock was economical. We could not afford to buy any new clothing. I was faced with having to remain confined to my home, perhaps even my bedroom, as far as they were concerned. A native might appear at our front door, expecting to be invited in. It was the most unreasonable thing we could imagine. We felt trapped and deceived, because we had not been warned at all before we came.

It was plainly evident that I would not be welcome to attend the services at church or even to work among people in the villages without sleeves to cover my arms. It was a terrible predicament and I'm sure Satan was snickering in the shadows.

After much pain and much prayer, we decided the only thing we could do was write our home church and try to explain the unbelievable situation. We hoped they would understand and not think that we were complaining or trying to take advantage of their generosity.

[That was one of the most difficult letters we ever had to write. I cried and we prayed. After many revisions your grandpa reluctantly went to the post office to mail the letter. I even fasted and prayed as we continued to seek divine guidance. It was a terrible crisis battle and I shudder as I recall that period of intense testing.]

When our home church in Illinois received the unexpected letter with details of the strange development, they were as surprised as we had been. The women in the church were touched by my sudden problem even though they, like me, couldn't understand why this had happened. When they looked for summer dresses or blouses with long sleeves, or even to the elbow, they found no such thing. They were laughed at for asking. There was simply no need for them during the hot humid Chicago summers.

As a last resort, the missionary society ladies in our home church decided the only alternative was for them to sew some lightweight jackets that I could wear over the things I already had. Guessing at a size that would be comfortable, they quickly made several long sleeved tops of light weight materials and neutral colors, and mailed them to me.

[I wore odd combinations everywhere I went. They were usually quite uncomfortable in the day time. In the evening, however, long sleeves were welcome and a blessing. We found the nights to be a bit chilly, although the natives didn't consider them so.]

The Culture Shocked Us

Another area which took us by surprise was the different sense of modesty and decency displayed by the natives.

Our first year there we walked most places because we didn't have a car. When working we did drive an old "san pan" type car which belonged to the circuit of little churches. We transported the elderly to church on Sunday and to do their shopping during the week. We did not however, have access to the vehicle for our own personal use at any time, as we should have.

One day we had to go to Kahului to take care of some business. It was too far to walk so we decided to try out the public transportation. We boarded an old dilapidated bus at Upper Paia, along with several other passengers. We were all eyes and ears to observe the interesting sights and the varied people all so new to us.

We were apprehensive about the safety of the old bus. It gave the impression of having been salvaged from the junk yard, and with great effort at that. The driver was also quite reckless. We were so concerned about our physical safety that we were quite unprepared for what came next.

We had just settled into our seats and started to feel a little more at ease as the noise and clatter began to let up. Suddenly, a Filipino couple seated directly behind us started to talk rather loudly in a very open manner. Today on television or in public you may hear foul gutter language and conversation about private and personal topics, but it wasn't like that then, especially not in rural areas such as where we had been raised.

We couldn't believe what was happening. Others around us didn't seem to notice. They were evidently used to such talk; we were not. We felt embarrassed as adults, but we were more concerned about our young sons. We didn't know what to do; we just looked at each other and prayed silently, hoping our little boys hadn't heard or noticed.

Perhaps the most disturbing aspect was that we had seen the couple in one of the churches. We later learned that in their native Philippines this type of talk was common. For some of the Christians, it took years before their behavior changed from when they didn't know Christ. We were convicted of the need to help them build a solid foundation to their faith, one that was based on the Scriptures. We are all powerless to make deep lasting changes in our lives, but God's Holy Spirit can, and the Christians there had not been taught of Him. It was the greatest desire of our hearts to be able to do this freely.

The Irregular Family

In many respects, the Hawaiians found us and some of our ways to be strange too. In fact our family was different to them in many ways.

Right away we discovered that their family units were structured differently. There might be as many as sixteen children in one home and in many cases the children hardly knew who was a parent and who was an aunt or uncle. Sometimes the children living in a home were not even blood relatives to that family. A household could include any child who wanted to be a part of that particular family and who chose to participate in their home life.

While they lived harmoniously in the home, they never went out together as a family. This was different from what we were used to. Whatever we did, we did together. A father, a mother, three fair-skinned little boys like stair steps, and a little blond-haired girl in arms. Everywhere we went, our family was on display. Whenever we walked down the streets in the little villages or along the trails, children, and even adults would stop and watch us with curiosity as we walked by. This was a totally new concept to them. When we first arrived in the Islands, I used to say I believed some people came to church just to watch our family.

Our children were usually with us unless they were in school. This was also new to the natives. Children there were allowed to go wherever they wished, anytime they wanted to. I had a hard time getting used to this and it always bothered me.

I was in constant fear of our children getting too close to the ocean. It's great expanse intimidated me and ever since my brother drowned I had been afraid of water. [Your grandpa sympathized with my concerns.]

The natives had no fear of the ocean. We were told that parents often pushed their young children, not yet old enough to walk, into the water so they would learn how to swim. We never learned if that was actually true, but we did observe that they did not fear water. I'm sure God must have watched over them in a special way; otherwise many of them would never have made it to adulthood.

Maybe I watched over mine too closely. As long as they were in my care I always did my best to protect them and to train them in the best way I knew how, in every aspect of their lives.

The Melting Pot

In our preparation for serving in Hawaii, we had learned that several different nationalities lived there.

I had been raised in the South where strong racial discrimination was prevalent, but I was not narrow-minded as many people I knew were, including some of my relatives. The prospect of living and working with people of other races neither disturbed nor frightened me.

(Your grandpa had grown up in New Mexico, where he went to school with Mexican children and had many as friends. I believe God graciously prepared us by giving us a special love for people who were different from us, long before we were called to serve Him on the mission field.)

Once in the Islands we found that many Japanese lived there. They were pleasant and those we came to know were artistic and studious. Many of the ladies were accomplished seamstresses. On Maui, all the barbers were Japanese women.

The Japanese tended to keep their thoughts and emotions to themselves. The true, peace-loving citizens who were living there at the time of the attack on Pearl Harbor and immediately following the war, suffered greatly because of the actions of some of their fellow countrymen. Our hearts went out to those who had not been in agreement with the military tactics of their country. We especially felt concern for Japanese Christians.

We enjoyed working with the Japanese Christians. We found them to be dedicated and sincere. They could be trusted and depended upon. They were true friends and sensitive co-workers.

It was sad to see so many Japanese living in Hawaii who still worshipped Buddha, just as their ancestors had back in Japan. Many temples and gardens had been erected, where they held their strange rituals. Their cemeteries were also involved in various ceremonies. The celebrations were loud and boisterous. They filled the night air over the whole central area of Maui with their satanic chanting and eerie music. The moist, salty air was a good conductor.

(I can remember nights when we could not sleep because of the loud, devilish disturbances from which we could not escape.)

The Chinese in the islands also carried out ritualistic worship, just as their ancestors had for hundreds of years. It was extremely difficult to reach them with the Gospel message.

Not nearly as many Chinese lived on Maui at the time we lived there. We got to know one Chinese man quite well. He was an excellent cook, and he loved to watch us enjoying the dishes he had prepared, often especially for us. There was also a Chinese-Hawaiian couple in one of our churches whom we loved. They were among the few Chinese who had embraced the Christian faith. One thing I remember well about Mr. Wong was his handshake. When he shook my hand he would almost crush the bones, and his "God Bless You" sentiment went through his strong body and into a firm handshake.

His precious wife always had a smile on her face. Even when praying about a great burden, her face emitted a radiant beam as she expressed her deep faith in God. The "smile wrinkles" were too deep to go away, even when she suffered despair. Her family had a lot of problems. Her reaction to such a hard life was a great blessing to us.

We also had some Chinese children in our Sunday Schools, but we were never able to make much headway with their parents. We appreciated the opportunity to teach the younger members of the family about God and His Word, even though their parents and other relatives were not responsive. If they resented our teaching or tried to discredit it when their children got home, we never heard about it. It seemed strange to us that they would so willingly allow them to come to learn from us. They were aware of what we taught and about the God we worshipped.

At the time we lived on Maui, there were quite a few Filipino people in the Islands. Several of the families had become Christians. Our senior missionaries had started a small mission near a camp where many of them lived and labeled it "The Filipino Church".

Some of the Filipinos we came to know were depressed and sad and lived in the meagerest homes, under the poorest conditions we had ever seen. But there were exceptions. One man we knew wore very flashy clothes which made him look like a colorful male bird. Raphael often turned up in church wearing strange combinations, such as bright green slacks and a purple shirt. Or he would be decked out in purple trousers and a bright yellow shirt with huge red flowers on it. It was as if he loved to be noticed and admired. Although there were indications that he was very poor, he somehow managed to strut about in a number of different outfits when he came to church. We suspected he didn't even have enough food to eat, though we never knew for sure.

We were impressed with the shoes Raphael chose to wear with his way-out attire. He wore sleek, shiny patent leather oxfords and shoes make of snake skin or alligator hide. We often wondered where he found such spectacular, outrageous clothing. We never learned. Although most of the Filipino people adhered to Catholicism which they had been used to in the Philippines, a number of them embraced the Protestant faith after moving to the Hawaiian Islands. Several families attended the churches we worked with and others we knew attended a little Baptist mission in Happy Valley.

[The Filipino people your grandpa had the privilege of working with loved him. He had the patience necessary to try to understand the broken English the people still spoke. He had an effective hospital ministry to a group of older Filipino men.]

Younger Filipino men who came to the churches listened gladly as he presented the Gospel message. They seemed to be at ease with him. Raphael eventually became a Christian and consequently sought less attention for himself. He never did completely lose his attachment to gaudy fashions though.

[One really young Filipino couple with two small children eagerly pursued the Bible study sessions your grandpa taught. They became solid, active Christians, with a strong witness and an effective outreach ministry to the members of their own race. They could reach them easier than we could.]

Domingo, who also graciously accepted the truth of the Gospel message, loved the Lord and enjoyed life in general. I will never forget him. He was so happy in his newfound faith. Domingo got a special thrill out of some of our peculiarities. He was often amused at me, especially when I kept asking, "Which way is north?" As far back as I can remember I always felt the need of being directionally oriented, no matter where I was. It was hard for me on that tiny little island, surrounded by such a mighty ocean. North, south, east or west didn't have any meaning in relation to the seemingly endless sea. The Island people described directions as windward and leeward. Windward means the direction from which the prevailing wind blows. Leeward means away from the wind, towards the sea.

Juan Moldera and his wife and three children were another family we came to know very well. Juan often did special things for us. When he learned that we liked frog legs he went out to the reservoir and caught a whole bucket full of frogs for us to eat. It was a kind and thoughtful gesture. We were so starved for meat that we really enjoyed them.

From the first day, it was interesting to observe the various races of people, blended together in the unique melting pot of humanity in the unique territory of Hawaii.

Who Are We Anyway?

Living among so many kinds of people sometimes put us on the spot. Everyone born or raised there knew what nationality they were. If they were a mixture, which most were, they knew the exact proportions; one half, one quarter or whatever. We could not say that.

I remember when we first arrived and attempted to register our oldest son in school. The office staff was completely frustrated, trying to help us answer the questions on the forms. We were all totally confused. We simply did not know who we were as they did.

My Grandma Adams had told me that I had German, Dutch, Norwegian and English blood in my veins, but I had no idea in what proportions. I knew my dad was French. [Your grandpa had no idea who his ancestors were.] We were really in an embarrassing predicament.

Finally, after considerable frustration the office staff decided we must be Caucasian, which means a member of the white race. I had never even heard the word "Caucasian" before. We accepted that and were happy to have that behind us. We had those office workers feeling really sorry for us, not knowing who we actually were.

The Illustrious Hawaiians

At the time we lived on Maui, there were not many full-blooded Hawaiians left. Most had mixed with other races. They still knew, however, what part Hawaiian they were and they were proud of it. It grieved our hearts to see these lovely people, people we were especially attracted to and loved so much, slowly losing their cultural identity.

One small island was still owned by a Hawaiian family and only pure-blooded Hawaiians were allowed there. This was a concentrated effort to preserve a pure remnant of their race.

The more we learned about the Hawaiians the more interesting we found them to be, and the more we loved them. The history of these people before Captain Cook's discovery of the beautiful Hawaiian chain on January 20, 1778, is still a mystery.

The earliest arrivals on these islands were Polynesians. Without navigational instruments or charts of any kind, they had sailed vast seas and survived to become a kingdom. Their knowledge of the ocean, the sky, and the birds which probably assisted them, enabled them to conquer the ocean in their crude canoes.

Because the Hawaiians were people without writing, it is highly unlikely that the exact date of their arrival on these volcanic islands will ever be known. Since information was passed on by mouth and told to succeeding generations, nothing is certain. Much of their early history died with the knowledgeable men and women as they themselves passed on.

Modern written history of Hawaii began with Captain Cook's discovery of the remote island chain in 1778. The English captain must have been quite surprised to find this unusual kingdom situated in the middle of the great Pacific ocean.

At the time of Cook's arrival, each of the islands was ruled by a separate king and they were often at war with each other.

A young Hawaiian man, only twenty-five years old at that time, lived at Kealakekua—on the Big Island—when Captain Cook's ship anchored there. He later became the king and conquered all the other islands and united them into one kingdom. He was the famous Kamehameha the Great, the first of an illustrious line of "Kamehameha"s.

The now written history of the royal kings and queens of those early documented years in Hawaii makes fascinating reading.

[I urge you to read as much about Hawaii as you can find in your local library. After all, our family did have a close connection with those interesting islands for a number of years.]

We were surprised to learn that foreign ships brought all trees, flowers, and other plants, as well as domestic animals and many other things to the Islands. The sad thing is that they brought social diseases, alcohol and firearms as well.

The Hawaiian people had little resistance to these new diseases when exposed to them. Many prominent dignitaries died young. Staggering numbers of common people also died. The population plummeted at an alarming rate in a short period of time.

Unfortunately, there were tragic victims of alcohol as well. And firearms were not a beneficial addition to their way of life.

The elderly Hawaiian people we knew remembered this aspect of their history with regret and resentment. Just to hear them tell about it made us sad.

The years we lived among them and worked with those precious people left no doubt in our minds that they are a loving, lovable and trusting people, sometimes too trusting for their own good. We often wished we could repay them for some of the injustices they had suffered. At least they knew we loved them and that we would not take advantage of them.

[Incidentally, the first missionaries arrived from New England one hundred years before I was born.]

Historical accounts tell how early missionaries took advantage of these generous Hawaiian people and managed to acquire large segments of their land through unscrupulous manipulation. We could see how these big-hearted, sharing people could easily become victims. It is unfortunate however that sometimes those who claim to be Christians stoop to such levels as these early missionaries were accused of.

* * * * * * * * *

"I love remembering all these interesting things about Hawaii for you. There is so much more I would love to tell you about but this story is about what God has done in my life. That is what I want you to know about. I have so much more to tell you."

Note of Interest . . .

There are only twelve letters in the Hawaiian alphabet:
They are a, e, h, i, k, l, m, n, o, p, u and w.
It's surprising what they have done with so few letters. The Hawaiian language is indeed very beautiful.

CHAPTER 14

Real Life Experiences On The Mission Field

"I sure miss Grandpa!" Marissa said sadly.

"So do I," agreed Barry. "We hope he gets a deer this trip, don't we Grandma?"

Nodding my head in agreement, I sank into the leather recliner as Andrea and Marissa each scrambled to get closest to me.

"Are you going to tell us more about Hawaii tonight, Grandma?" Gregory questioned.

"What would you like to hear about this time?" I asked, with a smile.

Barry was the quickest to respond. "Could you tell us about some of your experiences while you lived there? I'd like that!"

All nodded in agreement.

*** *** ***

A Little Break on the Big Island

When we first moved to the Islands, we were surprised at the slow pace around us. We had just come from a completely opposite climate and lifestyle, where people rushed around at a constant breakneck speed. As we observed all that needed to be done on our new mission field we couldn't help but feel impatient with those who seemed so unconcerned, even lazy. No one appeared to have any ambition. We wanted to take them by the hand and say, "Come on, let's get going!" We wanted to get on with the tasks at hand, but the senior missionaries advised us against rushing around the way we had before. The natives tried to explain to us that our hearts were beating "twice as fast" now that we lived in Hawaii. They said we would die too soon if we went too fast. But we were overwhelmed with the challenge and proceeded to get started on what we believed had to be done.

We soon began to feel frustrated with some of the responsibilities given to us by the senior missionaries. It seemed to us that we had to do too many menial tasks that didn't deal directly with the spiritual needs of the people we had come to serve.

After about nine months in Hawaii your grandpa's body just gave out from physical exhaustion. The doctor warned us we would have to slow down. I was concerned for his life. We both determined to do our best to let up on our activities and the fervency with which we went about them.

Everyone expressed great concern for "Brother Brown", who had by this time endeared himself to many. The news of his weariness and health problems quickly spread to everyone we had come to know in the Islands. Many were praying for him.

Some missionaries on the Big Island of Hawaii whom we knew planned a twelve-day vacation for our family on their island. I'm sure God was behind the scenes, directing their planning.

[The Big Island, so named because it was almost twice the size of all the other islands put together, is just across the channel from Maui.]

Our missionary friends planned several stops for us, from the airport where we would land first, all the way around to Hilo, and back on the opposite side of the island. We didn't realize that the trip would include a narrow cliff road on the windward side of the island. If I had known that, I probably would have tried to chicken out and find an excuse to avoid that part of the planned tour.

Our missionary friends met us at a tiny little airport just across the channel from Maui, and took us to a Christian camp already in session. It was an indescribably beautiful setting. Everyone was so gracious to us, and the food was delicious. The thing I remember most, however, was that the bloodthirsty mosquitoes were so bothersome it was hard for us to concentrate on anything else. They seemed to recognize us as fresh meat. No one else appeared to mind. From there we were driven from one attraction to another on their lovely island. It was as though people at each place tried to outdo the others with hospitality and personal attention. We were treated royally.

I remember we were overwhelmed with beautiful Kealakekua Bay. Captain Cook had first landed here and made contact with the island people. We could easily imagine his ecstasy upon discovering these Islands which defy description. [He first called them the "Sandwich Islands", for the Earl of Sandwich.]

The islanders at first thought Captain Cook was the god Lono, returned in fulfillment of an old prophecy. They later lost respect for the captain and his crew, however, because of their way of life.

[We were surprised to learn that Captain Cook was actually able to communicate with the natives by using a Polynesian dialect he had learned in the South Pacific. I imagine the captain was surprised about that also.]

The English captain was buried at a beautiful site there, following a battle in which he and seventeen natives, five of them chiefs, were killed.

On one of our outings on that vacation break, we visited a tiny village on the Kona Coast that had been set aside to retain the old way of life in Hawaii. A posted inscription described the simplicity of native life in bygone days. They had lived in thatched huts, using grinding stones and crude utensils for making poi, the staple food of the Hawaiian people for centuries. The marker indicated that the natives bathed in the shallow water in the nearby inlet; water that was so clear you could see the rocks at the bottom. It looked clean enough to drink.

Not far away, however, were remains of heathen altars where human beings had actually been sacrificed to the gods. That was shocking to us.

Peter, a dear Christian Hawaiian man on Maui, told us he vividly remembered witnessing those sacrifices, as well as other satanic practices. He recounted bloodcurdling accounts which made us realize that we were indeed on a foreign mission field, even though it was now a territory of the United States.

Peter's stories seemed all too real as we stood at the sites of what was left of ancient altars and temples, where those early day sacrifices had taken place. We were reminded of the Biblical accounts of the children of Israel and the types of heathen worship they found when they entered the land of Canaan in the days of Joshua.

We were quite surprised to find a place on the colorful Kona coast called the City of Refuge, with all the characteristics of the Biblical description of provisions made for those who unintentionally committed crimes, that we had read about in the Old Testament. The accounts of Hawaii's elaborate kingly dynasties are also strangely reminiscent of Old Testament days. [I have always wondered what the rest of the planet was like during the Bible's account of Canaan and the promised land.]

Hawaii is proud of the royalty and splendor of an era that is kept alive in the memory of its people as well as eagerly shared with thousands of tourists annually in the many museums found throughout the Islands. We saw plenty of their preserved mementos on that trip and lots more when we later visited Iolani Palace on the island of Oahu where it is said, "If you are very quiet, you can almost hear a king".

We will probably never know where these ancient people learned their primitive religious practices or where they got their ideas for such splendid kingdoms. Some have dared to suggest that the Hawaiians may have been influenced first by Cain and his descendants, and that later practices were probably a reflection of the times of David and Solomon.

While still in the Kealakekua Bay area, we saw real Hawaiian cowboys; "paniolos" as they were called. These colorful characters transported cattle from the Parker Ranch to the coast, where they would be shipped out by boat. We watched with interest and a bit of sadness, as they roughly loaded them onto a ship in the harbor.

[Your grandpa, an authentic cowboy himself, admired the attire, but not the methods, of the island ranch hands.]

The Wrath Of Madame Pele

While still on the Kona side of the Big Island we were taken for a tour of the volcanos we had heard so much about. In a tourist presentation at the park headquarters we learned that the Hawaiians believed volcanic activity was caused by the anger of Madame Pele, who was said to be the goddess of the volcanos.

When a sudden eruption would occur, the natives would cry out, "Madame Pele, she ees mad!" They sincerely believed this "female goddess" controlled the volcanos; the times of their eruptions, and the extent of their flow. Their warped beliefs were fed by the lifelong influence of weird superstitions, exaggerated by their distorted imaginations.

We learned a lot about volcanos from the films and the lectures, and by actually being there and seeing them ourselves. It was a bit scary to actually walk around the rim of a real volcano, even if it wasn't currently active. We were assured that it was perfectly safe but we still felt uncomfortable.

[I still tremble when I remember trying to hold back two inquisitive children who wanted to see over the crater's edge. Your grandpa was carrying our little girl in his arms and I was holding on to the youngest of our three boys so tightly that he kept complaining that I was hurting his hand. The adventurous older boys were watched closely, and constantly. The park ranger told us that some "daring ones" had indeed fallen over the rim and never been found. We felt greatly relieved when at last we were viewing the volcano from a safe distance. We were told that five major volcanos had formed the Big Island of Hawaii. Two, Mauna Loa and Kilauea, are still active. In 1845, Mauna Loa erupted so violently that a two mile wide flow threatened the city of Hilo, the Island's largest town.

It's a surprising fact that Mauna Loa, 12,000 feet high, receives enough snow on its towering slopes during winter to attract skiers. Mt. Kilauea erupts still today, although rarely is anyone hurt. Many homes have been destroyed but there always seems to be enough time and warning to spare people.

One of the most memorable natural formations we saw on our vacation tour of the Big Island was the Lava Tube. This is a long tunnel formed by the uneven cooling of past lava flows. As we made our way through the formation, we suddenly reached a place where it became very dark. The opening where we had entered the tunnel appeared as a tiny dot of light. I was frightened and wanted to go back. Our missionary tour guide, whom I trusted, assured me that if I took two steps forward in the total darkness, I would then be able to see the light at the opposite end of the tube.

Sure enough, based upon my faith in her word, I stepped ahead in the darkness and was soon walking confidently toward the light. That was a lesson of faith that I have never forgotten. So many times since then I have taken a step of faith according to God's trustworthy Word and it always enabled me to get through some dark tunnel of life and come out victorious, into the light of God's provision for me.

We also drove over large lava fields that covered a lot of land. There were numerous detours where recent lava flows had crossed roads and left lava barriers several feet high. Roads often had to be rebuilt around the obstructions which had so suddenly become a part of the landscape.

On the slopes of Mt. Kilauea are magnificent forests of giant ferns. The Big Island, known as the Orchid Isle, is said to produce 22,000 varieties of the beautiful flowers. They even grow wild in people's back yards. Numerous other beautiful and fabulous flowers, including African tulips, ginger plants, and the graceful anthurium grow there.

Our trip allowed us to experience the unique beauty and magnificence of that wonderful island.

Gifts To Take Home

On our twelve day vacation, we eventually reached the quaint little town of Hilo. Our friends there honored us with a thoughtful shower at one of the churches. They presented us with gifts of fruits and flowers to take home with us, as well as a financial gift which they had planned for us ahead of time.

Most of the missionaries on that island had at one time or another stayed in our home when visiting on Maui. They had slept in our bed when they stayed overnight, and everyone was aware of the pitiful mattress we had. They took a love offering at the little church while we were there, and added it to what the other churches and missionaries had given so that we could purchase a new mattress. They had decided to do this before they invited us to visit their island. [They felt that money for a mattress was especially appropriate due to your grandpa's serious health problems.]

We were overwhelmed by their generosity. Most had given sacrificially. Little did we realize at the time what a blessing that mattress would be. How good the Lord is.

[His ways are wonderful, Marissa and Barry. You can always trust Him to look out for your best interests; never forget that.]

As we departed the Hilo area, old and new friends gathered around to give us a big send off. In addition to the earlier gifts, they now added numerous smaller items to take on the plane.

I vividly remember the whole "hand" of vine-ripened bananas given to us. We had been intrigued to see bananas growing on stalks, so they insisted we take some with us. They gave us other fruits and flowers too. We then left for a drive around the Island and back to the airport, for our return flight to Maui.

It was a winding and narrow road which frightened me very much but we eventually reached the airport. As we waited to board the plane that would fly us across the channel to Maui, we were quite a spectacle, struggling with our luggage, four children, and an abundance of thoughtful gifts from caring people. We attracted some curious smiles from onlookers, but we managed to get everything on board, including the intact "hand" of bananas.

Our twelve-day vacation on the Big Island of Hawaii had been an interesting change, although not exactly restful. We were indeed grateful for the opportunity to fill our lungs with the expanded land air of a bigger island.

The Work Must Continue

As soon as we returned to Maui, we set out to find a new mattress for our bed. Despite the loving sacrificial gifts of so many, we soon realized that we would not be able to get a very good one with the amount of money we had been given, due to the high cost of everything in Hawaii. We struggled with the problem and prayed much about it. Finally, we decided that a new cheap mattress would be better than the old lumpy one we were sleeping on. We settled for the best we could get with the amount that had been provided.

[It wasn't long before your grandpa was as busy as ever, even though he tried hard to slow down as the doctor had ordered. So much was required by those we had come to help. This was a strain on us, as was the feeling of disappointment in not being allowed to do what we felt the Lord was calling us to do.]

Often we felt we were performing chores that were totally unnecessary and out of line with our real calling, yet we were helpless to free ourselves from the circumstances. In those difficult days, we longed to help the precious island people that we loved so much, to see Christ Himself rather than to be distracted by distorted teachings of a denomination.

Our hearts hurt as we watched those believers trying to cling to God for fear they were going to be lost. One moment they would be excited about their faith and the next moment they would be in despair, fearing that they were no longer Christians. We wanted to help these dear people find the peace that only comes when a person is assured of his or her salvation. Only then, we knew, could they use their strength and effort in living a victorious life.

While on the mission field, we learned to work under strained conditions. We learned faithfulness and perseverance. We also developed the characteristics of a missionary heart. Our ministry in the Islands, as painful as it was many times, was necessary training for the missionary service that was to follow. No doubt the greatest lesson we learned in those years was to totally trust the Lord regardless of circumstances or pressure. I thank Him for granting us grace and strength and insight to see us through that time.

Resistance To Change

The first year we were in Hawaii we tried to convince our senior missionaries that the new vacation Bible school concept, so popular in the states, would be very effective in the Islands.

We offered to do all the work and even provide the materials if they would agree to let us hold a two-week session. To our complete disappointment, they refused to even discuss it. We were very excited about the idea, but our spirits were quickly squelched by their resistance. The older missionaries declared that they did not intend to allow us to try some "newfangled" methods on the natives. Yet we knew the Island people would have responded positively. They were open and eager to learn, but our hands were tied. We finally gave up on the idea.

We were allowed to teach classes sometimes, but always under the critical, watchful eye of those over us, lest we discredit certain doctrines which they clung to. We only wanted to teach directly from the Scriptures, but they never learned to trust us.

After we had been there nearly a year, they finally called on your grandpa to preach in the different churches. Even then, the same critical, watchful, judgmental spirit hung over him. He knew every word was being scrutinized. They still required him to do so many menial tasks that there was little time for him to study consistently. They expected him to get up and just talk the way they did, with little or no preparation. However, he felt the necessity of being well prepared and making sure he spoke the message God gave him for the hour. It was hard enough for him to preach even when well prepared, knowing every word was being censured.

We were troubled because the youth in island churches were being treated like young children, not being allowed to handle responsibility or given an opportunity to use their talents and abilities. We soon had a following of Christian young people who wanted to learn more about the Bible because they saw how much we loved God's Word. They wanted to be productive and effective young adults, but they were restrained, restricted, and constantly put down.

God allowed us to have a significant influence on the youth of Maui, in spite of the negative conditions we worked under all the years we were there.

[I have thanked God so many times that we were "rooted and grounded" in the Word. With the help of the Holy Spirit we were able to withstand the constant badgering to try and change the basic truths we had been shown by God Himself, as we had prayerfully studied the Bible.]

Happy Valley

The second year we had an opportunity to become involved in a short missionary project that was more like what we had expected to be doing when we went out to Hawaii.

A missionary who was working in another area of the island had been sent there by a different organization than the one we were working with. When he told us they were introducing the Vacation Bible School ministry to the islands, in his little mission, we were excited. He needed help so we volunteered to assist him.

Our decision did not meet with the approval of our senior missionaries but we were convinced it was what we were supposed to do. At the time we desperately needed a change of pace and a time of rest. We knew from past experience that if we were going to have either, we would have to take it on our own. We asked for two weeks leave and told our new missionary friend to count on us.

For most who lived in Happy Valley, life was anything but happy. The boys and girls, and some who were older, who became Christians during those two weeks got their first taste of true happiness. The results of that concentrated effort reached beyond the tally of those who indicated a desire to follow Christ during those structured classes. The young people went to their homes and eagerly shared the marvelous truth of the Gospel message. Soon other members of their families came with them to the mission to learn more for themselves.

The joy we experienced as the result of that special missionary outreach and the evident results of the ministry of the Holy Spirit was indescribable. It was a genuine taste of what we had longed and prayed for when we had accepted God's call to be missionaries. We would have loved to have continued working at that little mission. It was so thrilling to see people coming to the Lord. We could not change our situation however. After the closing program of that successful Vacation Bible School, we went back to our regular ministry.

We considered those two weeks a necessary vacation. Even though we worked hard with our friend, it was restful and rewarding.

A Sudden Realization

During those crucial days there were many adjustments to make and we learned to simply face each new day as it arrived, with complete trust in God.

It was in this state of mind that I awoke one morning with a sudden feeling that there was something God wanted me to be aware of. I kept experiencing mixed feelings of joy and helplessness. No doubt God was preparing me for something. Even so, when I discovered I was going to be a mother again, I was overwhelmed. How could we possibly manage more physical and financial problems?

[I struggled for days before I could bring myself to discuss the matter with your grandpa. I felt he had all the strain he could hold up under already. When I finally told him, he scolded me for my lack of trust in the Lord. Had He not always helped us and wasn't He in control of our lives? He was right. I felt humbled.]

We kept our secret from everyone until we felt it was appropriate to tell them. On the first day of September, our precious little girl was born.

The Little Missionary

During the months that followed, the rainy season hit. Huge ocean waves lashed against the beach behind our house, whipped up by the seasonal winds. The overcast skies blocked out the sunlight. Our whole family felt cold, often chilled through to the bones.

In early February our baby daughter fell ill, at first with a cold, but then her condition developed into double pneumonia.

A little over five months after her birth, our baby was admitted to a local hospital, by this time very ill. All of our Christian friends rallied together and stood with us in prayer. Some cared for our other children so that we could stay with our suffering little one.

One of the attending nurses assigned to look after our baby was a relative of a couple of the young people who had become Christians during our Vacation Bible School in Happy Valley. Nona happened to be on duty the day our little girl's condition became very critical.

Our baby grew weaker and weaker, and finally the doctor approached us and told us there was no chance that she would live. My heart was filled with grief and sorrow, yet I knew that God was in control. I felt the little bundle that was so much a part of me was being lifted into the loving arms of a merciful Savior. His comfort seemed to surround me. I could only say, "Oh, Lord, You know best. Help me to understand."

Nona had often seen the hopelessness of many families facing the death of a loved one, and now she observed our faith in God during our ordeal. At that time, she did not know what I knew; that God does not allow nor require a suffering child nor its agonizing parents to suffer more than they can endure.

Death, for many, is hopeless. Nona and her co-workers looking on that evening had never seen anyone react the way we did. They knew something was different about us. Because of the hope we had found in Christ we were able to accept death.

Nona had already been wondering about the miraculous change in her brother's family since they had attended our summer school in Happy Valley. Now this life and death situation involving a mother and her dying baby made another strong impression on her.

At an opportune time, Nona approached the missionary from Happy Valley who was standing by with numerous others to comfort us. She told him, "I want what that mother has. I have never seen anyone indicate so strongly that they believe in life after death. I want that kind of faith." Our friend was able to help Nona understand the plan of salvation and she accepted Christ as her personal Savior that very night.

[I'm happy to tell you that Nona, that dedicated little Japanese-Filipino nurse, became a radiant Christian and an enthusiastic witness for Christ. She soon brought her husband and children to the Lord, then her husband's brother and his family, and several of their friends, all as the result of what happened in that hospital room the day our baby died. Can you imagine how that little mission in Happy Valley was affected by the beautiful tapestry God had woven through these various circumstances?]

Unity For A Day

The loss of a loved one is always painful. It can, however, be eased somewhat when you are among caring family members and longtime friends. Our families, however, were several thousand miles away. We knew it was also hard for them not to be able to share our grief by being with us. Unfortunately it was not possible for any of them to come to Hawaii. Instead, we had the complete support of the native Christians on the island.

During the period of our baby's illness and death, all squabbling between the denominational groups around us ceased. They all knew how much we longed to see harmony between them. Each one tried to help us through our bereavement. Our seemingly wasted efforts to bring our friends together in Christ were fully rewarded during that crisis time.

The day of the funeral service for our precious baby will always stand out in my memory as a day when God must have rejoiced at even a brief period of unity. Missionaries from the two main denominations on the island took part in the service. Though our hearts were grieved from our loss, we rejoiced to see the two groups sitting together and participating in the service so harmoniously in the little church where the service was held. It was a heavenly scene.

If only they had been willing to unite and cooperate for the sake of the Gospel, I believe nearly the whole island could have been won for Christ. But alas, how narrow and selfish people can be in their bigotry.

When we considered how many people came to know Christ as the result of Janet's short life, as well as the unity expressed at her funeral, we concluded that she herself was a real missionary in every sense of the word. Many who have lived to a ripe old age have not had the impact that she had in the short five and a half months of her life.

A V.I.P. Visits Maui

Life on a tiny little island can become terribly monotonous, especially to someone not born and raised there. You soon reach the place where you have seen and done everything possible. Nothing exciting ever seems to happen. We would get so bored we would long for something, anything, to happen.

Once, I remember, an elderly Asian Indian lady came to Maui and spoke to the denomination we were working with. She explained in her broken English, that she was a missionary to the American people. She had heard how much they needed the Lord and she was on her way to the United States to try to help them.

We were touched. It was quite a switch, the reverse of what we usually thought of when talking about mission fields. The United States was definitely a foreign mission field to this dear, consecrated lady.

[We identified with her concern for America. Today, so many years later, conditions are even in our country. Even at your age, you can sense how far our country has moved away from God and His Word.]

The event that really shook our island was when Dr. Bob Pierce, a well-known missionary to Korea, sent some representatives to Maui to arrange for evangelistic meetings and for his documentary film, *"38th*

Parallel", to be shown. We helped find accommodations and make arrangements for the meetings. We were delighted with the prospect of having a nondenominational speaker with a broad view of reaching all the island people with the gospel.

Finding an adequate building to hold the anticipated crowds was a challenge. We finally settled for a large quonset building which one of the denominations had found and hoped to eventually renovate and use for a church. It was the largest building of any kind that we could find on Maui.

Chairs were collected from every possible source. When all the preparation was complete and the advance promotion had been carried out, we were ready for Dr. Pierce to arrive.

We had expected an excellent response, but we were not prepared for the large percentage of the population of central Maui that turned out. The building was packed. As many people as possible were packed in, including those standing around the inside walls. Many stood outside the building, listening and watching through the windows and at the entrance.

The fact that a visiting speaker advertised that he would address all the people, not just certain denominations, appealed to many. They came to see and hear this man and his film.

I remember that many Catholics, including some priests, came to hear this broad-minded man speak. They were impressed that they were included in the invitation to attend.

The night the film was shown, two priests sat in front of me and my children. [Your grandpa and the other ministers who had planned the series were at the front with Dr. Pierce.]

The priest sitting directly in front of me was rather tall. I saw the film around the outline of his head, with his funny ears limiting part of my view. There was no way I could miss his reaction to the film. His emotional response ranged from amusement to amazement, as well as deep conviction. I could see that all the priests sitting near us were really frustrated. I think they would have left the room if it had been possible, but the building was too packed for anyone to get out. I'm sure none of them ever forgot that experience. We later learned that one of the Catholic priests became so convicted that night that he started searching the Scriptures. Later, it was reported that he was preaching Gospel sermons to his parishioners and that they loved them. They had a real revival in that church.

Only our all-knowing God was able to register the impact and record the true results of the visit of Dr. Bob Pierce on Maui.

Lost In A Sugar Cane Field

During our second year in Hawaii, we moved from Paia to Kahului in order to be more centralized to the ministries we were involved in. We were able to find a nice small house near the beach. Our back yard was right next to Kahului Harbor. Only a rickety fence separated us from the beach and the ocean itself.

[I know you remember that I had a natural fear of water, a carry over from when my brother drowned at age fifteen. From that time my mother tried to protect us kids from the danger of drowning. I tried not to be as fearful as she was, but the deep concern was always there. It surfaced anew now that we were living on a tiny island, completely surrounded by water. It was while we lived in this little cottage that our little girl was born. Before she became ill our whole family would head out each day in our old car to do the Lord's work.

Once a week we held classes for children and older youth in the town of Halimaile, up the slopes of Mt. Haleakala. We used the Boy Scout building in the community for the sessions. The inquisitive mountain residents would usually come early to watch us set up our flannelgraph board and then watch with interest as we presented the lessons, illustrated with pictures of Bible characters. They would often linger nearby, listening with interest to the stories, and sometimes joining in as we sang lively choruses. They were intrigued with the "magical" story board. We had numerous opportunities to witness to parents as well as their children.

Sometimes, after the class was over and everyone had left for their homes, we would stand in front of the building and enjoy the remarkable view down the mountainside and out over the ocean. It was spectacular.

On one particular trip we scanned the panoramic view and spotted a landmark that we recognized as being near our home. We suddenly got a brilliant idea. It appeared from looking down in that direction that we would be able to cut off a number of miles if we could just find a different road. The regular road to Halimaile was so far around, maybe there was a shorter route which would save us time and money for gas. We could see a number of roads from our vantage point. It seemed like such a good idea, we decided to try it. In fact, we felt so confident we didn't even bother to pray about it.

We knew that the roads through that part of the island had been built for transporting sugar cane and pineapple from the fields to the cannery and mills for processing. Most of them were new roads, built to accommodate the large machines called tourneauhaulers, used to transport sugar cane to the mills for processing.

Not dreaming that it would turn out to be a day we would never forget, we anxiously set out on our adventure.

We easily made our way across the pineapple fields because we could see for quite a distance ahead. Then we approached the larger farming area in central Maui, with large fields of sugar cane gently waving in the breeze.

The long straight roads, often alongside irrigation ditches, stretched out ahead of us. There were numerous crossroads but you could not see around corners due to the tall sugar cane plants. We could see only a short distance ahead. The stalks were growing close to the road, sometimes leaning across to the other side, so that it felt like we were driving through a tunnel. We became more and more concerned about the wisdom of our decision to seek a detour.

When we thought about the possibility of meeting a truck and realized that if we did, it would probably not be able to see us in time to stop, we became fearful.

We did think of turning around and going back, but there wasn't room to maneuver the car around. Besides, we felt sure we had to be getting closer to home.

By this time we realized that we were lost in a sugar cane field. Our idea had not been so good after all. We felt even worse when it occurred to us that we had actually embarked on the adventure without first asking for God's direction.

[I still don't know how we could have been so careless and foolhardy. We were in the habit of depending completely on God in every way.]

We were so ashamed that we found it hard to come to the Lord for help, but we knew there was no other way out of our serious dilemma. How wonderful that God knows our frailty, and that He is so quick and willing to forgive. How we appreciated His mercy in that hour!

By this time the children were getting tired and hungry. They sensed the tension we felt and our baby daughter was getting more upset by the moment.

Time too, was getting away from us. The prospect of being stranded in our awful predicament in the dark was scary. There was also the possibility that we might not even be going in the right direction. We had thought our bright idea would save us a lot of time; instead, we had already driven more than on our regular route.

In desperation, we began to panic. Guilt overwhelmed us. We became overly agitated. We knew it was not possible to find our way out of this terrible predicament on our own. We also knew that God was in control. Finally, with truly repentant hearts, we turned to Him in sincere prayer. We prayed like we had never prayed before; our only hope was in God.

When we opened our eyes and looked up, we saw the lights of the radio station towers in Wailuku. We had not noticed them before. With grateful hearts, we drove toward the landmark, our guiding beacon. It was easy to see that we would have to make a right turn at the next crossroad. We felt sure that road would at least lead us to one that was a little more traveled and one that would eventually take us home.

Sure enough, we soon came to a wider two-lane road. With great relief, we no longer had to worry about meeting a vehicle on a one-way road.

We actually wept when we came to the place where we were sure we were on the right road, one that would take us home. We were fully aware that it was a definite answer to prayer.

Our help truly had come from above. And God had used the towering lights of the local radio station to guide us out of our lost condition.

A New Home In Puunene

Following our baby's illness and death, our doctor insisted we move to a healthier location. He was so adamant about the necessity of us getting away from the cold, damp harbor that he contacted the senior missionaries we were working with at the time and told them to help us find accommodations elsewhere. Being aware of our financial limitations, the doctor suggested we check out the vacant officer's housing units at the Marine base on the leeward side of the island. It was called Airport Village because there was a small military airport near the marine base. We suspected the doctor himself had contacted someone on our behalf.

A house was made available for us. It was one of several that had been occupied by military officers following the Pearl Harbor crisis. It was much larger and nicer than both the old plantation home we had lived in at first, and the little cottage in Kahului.

The interior was roomy and featured modern fixtures and appliances, which we really appreciated. The exterior however, was a drab olive color and seemed really ugly to us. Dark green pull-down shades still remained at the windows as grim reminders of the blackouts residents of the islands had so recently experienced.

Overall, we were delighted with our new home. As the doctor has suggested, we were exposed to more sun and less moisture and wind right off the ocean. We knew it was a healthier location for our family. One of our problems was getting our children to and from school. It was several miles from the nearest facility, and there were no school buses. As with all of our other problems, we took it to the Lord in prayer. The nearest public school was in the little village of Puunene, about half way between our new home and Kahului where we had moved from.

While we were praying about the transportation problem, we learned about a new private school just starting near Kahului.

Getting the boys to and from school would be difficult with our schedule and the undependability of our old car. We also knew we could not afford the extra gas for the two round trips each day. It was evident we would have to trust the Lord to help us work the situation out.

When our friends the Hanley's, who had paid for our boys school lunches, learned that we were moving, they expressed concern for the children's education. Although we did not know it, they were working with those who were trying to start a private school for haole children living on the island. Our boys were included in their concern and they were planning on providing their tuition for the new school.

About that time, a woman from the states and her daughter, who was about the age of our second son, moved into a home near us in Airport Village. She too was pleased to learn of the new haole school but was also concerned about transportation.

One morning we were delighted to receive a call from our friends from Makawao, saying they wanted to pay for our sons' tuition to the new haole school if we could arrange for transportation. We knew the offer was God's provision.

We soon had a plan worked out with our new neighbor from the states, enabling us to share the driving and expenses. We were truly grateful to the Lord for His provision.

Our neighbor had an old dilapidated automobile that was in worse shape than ours. But that was not all that we were concerned about; we had observed that she was a nervous, somewhat careless driver. On her days to drive we felt constrained to really pray.

I remember one morning when she left with the children I felt so uneasy I got down on my knees beside the couch and began praying. I was still praying when I heard our sons at the door. They had been involved in an accident enroute to school and were terribly frightened, but fortunately unhurt.

I will never forget the look in their eyes as they stood there trembling, trying to explain what had happened. They knew I would be praying. I held them close and we thanked the Lord for answer to prayer, even while I was asking.

An Angel For A Baby Sitter

Another neighbor in Airport Village, was an oriental woman whose son Arlin played with our boys. Although the boy was well-behaved most of the time, we were concerned that his parents did not discipline him in any way. One day Mrs. Omata casually mentioned to me she had no idea where Arlin was. I expressed shock at her admission that she had no control over so young a boy. She was quite upset when I told her I didn't like to have my boys playing with Arlin for that reason.

"How could you be so unconcerned about Arlin?" I asked her.

"Oh," she exclaimed emphatically, "I never worry about him. You see, he has an angel that looks after him." I knew her family did not embrace Christianity. I tried to explain that God had given us parents the responsibility of looking after our children but it was hard for her to understand.

While it was true her son was alive and had been protected from physical death, he did show signs of rebellion which I'm sure were due to neglect and lack of discipline. I believe Arlin inwardly wished for some restraint from his parents, which he never received.

This poor mother sincerely believed in her philosophy of child rearing. I was terribly shaken by that woman's attitude. I suspected she was hiding behind her angel theory because she was simply too lazy to execute her motherly duties. I tried to explain to her that I, too, believed in angels, and that they had their assignments. I told her I even believed we all have a guardian angel, but that I did not believe God would excuse us of our parental responsibility on that basis.

A Ministry In Airport Village

Soon after we moved to Airport Village, we arranged to use one of the vacant military homes, like we were living in, to hold classes for children and adults in the area, and later for regular worship services.

Our happiest years of missionary service on Maui were in that setting. Our senior missionaries had finally softened to a point that they were willing to allow us to start and be in complete charge of a new mission work in the village.

We had free use of the building and could set up our classrooms and leave them. This was a great blessing because for some time we had been using a hall in Puunene where we had to set up for each meeting then tear it all down again afterwards. We appreciated not having to be constantly repeating this tiresome and time-consuming chore. At our new work in Airport Village we were allowed to teach and minister a little more freely, and more according to our convictions. I don't have the words to describe the thrilling fulfillment of being able to teach God's Word to those who have not heard it before and having them respond so enthusiastically. It was a rewarding experience. [Unfortunately, by that time your grandpa's health was failing fast. I tried to take on as much responsibility as possible to relieve him. We often talked about how nice it would have been to have had those opportunities when we first went there.]

I will never forget one Sunday morning I was teaching a class of eight and nine year old boys and girls. The children sat in a circle in front of me, listening intently to the story of the Good Shepherd. A picture of Jesus blessing the children of the world hung on the wall.

As I looked into the eager, anxious eyes of those youngsters, representing several nationalities, I wondered where else in the world could the picture of Jesus blessing the children of various colors be so realistically portrayed.

As we sang, "Jesus loves the children of the world", this truth was visually illustrated to all the children in the class. Those island children clung to every word as I told them about the Good Shepherd, and how He was willing to leave the ninety-nine sheep in the fold, and go out and find the one lost sheep and bring it in. They were impressed that the Good Shepherd loved His sheep enough to die for them. His concern for the one that was lost really touched them.

I noticed tears trickling down the cheeks of a young Japanese girl named Bertha. When I asked if anyone in the class would like to accept Jesus, the Good Shepherd, as their personal Savior, Bertha who was very shy, tried to hold up her hand but couldn't. When class was dismissed and the other boys and girls quietly left the room, Bertha stayed to talk to me.

"Mrs. Brown," she whispered, "I am that little lost sheep. I want to be found by the Good Shepherd."

I answered all her questions and made sure she understood clearly.

As the radiant Hawaiian sunshine streamed through the window that gorgeous Lord's Day morning, Bertha quietly and sincerely accepted Christ as her own personal Savior. The Good Shepherd had truly found a little lost sheep, there in that little makeshift chapel on the island of Maui. And there was rejoicing in heaven. From week to week the children learned more and more about Jesus, each at their own speed. In time, every child in my class accepted Christ. Their hunger to learn about the Bible and their response to the teaching of the Scriptures was most rewarding. Every previous hardship and trying experience on the mission field was forgotten during those days of concentrated, fruitful ministry.

For a time only elementary school age children came to our Sunday School. Then gradually, a few parents and some older youth came to see what the children were so excited about. Many of them were little missionaries to their own families. It was a notable milestone, the day we knew it was time to initiate a morning worship service for all ages. The older folk were much slower in coming to a place where they could accept a religious concept that was so different from their earlier training. We never ceased to wonder that these parents, who had not known much at all about Christianity, were so willing to allow their children to attend our classes regularly, without questioning what they were being taught.

Sister School Ma'am

After our move across the island, we became more and more concerned about our additional expenses. As usual, we prayed much and waited on the Lord for answers. To our surprise, I received a phone call one day from the public school system. They asked if I would consider working as a substitute teacher for the schools in central Maui.

A job offer right out of the blue appeared to be God's provision, but I earnestly prayed to make sure. I wasn't academically qualified to teach but they desperately needed substitute teachers. They approached me because they knew I worked with elementary age children. I didn't feel I was capable but I agreed to fill in until they could get someone else.

Initially I substituted for kindergarten through eighth grade teachers. They would call me early in the morning. I never knew when or where I would be needed.

At first I worked two or three days every week. Soon I was in great demand at the school in Kahului and worked there almost full time. Still later, when the fourth and fifth grade teacher had to take an extended sick leave, I was given her class.

Teaching the island children was an experience. The schools were quite a bit different from those I had attended in the South and the one our oldest son had attended in Illinois.

We were surprised to learn that the public school system in the islands was considered superior to mainland schools, particularly those in California. I was even more surprised that under those circumstances they would ask me to teach when I wasn't qualified. I was told that the school officials considered my methods of teaching, my experience, and the way I handled the children more important than having the required credentials.

When I first started substituting, I was not at all sure that I could do it. Soon, however, I felt confident and comfortable. Because the children loved and respected me, they gladly followed my instructions and were easy to manage. I really loved teaching children. By the time I was hired to teach the fourth and fifth grades, I was an old pro.

My experience in missionary work had prepared me to understand children who were poorly trained at home. I was already aware that in working with children in a Christian setting, as with secular students, motivation was a critical part of teaching. My classes were divided into three groups: A, B, C. I remained in one room, and each group would come to me in turn for their session.

Class C students would amble into the room and flop down into their seats, one foot sticking out into the aisle. Often they would lay their head on their desk. It was hard to keep their attention. I could easily see they would much rather be swimming, fishing, or anything other than studying in class. The B group was not quite as bad as the C class, but they were not as attentive and eager to learn as the A class. The A's were a pleasure to teach. Being somewhat familiar with their backgrounds, I could understand why some of the children were the way they were.

As I observed the three types of behavior of the children, I got an idea. One morning I discussed behavioral patterns with each of the three groups. Before this they had not realized why they were in their particular group.

When the C students learned how they appeared to me as I pantomimed their actions, they were ashamed. It was an experience I will never forget. Those lazy students were inspired and determined to do better. It was not easy for them to change, especially the most careless and inattentive ones, but I kept challenging them. In time they began to improve remarkably both in actions and grades.

While times were a lot different from today, we did have some restrictions in the public school system in Hawaii in those days. When I applied for the teaching job, I had to swear that I was not a Communist, and that I had no connection with them. It was also made quite clear that we were not to pray or mention God's name in the classroom.

The classes I taught were made up of students from various religious and cultural backgrounds, many unfamiliar to those of us who had been raised on the mainland. The largest percentage of my students were from Roman Catholic homes. They called me "Sister Brown". So did the children whose parents were in the Pentecostal churches. Most of the others followed along and called me Sister Brown too, hardly knowing why.

Being both a missionary and a haole lady earned me a great deal of respect from my students. None of my pupils viewed me with suspicion or skepticism; they all looked up to me.

When a controversial subject would come up I would pray silently, then handle the matter as best I could. I always tried hard to maintain a professional and spiritual balance.

I was often asked questions related to spiritual things and I had numerous opportunities to witness to my faith, not only to my students but also to fellow staff members. I was confident that my ministry there was God's will at the time. [Your grandpa and I were both convinced that my job was God's provision for our urgent financial needs. My evenings and weekends were still free so that I could carry out my regular duties.]

Many of the children I taught in Kahului also attended our Airport Village Sunday School, simply because they knew and loved me. I really enjoyed teaching the fourth and fifth grades in both Sunday School and public school. They were inquisitive and challenging. [As you can imagine, I learned a lot myself as I prepared to teach my daily classes. I'm not sure how much knowledge I was able to impart, but I am certain that I taught those children to study for themselves and to aspire to high goals. That meant a lot to me.]

Even my C group students became excited about subjects and goals they previously had no interest in. Their ambitions were stimulated and I'm sure many of them got a good start that year towards a brighter future for themselves. I loved teaching my favorite subjects, history and geography, to the island children. My enthusiasm for history, a subject that many boys and girls that age detest no matter where they live, rubbed off on them.

When it came to geography, they thought I was a genius. The only part of the planet they had personally experienced was their own little island world. Many of them had never even been to the summit of the big mountain that is the main part of Maui. Most of them dreamed of one day visiting the mainland. It was a delight to me to help enlarge their world.

One aspect of history we studied was railroads. Trains had been very much a part of my life, both in the North and in the South. But I found it difficult to reduce the information to their level of understanding.

At the time I was teaching about trains, the only train they had ever seen was sitting in a local park, a permanent monument to history. It had pulled carloads of sugar cane from the loading areas on the plantations to the mills to be processed.

[The tiny train's usefulness had been replaced by the huge tourneauhauler vehicles, designed and built by Mr. R. G. Letourneau, of Stockton, California, specifically for the sugar cane and pineapple industries on Maui. The huge machines were so much more efficient for getting the sugar cane to the mills to be processed, then to the harbor, where it was loaded onto Matson Lines freighters and shipped to Crockett, California, to be refined into white sugar such as we use in our homes today.]

The boys and girls loved the little engine and caboose that had been retired in a park on one of Maui's popular beaches, Baldwin Park. Playing on it was a favorite pastime for many children. When we studied about the great railroads across the United States of America, which they referred to as "the mainland", my students became so absorbed they didn't even want to take time out for recess. Hearing about those huge, fast-moving trains, and the almost unbelievable distances they traveled across the United States fascinated the children. It was to them, like science fiction is to you today, pretty farfetched.

When I knew we were coming back to the States, I promised I would try to get some large pictures of real trains which they could display in their classrooms. Once we had returned, I went to the Southern Pacific office in Crockett, California, to inquire about getting the pictures I had promised. The students had all heard of Crockett because raw sugar from Maui was shipped there to be refined.

The executive in the Southern Pacific Railroad office graciously invited me in and asked me to sit in a big chair across from him. He also knew where Maui was and listened with great interest as I told him about my promise to send the students at Kahului School some pictures of real trains. I left his office that afternoon with a series of beautiful oil prints of various types of one of the world's most romantic types of transportation—trains. There were pictures of the first trains invented, the fantastic steam engines, on through to the most modern stream liners. Those lovely pictures hung for many years in the fourth and fifth grade classroom in Kahului School. That special time of teaching school on the little island of Maui, before Hawaii became our fiftieth state—and a vital part of our wonderful United States of America—will always hold a special place in my heart and in my memory.

*** *** ***

"We've covered a lot tonight. I think we'd better get some sleep now. We still have a couple of days before you have to go home. We'll talk more"

CHAPTER 15

God Leads His Dear Children Along

"We've really enjoyed staying with you, Grandma, while Grandpa was deer hunting." Barry announced at breakfast on the last day of their visit.

"Most of all I've enjoyed hearing about when you lived in Hawaii."

"Me, too," Gregory agreed.

"Do you think you could tell us more before we have to leave?" Andrea asked hopefully.

Marissa hurriedly swallowed a bite of Belgian waffle so she could say, "Oh, Grandma, would you—please!"

"I'm anxious to see Mother and Daddy," Andrea admitted, "but I want to hear some more about how God blessed you and showed you what He wanted you to do."

Marissa was just finishing the last bit of food on her plate. Wiping her mouth with her napkin, she said, "I'm going to tell my Sunday School teacher about what you told us this week."

"I'm glad," I told her. "I'm going to miss all of you. I've enjoyed remembering and telling you about these treasured experiences. I've an idea—let's do the morning chores real quickly, then I'll tell you the rest of the Hawaii story, and how we came to California."

*** *** ***

When It's Time To Return

[Even though your grandpa was not at all well, we stayed on the field and continued to work as hard as we had before his health failed.]

We were very involved and busy in those days. Time passed swiftly. There were many times when we were so weary we feared we couldn't go on, but we did. We knew God was mindful of our physical needs and we trusted that He was in control. The senior missionaries were getting more feeble and both were suffering from serious health problems. They finally decided to give up the work on Maui and return to the mainland.

By this time they were finally convinced we were not going to give in and become members of the denomination they were a part of. They frankly told us they didn't feel they could trust the work to us since they knew we did not agree with some of their doctrines. They wrote to their denominational headquarters in the states and asked them to send a couple to relieve them.

It was a crisis time for us and I know I don't have to tell you that we went to the Lord in earnest prayer.

Because your grandpa was in such bad health, we questioned whether it might not be time for us to return to the mainland. I fasted and prayed, as I had done during so many crisis periods. This time, God clearly revealed what He undoubtedly had in mind for us all along. He not only showed us that it was time for us to return, but also that it should be by a certain date. The mode of transportation was also made quite clear; we were to return by boat.

Our faith was severely tested at that time. It grew stronger however, as we grew physically weaker.

Without any idea of where the boat fare was coming from, we called the steamship lines to inquire about specific sailing dates. To our surprise (though God knew), we were told that the very next departure after the date I was strongly impressed we should reserve, fares would be going up considerably. This indicated to us that God was indeed leading us in the matter.

We also realized later why the Lord had shown us we should return by boat. In His divine, all-knowing wisdom, He was aware that we were too weary to fly immediately back to the states. Our bodies could not have stood the strain. We needed the extra few days of rest to help prepare us for our reentry into the rigorous pace of the mainland.

Releasing Our Responsibilities

There was much to be done, and so quickly, as we prepared to meet our deadline to sail from Honolulu.

In God's mercy, the new couple who was to replace us arrived shortly. We observed with interest that they were fresh and inspired, ready to launch into the work with "mainland" energy and incentive, just as we had several years earlier.

The new missionaries had barely finished unpacking when they informed the elderly, retiring workers, that one of the first things they planned to do was to conduct a Vacation Bible School in each of the churches. "These fantastic schools are sweeping the mainland," they said enthusiastically. "They will be very effective here, too. The islands simply must take advantage of the phenomenon."

We noticed that the senior missionaries didn't even try to protest. They did admit to their newly arrived successors that we had been trying all the years we had been there to convince them of the merits of the concentrated classes. But they never apologized to us for having resisted our efforts so firmly.

The elderly missionaries were reluctant to let go of us. There were so many things they wanted us to do, and the newly arrived recruits endeavored to enlist our expertise and energy in order to have a "great" report to send back to their home church and to their denominational headquarters. But God was looking out for us. He gave us grace and strength to complete everything in time so that we would not miss our boat.

As our departure date drew near, we began to pack our meager belongings. Since we expected to be traveling by car from San Francisco to the Chicago area, we mailed some things that we didn't think we would be using for a while. It was difficult to decide what to send to Chicago and what to take with us on the ship.

When we looked at our scant wardrobe, we felt sick at heart. We knew we would be embarrassed on the ship as well as when we arrived in the states, yet we had no money to purchase other clothing. We were totally dependent upon the Lord to supply our needs.

When our haole friends in Makawao, who had so generously provided for our family during our years on Maui, heard that we were returning to the states, they came to our rescue once more.

[I'll never forget the day the Hanley's came to our home in Airport Village with a large box of good clothing, including some nice suits for your grandpa. They couldn't have fit better if he had had them tailor-made.] Among the lovely garments Mrs. Hanley shared with me was a beautiful coat, appropriate for the Illinois winters. She had worn it in Wisconsin before moving to Hawaii. She had also taken some pretty dresses right from her closet so that I could feel dressed up as I re-entered the mainstream of society.

And they hadn't forgotten the children. Over the years, they had been watching them grow and now, with their usual good judgement, they had shopped for each of them and everything fit beautifully. We never doubted that God often used those dear people to supply our needs, even up to the end of our term in Hawaii.

It Was Hard To Say Goodbye

During those last weeks before we left Maui, the native people sought creative ways to show their love for us; they had so much appreciated our years of service among them. Our precious Filipino friends, the Molderas, lived near us at the time. Juan Moldera was overcome with emotion when he learned that we were going to be leaving Maui. [He loved your grandpa dearly, because he had helped him so much spiritually.]

Mr. Moldera realized that his beloved Brother Brown was not well and he knew that we often survived on less than an adequate diet. Often he would take his sons and go to the reservoir, where they would dig a pailful of frog legs so that we could enjoy the meat.

Our dear Filipino friend was happy that Brother Brown was going to be getting a little rest and better provisions, he thought, and we hoped, although we had no assurance of receiving either. But Juan wouldn't have been more saddened at the loss of a blood brother, as the time drew near for us to go.

That dear Christian man was among the crowd that stood along the chainlink fence at the airport, waving to us the day we left Maui. [I can still feel the pain of seeing that dear man, suffering from the prospects of not having his best friend around anymore.]

There were lots of fragrant leis and an abundance of tears and sad good-byes, as we parted. We left a part of our hearts on that little island that day.

[Please excuse me, I can't help weeping as I remember again.]

We had lived there a long time. Our children had spent their formative years there, growing up among children of several nationalities. Leaving Maui was painful for all of us.

Aloha Oe

We flew to Oahu and stayed there a few days before our ship departed. A missionary who had visited our home invited us to stay with her for a few says so that she could show us around the island of Oahu. This was part of God's plan for us also, to allow us to unwind and get at least a little rest before making the transition.

We thoroughly enjoyed her guided tour of some of the out-of-the-way places around the island, as well as popular tourist attractions, including a breathtaking ride over the Pali road. We were overwhelmed with the panoramic view from the pullout overlook area. Our host explained that the tradewinds from two directions met and combined just below us, and that the force was so strong that if a car should fall over the cliff, it would be lifted up again by the wind. Legend has it that a prominent Hawaiian personality once jumped over the high cliff in a suicide attempt, but the force of the wind would not allow him to fall to the dangerous rocky area below.

We were blessed by the kindness of this dear lady during our visit with her. She also took us to the ship and waited to wave to us as we moved out to sea. While waiting, she outfitted each of us with beautiful flower leis, and took pictures that would enable us to retain our memories.

On that unforgettable May afternoon, we stood on the deck of luxury liner, the S.S. Lurline, waiting for it to sail for San Francisco.

[It was a touching scene, and I find it difficult to describe to you. It's impossible to keep back the tears when I remember that day.]

Leis were thrown overboard to see if they would drift back to shore. If they did, we were told, it was a sure sign that you would return to the Islands again someday, and that the passengers would have a pleasant voyage. We were reluctant to remove our beautiful, fragrant, fresh flower leis, which our host on Oahu had made and given to us.

Everyone wept. I don't remember seeing a dry eye. The natives were strumming their ukuleles. The haunting words and melody of *"Aloha Oe"* wafted across the waves. That melody is one of the most beautiful tunes I have ever heard. You'll even find it in some hymnbooks. The Christian words are entitled *"He's Coming Soon"*. It's appropriate because that tune, along with many others, was originally composed and sung in the Hawaiian language as hymns, long before secular words were written for them. Another lovely Hawaiian song which was played and sung as the famous ocean liner, the Lurline, sailed away from the harbor, was *"Now Is The Hour"*, also known as *"Maori's Lullaby"*. That song is also in many church hymnals, under the title *"Search Me, O Lord"*. We had often sung both of these songs, in Illinois and Hawaii.

Overwhelming emotion swept over everyone on the crowded deck of the Lurline that afternoon, as well as those on shore who had come to bid the passengers farewell.

Just as the boat started to move away from the dock, we suddenly became aware of a man pushing his way through the crowd on shore and waving frantically to get someone's attention. We could hardly believe what we saw, as we strained to try and make out who it might be. Then we recognized the familiar face of our precious friend, Juan Moldera. We later learned that the day he watched us leave the airport, he had bought a ticket to fly to Honolulu to see us off once again, on the boat. We kept our eyes on Juan, waving and weeping, until he was only a dot in the distance, as the Lurline was being towed out into the open sea.

Mr. Moldera later told a friend that as we were moving away from the shore, he saw in a vision that Brother Brown would indeed come back to the Islands someday, just as the floating leis indicated.

[Providentially, I went back—fifteen years later, and took our younger children who were born after we returned to the states. But by that time Juan's dear friend, your grandpa, had gone to another paradise, far beyond the great Pacific Ocean.]

Juan and his family were no longer living on the island when I returned. I checked several phone books for a listing, and asked everyone who might know about them. I was told they had moved to the mainland several years earlier. He may have still hoped he could find his friend.

The Ocean Liner

Once the big boat had cut loose from the island and we were moving slowly across the ocean we set our minds to unwinding and getting some much needed rest.

The first thing we did was explore the ship. It was all so new to us. We had never been on an ocean liner before. It was quite an adventure for all of us, especially our young sons.

We had no sooner completed a quick tour on our own when dinner was announced, over the loud speaker. We had heard so much about the food, we were anxious to experience our first meal. It was far beyond what we had imagined. We had never seen so much food, so exquisitely prepared and served. And we had never been entertained so royally or given such attentive service. It was more fantastic than we could ever have dreamed.

We were assigned seats at a table in the dining room and had our own waiter who gave us his complete attention. Although it was the normal, everyday procedure on the boat, it seemed very special to us.

After dinner, exciting entertainment was provided in a designated area. We could see from the ship's newspaper that many activities were scheduled for each day.

That first evening a talented trio of authentic Hawaiian singers entertained the captive audience. We were not sure what to expect and hesitated at first to take the children, but it turned out to be good family fare. I doubt if anyone on board enjoyed the performance more. We had lived and worked very closely with the Hawaiian people for several years and we truly appreciated their unique musical talent. There was plenty to keep us busy while traveling across the ocean. Numerous activities had been planned to keep the children occupied as well. Our children spent much of their time investigating and exploring the ship from the crow's nest to the hold. We had taken them out of school early to make our sailing date, but they learned a lot more on that five-day ocean voyage than they would have in a classroom.

[Your grandpa and I were a lot more interested in finding a quiet place to rest than in participating in the many available activities. I was also several months pregnant and needed even more rest for that reason.]

We found a little lounge that was tastefully decorated and provided perfect quiet and solitude. There were tables for writing and comfortable corners for reading, meditating, and praying undisturbed.

Our future was uncertain, as far as our knowledge went, but we knew that God was fully aware of what He had in store for us. The more we prayed, the more our faith was strengthened to trust God for whatever the future might hold. We had taken an inside cabin because we couldn't afford a suite or even an outside cabin with a porthole. The main inconvenience was having to share a bathroom down the hall. The cabin was also quite tiny and I felt cramped for air at times.

Our ocean voyage was extremely rough due to a storm coming down from Alaska. For two of our five days it was so rough that everyone on board, even the captain, was seasick.

The ship was designed to handle rough seas, however. Rims around the edge of the tables in the dining room and indentations for cups, glasses and plates kept most articles anchored. These built-in provisions were tested to the limit by the severity of that storm.

Some of the time I had to have food brought to our cabin because I was too sick to walk to and from the dining room. All passengers had to brace themselves along the walls of the hallways to maintain their balance as the ship rocked from side to side. We were disappointed that we missed out on much of the superb food, but during that time, food was the last thing we were thinking about. Few passengers were able to keep food down.

Many distraught passengers were lined up along the rail around the deck, throwing up over the side, lots of them so sick they could hardly stand up. There is something indescribable about seasickness and the despair one feels with it. We were reminded of Paul's adventures at sea recorded in the New Testament.

Our steward tried hard to give us special attention during the storm because of the children and my condition. We sincerely appreciated that.

Finally, after two days of turbulence, the ocean was again calm. As we neared the end of the voyage, we were told that the stewards and waiters were expected to be tipped generously for their excellent service. We had no money to tip them with and we knew we had to try and explain that to them. It was especially embarrassing since they had really tried hard to make our trip a pleasant one.

Steve, our waiter, insisted he did not mind at all. He assured us that our children had been the best behaved that he had ever served. (They were almost the only children on board.) We believed he was sincere in his response. There were plenty of well-to-do passengers to make up for what the personnel didn't get from us.

The Captain's Dinner

Each day while on board the Lurline, we received a copy of the ship's newspaper. Two days before we were scheduled to dock in San Francisco, the newspaper dealt almost entirely with details referring to the "Captain's Dinner". It was to be served the last evening at sea. Everyone was expected to be dressed in their very formal best.

[Your grandpa did have nice suits the Hanley's had given him, but because I was pregnant, I could not wear most of the things they had given me. We began thinking up excuses, so as not to have to attend the gala affair. We knew we would feel awkward and out of place with inappropriate clothes. Even though your grandpa could get by, he would never leave me.]

The day before the Captain's Dinner, I met a lovely woman on deck. She really took a liking to me and simply would not let me go. I'm sure the Lord sent her. She asked many questions about our work on the mission field and where we were going to be situated in the mainland. Finally, she brought up the subject of the Captain's Dinner. She soon caught on that I was not planning to attend. Very tactfully, she asked if I was concerned about what to wear. Explaining that she had made the voyage between California and Hawaii many times, she said she had several Hawaiian dresses which would be appropriate for the evening. She added quickly, before I could respond negatively, that they were long, flowing dresses and could be worn as maternity dresses.

"Wait right here," she requested, "I'll bring you a dress to wear." She disappeared before I could protest.

I was nervous about wearing a dress borrowed from a stranger but she soon put me at ease.

"It's fresh and clean," she insisted. "And it's not borrowed anymore; I'm giving it to you."

The dressy, formal Hawaiian evening gown, which she had made herself, was soft blue with white flowers and had a long train in the back with a loop which you put over your wrist to hold the train up as you walked.

The gown fit me nicely and I felt very dressed up. I also wore the fresh flower lei I had saved to give the couple who was meeting us in San Francisco.

[Your grandpa dressed up in the best of the suits the Hanley's had given him. It had belonged to a Japanese business man, now living in the men's home which the Hanley's operated in Makawao. It too, was fresh and clean. We were amazed at how well the suit fit him, and how nice he looked in it. It was a beige color with soft blue plaid, perfect to go with the dress the Lord had provided for me.]

Excitement ran high that last evening we were at sea. Because God had sent angels to provide for us, we fit right in and really enjoyed the Captain's Dinner, right along with all the others.

Our faces must have been beaming when my new friend introduced her husband to us and whispered to me how nice we both looked.

For that evening the children were served dinner in a special area and child care made it possible for us to enjoy the festive evening. Fortunately, the storm had subsided so that we could enjoy the delightful food.

I will cherish the memories of that evening as long as I live. It was a once-in-a-lifetime experience, that I thought at the time, would never happen again, but it did.

The Golden Gate

During our voyage, we were shown movies depicting the sights and sounds of San Francisco and the Bay Area. We saw pictures of the Golden Gate Bridge, and other interesting attractions.

They didn't tell us that the movies were all filmed on some of the few sunny days. They also neglected to mention how cold and foggy it is in San Francisco much of the year. In the films, everything was bright and beautiful like we had been used to in Hawaii. We were too excited to sleep much the night before we were scheduled to dock in San Francisco. We wanted to be on deck to get the first glimpse of the Golden Gate Bridge. After all the buildup in the films, we didn't want to miss it.

When the time came, we discovered to our dismay that the famous bridge and the San Francisco skyline were both shrouded in heavy fog, such as we had not seen since we lived near Chicago.

We had to use our imagination when told there was a bridge called the Golden Gate out there. In fact the fog was so dense, it was hard to imagine that there was land up ahead. As we neared the pier we could only vaguely make out the San Francisco skyline. It looked like we had collided with a cloud.

As we approached the dock that gray May morning, we were surprised to see a vast network of heavy wire along the roof tops. Some of the wires were fashioned in circles, others in various patterns. Most of the buildings had this wire network. We couldn't imagine what the purpose might be. We were later informed that they were television antennas. We had heard about this new invention but we had never seen a television set, nor known they had such a strange receiving network. It did not take us long to find out what television sets were and what effects the new invention was having on the family and on interpersonal relationships. It was more evident to us as we suddenly came upon the new phenomenon. Stateside residents were so involved with the fascinating new invention they didn't stop to think about its effects. I don't think we could ever have imagined the devastating results that years of satanic bombardment via television would have on our nation.

The State-Side Welcome

Friends of the missionaries who had come to replace us on Maui were at the dock to meet us. They had driven two hours from a community south of San Francisco to be there when our ship docked. We really appreciated that.

After a brief greeting we sought to retrieve our baggage from the hold of the ship. After a frantic search, only part of it could be accounted for. We were told we would have to come back for the rest of our belongings at a later date. This meant imposing on our new friends and we had not wanted to depend on them any more than was absolutely necessary.

These kind people worked very hard to give us a warm welcome. Most people aren't prepared or particularly anxious to suddenly have a family of six to feed and entertain as guests in their home. Our new friends had been told that our children were exceptionally well-behaved which put them a little more at ease.

We soon learned that they had also been told we would be available to speak in their church, and others of their denomination that were nearby. (It was the same group we had worked with in the Islands). This particular church wanted to be enlightened on the work to which they had so recently sent out a missionary couple.

In all their hospitality, this kind couple did not realize our need for rest. They took us to one church after another for prearranged speaking engagements—almost every night for a couple weeks. We were expected to tell about our work on Maui, the mission field they had just become interested in. This would have been fine if we had been up to the activity, but we were not. We desperately needed just to be alone and to get some rest. No one but the Lord could have understood how very weary we were. We had to trust Him for added strength.

As we met with these different congregations, we sensed that these churches had been forewarned that, through our years of ministry on

Maui, we had not gone along with some of their denomination's doctrines. We had the feeling that they may have been advised to try to make one more attempt to win us over. As much as we appreciated the outward hospitality and acceptance by the Christians in these churches, we felt quite uncomfortable at times.

In the providence of God, the little churches in which we spoke gave us generous offerings, which we desperately needed.

A lovely Puerto Rican family who had moved from Maui to a city north of San Francisco had invited us to stop off and visit them as we passed through Northern California enroute to Chicago. As soon as we had finished our speaking engagements and picked up the rest of our baggage, we went to the home of those friends we had known on Maui. We were not surprised to learn that they, too, had already made arrangements for us to speak in the large church they attended.

We were both so utterly exhausted it was only through the mercy of God that we had strength to keep giving out. No one had given us a chance to explain that we were not physically up to so many speaking engagements. They clearly did not realize how tired we were.

We soon made friends with numerous people in that large church. They were especially drawn to us and wanted to help us. Our stay with our Puerto Rican friends, was much longer than we had intended, however, and we began to feel we were imposing. We had hoped to buy a car and drive back to the Chicago area, but as hard as we tried to get on our way, something always seemed to prevent us from leaving. After what seemed like weeks, though it was only days, God laid it upon the heart of one family to lend us their nineteen-foot travel trailer to live in, until we were sure of what God had in store for us next.

The Littlest Home

Imagine, if you can, six people living in a space only nineteen feet long. I still marvel at our ability to do that. We actually lived in something that was built for temporary traveling use. But after living with our good friends until we had outstayed our welcome (as much as we had hated to have to do that), that little cubicle seemed like a miniature palace.

It was a glorious feeling to have our own home, as tiny as it was. God had provided the little compartment, through these alert Christian friends who insisted we were more than welcome to use their special little home.

There was a place for each of us to sleep, a tiny kitchen with a sink, a stove, and a small refrigerator. There was even a little bathroom, with toilet, shower and basin. What more could we ask for? We felt welcome and at home.

We were surprised at the amount of storage space in our little house. We had plenty of room for everything we had brought with us on the boat.

We rented space to park our new little home in a quiet trailer park where we could rest and be comfortable for a time. It was a sure sign to us that God was in control and that we were in His will. We were willing to wait and watch Him work out details of the next step He had in mind for us.

It soon became evident that we were not to proceed to Illinois at that time. Every door we tried to force open in that direction slammed shut. We couldn't even find a car we could afford.

[Our friend from Maui mentioned us our situation to his supervisor at work. Your grandpa was soon offered a civil defense job at Benicia Arsenal near Vallejo, California, not too far from the trailer park. Again, God had provided and we were extremely grateful.]

Many people who had come to California from across the United States during the war had stayed to work in the defense arsenals, such as the one at Benicia. We soon discovered there was very little housing available. As soon as your grandpa went to work and it appeared that God intended for us to stay in California, we applied for an apartment. Unfortunately we were placed at the bottom of a long waiting list.

With a heaven-sent cubicle to call home and employment which was a miracle with so many looking for work, we were assured that our strange set of circumstances were indeed arranged by the Lord.

A Surprise Ministry

We now struggled to determine where God wanted us to serve Him. We had dedicated our lives to Him and consecrated ourselves for His service. Our greatest desire was to be in the center of His perfect will.

We did not believe that working in a large church in the inner city with a denomination whose doctrines we could not agree with was what God had in mind for us, especially for long term. At the time, however, we were asked to conduct a large-scale two-week Vacation Bible School for all ages, and to help with numerous other projects such as assisting in the Sunday School ministry in various capacities.

Almost immediately, we were given complete freedom to conduct the summer school as we felt led, using materials from one of the leading publishing houses that we respected. That year they had a Hawaiian theme, comparing the Christian life to a voyage to Paradise. At that time the Islands were often referred to as the "Paradise of the Pacific".

The fact that we had just returned from serving several years as missionaries in Hawaii seemed to earn us the right to direct that specific school. We had the complete cooperation of our co-workers and we were respected and looked up to by the students, which included teens and adults as well as children. The school was held in the evening so that the whole family could attend. It was good arrangement and God abundantly blessed those two weeks of ministry to all ages. [Even though your grandpa continued to work on the job he was somehow able to get through those two weeks. God gave us both unusual strength for the challenge.]

We appreciated the opportunity to at last carry out a successful Vacation Bible School as we had longed to do for so long. God rewarded us for our long-enduring desire and our many prayers.

Many decisions were made to accept Christ during those two weeks and renewed dedications resulted in a spirit of revival in the church. It was overwhelming to see young and old converts begin their journey on the sea of life with the paradise of heaven as their destination. Many Christians were also challenged and inspired to have more concern for their families and friends, and especially those who didn't know God and who were traveling in the opposite direction.

Another church in the area heard about the success of our unique vacation school and asked us to assist them in a similar project. We had visited the Bible Church a few times so they felt they already knew us. A group of native musicians from Bolivia, where my sister and her husband were serving as missionaries at the time, had put on a concert at the church a few weeks earlier which we had attended. We were anxious to meet natives of Bolivia and to hear more about that mission field. This experience had introduced us to many of the members of that church. Since they knew us, they felt comfortable asking us to conduct a summer school for them. It was a rewarding experience and once again we were rewarded with a fruitful ministry. We did not doubt that we were where God wanted us to be at the time.

In the weeks that followed we divided our time between the two churches, doing special projects and helping out where we could.

Good News In A Box

Our summer schools had been so successful I decided to begin a weekly Good News Club in our home, which was still the tiny trailer.

Vallejo is a city of transient residents. This was particularly true in the trailer park where we lived. I was concerned that some of the children near us may not have heard the Gospel message before, and might not have an opportunity later. I was burdened to share this most important information with them while I could.

We were living in extremely close quarters and expecting our fifth child. I was busy with my family and teaching a class in Sunday School, as well as working with women in two different churches. Even so, I knew the trailer park project was something I had to do.

I went to each park space, inquired if there were any children, and left a flyer with details of the Good News Club I was starting, to be held each Thursday at 4 p.m. Parents and grandparents with grandchildren visiting them were enthusiastic about the idea and pleased to have the children attend.

We averaged seventeen children each week. As crowded as it was in our little trailer home, no one seemed to mind.

I set up my flannelgraph board over the sink. Wide-eyed children squeezed together, hardly conscious of the inconvenience, as they listened to Bible stories and sang songs about Jesus, many hearing them for the first time. They were fascinated with the way the Bible came alive with the cut-out characters which miraculously adhered to the background, and they loved the exciting stories.

Teaching these children to sing *"Jesus Loves Me"* and to recite John 3:16, with which we are all so familiar but which was completely new to them, made me realize that not all mission fields are across the ocean.

At every class session some children would accept Christ as their Savior. Often, they would come to me a few weeks later crying with the news that their family was going to be moving on.

I had to put them in God's hands and pray that He would arrange for them to have some spiritual contact at the next location where they would be living. I knew they belonged to Him. I prayed a lot for my little fluctuating "congregation". Every week we had new children, and almost every week we said goodbye to others.

In the classes I dispensed solid Bible teaching, in bite-sized segments. The children and young people soaked up these truths like dry sponges. It was surprising to me to find that these youngsters, in a city with so many churches, still knew so little about the Bible. I had discovered a new kind of mission field. Only eternity will reveal the true results of those concentrated classes, and my efforts on behalf of the trailer park children.

All too quickly the summer was over, and I realized that the harvest in that particular field was too. I was glad I had listened to God's bidding. Our baby was due soon. In answer to prayer, we were notified of an available apartment just in time. God has a wonderful way of managing time and schedules, when we trust Him.

A Happy Reunion

It was a great relief to be able to move into an apartment, even though it was in a complex of over twenty units. God was gracious to us and saw to it that it was downstairs, and at the end of a one block long building.

We had close neighbors only on one side and upstairs. A little fenced yard extended around the end of our apartment. We didn't know of any other unit with a fenced-in area; it gave our children a safe place to play and kept the neighborhood pets and uninvited children out. That was a bonus from the Lord.

Our loving heavenly Father is so good. Just as we were getting settled into our new apartment home, we had a long distance telephone call from my parents who lived near Chicago. They excitedly told us that they had been invited to accompany friends who would be visiting the West Coast, specifically Stockton, California.

"Where is Stockton?" they anxiously inquired. "Is it near where you live?"

"It's over in California's big valley," we told them, so excited we could hardly speak. "But we'll be happy to pick you up there."

I don't think I've ever been more thrilled and overcome with appreciation to God for sending such a precious unexpected blessing. I could hardly believe it was true. My mother and dad were coming to California! I knew it would be easy for Daddy to just decide on the spur of the moment to make a trip like that, but not Mama. She was always very cautious and slow to make that kind of decision. But I had heard her myself. She had said to me on the phone, "We are going to come to California to see you!"

We were again aware of the hand of the Lord. We had been heartbroken not to be able to go back to Illinois to see our family as we had expected to when we had returned from Hawaii. They, too, had been terribly disappointed.

When our church friends heard the good news that my parents whom I hadn't seen for several years were coming to visit, they scurried to help furnish our apartment with adequate furniture. A couple of families had given us some of the bare necessities. Now they all rallied to help make this a happy occasion for us. A second call from Stockton informed us that the couple my parents were coming with had decided to tour San Francisco and that they would be bringing my folks to our home. That was the Lord's provision too, because with the baby due any day, I was not up to making the trip to pick them up. They also came earlier and were able to stay longer.

Seeing their faces again, after such a long time, was one of the most beautiful sights I have ever seen. But it brought me an inner pain to see how much they had aged, especially my mother.

Every moment of our visit was precious. Heaven seemed to smile on our time together. We could feel the presence of the Lord during those few days. It was almost as if He was rewarding us for the sacrifice of leaving our loved ones to serve Him on a far away mission field.

When we knew my folks were coming to California to see us, I was not sure how my mother would react. She had been very upset when we agreed to go to Hawaii, but she had written to us every week while we were there. My mother's rejection was painfully difficult for me at the time, but I understood that she was attached to the children. Our oldest was her first grandbaby. [It's easy for me to understand now why she would feel the way she did. It would break my heart to have to be thousands of miles from my precious grandchildren.]

When I had time to think it through, I realized that our loved ones did not receive a call from the Lord as we did. While we knew we had to answer the call, they could not understand our dedication.

We had been gone long enough; we knew even the older boys wouldn't remember their grandparents. We earnestly prayed that they would behave well so that their grandparents would be pleased and think we were raising them well. Our prayers were answered. All of them were especially good the entire six days my parents were with us. It was unreal. I will always believe God blessed us in an unusual way during that time of reuniting with my parents. He could see the future and knew that we would have very few days to spend together with them in this life after that. During their visit my mother did not appear to have any of the resentment she felt when we took the children away and went to the mission field. Instead, she clearly expressed her gratitude to the Lord that we had been faithful in His service.

My parents had barely arrived home in Illinois when we called them with the news that God had blessed us with a healthy baby, our fourth son. How they wished they could have seen the newest grandbaby.

I Was Her Only Friend

We had just moved into our apartment and did not know any of the neighbors, when I began praying for someone we could trust to watch the other children when I had to go into the hospital. There were a number of people in the two churches we were working with that we could have asked, but they all lived far from us and most of them worked during the day. And we knew it would be hard to call on them if I had to go in the middle of the night. Once again we were in a dilemma, but as always God was looking after us.

I soon met the woman who lived in the apartment above us. She was alone most of the time with her ten-year old son and eight-year old daughter. Her husband was a military officer and was seldom home. I befriended Maryann and showed her loving concern, which was something she evidently had not experienced much of. It was plain to see that her husband was not as attentive to his family as he could have been.

Although Maryann was a loyal member, the church she belonged to offered nothing to help her and her children escape their terrible loneliness. Even so, she was strict in her belief and did not blame her church. She had not been exposed to the Gospel and was at first afraid to make friends with me. I continued to be neighborly, talking to her wherever we ran into each other. Finally, one day she accepted my invitation to come into my home for a visit.

We soon became close friends. She knew I was a Christian and that we had been missionaries. There were times when she expressed genuine interest in spiritual things, but she was too tied to family tradition to break loose from her religion. She saw in me, however, something she longed to have. I wanted so much to help her spiritually, and I tried. But she would only let me be her friend at a "safe" distance.

On one day I will never forget, Maryann told me in a sad tone, "Ardelle, you are the only friend I have." I held her close and wept, as I told her how much I valued her friendship.

My precious new friend tried to find ways to express her appreciation for my kindness to her. When she volunteered to keep our children while I was in the hospital giving birth to our baby, she did not realize that she was being used of God in answer to my prayers. Oh, how Maryann enjoyed our tiny new son. Helping care for him gave her an excuse to be with me more. She would lovingly cuddle our little boy close in her arms. Several times she told me she would have loved to have had another baby. My heart went out to her.

[One day I noticed Maryann watching your grandpa as he held the baby, then handed him to me and got down on the floor and played with the other children after working hard all day. She told me later that her husband never paid much attention to their children. They felt they hardly knew him. In fact, she said, they were almost afraid of him at times. It was as if he were a total stranger. It made me appreciate even more having a husband like your grandpa.]

Our baby was only a couple of months old when Maryann came running into my kitchen one afternoon, sobbing so hard I thought there was a death in the family, or that something drastic had happened to one of her children. She told me her husband had been transferred to another state clear across the country and that they would be moving soon.

Our parting was as sad as if we had been sisters. I will never forget the terrible pain of watching that lonely woman, who had told me I was her only friend, drive off in their car. It tore my heart out. Maryann moved many miles away, but not beyond my love and my prayers.

My heart ached because I had not been able to help her come to know Jesus, so that she would always have Him as her friend, no matter where she was. I have always hoped that God answered my prayers and sent Maryann another friend, and most of all that she became a Christian, so that she could enjoy the friendship and fellowship expressed only in God's family.

A Shower Of Love

A woman who had taken special interest in us observed that our growing family needed many things to get started in a new area, and invited me to visit the clothing closet at her church. This was difficult for me, but believing it was God's provision I humbled myself and took advantage of the opportunity to make our family members more presentable in public. Because of a baby shower at each of the churches we were working with, our infant son was very well taken care of, but we had not yet been able to manage the clothing needed for the older children and for ourselves.

[Several ladies in a group I had spoken to a couple times planned a surprise party for me. My friend, Lois, plotted with your grandpa to make sure I was there. When I arrived at the location, all the ladies called out in unison, "Surprise! Surprise!" I truly WAS surprised. I couldn't figure out who was being honored. When they assured me I was the one, I asked, "Why? It's not my birthday or anniversary, I'm not getting married, or going away . . ."

They explained that the party was indeed for me. It was a LOVE shower they said; something they wanted to do as unto the Lord. Different ones spoke up to say what a blessing I had been to them. I was overcome with emotion.

The "love shower" held in my honor that evening will never be erased from my memory. The personal items, many of them lovingly handmade, were generous and God's way of taking care of my great needs at the time. I had never before had such lovely things nor so many of them. I felt like a queen. [Well, at least like a princess. And, you know, as a child of the king, that's what I really am.]

The Little Artist

After living in a large apartment complex with five children longer than we had hoped, we were very happy to finally find a more desirable place to live, much closer to work and the various ministries that we were involved in. It was a downstairs apartment in a large home that had been converted into two living units.

My friend, Lois, stopped by to see our new place one day and excitedly told us about an art class she was taking at a nearby junior college. Lois knew that our oldest son was an artist. She had admired his work and had even told her teacher about him.

"Miss Polly wants you to enroll in our class," she informed me. "You need a diversion," she added. "I told her about your young artist," she said excitedly, "and she said you could bring him to class with you."

It was an evening class for adults only but a ten-year old could attend with his mother, the teacher told Lois.

[When we told your grandpa about the art class, he was delighted with the idea and insisted that I enroll.]

Lois glowed with pride when Miss Polly had my son come up in front of the class to demonstrate how to paint.

"Now, this is how you do it," she explained to the class. They all watched with delight as he quickly demonstrated his artistic expertise. Everyone was amazed. Lois and I were quite proud, of course.

All three of us really enjoyed our art class that year. I even turned out some work I was pleased with, but the exposure and encouragement it provided our young artist was the most rewarding of all.

* * *   * * *   * * *

"I have enjoyed our time together but I think we will have to break off our session for this time. This week has gone by so fast for all of us. It has been a pleasure having you with me while Grandpa was gone deer hunting. We've covered a lot of area and it has been a joy for me, remembering all the things I've told you about. There's so much more, but that will have to wait for another time. Thank you all for coming, and thanks for listening so attentively."

CHAPTER 16

Really Trusting

"Are we still going to target practice?" Gregory asked, looking around the table.

We were just finishing a late midday family get-together meal. At such times more than one suggestion for afternoon activities usually came up.

"How about pitching horseshoes? I get to play with Grandpa!" Marissa called out.

"Oh, let the grown-ups do that," Karl suggested. "I'd rather hear Grandma tell a true story."

"Your daddy says you have to go home early," I told him.

Karl looked so disappointed I asked, "Would you like to stay overnight?"

"Can I stay too?" Kathye wanted to know.

"What about me?" Andrea pleaded, "It's my turn!"

"You can all stay," I said, "if your parents don't mind. Right now, go have fun outside, while we get the kitchen cleared away. We'll have plenty of time for a story tonight."

"Will you tell us about when you first lived in California, and what it was like?" Barry asked. "I'll go ask my folks now if I can stay tonight."

"It's always a pleasure to tell you more about the things I want you to know about," I assured them all.

*** *** ***

Silverware and Souls

We hadn't been in California very long when it became quite evident that we were not supposed to go back to Illinois as we has planned. It was difficult not knowing what God had in store for us but we left it in His hands and exercised our faith as best as we could. We faced each challenge believing that He would show us His will. The first Christmas we were in California we received many cards and letters from relatives, church family, and friends both old and new. One came from a couple we had known in Illinois. They had attended our home church for a while and had, in fact, been in our missionary training class. They had left the church about the time we went to Hawaii. Their letter was addressed to us in the Islands and had been forwarded to our Vallejo address.

They informed us that they were now doing missionary work in California. The name of the town was not familiar to us, but when we looked it up on a map we were surprised to find it was less than an hour's drive from us.

We soon made contact with them and were invited to visit them and their little church. What a grand time of fellowship we enjoyed, exchanging news, blessings, burdens and aspirations.

The offerings at Carl and Marilyn's small church were hardly sufficient to provide for their family of five. At the time, he was involved in door-to-door sales in an attempt to supplement their meager income. A few weeks later, Carl stopped by our home in Vallejo to tell us about the "excellent" features of his newest product, which happened to be name-brand silverware. The "special" offer that day was two sets of service for six for what seemed to us a very reasonable price. The main advantage of this particular offer, he pointed out, was that we would receive two double sets of teaspoons. As I examined the lovely Oneida silverware that day, my love for beautiful things resurfaced.

We bought the pretty table service, partly because we really needed it but mostly because we wanted to help Carl and Marilyn. [That silverware proved to be a greater blessing than we could ever have dreamed. It served our family and our guests well, for many years. We did not use the beautiful tableware just for guests, though it served many of them in our home. We reasoned that no one was more important than our own family. We wanted our children to have memories of enjoying our best silver because they were so special to us. That lovely table service was still beautiful years later until it was destroyed in a dishwasher fire.

The most important thing that happened the day we bought the pretty silverware from our friend, Carl, was our discussion about the burden we both shared for the lost.

Carl's main purpose for stopping by our place that day was to ask us to help him and Marilyn pray for a needy community he had discovered while out selling. During his business day he had met an older Italian couple in the town of Sonoma. The woman had wept when Carl began to talk about the Lord as he always did. He considered his job a missionary venture. Carl asked about local churches as a means of opening the conversation to spiritual things. The elderly woman was overcome by that. Through her tears she told him of her concern for her grandchildren who desperately needed spiritual guidance. Although she herself was not a Christian, we found out later, she had a great burden for her family, particularly her grandchildren.

She had been very "religious". A few years earlier, however, she and her husband had been terribly hurt when the "church" they were involved in took advantage of them in a time of crisis after their only son was killed while serving his country. The church had taken much more money from them than they could afford and had not provided any spiritual support. They were smart enough to see that something was wrong. From that time they would have nothing to do with that church. Somehow, God had given this brokenhearted grandmother a desire for something better for her grandchildren. She had a great burden for their spiritual welfare.

Mrs. Astilli also revealed to Carl her personal heartache; having a husband who had been a "wino" for many years. Carl tenderly told her about Jesus, a true friend who can be trusted with every family problem. She listened intently, sensing a ray of hope for those she loved. Carl explained that the children should be learning about God and the Bible. She begged him to come back and teach them. He promised to pray that God would provide someone to come. He told her he could not come himself because he was already involved with a church in another area, but he understood the urgency of this little grandmother's request.

Carl related the whole story to us that afternoon while the demonstration silverware lay across our coffee table. We promised to drive to Sonoma and meet Mrs. Astilli and her family and also to visit some of the existing churches in the area to see if there might be one that we could recommend. We expected to find at least one church with an active Sunday School with some believers who would be happy to reach out to a seeking family. In the following weeks we visited each of the surprisingly few evangelical churches there, hoping desperately to find help for this concerned grandmother's family.

One church we dropped in on had no children or young people and, consequently, no Sunday School. It had all the symptoms of a dying church. It was just as well, because they weren't teaching what the Bible declares to be truth. The handful of older, sad members and their leaders were very evidently misguided and our hearts cried for them. They were themselves a mission field. We went home with a heavy heart that day. On another Sunday we attended a small newly planted church, a "mission", which a larger church in a nearby town was sponsoring. Since they were attempting to establish this work we thought they would be happy to have us tell them about a family who needed the Lord and was searching. We were somewhat taken aback when they made it plain that our visit and our request were intrusions. They expressed no concern when we explained the spiritual needs of this large family. Why should they be concerned about people like that, seemed to be their attitude. We thought their reaction was rather strange, especially for a church denomination that we had thought of as being solid and evangelical. We later learned that one of the reasons they had started the mission was that some members of the original church were secretly planning to split. This seemed to them to be a respectable way to divide the church. They certainly were not thinking of reaching the lost in a new community.

Each time we went up to Sonoma to visit a prospective church we also went to see Mrs. Astilli and talk with her about the Lord. We explained that we were trying to find someone who could help her grandchildren learn about God. One Sunday afternoon she began weeping as we talked. "Won't YOU come and teach my grandchildren about Jesus and the Bible?" she sobbed. We promised to pray about it, but this burdened grandmother would not let us go.

"Please come," she begged, "and tell us more about Jesus." She was squeezing my hand as tight as she could as if trying to hold on to me. A great burden gripped our hearts that week and it was all we could think about. We knew we had to do something.

We finally admitted to ourselves that God was calling us to a ministry in Sonoma. We called those we had been working with in the churches in Vallejo and explained that we were going to have to resign our duties, because we planned to concentrate our energy and time in an effort to establish an outreach in our new mission field.

On the following Wednesday evening after church, I explained to the Sunday School superintendent at the church where I was teaching that God was calling us to a new mission field in Sonoma. He tried to appear glad, but in reality he was very sad and this sophisticated business man actually wept when I told him I would have to resign my class of fifth grade boys.

As he pulled out his handkerchief and wiped tears from his eyes I realized he was not concerned merely for his class, he was expressing his own feelings. "Please forgive me, Ardelle," he begged. "There's something I have to tell you." He hesitated, then went on. "I feel trapped by the traditions of this church. I've watched you and Brother Brown since you've been here. You are free. I have admired your convictions and the way you have stood firm." He paused a moment, looking down at the floor. "I don't know if I can ever get free from some of these things that I'm convinced are not aligned with the Bible," he continued. "I was raised in this denomination, as was my wife. We could never break loose. Our families would never forgive us. I feel trapped. Will you please pray for us?" he pleaded.

I understood what that sincere man was feeling and trying to tell me. I can still see the look in his eyes. As I turned to go, he said, "Ardelle, I'd give anything to have what you and your husband have. Please don't forget to pray for me and my wife."

I never learned if he was ever able to break out of the chains that bound him so hopelessly. I do know that I have great concern for the many people who are today in that same situation.

A Most Unusual Chapel

I'll never forget the Sunday afternoon when we arrived in Sonoma to hold our first outreach service, to tell those who had asked us to come about God's love and mercy.

Our family, including three towheaded little boys and a little blond girl, were all seasoned missionaries and our baby son was in the process of being initiated.

We proceeded to unload our flannelgraph and easel, and the lesson material we had prepared for the day. Mrs. Astilli was standing in the yard waiting for us to arrive. Her grandchildren were all around her. The look of hope on that grandmother's face is indelibly impressed in my heart and mind.

"Where would you like for us to teach the class?" we asked as we walked toward them with our equipment. We had observed on our previous visits that there was no room in her overcrowded and cluttered home. Taken by surprise, she began to flutter about, trying to think of something.

Your grandpa came to the rescue and suggested we meet in the side yard. "We can lay planks across those boxes over there for the children to sit on," he told her.

She smiled with relief and ushered us into a small, fenced chicken yard; it was the only place with enough space for our flannelgraph board and seating for the children. We quickly set up some boxes we had spotted near the back door, and laid some old pieces of lumber that were piled nearby across them. Our own children led the way and sat down. Her grandchildren timidly followed them. Mrs. Astilli sat on the steps at her back door, carefully watching everything that went on. It was one of the most humbling experiences we had ever faced. You could not take one step without stepping in chicken manure and the stench was stifling. The fact that it was a hot day didn't help. We had never experienced such a smelly, messy situation. It was the exact opposite of what we had been used to in the Islands. We had rarely smelled anything offensive there. The fish markets did emit a fishy smell as did the seaweed that cluttered the beaches, but the odor was diluted by the seabreeze. And contrary to what we had expected, there was no such thing as body odor in Hawaii. Everyone bathed often.

That first Good News Club meeting in Mrs. Astilli's chicken yard made a "strong" impression on all of us. Even though we knew our children noticed, they never said a word. We prayed for patience and wisdom and guidance as we presented the Gospel message in that humble setting, which God had so definitely led us to. I'm afraid we cringed at the prospect of carrying on this ministry under such undignified circumstances.

[We kept "shooing" the chickens away from around our feet as I led the children in singing choruses, and your grandpa presented a Bible story. The attentive grandchildren and their grateful grandmother didn't seem at all distracted or disturbed.]

By the second or third week, the children's mother came with them to hear the lesson and to see what was happening. The mother and the grandmother both became so interested in the lessons that they ventured close enough to sit in the back so they could see and hear better.

We could tell Mrs. Astilli was a little embarrassed with the condition of her home and yard, but she begged us to keep coming. Soon the grandchildren began inviting neighborhood children, and their classmates from school. They were anxious to share the wonderful stories with their friends.

Before long, the boys and girls were asking if they could bring their older brothers and sisters and their parents. We prayed fervently for a more appropriate place to invite the community to come and hear the story of Jesus and His love and mercy. Our little missionary "church" was growing steadily. We suddenly awakened to the realization that God had given us our own ministry, just as we had asked Him to. But this was not exactly what we had envisioned. It certainly was not the kind of story that you would want to write about to your home church or to relatives that you hoped to impress.

For a while we felt disappointed, but then we prayed through our attitudes and letdown feelings and admitted that God was answering our prayers, even if not as we had expected. When we got our priorities in order, we saw the picture differently and it was easier for God to work through us. He began to bless our ministry tremendously.

We had only been going to Sonoma for a few weeks when something wonderful happened. We arrived as usual at the little farm on the outskirts of town where the elderly grandmother and her little flock were waiting for us. We saw immediately that Mrs. Astilli was unusually excited. She came running out to meet us.

We feared that her husband, whom we knew was not too happy about us coming each week, was not going to let us teach the class anymore. We hoped however, that she had some good news for us maybe that her husband was interested in hearing the message too. Whatever it was she could hardly wait to tell us.

"Please, I want to talk to you after the meeting before you leave," she insisted firmly. [Your grandpa clasped her hand, assuring her he would not rush off and would gladly talk to her.]

We both noticed that Mrs. Astilli listened to the lesson even more intently than usual. She seemed to be weighing every word carefully. Inwardly, we were grieving, fearing this might be our last opportunity to talk to the children or the grandmother or the others who now attended about the Lord.

At the close of the teaching session each week we always provided an opportunity for anyone in the class to accept Christ as their personal Savior or to make a decision about the challenge of the lesson. Several of the children had indicated that they wanted to follow Jesus and make Him Lord of their life. We always made sure they understood the plan of salvation clearly.

We emphasized that a person does not become a Christian by being good or by going to church or anything that they themselves could do, because the Bible clearly states that all of our righteousness is as filthy rags. And we were always careful to clarify the difference between religion and Christianity. Mrs. Astilli was very much aware of what religion was; we wanted her to understand that Christianity was not the same.

Our lesson that day was about Nicodemus, the religious man who came to Jesus to ask what he had to do to be saved. In John, chapter 3, Jesus Himself said it was necessary to be born again.

Mrs. Astilli listened intently as your grandpa explained the new birth. When the invitation was given and no one responded, we were surprised and disappointed, but we noticed that the dear grandmother sat with her head bowed and appeared to be heavily burdened. An occasional tear dropped onto her apron. The meeting was dismissed and the children rushed off to play as they always did while we were folding up our equipment. I went back and sat down beside the little grandmother. She was so still, I wondered if she had noticed I was there. I sensed that she was trying to get up courage to say something. Finally, she began to sob. When she could bring herself to speak, she explained to us that she wanted to know for sure that she belonged to God. She said she believed all that our friend, Carl, had told her but she was not sure she had understood correctly.

We had been watching for an opportunity to discuss her convictions and concerns and we were glad it had come to a head. She told us that she had an increasing uneasiness that she may not have understood clearly and she wanted to be sure about her salvation. She insisted that before we left that day we had to help her get it all straight. That was a great relief to us. We were also relieved she wasn't going to tell us that her husband had decided we couldn't continue coming. What a day that was.

We rejoiced in the radiant smile that illuminated Mrs. Astilli's face, as she expressed complete assurance of her salvation. She was very happy and kept thanking us again and again for coming to share God's Word with her and her family.

It was rewarding to watch our newest convert develop spiritually. She prayed often for her husband and tried to witness to him. She tried to reach out to her neighbors and friends as well. She began to read and search the Bible for answers to her questions, and for the sheer pleasure of discovering nuggets of truth. We bought her a beautiful leather-bound Bible which she loved dearly.

The Quonset Chapel

One Sunday afternoon a few weeks after her new-birth experience, we arrived at Mrs. Astilli's house to find her bursting with excitement. She had been praying, along with us, for a place to meet that was clean and more inviting. And fall was coming soon, bringing with it rain, cold and wind.

She ran out to meet us and before we could even get out of the car, she announced triumphantly, "My husband has agreed to let us use one of the quonset buildings on our property." We had noticed the two identical buildings just up the road, but had not realized that they belonged to the Astilli's.

We were so surprised and pleased we hardly knew how to react. She knew it had to be an answer to prayer. It was a great victory for her, seeing her husband agree to anything having to do with the Lord, and also experiencing the power of prayer.

Mr. Astilli was still not in agreement with what we were teaching, nor did he particularly appreciate our efforts on behalf of his family. Somehow, though, he had been impressed that we needed a better place to meet for our classes.

As we explored the unusual buildings and began to think of them in terms of a place for worship and classes, we could see the potential. We could also see that there would be numerous problems. Much material would be needed and considerable work would be required, to get the inside in sufficient shape for our purposes. We knew we would need to make the exterior more presentable also. We would need chairs or benches to sit on. It was going to be a major undertaking, but at least it was something definite to pray about and work toward. Because of the bad experiences this family had with their previous church we did not feel we could bring up the need for money for materials. Mrs. Astilli would have loved giving to this important project. She had mentioned several times that she wanted to contribute towards our expenses in driving to Sonoma every week, but her husband wouldn't let her.

We assured her we did not expect any monetary help. We were confident that God would meet our needs. This was such a touchy issue at that point. We did not want to spoil God's plan to reach this family and the surrounding community with the truth of His Word.

Mr. Astilli did not mind at all when she gave us extra eggs, and vegetables from her garden. She was grateful to be able to do that.

The Gift Of A Lamb

Mr. Astilli often supplied us with spontaneous generosity. On one occasion, he gave us a lamb to butcher for meat for our family. Mrs. Astilli was ecstatic. She knew he would not have done it if she had suggested it. It was also the prize lamb of his flock.

[Can you imagine how much that blessed your grandpa?]

We had never tasted lamb and didn't even know how to cook it, but we were overcome with gratitude the day this dear Italian man presented his love offering to us. It reminded us of Old Testament days when the best lamb was offered as a sacrifice to God.

We never knew what prompted Mr. Astilli's touching gesture, which was such a tremendous blessing to us. I wish I could tell you that he accepted God's gift of His Lamb, but if he ever came to Christ, we did not know about it. As time went by, however, he did become less and less hostile. He drank much less than before and we never stopped praying for his salvation and for his deliverance from alcohol.

Mr. Astilli was patient with our ignorance concerning lambs and sheep. He showed us how to properly butcher our lamb and Mrs. Astilli showed us how to cook it. Some friends of theirs from Italy operated an Italian bakery in San Francisco. They drove up to Sonoma often and always brought a large box of day-old bakery goods for the Astilli's and their daughter and her family. She always shared them with us. Many of the

Italian bakery items were new to us. We had never tasted such delightful pastries and cookies. It really thrilled Mrs. Astilli and her husband too, to see us enjoying Italian specialties.

The Offering Chest

Along with the blessing of a building to meet in, we were faced with a challenging fixer-upper project and the necessity for at least some finances. We knew something would have to be worked out.

[Your grandpa worked very hard to provide for his large family of seven. We gave as much as possible but we didn't believe it was God's will that we do it all, even if we could have.]

By now there were several children and young people, as well as a few adults coming to our weekly classes. We knew we should also be teaching them about the necessity and the blessing of giving.

With the prospects of actually having a place in which to worship and study God's Word everyone soon got into the spirit of helping, but it was evident to all that we needed to purchase paint and other materials. We prayed and waited for the Lord to show us how to handle this new financial situation.

[Your grandpa came up with an excellent idea for showing them what God's Word says about giving and offerings. I believe it was from the Lord. He bought a beautiful little wooden treasure chest, cut a slot in the top, and put a decorative lock on the clasp. He carved the words FREE-WILL OFFERINGS in the top of the chest.]

The first Sunday he brought the little box out, he set it on a chair near where he stood to give the message. He gave a lesson from the Old Testament, telling how the people gave willingly and generously, so that the temple of the Lord could be built. He read from the Bible how the people gave so much that they had more than was needed.

He described God's method of carrying on His work, as all listened reverently. He explained that money put into the chest should be voluntary and should be given as unto the Lord, and not to us, and that all of it would be used for God's work there in Sonoma.

Our little congregation surprised us. We were pleased with the manner in which each one gave. We soon had enough for the supplies we needed to renovate the building and enough to begin looking for folding chairs.

Everyone pitched in and in a surprisingly short time we had the inside of our new chapel cleaned and painted. We hung some pretty curtains over the freshly washed windows and laid large colorful throw rugs at the entrance and in front of the pulpit which your grandpa built. A family in the community who learned about our church offered us an old upright piano. When it was in place, along with some bought and donated folding chairs, our miniature sanctuary was ready to dedicate.

To our surprise and delight, and the sheer joy of his wife, Mr. Astilli insisted on painting the exterior of the building himself. When he saw what we had done to the inside, he wanted to help get the outside looking nice, too.

The week before the dedication service we painted and framed a large sign to put above the entrance.

It was difficult coming up with an appropriate name for our new little church. We finally decided against using the word "church" because our dear friends, the Astilli's, still had such bad feelings about their experiences with a church.

We finally settled on SONOMA GOSPEL CHAPEL. I was not very happy with that name because I feared it might lead people to believe we were a different kind of church than what we were. Sure enough, occasionally people would come and assume we were an emotional type of church. Our name suggested that we were interdenominational, which we were, but some would have liked to have influenced us to become charismatic as well. We had seen enough of that while living on Maui and no one could have ever have convinced us to become like that.

News of the new church spread fast. The warm, early September sunshine bathed the little makeshift chapel with a heavenly radiance as we conducted opening services that first Sunday. It was a grand day. While our own little congregation and our guests listened intently, the children sang all the songs we had taught them, as I accompanied them on the old piano which badly needed tuning. The adults sang along on some hymns they knew.

With a truly grateful and humble heart, their pastor, Reverend Brown, delivered an appropriate sermon. What a glorious day it was. Mr. Astilli could not resist being on hand, if just to see what would happen on that long anticipated day.

That service in an oddly shaped building was another milestone of a long, fruitful ministry in Sonoma that had really started in a stinky chicken yard, or perhaps further back still, in the heart of a silverware salesman with a love for the souls of mankind. It certainly was a true mission field.

The Next Move

As our little church grew we were assured that we were where God wanted us to be. We spent as much time as possible in Sonoma, visiting homes and tending our little flock.

[We began to pray about moving to the community. Driving all the way from Vallejo to Sonoma was tiresome, expensive, and time consuming. However, with his big family to support, your grandpa could not afford to quit his job yet. Driving all the way to Benicia to his work every day was beginning to take its toll on your grandpa. He still had not regained his health. He tired so easily and usually had me drive if I was along because he was so prone to falling asleep at the wheel.]

The little church was not yet able to support us. Most of the adults who were attending had large families and were barely able to support themselves.

As much as we longed to, moving to Sonoma seemed impossible. We knew God was in control, however, and that if it was His will He would work it all out.

One day, quite unexpectedly, we met a couple while visiting with people who attended church. The husband worked at Hamilton Air Force Base, north of San Francisco and was in a car pool in which each person only had to drive one day a week. He said that if your grandpa could get a transfer to Hamilton Field, they would be happy to have him in their car pool. [This was a new idea that we had not thought of.]

Upon immediate inquiry a transfer was made from Benicia Arsenal to Hamilton Field. He was soon working there, in a more desirable atmosphere and with an increased salary. And he did not have to drive at all; our new friends already had enough drivers in the car pool. We were so grateful for the new arrangement. It was better than we could have worked out ourselves. Once more, God had answered prayer miraculously.

Just as with the transfer, we soon found a house in Sonoma, near our church and the people we were working with. God even provided us with a bonus by providing a home that bordered on a little stream. It seemed like heaven to our children. Although we were inside the city limits of the small town, it was more like living in the country. The children loved the school there. They had no difficulty adjusting. They already knew some of the students from church, which made it much easier for them.

The climate in Sonoma was also better for our health. We were grateful for such a pleasant place to live, but most of all that we had our own little spot to serve God, which we had longed for, for so long. Our enthusiasm for the ministry was increased even more.

Church attendance grew steadily and we soon had a new problem— we had outgrown our little chapel. We were holding Sunday School classes behind the piano in compartments divided by screens or curtains, and even inside of cars parked near the building. During the worship hour, latecomers had to stand in the doorway.

Fortunately, we were able to use the Community Center in town, where there was adequate room to grow. God also blessed our ministry in that location. We were there for several years. During those years our happy, healthy family was growing up. There was never a dull moment around our house, what with juggling our time between church and school functions.

Our children all did well in school and in sports, music and art. There were many times of special achievements and accomplishments. [How do you describe the thrill of seeing your son's picture in the local newspaper and reading the caption underneath, rating his performance on the trumpet as "flawless".]

Each of the children excelled in one or more areas. We had so much to thank the Lord for.

The Trip Back East

Even though happy, we were so involved in our ministry in Sonoma that without realizing it, we had been working relentlessly and not getting enough rest.

[Despite his continuing health problems, your grandpa was working at a full-time job and carrying the heavy load of a growing young church as well. The doctor had warned us that it would be necessary for him to occasionally take a break from his responsibilities. We both were aware of his advice but there just didn't seem to be any place to break off and get away.]

Finally, we saw we had to take a vacation. Each time we heard from either of our families they would ask when we were coming back to see them. By that time your grandpa had accumulated enough vacation leave that we could make the long trip back to Illinois, and on down South.

Since we knew I would have to do most of the driving, we planned to stop early each night and get an early start the next morning.

Our whole family was excited about the trip across the country, and especially about seeing grandparents and other relatives after such a long time. There was so much to do to get ready for the long trip but anticipating a vacation spurred us on. Arrangements were made for someone to care for our church family and be in charge of the services while we were gone. Finally, the old car was packed and we were ready to go. The day school was out, we took off. At times it had seemed like that day would never come. When we had arrived in California from Hawaii, we had thought we were enroute to Illinois, but God had different plans for us. That was difficult to understand at the time, but now we had a different perspective. We were going back now, as we had so much longed to do, for so long, but we were going to be returning to the home missions ministry which God had so graciously given us in California.

[Every day of that momentous trip was an adventure. Your grandpa was content to let me do the driving in order to let his weary body rejuvenate. When he would insist that he should drive for a couple of hours, the other children would beg him to "let Mother drive". He was so weary in body that he just could not keep from becoming drowsy. I was concerned about his continuing poor health and felt that getting completely away from the area and all the responsibilities was the best thing we could do for him. He was excited about seeing all the family and about speaking in our home church.]

We enjoyed the trip as a family. On the long stretches between towns we would sing choruses, quote Bible verses, and count our blessings. We also played travel games to help keep the children occupied. They were good travelers. The baby did exceptionally well, especially with his mother being so occupied with driving and traveling responsibilities.

What a happy reunion we had with our families. It had been years since we had seen them. When we saw how much my parents—especially my mother—had aged, we knew we had made the right decision to make the trip that year.

We tried to get in as much visiting and "loving" as possible in our limited time.

A Faithful Warrior Returns

Friends at our home church, near where my parents lived, greeted us warmly and could hardly wait to hear from the missionaries they had sent out to Hawaii several years earlier.

The church was crowded to hear Reverend Brown speak. It was the first time any of them had seen us since we had returned to the states. They had asked me to also say a few words so I talked first. I told them about the aspects of our ministry that we had earlier agreed upon and briefly shared how the Lord had led and blessed us.

Then it was your grandpa's turn. After about fifteen minutes, I noticed he seemed to be tiring, and was grasping for the edge of the pulpit. When I saw him turn pale, I gasped and prayed, "Oh, Lord, please help him."

Suddenly your grandpa slumped and fell to the floor. A fearful silence fell across the room. Fortunately a doctor friend we had known before we left for Hawaii was in the audience and rushed to his side. I could sense that everyone was praying as I ran to the front of the church. Some who were sitting nearby tried to ease the children's fears. No one left the room. After carefully examining your grandpa, the doctor stepped to the pulpit and announced that it appeared that Reverend Brown was simply suffering from sheer exhaustion.

The pastor took over at that point and talked for several minutes about the faithfulness of their missionary, who had given himself so sacrificially on the mission field and explained to those who were new in the congregation that he had suffered the loss of his health as the result. Everyone was challenged to pray for him and his family.

The Old Fashioned Way

After our time in Illinois, we visited with our family in the South and had a memorable time, especially for the children. Their paternal grandparents lived in an old farmhouse with no electrical appliances. Both of us had been raised that way. It brought back a flood of memories and made us realize how far we had come. It was educational for the children. They were intrigued with conditions they had never even heard about.

Lamplighting time fascinated our youngsters; they had never seen kerosene lamps in actual use. They watched curiously as their grandmother filled each lamp with oil and cleaned the chimneys so that a bright, clean light filled the room.

The one thing that made the most lasting impression on them was the source of their water supply. They looked on in disbelief as their Grandpa Brown primed the old-fashioned pump by pouring water into it which they had saved in a can specifically for that purpose. After a number of "pumps", a stream of clear, cool water finally poured forth from the old pump into a large rust-stained bucket.

I stood by, almost holding my breath, as he offered each one of them a dipper full of freshly drawn water to drink. I was so germ conscious I could hardly stand to see everyone drinking from the same dipper. Of course our family had shared water that way too, but even as a child that unsanitary practice had caused me great concern. This brought it all back. I was also afraid that the water had not been tested and that it might contain dangerous impurities. Despite my lack of trust in the water, I had to admit that it was tasty and cold. The children were all eyes as their grandma fired up the old woodburning kitchen range and began cooking food that was somewhat different from what they were used to. Nothing was new and unusual to us but it was interesting to watch it all through the eyes of our children, as they experienced it for the first time.

[Your dear grandpa was so tired that he had to suggest to his folks that we all go to bed much earlier than they would have liked. As much as he loved seeing them again, the visit was taxing for him. He was just too tired to talk and was barely able to sit up.]

All too soon we had to be on our way. Many miles separated us from our home in California. We knew we had to limit the distance we traveled each day so that I wouldn't get too tired driving. [On the return trip we planned to stop in New Mexico to visit with your grandpa's uncles there, his dad's brothers. He also wanted us to see the old home place where he had been born and raised. His grandfather had homesteaded several 640 acre sections of land there and when he died he left it to his four sons; your great grandfather and his three brothers who still lived there. The three brothers had remarkably married three pretty Mexican sisters. They were your grandpa's Aunt Alice, Aunt Bennie, and Aunt Ramona. I admired them all.

We all enjoyed the uncles too. Uncle Charlie held us all spellbound with his animated tales of the Old West, while his beautiful brown-eyed wife gently rocked in an old rocking chair, all the while smiling approvingly. We could have listened all day.

[Your grandpa was closest to his Uncle Homan and his Aunt Alice, because he had lived in their home and attended high school in Santa Rosa, New Mexico, before moving to the South and being transferred to the high school I was attending and where we met.]

Uncle Addison (they called him Ad) and Aunt Ramona lived far out on another part of the range in the direction of Ft. Sumner.

A storm was brewing as we drove out across some authentic "Old West" pasture land to accept an invitation to have a meal with Uncle Ad and Aunt Ramona. Their place seemed to me to be as much in the middle of nowhere as anyone could have access to. Dusty, unpaved, trail-like roadways lined on each side with cactus and sagebrush seemed to go on forever.

By the time we arrived, an electrical storm such as I had not seen since I lived in the Midwest, lowered on us. The sky lit up with tongues of forked lightning, followed closely by loud claps of thunder. I was terribly frightened but the children thought it was fascinating.

While Aunt Ramona was finishing the salad and dessert, Uncle Ad was busy getting the steaks ready to cook, hardly paying any attention to the storm in progress.

[When Uncle Ad finally served the steaks, your grandpa smiled knowingly as I stared in amazement at the size of them. Each individual steak was as large as one I usually served at home for the whole family.]

"Hurry up," Uncle Ad urged, "eat 'em while they're hot!"

I blinked and slowly picked up my fork. We recognized the look on the children's faces as a mixture of disbelief at the size of their steak, and concern as they realized they could not possibly eat all of it. We had taught them to take only what they could eat and to eat all of whatever was on their plates. They looked at me, then at their daddy, then back to me. We knew they were grappling with how to handle the situation and we didn't want to offend our gracious hosts. They had already been eyeing Aunt Ramona's dessert and were certain they would never get to taste it because there was no way they would be able to clean their plates.

[Your grandpa and I were almost in the same predicament. He couldn't eat even half of the thick steak on his plate. I could only eat a small amount of mine.] Uncle Ad quickly sensed our uncomfortableness. He tried to set everyone at ease by saying he wanted us to remember that when we visited them, he served steaks the size of his big heart.

"It's called hospitality," he drawled, the way they do in Western movies. "Real western hospitality!"

After a good laugh he announced, "Of course you would insult Aunt Ramona if you didn't have a large helping of her yummy dessert."

With that he began picking up everyone's plate. When he got to the children he said, "When we're all finished eating, how about a nice hay ride for these fine boys here and that pretty little blonde gal over there by her daddy." He looked straight at a very tense little girl and said, "Now, you won't be afraid, will you?" Already shaken by the electrical storm, she glanced around to get my reaction. When she looked back at Uncle Ad, his big, friendly smile braced her courage. She sat up straight and assured him she would not be the least bit frightened by the horses.

He put his hand on her head and whispered, "That's a good girl."

When the dessert—which was just as delicious as Uncle Ad knew it would be—was finished, the hay ride was on. That gave Aunt Ramona and me a chance to become better acquainted while clearing up the kitchen.

The next day we were invited to Uncle Homan and Aunt Alice's home. I had heard so much about them, I felt I already knew them. They all enjoyed remembering old times when their nephew had lived with them while attending high school in Santa Rosa. It was almost as if I had been there, too.

After lunch they took us out to see what your grandpa referred to as "the old home place" where he had been born and lived as a child. It brought back many precious memories for him.

[Meeting and getting to know your grandpa's relatives and experiencing a bit of the real Old West was a great awakening for both the children and myself. The entire visit to New Mexico was pure pleasure for your grandpa and I still love to recall those vivid memories.]

When we left Santa Rosa, we went to Albuquerque where we visited one of my second cousins. Like Uncle Ad, Uncle Homan, and Uncle Charlie, my cousin had also married a Mexican girl. They proudly prepared for us their best Mexican dishes. We were impressed and appreciated it but, unfortunately, we had a problem. We were totally unfamiliar with Mexican food and our stomachs were not used to such highly seasoned cuisine. The children were looking at us pleadingly. They had never been exposed to such hot food and they simply could not swallow it. Like at Uncle Ad's, we did not want to offend our hosts. I silently prayed that we could get out of this one gracefully. Finally my cousin asked, "Is the food too hot for you?"

"We're not used to highly seasoned foods," I explained apologetically. "The children have never eaten Mexican food and we both have uneasy stomachs and have to be careful about what we eat." I felt very awkward.

They tried to be very nice about it, but we felt they didn't understand. That was the only kind of food they ever ate.

He Walked Across The Screen

From Albuquerque we headed north to Colorado for a scheduled conference for pastors. We arrived in the little town of Manitou Springs in late afternoon and were able to find a place to stay in an older home with a "Rooms for Rent" sign in a front window. A matronly lady and her heavyset bachelor son owned and operated the place.

While we were unloading our luggage we were introduced to an interesting gentleman who was evidently renting a room by the month. He was quite friendly and made us feel comfortable.

When we returned from eating at a little restaurant down the street, we joined other guests in the living room where the landlady had instructed us to "make ourselves right at home." The television set was on and those in the room were watching. TV was a novelty for our family. We didn't own a set and we didn't want one. Here, however, there was nothing else to do so we all sat down and watched.

Following few commercials, we were surprised to see the friendly man we had met earlier in that very same room, walk across the screen. He was a local television personality who just happened to be living in the rooming house we had checked into for a few days. It was an exciting and unexpected experience.

While in Colorado the children and I tried to find interesting things to do to occupy our time while your grandpa attended the conference. We went to the park, a museum, and investigated the downtown area of the little town. I mainly rested so that I would be up to driving the last lap of our journey home.

Mountain Driving

Soon after we headed out again we found ourselves in a mountainous area. [I had to insist that your grandpa drive through the mountain passes that took us out of Colorado. I knew my fears would be enough to keep me on the edge of my seat and that certainly would keep your grandpa awake.]

We were not aware that there was a better highway we could have taken and avoided the worst curves and passes. We would have missed some beautiful country, but as we pulled a small, rented trailer around those switch-backs, I'm sure we would have been glad to have settled for a more direct, and less mountainous route. When we finally came down to a normal highway again, I breathed a sigh of relief and took the wheel again, assured that we had endured the most difficult driving of our trip.

We approached our home state of California with anticipation and relief. The trip had become very long and tedious by the time we reached the state line. I was weary of driving but determined to make it the rest of the way home. Little did we realize that our biggest surprise, and our greatest hurdle still awaited us.

We had never been through the Sierra Nevada Mountains. All of us were anticipating seeing the beautiful country we had heard so much about. Our map indicated that we would be going through them that very day and then we would be home. This was before the old two-laned Highway 40 was replaced by Interstate 80, a large multi-laned freeway.

As we drove around a bend, the breathtaking mountain range came into view. We soon found ourselves on a winding highway that was even more frightening to me than Rabbit Ears Pass in Colorado. [Once again your grandpa mustered up strength to do the driving. One thing that really scares me is mountain driving.]

We could see on the map that we would be coming down into the foothills in a matter of a few hours. The prospect of reaching home before bedtime was most comforting to each of us.

An Interlude In The Wild

Soon after returning to our home in Sonoma, our extremely busy schedule was interrupted by news that the house we were renting was being put up for sale. This meant keeping the house ready to show, finding a place to move and being ready to move on short notice if it did sell. We had already been discussing the possibility of buying our own home so that the children would feel they had roots. We would also be building equity which would enable us to buy in another area should the Lord see fit to move us on. It was enough to make us start seriously scanning the ads in the newspaper and to pray in earnest.

[Your grandpa wanted very much to get his family out of town and into the country, so we began watching for ads "with acreage".] One particular five-acre parcel was located just over a small mountain range above Sonoma. It was raining the day we eagerly drove up the narrow, winding road through a wooded area we hadn't known existed. It felt as if we had been suddenly transported into another world.

The quiet beauty almost hypnotized us. The sound of falling rain, was accented by the occasional movement of some little animal darting about. We were too overwhelmed to break in with words.

We soon found the landmark we had been told to watch for, then the real estate sign assuring us we were in the right place.

Up ahead, a small cottage could be seen now and then as we made our way through the trees, which were so close together in places that they often intertwined. What a beautiful scene; the natural forest, dripping with a sudden summer rain, the stately trees so shiny and clean.

The downpour let up just as we were parking the car near the little house. We could imagine calling a place like this home.

The boys scurried off to investigate the trails as I called to them to be careful and not get lost. Our little tomboy daughter begged to follow them but I insisted she stay with us. We would check the hills around the place as soon as we explored the house, I promised her.

We soon saw the little cottage was not adequate for a family the size of ours. It was more the type of house that people build for a second home. We could dream anyway, and we did. We even discussed how we might add on to the existing structure.

By that time it was getting toward evening so we hurried out to keep our promise and explore around the house.

Some five hundred feet up the hill, at the end of a path leading up from the back door of the cottage, someone had built an arbor with a trellis on each side—something like a gazebo. We guessed that when it was clear you could probably see for miles over the valley from that vantage point. There was a small built-in table and bench inside the fascinating little structure. In my mind I saw it as a prayer retreat. I could see my Bible on the table, opened to a Scripture reference that was momentarily speaking to my heart. [Your grandpa found a good place for a garden and envisioned killing a mountain lion, as they had been reported to be on that mountain.] Each of us had our own thoughts and ideas as we scouted around the unusual setting.

As the twilight closed in, I began to imagine the reality of having to stay there alone at night. Secretly, I decided I wouldn't even want to be there alone in the day time. (It would be the perfect hideout for an escaped criminal.) As much as we were enjoying the dreamlike haven, I knew I would never feel secure living there.

It was starting to get dark but no one wanted to leave. We had all thoroughly enjoyed our brief respite. It was like a fleeting dream. All too soon we had to get back to work, and school, and life as it existed in the web we had woven ourselves into. Almost with reluctance, we returned the key to the realtor and steered our hopeful search toward a more practical home for our growing, active family.

A Pink Home Of Our Own

We kept our eyes and ears alert, hoping and praying for a home to buy. When a new subdivision in an area we liked and which was easily accessible to schools opened up, we entertained the idea of possibly buying a brand new house.

We found a new house that was in the process of being built and decided to buy it. We liked the idea of choosing colors, carpet, and other important incidentals which we ourselves would be living with. And I knew it would be clean.

Our congregation rejoiced with us as we watched the progress of our new home, anxiously awaiting the day when we could move in. I think they were all a little shocked the day they saw the house being painted pink, of all colors. It was my choice; others had to get used to it.

It was a joyous occasion the day we moved into our own pink home on Arroyo Way. It was a dream come true. It wasn't in the country, but Sonoma was a country-like town in those days, so it was right for us.

While construction in the new subdivision continued, a new hospital was also being erected just across the ravine in back of our new house. We liked the idea and it was timely; we were expecting another child. The old hospital was located up the mountain side. I was relieved to see the new one nearing completion. I helped initiate the new maternity ward at the hospital. Our number five son was the second baby born in the new medical facility. It was comforting to me to be able to look out the window of my room and see our home. [Your grandpa would walk over with the other children and let them peek through the window at their new baby brother and their mother.]

What a wonderful time that was. God was blessing our family and our church. The memories of those years fill large compartments in the archives of our memories.

Castles Of Gold

When we first began our ministry in Sonoma we did some canvassing in the area where we were holding our weekly classes to invite people to come to church. One of the contacts we made was an elderly couple who owned several acres next to the Astillis.

The Bakers had moved from Southern California several years earlier to retire. They were Christians and they told us they had been praying for a solid church in the area. They were thrilled to learn of our missionary efforts and offered to help us in various ways. We especially enjoyed their friendship and the Christian fellowship which we desperately needed, and so did they. They often asked us to their home for a meal and to pray with them. We had them in our home many times as well. The children thought of them as second grandparents.

The Baker's had a walnut orchard and a vineyard too, which was common in the Sonoma wine country. Their grapes did not end up in wine however, but in grape juice.

They also had dairy cows, a number of beef cattle, some horses, goats, ducks, and many chickens. They kept us supplied with fresh eggs and often meat too. When they had more milk than they could use, they insisted on sharing it with us. They were blessed as much in giving as we were in receiving.

A couple of times each year these good friends would spend three weeks in Kokomo, Indiana, with their children. At such times, they appreciated having us take care of their animals, watering their plants and generally looking after their place.

They were always looking for special ways to express their appreciation. Once when they returned from the Midwest, they brought us a beautiful set of dishes. It was the first complete set of dinnerware we had since the one given to me by my aunts when we were married. Now, when we bought our first home, the Bakers were excited along with us and insisted on helping with something we needed.

Mrs. Baker asked if she could go shopping with me and she suggested we look for drapes. She said she would pay for them but she wanted me to choose them. It was a difficult situation for me. I hated to choose the more expensive ones and I didn't want the cheapest ones. We had planned to wait until we could get what we really wanted. Mrs. Baker was sensitive, however. She could tell which drapes I liked, even though I had tried not to admire them too much. I loved them the minute I saw them. I had never seen such beautiful drapes. They were distinctive, unique, and quite expensive. I imagined how perfect they would look in our new living room and on the sliding glass door, opening onto the patio from the dining room. But they were far too expensive for me to wish or pray for—I thought.

My heart beat quickly when Mrs. Baker said to me, "Let me see those measurements." With hesitation I handed her the slip of paper I held in my hand. She in turn gave it to the clerk.

"See if you can fit these windows," she said with firmness, "with those pretty gold and green drapes. I can see she likes them."

"Oh, no", I protested. "They cost too much. I'm sure we can find something nice that's cheaper."

She didn't respond, although I was sure she heard me.

The clerk checked the sizes and soon my dear friend was paying for the lovely drapes that had seemed impossible for me to have.

As much as I tried to tell her she shouldn't have done it, Mrs. Baker assured me it was what the Lord wanted her to do. She was sure, she said. I thanked her, and I thanked my Heavenly Father, who had so many times given me the desires of my heart.

The Sonoma Valley Round Up

We were busy but very happy living in our pink house in Sonoma. In addition to our church and school activities everyone seemed to have their own projects going. There was no time for anyone to get bored and we never heard complaints that there was nothing to do. Music, art, sports—something challenging was always going on. One son decided to take a paper route to earn a little money for himself and learn some business tactics. The newspaper was published in another town and each day enough papers for his route were delivered to our home.

One day the circulation manager delivered the bundle of papers and stayed to talk with me.

"We need a correspondent for the valley," he told me. "Would you be interested in writing for us?"

It was so sudden, I didn't know how to answer. I told him I would have to think about it and discuss it with my husband.

While my interest in writing dated back to elementary school, my actual experience was limited to writing weekly promotions about our church for the local newspaper. The idea intrigued me. I decided to try it. After all, I did know a lot of people and I liked keeping up with what was going on.

The very next day when the circulation manager brought the newspapers, he gave me a small booklet with journalism guidelines, and suggested form. It turned out to be a very valuable source of help. He also brought me a stack of grayish newsprint to type my news items on. I was on my way. I was given a designated area that included several communities. I called my column *"The Sonoma Valley Round Up"*.

In addition to my regular roundup of news, I was asked to be on the alert for newsworthy feature stories, as well as "big ones" that could be used on the front page. I also furnished pictures and got paid for them by the column inch, just as I did my news copy.

The next morning, after I turned in my first batch of "newsworthy" items, including a couple scoops that I was really proud of, I received a call from the circulation manager.

"Mrs. Brown, are you sure you've had no experience writing for newspapers?" he asked. "Your work is good enough to print 'as is'. It needs no editing." He assured me I had journalistic ability. That was all the encouragement I needed. It launched me into the field of newspaper journalism. I was soon covering special events, fires and other emergencies, as well as the normal "who's doing what, when and where" type of community news that regularly filled my column.

I kept a pad by the phone and never picked up the receiver without a pen in my hand. I immediately began getting regular calls from various sources up and down the valley. There was always plenty of material for my column. It just sort of fell into my hands. And I almost always had some front page copy.

My own family made front page news for being the first to spot and report seeing Russia's startling scientific feat in space in the late fifties: an artificial satellite circling the earth. The editor played that one up big. Large headlines read, "OUR SONOMA VALLEY CORRESPONDENT AND FAMILY, FIRST IN AREA TO SEE SPUTNIK I". Others may have seen it first, but I was the first to report it to the newspaper for which I worked.

At first, the circulation manager picked up my copy when he delivered the newspapers to our home. After I had been writing for the newspaper for a few weeks, they notified me I would have to bring my copy into the office in person and by a specific deadline. I would present a scrapbook of my newspaper stories and pictures. They would measure them and pay me by the column inch, including headlines.

The *Petaluma Argus Courier* was published in Petaluma, a good half-hour drive from where we lived. Getting my material there on deadline was not easy but I always managed. The newspaper appreciated my dependability. They always gave me flattering headlines and seldom changed even one word of my copy. This gave me confidence in myself and challenged me to do my best. I worked for that newspaper for a year, until we moved completely out of the area. It was a good experience for me. It sharpened my writing skills, and taught me how to deadline, something the Lord knew I would be able to profit from later, in another ministry He would give me.

Please Send Someone To Help Us

Soon after we began services in our newly renovated chapel, we realized we were going to be needing teachers so that we could divide into classes for Sunday School. We had no one in our little congregation who was capable of teaching. The adults coming were all like a nest of hungry birds, waiting to be fed.

We also needed someone to lead the singing and a woman to help with the small children so that the young mothers who were starting to come could give their attention to the sermon and Bible teaching.

When God answered our prayers for help He sent us the perfect couple. They were able to teach classes during Sunday School and then assist us with the worship service.

We had met Doug and Mildred Cooper at one of the churches where we had conducted a Vacation Bible School. They had assisted with teaching there. When they came to Sonoma to visit our church, they recognized our need immediately. They went home and prayed about it, then called and offered to help us.

The Coopers were capable, cooperative and faithful workers. They drove many miles from their home in Vallejo to help us. A few years later Doug's health failed and they were unable to continue; we felt a great loss. Doug eventually died of a heart attack, at a fairly young age. By that time there were others who had started attending, and some who could help. Every week we had visitors from the community who had heard about our church. Sometimes they had just moved to the area and were seeking a church to identify with. Usually, they would start coming regularly.

When these new friends proved themselves and we felt comfortable with them, we would engage their help in Sunday School and other areas.

From time to time we had guests whose motives were not always pure, people who would try to influence our church away from the truth God had given us. He had given me the gift of discernment and I would sense the problem right away. I was well aware of the tactics of such people and prayed constantly that God would protect those He had given us charge of. [Your grandpa trusted my intuition and my prayers. We both knew we were vulnerable and we watched faithfully over our little flock, lest wolves sneak in among them and try to inject false doctrines.]

More than once we recognized threats and dealt firmly and quickly with the issue. Unfortunately, this was an ongoing problem which required persistent prayer and constant alertness. We also taught our people what the Bible says so that they would recognize error and the counterfeit. But we still watched out for them because they were young Christians and the evil one is so subtle.

It was thrilling to observe the growth and maturity of some of our young people. I remember one girl in particular. Dorothy came from a large family and had learned responsibility at home. She readily accepted the message of the Gospel and quickly blossomed into a beautiful and effective young Christian woman.

Dorothy asked if she could teach a Sunday School class of young children and studied hard to prepare the lessons. We knew she could not have learned more sitting in a class than she did preparing to teach. We were really proud of her. She was one of the rewards God gave us for our efforts in that needy field.

I was always aware that Dorothy admired me and I tried to be a good example to her. One of the things that intrigued her was the way I played the piano. She didn't know and I'm sure she wouldn't have cared if she had, that I never had a piano lesson. I didn't play that well and my timing was sometimes off.

One day Dorothy timidly asked me, "Do you think I could learn to play the piano?" She hesitated, then cautiously ventured, "Could you teach me?" It was an honest, straightforward request. I hesitated, not knowing what to say. But Dorothy quickly responded, as if she could read my mind.

"I'll help you with your work," she offered. "I could do your ironing maybe."

"That's sweet of you, Dorothy." I replied, smiling to break the tension. I could see it was very important to her.

"Sure," I promised. "I'll be glad to teach you as much as I know."

She was determined and dedicated. In a short time Dorothy could play the piano better than I could. Her parents were pleased. They scraped the money together to buy her an old upright piano. She was soon playing for Sunday School and then for the worship service. Her folks, who by that time were attending regularly, beamed with pride at Dorothy's accomplishment.

Dorothy was the oldest child in her large family and heavily depended upon at home. We sometimes felt she was required to assume too much responsibility. Dorothy was a jewel in God's kingdom and in our church. We thanked the Lord for her progress and for her contribution to the work in Sonoma.

The Captain Of The Lord's Host

Your grandpa worked very hard at his job at Hamilton Air Force Base and even harder in our ministry in Sonoma. I was greatly concerned that he had to work two jobs when he was not physically able to handle one. He would have loved so much to have given his entire strength and time to the ministry which God had assigned to us. His heart was in the ministry and God was blessing it. Unfortunately, our little church was a missionary project and the congregation was made up of families who could hardly support themselves.

They were willing to give, and they did, but they had very little to give. If there had been only the two of us it would have been different. But God blessed us with a large family. [Your grandpa knew it was his responsibility to provide for them. He was never resentful; he simply went on working and serving the Lord with all the strength he had.]

Upon the advice of his doctor, we tried to make sure your grandpa had at least a two week break from his job and the ministry every year. However when he had built up vacation time there was always the temptation to get caught up with things around home. It was a constant battle.

He loved to attend pastor's conferences and seminars. It gave him an opportunity to fellowship with other ministers and to pick up some new ideas, as well as to rest his weary body. It was the kind of vacation that was most refreshing for him. I tried to see that other things did not interfere, even though it was very difficult for me.

The first time he left us at home alone, it was a real crisis for me. I wanted so much for him to go for his sake, but I was afraid to stay alone because we lived outside of town and there were no near neighbors. We were surrounded on three sides by vineyards and across the road from a world famous winery. I never liked that. It was lonely and frightening at night. Now that I was facing the prospects of staying alone with the children for a whole week while their father was in another state, I was paralyzed with fear.

The morning he left and we said goodbye I kept a brave front, for his sake and the children. But as soon as he had gone I fell into a chair, clutching my Bible and praying for strength to overcome my fears.

My Bible fell open to the book of Joshua. I began reading in chapter five, verses 13-15. Suddenly I was standing beside one of my favorite Bible characters—Joshua. I felt like I was on holy ground; that God was there with me, just like He was with Joshua. I worshipped along with Joshua, realizing that God was indeed with me. I believe it was Jesus Himself who declared to Joshua that He was the Captain of the Lord's hosts, or the Lord's army as some Bible translations say. Joshua no longer had need to be afraid of what the enemy might attempt to do. Oh, how that spoke to my heart. [That's what I love about this wonderful treasure we have—the Bible. It comforts, guides, and quiets our fears in any situation. Oh, how I love it!] God seemed to be showing me that the Captain of the Lord's hosts was likewise watching over me and my children and that I did not need to be afraid.

The experience was so real I felt brave and strong from that moment on. I slept peacefully that night which for me was a miracle.

The next morning I was amazed to find that I had not only forgotten to lock the front door, I had not even closed it completely. We had slept safely all night with the front door in such a position that someone could easily have pushed it open without making a sound. I thanked the Lord for His protection that night and for taking away my fears. [The rest of the time your grandpa was away, I was a braver wife and mother, as I held down the fort at home.]

Andy and Roancy

[When your grandpa called from Colorado I could hardly wait to tell him about my experience. He also had something exciting to tell me. We both wanted to talk at the same time.]

He was having a great time and had met some interesting people. It made me happy to hear him sound so refreshed.

"I met this neat guy named Andy," he told me. "And guess what? He's from Sonoma."

What a wonderful coincidence. Andy's parents and brothers lived on the same street our little church was on. We had been by their place many times.

Andy was working with a group called The Navigators headquartered in Colorado Springs. The Navigators was a fairly new organization at that time. It's purpose was to follow up on people who had become Christians through the Billy Graham crusades, which were becoming increasingly popular across the country.

[During time off from the conference at Manitou Springs, Andy took your grandpa to the Navigator's facilities, called Glen Eyrie, near Colorado Springs. He was given a grand tour of the beautiful old mansion which the Navigator's had purchased and developed into offices, a training facility, and a conference center. Your grandpa had so much to tell me about Andy and about the conference, he almost forgot to ask how we were doing at home. I thought I was never going to get to tell him about my "meeting" with Joshua and the Captain of the Lord's hosts. He was delighted to hear what I was so anxious to tell him. There was so much we wanted to say but we couldn't afford to talk too long, long distance.]

"I mailed you a long letter today," he told me as we said goodbye. I knew writing letters was a real chore for him so I really appreciated him making the effort and taking the time to write me.

In his letter he went into detail about the conference. He was particularly impressed with a Jewish rabbi who had come to speak to the ministers. The rabbi explained what the Jews believed and why, from the viewpoint of a modern Jew. It was an enlightening experience for the Protestant ministers attending the conference and it helped them to understand the Old Testament Scriptures better. The rabbi enjoyed his contact with the ministers as well. [Your grandpa also wrote that they had a great opportunity to discuss the New Testament with him, and at times it almost seemed that he was convinced that Jesus was indeed the Messiah. His fat, newsy letter from Colorado contained still more about his new friend Andy and the Navigators. And I knew he would have a lot more to tell me when he got home.]

From the time of that eventful week in Colorado, whenever Andy came to Sonoma to visit his family, we always spent a lot of time together. The three of us enjoyed many precious hours of sweet Christian fellowship. We would sit up until after midnight talking about the Lord and His work and discussing the Bible.

Andy enjoyed our children and they loved him. He looked forward to someday having children of his own. Some friends of his dubbed him an "old bachelor", but he wasn't planning to always be that way. He was praying for a special wife and he was willing to wait for her. Andy expressed his desires freely with us, and we prayed often with him about this important matter. The three of us prayed together for his requests and for ours. Our fellowship in prayer was rich and powerful.

A few years later, Andy took a teaching job in Watsonville, California. He liked the area and decided to build a home there in anticipation of sharing it with the wife he was trusting the Lord to provide. It was during that time that he met Roancy, a young woman from the Midwest who was also teaching school in the same area.

Roancy was the one God sent in answer to our prayers. She was above and beyond the dreams and expectations of Andy and us. They fell deeply in love and were married and lived happily in the home that Andy had built, believing his prayers would be answered. Their story was a great example of how God works—in His time, and in His way, when we put our trust in Him.

Andy and Roancy and their lovely family now live on the old home place in Sonoma, not far from the old Astilli ranch.

Those busy, fruitful years in Sonoma included some of the most challenging experiences in our life and ministry, and certainly many of the most cherished memories as well as the most rewarding answers to prayer.

* * *   * * *   * * *

"Oh, look what time it's getting to be. We've been talking for a long time. You've been good listeners, but I can see you're getting sleepy now. So am I. There will be other times for me to tell you more. Goodnight all!"

CHAPTER 17

Hoen Home and Horizons Beyond

"This is a very interesting room, Grandma," Karl observed as he came into my office studio. He was interested in anything having to do with electronics. He knew something about the ministries God had given me, but he didn't know how they came to be.

"I can't believe you know how to use all this equipment, Grandma," he said, partly teasing but serious too.

"Well, I do," I assured him.

"Could you please tell us about how you learned," his sister Tania asked as she sat down in a chair nearby.

"I'd love to," I told them, "but it's a long story. This all happened after we moved to Santa Rosa."

"Please, can we talk about that right now?" Karl wanted to know.

"Bring in another chair and make yourself comfortable," I invited. "I think you'll be surprised at some of the things I want to tell you."

*** *** ***

From Sonoma To Santa Rosa

During our busy years of missionary service in Sonoma we made many friends among pastors and Christian workers in the surrounding areas. We needed the fellowship that we enjoyed as we shared each other's triumphs and special needs in prayer. We took urgent requests given to us in strict confidence to heart, and prayed for the crisis situations.

Our good friends who headed up the American Sunday School Union ministry in Santa Rosa often asked us to pray about some critical request. When the Sunday School they had started in the Santa Rosa area became large enough that it needed to be organized as a church and begin holding worship services, they naturally asked us to pray with them about it.

They invited your grandpa to visit the Sunday School and discuss the advantages of being organized. We were sincerely praying with our friends that God would help them find the right pastor. It was evident to us it needed to be someone with a missionary heart. Just as we had observed in Vallejo and in Sonoma, we could see that part of Santa Rosa was just as much a mission field as Hawaii.

Since we were in on the need and asked to pray, we diligently did so. Unbeknownst to us, our friends were praying differently. They were asking God to lay it upon our hearts to come to Santa Rosa and help organize the church. The Sunday School group at Santa Rosa loved us. They too were praying a similar prayer—that we would be willing to come to Santa Rosa and become their first pastor. We had not actually considered the possibility that we might be the ones God would choose to use in the work there.

[Your grandpa and I had discussed the idea between ourselves that the Sonoma church might benefit from having a new pastor. We felt that after the number of years we had been there they sometimes took us for granted. We were faithful and really had no secret motive to leave Sonoma, but at times we did wonder if God was not preparing us for a new challenge.] Just at the right moment, our American Sunday School Union friends approached us with the direct question, "Would YOU ask the Lord if it is His will for you to come to Bellevue?"

At that point we began to consider the proposal objectively. Finally, after much prayer, we had the assurance that God was indeed calling us to organize and pastor the new church in Santa Rosa. As had happened so often before, we began to see God work in such a definite way, we couldn't doubt His will.

The Hoen Avenue House

Our congregation in Sonoma was shocked when we told them we were going to be leaving. We tried to explain to them that they would soon learn to love a new pastor and that they would find that God would bless their church under fresh new leadership.

It's always difficult to leave a flock that you have shepherded for several years. Many deep friendships develop. Parting is always painful. We dreaded leaving, but we knew it was a necessary part of following the Lord in His service. We had to sell our house in Sonoma and find a place to buy in Santa Rosa. It was all too much for us to handle in our own strength so as always, we put it in God's hands and waited for Him to work in His usual wonderful way.

We had a real estate agent help us sell our home in Sonoma and another one show us around Santa Rosa. In our prayerful search we found an older home situated on one and a half acres, but still inside the city limits. There was a creek running across the back of the property and another across the road in front. The two small streams merged as they flowed into a city park, a block and a half up the street.

The house was conveniently located close to elementary and junior high schools, and a brand new high school was nearing completion next to a nearby shopping center. There was also a junior college on the opposite side of town. It seemed like the perfect place to raise our big family.

We loved the older home at first sight. It was situated near the center of the property and back from the street. It had a spacious porch across the front. A window in the front gable gave the false impression that there were rooms upstairs.

The closest neighbor on one side was a widow lady with orchard acreage which she insisted on holding on to, even though the city was growing around it. On the other side of the driveway was a small, neat cottage which sat quite far back. An elderly German man lived there alone. I'm sure neither of them exactly relished the idea of having a large family of children move into the big house in between them. An older gentleman whose wife had died the previous year lived in the house we were looking at. As we approached the house, we noticed the welcome atmosphere about it. The place had clearly been loved and taken care of.

We couldn't help noticing the sad countenance of the man who came to the door. He stood quietly by as the real estate lady showed us through his home.

As we went from room to room I commented on the unusual fireplace, the interesting bay window, and the unique risers for flower pots in front of it. I admired the kitchen and breakfast nook. I expressed my admiration for the beautiful hardwood floors and the lovely oriental rug in the living room. A huge, ornate grandfather clock stood imposingly in the corner of the living room. I had never been so close to such a beautifully crafted clock. The owner was obviously pleased that I liked his house so much. He was touched when I expressed sincere admiration for the things that had meant much to him and his late wife. I noticed that now and then he would attempt to thwart impending tears with the back of his hand. This house was precious to him. He had spent many happy years there with his family. The exquisite clock had ticked away many hours of pleasure as well as pain as he and his dear wife reared their children there. We could see that the thought of leaving was difficult for him. His son and daughter insisted he sell the place and move to a guest home where he would be looked after and assured of regular meals.

Until the day we showed our appreciation for the things that meant so much to him, this dear man had been reluctant to discuss selling his home. From that day on he responded differently.

On another visit to see the place because I wanted to check it out further, he was anxiously awaiting our arrival. He told me he would like to give me the lovely grandfather clock that I had been so enthralled with.

I hardly knew how to react, but he was serious. When he mentioned his intentions to his son, however, the matter ended. His son had other ideas for the clock. The lonely old man was terribly disappointed. I hugged him and told him it was all right, I understood. I can still see the hurt in his eyes. I knew it was painful for him not to be able to make his own decisions anymore nor to be able to keep his word. Our hearts ached for him.

The real estate lady told us he had not wanted to sell to a couple with young children until he met us. He was impressed with our well-behaved children. When she saw his reaction to us and how much we liked the place, she was sure she had a sale. We discussed the property at length in her office. She kept figuring numbers and preparing papers for us to sign, not doubting that we would.

[As you've gathered from things I've told you before, your grandpa and I never acted impulsively on decisions of such magnitude. We knew we could not do so in this instance either.]

When we told her we would have to pray about it, she insisted a "buy" like this wouldn't last. Someone was sure to grab it. We assured her that if it was God's will that we get the house, it would still be available; no one could possibly buy it out from under us.

When we went in a few days later to sign the agreement, the real estate agent told us she had been selling properties for more than fifteen years and never before had she had anyone tell her they had to pray about the decision before buying a home.

Several weeks later when all of our real estate transactions were completed, we moved from Sonoma to Santa Rosa. On a beautiful Memorial Day weekend, the men in our Sonoma church sadly helped us move our furniture and belongings to our new Hoen Avenue address. We had mixed emotions ourselves. We loved those precious people dearly. We shed many tears in parting.

[Your grandpa was impressed with the large commercial-size garage on the property, where he would be able to work easily on our forever-ailing automobiles. There was also a barn on our new property and a small smokehouse between the house and barn. Next to it was a small cottage that had once been used as maid-quarters, evidence that wealthy people had once lived there.]

We were all happy about the creek at the back. I was glad to have it separate us from our more "citified" neighbors on the other side. Our active young sons and our little tomboy daughter anticipated many happy hours of fishing in the stream. [Your grandpa and I were both thrilled with the large, fenced garden plot. We noticed the rich, black adobe soil which we had heard was difficult to cultivate, but conducive to good plant growth.]

The well established grapevines growing on a pretty trellis and the numerous fruit trees awaiting our identification were other special bonuses. Perhaps the most thrilling of all were the eight large English walnut trees, two of them with more than a fifty foot spread.

[Those huge, healthy walnut trees became your grandpa's most prized possessions. He loved to show them off when friends stopped by to see our new home in Santa Rosa.]

The information sheet describing the property stated that the walnut crop from one or two of the trees had been sufficient to pay the taxes on the place in previous years. We liked that idea.

We discovered many pleasant surprises after we moved into our newly acquired acreage on Hoen Avenue. We quickly saw that it would be a long time before the children would have reason to become bored, there were so many things to do on the property. But if they did, there was a wonderful city park just up the street. We were thoroughly convinced that God has led us to the house we were supposed to have and we never ceased thanking Him for the answer to our prayers.

A New Church at Bellevue

We could hardly wait to get settled in so that we could get on with our new ministry in the rural area of Bellevue, a part of Santa Rosa.

We arrived on the scene with a vision of organizing the thriving American Sunday School Union group into a church and beginning morning worship services following the Sunday School hour.

The people in that community were eager and anxious to learn more about God and the Bible. Serving them was a pleasure. They had not had a regular pastor before and really appreciated us.

[Your grandpa had a special way with people. He would endear himself to them almost immediately. His success with this group was inevitable.]

They loved me also. There was a lot for a pastor's wife to do. I worked with the women, taught a Sunday School class of fifth grade boys, and played the piano for both Sunday School and church. The young people were drawn to me, too. Often, they would gather around the piano to sing favorite songs and learn new ones.

I particularly enjoyed my class of boys—future young men, if you please. I poured my heart into the study of the Scriptures and teaching those precious boys. And I tried to inspire them to study the Bible for themselves. It was thrilling to the whole class when they would share their startling discoveries in God's Word with their classmates and their teacher.

Two of the boys were brothers. Their mother was an alcoholic but their father, who was of Russian descent, saw to it that they came to Sunday School and church. He took great pride in the fact that his sons were learning to be students of the Scriptures.

The father sometimes talked with us about his concern for his wife. He told us more than once that he did not want his sons to follow in the footsteps of their mother. He would express his faint hope that she would find her way out of the maze of alcoholism that she was trapped in. She herself hated the way she was but considered herself hopelessly bound. We talked and prayed with her. We longed to help her get free. She would weep and tell us how sorry she was about the way she was hurting her family.

"I'm never going to touch a drop of the stuff again," she would vow. And she meant it too. She really and truly wanted to stop drinking and living the dangerous lifestyle she was caught up in. The poor lady would go off to a bar for one drink and be gone for days. Her family would have no idea where she was. Then, one day the inevitable happened. Late one night while driving drunk, this poor woman whose life was completely out of control crashed into an oncoming car. The driver of the other vehicle and his passengers were all seriously injured. Another enslaved life ended in tragedy. How my heart hurt for the young brothers in my Sunday School class. It was a terrible experience for such young boys. I was thankful that God had allowed us to be there when this family needed us so much.

I had the thrilling privilege of leading each of the boys in my class to the Lord. In this difficult time of bereavement, the young brothers were comforted by the Holy Spirit. They were also able to help their father and their older brother through the difficult time.

The Visitor

The first summer in our new home in Santa Rosa we were extremely busy with our new church and our big family, but those were memorable days and we loved them. It seemed there were never enough hours in the day to accomplish all that we wanted to get done. In addition to our Sunday services at the church, we held a midweek Bible study in our home. We encouraged neighbors and friends as well as our parishioners to attend.

A missionary friend who was home on an extended furlough to care for her aging and ill mother taught the class for us. She had spent twenty-seven years in Venezuela. In addition to being an excellent Bible teacher, she shared many of her experiences on the field with us. No one wanted to miss a single session. It was a good missionary exposure for our people. God richly blessed her ministry in our home.

Of necessity your grandpa still had to commute daily to Hamilton Air Force Base after we moved to Santa Rosa. He was fortunate to be able to get into another car pool but he was always weary by the time he got home. He could not possibly manage time to prepare to teach a midweek class. He did well to get his Sunday messages ready. You can understand how we appreciated the help of Miss Ruth Battey for our Wednesday night class. We were unable to carry out a satisfactory visitation ministry as we so much longed to do. He did manage to handle emergency situations as they arose, but as I look back I don't remember how. I know I tried to help as much as I could, and I was constantly coming up with ideas to make it easier for him and to get more done.

One of the heaviest burdens on our hearts was to be able to contact people in the community and to make a spiritual impact on them, regardless of whether they would attend our church or not.

[Your grandpa was thrilled with my idea to help accomplish that goal—a newsletter which we would mail on a regular basis to as many in the community as the church could afford to.]

We called our new publication "*The Visitor*", an appropriate name we believed, because it could go where we wanted to go in person but couldn't. In fact it could get into some places we could never go. It proved to be quite effective. I hatched the idea, created the format, chose the content, and did the layout. [Your grandpa printed *"The Visitor"* on our pitifully antiquated and dilapidated mimeograph machine.]

In those days, I had to type the master on those old-fashioned blue stencils, which I doubt if any of you have ever seen. The process was extremely hard on my eyes. Just typing was difficult for me. I couldn't type fast and I made many mistakes, which had to be corrected before we could print the stencils. I had to draw the illustrations, and I am not an artist. Overall, it was an amateur effort but it was a step in the right direction. Printing and mailing the little publication was costly and time-consuming, but we were convinced it was the next best thing to personal contact.

At first we printed the newsletter on both sides of letter sized paper and folded it twice into a convenient mailing size. We sent *"The Visitor"* out every week for several months, then decided to mail it out every other week instead. Some time later we began printing it on legal size paper, added a sheet, and started mailing it monthly. It turned out to be an attractive eight-page publication which we were happy to take credit for. We soon began getting response through the mail and by telephone.

Over a period of time we made numerous contacts, some of which resulted in people attending our church. Only eternity will reveal the results of that concentrated effort. We attempted to make each issue thought-provoking, always trying to keep our church announcements to a minimum and include as much interesting, soul-searching material as possible.

A Wonderful Door Opens

As autumn approached, your grandpa decided I needed a little diversion from my heavy schedule. He knew my interest in writing was not being fulfilled, so he insisted I enroll in a writers' workshop class at the local junior college.

When a brochure arrived in the mail with details about a writing class, we were reminded of the art classes I had taken in Vallejo and how much I had been refreshed by the experience. I hated to leave him with all the children after he had worked hard all day, but it was his idea and he did not give in when I tried to refuse to go. He argued that it would give him an opportunity to do things with the children. Often he would ask me to let him prepare dinner too, with the children's help, so he could do something with them. He was a good cook like his mother had been. He had learned the skills of cooking while helping her as a boy. He knew how much it would mean to the children. And mother's night out proved to be all he had hoped it would be.

The class was interesting and informative. Our teacher knew how to bring out the best in each of us and she was patient with new students, which I appreciated. I discovered that it was an ongoing class; some of her students had been taking the course every semester since she started teaching it. It was open to anyone interested in any type of writing—

fiction, nonfiction, poetry, play writing, anything anyone wanted to write.

Students were required to write something fresh for every class. During the hours from 7:00 to 10:00 p.m., someone, usually our teacher, would read as many manuscripts as possible. We never knew from week to week whose work would be read or whose might be left out, due to lack of time. It kept us all on our toes.

It was difficult for me to manage time to write or to attend the class each week. I had to learn and practice time management. My experience in writing for a newspaper had been good preparation for future endeavors. It sharpened my skills and taught me to deadline.

Our teacher insisted we try various types of writing. With practice I found I could write fiction and nonfiction and I had my appetite whetted to someday write a book. I learned how to pull ideas from the air and to develop them on paper. Learning by doing was very effective. I found creative writing to be stimulating and fulfilling.

One of the interesting things about our class was the variety of the people who attended.

One young Russian woman wrote fascinating and refreshing humor. She always kept the class roaring with laughter. Goldie, an older woman who had been coming to the class for a long time, wrote and read her own monologues. We all looked forward to her presentation each week. Her unique, droll style of reading made her writing even funnier. She derived a great sense of accomplishment and satisfaction from her writing class, even though she never achieved her dream of being published. Then there was Linda, a young mother with two babies. Her husband, like mine, had insisted she enroll in the class, but for a different reason. Linda had a drinking problem and her husband hoped she would develop her slight interest in writing and be able to escape the boredom at home which he felt was driving her more and more to drinking.

Linda had a great deal of talent but unfortunately, her addiction had enslaved her. Her search for fulfillment in creativity lost out to her craving for alcohol. I prayed for her, talked to her, befriended her and tried to inspire her to write more but it was no use. She finally had to drop out of the class. We were all disappointed to see her go. I never saw Linda again. It made me sick at heart to think about what may have happened to her.

We had some men in class too, but more women. One man wrote intriguing short stories with surprise endings. He started getting his stories published soon after he enrolled in the class.

Many students wrote poetry, some of which was quite good. Others just tried to get a few lines down in order to make them eligible for class. One of the most fascinating people in our class joined the following spring, after I started in the fall. She was a retired female doctor from Southern California. She had just moved to the area and at the time was experiencing marital problems. A teenage son, born to her late in life, was also generating tremendous stress in her life. She was not coping well.

A friend suggested Clara enroll in Mrs. Goodrich's writing class, more for therapy than anything else. She had never written anything in her life, and was not the slightest bit interested in writing. But when she learned that to be eligible for the class she would have to write something each week, she accepted the challenge, thinking it would keep her occupied and distract her from her problems.

Dr. Coleman happened to be an avid gardener. Our teacher suggested she write about things that interested her most, so she chose gardening. By the time the first semester was over, everything she wrote was being accepted by an organic gardening magazine and they were begging for more. It was almost instant success for her.

Although Dr. Coleman was quite a bit older than I was, we became good friends. I appreciated her talent, and she was a vibrant, interesting person. She desperately needed a caring friend and often confided in me the details of her complex problems. I tried to help her spiritually but I never knew how effective my efforts were.

As a minister's wife and mother of a large family I found plenty to write about. I was one of the few in class who attempted several different types of writing. Classmates liked me but they hardly knew what to expect from a minister's wife. I was always aware that I was somewhat in question and perhaps suspect in many ways. Even so, I was actively engaged in the sessions and tried to take advantage of all the class had to offer.

Learning By Proxy

Not long after I enrolled in Mrs. Goodrich's class, I discovered an advertisement in a Christian magazine describing a correspondence course on Christian writing. I was intrigued since that was the kind of writing I really wanted to do. I felt I could handle the two courses at the same time and hopefully they would overlap, so I enrolled in the Christian Writer's Institute of Chicago.

The initial course consisted of ten basic lessons. As each lesson was completed I would write my assignment and have it read in my writer's workshop class. My classmates who knew me would evaluate and criticize it before I would send it in. This feedback was invaluable. Inevitably sharp ears would catch something I had missed.

That first year of intense study, combining the two classes, was a true test of time management for me. I had to juggle all my responsibilities and constantly pray for God's help in keeping my priorities in focus. As much as I loved writing and learning in school, my greatest desire was to be a good wife and to assist my minister husband with our Christian outreach in the community. Fortunately I was young and healthy and able to do more than some people believed one person could do. Maybe I tried to do too much but it was my nature to be busy, ambitious and creative. And I loved meeting challenges. There were highlights and rewards along the way, and each one beckoned me on to higher heights. One of those was the day I received a check for an article I had submitted to a leading Christian magazine.

Since it was the first article I had ever submitted, I was braced for another rejection slip to add to those I had received for some short stories which had been returned. I was reluctant to open the letter when I took it from the mailbox.

Imagine my surprise when I saw a check for $30.00. I let out a squeal and ran to find your grandpa to tell him the exciting news. My joy knew no bounds. I was elevated above the earth's atmosphere, floating on clouds. Your grandpa was really proud of me. He wasn't a bit surprised. He thought I could do anything.

While I was bouncing around with excitement he ran for the camera and took my picture holding the prized check so that I could capture the success I felt at that moment. This was the biggest boost I had received in young writing career.

My classmates at the college were also thrilled for me. They too assured me that they were not surprised. Dr. Coleman was so excited she kept wiping tears from her eyes. My success thrilled the whole class.

A Mother At Forty

Although I worked hard at my writing, I never felt I was letting my children down or failing my family in any way. They all knew how much I enjoyed writing and taking classes, especially at their daddy's insistence.

They were also pleased to have that special time with him. We were busy and happy and not at all prepared for the big surprise when I discovered that I was pregnant again. It was the furthest thing from our thoughts, especially mine. [When I mentioned my suspicion to your grandpa he thought it was highly unlikely, but it wasn't long until we knew for sure. Then we broke the news to the rest of the family.]

The initial surprise soon became a shock when I began thinking about having a baby at my age. I would be forty when the baby was born. Even so, everyone was terribly excited and could hardly wait.

We waited as long as we could before springing the news at church. Some people feel sorry for you when you have several children. Often they make remarks that are well-meaning but sometimes come across badly. We were not ready for that. It really hurts when others suggest you already have enough children. We kept it our family secret until we could keep it no longer. When we did tell our church family, they too were surprised but most were pleased and supportive. When I finally got up nerve enough to make my announcement during the spring semester of my college class, those who hadn't already suspected looked rather amazed. After the initial look of surprise on some faces, all joined in to wish me well. I debated whether to drop out of the class but decided not to when everyone begged me to stay. They thought it would be special to have a new baby in our writer's class family. My baby was due soon after school would be letting out for the summer.

As the months dragged by, my concern about having a baby at my age intensified. I had heard so many scary stories, it was hard to keep from thinking about them. A respected doctor I knew told me that such babies are often mentally deficient, but that I shouldn't worry about it. Sometimes, he said, they are exceptionally intelligent. I would simply be taking that chance.

I had plenty to pray about during those months of waiting. I tried to keep my mind off the negative and kept very busy with church work, duties at home, and my writing projects. I found writing helped alleviate the stress of living with an uneasy outlook. Certain "knowledgeable" students in my class assured me that keeping active mentally was very important. It would contribute toward a healthy, intelligent baby, they promised. Their encouragement was welcome and helpful. My teacher kept telling me, "Ardelle, be sure to name that baby a good name for a writer. It will no doubt be a creative child."

I managed to complete the spring semester. Then, in June, our wonderful baby boy arrived. At first sight, it was evident he was a normal, healthy child. I thought he looked "smart" from the very moment he was born. The doctor commented that he was certainly a fine baby and we didn't have anything to worry about. I thanked God for answering my anxious prayers. Soon after he was born I found myself crying constantly. I could not seem to stop. I thought it was because I was so relieved that my baby was all right. I had already had seven babies but I had never experienced what the nurse referred to as "baby blues". I was not aware of what was happening to me. The feelings I was experiencing were frightening. I didn't realize I was undergoing a complete hormonal change.

When I arrived home with our new little son, I had the undivided attention and support of the rest of the family. There wasn't a hint of resentment. I don't think anyone felt there were too many of us either. Everyone was too busy loving the new baby and helping care for him.

Seven Plus Three

One day when our baby was about one year old, a crisis situation in the community challenged our entire way of life. Three teenaged boys, friends of our older sons, suddenly had to be removed from the foster home in which they were living at the time.

When a place for them to stay could not be found, we were approached. We knew they were well-behaved youngsters. They had been in our home many times. Now they were asking pleadingly if they could come live with us.

We hurriedly called our children into a family conference session and explained the situation to them. We really didn't have room in our house but we quickly made room in our hearts. We knew we could manage it somehow, even though it wouldn't be easy.

Without the slightest hesitation, the children begged us to let Art and Harry, two Mexican brothers, and Jerry, a full-blooded "California Pomo" Native American Indian, come live with us. Since most of the work and responsibility would fall on me, your grandpa insisted the final decision should be mine.

It was a difficult decision to make. The plight of the boys with no place to go tugged at my heart. I knew they needed a family atmosphere. But I also had to think of the welfare of my own family. I was sure our children could not foresee the changes having these three boys come to live with us would create in our household. I knew we, as parents, were responsible for making a wise decision.

We had to pray fervently and quickly. An answer was needed at once. We finally decided we could not turn the boys away, so we took them in, hoping a place could still be found for them.

Our new family now consisted of our own seven, the youngest an infant, our oldest a teen in high school, and now three more teenagers who looked to us as foster parents. All were boys except one. Our daughter had three older brothers and three younger ones, and now three older foster brothers as well.

There were drastic adjustments and plenty of work involved, but we had wonderful, rewarding times together. Jerry was quite a comedian. We realized his acting was probably a front which he put on, an outward attempt to keep those around him laughing so they wouldn't suspect his inner pain. It was a safety valve that enabled him to let go of some of the pressure inside of him and keep him from exploding. He had been taken from his mother because she was considered an unfit parent. Even so, he still loved her. Jerry had so much love to give and he made me the recipient. He not only loved deeply, he had a great need to be loved in return. He absorbed our family's love like a sponge.

I somehow managed to stretch my love to go around. A conscious effort was required to keep my own children from being jealous. Fortunately they were understanding and helpful. Their hearts went out to their foster brothers who had not had loving parents and a supportive family like they had. Our whole family worked hard to make these displaced boys feel loved and a part of us.

Learning and Doing Things Together

Every day was filled with new activities and experiences.

Your grandpa taught all the children how to cut hair. He volunteered himself as a guinea pig for each to learn on, then he supervised as they cut each other's hair. This procedure really tickled Jerry. He never stopped laughing about how brave "Brother Brown" was to let an Indian "scalp" him.

When we took the boys in, our home was really inadequate for that many children. There was room, however, in our attic for a couple of small bedrooms. When we had first moved in we discussed the possibility of remodeling to include upstairs rooms but we had always been so busy we kept putting it off. Now that we desperately needed the space the project was undertaken. [Your grandpa enlisted the assistance of a bunch of eager-to-learn boys and an inquisitive little girl.]

The enormous project was quite a learning process for all of us. Over a period of time, we all learned how to turn space into bedrooms and how to construct stair steps to access them. We also moved the two-room cottage on the property and attached it to the house. This provided two additional bedrooms and gave us all the room we needed. All of the children were good workers. Our foster sons especially enjoyed helping with the regular chores. At the time we did not have a dishwasher. The boys almost fought for the privilege of helping me in the kitchen. We had to come up with a schedule so that each of them felt they got their fair share of time with me. No one ever complained that there was too much work, only that they didn't get to be with me enough. [Can you imagine fighting to get to wash dishes?] Mealtimes were fun. We had a large, round table that could accommodate all twelve of us with the extra leaves in. Our foster sons loved everything I cooked. I always tried to include foods they enjoyed in the menu. Jerry loved artichokes. He actually taught our family to eat them. He was delighted to see us enjoy them.

[Your grandpa insisted that dinner conversation be pleasant. No bickering, quarreling or complaining was allowed. Any troublesome situation had to be dealt with away from the table.]

After we prayed and while we ate, each one had an opportunity to share about their day. Sometimes we would get so involved in mutual sharing that we would run over into dessert time. Usually, however, one of the children would be eyeing the peach cobbler or lemon meringue pie and when they could stand it no longer, they would call out, "It's time for dessert!" This always brought everyone to rapt attention. No one wanted to wait any longer than they had to for the special dessert I always planned because I knew it meant so much to them.

We shared the good times and we shared the bad. When one of our foster sons felt "down", as they often did, everyone rallied to cheer him up. Jerry, especially, fought that problem. He mourned for his mother because he was not allowed to see her. Sometimes he would tell me all he remembered about her. Even though he was a teenager, he would cry and confess to me,

"I love my mother and I want to see her." That would tear my heart out. I would give him special attention to help him through those rough times.

During the time Jerry lived with us, he got the mumps. We were aware of how dangerous this was for him. Our whole family rallied around and gave him the best of care. He also got chicken pox that same year. I'm sure he wouldn't have received better care anywhere, or received more love. I know the Lord blessed him by letting him suffer those two illnesses while living with us.

All the boys accepted the Lord Jesus as their Savior and they gladly attended church with us. They loved Sunday School and enjoyed even more hearing their dear "Brother Brown", whom they loved and respected, preach. His words carried weight with them; they knew he practiced what he preached and taught. The church congregation took our "added" sons to heart, too. They were made to feel very much a part of the church family. I'm sure that was one of the reasons they loved to go to church so much.

The following year Harry and Art went to live with an uncle. Jerry continued to live with us. He begged to stay. I really don't remember exactly how long he ended up staying with us but he truly endeared himself to us during those years.

For a while we lost track of Jerry. At one point we heard that he had been killed in a Greyhound Bus accident. Much to our surprise and our gratitude, several years later we learned that he was still alive, had a large family, and that he was a minister of the Gospel. Still later, I received a letter from his wife Nancy saying Jerry had died from an illness.

Given An Amplified Voice

During the time we had our foster sons I continued with my classes at the college, and my lessons by mail. I completed my ten-lesson course during the spring semester. The last lesson included a brief section on each of several types of writing and called for an assignment in whichever particular field I found most interesting and might want to pursue. I chose script writing. I was instructed to write a sample radio script, whether I was really interested in going on the air or not, and to take it to a local radio station and get their reaction.

After spending considerable time writing and rewriting, timing and checking my manuscript, I took it to my class at the college for their unbiased input and criticism.

Since I would be reading it if I went on the air, my teacher insisted I read the script in front of the class. I'm sure I learned a lot by doing that. I asked to be critiqued on my delivery, as well as the content of my manuscript. I needed to learn the correct techniques.

My fellow classmates could always be counted on to voice their honest opinion. I felt it was a fairly good test for the reaction I could expect later from a radio audience.

I always typed my work as neatly as possible. It wasn't easy for me since I hadn't had an opportunity to take typing at school. I would always send my assignments in early, then wait for the comments of the institute's teacher assigned to evaluate my work. I worked especially hard on that last lesson of the series. As instructed, I prepared it with the idea of having it scrutinized by the staff at a radio station.

I will never forget the day I took my script to a radio station. I was quite excited and yet very nervous. To calm myself, I sat down and gave myself a stern pep talk.

"Just pretend that you are experienced," I advised myself. "Act as though you are. Walk in with confidence."

My family was almost as excited and as nervous as I was. My Indian son, Jerry, asked if he could ride along with me to the radio station. He said he would stay in the car and pray while I went in. I needed his support and I was happy to have him come along. It was precious to me to have Jerry realize the importance of prayer and to have him approach God on my behalf.

Off we went to the largest radio station in the area. KSRO's offices and studios were located upstairs above the Flamingo Hotel. I had not been there before and was surprised at how narrow the steps ascending to the second floor were. I wondered how they ever got their office furniture and broadcasting equipment up the narrow passageway.

Somehow I managed to retain my composure as I struggled to walk up the narrow stairs, wearing my best high heeled shoes.

I was apprehensive, not knowing what to expect or who I would see first as I approached the door. When I opened it, the slim, attractive receptionist smiled and blinked through shell-rimmed glasses.

"What can I do for you?" she asked pertly.

"I would like to speak to the station manager, please," I told her. "Is he in?"

"No, he isn't right now," she said. "Could someone else help you maybe?" Her questioning look told me she was curious about what I might want to speak to the manager about.

At that point I prayed silently for the right words. I had a speech all memorized to recite to the man in charge, but I hardly knew what to say to the inquisitive young lady who obviously wanted to know what I was there for.

"When will the manager be in and, by the way, what is his name?" I ventured.

Instead of answering my double-barreled question, she said, "Maybe someone else would be the person you should talk to."

"Well," I told her hesitantly, "I would like to speak to someone regarding a radio program . . . "

"Oh, I see," she brightened, "you want to talk to the program director. Let me check, maybe he can see you now." I was soon sitting across the desk from the person I was supposed to see, explaining that I would like him to check my radio script and consider my idea for a program on his station. He was a pleasant man, who struck me as being in his mid-thirties. I watched him carefully and studied the expressions on his face as he scrutinized my script, trying to determine if he was pleased, puzzled, or disinterested.

I tried to give the impression that I was experienced, but as we discussed the suggested program I finally just told him I was studying with the Christian Writer's Institute of Chicago and that this particular script was an assignment. "It's really your reaction to the script that I came for," I admitted. "But I would also like very much to have a program on your station."

After thoroughly assessing my lesson assignment he said politely, "This is an excellent script. I'm sure you'll get a good grade on it." After a long pause he said, "I wish I could offer you a spot on the air. However," he explained with apology, "a station this size is not allowed to use inexperienced personalities in it's programming."

I stood up to go. Before I could thank him for his time he handed me the script and said, "This is a great idea and you've done a good job on it. If you'll take it to the new radio station here in town that just went on the air, I think they might give you a chance at it."

That was a development I hadn't expected. I wasn't surprised that he didn't offer me a spot on the air, but to have him suggest another station gave me an unexpected thrill. I was fairly trembling as I asked where the new radio station was located. As I got up to go he said "When you've had some experience, please check with us again." I was overwhelmed.

Jerry was waiting prayerfully in the car. I explained all that had happened as we drove straight from that radio station to the new one. Together we thanked the Lord for what we believed was a direct answer to our prayers. As we approached the new radio station we prayed that God's will would be done.

The road we turned onto was merely a wide, graded path. The building also was just in the process of being built. There wasn't even a front door. We parked in the only spot that was cleared sufficiently alongside two other cars.

Encouraged by the positive response I had received at the previous station, I walked confidently across the soft dirt (trying hard not to be too disturbed about getting my best shoes ruined) and into the open entry way.

As I walked in I saw two men sitting at a desk. One looked up, surprised at having a visitor. "Well, what do we have here?" he said to the other.

I decided not to make any pretense about having had experience in radio but instead to try a different approach.

"Good morning!" I greeted them and then introduced myself. "I'm Ardelle Brown, an aspiring radio personality," I said confidently. "I've come to offer my talents to help make your station famous and successful. Would you like to be the one to discover me?"

One of the men introduced himself as Tom and the gentleman next to him as Joe. Tom had the strangest look on his face. He glanced at a third man who had just appeared in the doorway of the adjoining room. "This is Bob," Tom explained. "I'm sure he will be happy to talk to you." Bob was the program director and business manager. He seemed interested in the script I held reverently in my hand. He began surveying it with a critical eye as he asked me to come in and sit down. He asked numerous questions about my status and motives, and responded with respect when he learned I was a minister's wife. He said he admired my initiative and my efforts to further my ambitions. Finally he paused. "This looks like a professionally done script," he said. "I'm really impressed but we are new on the air. We're not quite ready for a woman's program but I'll tell you what we are looking for—religious programs for Sunday morning. Would you be interested in doing something like that?"

Would I? I thought to my self. I almost said "Thank You Lord!" right out loud. Yes, I would be interested in doing a Christian program. I would like that more than anything. My heart was racing; this was too good to be true.

"I would love that!" I told him, trying not to appear overly anxious. The proposal was so new I was staggered by it. Bob suggested I work on some ideas then come back and discuss them with him.

"Be thinking of a time slot also," he said as I was leaving the station, so exhilarated I was walking on air. When Jerry saw me walking back through the unfinished doorway he could tell something wonderful was in the working. I must have had the look of success on my face and the spring of victory in my step. I couldn't wait to tell him and the rest of my family that I WAS GOING TO BE ON RADIO!

As we drove away from the radio station, I recounted all that was said while I was with Bob. Jerry was almost as elated as I was. He had been praying the entire time. We rejoiced together and thanked the Lord for answering our prayers beyond our wildest dreams.

[Your grandpa was surprised and thrilled when I broke the news to him, as Jerry stood by fairly beaming. The rest of the family found my potential fame hard to believe, but Jerry was a firsthand witness.] I prayed a lot as I searched for ideas for a title, format and an appropriate time to suggest. The door was wide open and the opportunity so great; I wanted to do this new project well.

I could hardly wait to tell my classmates at the college what had happened. I also wanted their input. I knew that I would have to venture far beyond their suggestions since it was going to be a Christian broadcast. Few if any in that class had any inclination toward Christianity. I had never tried to hide my position but the message of the Gospel was beyond the comprehension of most of them.

When I told them the good news they all shared my enthusiasm, even though they were a bit subdued because it would be a "religious" program. I felt like I was riding high, holding on to the string of a big, beautiful balloon with the word SUCCESS written in large letters on it. Everyone was excited along with me.

Then my balloon popped. I suddenly became very ill and was rushed to the hospital in great pain. I had never experienced anything like this attack before. [Your grandpa was upset and the children were scared and nervous. I prayed desperately, all the time trying hard to put my complete trust in the Lord.]

My problem was diagnosed as kidney stones. When all attempts to dissolve them failed, I was scheduled for surgery.

My family prayed and our church family prayed. I wanted to be spared the knife, and God heard and answered. Shortly before they were going to take me to the operating room, the stones passed. Oh, how I thanked the Lord. All those around me, including the doctors and nurses, knew that I believed God had intervened; I think they believed it too. When the doctor came in to discuss my release, I cautiously mentioned that I was anxious to get back to my family and to get on with my new project. He listened with interest as I explained the radio program.

"Well," he responded firmly, "you tell them your doctor won't release you for at least a month." I was crushed. "They will wait." he assured me.

"You should not take on anything that is not absolutely necessary at this time." With an "I mean it!" look he added, "Don't worry, the time will pass quicker than you think, then you'll be up to your new challenge." I was disappointed but he was an excellent doctor and God had definitely led us to him. I didn't know if he was a Christian but we were aware that he had great respect for God. Someone told us that he had at one time been in a serious accident and had realized that God had spared his life. From that time on, he had treated many ministers' families without charge.

I really did need the extra time to recuperate and get ready for the program I had been promised. While waiting, I developed ideas and made notes. I rehearsed programs, pretending I was on the air.

In working out a format, I kept remembering two specific programs that I had been impressed with and considered effective. One was a children's program which a Baptist woman in Hawaii had produced and the other was First Mate Bob's *"Haven of Rest"* broadcast, which originated in Southern California. Whether consciously or not, I'm sure I copied some of the format of both.

I got things under control at home, just as the doctor had ordered, and finally felt rested.

On The Air Live

In July of 1962, I went on the air live with my very first radio show. It was a day I will never forget.

I was at the station early to get braced for my debut as a radio personality. *"Wake Up Time"*, which was what I decided to call my program, went on the air Sunday mornings at 8:00, the time I had chosen. I thought both children as well as adults would be able to hear the program.

I felt very confident. I had carefully written my script and determined the exact time the songs and music would require. I had read aloud and timed everything I would say, over and over many times. But in spite of all the preparation, I was still terribly nervous. I was not at all familiar with the microphone, even though one of the operators had taught and drilled me regarding hand signals and what to expect from him (or whoever was on duty) as they communicated with me through the glass wall between the small studio where I would be and the control room.

I felt panicky in the tiny production room where I would be separated from the on-air operator. I was scared I would forget the signals and do something wrong. I certainly didn't want to "mess up" on my very first broadcast. I prayed desperately as the time drew near for me to say my first words above the background music which the operator engineer was to play as I came on. As instructed, I had made a carbon copy of my entire script and had carefully marked both copies with instructions so the operator would know exactly what I wanted to have happen.

It was eight o'clock on the dot! Bob, the morning engineer, began by saying, "We're delighted to introduce a new family program called *'Wake Up Time'* and here is the lady who makes it all possible . . . Ardelle Brown. Ardelle, it's all yours . . ."

"Thanks, Bob," I said, as bravely as I possibly could. I wasn't even sure if my voice was reaching beyond my lips.

[I'm sure you will believe me when I tell you I was terribly scared and so nervous I was trembling.]

Trying hard not to think about what might happen, I read my script exactly as I had written it. I could see that Bob seemed to be bringing the music in at the right places, but I couldn't actually hear the music myself. The second time Bob signaled that it was time for me to read, I was not nearly as frightened and nervous. By the end of the half hour, I was performing like a pro. I felt like a celebrity.

When Bob got me off the air, and after a station ID and a couple commercials, he hurried in to congratulate me. "You did great!" he said. I could tell he was proud of me and pleased with the way I had prepared my script and followed his instructions.

The phone rang. "It's for you," Bob said as he handed me the receiver. It was my teacher at the college.

"Ardelle," she said breathlessly, "that was electrifying. It was wonderful! You came across really great. I loved it! I'm so proud of you!"

On that first broadcast I shared a story entitled *"Echo Valley"*. It was about a man who found that his attitude echoed back to him. When he expressed love as he entered the valley, the people he met happily responded, "We love you too". Likewise, when he expressed disgust, people came back with the exact same attitude.

Later, when I shared the true Gospel on the air, my teacher expressed disappointment. She, as a "Christian Scientist", could not agree with my views. She sat me down and gave me a teacher-student pep talk. She strongly urged me to keep the broadcasts more inspirational and not so focused on Christianity.

The message which I knew I had to get across—that Jesus is God's Son and that He died to save us, and that there is no other way we can be saved— was repulsive to her. I knew she could not understand that I had to do what God had called me to do. I don't know whether she continued to listen to my broadcasts. I suspected she may have, at least out of curiosity. But she never commended me again. I understood why.

Unfortunately I had to solicit sponsors to pay for the radio time for my program. That meant that in addition to planning, writing and producing the programs, I had to sell the time, write the advertising copy, and produce the commercials as well.

There were advantages, however, in being required to have financial sponsors. During the week when their spots were aired, as part of the advertising package, the announcer would say after each commercial, "We invite you to listen at 8 a.m. on Sunday for *"Wake Up Time"* with

Ardelle Brown." Since I had four to six sponsors at a time, their spots and the promos were heard throughout the day, all during the week. That particular station was one of those whose listeners were referred to as non-dialers. I had a captive audience. My name became a household word in many homes.

When I went on the air each Sunday morning I was also expected to promote my sponsors and I was glad to do so. I tried to make sure that each one got their money's worth for their advertising dollar. I knew each of them personally and had a good rapport with them.

I had to "sell" them the idea of helping pay for the radio time for my program for three months at a time and get what the station referred to as a thirteen week contract. Then I would find out what aspect of their business they wanted to promote on radio, write the commercials and incorporate them into the program—something like Paul Harvey [I know you've heard him] does for his sponsors.

Some of those I persuaded to advertise with me were businesses such as a mobile home distributorship, a mortgage and insurance corporation, a hearing-aid center, a real estate firm, a neighborhood supermarket, and a leading downtowm department store. Some of the owners or managers were Christians, some were not.

A Surprising Change To Cope With

Those were tremendously busy days for me. I was a busy pastor's wife, mother of seven—plus three foster children, and I was continuing with my writing class at the college.

All during the week I was planning my half-hour program for the following Sunday. Here and there, in between other things, I somehow managed to get my script written.

[Can you imagine my reaction when the station managers called me into their office one morning and informed me I would have to start producing my broadcasts ahead of time, and bring them into the station pre-recorded, and ready to air? Tom explained that their Sunday morning operators were often inexperienced with the techniques of doing live broadcasts and that some were unwilling to perform this extra service which they did not feel they should have to do. I was shocked! I had no equipment and no money to buy an expensive tape recorder and all the other things I would need. And I had no technical knowledge to operate them, even if I had them.]

Complications certainly were evident. I had already run into some resentment from a couple of the young guys who turned up on Sunday morning. This had troubled me. It was hard enough to do the program live when the on-duty operator was enthusiastic and helpful.

Tom told me that he and the other employees I knew well by then would try to help me as much as possible with learning how to produce my programs at home. He assured me it would be a lot easier once I learned how to do it myself, and said I would thank him later, although at the time he realized how traumatic it was for me.

As soon as I left the station I began to cry and pray. It was almost too much for me. Then I tried to get ahold of myself. I had faced numerous crisis situations in my lifetime. I knew I should put such matters in God's hands and that was just what I decided to do. I truly believed Romans 8:28 which says, *"And we know that all things work together for good to them that love God, to them who are the called according to His purpose."*

At that time I could not see the good I was told was in it, but God could. I resolved to trust Him.

By the time I arrived home I had prayed through the situation and had come up with some ideas. When I shared my alarming story with my family, I was able to temper the seemingly insurmountable obstacles with some suggestions and possible solutions. I convinced them and myself that it was not the end.

I did not doubt that it was God's will that I continue on the air or that He would come to my rescue. I truly believed that the matter could be resolved in a way that would honor God and bring glory to His name. And it would certainly be another lesson in trusting the Lord.

My Own Studio

Tom and Joe's suggestions for setting up a small recording studio in my home filled my thoughts. Questions and answers surfaced intermittently. I was eager and confident and at the same time fearful and unsure of myself. I believed I could do it, but I was completely untrained and inexperienced. The uncertainty of it all overwhelmed me at times.

There were many questions. How could I possibly finance even one piece of equipment, such as a tape recorder? I knew I would also have to have a microphone and other items in order to produce my program broadcast quality. Where could I find room to set up the equipment, if I did have it? Many uncertainties challenged me.

I considered various possibilities. The idea of giving up kept surfacing, but I am not a quitter so I refused to consider it further. When I thought about my listeners I knew I could not let them down.

Never once did I doubt that God had opened the door to this ministry. Who was I to stand in the way of His provision so that the broadcasts could continue. I simply could not believe that He would allow the ministry to come to an abrupt end. It would not honor His Name.

I knew I had been careful to give God the credit and all the glory for every part of the radio ministry. Why should I worry now? Hadn't He worked out each crisis thus far in this special project and in everything else I had ever attempted to do for Him?

As I prayed and read God's Word, the impending pressure of possible failure began to fade away. New and fresh ideas flooded my thoughts.

I was sure we would be able to find some spot in our house to set up a little recording studio. The biggest hurdle was going to be getting the necessary equipment.

The men at the radio station told me that in addition to a professional tape recorder I would need at least one turntable to play records on. And they said I would need a good microphone, and a "mixer". I had no idea what that was. The only mixers I knew about were the ones I used in the kitchen to mix cake batter, and the one our friends used for mixing cement. When it came to technical terms and technical equipment I was completely ignorant. I had to rely on those who knew about such things.

Tom and Joe suggested I contact a dealer and determine exactly what I would need and then have them help me set up my studio.

My Christian real estate sponsor was pretty knowledgeable about such things. When I told him what was happening he hesitated a moment, then made his suggestion.

"There's a new electronics dealer just down the street from my office", he said. "It's called The Golden Ear".

He offered to go with me to inquire about the equipment I would need and told me he would pay for a suitable tape recorder himself. I had no idea how much one would cost and I don't think he did either. I was thrilled at the way God was starting to answer my prayers. Each step seemed to reveal another miracle.

The owner of The Golden Ear was a bit intrigued with our story. His store had opened so recently that he didn't have as much inventory as he would have liked to have, but he assured me that he could get anything we needed quickly. Naturally, he didn't have a full track, professional-type tape recorder in stock, but he showed us one in a dealer's catalogue. The outlined specifications indicated it was one that was used by numerous radio stations across the country.

Tom had told me that he had produced the *Old Fashioned Revival Hour* broadcast for Dr. Charles Fuller when he lived in Southern California. From his experience he advised me to make sure I bought a tape recorder with a full-track head. At that time, I had no idea what that meant. Fortunately the man at the Electronics firm did. He pointed out to us in the book that the Roberts "Workhorse" was indeed the one I would need.

When we inquired about the price he showed us that it was over $400, which he pointed out was very reasonable for that type of equipment.

I'm sure I appeared a bit shocked at the price. The proprietor hastened to say he would give me a good deal on it. He went on to explain that with proper care it would provide many years of service.

I glanced at my realtor friend to get his reaction. He knew I was praying and trusting God to help me comply with the radio station's suggestions.

"We'll take it!" he told the electronics dealer without a moment's hesitation.

"Let me know when it arrives," he said to me as he excused himself to get back to his office for an appointment.

After pricing the microphones and other items, I said I would have to discuss the purchases with my husband before ordering them.

The owner of The Golden Ear told me he would call me when the recorder came in and we would decide then what else would be necessary. He was obviously excited about helping a radio personality set up a recording studio. He assured me there would be no extra charge for setting up the production room and getting it operational. I felt relieved as I left for home.

Something Beautiful

A couple of days later the man at the electronics store, who asked that I would please just call him Jack, called to tell me that KSRO, the large radio station I had first gone to, was replacing the turntables in their mobile unit which they used at the county fair each year and for other remote broadcasts.

Jack said he thought he could get the two turntables and the console they were mounted in for $50 if I was interested. I had to tell him I would have to pray about it.

[I'm sure Jack didn't understand that I had to trust God for everything, including money to buy what I needed for my recording studio.]

When I remember those days, now, I marvel at the way God was already answering prayers, before I even prayed. That very afternoon our good friends, the Bakers, from Sonoma, stopped by to see us. When they mentioned how much they enjoyed my broadcast I told them about the emergency. They handed me a check which they had already made out—for fifty dollars.

"Here," they said with conviction. "God must want us to pay for the turntables.

The Lord was definitely showing me that He was working everything out and that I should simply trust Him.

My heart was still rejoicing with gratitude when, a few days later, Jack called. "Ardelle," he said excitedly, "please come down. I have something beautiful to show you."

When I got there he was smiling from ear to ear, like a young boy admiring a fantastic new toy. "Look at this machine," he said. "I've never seen anything like it." [I assure you, it WAS beautiful.]

We could hardly believe how well the Workhorse was constructed. Though an amateur, knowing nothing about tape recorders, I could see that it was an excellent piece of equipment. Jack knew, and he was absolutely overwhelmed with the workmanship of it.

[Neither of us could have dreamed that day that this professional tape recorder, manufactured by Roberts Electronics, would almost miraculously perform for more than twenty years.]

Testing—One, Two, Three . . .

My family was almost as excited as I was as we looked for an appropriate place to assemble my little production room. We finally decided to use the breakfast nook. We hung a heavy drape over the entrance to the kitchen and over the window in the tiny room. These absorbed the sound just fine.

I think Jack was as thrilled as I was as we set up the new tape recorder between the dual turntables on the console. He hooked up the new Electro Voice directional microphone and connected them all with a small Bogen mixer which he said required some sort of adapter. [I didn't know what he meant at the time but I clearly understood later.]

Jack efficiently wired, tested, and adjusted, until everything was ready to operate. He was beaming when he had me sit down beside him so he could show me how to operate each button and knob. I was apprehensive at the thought of operating all that strange equipment by myself. I knew I had to learn, however, so I asked the Lord to help me and then plunged wholeheartedly into the project.

[Your grandpa and the "seven-plus-three" children in our home stood by in disbelief as they watched me record and play back my voice. Of course each of the children wanted to hear themselves talk, so I practiced the controls on them. As you can imagine I had to teach all ages not to touch or fool with my business equipment. It wasn't easy trying to educate the older children, especially the boys, it was so intriguing to them. However, they soon learned that this was my private little room where I served the Lord, and that it was strictly off limits for them.]

Our youngest was only two years old when I first went on the air, and only two and a half when the little studio was installed. Everyone knows how active and noisy a child that age can be, but my precious little boy quickly learned to play quietly on the floor by my feet or in the adjoining room when I was recording. I don't remember ever having to record something over because my baby acted up and accidentally got recorded. He actually helped me by not disturbing. Somehow he seemed to sense when it was all right to make noise and when it was not. He grew up with me producing radio programs. It was a real challenge to find time to do my recording undisturbed. Many times I would do it in the middle of the night or very early.

At first I was frustrated and aggravated at having to set up my own studio and having to learn to do my broadcasts all by myself. But, as Tom said I would, once I caught onto it, I found it much easier and less stressful than doing the programs live. What at first had seemed so terrible, actually turned out to be a blessing.

The next thing I had to learn was how to translate my script onto tape and to do it well enough to be broadcast over the air. I think my biggest problem was timing. At first I didn't have a stopwatch and I tried to work with an old wall clock. Then I bought a good stopwatch that I am amazingly still using for the very same purpose after more than thirty years. The Lord helped me learn to coordinate voice and music, volume and time. At the beginning I had absolutely no expertise, but I had determination and I followed through.

God opened a door for the message of the Gospel to go out over the airwaves. He provided the equipment I needed and the ability to use it. That's how it always is when we are willing to follow through as He leads.

The New Method

That first recorded program took me hours to complete. I was scared to listen to see how it would sound over the air. Actually, I don't think my listeners knew the difference. Later when I mentioned to my classmates how concerned I was, they all said they didn't detect any problems.

The operator at the station who played my tape complimented me highly. I often wondered if he had played it first to make sure it was good enough to broadcast. He assured me he hadn't. He said he trusted me.

I realized right away that through it all God was looking after my best interests. When I was informed that I would have to produce my own broadcasts, it seemed like the worst thing that had ever happened to me. But it turned out to be one of the best.

There were numerous advantages. If I made a mistake I could do it over, as many times as necessary, until I was satisfied with it. And I could time it before taking it to the radio station. Dealing with my own microphone was less stressful.

I was rewarded for all my hard work and my insistence on doing each broadcast the best I possibly could. The men at the radio station often complimented me on my "professional productions". It was encouraging to be told my work was "tight" and free of "dead air", as they called it. I loved their approval. It inspired me to strive toward perfection. To be told they could trust my tapes without checking them caused me to try very hard to maintain my reputation.

At that time I knew of other Christian broadcasts which were sometimes not broadcast "due to technical difficulties beyond our control", as the announcer would comment on the air. I was determined not to have them say that about my tapes.

Completely On My Own

I found out that Jack, the man who helped me set up my studio, usually came down to his store early on Sunday morning and I believed he listened to my broadcasts. His comments and suggestions indicated so. I strove for his approval as well as the operators and management at the radio station. He had helped me so much I wanted him to hear the results of his efforts—on the air. It was comforting to know that Jack was concerned about the technical quality of my tapes and to know he was standing by in case I needed assistance.

Early one Tuesday morning, my real estate friend called to tell me that Jack had died suddenly of a heart attack. The news shocked me. The first thing I thought of was how I had refused to listen to my teacher at the college when she urged me to make my broadcasts merely inspirational. I had insisted on giving out the Gospel message as I believed the Lord had intended for me to do. I wanted desperately to believe that Jack had heard and understood what I had been saying and that he had accepted Jesus as his Savior. I was so glad I had been faithful to the Lord, and to Jack and all my listeners.

When Jack died, I felt a great loss. I hadn't realized I was depending so heavily on him. Suddenly I knew I had to rely solely upon the Lord for wisdom to do my broadcasts and keep things running smoothly in the studio. I learned quickly not to take things for granted; to never try to produce a program without praying for divine assistance and protection. I knew I had to trust God to keep my equipment functioning.

When there was a problem, I would get down on my knees in front of the console and acknowledge my inability and my dependence on God.

[Through the more than thirty years of broadcasting, it has been the Lord and me. I could never have done it myself. I give God the glory for anything we may have accomplished together. Never once did I believe I was doing any great feat; it was God, working through me.]

A New Salesman

When I had been on the new Country and Western station for about a year, I faced my biggest crisis situation. Until that time I had the highest respect of the managers and had actually been asked for my input as the station developed and grew in popularity in the community. I had been there almost from the beginning. The men who had helped me so much had taken me into their confidence many times. I was in and out of the station constantly and was in on what was going on most of the time.

One day I stopped by as usual to leave my taped broadcast for the following Sunday. Tom met me at the door and rather sheepishly told me that they had hired a new sales representative from back east. About that time a man whom Tom introduced as Rex walked into the room.

I immediately sensed that Rex was not going to like me. Somehow I made him nervous. He seemed almost afraid of me. In the weeks that followed it became quite evident that Rex was jealous of me and uneasy about the way Tom and Joe respected and confided in me.

Rex was a "hard sell" type of personality and I couldn't imagine him fitting into the scene at KVRE. I wondered why Tom and Joe had hired him and why they hadn't said a word to me about him before. Not that they were obligated to me in any way, they just usually felt free to discuss such matters with me.

Things were not the same after Rex came. For one thing, Rex insisted that the station would never make it without advertising local night clubs and running liquor commercials.

I soon realized why Tom and Joe had not even mentioned Rex to me. They knew I would not approve of his philosophy. They also knew that our community of faithful listeners would also disapprove. I prayed for Tom and Joe. They were so distant towards me; I was really concerned. Then one morning when I stopped by Rex met me at the door. "Ardelle," he said, quite arrogantly, "I sold your time to somebody else."

I looked at him in astonishment. He had bumped my time, the time I had chosen as an appropriate hour for my program.

"You can't do that!" I challenged, fairly shaking. "I have paid sponsors." He knew that.

"Well, I have!" he assured me emphatically. And he had.

I quickly sat down, lest my knees give way beneath me. I was shocked, hurt and disappointed. When I could stand again, I hurried to my car, trying hard to regain my composure. As soon as I closed the door I began to cry out to the Lord, asking Him to help me.

How could Rex do that to me? Why would Tom and Joe let him? Why would they ever listen to this indiscreet man's council? They simply fell for his line that extra money would be forthcoming. They knew the impact it would have on the station. It was hard for me to understand.

But what about MY sponsors? They were good, honest, hard-working business men and women with whom the station's audience could identify. And how could I explain this to them?

And what about my listeners? They would have no way of knowing what was happening. I would just suddenly be gone without any explanation.

I rushed home crying, utterly confused, and completely devastated. How could such an awful, underhanded thing be taking place?

"Lord, why?" I pleaded, "when everything was going so well."

A Brighter Light

The following Sunday morning, after my encounter with Rex, *Wake-Up Time* was off the air—without a word of explanation. But I was on my knees praying. I was so upset and had cried so much I couldn't even go to church. All I could do was continue to cry, and pray.

When my sponsors inquired about what had happened, it was hard for me to explain. They each had unexpired contracts. Until that time, they had held the radio station in high regard. Now they too became upset with the way we were all being treated.

When the commercials promoting questionable "night spots" in the area, and some glorifying the merits of a specific brand of beer were actually broadcast on our hitherto "clean" radio station, I cringed. It just broke my heart. Those of my sponsors who were Christians felt the same pain.

The dedicated audience now hearing these questionable commercials were MY former listeners. They had been able to hear the Gospel message because of the kindness of my good sponsors. I did not believe that they were the kind of people who would be unmoved by the sudden change in our local radio station. I was convinced that the ads were an insult to the ears of most of the listeners who loved the radio station.

I was off the air for two Sundays, but I was not defeated. I still had a lot of fight in me. I was praying too. And I was trusting God to make it all come out right for His honor and glory.

One morning when I was praying I remembered that the program director at KSRO, the larger station I had first gone to, had told me to come back when I had gained some experience. Right away I came up with a new program idea and rushed over to KSRO with a confident spring in my step.

As I came up the stairs, the man I had talked to the first time I had come was standing in the doorway. When he saw me his face lit up. He remembered me and our conversation.

"Come right in." he said with a smile.

"Do you remember me?" I asked.

"I sure do." he replied. "Tell me, what happened. Did you get on the other station?"

"Yes, I did." I told him. "I've been on for a year. I'm wondering, am I eligible now to go on your station?"

"You certainly are!" He answered so quickly, and so firmly, my prayerful hopes were bolstered.

"What would you like to do?" he graciously asked.

I suggested a *Radio Sunday School* program. He thought the idea was great and asked what time slot I would like and when I could start. He said it wasn't necessary for him to check the sample script I had prepared. He knew I could do it. I suspected he had heard me on KVRE.

When I told him I had my own studio and in fact worked with turntables and a console that had once belonged to KSRO, he seemed delighted.

I chose 8:00 a.m., the time my *Wake-Up Time* program had aired on the other station, for my new *Radio Sunday School* program. They scheduled me to start the following Sunday.

I went home feeling like I was walking ten feet above the ground. Even though I had suffered great pain as the result of the injustice to which I had been subjected, I could see that God was in the whole situation. It was evident that He was being glorified in the midst of what had seemed to me to be a terrible disaster. God had no doubt answered my prayers. Rex had intended to put my candle out. But, as it turned out, he had actually been instrumental in making it burn much brighter. He would sure hate that, I knew, if he found out about it.

I was thrilled to now be on a much more powerful station, but I had to start from scratch again and build up my audience. And I also would not have weekday promotion as I had on the other station. Even so, I was thrilled with my new program and the prospect of having an even larger audience. KSRO was the largest station in the area. I mourned the loss of my previous listeners, but I put my heart and strength into producing the best possible programs to meet the standards of the larger, more sophisticated station, and designed to please my new audience.

Faith For The Family

I was only off the air on KVRE for two Sundays. Early the next Monday morning, Tom called and asked if I could come to his office. He said he wanted to talk to me.

When I arrived, both Tom and Joe were waiting to see me. They humbly apologized for what had happened. They admitted they had made a mistake in hiring Rex. They now realized they were wrong in listening to his unwise advice. They did not deny that Rex had been inconsiderate and unkind to my paid sponsors. Not to mention the unethical aspect.

"We let Rex go," they told me with relief.

I was pleased, but a lot of damage had been done. Rex had sold my 8:00 a.m. time slot to a modernistic church. I was sick about that, as well as having my well established program time taken. He had also been responsible for the station lowering its standards regarding who would be allowed to advertise. Both Tom and Joe realized it afterwards and were sorry they had not been more careful.

"We want you back on the station," they said. "You can choose any time you wish and do whatever type of program you would like to do."

After prayerful consideration, I decided on 8:30 a.m. It seemed to me that was a little late for a program called *Wake-Up Time*, so I came up with a new title *"Faith For The Family"*.

I chose a family-oriented format that included all ages. It would include a story for the young and the young-at-heart. In those days I wrote and produced the stories myself. As time went by I built up a good library of Bible stories, and other appropriate stories, on records and tapes.

During the second part of the thirty-minute program, I planned something for adults that expanded on the same theme as the story and children's music. In later years I began to include a five-minute sermonette by a local minister.

[That program was on the air on various radio stations for more than twenty-five years.]

After Rex's dirty trick, I now had two programs and I was on two different radio stations. Just as with Joseph of old, what Rex had intended as evil, God had turned into good. My *Radio Sunday School* program on KSRO was similar to *Faith For The Family*. I chose various themes and treated the subject matter much like in a coordinated Sunday School. I presented a story and music for the younger age groups early in the broadcast, followed by corresponding material and music for older listeners. It wasn't easy producing two programs that much alike to be heard in the same area. I kept careful logs of each, precisely noting each song, story and feature so that I wouldn't duplicate them. With practice I soon became more proficient and was able to do the two programs more easily than when I had only one to do.

A few months after the second program began, one of the engineers I had worked with on KVRE called to ask if I would be interested in having a program on a new station that had just gone on the air in the area. He had recommended me to the station manager who had expressed a desire to have a Christian program produced by a local personality for their Sunday morning schedule. I told him I would love to be on that station. I was pleased to be asked. I began dreaming up another program idea. The new station was referred to as a "good music" station, playing classical and semi-classical music.

It had a wonderful sound and catered to a different musical audience. Listeners with refined musical tastes were attracted to it. Again, as for each of the other broadcasts, I prayed about an appropriate title for the half-hour program which I had been offered on this new station. I decided to call it *"Music With A Message"*. I used sacred music that conformed to the station's policy and format, and short talks between songs. By that time I had collected a considerable amount of source material. I never seemed to run out of ideas. People often asked me how I could possibly fill up an entire half hour on the air. If that had been a problem for me, it probably would have been time for me to stop. Usually I did not have time enough for all I wanted to use.

I never learned to say "no" when offered time on the air. One day when I was talking to one of the managers at KVRE about my various programs, how I came up with names for them, etc., he asked me what other ideas I had up my sleeve. I told him about a couple of them, including my desire for an educational broadcast. "You know, I like that one," he said. "How would you like to do it for this station?" I thought he was joking.

"No, I mean it", he smiled. "What time of day would be good for that type of program?"

I had already thought that through, though I had not dreamed I would have an opportunity to carry through on it so soon.

"In the afternoon, after students of all ages are home from school," I told him.

"What would you call the program?" he asked. "I suppose you've thought that out too."

"Yes, I have," I admitted. "I would call it: *Our Land U.S.A.*"

"That's a wonderful name," he said. "I like it. When can you start?"

I didn't know how soon I could get the first program together. After all, I already had three different weekly half-hour programs.

It didn't take me long to work out a format, but it did require some time to do the necessary research and get together some good material. I ordered several excellent story albums from a company the manager had told me about. While preparations for the new program were under way, I was busy with my other three broadcasts, taking care of my large family of seven plus three, and of course my duties as a busy minister's wife.

One morning I received a call from my friend, Bill, at KHUM, the good music station.

"Sorry to have to tell you this, Ardelle," he apologized. "But KHUM is folding. We're going off the air in two weeks."

The news was disappointing. I was saddened at the thought and actually wept. On the other hand though, I was relieved. I knew I would have more time to devote to the production of my new patriotic program. But still another surprise was in store for me.

A friend who was disappointed to see my *Music With A Message* forced off the air told me about a powerful 50,000 watt radio station in San Diego and suggested I contact them. He said my broadcasts would be perfect for that station and I would have an opportunity to reach out for hundreds of miles. I liked that idea.

Encouraged by my friend, I wrote the station, but I honestly did not expect a positive answer. They replied promptly however, and asked for audition tapes of the two programs I had described to them: *Faith For The Family*, and *Music With A Message*. They then called and expressed their desire to air both of the programs.

I now had two programs on XEMO, two on KVRE and one on KSRO. This involved producing only four shows, since *Faith For The Family* was heard on both KVRE and Xemo. I had already had my *Music With A Message* program on the air for almost three years. For a long time I was able to send XEMO the previously produced programs.

It was necessary to keep accurate records of which tapes had been sent, when they had been sent out and where. That was more work than the actual production. I bought film mailers to send them in and a friend printed cards for the address compartment. To return the tapes, all the station had to do was simply turn the card over and mail the tapes back to me.

It took plenty of discipline and management to keep that many broadcasts produced and delivered to the three different radio stations every week. God in His mercy had seen to it that I had learned to meet deadlines. One way or another, I was always able to get the tapes there. I soon learned to always have backup tapes for each program on hand at the radio station, in case one of the tapes got lost in the mail. It only happened once or twice over the many years, but I was always prepared just in case.

[Meanwhile, we were extremely busy with our missionary work at Bellevue, our second church in California, and the Lord was blessing our concentrated efforts. During this time, your grandpa still had to work at his secular job at Hamilton Air Force Base to support his large family. God in His graciousness gave both of us added strength. As I look back now, I wonder how it was possible for us to do as much as we did.]

Still Another Outreach

One day one of the students in my class who had just started coming to our church told me about her friend who was a missionary in Portugal. She was due home on furlough soon, she told me.

When we invited Palmyra to come speak at our church and tell us more about what was happening in missions in Portugal, I was surprised to learn that she, too, was a writer. Her unique ministry in that far off land, which was actually her homeland, partially entailed writing the true stories of converts among her native people and having the testimonies published in books for distribution. That was one of her unique methods of evangelism.

We found her work intriguing. We were greatly burdened to pray for her ministry in that spiritually needy country. She was encouraged by our friendship and concern.

When she was ready to return to the field, Palmyra asked me to pray about her specific need for someone to be her home secretary in our country, as well as her power of attorney. She desperately needed someone she could trust, and who would be willing to take care of depositing her donor's gifts and forwarding the modest amount she received each month from them to her in Portugal, as well as to send receipts to her donors.

We had just incorporated our several ministries into what we called Word and Witness Ministries, Incorporated. After much prayer about whether I should take on additional responsibilities, we decided it was what God wanted me to do, so I became her partner as a co-missionary to Portugal. I was Palmyra's home secretary for quite a few years. She returned on furlough a number of times during that extended period.

It was always rewarding to hear about activities on OUR mission field.

Apron Strings and Heartstrings

We were unbelievably busy with our work and the ministry God had entrusted us with, yet all the while very much aware that our most important ministry and our greatest responsibility was our children.

They were all actively involved in the various stages of growing up. There were school and homework, sports and recreation, art and music, doctor and dental appointments, and of course, church functions. It was a never ending chain of activities. With children in elementary, junior high, high school, and college, all depending on mother for transportation, at least for special activities. It was like I was operating a taxi service.

In my heart I wished for those wonderful days to last forever, but slowly and in a quiet sort of way, our older children were beginning to exhibit an independence of their own.

When the boys started to express an interest in cars and then girls, I sensed that our hitherto close family circle was changing. Our tight bond was being threatened by the normal growing process. The little boys who had always been within my reach were moving from my grasp.

When school was out that year I began to feel the earth shaking beneath my feet—the three oldest boys all got jobs and we watched them become more independent every day.

There were still many happy times, when they would bring their friends home and we would all enjoy time together around the dining room table for dinner or for games. There were always jokes about mother's cooking; about how everything always had to be "well done", or teasing me in front of their friends, like saying you could eat anything "Mother" cooked, with a little catsup on it.

There were also very painful days when I could see the evil one attempting to reach into our happy nest with his ugly fangs, in an effort to snatch one of my precious ones away. I was well aware that my fine, young sons, and the sons of one of God's faithful servants—were his prime targets.

Many and fervent were the prayers of my heavily burdened heart during those years, as well as those of their equally concerned father. We knew we had done our best to raise them according to our convictions based on the Scriptures. From that point we simply had to put them in God's hands. We had given them back to Him from the moment we knew they were coming and dedicated them back to the Lord as babies. Now, we had to let them go. [Memories of those painful days still remain. I'm sure they always will.]

I was just beginning to learn to trust God in a way that would continue the rest of my life. A mother's prayers for the protection of her beloved children must constitute a private line right to the throne of God. And it must always continue.

When it seems God is putting us on "hold" and we have to wait so long for the answer we're trusting Him for, it is not that He is taking care of other business and is too busy for us. I believe it's because He wants to keep us trusting Him in their behalf.

God knows even more than we do, how strong the power of evil is and how persistent Satan is in trying to entice our children and grandchildren away from the right way. We just have to let God handle the situation.

A Heart-Rending Experience

Fortunately, Santa Rosa had a junior college so we didn't have to deal with the "going away to college" ritual quite as soon. But the day did finally come and I remember well that inevitable hour. As thrilled as I was that our oldest son wanted to further his education, I was fearful at the thought of having my precious son out of sight and out of reach. I would have no way of knowing if he was safe. Watching him go was like having my heart torn out.

[I knew I wasn't the first mother to experience those awful pangs and I also knew I wouldn't be the last, but they were painful for me at the time.]

We were so proud of our son when he was able to get a transfer and continue his job as a checker at a supermarket in the town where he was enrolled in college. In this way he was able to pay his own way in school. That was a blessing from God and an answer to our prayers. Even though he was away, college was only a couple hours' drive from our home. We knew he would be coming home often. Even so, I was terribly frightened and imagined all kinds of things that might happen to him. I knew, however, that the time had come for me to turn him loose and let God take over. But in spite of all the reasoning, I had a difficult time for the first few weeks he was away from home.

When my tall, handsome son came home the first time for the weekend, I didn't really mind that he barely gave me a quick hug and the rest of the family a passing smile as he made his way to the piano. The sound of music ringing through the house once more was like a symphony to me, tying memories and current realities together.

All of our children had been bathed in prayer and saturated with spiritual training since infancy. How I longed to keep them all in a protective bubble, away from the temptations I knew they would face. I was well aware of the concentrated effort of the evil one toward young people, particularly ministers' and missionaries' children. I longed to protect mine from the wiles of Satan. I realized however reluctantly, that I could only try to prepare them to the best of my ability while they were still under my influence. I naturally turned to the Scriptures and prayer. When one day I read the account of Moses and how his mother reacted when her son was in danger, I was overwhelmed. She had entrusted her beautiful, helpless, infant son to a crude basket with a tar-patched bottom, and placed in a filthy river. I could imagine how the dangers of the hour must have troubled her. Reading the account really spoke to my fearful heart. Surely, I could trust the Lord to take care of my children, just as Moses' mother did. If I could not trust God, who could I trust?

There would be temptations, I knew. The battle had just begun. I was thankful I knew God, who was aware of the nature of my burden, as well as all the struggles, and concerns of a loving, caring mother.

Stretching My Concern

When son number three announced that he was going to take off across the country with two of his friends to visit the parents of one of them, it caught me by surprise. It really concerned me that on the day they wanted to leave, all the boys were extremely weary from working long hours in a local fast-food restaurant.

Observing how tired they were, I begged the boys not to go, at least not to start out on such a long journey until they were able to get some rest. They had finalized their plans, however, to leave at a certain time. They refused to listen to my reasoning and took off against my protests, tearing at my heart and pulling a part of me along as they went. As they set out on their cross-country itinerary, which included a dip into Mexico, they stretched the apron stings and the heartstrings attached to this mother, to the breaking point.

The first night they were gone was one of the longest nights in my life. I was terribly concerned about their physical welfare and their safety on the highways. And I feared for a million imaginable threats. Up until that time we had almost always been aware of the whereabouts of our son. He was good about telling me where he would be and with whom. Now, for the first time I did not know where he was. I knew that he and his pals were out there somewhere on a dangerous highway, battling the merciless traffic, driving further from me every hour.

I did not know either of my son's friends very well. The boy from Iowa was staying with his sister in Santa Rosa and working for the same fast-food restaurant as our son. The other boy I had only seen a couple times. The whole situation concerned me a great deal.

That first night I tossed all night long, not sleeping at all. By the next night I could not even lay down. All I could do was pray. While the rest of the family was sleeping, I retreated to my little studio and tried to do some recording that had to be done. I knew I would not be able to concentrate later.

Prayer In The Night

All night long I sought comfort and peace from the Scriptures when I wasn't recording. I cried out to the Lord for protection for my precious son and his friends. Waves of deep concern swept over me. Something seemed to compel me to pray.

Finally, I completed my radio production. With my Bible in front of me I knelt by my old swivel chair and cried out in behalf of the boys. Only God knew where they were at that moment. It was almost daylight. I was trying to read the Scriptures through swollen eyes from crying through the night hours when suddenly the phone rang. I was too alarmed to move. Then, almost mechanically, I reached out to catch the receiver before another ring could awaken the family.

"This is the hospital in Marshalltown, Iowa, calling for Mr. or Mrs. Brown", the far away voice said. "Your son has been in an accident . . ."

"Oh, no!" I cried.

I could hear someone in the background begging the nurse, " . . . let me talk to her. Please let me talk to her . . . "

"What happened?" I asked the nurse. "Is he all right?"

"Here he is," she said. "He wants to talk to you."

"I'm all right mother," he insisted. "Don't worry about me."

The soft-voiced little nurse came back on the line and explained that the boys had collided with another car in heavy fog on a dangerous curve.

My son had been asleep in the back seat when the collision had occurred. It turned out that his back had been broken in several places but he was alive and he didn't have any head injuries. How I thanked the Lord for an answer to my prayer.

At the time they called me, the full extent of his injuries had not been determined. I will always believe my persistent prayers were responsible for his life and his friends' lives being spared. I was convinced that the urgent need for special prayer had been transmitted to me over the many miles. The parents of our son's friend, who lived in Marshalltown, looked after our son like he was their own. They called soon after the nurse had contacted us from the hospital to try to assure us that he was going to be all right, even though he had suffered serious injuries. Since we could not go back to Iowa, these kind friends promised to take care of our injured son's needs and to visit him in the hospital. We great appreciated their thoughtful kindness. We talked to our son daily in the hospital and kept up on his progress.

A couple who owned and operated a pancake house in Marshalltown read about the accident in the newspaper and said to themselves, "If our son were injured in another state, we would appreciate it if someone would visit him in the hospital." So they went to see him, and they went back many times. They expressed true concern for him and for us in many ways. Following careful examination, the doctor called to tell us that our son's back was broken in several places and that he would not be able to fly home. He was encased in a plastic cast and would not be able to sit in an upright position.

When he was finally able to travel, arrangements were made for him to return to his home state on the train. We met him in Oakland, California. Naturally we were apprehensive as we approached the train depot, not knowing what to expect. Our fine young son in a body cast? But I kept telling myself, "at least he is alive, and he will recover." He was as glad to see us as we were to see him and to take him home. He had been delivered back to us from a brush with death in answer to prayer. We never doubted that.

During the period of his recuperation, my father passed away. In addition to caring for my son, I was ill with influenza at the time and unable to go back east for the funeral. It was a particularly difficult time.

Flowers and New Daughters

Changes in our family came in rapid succession after that. First one and then the second of the two oldest sons got married, each with a lovely church wedding. I now had two beautiful daughters-in-law to bless my heart. I almost burst with emotion as each son walked out of the church with his lovely bride on his arm. Each time, I did not grieve at losing a son; instead I rejoiced at gaining a daughter. I loved "my girls", as I called them, as I loved my own daughter. [I have still more now, and I love them all.]

I'm sure the prospect of my sons having their own homes and families set my mind at ease to a certain extent. I felt they would be more out of the reach of certain questionable friends who had no respect for God and whose influence on my beloved sons I feared.

With all the loving care, training and prayer I had invested in them, I didn't want to believe my children could go astray. But I was often reminded that the enemy is strong and that he forcefully goes out to entrap all young people, even more so those brought up in Christian homes.

I knew that my sons were intelligent and enlightened concerning wrong and danger, but I also knew what all of them were up against. I tried to stand upon the Scripture, *"Train up a child in the way he should go: and when he is old, he will not depart from it."* Proverbs 22:6

Just Following Charlie

While the older children were growing up and leaving home, the younger ones were receiving our concentrated attention as well. With all that was going on, I always managed to watch after each of the younger children closely. I was sometimes accused of being overly protective, especially when they were very small. Maybe I was, but I loved them and I didn't want anything to happen to hurt them.

One day my youngest, who couldn't have been more than three years old, was playing in the driveway by the front porch steps. On that sunny morning I had given in to let him play outside with our little cocker spaniel, Charlie.

"Stay right here by the porch," I cautioned. "Don't dare go out by that busy road. You might get run over by a car."

Charlie's tail wiggled with delight as my sweet little boy occupied himself with his toys and our pet. I sat down to enjoy the fresh air before getting back to tasks inside. Every few minutes I checked on them from the bedroom window as I made the beds and prepared to do the laundry. Suddenly I looked out and he wasn't there. I flew out the door, calling his name frantically, louder and louder, as if to draw him to me. He couldn't be very far away; I had just checked. A gnawing fear gripped my heart as I ran towards the road, then back to the barn and the creek that represented our back property line. I looked in the garden, in the neighbor's orchard, and our large garage where his daddy worked on our ailing automobiles, but he wasn't there.

"Oh, dear Lord," I prayed. "Where is my baby?"

I was so distraught I was beside myself. Where could he be? Had he just wandered away? Had someone kidnaped him? I imagined everything.

"He must be around here someplace," I cried, growing more uneasy every second.

After looking every place I could think of and checking with my neighbors, I was getting weak and nauseated.

"I think I had better call the police," I told the elderly man next door when he offered to help me look for him. I ran towards our back door to make the call.

"No, we have no report of any found child," the police dispatcher said as calmly as she could, sensing my fear. "Please give me all the details and your phone number."

Now, I had to stay by the phone and couldn't hunt for my lost child anymore. I was practically frozen in my frantic fear. Pray! That's what I could do. Really pray. God knew where my little boy was. Only He knew.

After what seemed like hours of walking up and down and calling out to God for mercy for my small son, I heard a car in the driveway. When I saw it was the police I just knew they had come to tell me something awful had happened. However, by the time I got out on the porch, they were opening the back door to release a small, scared little boy and his puzzled puppy.

I ran to put my arms around him, hardly noticing the presence of the officers.

"Where have you been?" I cried. "Why did you run away?"

Turning to the two officers, I asked, "Where did you find him?" By that time I was crying from relief.

They explained calmly that he had climbed a tree and was hanging tightly to a limb above the creek that ran behind our house, in an area where there was enough water for him to drown if he had fallen in.

"Just after you phoned our office, a lady called to say she heard a small child crying," the other officer explained. "When she went out into her back yard she could tell the cries were coming from the vicinity of the creek."

As soon as the woman called the police, they rushed to rescue our little boy. Then they brought him and Charlie, who was waiting under a nearby tree, home.

Through grateful tears I thanked them for their efforts and they drove off to answer another radio call.

"Why did you run away?" I pleaded with my scared little boy.

"I was just following Charlie . . ." he said fearfully, knowing he might be punished for causing me so much concern.

"Well," I said firmly, surprised at the tone of my voice, this will teach you never to wander away again."

Just as he expected he did indeed receive a spanking that he never forgot. Then of course I quickly took him in my arms and lovingly hugged him, as I sobbed, "Mother was terribly scared, I didn't know what had happened to my precious little boy. When I prayed, God let me have you back again."

I held him tightly and wished with all my heart that I would never have to let him out of my sight again.

* * *   * * *   * * *

"As I sometimes say on radio, 'I'm afraid my time is gone for now'. There's so much more I want to tell you but that will have to wait. You've been good listeners.

"Now you know about my little studio, and about what life was like with our big family in those busy days when we lived in Santa Rosa, California."

CHAPTER 18

The Biggest Adjustment of All

"Grandma, can you tell us another true story?" Karl asked as we finished our afternoon watermelon break.

"Please do," Tania begged. "We have to go home tomorrow."

"Remember you promised you'd tell us about Grandpa Brown . . . and the accident . . . " Karl reminded me almost apologetically.

"Oh, yes, I did promise—and I want to tell you," I agreed. Why don't we sit on the front porch. The shade from the big oak trees should make it cool and comfortable out there by now."

"I get to sit with Grandma in the porch swing," Tania called back as she ran outside.

"Fine," I told her. "Karl, why don't you pull up one of those white metal chairs there."

***   ***   ***

There's Music In The Air

While still living in Santa Rosa we were busy with our church, the radio broadcasts and other projects.

[I think you remember that Grandpa was pastor of the Bellevue Community Church, west of town.]

Two of our older children were married. Those approaching adulthood had their various interests.

The Christian and Missionary Alliance denomination had built a lovely church near our home. We became acquainted with the pastor and his family who lived just up the street from us. Our daughter's closest friend was the pastor's daughter.

As is usually the case in smaller churches, we didn't have a large group of young people. Our children were drawn toward the youth activities at the nearby church. We were happy to have them attend and we often went there ourselves on special occasions when we didn't have anything going on at our own church. They often scheduled outstanding singing groups and recording artists. We enjoyed these along with our teenagers.

When one of the gospel quartets that performed learned that I had several radio programs, they gave me a number of their albums to use on the air. Their music was very appropriate for my broadcast on the Country and Western station. I was soon receiving favorable response. The Claiborne Brother's Quartet became well known in that area.

In corresponding with them I mentioned that my fan mail indicated our listeners would like to hear them in person if they ever came back to Santa Rosa. They called immediately and asked if I would be interested in planning and promoting a concert if a large local auditorium could be found.

This was a new challenge for me. My family and many of our friends in the area enjoyed their music. I was hearing from more and more radio listeners. There was no doubt in my mind that we could generate plenty of interest for a concert.

I began to scout around for an appropriate place to meet. There weren't many choices: the high school or the Veteran's Memorial building. I prayed about the right place and date, and that the whole affair would be something that would honor the Lord. We decided to hold the concert in the Memorial Auditorium.

When arrangements were completed, I proceeded to promote the concert on the air, in the local newspaper, and in our own publication, *The Visitor*. And I wrote letters to all the local churches. By the time the date for the concert rolled around, just about everyone in listening distance had heard that the Claiborne Brother's Quartet was coming to Santa Rosa.

I was really nervous as the date of the event approached. So much of the success of the concert depended upon me. What if only a few people came? I had ventured out in faith and rented the largest auditorium available for the concert. How embarrassing it would be for me if only a handful turned out.

My worries were needless, however. The place was packed and people were standing around the walls. The enthusiastic crowd was ecstatic as the quartet and their lively pianist performed. Many said they had never seen anything like it in Santa Rosa. Some of those who attended had driven quite a distance to enjoy the concert. At that time, gospel music was a new phenomenon in that part of California.

One couple who were avid fans drove all the way from Walnut Creek, which was at least a two hour drive, to hear the quartet. They were impressed with the performance, the attendance, and the way I handled the promotion. At the time, they were working toward publishing a gospel music magazine.

The night of the concert the couple asked me if I would consider editing the new magazine. The problem was that they were in Walnut Creek and I lived in Santa Rosa, but they didn't give up on the idea. They called and wrote asking if I would consider moving to the Walnut Creek area.

We at least knew where Walnut Creek was. A few years earlier we had driven through it on our way across the country. We remembered it as a quiet little town in a lush green valley east of Oakland and San Francisco, often referred to as the "East Bay" area.

The town was named for the walnut orchards that at that time flourished there. They were just starting to disappear due to the growth of the area. We remarked at the time that it would be a nice place to live. However now, with this businessman's proposal, the possibility of actually moving there seemed pretty farfetched. Many things would have to be taken into consideration.

Your grandpa would still have to commute a long distance to his job, just from a different direction. He was weary of commuting, spending hours of each weekday on the highways. [In previous weeks he had said to me, "I wonder if there would be a chance that I could find work locally. I'm so tired of all the driving." But there wasn't any work in Santa Rosa. We dismissed the idea from our thoughts.]

So often we had wished the church could support our family so that he could spend most of his time among the people, looking after their welfare and promoting the growth of the church. But it was a struggling missionary work and most of those who gave had hardly enough for their own families.

[Your grandpa knew it was his responsibility to provide for our large family. He often referred to the Scripture reference in I Timothy, chapter 5, verse 8, which says, *"But if any provide not for his own, and specially for those of his own house, he hath denied the faith, and is worse than an infidel."*]

A Big Decision

By this time he had been pastoring the church at Bellevue for about eight years. There were times when we considered the possibility of moving on so that another couple, who could perhaps spend more time in the community, could replace us. We had in fact prayed about it and left the matter in the hands of the Lord as we continued our ministry there.

When the idea of moving to Walnut Creek surfaced, we couldn't help wondering if God might be directing us there. We were careful not to dismiss the possibility, and yet not to push it. And we continued to pray, and trust Him to show us His will.

When we discussed the matter with our children, we naturally received a negative response from the older ones. The oldest at home was working and had his circle of friends, including a special girl friend. Our only daughter, who had just finished her junior year in high school, announced defiantly that she was not going to leave Santa Rosa. She intended to graduate with her friends, she said. She was not about to move to a new school for her final year. Her three older brothers had all graduated from Montgomery High School and she wanted to also. We understood their feelings.

The younger children were more open to change. We did a lot of praying. There was so much to take into consideration. In addition to our church, there was our own publication and my broadcasts to consider. I was on two local stations and the large station in Southern California at the time.

When I thought it through, I couldn't see that a move to another city would make that much difference as far as my radio ministry went. I had my own recording studio and I could easily mail in all the programs. The same was true of our publication, *The Visitor*. While we wouldn't be mainly promoting the Bellevue church, we could certainly use this tool as part of the ministries that we would want to continue wherever we were.

Then there was our home. If we moved, we would have to sell it and buy another in our new location. There was always the possibility that it might not sell, or it could take months, if we decided to put it on the market.

There was so much to consider, we felt frustrated. It would have been easier just to have said, "Forget it, there's too much involved." In fact, we actually tried to do that. But we knew from previous experience that God moves His children and guides them in His own ways, because He can see the future while we can't.

At that point we simply stopped grappling with the decision; to just trust the Lord and let Him work it out the way it should be.

At the urgent invitation of our new friends in Walnut Creek, we went over to visit them. We also attended a church in nearby Lafayette that we had been told about. The pastor, an older retired Army chaplain, indicated he could use some help in the work there. It was a Christian and Missionary Alliance church like the one near our home in Santa Rosa. Lafayette was not far from Walnut Creek where the Sabatka's lived and where their business was located.

[Our music-loving friend in Walnut Creek gave your grandpa a tour of his specialty business, Sabotka Specialties. He owned various types of equipment, providing a variety of services in a broad area surrounding Walnut Creek.

"By the way," he said to your grandpa, "would you be interested in working with me?"

That was a sudden twist in events.

"I couldn't pay you as much as you make where you are, I'm sure," he said, "but you would be working locally."

The offer was tempting to your grandpa.]

After carefully assessing the area we told our new friends we would have to pray about the matter and that we would have to be completely sure it was God's will for us to move to Walnut Creek. They seemed pleased with our convictions and attitude.

We certainly did not have to be sold on the idea of living in Walnut Creek. We loved the area. While there we drove around town checking out the various housing developments and the schools. Like Gideon, in Old Testament days, we decided to let our home in Santa Rosa be the focus of a fleece before the Lord. We believed that if it was God's will that we move, He would help us find a place in Walnut Creek quickly, as well as a buyer for our home.

We came to the conclusion that our oldest son was old enough to make his own decisions and to be on his own if he chose to do so. He would probably not be living at home much longer anyway if we stayed in Santa Rosa. It was a little more difficult to deal with the situation regarding our daughter, but it wasn't long until she and my retired lady doctor friend had worked out a plan. Dr. Colman lived alone at that time. She insisted she would love to have our teenage daughter live with her and finish high school. I hated the idea of leaving her behind in Santa Rosa, but it didn't appear to be my choice.

The next step was to investigate the real estate possibilities in Walnut Creek. We drove over for another look at the area. This time we engaged a real estate agent to show us around.

By early afternoon we had found a home we liked very much near schools the children would be attending if we did move. We made an offer on it, contingent on the sale of our home in Santa Rosa.

The job offer was waiting and all the other aspects seemed to be falling into place. Now, we would see. If our Santa Rosa home sold, we would be assured of God's guidance.

We listed our house with our realtor friend and he began showing it right away. He told us he liked the place with its acreage in the middle of town so much, he would buy it if someone didn't scoop it up soon.

Believing we were doing what we were supposed to do, we agreed to pay rent on the Walnut Creek house, while waiting for our Santa Rosa house to sell, and with the younger part of our family we moved to Walnut Creek.

Open Windows

The move to Walnut Creek was a big step but there were many indications that God was leading us. Physically, we were exhausted.

[Your grandpa's health had been deteriorating over a long period of time. He had never fully recovered from the rigors of our years on the mission field. He was extremely anxious to get the move over with and to begin work near home.]

It didn't take us long to get settled into our new home on San Benito Avenue, in the San Miguel subdivision.

[Your dear grandpa found his new job a welcome relief from the endless hours he usually spent on the highways. In an effort to regain his health, he purposely avoided becoming too involved in the church we were attending. He was available however, and helped when he was needed.]

We had hardly unpacked the studio equipment when I approached a radio station in nearby Concord about getting a program on the air locally. The handsome young station manager was active with the Youth For Christ ministry in the area. He was impressed with my idea for a 30 minute program which we would call *The Open Windows Chapel Hour*. I explained that I would like to include a five-minute sermon featuring the retired Army chaplain who was pastoring the church we were working with. He had also had radio experience. Chaplain Harry Webster would come to my studio and record his short sermonettes and I would produce the programs. As I did on my *Faith For The Family* program, I included a story that fit in with the sermon and music. It was the beginning of a radio ministry that would continue for many years on that station.

I was very busy with the various broadcasts and with the new music magazine which I had agreed to edit. The magazine, however, although it started out with a bang, fizzled out after a few months. I believe that the idea of its existence was a link in a chain of events which God used to further His purpose in our lives at that point. Working on the magazine led to a number of other opportunities that would not have been available otherwise.

It didn't take me long to work out a routine so that I was able to do a number of broadcasts more easily than when I had only one.

I worked several hours each day in my studio and devised a chart and logs to help me keep track of what I used on each program and which tapes were coming and going. At times, it was pretty confusing. I had to really concentrate to keep it all under control.

San Benito Avenue

The children adjusted well to their new schools. I became involved in their activities, as I had always tried to do with the older children.

[Your grandpa was now able to attend school meetings with me. He got to know the teachers and sometimes participated in school activities with them. Sometimes he helped the children with their homework. Always before he had been too busy and too tired. It was a blessing to him and for us, to be able to have him with us more; and to be able to have dinner together at a reasonable hour most times. The extra rest during the early morning hours gave him a little added strength for the day's challenges.]

Having Daddy home more was wonderful, but there were adjustments. A considerable drop in monthly income made managing the budget even more difficult than we had anticipated. After struggling with the problem for a period of time, we decided to look for a more modest home, but "moving down" was a difficult experience for me. While our new home was not as big, and less attractive, it was comfortable.

The developments that resulted from moving to a new area were very rewarding. For a long time we had been burdened regarding our ministry. We believed that God was leading us toward another missionary project. We had no idea where, but we recognized the feeling; an impending sensation that we had experienced more than once before.

When we drove around the outlying areas, checking them out for a place to live, we prayed for God's perfect will in every aspect of our lives. In the Clayton area, east of Walnut Creek, we discovered an old church which we learned was being used for a community club house. There were several homes and a post office, as well as a large subdivision nearby. We talked to people up and down the street near the old church. We observed that there were lots of boys and girls and some teenagers in the vicinity. We immediately felt love and compassion for them.

It was easy to detect the lack of knowledge or concern regarding spiritual matters among those we talked to. We suspected it was a pretty good indication of the condition of the general area. We began to pray about the situation.

The Highlands

Once again, we sought out a real estate agent to help us find an affordable home. When he called to tell us he had chosen a few to show us, we told him we were praying about it and trusting the Lord to help us find the right house and the right community. He told us he too was a Christian.

He showed us a couple of houses which we examined with great interest and

then he said, "I have one I think would be a good deal for you, and the nearby school is highly recommended." After a moment of hesitation, as if waiting for our reaction, he went on, "I don't know if you want to look at it, it's a bit further out."

To our surprise, he drove us to the very area we had been praying about—the subdivision in the vicinity of the old church.

Even though the house was not as nice as the one we were living in, we liked it and the price was down in our range. Because of the location, we believed it to be the direct leading of the Lord. In a way, it would be like moving to a new mission field.

We made an offer on the house we had been shown, and our concern was suddenly shifted to a burden for souls in Clayton Valley Highlands.

Soon we were settled into our prayerfully chosen home in the new location and the children were registered in the new school. Our thoughts and prayers turned toward reaching out to the people who lived in homes surrounding us.

When we inquired about the availability of the old church that was currently being used as a community clubhouse, we learned that the structure was close to one hundred years old and that it had been built for and used as a church for many years. The woman in charge of renting it for various functions wasn't too sure about letting it out for use as a church again. She wasn't nearly as enthusiastic as we were, anyway.

The building was very run down. We offered to clean and paint it on the inside so that it would be acceptable for worship. This impressed her. While waiting for permission to use the building, we began talking with people who lived near the old church, as well as those around our home in the nearby subdivision.

As we always did wherever we lived, we opened our home for children's meetings one afternoon each week, and I taught the classes myself.

The new mission field turned out to be a fertile area for a Good News Club. Boys and girls came from all around. Our living room was packed every week. The eager young people, hungry to learn about God, reminded us of our missionary experience in Hawaii.

A large percentage of the children who attended the classes had never even heard the popular children's song, *"Jesus Loves Me"*, nor the Scripture which so many children can recite so easily, John:16: *"For God so loved the world, that He gave His only begotten Son, that whosoever believeth in Him should not perish, but have everlasting life."*

This verse, which is sometimes referred to as the "Gospel in a nutshell" was truly good news to that young congregation meeting in our living room. They had never heard that God loved the world nor that He loved them. Their parents did not know or care about spiritual things themselves, consequently the boys and girls had not been exposed to the Bible at all. Most of the children were at least three generations removed from any association with Christianity.

In God's wonderful, quiet way He had led us to this unsuspected mission field, only minutes from a number of Christian churches. These completely unchurched people were American heathen, living in the shadows, in the midst of a nation founded on Christian beliefs.

We were finally granted permission to use the old church, though rather reluctantly. We immediately began to transform it into a place of worship. We cleaned and painted the inside, and found some chairs that we could use in the "sanctuary". As soon as the interior was in sufficient condition we began Sunday morning worship services.

Someone who was impressed with our missionary effort gave us an old upright piano to accompany the singing. Neither of us could sing well enough to lead others without accompaniment. I was having the same problem in our Good News club sessions at home until God also answered our prayers regarding that need. We were given a small Wurlitzer electric piano which I could use in our living room. It was low enough so that I could lead the children in singing as they sat in front of the piano.

In time we were given permission to give the old church an exterior facelift. Your grandpa squeezed in many long hours painting the badly deteriorated old building so that it would attract community residents to come and worship and study with us.

[Before the job was completed your grandpa became very ill and was diagnosed as having lead poisoning. How well I remember how weak and sick and tired he was.]

We were proud when at last we were ready to mount our sign: CLAYTON COMMUNITY CHAPEL, on the front of the newly renovated building.

[In spite of being so sick, your grandpa looked radiant the day he stood on the ladder, smiling back at me as he held up the new sign to decide where to put it. "Is this about right?" he asked me.]

With the cleaning and painting completed, we began a door-to-door survey and invitation campaign to publicize the beginning of regular services. We designed a Sunday School program to meet the needs of each age group. Most of those who came knew very little if anything about the Bible.

At first we divided into only two groups, since we were the only ones available to teach. Your grandpa took the adults and teenagers and I taught all the younger ones. We planned and coordinated the lessons so that all family members could share and interact at home. Later the Lord sent us a family to help teach and we were able to divide into regular classes.

[Since everyone who came was so unfamiliar with the Scriptures, your grandpa decided to begin at the beginning when planning for the worship services. He started with the book of Genesis, and proceeded right through the Bible.]

It was remarkable how the Lord helped our pastor with sermon preparation. His work, though local, was an eight hour job, and he sometimes worked overtime. His health was still below par and he needed much more rest than he was able to manage. Somehow, even with so little time to prepare, he was able to preach sermons that were profound. They always challenged me and yet they were clear and simple enough for everyone there to understand. I know they were straight from God.

You Can Make It

Since we were meeting in a building that was used by various groups, we had to set up chairs for every service and them take them down again afterwards. [This was hard on your grandpa. It seemed like he was always weary by the time he got to his pulpit, even though many people helped him.]

In addition to working a full-time job, there was always one of our cars needing attention. We simply could not afford to hire someone else to do it. Fortunately, he was a good mechanic, but diagnosis and repairs required many tedious and frustrating hours. He often worked late into the night, and sometimes into the early morning hours in a desperate attempt to keep at least one of our old cars running.

One particular Saturday night it was eleven o'clock before we finished getting the chairs in place. Our whole family was weary from the process and the lateness of the hour. When we were finally ready to go home, the car wouldn't start. Your grandpa tried everything he could think of to get it started but to no avail. Finally, I suggested we just leave the old car and walk home.

It was over a mile to our house and uphill all the way. I had been having trouble with my hip and your grandpa didn't think I should try to walk that far. There was no other way though, since it was almost midnight and we didn't feel we could call anyone for a ride home.

"Let's go!" I suggested, "we can do it!." [But I was terribly concerned for your grandpa. He was extremely tired.]

Maybe someone will come along and give us a ride," he said, hopefully, thinking of me. But no such luck. No one was out on the road at that late hour. If they had been, we would have been afraid to ride with strangers.

We plodded along in the warm, middle of the night summer air, ascending each grade as best we could. It was slow going and hard on all of us, but it was an emergency that couldn't be avoided.

It occurred to me that this midnight crisis would not have happened to us if the Lord had not allowed it. I mentioned this to our company of weary travelers and suggested that each of us try to think of some reason why God had let this happen to us at this particular time. Some of the reasons we imagined were really quite funny.

We were soon laughing and intermittently thanking God for allowing us to enjoy such a unique experience, whatever the reason. By the time we reached the street we even felt refreshed. [Your grandpa kept reminding us not to talk too loudly lest we disturb our sleeping neighbors.]

The boys quickly fell asleep from utter exhaustion. Your grandpa sat down beside our bed on a small stool where he always took off his shoes. After a few minutes he began to weep. I put my arm around his shoulder and softly asked, "What's the matter, sweetheart?"

He squeezed my hand and sobbed, "The way you handled this emergency tonight, I know you could take care of yourself if something should happen to me."

I had no idea how prophetic his observation would turn out to be.

A Heavenly Break

The taxing car problems did not let up. [The following weeks were tiring and distressful for your dear grandpa. His boss was a sensitive person and concerned about our problems. He knew it was a constant heartache to your grandpa to have so many things that kept him from being able to spend time with his children.] To our surprise Mr. Sabatka arranged for our whole family to take an all-expenses-paid vacation to Disneyland, which at that time had only recently opened in Southern California. At first, your grandpa thought Disneyland sounded terribly juvenile. He wasn't at all excited about going. Then he decided the children would enjoy it, and that was what he wanted anyway.

[Of course we didn't have a car that would make the trip, but his boss handed your grandpa the keys to one of his newer cars, along with a credit card for gas and money for our meals.] This kind man and his wife had already made motel reservations for us and they had purchased a book of tickets for our family to enjoy the attractions at Disneyland in grand style. With everything arranged, we were on our way.

I will never forget that trip. [At first your grandpa had a hard time unwinding. He was so used to working all day on the job, then half the night on an old car. Switching gears was not easy for him. I don't think he actually felt full release until about the middle of the second day.]

We found our motel, checked in, and tried to rest from the long day's drive, and fighting the city traffic. We went to bed early so that we could get up and be at Disneyland when the gates opened the following day. We had heard so much about this amusement park; we wanted to spend as much time there as possible while we had the opportunity.

We were not prepared for how clean and healthy the environment was and the delightful surprises that awaited us there. [This was before some of the later additions which we would not have cared for were added.].

What fun it was for the children, doing such delightful things with their daddy. I can still see his expression as he began to loosen up and forget the old crippled cars at home, the things that he "needed to be doing", and the people in his church who depended on him so heavily.

It had been years since I had seen him so rested and refreshed. It thrilled my heart. I think that was the best part of the vacation for me. It was so wonderful to hear him laugh with the children as they enjoyed the antics of the Disney characters walking up and down the park. He watched as they went on all the rides and gave in when they begged him to come with them on some of them. They all encouraged me to go along and I finally gave in. I got up enough courage to go on the scariest ride they had at that time. But just when the children were all on and your grandpa right behind them, the little man who operated the ride stepped in front of me and announced, "That's all for this time!" You'll be the first on for the next run."

When I saw the frightened looks on the faces of those who got off the ride, including my own husband and children, it was evident that ride was not for me. [Your grandpa marveled at how the Lord protected me from something he knew I would not have liked.]

We all enjoyed such attractions as It's A Small World, the underwater submarine, the jungle trip and the river boat ride. But the one thing we all liked best was the speech of Abraham Lincoln, performed by a realistic, animated mannequin, complete with tears forming in his eyes and dropping onto his cheek at the appropriate time. It was so real we could hardly believe it wasn't. It really took us back in time and made us feel like we were back in the days when Mr. Lincoln was alive.

We went back the second day to let the children enjoy the rides they still had tickets for. I decided to go to the business office and see if I could influence them to do some advertising up in Northern California.

When they learned I was a radio personality, they gave me ticket books enough to insure that the children could go on every ride as often as they wished. The told me they were not doing any advertising at the time and that what they did was arranged for in a different office. I was also told that at that very moment, Mr. Walt Disney was critically ill with cancer. (Shortly after we got home, the world was saddened by the news of the death of this famous man who had become a symbol of good family entertainment.)

The third day we were in Southern California we visited Knott's Berry Farm where we discovered several interesting things to do. [Your grandpa especially enjoyed the authentic Old West reproductions, which took him back to his childhood days when he was growing up in New Mexico.]

We spent three unforgettable days at Disneyland and Knott's Berry Farm before we had to start thinking about returning to the real world.

At the insistence of the couple who paid our way, we ate several meals at restaurants that were nicer than we had ever been able to afford. The rest of the time we dined at places that were at least better than "fast food" restaurants. It wasn't easy for us to spend money that someone else had provided for food. [During that pleasant time of relaxation, your grandpa forgot that he had at first been reluctant to go to Disneyland because it was for children.] As we drove home he remarked, "If we can enjoy a place with good, clean entertainment like that so much here on earth, what must it be like in heaven." We had no idea then, but that statement was also prophetic.

[Your grandpa had never had an opportunity to become so completely involved with the family in an atmosphere that crowded out the normal cares of daily living, like he did during that short five-day vacation. It was a heavenly diversion for him.] That trip to Disneyland was an experience none of us would ever forget. I truly believe the idea originated in the mind of God and that He moved a thoughtful, sensitive couple to cause it to happen. Your grandpa was refreshed and ready to get back to work and to his duties as a pastor when we got home. I could hardly believe what a difference such a short period of change could make. Our boys enjoyed the trip very much. We had taken them out of school to go. When we went in May, they were almost the only children there. They received a lot of attention everywhere they went. And it was almost as if the Lord had planned for them to have that special time with their daddy, and he with them. They enjoyed telling their classmates about their special vacation when we returned. I was also greatly refreshed. I was able to re-enter my routine and resume my difficult schedule and was soon back where I had left off.

Dial Faith For Living

We had enjoyed our brief respite in Southern California and were now back in the swing of things and happily involved in the ministries God had given us. Each day was filled with a prayerful outreach on behalf of those within our range of influence. One day when I stopped by the radio station, the manager explained to me that they were installing a unique new telephone service. It would enable them to record the latest news headlines and weather forecast when they went off the air at sunset. Throughout the night while no one was in the office, callers could receive the pre-recorded message just by dialing a particular number. I was intrigued by the idea, as I always am by any aspect of any new idea in advanced communications.

"What a wonderful idea!" I exclaimed.

I couldn't get over the creative innovation and its potential. At dinner that evening I described the clever device to my family. [Your grandpa was impressed with my description of the new device.]

That night I kept waking up, thinking about the tremendous potential that new telephone apparatus could have. During the following days we kept thinking about it. We called the new recorded service at the radio station over and over after they had gone off the air, to try to determine how the system worked. It occurred to us that if such a device could be used so effectively for communicating regular news, most of which was not good, why couldn't it be utilized to give out the Good News of the Gospel of the Lord Jesus Christ?

We continued to pray about it and decided to call the telephone company and find out more about the service. We had no idea how much it would cost to install or to operate the innovative new telephone.

Informed with all the details, we continued to pray. We couldn't seem to shake the idea. Toward the end of July we decided it was God's will that we launch a telephone ministry.

Our target area was heavily populated and growing rapidly. The potential was overwhelming. We began to feel the burden of reaching several closely connected communities with a high concentration of people, each person with a soul for whom Christ died. Our concern for the lost had never been greater. When I called the telephone company's business office to tell them we had decided to initiate the service, I talked to an operator who told me she was also a Christian. She became very excited and was thrilled that someone had come up with the idea of putting the new device to use as a Christian ministry.

We had been thinking and praying about what we should call the service. After getting helpful input from the enthusiastic operator, we decided on DIAL FAITH FOR LIVING.

The man who came to install the service also thought it was a great idea to use the new phone for spiritual purposes.

We chose the machine with a recording capacity of about four minutes. I proceeded to write messages of that length in a notebook. Each morning one of us would dictate a new and appropriate message onto the disk. Once we hung up it was ready to be received by a caller. When someone would dial the number we would hear a click and a small light would come on, indicating someone was calling the recording.

We decided to run a continuous ad promoting the service in the personal column of the local newspaper. Very quickly, the phone began to be used almost constantly, both day and night. We reasoned that if we changed the message twice a day, callers would soon realize they could dial two different messages every day, so we began to do that. [Your grandpa would dictate one message each day and I would do the other one. There were many days when I had to do both. He simply could not get to it. I always managed to fill in for him whenever he needed me to, in each aspect of our combined ministry, with the exception of his sermon for the Sunday worship service.] As you can imagine, much was going on at our address. We both had to practice strict time management and keep on schedule. Even minor interruptions were difficult to adjust to. But we loved being deeply involved in ministries that were visibly effective and that we knew we were supposed to be doing.

A Strange Lapse In Time

Soon after we moved to the Highlands, I encountered problems in the studio. I started picking up conversations which were being broadcast and received by a ham operator who lived across the street.

The interference made it impossible to get my broadcasts done without interruption. I finally had to inform the man and his wife of the problem. They were surprised to learn I was hearing all they said. Soon after that I no longer received their transmissions and we learned that they had moved. A week or so later we watched as a new family moved into the house immediately across the street from us, but we did not meet them right away. From experience I had learned to be cautious about being overly friendly with my neighbors, lest I run into problems. Too many interruptions could easily result. I had to protect my time for the sake of the ministries I was responsible for.

One day, a month or so after our new neighbors had moved in, I was out in the yard watering our flowers and shrubs. I noticed an older couple across the street. They appeared to be visiting our new neighbors, whom I still had not met.

Can you imagine my surprise, when I heard someone call my name?

"Ardelle, is that you?" the pretty, gray-haired lady called to me from across the street.

I looked up, wondering how this elderly woman knew my name. She came running across the street with a pleasant looking older man limping behind her.

By this time the lady was crying. "Ardelle," she sobbed, "do you remember me? I'm Mrs. Winnie. You're Bill and Thelma Chappell's daughter, aren't you?"

Now I recognized them. They had been my parents' best friends over thirty years before, when I was growing up in the South. Their last name was Thomas. My head swirled as memories came flooding over me. In just a moment's time I was suddenly transported back to my childhood; it was a strange sensation.

My dear parents had been dead for many years. Their friends had moved to another state and they had lost contact with them. They didn't even know my parents has passed away. When they came to visit their son and his family who had just moved in across the street from us, they never dreamed of seeing someone they had known in the past. They were as surprised to see me as I was to see them. It amazed me that they could recognize me as a grown woman when they hadn't seen me since I was in my early teens.

They were both getting up in years and Mr. Dewey, as we always called him, was in very poor health. Mrs. Winnie was a nurse. Fortunately, she had been able to continue working as well as take care of her husband, but it was obvious that she too was feeling the effects of her age. We had so much to talk about to get caught up on the events of the lapsed years. Many tears were shed as we visited, before they left to return to their home in the Midwest.

I wanted to believe my precious parents were watching the unlikely reunion from their portal home with Jesus, where they were awaiting the great reunion in heaven, when all of us who belong to the Lord will have eternity to remember God's bountiful blessings of family and friends, and special friendships, so highly treasured in this world.

The Accident

The events of the next few weeks still stand out clearly in my mind.

It was now September and your grandpa insisted that I enroll in an advanced electronics class at the local junior college to continue my studies. I tried to refuse to go because I was needed more at home but he would not let me drop out. It required two evenings, one lecture and one lab. I felt guilty about being away from him and the family for two evenings every week, but he insisted. The math associated with that course was extremely difficult for me. It had been so long since I had been in school, I had lost my knack for it. But your grandpa encouraged me and took time to sit down and try to help me. He had been exceptionally good in math in his younger years, but he had also been out of school for a long time. To his utter frustration, he found the formulas I was supposed to learn and the problems I was supposed to solve too complex for him to understand. Being forced to admit that he couldn't help me that much, especially with a subject he had excelled in, really threw him. I felt guilty about bringing a difficult situation about, and wished with all my heart that I had simply refused to take the course, even against his wishes.

I did the best I could in the class and tried to believe my instructor when he insisted the mathematical aspect of the course was really quite easy. It WAS easy for him, but I still struggled.

Early in October, the first rain took us by surprise. Your grandpa had gone to work unprepared for it and came home soaking wet. He built a fire in the fireplace and hovered close to it, sitting on the hearth. He looked so cold, so tired, so thin; I was deeply concerned about him.

On Monday night he was too weary to work on our cars. We went to bed early but we didn't go to sleep. Instead, we talked for hours about the wonderful way the Lord had worked in out lives. He recalled things from his childhood that he probably hadn't thought of since, until then. He shared thrills and heartaches he had experienced over the years; things he had never mentioned to anyone.

He talked about how his mother had looked to him for help and understanding during the trying seasons of her life. She had shared unbelievable heartaches, disappointments and hardships to help relieve her burdened heart. His dear mother had been with the Lord for many years.

He had not told anyone before, keeping it in strict confidence, and it seemed to relieve him a great deal to tell me.

He remembered and related to me how he had helped his mother with chores that were too much for her, especially when her health began to fail. And he recalled sadly, how he had been dubbed by his friends, classmates, and even family members as a "sissy" because he knew how to cook, wash clothes and iron.

Often in those days, he would work late into the night helping her, because his slave-driving father made him work extra long days in the fields and doing outside chores. Many times he felt he was helping his mother against his father's wishes.

His dad was a typical example of a pioneer man who expected women, especially his woman, to do all the work in the house and take care of the children, and work alongside him in the field as well. Many women in those days received little respect from their husbands, or consideration for having been born a woman. That's the way it had been with those who had gone before, and that's how it was with them.

That night as we lay there in bed, your grandpa recalled again his conversion experience, which he had told me about when we were courting and contemplating marriage. He often referred to it for it was very real to him. As he remembered one more time, he relived that vivid memory all over again. He wept as he thanked me for praying for him and for standing with him during the years of our ministry together.

"I could never have done it without you," he said, holding me close. "I know God brought us together. He knew I needed you . . . you have been the best wife any man could hope for. I love you so much!"

It was very late when we finally fell asleep.

The next evening he got home late and I had to rush to class. I had a good hot dinner waiting for him and I left with a picture in my mind of my family, sitting down to a dinner I had prepared for them with love. It was an image I will never forget. As I went out the front door I heard my children eagerly sharing the events of the day with their daddy. He always listened carefully to each trial and triumph while he enjoyed the nourishing food before him. Everyone was glancing at the lemon meringue pie sitting on the counter nearby. The following night, your grandpa hurriedly left the dinner table with apologies to his family to get to the garage in an effort to get our second car running. I needed it badly. I kept asking him if there was anything I could do to help.

"Please come to bed," I pled with him as midnight approached. "You need the rest," I insisted, "We'll get by somehow."

"The motor seems to be frozen," he told me. I didn't know what that meant and I couldn't do anything about it except pray. I did a great deal of that.

It was hard for us to understand why we just could not seem to have two cars running at the same time, and sometimes not even one.

That night your grandpa urged me to go on ahead to bed, he wanted to make progress on the car he was working on before calling it a day. I finally did, but I couldn't go to sleep. My heart ached so for him. When he at last came to bed he felt he hadn't accomplished anything, and he was too tired to sleep. He wanted to talk about our daughter who was attending college in San Francisco. She was so precious to his heart. We were both terribly concerned about her. Having her away from home and living in a big, wicked city was a constant burden on our hearts. The bad influence of college atmosphere worried us, even when she was in a Christian college. When she decided to transfer to a secular college, we were sick at heart.

That night he imagined every awful thing that might happen to her. He even mentioned his fear that some communist front youth organization might try to entice her. We felt a great burden to pray for her.

When he finally fell asleep, it was almost time for him to get up. They were going to be working out of town that day, and I was really troubled about his weariness.

It was late when they got back to the equipment yard that night. By the time he got home I was late for class. Before I got into the car to leave he held me close and said, "Sweetheart, I love you—so much!"

As always, he kissed me through the window. I had to go. Road construction near the campus made local travel stressful. By the time I finally got home after class, it was past eleven o'clock. Your grandpa was already asleep. I knew he had to leave earlier than usual the following morning because it was Friday and they wanted to finish the project they had started the previous day.

I set my mental clock to get up and see him off but when I awoke, he had already gone. I wept and prayed as I tried to do the things I had to get done. My heart was heavy. I had only seen my precious husband a few minutes the night before and missed him entirely that morning.

The day seemed to drag on. I went about preparing dinner on time because I knew your grandpa would be very tired and hungry when he got home. When he didn't get home at the usual time, and it kept getting later and later, I thought perhaps the project had taken longer to complete than they had anticipated, or that he was having car problems. I knew if it was possible, he would call me if he saw he was going to be very late because he knew we would be worried.

When he hadn't come home or called by seven o'clock, I became very uneasy. By eight o'clock I was frantic. I knew something was wrong. Then the phone rang. It was your uncle, who had been working with him.

"Mother," he said. "Daddy has been in an accident. Can you come to the hospital?"

Then he told me which hospital he was in and a few more details. He knew I had no transportation so he had called the bookkeeper for the firm he and his dad worked for and asked him if he could take me to the hospital. His wife offered to keep the children.

I was trembling when I hung up the phone. The first thing I had to do was tell the boys the terrible news and then hurry and get dressed before the bookkeeper got there. The drive from our home in Clayton Valley

Highlands to San Jose was further than I had remembered. It seemed like we would never arrive at the hospital and I knew they would be waiting for my signature before they could operate if needed.

I did not know what to expect when I got to the hospital. I had been told that he was being transferred from a smaller medical facility in Fremont, where the accident had occurred, to a large hospital in San Jose, where a well-known neurosurgeon was available. I knew this meant the situation was very serious.

"Come this way," the nurse instructed, as soon as I entered the hospital. "The doctor wants to see you as quickly as possible."

He explained that your grandpa had been very seriously injured when he fell from the back of a slow moving truck, hitting his head on the cement road surface.

"We can operate," he said, "but it won't do any good. He's too far gone. I don't advise it."

He told us it was just a matter of time and that he was only being kept alive with the help of life-support machines.

They took me into the intensive care unit where he was fighting a losing battle for his life. I could hardly bear to watch him lying there in that awful state. Silently, I asked the Lord for strength.

It was just the beginning of a long period of waiting. I stayed by him as long as they would let me, then sat in a nearby waiting room where I was asked to remain so they could find me if I was needed.

I was weary but unable to sleep. A nurse brought me a pillow, trying to help me get comfortable enough to at least rest. I could not. Later they told me they had prepared a bed for me and urged me to try to sleep for a while. They knew what I was facing and that I would need the added strength. As hard as I tried, I could not sleep, but I really appreciated their thoughtfulness.

On Saturday morning someone brought me a San Jose newspaper. I thought perhaps reading would help me get drowsy enough to at least doze. I thumbed through the newspaper, mostly looking at the pictures. My eyes were too tired to read. Then a headline caught my eye. "What To Do When A Loved One Dies," it said.

How strange, I thought, that an article like that would just happen to be in that paper and on that particular day. I later realized why. It was there for my benefit. It offered helpful insights and suggestions that would help me handle the crisis period I was approaching.

Early Sunday morning, before it was time for my broadcasts to go on the air, I called the different radio stations in Northern California and asked them to please just play appropriate music at the time I was scheduled to be on the air, since my husband was near death in a San Jose hospital.

One of the reasons I chose to do that was because so many people believed I was actually in the studio at the radio station, for every broadcast. I didn't want anyone to think I had not been with my dying husband when they would hear of his passing later. Between selections, the operators suggested listeners pray for my husband and for my family and me.

Calls began coming into the hospital from many areas. The lines were soon jammed. Finally they called me into the business office where they insisted calls would have to be limited.

When the switchboard could no longer handle the calls they told me they would only be able to accept them from those who identified themselves as family. Others would be asked to leave a message for me. They could not afford to have their lines tied up to that extent, they said.

Death Of A Warrior

At eleven o'clock that Sunday morning, they came to the room where I was waiting to tell me your grandpa had died.

The older children had come to the hospital and were nearby to stand with me as the full impact hit me. Even though I knew it was coming, it was extremely difficult. [I called your grandpa's father who lived in the eastern part of the United States to inform him that our loved one was gone. We all knew he didn't have a chance, despite our hopes and prayers. He was too far gone. Your great-grandpa Brown informed me that they were ready to leave to come to California for the funeral.]

I decided to wait until I was back with the younger boys before telling them that their father had died. My head was swirling with thoughts of all I had to do. There were so many decisions to make and I was so weary. While trying to get arrangements under control at the hospital a priest came and asked me to go for a walk with him. (It was a Catholic hospital).

As we strolled across the grass expanses surrounding O'Connor Hospital that balmy October morning, the whole world took on a different hue for me. I was just awakening to the realization that the earthly sun would never shine on my loved one again. But I knew he was in heaven, with his Savior and Lord whom he had loved so much and served so faithfully.

As we walked and talked, I told the priest that it was the hour when he would have been preaching to his congregation. It was precious to me that he died at the exact time that he would have been going into his pulpit for the Sunday morning worship service.

Later, it occurred to me that the accident happened about five o'clock on Friday, at the time when he was just getting off work from his secular job.

The priest was kind and thoughtful. He let me talk, then he told me how fortunate I was to have had such a kind, loving, and caring husband for twenty-eight years.

During our stroll together I told the priest about our ministry together down through the years and also about my radio ministry. He said I appeared to him to be the type of person who would be able to carry on and he wished me well.

I was taking my first steps into widowhood. The responsibilities and burdens of a large family, three of whom were still at home, and the concerns for all of them were just beginning to settle on my shoulders. I expressed no doubt about my faith in the God I served and trusted and that He would give me the strength to make it through all the hurdles that would be coming my way.

Making The Big Adjustment

One of the most difficult aspects of the whole ordeal was having to tell my young sons that their father would not be coming home. I was relieved that they felt as strongly as I did that he was not actually dead but that he had just gone to be with Jesus.

I remember when a few days later a friend mentioned his "death". My ten year old looked at him with an expression I will never forget. His eyes were saying, "He's not dead", and I knew his faith was strong. Knowing what the Bible says and being assured of their daddy's faith eased the pain for all of us. The children and I decided to have the funeral service in Santa Rosa. We thought it was appropriate to bury him there. We had lived there longer than any other place. (Our oldest son still lived there.)

Wearily I pulled myself together and assembled the necessary papers so that we could make the funeral arrangements in Santa Rosa. The Lord had to help me. I was unable to sleep or eat for such a long time, my body was exhausted from the strain. I will never forget the comfort my children gave me during that time.

While in Santa Rosa we stayed with my oldest son and his family. They took care of such details as buying new outfits for the boys to wear for the service, and they took me to a nice department store and bought me a nice black suit along with some good shoes.

I tried hard to be brave for the children's sake. We asked a minister friend in Santa Rosa and the retired army chaplain we had worked with in Lafayette to share in the service.

The lovely weather held out and on the day of the funeral, the autumn sun streamed through the stained glass windows of the chapel as people came from near and far to pay their last respects to a man who was loved by all and to share with his family in their time of bereavement. It was as though a bit of heavenly light was filtering down to assure us all of the safe arrival of our loved one.

How fitting were the beautiful words of the ministers as they voiced for everyone present what each would have liked to have said themselves. It was a precious and fitting memorial service.

A good friend of ours told me later that he had also gone to another funeral that day, for a man who did not know the Lord. He said it was the saddest funeral he had ever attended. There was no hope for the deceased. The contrast was indescribable.

Our friend told me he had never attended a more beautiful service than ours. "It is perhaps the greatest testimony for Christianity," he said, "to compare the hope we have in Christ to the hopelessness of those who do not acknowledge God, when death comes."

There were many beautiful floral arrangements, though many chose to give instead to a fund that was set up to help us adjust financially. The staff at the Chapel of Roses funeral home helped me with many details I had not anticipated. Since your grandpa had served in the armed forces, his children were eligible for veteran and social security benefits. I knew absolutely nothing about setting these in motion. Those kind people helped me fill out each form and made the contacts for me. By the time we left Santa Rosa the process was underway. When we got back to our county, however, I found I had many more things to do before we could receive any financial help. For one thing, I did not have birth certificates for every member of the family. These had to be sent for and as it turned out, acquiring them took a long time.

When we moved to Walnut Creek from Santa Rosa, the insurance agent who came to our home to help us transfer our homeowner's policy had asked your grandpa a straightforward question.

"Don't you think you should have mortgage insurance, in case something should happen to you?"

I'll never forget the look on your grandpa's face when that possibility was brought to his attention.

"You know, I think you are right," he admitted. "How much would it cost?"

The agent explained two different plans. We decided on the one that would pay eighty percent of the balance of the loan in case of death. It was all we felt we could do at the time.

Now, at the time of his death, I notified the company right away, hoping to save our home for which we had worked so hard.

It didn't take long for me to see that they were going to do whatever they had to do to keep from paying my claim. What they didn't realize was that I had a heavenly attorney who was looking after me to protect me from unscrupulous people. I referred to my "attorney" in all of my correspondence. When they asked for his name and address, I knew I had to employ an earthly lawyer also. It soon became clear that this case would have to be fought in terms they could understand and it wasn't until I obtained an attorney that they finally gave me the money I had coming. I had always heard that widows were prime targets for all kinds of unethical dealings and I was now learning that it was true.

My second and third sons helped me get my transportation problems under control. They did most of the work to keep my car going and when it needed repair work that they could not do, they made the arrangements for me and saw to it that I was not taken advantage of. Fortunately, they were both talented mechanics, something they undoubtably inherited from their dad.

It didn't take long for me to learn how to hold my own in new situations in which I found myself. Anyone dealing with me soon saw that I was not going to let myself be pushed around and when they learned that I trusted God to protect me, most didn't want to tackle Him.

One of the biggest adjustments I had to make was learning how to handle the finances. I had not been the one who wrote the checks or paid the bills. That posed a fearful responsibility for me.

Aware of my complete ignorance in that area and knowing I still had to do it sent me to my knees in prayer. I cringe to think of what I would have done if I had not known the Lord or how to pray. I would lay my paperwork and checkbook on the bed, and kneel and ask God to help me.

We would never have been able to make it financially if I had not been frugal and we had not had a heavenly Father looking after us. It was months before we received the first checks from Social Society and the Veterans Administration, or the insurance companies.

God knew our predicament and our trust in Him. He saw to it that help came from various sources, often completely unexpected. We would hear from someone who would say, "the Lord laid it upon my heart to send you this", and a check would be enclosed. We always had enough to just barely get by. We didn't go hungry but when the money we were supposed to get did start coming from the sources we certainly knew how to appreciate it. It was still a meager amount to live on but at least we could depend on something coming in regularly each month.

I was often reminded of God's faithfulness to us and how He had always proven to me that I could trust Him, even during times when it seemed like He was making a mistake. I vividly remembered how all of us—myself, my parents, my church family—had doubted God's wisdom in seeming to fail to answer our prayers to prevent your grandpa from having to enter military service so many years before. But God could see ahead and we couldn't. He knew the benefits we would receive later and that they would be especially needed at that time.

I considered working but quickly decided my children needed me more than we needed what I could make. I would still have to pay for their care. In the years ahead we never doubted that I had made the right decision. Trying to be both father and mother to young children is a full-time, twenty-four hour a day job. They were my divinely appointed responsibility, as well as my blessing, and I wanted to be available when they needed me.

Even though my boys often had less than their friends, they never complained. They were assured of my love and they knew they could depend on me to take care of them the best I knew how.

The lack of money and possessions was the least of my children's concerns as they learned to go on living without their daddy. They missed him terribly. My ten-year old actually developed physical symptoms which kept us running to the doctor. One day our family physician told me, "The only thing wrong with this child, I believe, is just a ten-year-old boy's adjustment to losing his father."

In my feeble attempt to help them I tried to fill in as many of the voids as possible. I knew how much they had enjoyed hearing their father tell of his boyhood experiences as a cowboy in New Mexico, I arranged for riding lessons for them, but that didn't work. I tried to get them out of the house by going places and doing things with them to help get their minds off of their loneliness, but they still were not consoled. Family and friends gave them special attention, especially the older one who seemed to be suffering the most. I think we all took it for granted that his younger brother was fine. I'm sure I hadn't been as alert to his feelings as I should have been, as hard as I had tried.

We were coming home from someplace one day when my seven-year old suddenly burst into sobs. Trying to comfort him didn't help. I pulled the car off the road and gave him my full attention. I begged him to tell me what was wrong. When he finally stopped crying enough to speak he said, "I miss Daddy, too."

That was when I realized that all of us had been giving his older brother more attention and sadly neglecting a little boy who didn't express his emotions as much. From that point on, I saw to it that that particular oversight was not repeated.

Their next older brother had moved out of the home by this time. He was a constant concern for me. I did not realize until much later how much his father's death had affected him. I did what he would allow me to do for him at the time, and I prayed for him constantly.

I suffered a lot of pain myself, trying to help fill the void in my children's lives. In addition to my own battle of loneliness, I experienced constant feelings of inadequacies and fear of failure as a single parent. It took me a long time to get over feeling guilt for failing my husband by going to school two nights a week and being away from him so much the last few weeks of his life, even though I knew how much he insisted that I go. Sympathetic friends who had worked with him assured me that he was proud of my efforts to learn and enhance my ministry. They were sure he would have had it no other way, they told me.

"He was pleased that you have talent, ambition, and persistence," they said. "He always spoke of you with pride."

Understanding friends expressed their love and thoughtfulness during those lonely weeks and months when I was experiencing the pangs of sorrow. Many wrote notes and sent cards of encouragement. I had been warned that at first I would be inundated with condolences and consideration but that soon it would all cease, but many of my friends near and far never did let me down. One friend, who was also widowed, sent me a copy of Catherine Marshall's book, *"To Live Again"*. I found comfort and encouragement in her understanding words, as she shared her experience of trying to cope with the loss of her husband, Peter Marshall. Fortunately I was deeply involved in various ministries. It would have been much more difficult if I had had time on my hands. It helped that I knew I was serving the Lord as He had called me to do, helping people with their spiritual needs. I was indeed thankful for my radio ministry, which was far reaching and fulfilling. Then there were the ministries we shared: the church and the telephone ministry. I was grieving along with our congregation in the loss of our pastor, mine as well as theirs. Our precious church family was dazed by the sudden loss of their pastor we all suffered. Each of the adults tried to show me special concern, their way of expressing their love and respect for him. The young couple whom the Lord had sent to help us when we needed Sunday School teachers so badly were especially saddened. They had grown to love the people they were working with and had the highest respect for their pastor.

[A short time before the accident, Tom and Agnes had bought your grandpa a beautiful new suit, which he desperately needed. He looked handsome in the stylish suit after wearing donated missionary clothes for so many years. Now, they asked me if he could be buried in it. It seemed appropriate to them and I agreed.]

The boys and girls who attended our church services and Good News clubs were not sure how to take the news of the accidental death of Reverend Brown. For most of them it was their first experience with death. They had many questions.

One day after I resumed my weekday club classes in our home, one bright young boy looked straight into my eyes and said, "You really do believe what you teach, don't you?"

I think the children in the club expected me to be mourning and crying like they do in the movies, where people who have no hope are depicted.

I taught a lesson specifically to answer their questions about death. It was evident that some of their inquiries had originated in family discussions on the subject at home. What a wonderful opportunity for me to minister to their families, I realized. I knew they would repeat what I told them when they got home. Our sudden tragedy had certainly caused the parents of the children we worked with to be at least momentarily sensitive to the reality of death and life hereafter. Some of the boys and girls had a hard time believing that Reverend Brown was really gone, and that he would never return. Our assurance that he was actually more alive than ever with the Lord Himself helped them sense the victory of the resurrection, and eternal life for Christians.

One day, shortly after the funeral, I ran into the mother of one of the children at the local supermarket. [Your grandpa had been in their home a few times and had been especially burdened about their spiritual welfare.] When this mother saw me, she was reminded of his efforts and quite obviously convicted of her lifestyle. She apologized for not coming to church as she and her husband had promised to do. She told me that they had wanted to come but just kept putting it off. I understood.

A few weeks later I was pleasantly surprised to see this mother and her husband coming into the church. Their son was walking beside them, his face beaming with pure pleasure. He could hardly wait for me to greet them. He wanted them to feel welcome. My heart leapt for joy as I shook their hands. [I knew your grandpa would have been thrilled to see them there.]

The responsibility of our pastor-less flock rested heavily upon my shoulders. I was able to arrange for different speakers each week, often inviting missionaries home on furlough, until we were able to get a regular pastor.

[We had only been involved with our Dial Faith For Living telephone ministry a little over two months when your grandpa was taken from us.]

A missionary, home on furlough, who happened to be living up the street from us volunteered to change the messages for me while I was in Santa Rosa for the funeral. When I returned home he sat down with me for a heart to heart talk.

"Ardelle," he pointed out gently, "I suggest you only try to change the message on your phone once each day. I don't think you'll have time for more than that."

He was right and I took his advice. There were more things to demand my time than I could have imagined. Each day I consciously attempted to keep my priorities in order. My children were my first and most important responsibility. They deserved much of my time and I didn't begrudge them of it. But I don't believe I failed them by continuing my ministries. Instead, I think it only helped me to be a better mother. Certainly their father would have felt that way.

I made every effort to get my broadcasts produced while they were in school or early in the morning when they were sleeping, so that I could spend as much time as possible with them. We often took short trips, sometimes to visit their sister in San Francisco or their brothers in Santa Rosa. And we went to the cemetery in Santa Rosa as often as we could. Once we went to Sacramento to visit the state capitol. It was a fun time for us as a family. (I also made notes and later took my radio listeners on a proxy tour on my educational broadcast.)

In the evening when the homework was done, we would watch television together. When our old black and white TV finally quit, I loaded the boys in the car and we went shopping for a "new" used one. We wanted color but we couldn't afford it on a new set, so we looked at some used television shops. The boys were amazed as I bargained with each proprietor for a good deal. Finally we decided on an older set in a really nice cabinet for what I considered a good price. I think the salesman felt sorry for us as we tried for something better than we could afford.

When we got home, your uncle, who has a knack for that sort of thing, gave it his magic touch. It worked better than any of the new sets we had admired in the stores, and it lasted for a number of years. Watching programs together was much more interesting in color.

My older children and my first grandchildren were a rich blessing to me during the time after your grandpa's death. Their understanding and thoughtfulness helped to ease my loneliness and provided the needed support to help carry me through that difficult period.

The Listening Ear

Spending time with my children was satisfying, and I appreciated my family but I was thankful for avenues of ministry which the Lord had given me. I needed the association with other adults also, and the Lord saw to it that I had that. The several broadcasts God had given me occupied much of my time and the telephone ministry was especially close to my heart. I carried the burdens of those who called, even though I did not know them, and I spent a lot of time in prayer.

From the time I began dictating only one message each day, I felt there must be some way to accomplish more through the ministry, but I didn't know how.

Then I read an article in a Christian magazine written by a man who had discovered a way to use his telephone as a ministry with a device similar to the answering machine which is so common today. I doubted if those who were calling my Dial Faith For Living service would leave a message, but the article set me to thinking and I believe the Lord gave me an idea.

I decided to give my personal telephone number at the end of my four-minute message and invite anyone who had questions or spiritual needs that I might be able to help them with to call me—anytime day or night. I also mentioned that they need not identify themselves. I had a spill-over number, so that if someone called and I was on the line, the other number would catch it. On the very day that I first invited callers to dial me personally the floodgates opened. An unbelievable amount of pain and grief was brought to my prayerful attention. All day and half the night a steady stream of calls representing the concentration of troubled humanity in that metropolitan area continued to light up that phone. A large percentage of them would call me to express their personal needs anonymously. I was often interrupted while working, but the Lord seemed to help me make up the time. Somehow I was always able to make my deadlines. I made every effort to deal with the troubled callers in an unrushed manner. I always answered the phone very graciously and tenderly because I never knew whose broken heart might be trembling on the other end of the line.

I often picked up the phone and would hear only soft sobbing. The caller had finally gotten up courage to dial my number but couldn't even speak, so I would wait until they could. People from all walks of life called me. All kinds of people; frightened children, troubled and frustrated youth, young marrieds and older people called, and most felt free to call again when they needed to. They would tell their friends who would also call. Just about every type of problem you could imagine was represented.

Many men and women with marital problems would call and unburden their hearts anonymously. Sometimes they would reveal great personal pain because of unfaithful spouses. I even listened to confessions of some who were themselves involved in an affair and whose spouse was unsuspecting. I could sense their guilt right over the telephone. Women with midlife difficulties would often discuss their real or imagined problems, which usually looked different when voiced, they would admit. Often when people shared, I would simply listen, not saying a word. At times my heart was so full of other people's troubles it almost burst. God gave me an understanding heart, a sympathetic, listening ear, loving concern and a soothing voice.

I was aware that the Lord had entrusted me with a gift of discernment. Very few tried to fool me by making up problems. When they did, I could detect it and would confront them. Usually that person would apologize, often admitting even more bizarre stories that WERE true; confessions they had never revealed to anyone before. They would often break down and cry when they realized they were caught. When they recognized my true concern for them, they would feel ashamed to admit they had tried to fool me.

It was the decade of the 1960's: San Francisco and outlying areas were being invaded with "hippies" and "flower children". Many of them were runaways, determined to keep their whereabouts undetected. When these frightened young people discovered they could talk to me anonymously, they would cry their hearts out over the phone. I often felt I was the only real contact they had with another caring human being at the time. (I never once betrayed one individual caller, or violated anyone's trust.)

These young people would often tell me how much they would like to go home. Just saying the word "home" would cause some to break up. But they honestly believed their parents didn't understand them, or want them with them, and in many cases this was undoubtably true.

There were times when I was able to help them see the situation from their parent's viewpoint, as well as their own. But many of them were indeed not welcome at home.

Some were from broken homes, with pitiful stories to tell of relationships that appeared to be beyond repair and without hope. Many of these young persons had actually been pushed out by their parents who simply could not cope with adolescent problems in a modern world.

A large percentage told me that one or both of their parents were alcoholic and some admitted that they themselves were already enslaved by substance abuse. Some confessed that they stole or engaged in other crimes to feed their habits. As they shared their intimate lives, my heart would break. I cannot describe the pain I suffered in those days.

I know God honored the time I spent with these dislocated, troubled youths, and the prayers I lifted up to Him in their behalf. Often, a call would end with the young person sighing, "Oh, I feel so much better after talking to you."

Some had left home for a trivial reason, only to realize later that what had seemed to them a bad situation had turned into something much worse. Once in a while a teen would say, "I'm going to call my parents right now and tell them where I am." That always made me feel good. I could sense the effect it would have on both them and their parents. Times like that were rewarding.

Occasionally I would get calls from people who wanted to challenge me. Two students from Berkeley thought they would have some fun at my expense. One would get on the extension phone and between the two of them, they would fire Bible questions at me. Often they would bring up what they considered contradictions in the Bible, but they soon would realize that they were the ones who were stumped. God always gave me the right answers to their questions.

Before long they would begin asking serious questions about God and the Scriptures. Then I would have the opportunity to explain God's wonderful plan of salvation. Only God knows if those two young men ever accepted the Savior. I witnessed faithfully to them many times on the phone and they even told me that they believed, but I had to leave that up to the Lord.

One thing I know for sure, neither of them could ever stand before God and say they didn't know Jesus loved them or that He died for them. I would not be surprised to meet them in heaven someday.

During the five years that I carried on that ministry until I moved from the area, I dealt with almost every problem you could imagine. I even had individuals tell me they could not talk to their minister about the issues they were sharing with me. They didn't believe he would understand and they didn't think he would be willing to listen to their problems. They were convinced he would condemn them without hearing them out. I never agreed with them regarding such accusations even though I knew what they were imagining was probably true. I knew some ministers myself who were hard to approach.

The physically handicapped and homebound were frequent callers. I remember a young blind man who would call me every day. He had hours of time on his hands with nothing to do. When I told him I was moving out of the area and would be turning the ministry over to someone else, he was devastated.

There were times, I have to admit, that the ministry was almost too heavy for me, but God gave me extra strength. It was not unusual to have someone call me in the very early morning hours. That's when desperate souls find it difficult to sleep. I would suddenly be awakened from deep sleep by the phone ringing and quickly answer so the boys wouldn't wake up. The mumbling voice at the other end would apologize, then pour out their sad story.

It might be a frightened wife whose husband had not returned home. She knew that when he did, he would be drinking and possibly a threat to her and the children. She was calling to fortify herself against the inevitable. Many of these "wee hours" callers were alcoholics. They hated the way they were and wanted to be free of their terrible addiction. They often asked me to pray for them over the phone. Sometimes they would talk for an hour or more. When they would finally hang up, I would put their case in God's hands and fall asleep quickly. Miraculously, I would feel no loss of sleep the next day. I know it was the Lord's mercy. I do not doubt He gave me added strength.

Whatever the problem or its severity, I always pointed the troubled one to Christ the Savior. He alone could provide the help they needed. My part was to lend a listening ear and to tell them of the only One who could help them, really.

I will never know in this life, the actual results of that unusual ministry which I carried on for more than five years. I'm sure suicides were prevented, complex problems eased if not solved, and I have no idea how many sincerely accepted Christ as their Savior. Many said they did but I am satisfied to leave that in God's hands. We can't save anyone, we can only bring the lost to Christ. Only God knows when its real.

Trying To Carry On With Daddy Gone

One of my deepest concerns in trying to raise my sons alone was my fear of having them grow up without masculine influence. Friends suggested it would be good to have them in a Christian school where they would get special attention because they were fatherless.

The two boys still at home were now eight and twelve years old. They welcomed the idea of attending a Christian school. [Your grandpa and I had earlier observed disturbing concepts that were being taught in the public schools. My concern had intensified when I was faced with the full responsibility of raising the younger children by myself.]

I wanted desperately to get them out of the system but I knew we could not possibly afford the tuition, no matter how much we tried to sacrifice. The problem appeared too big for me to handle and impossible to solve. But I knew how to pray, and pray I did.

Because I had no idea how much it would actually cost to send them, I inquired at the office of a reputable school which was sponsored by a local Baptist church. When I explained my situation they told me they had a policy of taking children of pastors and missionaries in their denomination on scholarships. We were not members of their denomination, but the pastor of that church and also the Sunday School superintendent knew about our missionary work in Clayton, as well as our telephone ministry and my broadcasts. They told me they were impressed with my efforts to continue the various ministries while raising my fatherless children alone.

To my complete surprise, the executive board agreed to accept my two young sons free of tuition on my part, even though we were not Baptists. It was a remarkable answer to prayer. As He so often does, God answered in a way that I could not have imagined.

In those days I was always conscious of God's protection and care for our little family. We didn't have an earthly father to depend on, but our heavenly Father was always there. We learned to trust Him.

Mother Gets A Break

During the weeks and months following the untimely death of your grandpa, I kept extremely busy with the ministries and my children. Friends and relatives observed that I needed a break. One couple volunteered to look after the boys so that I could attend a weekend Navigators conference at Mount Herman, a popular Christian campground, a four or five hour drive from our home. I went with three other people I knew.

While at the conference I met many lovely Christians and thoroughly enjoyed their fellowship. I hadn't realized how much I needed to participate in adult activities. The sessions were inspiring. The keynote speaker emphasized our responsibility to witness to the unsaved.

"We are ambassadors on earth," he challenged. "It's easier for some to share the good news of the Gospel because they have a natural charisma."

I was sitting in front of a lovely young couple I had met at the conference. The wife leaned over and whispered to me, loud enough that others turned to look at us, "You have that charisma."

I was embarrassed but I also realized that God had given me a gift for sharing Jesus and working with people. That weekend conference was like a springtime tonic. I was refreshed and ready to get back in the harness again. As I juggled my projects and family and duties, I promised myself that I would try to arrange for another "mother break" soon.

The Tired Tour Guide

Early the second year after the accident, two of my single aunts who lived in Washington D.C. where they worked for the government wrote me that they would like to go to Hawaii on their next vacation. They asked if I would consider coming along as a tour guide. They had friends who also wanted to go. They offered to pay my way if I would be willing to plan the itinerary, make the reservations, and give them a personalized tour when we got there. They knew I was familiar with the Islands and knew my way around.

My three youngest sons had never been to Hawaii. You can imagine how the idea affected them. They knew that your grandpa and I had talked about it and dreamed of one day taking them to the beautiful islands where their older sister and brothers had lived and played and gone to school.

This seemed like the perfect time for me to go back to Hawaii and take the children. However I knew I had to pray and make sure it was what I was supposed to do.

When I was convinced that the timing was right and the proposed vacation was indeed God's will for us, I went to a local travel bureau and picked up some brochures. I also mailed some back to Washington and asked my aunts to come up with some appropriate dates so that I could make travel arrangements and reserve accommodations. I suggested we fly one way and take an ocean liner the other. From my experience, I knew everyone would enjoy that. Since I was so heavily involved and had so many radio programs, I knew I would have to work many extra hours every day to meet my broadcast deadlines for the time I would be gone and for the week after I got back. The aunts and their friends were going to be with us for an additional week after we returned so that they could take a closer look at California.

With meticulous care I worked up a chart showing the number of tapes I would need for each program on each station, then I began working toward my goal. It was a tedious, time-consuming procedure. At times I wondered if it was worth all the effort just to go to Hawaii. A few times, the pressure was so great, I actually wished I had never even considered going.

As anticipation ran high, however, and as the date of departure drew near and everything started falling into place, I knew it was indeed worth all the extra work.

As I completed the necessary number of broadcasts and boxed the cartons of tapes to be mailed to each radio station, I began to feel some release. By the time our guests from the east coast arrived, I had tickets and travel bags in hand and everything under control. No one suspected what an accomplishment it had been for me or how much I needed that seemingly "casually planned" vacation.

Since I was in charge, tight scheduling was necessary for me, right up until the moment we arrived at the airport. The night before we were to leave, my body was pleading for rest. I begged my family and our company to get to bed as early as possible so that we wouldn't be too tired to enjoy the trip. But everyone was dizzy with excitement.

Finally, just as the household began to settle down, later than I had hoped, the telephone rang. It was a long distance call from Hawaii. The ministerial association on Maui had planned a Memorial Day service and asked if I would be willing to speak to the combined churches.

Naturally, there had been many changes during the almost twenty years since we had lived there, but our ministry among them had remained very much alive in their hearts and in their memories. (The younger ministers had been told about your grandpa. The whole island had felt the shock of your grandpa's accidental death two years previously. They were anxious to hear more about the tragedy and hear how his family was doing.) The loving and gracious island people were planning a "love offering" for us. I didn't know about this until later.

I could never have refused their pleading invitation, but my body was extremely weary and the responsibility of a group of tourists looking to me for guidance was resting heavily upon me. I cannot describe the inadequacy I felt that night, as I wearily accepted the invitation to speak on Maui.

There was no time to prepare. We were leaving in a few hours to catch our plane and I needed rest desperately. I tried hard to think about what I should speak about, but my brain wouldn't cooperate. Reasoning that I might be able to concentrate while flying across the Pacific Ocean or that maybe my subconscious would come to my assistance while I slept, I attempted to relax. I finally fell asleep in a prayerful attitude with my Bible open beside me.

A few hours later I awoke abruptly, somewhat disoriented. I sat up quickly. Where was I? Why was my Bible open and a clean sheet of paper laying nearby? My uncapped pen was laying on my open diary. Several sheets of folded paper with Scripture references and notes scribbled on them were falling out of my Bible.

The reference on one sheet, John 3:16, seemed to grab my attention. A few months earlier, on New Year's Eve, I had been given that verse as my Scripture for the year. As I did every year, and I still do, I had spent the evening reading my Bible and praying. I always expected and received a verse that would be applicable for my life that year.

I was often amazed at the way a particular verse would take on special meaning for me during the following months. Each day I looked at the verse that I believed was mine for that year. Soon I began to see depths of meaning I had never seen before. Every day I would jot down new insights. Sometimes they were overwhelming.

John 3:16 is an important passage. In fact, it is so comprehensive it is sometimes referred to as the "Gospel in a nutshell." Even so, the words, *"For God so loved the world, that He gave His only Begotten Son, that whosoever believeth in Him should not perish, but have everlasting life"*, are so well known they seem almost meaningless. I couldn't see on that New Year's Eve how that verse could become very special to me that year.

When I awoke suddenly that night, so desperate for a response from the Lord as to what I should speak about when I addressed the native ministers on Maui I picked up the notes I had written and began to read them.

Then it dawned on me. There was my message, all outlined and ready to share with the audience that God knew all along I would be speaking to. On Memorial Day, everyone would be remembering our service men who had given their lives for their country, so that the rest of us could continue to enjoy freedom. It was even more wonderful that God gave His own and only Son so that we could be set free from the bondage and threats of Satan, the worst enemy of all. Jesus had won the complete victory over the enemy in our behalf.

I will never forget the impact of that heavenly revelation in the middle of the night. Long before I ever dreamed of going to Hawaii, God was preparing me. I was reminded once again, that He wanted me to always be alert to His method of leading and instruction.

I slept peacefully the rest of the night and was actually somewhat rested when we got to the airport. Knowing I had been given a message to be delivered in Hawaii gave me the assurance that I would have a safe trip there.

Aloha Hawaii

It was hard to tell who was the most excited that day we boarded our plane for Hawaii. I was going back to visit the island that after nearly twenty years, still held a special place in my heart. The boys were going to check out an island they had heard so much about from the rest of the family. Aunt Leton and Aunt Vauntee were fulfilling a dream come true for them, vacationing in the romantic tropical islands. Their friend Evalene was thrilled about having been asked to come along. (Two other friends who had been invited backed out during the early stages of planning for our Hawaiian tour.)

On the good advice of a helpful travel agent I chose a flight from Sacramento rather than San Francisco, where most flights to the Islands originated. We flew to Hilo on the Big Island, instead of going to Honolulu on Oahu. From Hilo we planned to fly to Maui, where we would spend most of our time, then on to Oahu before boarding our luxury liner, the S.S. Lurline, for our return trip.

Although it had been many years since I had lived in the islands, it was still like going home. I hardly knew what to expect but I was sure it would be different. I knew how beautiful it was and I knew that wouldn't change. I would now see Hawaii through the eyes of my children who were seeing it for the first time. As we flew across the Pacific Ocean I tried to remember some of the boys and girls we had worked with and imagine what they would look like so many years later. I knew many of their parents and grandparents would not still be living. Going back after all those years gave me a strange feeling. After what seemed to the boys a very long time, we finally began the descent to Hawaii. Everyone was wide awake, straining to see as much as possible as the stewardess walked down the aisle, explaining what to watch for.

A romantic Hawaiian welcome waited us at the airport in Hilo. My group was delighted with the fragrant leis placed around their necks by a native. [It was a surprise I had planned for them.] And that was just the beginning of an unforgettable vacation. Our bed and breakfast type inn turned out to be a small, Hawaiian-style motel, very picturesque, quiet and clean. As suggested by our travel agent, I reserved smaller out-of-the-way accomodations that would give us the true feel of the islands as well as save money. The aunts never stopped thanking me for that.

There was so much to see and do on the Big Island and I really wanted to please the three sophisticated businesswomen that I was accountable to.

Determined to make the most of this once in a lifetime opportunity, I programmed myself to forget schedules, deadlines, and telephones, but I will have to admit, it took me a couple days to start to unwind.

My aunts and their friend from New England were immediately delighted by the bright Hawaiian sunshine and the soft, floating clouds. They were fascinated by the tropical flora and the vibrantly colored flowers. Everyone was impressed with the island trees, swaying in the strong but gentle tradewinds. The blue-green ocean, leaping playfully on the warm beach sands, took their breath away. The boys were anxious to investigate the inviting beaches. I was constantly bombarded with questions and blessed by my appreciative group's observations. They helped me to see again many things I had forgotten.

With the assistance of brochures and the helpful advice of friendly natives, I was able to keep my little group "informed" and "instructed". I had taken the boys out of school early, believing the trip would be more educational than what they would have learned the last two weeks of school.

As soon as we found our accommodations on the first day, we decided to investigate inviting places to dine. I knew this was going to be an experience. My aunts and their friend had already expressed some apprehension about what foods might be available.

As we examined the brochures given to us at the airport and scanned the lists of restaurants and eating joints, Aunt Leton observed, "It sounds like all they have is pineapple, and dishes made with pineapple."

About that time, the host of our temporary home knocked softly at the door.

"Something for you!" she announced with a smile as she set a lovely platter of yes, you guessed it—fresh pineapple in front of us. I led the way as I sampled a slice of beautiful fruit. Soon everyone was enjoying the delightful refreshment. Everyone, that is, except Aunt Leton.

"This is wonderful!" Aunt Vauntee remarked. "Leton, you'll have to at least try it," she urged. "It doesn't taste at all like what you've tried at home." And it didn't.

That was just the first of our adventures with Hawaiian pineapple. We ran into it everywhere we turned. For Aunt Leton's sake, we tried to find something to eat besides pineapple. I remembered some Hawaiian dishes and some Oriental foods that our family had enjoyed. We stopped to inquire of some natives where a good restaurant could be found.

The occupants of our crowded car were strangely silent, waiting for me to interpret the unfamiliar English.

As we drove away from our informers, the boys began to giggle.

"What were they trying to say?" Aunt Vauntee wanted to know. I explained that they were not speaking a foreign language, just pidgin English.

We took the natives' advice and soon found a busy little outdoor restaurant which, we were informed, was popular with tourists from "de mainland".

Each one chose from the menu and by the time everyone was hungry enough to try some new foods. And the fresh, clean air helped to increase our appetites.

I was surprised at how well each one of them adapted. They seemed to find it exciting to choose foods they were totally unfamiliar with. By the second day, I was learning from them. They hardly consulted me anymore. I was really proud of my "tour" family.

Hippies In Paradise

We didn't have any time to spare so we got right on with the itinerary I had planned for us on the Big Island.

We took in the Hawaii National Park, with its interesting volcanos. All of my group viewed the films explaining past and recent volcanic activity with great interest. I was able to help fill in some details that I remembered, from the eruptions they had when I lived on Maui, which is just across the channel from the Big Island of Hawaii.

While on the Kona coast, we took in beautiful Kealakekua Bay, which was just like I remembered it—unbelievably picturesque.

My group was impressed with Captain Cook's monument, and the magnificent beauty that surrounded that area. And they were anxious to visit The City of Refuge, that I had told them about. A local plaque stated that it was patterned after the Old Testament concept, which you can read about in the Bible, in the book of Numbers.

They could hardly believe the natural beauty of the nearby spot that was being preserved—just as it was in the early days when the Hawaiians had the Islands all to themselves—undisturbed by tourists or other nationalities who had come to live in their lovely island paradise.

I knew when I had planned our itinerary that we would only be able to hit the highlights, so I put the emphasis on what I thought my group would enjoy most. When we met a commercial tour bus driven by a careless native—at one of our stops, and saw the fear on the faces of some of the passengers, I was reminded of other special care and consideration my "charges" were receiving on their personalized tour, even if they didn't realize it. The bus had just come over the road ahead of us. I knew why they were frightened. I was not anticipating the winding route around the windward side of the island, that we were headed for. I had really prayed about it. I also knew our chauffeur—Aunt Leton, was a careful, composed driver. If we wanted to see the rest of the Big Island that we had planned, and be able to say that we had driven around it, we couldn't stop at that point.

By the time we had completed our hurried, one day tour around the so-called "big" island, my little group knew I had protected them from some of the unnecessary stress they might have encountered; and shown them some extras, but I doubt if they ever realized how much money I saved them.

All too quickly it was time to leave the Big Island of Hawaii and fly to Maui, our anticipated destination.

We arrived at the airport in Hilo early in order to check our tickets out. While waiting for our flight everyone enjoyed watching the variety of natives, in and around the airport. I tried to explain to my tour group how different nationalities had come to live on the various islands. I rather enjoyed telling them what I remembered being told when I lived there. I was not prepared for the shock of seeing some "hippies" from the mainland invading that tropical paradise. When our family had lived in the Islands, cleanliness was very evident. The poorest person you would ever see was clean. That was probably one of the things we were most surprised about when we first moved there. Now, it was as though these two dirty, mainland type hippies loitering around the terminal at the Hilo airport were invading my memories. It gave me a sickening feeling in my stomach.

That little incident was my rude awakening to the fact that the sick mentality of the 60's had migrated to the islands I loved. Imagine how horrified I was when these uncouth characters got on the plane we were scheduled to take to the island of Maui. I cringed. My boys had often seen this type of character in the mainland but they, too, were surprised to see them there. They were not what we had come to Hawaii to see.

Our relatives and their friend form the east coast could hardly believe there were actually human beings living in such an unkempt condition. Their clothes were so filthy they were stiff. We felt dirty having to be confined to the same plane with them, even for the short flight. The incident put a damper on our plans for that day.

We picked up our second rental car at the Kahului airport, which to my surprise had been relocated since I lived on Maui. Once more all seven of us managed to get inside our temporary transportation. We sped away to our "condo with a kitchen", overlooking the ocean.

It was soon evident that everyone was going to love "my" island. We found plenty to do the first day. That evening I met with my missionary friends who were still living there. They quickly brought me up to date. When I mentioned some of the changes I saw, including the presence of the castoffs form the mainland, they sadly informed me that my beloved Maui had been inundated with them. They told us that the wealthy parents of many of these unsavory rebels, actually sent them money to live on in these far away tropical islands, so they wouldn't have to be near them. It was worth it to have an ocean between them so that they wouldn't be embarrassed by their lifestyle and behavior.

There were many things to enjoy on Maui, despite my unexpected disappointment. One day we went around the island to the historic old town of Lahaina, which at one time had been the capitol of the Islands. I was relieved to discover the road had been significantly improved since the days when I lived there. I had really dreaded that road.

Our trip to the rim of Haleakaka Crater was the experience of a lifetime for my tourist group which ranged from age nine to definite maturity. The trip up the mountain and down again was in itself exciting for all of us. I remember how chilly and invigorating the air had been at 10,000 feet on that tiny island. It had snowed on the summit several times during the years when we lived on Maui.

Viewing the seventeen square mile crater from the rim was definitely something to tell the folks back home about. And the trip back was unforgettable. My group could hardly believe how the ocean appeared to slant downward toward the shoreline, around the island, when viewed from the winding descent road.

I pointed out to my tourists a place on the map called Hana, and told them how beautiful it was. But in my loving concern and thoughtful consideration for them, and selfishly for myself also, I purposely left it off our itinerary. I remembered all too clearly the frightening road around to Hana, along the windward side of the island. Much of it was like a narrow shelf, built out over the mountainside. The only way I would ever include Hana in a tour would be to go by plane.

A Hawaiian Reunion

After a busy day taking in the beautiful beaches of Maui, I was looking forward to seeing my friends, whom I had not seen for so many years, that evening. I wanted my children to meet them, and my guests also, but the boys were suffering from intense sunburn which I had thought we were avoiding. They were not able to go so the aunts and Emalene stayed with them. It was evident they were going to need considerable nursing care. It was an emotionally taxing evening for me. I was looking forward to seeing precious friends but I was afraid I wouldn't know some of them after twenty years. The young people we had worked with would have changed dramatically and the older people still alive would look a lot different. I would also be changed. They, too, would not know what to expect. All of this was going through my mind as I drove to the church, and concern for my sunburned sons kept pulling at me. Then I had the responsibility of speaking and they would be expecting so much from me.

I purposely arrived just before the meeting was to begin so that I could visit with them after I had delivered my message. The missionaries had attempted to round up everyone who had known us. I could see that a large group had gathered.

I quickly made my way to the front where I was seated. Everyone was anxiously waiting to see what I would look like and if they would recognize me. While waiting to be introduced I looked out over the audience and noted how changed everyone looked that I remembered, and among them were many younger ones who looked familiar in a strange sort of way. These I realized were the children of those who were their age when we worked with them.

I was given a very sentimental introduction by one of the native pastors we had known well. He had loved "Brother Brown". His voice broke as he recalled specific incidents that had happened while we lived there.

When he spoke of the loss they all felt when they learned that their friend and co-worker had been called home so young, a hush fell over the room. It was an emotional time for me.

I spoke to an unusually receptive audience, as I delivered the message God had given me in such a unique way. And it was as if He spoke the words, through my lips. We all reflected on the significance of the occasion, that Memorial Day, when the nation and the island territory of Maui was commemorating the death of our service men who had fallen in battle, many of them on Hawaiian soil. Pearl Harbor was still fresh in their minds, even though it had been many years since the tragedy.

I talked about how much more important it was that God had sent His Son into our wicked world to fight an even more fearful enemy, and reminded us all of His sacrificial Gift and the loss of His only Son. And I challenged each of us to revive a memorial of Him in our hearts on that special national holiday.

"Let's all determine afresh to remember the One who died to save us and consider giving ourselves in a sacrificial way in behalf of those who are in spiritual jeopardy."

We all remembered that their beloved Brother Brown had sacrificed his health and several years of his life for them.

As the meeting came to a close, an opportunity was given for each one to bring their special love offering for me. One by one, they walked to the front of the large hall, lovingly and reverently, placing their gift of love in a special receptacle. Soon everyone was crowding around me.

"Do you remember me?" many asked.

We had worked with many of them as children. Now they were grown up and were there with their children to greet me. I tried to acknowledge each one in a special way.

Many memories were revived that evening. My heart rejoiced as I listened to their accounts of how God had been with them since we had led them to the Lord so long ago. It was a touching picture as I was introduced to their children and spouses. It blessed my heart to see that they were bringing up the children to love the Lord. Tears of joy flowed freely. The memories of that special reunion will always remain with me.

On To Oahu

When I got back to our Maui condo that night, the boys were suffering in agony as a result of their sunburn. I had tried to protect them with sunscreen and had limited their time in the sun but I had underestimated their resistance to exposure since it was so different where we lived in California.

We were scheduled to fly to the island of Oahu the following day. Neither of the boys thought they could endure wearing regular clothes for the flight. They ended up painfully suffering through the ordeal by wearing their softest shirts.

By the time we checked into our hotel I could see we would have to find a doctor. The front desk directed us to the emergency room of a nearby hospital. Because of his extremely fair skin, my twelve year old appeared to be the most severely burned. The doctor looked at his face, back and shoulders, then called other doctors in to observe his condition.

They all agreed they had never seen such a bad case of sunburn. They asked for permission to take pictures for a medical journal. You can imagine how I felt for having allowed them to burn so badly. Even though I thought I was taking ample precautions, it obviously wasn't enough. I was instructed to check with the ship's clinic as soon as we got on board. Since the boys couldn't be in the sun we wouldn't be able to travel around the island of Oahu as planned. It was a good thing we had hotel rooms near a number of attractions and souvenir shops which were what the ladies from the East were most interested in at that point.

My patients and I resigned ourselves to remaining in the hotel, nursing the after effects of earlier pleasures. There wasn't much to do but sit inside the lobby and watch people. As I sat here, hotel-bound, I thought how neat it would be if someone I had known when I lived in Hawaii would just happen to come by and recognize me. I knew it was highly unlikely, especially since I had lived on a different island and it had been such a long time ago.

"Oh, well", I said to myself. "Who knows, someone might just happen to be here from Maui."

Imagine Seeing You Here

I began casually observing the "human parade", coming and going through the lobby, stopping here and there to shop a little or to inquire at the information desk.

I was soon engrossed in watching people. Attire, in most cases was pretty scanty, and people's actions sometimes a little strange. Most scurried by, seemingly in a world to themselves.

Mainland tourists could be spotted easily. Some appeared to have abandoned all serious thoughts, while others seemed preoccupied with problems back home. I imagined all kinds of situations, and jotted down numerous character ideas for my writer's notebook.

Suddenly I hard someone call, "Ardelle, is that you?"

Looking around, I saw a man who was as surprised to see me as I was to see a person I knew. It was a friend from California whom I had met through the activities of a church-sponsored single adult group I had been attending.

"Alex!" I cried, "what are you doing here?"

He explained that he was on a business trip, but getting in a little fun on the side. We had a great time chatting and laughing about our chance meeting in an unexpected setting.

Before he went on his way, Alex insisted on treating us to ice cream. His little unscheduled visit added a special thrill to our limited activities that day.

Our time on Oahu was fast running out. We saw we would not be able to do all the things we had planned to on that island. We decided however, to load our sunburned patients into the car, and take in a couple nearby attractions.

Alex had said we shouldn't miss the dolphin show at Sea Life Park, so we went there. We also drove to Pearl Harbor to view the Memorial and to remember those who died that fateful day.

We went to the military cemetery at Punch Bowl Crater and viewed the sobering, seemingly endless rows of graves marked with white crosses, reminding us of the terrible cost of the Pearl Harbor tragedy.

All too soon, we had to get back to our hotel and get started packing for one of the most exciting segments of our tour—our trip back across the ocean aboard the luxury liner, the Lurline.

Tour Afloat

It was a day for all to remember, that day we set sail from Honolulu on one of the world's most popular steamships, on a voyage that would bring us back to the mainland. It would take much longer than flying, but we had planned these days as part of our special vacation.

Traveling by boat was a repeat adventure for me. For my tour group, however, it was a fantastic first. For the conservative ladies from the East Coast, to the brave young California lads, it was a bit overwhelming at first.

As instructed by the doctor in Honolulu, I took our sunburned patients to the ship's clinic, then I turned the three boys loose to enjoy themselves on the boat. There was no place for them to get away and I knew I could trust them. As might be expected, they explored the vessel from the "crow's nest" to the hold of the ship. It was a real education for them.

The ladies in our group had no trouble entertaining themselves. They, like me, chose to rest as much as possible. We all managed to get in some exercise, taking a brisk daily walk up and down the deck. The workout was invigorating, and the moist marine air refreshing.

One of the highlights on board the ship was mealtime. We were assigned a table and our own steward. When we sat down to our first meal, everyone in my group was flabbergasted. They had never seen such an extravagant display of food. My teenager got the biggest kick out of it. He joked while everyone else sat almost speechless.

The variety of food was indescribable, especially in contrast to some of the island food, which really hadn't impressed my group. This was truly a feast. If you could have resisted the temptation to eat more than you needed or wanted, you would have felt full just looking at all that delicious food.

At every meal, including breakfast, there was always a large dish of artistically prepared . . . fresh, ripe pineapple. By that time, Aunt Leton, who had declared so emphatically that she "did not like pineapple", was enjoying it more than any of us. Everyone kidded her about it, but she just laughed and went on eating the delightful pineapple.

On alternate voyages, the Lurline would return to San Francisco via Los Angeles. We happened to be on its triangle trip, which included a bonus cruise up the coast from Southern California.

We had mentioned this to a lovely couple we met in Hawaii. They said they lived on top of a hill overlooking the ocean and that they were familiar with the Lurline's regular schedule. They always watched the steamer make its way up the coast. They had told us to watch as they waved to us. As we came close to the landmark they told us about, we strained our eyes to see where they lived. When we finally spotted the location, we could see them waving frantically, trying to get our attention. They had remembered! We all received a thrill from the unusual contact. I even corresponded with the friendly couple after we got home. All of our group had enjoyed an unforgettable vacation, but the gray outline of San Francisco's Golden Gate was a welcome sight as we approached. We were all glad to be back in California again.

* * *   * * *   * * *

"I could talk all night, but it's getting late so I think we'd better save the rest for another time.

I'm glad I could share these incidents with you. Now, you know more about your grandpa Brown, including the accident and the changes that his sudden death brought to our family."

CHAPTER 19
Moving Events

"Grandma, remember you promised to tell us about when you moved back to Walnut Creek after Grandpa Brown died," Karl reminded me as we finished eating lunch. "I'd like to know why you moved and how you knew where you were supposed to move to."

"And I would like to know what it was like living in Walnut Creek. Isn't that a big city?" Marissa asked.

"Where did you move to after that?" Kathye wanted to know.

"Wait a minute," I cut in. "Not so fast. That's a long story. Let's start at the beginning. Your grandpa Darrell won't be home until late. If we begin now I think I can cover most of it before he gets here.

* * *   * * *   * * *

Where He Leads I Will Follow

When we returned to our home in the Highlands following our trip to Hawaii, we found ourselves practically overwhelmed. My two aunts and their friend from New England were with us for the first week. We showed them around parts of northern California which they were as anxious to experience as they were to see Hawaii. Fortunately I had allowed for the time I knew they would be with us. My deadline work didn't begin again until after they had gone. With plenty of prayer, some innovative time management, and a lot of hard work, I was able to get my schedule back in order again and things under control in an unbelievably short time.

During the summer we had decided to sell our home in Clayton Valley Highlands and move back to Walnut Creek. There were several factors involved in the decision.

First, I could see that the pastor who had agreed to come to our church felt he had to do everything to please me. I did not want him to be inhibited by my presence. I knew it was time for me and the children to move on. [It had been two years since your grandpa had died.] I also wanted to get the boys into a larger church so that they could be involved in a youth group. We had visited a church in Walnut Creek and found it to be the kind of church we wanted to be a part of. The Christian school the boys would enter in the fall was also located in Walnut Creek.

We all set to work getting the house and yard in order so we could put it on the market. We cleaned, fixed, and even painted the house, both inside and out. We did things I didn't realize we were capable of doing. The place really looked sharp.

"We'll be glad to show it now," we told each other as we finished the projects. We prayed that God would send the right people to buy it. I called a Christian realtor friend and told him we wanted to list our Highlands home and asked him to also start looking for a home for us in Walnut Creek.

He quickly worked up a list of prospective homes to show us, taking into consideration the location, price, proximity to the school and church we had indicated, as well as the features we wanted, such as four bedrooms so that I would have a studio. One day, as he took me on a look-see tour of available homes, he said "I have one house in a very nice area that I believe will fit your needs exactly."

As we drove down Citrus Avenue that early summer afternoon, observing the side streets and courts, we crossed a water service canal that divided the homes. On one side we were in Concord, on the other side we were in Walnut Creek. The boundary between was hardly noticeable. We had specified that we wanted a house in Walnut Creek.

All the homes in the area were large, well-built, and beautifully landscaped and cared for. It was obviously not an ordinary subdivision.

The real estate agent, who knew I was trusting the Lord for guidance, was watching my reaction. He could see I was impressed with the prestigious area which I had not been in before. I thought we were just driving through, enroute to some other part of town.

When we stopped in front of a picturesque Mediterranean style home with a beautiful yard. I looked at him in surprise.

"Are you going to show me THIS home?" I asked dubiously. "I could never afford it."

"Let's take a look anyway, okay?" he quipped, as he opened the car. It was so attractive and inviting it almost took my breath away. As we walked toward the entrance, we met a sophisticated young couple and their real estate agent coming out.

The minute we were inside and I saw the floor plan, I could see what could be accomplished for the Lord from the premises of that house. But it was so elaborate and expensive-looking, I hardly dared to dream.

The deep luxurious gold-colored carpeting was so lovely I hardly had the nerve to whisper to the Lord, "Do you think I could have this one?"

The matching custom-made, fan-folded drapes exhibited a heavenly effect, I thought. The lady of the house was an interior decorator and had made the house look beautiful. The formal dining room was one step above the sunken living room and a family room just off the other side of the ultra modern kitchen. Next to the central living area was a hallway leading to three bedrooms and two baths.

Before we had stopped to see the house the real estate agent had explained that there were only three bedrooms, and I had indicated I wanted four. He said he was sure there would be room somewhere for my studio.

I was surprised at how small the bedrooms were in comparison to other parts of the large home. A sliding glass door in the master bedroom opened onto a patio, flanked by a large fenced back yard.

After checking out the yard, we went back to the front of the house. I kept holding myself back, thinking, "I could never afford this house." But the potential was so great. It was like it was built especially for us.

As we walked back to the car, the realtor asked, "Well, what do you think?"

"Oh, I love it!" I told him without hesitation. "It's the one I would choose, but I know I could never afford it. It was fun looking, though."

"This house," he announced with an assuring smile, "is more accessible to you than any I've shown you today."

"What do you mean?" I asked earnestly.

"It has a good, assumable loan and you will have a sizable down payment from the sale of your present home. Your payments would be well down within your reach. This house would be a good investment for you."

I stared at him in awe and disbelief.

"Besides that," he added, "I think they're asking a very modest price for this home. And of course we can offer them less."

I automatically bowed my head and prayed, "Dear Lord, please help me to know your will." When I opened my eyes, I saw the realtor had bowed his head also.

"Shall we make an offer?" he asked cautiously. "I think that young couple we met as we went in liked it also."

I was certain it was too good to be true. As I tried to decide what the Lord would want me to do, it occurred to me that if the house was not for me, I would not want it anyway. If it was, I would get it. I believed God would protect me from making a mistake.

"Let's try for it!" I heard myself saying. "What a wonderful place that would be to live in and to serve the Lord from." The realtor agreed.

As my realtor had predicted, the couple ahead of us liked the house too. They also made an offer through their agent. I just knew we didn't have a chance. They appeared to be well-to-do and I was just a poor widow with little resources. My hopes fell. I braced myself for the disappointment I feared was inevitable.

"It's in the Lord's hands," I told my agent. "If this one is not for us, I believe He has a better one waiting somewhere else."

I arrived home just as the boys were returning from school. There was so much to tell them. What a day I had experienced!

With forced hesitation, I told them all about the house and that I had made an offer on it. I quickly explained that someone else had also made an offer on it. I didn't want them to get their hopes too high either. They knew I would make the best choice possible and that I would make every effort to determine God's perfect will. Within an hour after I got home, the telephone rang. It was my agent. I was hesitant to hear what he had to say.

"Guess what?" he said, "They accepted your offer. You got the house."

The boys were at my elbow, listening to every word and watching my reaction.

I didn't believe him, but he insisted. "The young couple ahead of us made an offer almost identical to yours, but the owner's wife was impressed with you and wants you to have the house."

We were elated and the boys could hardly wait to see their new home.

The young Swedish homemaker, I later learned had many problems and heartaches. I sensed it at the time and wished I could tell her about the Lord. I couldn't of course, but I gave her a look of compassion and loving concern which she seemed to understand. I later learned from newspaper reports that her husband was in deep financial trouble where he worked.

I had a few very brief opportunities to talk with her during the transition. She was extremely thoughtful. She wrote down detailed instructions on how to operate the furnace, how and where to have the beautiful drapes cleaned the next time they needed it, and a carefully outlined routine for caring for the "maintenance-free" landscaping.

I longed to help that dear lady and I prayed a great deal for her.

Notable Guests

Moving without any adult men but plenty of help from two very enthusiastic boys was an experience. My recording studio was the most complicated aspect to move. My technician later helped me set the equipment up in the formal dining area which we had chosen to use for my studio.

To help improve the acoustics, we hung the lovely drapes our friends had bought for our first home in Sonoma just inside the wrought iron railing, between the dining area and the sunken living room.

The drapes had a castle design against a green forest on a cream colored background. Gold flecks on the staggered castles, here and there, glistened in the sunlight by day and lamp light at night.

They blended perfectly with the exquisite gold drapes in our new home, and made an attractive divider between the two rooms. It was as though the drapes had been meant for that purpose. The old drapes I had kept for so long were such good quality they looked like they would last forever. [I still have those drapes, after more than thirty years, and they're still in pretty good shape.]

Those incredible drapes royally accented my studio as well as the living room where I entertained special guests that I invited on the broadcast from time to time. I was now working six to eight hours a day in the studio, five days a week. [I tried to spend evenings and weekends with my boys.]

During the wonderful years that we lived in that home, I had the pleasure of interviewing many notable guests as part of my broadcasts. There were missionaries, evangelists, and recording artists who had come to the area for special meetings. It was a pleasure to invite God's servants to our beautiful home.

One of the most exciting experiences for me was the series of programs which I produced with Lambert Dolphin, Research Physicist at Stanford University.

At the time I was active in the ministry of the Christian Women's Club. I had helped organize the work in Walnut Creek, a few years earlier. We had been fortunate to be able to engage some outstanding speakers and to attract large audiences. The executive board, of which I was a part, had heard of Mr. Dolphin's remarkable conversion and asked him to come speak to our club. He lived only a few hour's drive away in Palo Alto.

We practically jumped for joy when he agreed to come. As expected, many came to hear him. His testimony was powerful and convincing. This brilliant man, who had only been a Christian a short time, had cultivated a tremendous ministry already. It was easy to understand why. God had used the witness of a dedicated pastor to show him the way to Christ, and to help him take his first steps as a Christian.

Mr. Dolphin told about his work on college campuses, where the cults, occultism, and Eastern religions were so prevalent at the time, and he had worked with the "hippie" culture of the "60's". As he spoke, I envisioned how far-reaching and effective his ministry would be on radio. As I listened to Mr. Dolphin speak to a spellbound audience, I began working up the courage to ask him if he would be willing to do some messages and interviews for my broadcasts.

I could just hear him saying, "I'm sorry, but . . ." I was sure he was very busy. Even so, I finally decided it was worth a try. The worst he could do was to say he couldn't come. I certainly would understand if he did, I told myself.

As soon as the meeting was over, I was right up front, before people could crowd around him as they always did in response to good speakers. I shook his hand and thanked him for coming and sharing his testimony. I told him I was a radio personality and that my broadcasts reached into numerous areas. Then I asked him if he would be willing to work with me on some specific programs.

To my surprise and delight, he said without hesitation, "Why, I'd love to," and pulled out his calendar. I was delighted.

"Please come at your convenience," I told him. I'll work around your schedule."

I walked out of that room shaking my head. "I don't believe it!" I said right out loud. "He's actually coming to my studio." I didn't fully realize then what a tremendous day was in store for me.

Mr. Lambert Dolphin arrived early on the day we had arranged and stayed until late afternoon.

We talked and we prayed. We discussed the Scriptures and prayed some more. He was hungry to talk about God's Word and I enjoyed it as much as he did. He loved the Bible, and so did I.

We talked about his conversion and about his ministries and about his trips to the Holy Land. Then we talked about my ministries and my family. He was so dedicated and so vibrant in his new Christian walk, I felt as though we had been entertained in the wings of heaven with Jesus as our host. The Holy Spirit had afforded us both a day of the sweetest fellowship this side of heaven.

He talked on tape for hours about the problems and challenges modern youth were facing. His discussion regarding the drug scene and the hippie lifestyle was timely and appropriate.

We recorded Mr. Dolphin's remarkable testimony for radio. Hearing it the second time, I was even more impressed. It was so powerful and compelling, I knew no one would be able to turn him off.

Lambert Dolphin was intrigued with God's wonderful plan of salvation. As a new Christian he devoured the Scriptures relentlessly and with his research-oriented mind he had developed some deep insights.

I was amazed as we talked, first with his abounding love for his Savior and the Bible, and then at the way the Holy Spirit had enabled him to understand the Scriptures. He had a healthier grasp on the important doctrines of the Christian faith than many ministers I knew. The minister who had led him to the Lord had helped him become grounded in the Scriptures.

Mr. Dolphin had the highest regard for the pastor who had been so sensitive to his spiritual need, and so willing to take time to share the Gospel message with him. He told me he wanted to be that kind of Christian himself.

As he studied the Bible, he was amazed at the way the Old Testament prophecies were fulfilled in the New Testament. That remarkable fact gave him the unshakable assurance that the Bible was indeed the Word of God.

The alarming increase in the acceptance and teachings of Eastern religions on the campuses in America was a great concern to Mr. Dolphin. He was saddened to see young people from all walks of life, many from Christian backgrounds, embracing these dangerous religions.

To his dismay, he also observed intelligent young people experimenting with mind-altering drugs and actually believing it was a legitimate method of divine pursuit. He had heard them say it was their way of seeking something that would satisfy their spiritual hunger. Unfortunately, in most cases it merely opened their minds to Satan's deceptive power, rendering them easy prey for occultic and mystical religious persuasions. In many instances, it even opened their minds to demonic possession. The idea of being involved with some sort of "religion", however wrong, seemed to make them feel secure and comfortable. He felt helpless on seeing minister's children, away from home in college, sometimes falling into this dark chasm as well. Lambert told me he had found however, that very few young people who had good Christian training played around with the cults and Eastern religions for more than two years. They soon saw the fallacy. Few were foolish enough to continue for long periods of time.

He concluded that the devil must have derived a great deal of pleasure from observing all the damage done by means of his traps, set purposely to ensnare intelligent, inquisitive, and particularly Christian youth.

I was grateful to have such a tremendous opportunity to get to know Lambert Dolphin and to record and share his insights with a wide audience.

I didn't take time to edit or time any of the material I recorded that day. I just captured as much as possible to share on numerous broadcasts.

It was a "mountain-top" experience for me to spend an entire day with Lambert Dolphin, a man who had a message worth hearing.

Those Who Walk Alone

When we moved to Walnut Creek we started attending the Evangelical Free Church that we had visited. We believed it was where the Lord wanted us to be.

Some single adults whom I had met through the Icebreakers, a singles ministry sponsored by the local Presbyterian Church, were members of the Evangelical Free Church. Being single myself, I soon met other men and women who were also alone.

Since there were so many single people in our church, some of us felt we should have our own singles ministry. There were certain aspects which we wanted to see emphasized more, such as Bible studies, and other Christ-centered activities. Being single, an organizer, and having a great burden for other lonely singles, I decided to act on my convictions. I invited the single people in our church to my home for an evening of fellowship and discussion about starting a singles ministry in our church. A surprisingly large group of single men and women showed up. We got to know each other better and talked about what we would like to see accomplished. Everyone agreed on a weekly Bible study and a monthly fun and fellowship evening. Two other enthusiastic ladies and myself volunteered to look into what would be involved in organizing such a group as a special outreach ministry to our community.

We visited a successful group we had heard about in San Jose to see how they operated. We combined what we picked up with our own ideas and decided to look into acquiring the use of a local restaurant for a Sunday morning Bible class. Following the class session, we would invite guests to attend the morning worship service with us at our church. We also planned a weekly Bible class in my home on a Tuesday or Thursday evening. A single man we knew, who was an excellent Bible teacher, agreed to teach both classes. It was a perfect setup.

All of us believed that a fun and fellowship time each month was a much needed outlet for those who rarely left their home. They were lonely and isolated. We saw this problem as a challenge.

A number of us who were deeply concerned about the need and enthusiastic about the possibilities spent time together praying and discussing plans.

As a member of the local church, I was asked to approach the pastor with our ideas, believing that he in turn would present them to the executive board. We felt sure our plan to reach the unique and sizable mission field that we were so interested in would go over well with the church officials.

To our complete surprise and great disappointment, we soon realized that individuals with spouses—even church leaders—don't understand or empathize with those who walk alone, for whatever reason. Some even regarded the widowed or the never married with the same contempt as they did the divorced. This was painful for me. I had been a pastor's wife for quite a few years and had been sensitive to all single people, no matter the circumstances. I had observed that they were often treated differently by others, however. Because I was able to get close to them, I was acutely aware that many divorced persons were actually helpless victims of circumstances, but they were often treated worse by other Christians than if they had committed murder.

I wept many tears because of the lack of understanding and concern for this growing segment of Christian singles which I saw in my church and in the surrounding community.

We had tried to go about organizing a single adult ministry in the proper manner and through appropriate channels. Now we were thwarted and could only pray. No doubt our burden for these people was intensified because of the apparent snag. We knew it was something that only the Lord could work out. We did not organize the singles group at that time because we did not have the support of the church. I did however, feel at liberty to invite the single people I knew and their single friends to my home for a fellowship dinner. My two like-minded lady friends and I tried to answer questions as to why we couldn't have a Bible study class by saying perhaps the time was not right. This seemed like a feeble excuse, but we assured them we expected to start one later.

We went on praying for our single friends, and for the church leaders as well. Then one day, out of the blue, I received a call from my pastor. "Ardelle," he asked, "can I come over for a few minutes? There's something I want to talk to you about."

I was somewhat apprehensive as I waited for him to arrive. What now, I wondered. I was really baffled and hurt over the church's reaction to our request for approval for a much needed ministry. I simply couldn't understand why they would want to suppress our efforts.

When my pastor arrived he got right to the point, even before he sat down.

"Ardelle, I want to apologize for the misunderstanding that has resulted from your sincere request to the church to sponsor a ministry to the single people in our church and in the community."

He paused, took his handkerchief from his pocket and went on.

"There are those who do not have the same burden that you do. They just don't understand. I have to admit," he said apologetically, "at first I didn't see the project as something we should sponsor at the time."

He paused again and became strangely silent, dabbing his eyes with his handkerchief.

"I've been really convicted about my attitude," he went on. "I want you to know I'm sorry."

By that time I was crying. I sensed that God was working everything out for His honor and glory.

After a few moments of silence, while we waited in the presence of the Lord, my pastor told me he was now convinced that a weekly Bible study outreach in the community at a restaurant was a great idea. And especially since we had a good Bible teacher lined up who was capable and willing to lead our studies. He also agreed that a midweek Bible study in my home had his approval and that finally, most of the executive board was now in agreement. We could proceed with our plan.

We prayed together. As he left my home I assured him we would attempt to do everything to honor the Lord and try not to disappoint him and the church officials. I could hardly wait to call the other two ladies who shared my burden. They were almost as thrilled as I was. We soon had arrangements worked out with a local restaurant, allowing us to conduct a Bible study from nine to ten a.m. in the main dining room, before they opened for business. This gave us time to get to our own church worship service, and our guests to theirs. (Those who had no church were invited by those who did and usually went along, feeling comfortable in our company.)

We also started a Bible class in my home right away, first on Tuesday night, then later we switched alternately to Thursday night for a few weeks at a time in order to accommodate those who could not attend one or the other evening.

Everyone loved Dave, our excellent Bible instructor for both classes. They were both well attended from the onset. Everyone was hungry to learn more about the Bible. Timid men and women and those not used to going to church, usually came to our monthly dinners first before they felt comfortable in a Bible study or church setting.

We were able to touch more lonely, isolated lives than we ever imagined. Being assured that they were understood and loved by those who shared their loneliness and frustration gave these often friendless single people a new lease on life. Many who had completely dropped out of church started attending with us. Some who had never gone before, got brave enough to come along after they started attending our Bible classes.

Our new home, which I believe God opened to us, became a chapel of worship, a school for Bible study, and a haven of fellowship for single men and women from our community and for miles around. When we planned a special banquet at the church, nearly one hundred people attended.

I Hosted The Staff

As busy as I was working with single people, I still had numerous broadcasts and an active telephone ministry, as well as the care of my fatherless sons and my married children, and the grandchildren to love and enjoy and pray for.

Because of my broadcasts I was around the local radio station so much that they started inviting me to their evening staff meetings. I felt honored but I was always rather uncomfortable that everyone except me always drank alcohol.

One month I decided to ask them to my home where I often entertained groups. I offered to prepare the dinner with the understanding that no liquor would be brought or served. I wanted them to see that they could have a good time without drinking.

I'm not sure what they were each thinking as they sat down to dinner, but they were soon enjoying themselves immensely and commenting on how good the food tasted. Everyone was talking sensibly, unaffected by alcohol. When it was time to go, everyone thanked me for my hospitality, commenting on what an enjoyable evening it had been. The station manager himself admitted he had never experienced such a pleasant staff meeting. Everyone was with it, and knew what was taking place. He thanked me for opening his eyes to see that life can be rich without the aid of a stimulant. Because of the nature of my broadcasts, they all knew that I was a Christian. I doubt however, if any of them suspected they were sitting in a room that had been dedicated to the Lord to be used for His honor. They all felt the peaceful atmosphere without realizing why. Much prayer and many hours of fellowship around God's Word had sanctified that area.

A Neighborhood Threat

With all my activities, I somehow managed to spend considerable time with my young sons. During the summer months when there was no school to keep them occupied, though, they had difficulty finding things to do. They attracted many friends to our place because I didn't let them run all over the neighborhood as many parents did. The year we moved to Walnut Creek the boys both joined the Boy Scouts of America. The meetings were held at our church and were led by Christian men who were willing to work with the boys. They sometimes went on nature trips to the mountains, lakes and streams where they often had a chance to do a little fishing.

They loved these outdoor jaunts in the country in the company of their Sunday School friends and Christian leaders. They always came home talking about how wonderful it would be to live in a rural area.

I loved the idea too, but I had some reservations. I often longed to be away from the noise and bustle of city life, but I knew I would be afraid to be alone at night when the boys were not home if we lived in a remote area. They were growing up and I realized they would not always be with me. It was just a thought and a dream, but it grew and we couldn't get away from the desire to be out of the city, and into the country.

The last year we were there, the summer dragged by so slowly; the boys had far too much time on their hands. So did all the boys on our street and in our neighborhood. I became increasingly aware that some of them were pretty rough. I realized my precious sons were being exposed to some bad influences. It was not possible to keep them in the house all the time. I did not doubt at all that God would answer my prayers regarding this situation. I simply waited, anxious to see what He would do.

The Safe Place

The time came when I prayed more and more fervently. When I finally asked the Lord specifically for a "safe place" in the country, I knew it was a strange request, but He knew what I meant. The "safe" aspect was very important to me. I knew there must be some place like that, even though I had no idea what kind of situation I was really praying for. I didn't even try to imagine how God might provide an answer to my prayers. I just trusted Him. Even though my personal request would have seemed selfish and perhaps unreasonable to some, I knew God understood. I had no apologies.

For the boy's sake, I asked the Lord for a place close to nature, maybe where they could go fishing sometimes. They so much longed for the kind of environment they had heard their dad talk about, where he had grown up in New Mexico.

I also wanted to be near a good, solid church, and also to have access to a Christian school. I was sure these were both legitimate requests which would please the Lord. I did realize that the combination was quite an order but I didn't doubt God's ability to answer.

Early one August morning, I fell on my knees before the Lord and carefully laid my petition before Him. I did not leave my position until my burden lifted. I felt something wonderful was going to happen soon.

He Answered While I Was Praying

I went about my busy day expectantly, alert to the doorbell and the telephone. The postman greeted me in his usual friendly manner, then went on his way.

Glancing quickly through the day's mail, I noticed a letter with the words, "You are invited" on the outside of the envelope. What could that be, I wondered. I opened the letter and read, ". . . a friend has suggested you might be interested in touring a new recreational community called LAKE WILDWOOD."

The enclosure explained that the unusual, exclusive development by

Boise Cascade was in Nevada County, in the foothills of the Sierra Nevada mountains. I had no idea where Nevada County was nor what a "recreation" community meant. Some of the features mentioned were a lake, a golf course, and a "security system". Well that certainly was something I wanted to know more about. The offer, a free tour of this so called "private" community, was extended to me and my family. I just had to fill in the information requested and mail it to the address given. I would be contacted regarding a date and a time for the tour. The boys were away on a Boy Scout outing so I had plenty of time to think and pray before they returned later that evening. When they got home I excitedly showed them the letter I had received. After thinking about it, they realized that one of their scout leaders owned property in Nevada County. That was one of the places they had been.

"Oh, Mother," they said with delight, "it's beautiful up there. Let's go see the place!"

Since the letter insisted there was no obligation, we decided even if it was something we wouldn't be interested in, we would at least have a one day vacation. Besides, this could possibly be the answer to our prayers, especially my early morning prayer that very day.

As we waited for an answer to our reply, I earnestly prayed that God would protect us from pressure to make a decision outside of His perfect will for us.

A couple of days later we received a phone call and soon afterwards a personable young man was at our door to tell us more about Lake Wildwood and to take us there for our tour. Mr. Moore, who insisted we just call him Larry, told us much more about Lake Wildwood as we drove along, enroute to the community. By the time we reached Nevada County, we felt like we had always known Larry.

I knew we would be presented with a persuasive sales pitch, but I also knew I would never make a quick decision. I would let the sales representative know that I would have to pray about any action. I had already told Larry that we were Christians and would have to be certain that we were in God's perfect will before I would ever sign any contract.

Larry insisted that we were under no obligation by going to see the development. He said they had a good motive for taking interested prospects on the tour. "We know that if you find you're not interested, or if its something you just can't do, you'll still tell others about your discoveries." I thought that sounded pretty reasonable.

It was a pleasant day in late summer when we first laid eyes on Lake Wildwood. Shortly after we turned off the main highway onto the road that went by Lake Wildwood, we were awed by the beauty of the pine trees and the large, varied oaks scattered here and there. I was struck by the beauty and quiet of these wooded hills.

Before we reached the entrance, we could see some of the administrative buildings and a couple of the houses that had been constructed as model homes. Patches of the beautifully groomed golf course could be seen here and there through the trees.

As we approached what Larry referred to as the "guard gate" at the entrance, we could see a uniformed man checking cars in as they went through the security gate. I liked the idea of that kind of safety. The first buildings we saw as we drove through the gate were the sales offices. "If it's all right with you, I'll give you a little tour now." Larry said, "we can look some more after we get back and have some refreshments in that building right over there."

When we went inside the sales office he showed us some very impressive maps. He pointed out some places he wanted us to see more closely when we had finished with our soft drinks and cookies.

He first pinpointed an attractive, rustic type structure which he called the "clubhouse". I wasn't sure at first what he meant, but I thought perhaps it was a place where people who live in rural areas can get together and share the joys of country living. Larry suggested he show us that building first.

The clubhouse, I soon saw, was a restaurant with an adjoining bar. I marveled at the rustic effect. The colorful decor of the dining area and even the rest rooms were done in rich earth tones. The whole color scheme blended tastefully with the fresh, new lawn. What a view; so restful to the eye, body and soul I thought. The dining room overlooked the attractive golf course, stretching out across the rolling hills.

When Larry called our attention to the pro shop, we kept quiet and didn't admit that we didn't know what a pro shop was. We soon saw that it was a convenience shop for the golfer. I was sure it was a big attraction for participants of the sport, but I couldn't see myself wearing the clothes displayed there.

Then Larry took us on a scenic drive over the beautiful roads around the large lake. Everything about the development was spacious and impressively done. The few houses that had been built were not just small, country homes. They were large, sophisticated country club estates, designed to blend in with the tree-covered hills surrounding the manmade lake. They were designed to attract a certain type of customer.

Coming from the city, this was like an illusive dream to us. We hadn't imagined there was a place like that in the world, certainly not within a two and a half hour drive from where we lived in Walnut Creek. It was a magical woodsy domain; a definite attraction for the leisure-minded retired set. I wasn't exactly in the "retired" category though, and I did have two young sons twelve and fifteen.

As we were exposed to this unusual development, it was difficult to determine who was more excited, the boys or me. I'm sure we were all trying to imagine what it would be like living in such an enchanting atmosphere. Even the roads were named to fit the area, with names like Woodchuck Court, Huckleberry Drive, Badger Court, Cottontail Way, Sun Forest Drive and Chaparral Circle. Just reading the road signs gave us a thrill.

During our tour we saw a great deal of wildlife, including squirrels, deer, wild turkeys, quail, and peacocks. The boys loved all of it and it touched my heart to see how much they wanted to stay in such an atmosphere.

Larry quickly saw that fishing was something they were interested in. He stopped by one of the bridges and let them walk beside the stream and watch the fish dart about playfully.

While they basked in outdoor pleasure I sat in the car and prayed. "Dear Lord, this place seems too good to be true. I know it's geared for retirees and not necessarily planned with children in mind. We don't play golf and we're not interested in a life of leisure. Far from it!", I reminded God, and I knew He understood my heart.

"You know Lord," I continued, "mere pleasure does not attract me in the least. And you know I don't want my children to be merely fascinated by fishing, hunting, and other recreation alone. But I do want them to have a chance to be close to your creation and to have an opportunity to be occupied with a certain amount of harmless recreation, away from city vice and temptations."

I paused and looked up to see if Larry and the boys were coming back. I closed my prayer. "You know that I don't know what the future holds for any of us, so we'll just leave all this in Your hands. Please don't let us be overcome with something that would not be for our overall good."

The happy laughter of my sons brought me back to the local scene. As we drove on around the lake we enjoyed seeing more squirrels and quail. A small herd of deer on a hillside appeared to be planted there to help impress clients. We were fascinated with them. Later we learned that it was normal to see deer grazing on the golf course almost any time of the day. The graceful creatures were very much at home.

"Let's go get something to drink," Larry suggested as we drove up to the sales office. It sounded like a great idea. We were getting thirsty.

I couldn't help suspecting that this place could be the answer to my fervent and sincere prayers. God does answer prayers quickly sometimes, even before we speak. I knew only God would make things come out right.

While we enjoyed cold sodas from glass bottles, Larry pointed out some statistics and described the features and advantages of the development in detail. There was a large map on the wall, with colorful pictures depicting the flora and wildlife. It also showed the lot boundaries. Bright flags dotted the map, indicating the lots which had already been sold.

I could see Larry wanted to put some pressure on, regarding specific lots he had pointed out to us on the tour, but he knew me well enough by then to restrain himself, to go slowly and tread softly.

Questions And Answers About Lake Wildwood

During the previous weeks I had carefully weighed the many considerations of everything that would be involved if God should move us out of the area, in answers to my prayers. And I fully expected Him to.

There was the telephone ministry, and my work with the single adults. I was more aware than anyone else of the importance of each one. Yet I realized there was one thing even more important than the others. That was my fatherless boys that I was raising alone.

During that time the ominous threat that had prompted my concern and prayers was hovering over me with increasing pressure. I knew some changes in our lives were inevitable. I was positive God was going to answer my sincere prayers. Every morning I awoke alert and sensitive to each possible indication of God's leading. I was very aware that He knew my heart and understood my concerns. Because of this, I was determined to find His will and to comply with His leading.

As we sat there in the sales office that September afternoon, many things I had already thought through were swirling in my mind. It was hard to concentrate on Larry's sales presentation. He could plainly see that I was determined to move only if I believed it was God's will.

"What about churches and schools?" I wanted to know.

Churches? He was taken aback. The salesmen were not prepared to answer this one. There were definitely no churches in the subdivision. Larry said that he had heard there was one in a nearby community.

He picked up a recent edition of the Grass Valley Union, a local newspaper, and flipped through it until he came to the local church section.

"Here," he said as he handed me the newspaper. "Take a look and see what you think."

I noticed that there was a Bible Church listed in Grass Valley and a community church nearby, as Larry had mentioned. These were two we could check out. "And schools?"

I waited to hear about the public schools, just as a matter of information. I knew I had asked the Lord for a Christian school and not just any one, but an excellent one that I could accept as a specific answer to my prayers.

Because Lake Wildwood was a retirement community, Larry hadn't had many inquiries about schools. Most people considering a private subdivision such as this had long ago released their children from the nest and were by now grandparents.

Larry was stumped. He didn't know about the schools in the area. He thought there was a school bus that picked up children along the rural road which passed in front of the guard gate, but he would have to look into what school it serviced.

I asked if he knew of any Christian schools in the area. No, he couldn't recall having heard of one. However, he vaguely remembered hearing someone in the office mention a private school. He wasn't sure if it was a Christian school.

I glanced through the Grass Valley newspaper again to see if one might be mentioned there but I didn't find anything. Larry made a note to inquire further as I had made it quite clear that there would have to be a good one available before I would consider moving to Lake Wildwood.

"Why don't you take this newspaper with you," he suggested. "It will give you an idea of what is available in Grass Valley in the way of shopping and other services."

On the map, Larry pointed out how close Grass Valley, Nevada City, and Marysville were. We had driven there by way of Marysville and had concluded that it was too far for me to drive very often to get to that town, in our old car anyway. I knew if we should move to this seemingly remote place, I would still be very busy with my many projects and I wouldn't have time to drive long distances.

I also asked Larry where the nearest post office was. I would mail my taped broadcasts and I was the stateside secretary for a missionary in Portugal. The U.S. Postal Service was vital to my ministries.

By that time we were saturated with excitement and information. Larry sensed this and proposed we head back towards Walnut Creek. We could carry on any further conversation enroute he said.

"We'll go back another way. I want you to see the Grass Valley area."

Soon we were on a winding road locally called Rough and Ready Highway because it went through the tiny historical town of Rough and Ready. (That crooked narrow road has since been rebuilt into a straight new highway, Route 20.)

The closer we got to Grass Valley, the more beautiful it seemed to us. As we approached the city limit, Larry described some of the colorful history of the Gold Rush days when Grass Valley and Nevada City had both been booming gold rush towns in the mid 1800's.

"In some places around town," he explained, "some of the equipment used in the mines still stands just as it was left the day they stopped mining." He told us that many people travel from all over the country to tour the "gold cities".

We could see, as we came into the nostalgic old town of Grass Valley, that some of the old structures clearly reflected a lively history. I thought Grass Valley was the most interesting historical area I had ever seen. Nevada City was over the hill. We thought it was funny that Nevada City and Nevada County were in California and not in the state of Nevada. We wanted to see it also but it was getting too late. "Another time," Larry promised.

We knew there would have to be another time. We were hooked on Lake Wildwood, the beauty of the pine trees, as well as the historical attractions in Nevada County.

From Grass Valley we took Highway 49 south, towards Auburn. The gorgeous pine trees growing on each side of the road gave us the feeling of being in Colorado. There were also large areas of manzanita growing beside the highway. The boys listened wide-eyed as Larry told us about the mysterious legend that says that wherever manzanita grows, there's gold in the earth beneath. Larry smiled and told the boys, "Of course, if you're really interested, I should tell you that people pan for gold all the time in the Yuba River. You remember the one with the narrow bridge that we crossed over on our way to Lake Wildwood. There are many places along the river where gold panning is popular." He let them think about that for a few seconds and then added, "and every once in a while someone finds a real nugget, too."

I think the highlight of our trip that day reached its climax on that road. The beauty of nature and the outdoors simply captivated us. Even the brick-red soil which was exposed where the highway had been widened thrilled us. It reminded me of the red volcanic soil in Hawaii.

As we approached Auburn, I remembered why the name of the town sounded so familiar to me. One of the donors who contributed monthly to the ministry of the missionary in Portugal lived there. Then it occurred to me. I would write the lady who lived in Auburn and ask her if there was a Christian school in the area. And I could also ask her about any local radio stations.

As we turned west toward Walnut Creek, Larry pointed out that the Sierra Nevada mountains were less than an hour away in the opposite direction. It would take us two hours or more to get home, he said. That told us about where we were on the map.

It was dark by the time Larry reached Walnut Creek with his weary passengers, but it had been a day none of us would ever forget.

A Dream To Relish

Back at home we had to come down considerably to get our feet back on the ground. We had so much to think, dream and pray about for the next few days.

The city seemed more complicated, the houses more crowded together, the noise level louder and the traffic even more congested. We knew we would never be content there again.

As we promised Larry, we prayed much about Lake Wildwood. And we went back up again. This time we found a parcel we liked on Sun Forest Drive. Numerous manzanita bushes grew on the back of the lot. It was located near the bridge over Deer Creek, with the fish underneath which had made such an impression on the boys.

We imagined our own house on that spot in Lake Wildwood and our hearts thumped in our chests. What fun my young sons would have working their way around the dark trunks of manzanita that had obviously grown there undisturbed for many years. There was no end to the places that could be explored in this unique setting.

We told Larry we would inform him regarding our decision soon. We knew without a doubt what we wanted, but we also knew that we had to determine God's will before taking such a big step.

With a great deal of enthusiasm we contacted other members of the family and gave them the startling news that we were considering and praying about moving to the foothills of the Sierra Nevada mountains. It was especially surprising to my married children. Their unpredictable mother had revealed another unusual possibility. This one was a whopper.

I couldn't read their minds of course, but I suspected they were secretly pleased with future "get-away" possibilities.

Our church family and our neighbors had varying responses. Our next door neighbors told us that they had purchased a lot in a similar community near Auburn called Auburn Lake Trails. It was promised as a future lakeside resort since the proposed Auburn Dam was going to be built there within a few years. (To this day, twenty years later, there is still no lake.)

A man in our church tried to discourage us. He had been disappointed by a real estate promise in the foothills also, at Alta Sierra. But some of our friends practically held their breath in awe as we described our discovery and our serious consideration regarding such a move. Most however, said they wouldn't risk it.

Everybody had an opinion regarding the wisdom of moving here. But we couldn't listen to people. Our decision had to be in accordance with God's will. I did listen carefully to each voice, however, in an attempt to discern God's direction.

I waited until our singles group had finished a Bible study session before mentioning to them the idea of me moving away.

"Oh, you can't do that!" they moaned. "We can't get along without you!"

A few expressed envy that I had been presented such a marvelous opportunity. But most of them were thinking about themselves and the club. I was thinking about them too, but I had an even greater concern to take into consideration—my children.

Nevada County and Forest Lake

A reply to my letter to the lady in Auburn regarding the schools and radio stations came quickly. Even though we had never met, she was happy to answer my questions. She was sensitive to the urgency and sincerity of my inquiry.

There was indeed a Christian school and a very good one, she wrote. It was located about halfway between Auburn and Grass Valley, Forest Lake Christian School. [What a beautiful name, I thought.] How heavenly those words sounded as I read them. I realized at once that this was our answer. We had prayed that if it was God's will for us to move, there would be an excellent Christian school available.

I read the rest of that dear lady's letter through tears of gratitude to the Lord for the way He had faithfully shown us His will.

She also told me about the radio station and the Auburn newspaper, but all I could see at the moment was the information about the school. As I sat entranced with the letter, the telephone rang. It was Larry. He wanted to know if we would like to meet him at Lake Wildwood and look around some more, and maybe make a decision.

With unabashed emotion, I told him about the letter I had just received and how God was answering my prayers so that I could be assured of making the right decision. He was so quiet on the other end of the line, I thought I had lost him.

"That really impresses me," I finally heard him say. "I'm thankful I got to work with you and your fine boys."

I confidently made an appointment to meet Larry at Lake Wildwood and told the boys about our wonderful answer to prayer.

We piled into the car and could hardly contain our excitement as we drove toward the foothills. It already felt like we were going home.

I decided to wait about calling Forest Lake School until we got to the area, so I could talk as long as I wanted for free. When I called from a phone booth in Grass Valley, Mr. Willard Schollerman, husband of Jean Schollerman the school principal, answered. He cordially explained the history of the school which he and his wife had founded because of their concern for their own children. They, like myself, had observed the decline of the public school system, both academically and morally. Their response was to start a Christian school themselves.

As I talked, Mr. Schollerman realized that God had surely answered my prayers and put me in touch with them. The more he told me about the school, the more I rejoiced because of the assurance God had given me that this was His perfect will.

One of the great surprises of the entire scenario, was when Mr. Schollerman told me he was project chairman for Lake Wildwood. That wonderful place that we had fallen in love with had been designed and engineered by a Christian man! It was almost an unbelievable story.

After a long telephone conversation with him, we were on our way, assured of God's goodness, guidance and protection. By that time I had no hesitancy about completing papers to purchase Lot 300 on Sun Forest Drive.

We learned a lot more about Lake Wildwood on that visit, the first of many during the following months. There were family excursions with the older children and sightseeing trips with friends who just wanted to see what we had been describing so enthusiastically.

The next spring we drew up plans for our house and dreamed constantly of the day when it would be ready to move into. We planned for lots of decking to accommodate outdoor living. One section would include two levels with unique steps winding down. We had fun working around an oak tree we wanted to keep for shade. We ended up planning a deck around it. From the architect's drawing it looked as if the tree was growing out of the deck itself.

At home in Walnut Creek, we continued to carry on our various activities, all the while dreaming of the day when we could move out of the city and into the country; into our new home in Lake Wildwood.

We Discover Lake Of The Pines

During the following summer, after we purchased our property in Lake Wildwood, my youngest son was invited to spend a week with one of his scouting friends and his mother, with the boy's grandparents who lived at Lake Almanor, still further towards the mountains than our new place in Lake Wildwood.

This left his older brother and me alone. That week I fell victim to an outbreak of influenza in our neighborhood. Flat on my back, I had plenty of time to think and pray. Naturally, I thought through what it was going to be like living at Lake Wildwood.

The more I thought about how difficult it was going to be to get the boys to and from the Christian school every day, the more troubled I became. I realized it was something that would have to be dealt with.

My serious-minded son and I prayed about the problem and decided to drive up and take a closer look at the situation. It seemed to me that it would be best to talk to Mr. Schollerman about it, since he was familiar with both the school and the Lake Wildwood project. I thought he might have a suggestion that would help.

Even though I didn't feel like driving, the urgency of the problem spurred me on. The two of us headed for Nevada County.

Few fifteen year old boys know how to really pray or even want to, but I knew I had one in the car with me who did. We both knew that we could trust God to work everything out. What seems insurmountable to us is simple for God to handle.

The road to Nevada County seemed twice as long that day. I'm sure it would have seemed even longer if we had not had such sweet fellowship together, and with the Lord, as we made our way up the freeway.

Finally, we headed north from Auburn on Highway 49 towards Grass Valley and the road that Mr. Shoellerman had instructed us to take to get to the school. We wanted to see where it was located. To our surprise, while watching for Combie Road, we saw a sign that read LAKE OF THE PINES, with an arrow pointing in the direction we had been instructed to take to get to the school. Strangely, we had not noticed the sign before when passing through. We must have been looking the other way.

On that corner sat a tiny little building with a sign in front that said, "Lake Of The Pines Sales". We wondered what Lake of the Pines was like, and why we hadn't heard about it before. Since Lake of the Pines was in the same general direction as Forest Lake Christian School, we decided to stop at the little sales office and inquire further. A pleasant lady invited us in, introducing herself as she offered us something cold to drink. We gladly accepted. We had some questions and this kind woman with the beautiful name of Franceline (Fran for short, she said) was eager to answer them.

We learned that Lake of the Pines was a recreational community, similar to Lake Wildwood only not as large. Fran said Mr. Schollerman had also been project manager for Lake of the Pines, before going to Lake Wildwood. Another interesting quirk in the story.

The wheels began to turn. We reasoned that if the two developments were similar, except that this one was close to the Christian school, then maybe we should be at Lake of the Pines instead of Lake Wildwood. Fran insisted she would be happy to give us a quick tour of Lake of the Pines and to drive us by the Christian school. This latest surprising development seemed to be one more indication assuring us of God's approval regarding our proposed move.

We were impressed with the beautiful setting of Forest Lake Christian School and its proximity to Lake of the Pines. Fran drove us around the lake and pointed out some interesting lots that were "For Sale", including one that we were especially attracted to on Singing Hills Court. (That name was even more beautiful than the names of the roads in Lake Wildwood, we thought.)

We were very excited and full of still more questions by the time we got to Mr. Schollerman's office at Lake Wildwood, where we had an appointment. He seemed very understanding of our problem. We had property in Lake Wildwood and wanted to take advantage of the school that was almost thirty miles away from where we were planning to build our new home.

After listening carefully to the details of our plight, this kind, wise man suggested we might want to exchange our lot in Lake Wildwood for property in Lake of the Pines since it was near to the school. We had mixed emotions about that. We loved Lake Wildwood. It was, however, too far from everything for us, especially the Christian school. We had an older Valiant station wagon at the time and we couldn't afford to buy a new car. I was also concerned about the time that would be involved if we were to live at Lake Wildwood, and have the boys attend school so far away. The more we thought about it the more comfortable we were with the idea of living at Lake of the Pines.

Mr. Schollerman told us we would have to trade "up" and not "down", meaning we would have to choose a lot in Lake of the Pines that cost a little more than our Lake Wildwood property.

Armed with his advice and suggestions, we went back to the Lake of the Pines sales office to talk to Fran about making an exchange. When she checked again, she found that the lot we liked so much was just slightly higher than what we had paid for the one in Lake Wildwood. She checked with Mr. Schollerman to make sure it would work. The result was unbelievable. In one day, since we had left our home that morning, praying all the way, the whole picture had changed. We had a new focal point from which to dream and plan and work.

The transaction was begun and we went on our way home, praising the Lord all the way for the continuing chain of events in answer to prayer. So much had happened so quickly. It could only be the Lord's doing. It was a good feeling to know that we were being propelled along by the providence of God.

A Complete Shake Up

That one eventful day set in motion a whole new set of developments. Fran and Mr. Schollerman worked out the business aspects while I prayed.

In a surprisingly short time our plans had changed completely. Our lot number changed from 300 to 135, and our street from Sun Forest Drive to Singing Hills Court.

We tried to make our house plans fit the new lot but that didn't work. We had to start all over again.

We decided to lease a house in Lake of the Pines while ours was being built. Fran was able to help us find a rental almost immediately. I enrolled the boys in Forest Lake Christian School and we began making plans to move so they could begin with the fall session.

The pastor of the church which sponsored the Christian school the boys attended in Walnut Creek agreed to take over my Dial Faith For Living telephone outreach ministry, which had continued for over five years. When I announced to the singles group that I was definitely leaving the area, a number of them were disheartened that I would actually leave them. Some thought I was brave to take a step like that, others that I was foolish, while still others envied me. Many of the lonely ones mourned what they considered the loss of my close friendship. Very few seemed to be able to understand that I had to look after the best interests of my fatherless children.

It was difficult to leave the group that I had organized and loved and nurtured. I wept many tears, but I never doubted that I was doing the right thing. I was doing what I had to do which is sometimes very painful.

I arranged for someone to take charge of the singles group. Our excellent Bible teacher would continue but there had to be someone who was willing to take the responsibility of the group. Very shortly another crisis arose in the group. When our teacher heard about the Christian School in Nevada County, he applied for a teaching position and was accepted. That meant that he and I would both be leaving at the same time. Everyone was terribly upset. My heart went out to them. Fortunately, our church was able to provide another good Bible teacher.

Continuing my broadcasts from another area and address didn't really constitute a problem. I simply bought additional mailing cartons and reversible address cards. In fact, a friend printed some new ones which made it easier for me to keep the tapes going to and from the various radio stations. Wherever I lived, my recording studio would always be a part of my home. When they learned I was leaving the area, our local newspaper called to ask if they could send a photographer out to get some pictures and do a story about my ministries and me leaving the area.

To my surprise, the half page feature story had pictures and a huge headline that ran all the way across the page. I was actually embarrassed that they made so much of it.

The Big Move

One obstacle still to be hurdled was the selling of our home in Walnut Creek so that we would have money to build our house in Lake of the

Pines.

The manager of the local radio station where I was involved was also a real estate agent. He was surprised to hear that I was really going to be leaving Walnut Creek but agreed to help sell our home.

About that time, still another crisis arose. I realized I had a serious health problem that would require major surgery. The situation was further complicated by the fact that we had no insurance. We just couldn't afford it. I desperately appealed to my doctor for help in getting the medical attention I needed. I continued to check out every avenue for possible financial help. To my utter distress I discovered I could not even be admitted to a hospital unless I had insurance or money to pay cash for all the services.

[It was the worst crisis I had ever encountered. My prayers didn't even seem to be getting through, but I kept praying and trusting. I reasoned that sometimes we just have to go through certain dark tunnels when our faith is being tested.]

September and school time were fast approaching. We started planning and packing, hoping to get moved so that the boys could start school on time. The doctor, who had at least accepted me for regular office calls, advised me to avoid all lifting and straining.

[Can you imagine that, when we were facing a major move shortly? It was an almost impossible situation.]

My two boys, who always tried to look after me, stepped in and helped me in a remarkable way. The older, who had just turned fifteen, took the packing situation in hand. He efficiently packed every item, from the kitchen to the studio, while I sat in a chair nearby, almost helpless but giving my support and helpful instructions. The move was a monumental project for one so young, but like his father, he was not one to view any problem unconquerable. He just did it because it had to be done. His twelve year old brother tried to help as much as he could but the whole moving matter seemed overwhelming to him.

Naturally we couldn't afford a mover so we had to pray about how we were going to handle that problem too. It had been almost five years since the children's father had died. During those early days of adjustment we had made many new friends. Among them was George the barber. Their dad had always cut the boys' hair, but when he was taken so suddenly a friend who worked at the radio station told me about George. He assured me that George was a good barber and that the boys would like him. They did. I was pleased that he cut their hair almost as well as their dad had.

In time, we came to know George quite well. He was a single man who seemed to enjoy our occasional visits to his barber shop. After a few years, George got up courage to ask me out to dinner at a nice restaurant. He knew it was something I didn't get to do very often. George was not a Christian but he knew I was and he always treated me with great respect. Our relationship was very casual, we were just good friends.

When we told George we were going to be moving, he expressed considerable interest in helping us. He knew we couldn't afford a moving van so he volunteered to drive a U-Haul truck and help us move. The offer came as a complete surprise to us. We were trusting the Lord regarding the huge transportation problem, but we hadn't expected our barber's response.

Our neighbor around the corner on the next street, who was a Christian, also offered to help load the truck.

By the time we got the truck and our car loaded, then drove the more than one hundred mile trip and unloaded them, we were all extremely weary. Even our healthy barber friend was completely exhausted. The boys gladly surrendered their room so that he could spend the night with us.

The next morning George lingered for a short visit after breakfast before leaving to return the rental truck to the Bay Area and get back to his barber shop. As we talked over lingering coffee, he admired our gorgeous view of the lake from our dining room. Closer at hand, he was fascinated with the tiny hummingbirds that flitted around the feeder which our landlord had left for us to enjoy.

When the little creatures began drinking the red liquid in the hanging feeder while hovering in the air, George could hardly believe what he was seeing. The colorful birds, who seem to defy all the laws of aerodynamics, never seemed to get full.

George smiled as he watched them and quietly suggested that one particularly beautiful hummingbird, who kept drinking and drinking, reminded him of his co-worker Ernie. We all had a good laugh about the comparison. (Ernie's drinking problem was not funny, however.)

We could see George was reluctant to leave our newly adopted setting in the beautiful Sierra Nevada Foothills. We couldn't thank him enough for his time and hard work in helping us get moved there, and we invited him back up to see us anytime he could get away from the rigors of city life.

When he had left, we felt the full impact of cutting off completely from the complicated life. We were momentarily overwhelmed with the realization that God had done a wonderful thing for us. With great anticipation we looked forward to a refreshing new beginning, and a remarkably different way of life.

* * *   * * *   * * *

"Now you know about some of the ways God took care of me, and those I was responsible for, after your grandpa was taken from us. He led me step by step, as you have seen, and answered prayers beyond all expectations. Maybe we can talk some more tomorrow."

CHAPTER 20

A New Life at Lake of the Pines

"Grandma, this is the day you promised you'd tell us what it was like moving from the big, noisy city to the quiet country!" Marissa chirped, as she flung open the door, announcing her presence. "I can't wait!"

"And Grandma, you said you'd tell us about when you built your big house on Singing Hills Court." added Gregory, following close behind her.

Before I could answer them, Kathye appeared in the doorway.

"You told me you'd tell us sometime about the snow storm here at Lake of the Pines. Did that really happen?" she wanted to know.

"Well, I see none of you forgot what I said." I told them. "And I'm glad you're right on time. I have a lot to tell you about, including some surprises I don't think I've mentioned before."

* * *   * * *   * * *

A New Lease On Life

The first order of business, after getting all of our belongings moved into the house we leased on Poplar Road in Lake of the Pines, was to find a doctor. I knew I had to get help with my medical problem. It couldn't be put off any longer.

I called the number of a doctor's group in Grass Valley that was listed in the telephone directory and was referred to a new doctor who had just joined them. He was fresh out of school, very young, and just beginning his practice. In contrast to my discouraging experience in Walnut Creek, this youthful physician, about the age of one of my own sons, was pleasant, kind, and considerate. He gave his undivided attention to my urgent need.

After examining me, he called a specialist and made an appointment for me to see him, that very same day.

It took a great deal of courage and stamina for me to face two brand new doctors within hours. Knowing I didn't have money for surgery or a hospital bill added to the strain.

That morning, before I went to get medical help, I put the situation in God's hands. I realized my utter dependence on Him. I was thinking beyond an earthly physician.

The kind gynecologist, who was somewhat older and with years of experience, acted quickly and firmly.

"You must have surgery immediately," he told me.

When I explained my financial status and that we didn't have insurance, he said, "As far as I'm concerned, we'll work it out. I'll call the hospital. I'm sure that can be arranged too." This was very different from the way my doctor in Walnut Creek had reacted.

I had the assurance that at last I was going to receive the help the Lord knew I had to have. This time I wasn't going to be turned away.

That understanding doctor scheduled me for surgery immediately. As much as I dreaded the operation, I was greatly relieved to know that at last I was going to get help. Soon I would be on the other side of this, looking back. My only daughter rushed up from San Francisco to stay with the boys and look after things at home.

It was frightening for the boys to have their only parent confined to a large, unfamiliar hospital so soon after we had moved to a new area. We had not been separated since their father's death. I was concerned about their feelings of fear of loss. We hardly knew anyone in Nevada County. There were Larry and Fran, the salespeople who had helped us, and Mr. and Mrs. Schollerman at Forest Lake School. We had also visited a church in Grass Valley and met the pastor and a few people. But we didn't know anyone very well.

I expressed my concern for my young sons to one of the nurses. She realized I was particularly troubled about the youngest; he had been quite upset when I was leaving him to be admitted to the hospital.

"But mother," he had questioned, "what would I do if something happened to you?"

The crisis of the hour was very real to him. That kind, sensitive nurse was touched by the concern of my little boy. As she straightened my pillow, she said softly, "Have your daughter bring him around to that side door down the hall. I'll wheel you there to see him. He can see you and talk to you. That will help him realize that we are taking good care of you and that we care about him."

I later learned that nurse was a Christian. I know the Lord put me in that particular hospital and gave me that nurse and that doctor. That's how the Lord had always taken care of me.

I tried to look beyond my hospital stay to the time when I would be home again with my family and back to my ministries. For several weeks I had worked on a moment by moment basis, knowing surgery was inevitable and that I might have to go into a hospital at any minute. Now I could finally look beyond this uncertainty.

While I was in the hospital I decided to make the best of the situation. My faith was strong and I was determined not to hide it.

The doctor explained that the operation he was going to perform had been proven highly successful. His positive optimism was encouraging. I trusted his wisdom, his skill, and his word. But I knew my life actually rested in the hands of God, that He would be giving the doctor the ability to deal with my problem.

My surgery was urgent. Because of my age and other reasons, the doctor decided to also do a hysterectomy at the same time. That meant that my child-bearing days would be over. I was too old for that anyway, if I should ever get married again. I had had eight babies already, which had no doubt contributed to my loss of bladder support problem.

The last thing I remember in the operating room was being cold and begging for something on my feet. A nurse hurriedly brought surgical stockings. The warmth was unbelievably soothing. I felt like the sudden assist to my circulation was saving my life. That's where I exited.

When I re-entered the real world in the recovery room, the nurse was asking me if I would like to talk to my daughter.

"Are you all right?" I faintly heard my precious daughter ask.

"Where am I?" I wanted to know.

"You're in the hospital in Grass Valley and your surgery is over," she answered. I could see she was smiling. "You did really well, the doctor said. You're going to be fine."

"Dr. Waechter was pleased with the way the operation went," the nurse added. Feeling half "out", and half "in", I prayed, "Thank you Lord."

When the doctor came by later he was surprised at how alert I was.

"You're doing great, Ardelle," he said, reassuringly. "You're going to be surprised at how well you're going to feel now."

My heart was bursting with gratitude—to the doctor, to the hospital, to the nurses, but most of all to the Lord. I was acutely aware that God was in control of my life. I believed He still had a specific work for me to do and I highly anticipated getting on with my life and my ministries, for His honor and glory. I was thankful, too, for all my friends in different areas who had been praying for me.

The pastor of the church we had visited, and where we planned to be attending, came to see me every day. He assured me that church members and friends were praying for my speedy recovery. Being so far from most of my friends and family, this helped me feel less alone. Everyone was amazed at how quickly I recuperated. My thoughtful daughter stayed with us as long as possible, taking excellent care of me until I was able to take care of myself. Her kindness will never be forgotten.

As the doctor had predicted, I felt like a new person. It was like I had been given a new lease on life—a new beginning.

Forest Lake Christian School

Very soon I was able to resume my radio rigorous schedule. In addition to my in-home ministries; my radio broadcasts and our publication, I began working part-time at the Christian school to pay the tuition for the boys to attend. I was extremely grateful to be able to take care of it that way. Since the school was so new and it was not church-sponsored, they were unable to provide scholarships.

During the following years I was able to work several hours each week for the school. I recognized the opportunity as God's provision.

Country Living On Poplar Road

When at last things had settled down to normal, we were very happy in our new foothill home. We thoroughly enjoyed the outdoor beauty, the wooded area around us, the lake, and the gorgeous sunsets behind the dam. It all seemed heavenly to us. We appreciated the quiet, peaceful atmosphere—no sirens, no low-flying airplanes, no blasting radios or television sets.

We especially enjoyed the wildlife, so new to us, having moved from the big city. Birds of numerous varieties frequented our deck and window sills, begging for our attention. They appeared to be coming down from higher elevations to investigate our country haven. We longed to be able to identify them and searched in vain for bird books in the local libraries.

We never ceased to thrill at the unreal antics of the many delightful hummingbirds that fed constantly around our hanging feeder. From our vantage point in our kitchen, the sunlight reflected off their wings and breasts at just the right angle, revealing dazzlingly brilliant colors, usually hidden beneath their outer feathers.

Squirrels loved to play in our driveway, and in the trees. Sometimes raccoons and skunks would climb the steep steps of our back deck. Occasionally we would see a fox. It was all a bit frightening for me but my country kids loved it. All the time we lived in that house at the back side of the lake, the boys slept in their sleeping bag on the deck, from early spring to late fall, moving inside only when forced to by the rain and cold. It was sort of like perpetual camping for them.

A Mirrored Scene

To my amazement and delight, my electronically inclined fifteen year old son set up my studio in one of the bedrooms. He did it as confidently and as efficiently as my technician had done when we moved to Walnut Creek. In order for me to see the steps leading up to the front door, we hung one of our lovely antique mirrors on the wall above the console where I worked. This also gave the room a more spacious effect. It was a pleasant place to spend long periods of time working in my new studio.

One morning I was concentrating intensely on what I was doing. Suddenly, a beautiful scene, almost like a vision, caught my attention. The mirror was filled with beautiful deer. A whole herd had wandered onto the hillside next to our house; I could hardly believe what I was seeing. I tiptoed to the window and looked out upon a live picture that practically overwhelmed me. The deer gazed contentedly just outside the window. Breathless with awe, I prayed, "Thank you Lord!", as the tears rolled down my cheeks.

I was careful not to make any noise as I counted the deer, oblivious to my admiration. There were at least thirty-five of them; the animals that I consider among the most precious of creatures that God has blessed us with. It seemed to me that He had led them there, as they wandered down from the higher hills and were enjoying the green grass, just outside my studio window. It was like a special show that He had staged just for me.

I completely lost track of time as I watched that almost sacred scene. Finally, when they were satisfied, they wandered on down toward the lake.

It was hard to get settled back into my recording routine, after such a thrilling interlude. When the boys came home from school, I had quite a story to tell them. They got excited just hearing about it. Some time later, they had one to tell me that topped mine. One afternoon as they walked home from school with a friend, they were all surprised to see a large herd of deer grazing together just off Combie Road. Each of them counted and agreed that there were forty-eight deer altogether.

What a blessing to live in such a natural area. Forest Lake Christian School was also located in a beautiful rural setting. Deer often lingered near the playground, watching the boys and girls playing at recess. There were many squirrels and other animals too, such as foxes and skunks, in the area. One day I drove to the school just before noon to deliver to the boys their lunches which they had forgotten that morning. While waiting for them to be dismissed, I heard a coyote very near the school. What an exciting incident to write to the rest of our family about.

Every day was a new adventure and each seemed to yield more thrills and surprises for us. We were convinced that God had placed us in His chosen spot.

The Sentinel Singles' Club

We had a lot to keep us busy and entertained in our new location but we missed our friends in the Bay Area. It helped that we were making many new friends at the church we attended in Grass Valley and at Forest Lake Christian School.

I also missed working with people in a ministry. For the first time in a very long time I didn't have a Bible study going in our home. I really missed that. The man who had taught our Bible class for the singles group in Walnut Creek was now teaching at Forest Lake. Dave also missed a teaching ministry to adults. We both observed the surprising number of single people that we kept running into everywhere we went in our new location. There were also a number of them at our church.

We became more and more concerned, and wondered how many single men and women there actually were in the combined population of nearby small mountain towns, and surrounding countrysides.

I continued to think about and pray for the group I had organized in the metropolitan areas of Walnut Creek. They missed me a lot too. They knew I loved them and was concerned about them. Sometimes one or two, or even a car load of them would drive the two hour trip up to visit me.

My burden for local single people grew. I began praying and earnestly considering whether the Lord might want me to launch a singles ministry in my new location.

I talked with the pastor and executive board at the church about my concerns. Just like in Walnut Creek, they were all married. They too expressed little interest or concern for the single people of the church or the community, even though I tried to point out to them that this group constituted a definite mission field in our country. But I guess I should have realized that it was difficult for them to understand what it's like to be lonely, and often left out and neglected. The time came when I knew I had to do something myself about the situation. I decided to make a stab at starting a singles ministry on my own. That was not the way I had hoped it would be, but it was the way it looked like it was going to have to be.

I came up with a name I thought would be appropriate for the group. I would call it the Sentinel Singles Club, the idea being that I would watch over their spiritual welfare like a sentinel.

I ordered attractive business cards, printed in black and red, with the club's name, and both my phone numbers' one for Nevada County and one for Placer County. I hoped to work with singles over a wide area. It seemed to me that Lake of the Pines was in the middle of everywhere.

On the card I also mentioned "Bible study and fellowship," and the words "with Christian emphasis". I hoped the idea of Bible study would eliminate individuals who had no intention of pursuing the Christian lifestyle.

I made plans and set a date for an introductory meeting so that I would have something to offer those who called in as the result of the promotion I planned to do on radio and in local newspapers.

I had no idea what the response would be. At that point I was glad I lived in a closed community with a security gate. The only way anyone could get in to see me was to make reservations so I could notify the security guards. I really appreciated this safety feature. As the calls began to come in, I prayed that everything would work out right.

With plenty refreshments standing by, I anxiously awaited my guests. When everyone had finally found their way around the lake to my home, we had forty-three brave single people (to my surprise, more men than women). Few had met before, so we went around the room, giving each person an opportunity to introduce themselves. There were single men and women from many different backgrounds. It was interesting to hear about the various occupations they represented. I had not realized how many professional people were single. We even had a well-known cartoonist present.

It was evident early in the evening that everyone was enjoying the fellowship and the refreshments. I was sure that out of the many people there, several smoked cigarettes and some would expect to be offered a drink. However, no one seemed to mind that there were no ash trays out and that the strongest drink available was coffee. Most chose to drink punch.

The meeting was lively and I don't think anyone felt any need for a stimulant. I had learned from experience, as a minister's wife, how to help a group feel at ease and comfortable with each other. From the onset I made it clear that our principle functions would be weekly Bible study sessions and a monthly fellowship time. No one expressed any resistance. I was pleased with the interest shown in those areas. Dave and I both realized it was time for us to get on with the ministry. I had prayed so much during our initial efforts, I accepted the favorable response as a green light from the Lord.

I immediately made arrangements to meet for a weekly Bible study at a local restaurant at 9 a.m. on Sunday mornings before they opened for business. With the promotion I was planning for the new club, the restaurant owner thought he was getting a pretty good deal. He even agreed to make coffee and doughnuts available.

My good friend Dave was to teach the class. He, like me, felt strongly about the need and wanted to follow God's leading. We were both anxiously awaiting His marching orders.

We were surprised and pleased with the interest and response to our Bible study sessions. I began running an ad in both local newspapers regularly and received many calls each week. Most inquirers turned up in the Bible class the following Sunday morning. Just as we had observed in our group in Walnut Creek, many single men and women had cut themselves off from all social interaction.

We started meeting one evening each month for fellowship and fun. Sometimes we would meet in my home, other times we would go to a local restaurant and enjoy dinner together. There would be so many of us I would reserve a banquet room. I'm sure the eateries appreciated all the business I brought them. I had in mind, however, the spiritual welfare of the "family" God had given me the watchful care over—the Sentinel Singles Club. They looked to me for encouragement and advice.

In addition to local activities, there were times when we would plan something with the Walnut Creek group. They would come up to Nevada County, or we would go as a group to the Bay Area to participate in their activities.

One particular event was a banquet in the Lake of the Pines clubhouse. After considerable persistence on my part, and plenty of resistance on their part, I was finally able to convince the Lake of the Pines management that there was a significant percentage of single residents living in our closed community. I tried to help them see that we had as much right to use the facilities that belonged to all of the members as anyone else. The functions that were important to us were just as important as those of interest to the other members.

While attempting to make arrangements for use of the "gun club" building, which was not being used, I attended several business sessions of the Lake of the Pines Association and got to know the general manager and the governing board. At one meeting where my request was discussed, the general manager took sides with me. Members of the board, all married, disagreed with my reasoning that those of us who were "single" residents ought to receive some consideration.

I was pleasantly surprised to find the manager so congenial and understanding and willing to stand up to what seemed to me to be a stubborn, narrow-minded board. I had the impression that they were mainly concerned with the interests of the drinking and golfing crowd.

During the process I learned that the manager and his wife had only been married a short time. He could understand my point of view. Once, when the opposition became fierce he spoke up, "I think this matter has gone too far," he told the board. "Ardelle is asking for something that is fair and reasonable. It is my feeling that she should not only be given permission to use the gun club regularly for the group she is working with so faithfully, but I believe she should also be allowed to use the clubhouse occasionally. You all know that outside groups are allowed that privilege."

By that time my emotions had erupted and I was crying. I got up and left as quickly as I could. On my way out the manager said to me, "I'm sorry, Ardelle, about all that has happened here today. I'll be over to see you later." He kept his word too. By the time he knocked on my door I had cried my heart out. He apologized again for the lack of consideration I had received and the embarrassment I had suffered. He commended me for all my efforts working with a lonely segment of society; single people. He told me he and his wife both knew where I was coming from.

At the time, his wife was the cook at the clubhouse. She was highly regarded because of her ability to prepare delicious food and also to serve it attractively. The general manager told me he had insisted I be given permission to use the clubhouse dining room occasionally for my singles group. He said he and his wife had discussed it before he came to my home. They suggested I plan a banquet and he and his wife would work out a menu with me.

I was overwhelmed. I had not believed it possible to get permission to have a singles function at the prestigious Lake of the Pines Country Club. I had not eaten there and I don't even know anyone who had. I had only dared to ask to use the gun club. What an unexpected blessing!

When I told the singles group, they were really surprised that I had been willing to do battle in their behalf. They were excited at the prospect of attending a banquet at the clubhouse. Everyone rushed to make reservations. They called their single friends and invited them. No one wanted to miss it. We also invited the Walnut Creek group. We soon had over one hundred reservations.

I was sure God had made it all possible and I was determined to see that everyone understood that we were indeed a group "with Christian emphasis", as our slogan stated. We planned special music, a talent show, and invited an interesting Christian speaker. I wanted it to be an evening none of us would ever forget, and it was. I also wanted my "opposition" to see that I could plan and carry off a successful event.

The whole evening turned out to be a wonderful experience for all, far beyond my hopes and expectations. I had heard about the good reputation the restaurant had, but words were hardly adequate to describe the delicious food. We were very pleased. I remember thinking that it was probably the first time prayer had ever been offered in that room.

I had never seen such an attractively laid out buffet. I doubt if anyone else there had either. We had invited the manager to sit at the head table with us. He seemed very pleased with the response. He and his dear wife, the very much appreciated cook of the hour, were rewarded with adequate praise when I asked her to come in for our applause.

After dinner, the talent show and special music went well. Our speaker, a single minister from the area, was definitely anointed by the Holy Spirit. The entire evening was blessed by the Lord.

Soon after that delightful evening, the manager and his wife moved back to the Midwest where her relatives lived. I know they never forgot their experience with the Sentinel Singles Club back at Lake of the Pines.

The following year we were able to hold another banquet in the club house. And we had the regular use of the gun club building for our fellowship potlucks over a period of several years—all because of the persistence of the sympathetic club manager and in answer to my many prayers.

The Initiation Snow Show

We were all very happy in our new location. The boys enjoyed Forest Lake School and their many new friends. They spent hours fishing, swimming and snorkeling in our wonderful lake. They watched the golfers and even got paid for hunting down errant golf balls. There was always something to do. Sometimes they just enjoyed being at home where it was peaceful and quiet. We all liked not having to worry about what our neighbors would think if we played our favorite music or hung our laundry on the clothesline outside. It was heavenly, living quiet, peaceful days and undisturbed nights in the safe place God had provided for us in the country, next to God's beautiful nature.

The changing seasons in the foothills were wonderful. Looking back now, I think God may have been amused at our fascination with the trees as they changed in the spring and fall and all the interesting flowers that we weren't used to. We even enjoyed the clouds.

When we were being shown around Lake of the Pines, Fran told us the location was "above the fog and below the snow". I liked the idea of being above the fog. I'd seen too much disruptive fog in Illinois, and in the San Francisco Bay Area.

To many potential buyers, the idea of snowless winters was a good selling point. We, however, were disappointed to hear that the snow that we had heard so much about was not expected. That's one thing we had anticipated when we considered moving to the foothills. I had enjoyed the abundance of snow in Illinois and had often told the children about our experiences there.

When we expressed surprise that there would be no snow to look forward to, our real estate agent quickly responded, "Oh, it does snow here—sometimes." That was music to our ears, but I was afraid she was just telling us that to make us feel better. Of course our decision to move to Lake of the Pines had not depended on whether or not it might snow here. There were so many positive aspects about it, we almost forgot about the snow issue.

The first few months in our leased home at the back side of the lake, we drank in the autumn beauty and enjoyed our new country freedom, and the amenities of our new recreational community.

Then, one gray November afternoon while the boys and I were in Grass Valley doing our grocery shopping, it started to snow. We had been told that Grass Valley, which is fourteen miles north of Lake of the Pines, did get snow and sometimes plenty of it.

We were in clear view of a bank thermometer when the flakes began to fall. While in the supermarket we had overheard someone remark that when the temperature reads 38 degrees, you can expect snow. We were thrilled to see the temperature and then to observe the huge snowflakes start to fall, slowly at first and then faster and faster.

[You can imagine how surprised we were to hear people around us on the street grumbling about the predicted snow.] We soon discovered that many locals hated snow. That was one way you could tell the newcomers from the "natives".

We didn't want to leave Grass Valley and miss the beautiful snow, but we didn't want to stay and get stuck in it either. A man walking by looked at us, shook his head and remarked, "this is going to be a big one." We didn't have tire chains or snow tires so we quickly decided to head south and try to keep ahead of the storm.

To our utter delight, the snowflakes were soon falling furiously as we cautiously made our way down Highway 49 toward Lake of the Pines. We had been informed that the snow would probably stop by the time we reached the 2,000 foot elevation, just south of the entrance to Alta Sierra. (Our home was at about 1,900 feet.)

When we reached Lake of the Pines, it was still snowing so hard that the wipers could barely keep the windshield clear enough for me to drive safely, and the roads were becoming quite slick.

We stopped at the guard gate and shared some of our enthusiasm with the officer on duty. Len had been born and raised in Grass Valley. He had been telling us that we could expect plenty of snow in Grass Valley. He had also been negative about it. He couldn't believe that we were actually hoping for snow, but when we drove up and excitedly began to discuss the beauty and the prospects of getting a lot more snow, he began to smile at our excitement.

"Is this what you've been telling us about?" I asked, bubbling over with delight. "You had better believe it!" he replied with a strange knowing expression.

To our surprise and indescribable thrill, the snow did not let up. Everything was dry so it started to stick immediately. In the short time we had been on the road, everything had turned white. I could hardly see to drive. By the time we got around the lake to our home, the roads were becoming quite dangerous.

The boys had never seen so much snow. They were ecstatic. It took me back to the thrilling memories I had of Illinois and still further back to my childhood in the South, where we enjoyed plenty of snow every winter.

We were all overcome with gratitude to the Lord. The boys thought we must surely be in heaven. I was convinced that the Lord had sent the surprise snow show for our benefit. We accepted it as a heaven-sent gift.

When the snow stopped falling, it turned very cold. Water pipes froze and burst. For over a week no running water was available to drink or to cook with, or to flush the toilet. During this emergency we learned that it takes an awful lot of melted snow to make a few drops of liquid water. It was next to impossible to melt enough snow to work the toilet. We also suffered a power outage. There were more problems than we could ever have imagined. With no power we had no heat. And we didn't have lights at night because we didn't own a lamp or lantern. I scrambled to find candles which I knew I had somewhere but couldn't remember where as we hadn't unpacked them yet. I hadn't expected to need them. The crisis revived childhood memories of kerosene lamps, woodstoves and fireplaces.

With no electricity, we couldn't keep food in the refrigerator. I was reminded of the way we improvised an extra "ice" box during the winter in Illinois. The boys quickly put one together as I described it to them and we set it on a table on the back deck. It worked really well during that time when it was so cold.

It didn't take long for milk and other perishables to run out. No one expected the unusual storm and the ensuing freeze so we hadn't prepared for an emergency. We had enough food for three days, but not a week.

My responsible young sons refused to just sit around and not look after our family. They decided to set out and walk the two and a half miles to a little country store and buy the things we needed. We had heard on our battery-powered radio that the snowplow had cleared the main road beyond the store, so that service trucks could get through with milk and other items.

The fellas enjoyed the challenge and the walk to the country store. I was proud of their willingness to look out for our needs and welfare.

When we began to really suffer from the chill and I felt our health was being threatened, I began to pray in earnest. It had become evident that along with the beauty, God intended to teach us some important lessons from the storm. He wanted to remind us that we still had to trust

Him and that He was in control of a situation that was about to get out of hand for us. And what a lovely surprise he had in store for us!

We had burned the small amount of wood that we had been able to find here and there, in our very inefficient fireplace. Now, we were completely out of fuel and there was still no electricity to operate the heating system. We really began to pray. It was several days before we could get our old Valiant station wagon down our steep driveway in the snow. To our utter surprise, one afternoon our real estate friends, Fran and her husband Jim, laboriously blazed through the snow and ice-packed roads with their truck and appeared at our door with a load of wood for our fireplace. They wanted to make sure we didn't freeze. It was a kind, thoughtful thing to do. We knew they were being used by the Lord to answer our prayers.

At first, we had been like children carried away, jumping up and down with glee, thanking the Lord for the snow that we were enjoying so much. Now we were lifting our hearts in praise to Him for taking care of our personal needs during what had turned out to be an emergency.

Our heavenly Father knew that we were enjoying the extra blessings He was sending, like children whose parents provide pleasant surprises. He also knew that we were learning to trust Him for sudden needs as well as for our daily provisions.

Singing Hills Court

While living in the house we had leased on Poplar Road, which was at the back side of the lake, we kept a close watch on our new home being built on our own property just up from the guard gate.

We loved the location. We had been thrilled with it since the moment Fran first showed it to us. It was on one of the highest hills in Lake of the Pines with a breathtaking view in every direction. To the east we could see the gorgeous Sierra Nevada range. One day we spotted Mount Lassen to the northeast. We were even able to make out the outline of the coastal range to the northwest. And one especially clear day we were almost certain that we were seeing the peak of Mount Diablo in Contra Costa County, beyond the Sacramento Valley. We were delighted with our range of view. When we first bought the property, I took my precious friend Ginger to see our future home site. As much as she had loved the time she had been able to spend with us at Lake Wildwood, she agreed that our new location was even better. Several of my associates from the Bay Area and from as far away as San Jose drove up to see our new property. A few were doubtful about my vivid description but those who came up to see for themselves also reported back how wonderful it was. One of my close spiritual advisors told the singles group, "I believe God is definitely leading Ardelle to make this move, as much as we hate to see her go." After we moved to Nevada County we never doubted we were in God's perfect will.

During the actual building of our home, we learned a great deal about construction and monitored every stage with great interest. A few times I had to fight for what we had been promised and actively ward off some shortcuts the contractors were tempted to take, which they thought they could get by me. When it was time to install carpet, I would not settle for an inferior grade. More than just a house was at stake—it was our home, as well as a base for our outreach ministries for the Lord. I knew we would host Bible studies and get-togethers, and I was determined to have a place that would honor the Lord. I stood my ground.

"You have built such a beautiful home," I reasoned with them, "it would be a shame to install cheap carpet." I prayed as I battled for fairness. God heard and answered, and I won. They installed a beautiful, good grade of gold colored carpet in the living room, dining room and three of the five bedrooms, two of which we would use for offices for our ministries. The morning sun flooded the boy's rooms so they chose a pretty rust color carpet.

Finally, as a result of my insistence, deadlines were met and we were able to move into our beautiful new five bedroom home at the beginning of September. When everything was in place and we were settled in we were pleased with the effect. It was as nice as our Walnut Creek home had been, we thought. We had the same furniture, and almost the same gold carpet. But this time we were in a rural setting with many advantages over the city.

We held many inspiring Bible study sessions in our pleasant living room. We also had numerous potluck dinners on our huge deck which we had built so as to insure afternoon and evening shade.

One of the rooms became my office, and another my recording studio. My now sixteen year old son took full responsibility as my technician and set up my new studio. Once again he proved himself, just as he had when we had moved to Lake of the Pines the year before.

[What a blessing to have my own personal technician. When problems arose, he and I would track down and troubleshoot, until we were able to remedy the situation. I thank the Lord that over a period of more than thirty years I never missed one broadcast due to malfunctioning equipment. I learned early on to pray and to trust the Lord a lot.]

The Print Room

As I've told you before, your Grandpa Brown and I had a printing ministry over a period of many years. After his death we attempted to continue the printing projects because of my conviction that the printed word is very effective.

When we moved to Lake of the Pines our publication that had been called *"The Visitor"* now became *"The Sentinel"*. We had decided not to try to move our huge offset press. One of our neighbors, who was also one of the ministers at the church we attended, wanted it for his Bible study ministry. He offered to buy us a new and much simpler to use system, which the boys and I could operate, in exchange for the offset press. We accepted the offer as from the Lord.

Soon after I started the singles ministry, a Christian businessman from Sacramento who had started attending the meetings became interested in the printing ministry. He became aware of an expensive piece of equipment which he knew would help us, an electronic scanner, and purchased it for us. He also contributed toward needed supplies when he learned how small our budget was. He was greatly impressed with our faith in the Lord, which we exhibited for everything from our daily bread to the ministry which God had given us.

[That tremendous equipment served well for many years. About fifteen years later that dear, dedicated Christian businessman went to be with the Lord, but his faithfulness and generosity are still evident in our ministry.]

* * *   * * *   * * *

"There are many more things I want to tell you about but they will have to wait for another time. I hope it can be soon."

CHAPTER 21
Life With Grandpa Darrell

"Hi, Grandma!" Joanna greeted me as I answered the door. "Thank you for inviting me to come stay with you while Grandpa is gone."

"Oh, I'm really looking forward to our visit," I assured her. "I'm sure we can find some fun things to do."

"You know what I would like most?" she asked, then went on. "I would just like to talk."

"I would like that also," I told her.

"For one thing," she said as if she had been thinking about it, "Could you tell me how you met Grandpa Darrell. I'd like to hear more about him. You know how we all love him."

"I would love to tell you about him," I told her, smiling as I hung her coat in the front closet. "After dinner we'll have a nice, long fireside talk."

* * *   * * *   * * *

Catching The Signal

When we first moved to Nevada County we attended a church in Grass Valley. It was somewhat similar to the church I was a member of in Walnut Creek, but not quite the same. A few years later we learned about a church in Auburn, in the opposite direction of Grass Valley, which was affiliated with the Evangelical Free Church of America, the church we had belonged to in Walnut Creek. Someone had told us it was a small, struggling group. The boys and I thought we would check it out for ourselves.

Before we left for church I prayed, "Lord, please let us know if this is the church we should attend and become a part of. If it is, let us be needed there, so that we can be assured it is your will." In my missionary heart I think I was longing for an opportunity to serve the Lord in a small church.

During the morning service the pastor expressed appreciation to the young, single girl who had been driving all the way from Grass Valley every Sunday morning to play the piano for them. He mentioned that it was her last Sunday and asked the little congregation to pray for a replacement for her. No one else there that morning suspected anything unusual, but I saw it as an answer to my prayer. It was a definite indication of a need and an opportunity for me to serve the Lord in a small capacity.

At an opportune time I volunteered to play the piano and from that Sunday I became very active in various ministries of the church. I continued to play the piano as the church grew, until other pianists who could play better than I started attending. I also served on the church executive board, taught Sunday School, and did the church bulletins. The boys and I printed them in our print shop; it was something we enjoyed doing together.

We also began a Bible study class in our home for Lake of the Pines residents and others from outside the development who wanted to come. For a period of time our Auburn pastor drove up to teach the class. Later, when he had to discontinue, I became the leader of the group. Those were happy, productive days for us as we served the Lord in our church and in our community.

New Friends

How well I remember the Sunday morning an especially nice couple visited our church. They had recently moved into the area and had been searching for a church that was right for them. My pastor's wife instinct drew me to them. I tried to make them feel comfortable in church and later invited them to attend Bible study sessions in my home. I was pleased when they came. Their names were Darrell and Patricia Hopkins.

Darrell was a California Highway Patrol officer, working out of the Auburn office. He had been transferred from the Placerville office a short time before. His wife Pat was not very well. She and I were drawn to each other and I wanted to help her.

Pat would call me and talk for long periods of time, earnestly expressing her deep need and pleading with me to pray for her special requests. I rejoiced at times when she seemed to improve physically, and appeared to be experiencing a sense of victory in her life. Then my heart would ache when it became evident that she was getting worse. I was aware at the time that she was spending a lot of time reading and studying the Bible and truly appreciated the Scriptures.

It was a great blessing to have Pat and Darrell coming to church regularly, and also attending Bible study sessions with us when she was able to come.

One week Pat called me many times when Darrell was at work. She opened up to me in a way which I doubt she had ever done with anyone before. From her heart, she poured out to me her highest hopes and her deepest heartaches. She had experienced a great deal of mental pain in her life. I was glad she felt free to unburden her heart to me. She really needed that release. I have her secrets locked safely in my heart, along with those of others, entrusted to me over the years. I will never betray their trust.

One day I was convinced that my precious friend Pat was truly doing better than usual. She told me she believed she could now somehow overcome her major health problems with the help of the Lord. She felt confident that God was going to help her conquer some of the barriers she was struggling with. I was thrilled and encouraged.

Then, to my utter dismay, the following Saturday morning, our pastor's wife called with the shocking news.

"Ardelle, I hate to have to tell you this, but Pat died last night at Auburn Faith Hospital."

I was stunned, and sick at heart. I couldn't believe she was gone. I had so much wanted to help her and I had believed there had been some definite progress. Now my precious friend was dead. She had been sicker than I had realized. Overcome with grief, I cried for hours.

My heart also ached for Pat's husband, Darrell. I prayed a lot for him. I understood his pain and sorrow because I had also experienced the loss of a mate.

I tried to express my sympathy by sending food to his home. I went to Pat's funeral, met other family members and truly grieved with them. She was my precious friend. In the weeks and months following Pat's death I continued to pray for her husband and children. I knew it was going to be hard for him to adjust. None of his family lived nearby. One son lived in the northern part of the state; the other on the East Coast.

I was glad Darrell continued to attend church and also come to the Bible class in our home. I had true concern for his spiritual welfare and I considered him a close friend.

In time, I invited him to our singles club functions because I knew he was very lonely. Then, suddenly, I found myself experiencing pain in my heart when one of the ladies in the club would cast an admiring glance at him. I soon realized I was jealous. I liked him a lot myself. And I guess I also felt I was watching out for him, for Pat's sake.

"Dear Lord," I prayed, "please protect Darrell. He is so vulnerable right now. I don't want some unscrupulous woman taking advantage of him." Our church family had taken Pat and Darrell into our hearts. We were touched with the tragedy that had suddenly hit the family. Pat was only 47 when she died and Darrell was young too. Everyone was holding him up in prayer. I think he could feel it too.

I thought Darrell was pleasant, handsome, and intelligent. I admired the self-discipline he had developed as a law officer, having been with the California Highway Patrol for more than twenty-five years.

When I first met him and Pat, he had just been diagnosed with diabetes. He had been able to bring it under control by diet and discipline. That really impressed me. When the emotional stress of bereavement and the months of adjustment threw him off balance, his doctor put him in the hospital for more tests. He was placed on an insulin regimen at that time.

I was concerned about him being in the hospital and so alone during such a trying time. He was in a hospital in Roseville, which was about 30 miles away, but I worked up the courage to drive there and find my way around in a town I was not familiar with. I wanted to show him I cared that he had health problems, and especially since he had no relatives close enough to visit him.

As soon as he was home again he was back in church and Bible study sessions. I anxiously looked forward to seeing him at every opportunity. I had no idea how he felt about me, but I was increasingly aware of my deep feelings for him. It was hard for me to know how to react around him. I certainly didn't want him to think I was foolish.

I remember one Sunday morning in particular when I watched him walk into church. I felt an overwhelming sense of love for him. I wanted to hold him close and tell him, "I love you and I care about what happens to you." But of course I could not do that, at least not yet. I prayed and cried all that week. I asked the Lord to take away the ever increasing sensation of love I felt for Darrell if it was not pleasing to Him. But it didn't go away. I was almost afraid to be near him for fear I would do or say something that would spoil it all.

In spite of my fears and prayers, Darrell started to attend the singles club meetings regularly. I remember one Saturday night when we ate at a restaurant as a group, he paid for my dinner and sat next to me. I was so overcome I could hardly eat. Could it be that he liked me too, I wondered. If not, why would he have bought my dinner? Oh, how I hoped!

He also began attending the Sunday morning Bible study sessions of the singles group held at the same restaurant.

[Joanna, I will never forget one morning when he sat across from me. I could hardly contain myself. At one point his knee touched mine underneath the table, sending a tingling sensation throughout my entire body. For a moment I couldn't even speak. I wasn't sure he even noticed that we had touched ever so slightly.]

Another Sunday morning I arrived at church before he did. When he came in, he walked right down the aisle and sat down beside me. It was a heavenly feeling. He had chosen to come sit with me, right in front of everyone. We stood to sing and when we sat back down he moved closer, which I discreetly noticed.

When he sang with the congregation his magnificent voice engulfed me. I closed my eyes and silently prayed, "Thank you, Lord!" We shared a hymnal but I only moved my lips to make it look like I was singing. I didn't want to miss any of the notes he sang. I couldn't tell you what the pastor preached about, or anything else that went on that Sunday morning. All I could think of was that the man I had come to love very much had chosen to sit with me. What a fulfilling experience! But I have to admit, I almost felt guilty of neglecting the Lord.

Our friends who attended the Bible study sessions in my home began noticing that we were attracted to each other. Later they smiled when they remembered how at first we sat on opposite ends of the couch, then each week a little closer, until finally we were sitting together. Of course no one said anything.

I will never forget the night when Darrell stood with me at the door as everyone left, then he sat beside me on the couch. My heart was racing. He had just returned from a hunting trip in Wyoming. I can still see the expression on his face as he brought out a picture of the "buck" he had killed. I admired his catch, but most of all I noticed the genuine pleasure in his smile. He also showed me pictures of his two sons and of his infant grandson. And he had a picture of Pat too, of course.

Pat was my dear, precious friend. Now I felt a strange sensation when I saw her picture. I didn't want to betray her, but the more I thought about it, the more I was inclined to believe I was doing her a favor by taking care of Darrell. It was an issue I had to deal with.

After the wallet pictures were put away, we continued to talk about various things. Then, after a brief pause he looked me straight in the eye and asked me a very unexpected question.

"What do you think of my hair, the way it's cut?"

I was so surprised and taken aback I couldn't answer at first. He wore his hair really short. I had wondered why he had such an old-fashioned haircut when he seemed so up-to-date in every other way. But I would never have mentioned it at that point. I am seldom at a loss for words, but I was at that delicate moment, and I didn't want to flub it. I believed he was asking for an honest answer. Evidently he was self-conscious about his hair in my presence. I knew I had to answer him.

"Well," I sort of stammered, silently praying for the right words. "This is a different era . . ."

He smiled at my reply and I felt it wasn't too far off from the answer he was looking for.

The following week Darrell came early for Bible study and again stayed after everyone else had gone. That night he sat very close and put his arm around me.

"I think I'm falling in love," he ventured, very sincerely, again looking me straight in the eye.

I KNEW I had fallen in love. Deeply in love. During the previous weeks I had struggled with my out-of-control emotions. I would cry and alternately pray that the Lord would please help me know His perfect will. I did not want to displease Him. Not knowing exactly how Darrell felt about me when I loved him so much, was tearing me apart inside. It was such a relief to have him reveal his feelings.

From that time on we went to church and most other places together. We spent many happy hours sharing and doing things we both enjoyed.

He helped me with the singles ministry. No one could doubt that we were in love. Everyone seemed to rejoice with me but I was aware that a couple of the ladies were a bit disappointed that I was the one who was so fortunate. I truly wished that they too, could find someone as wonderful for themselves, but I was not willing to relinquish the man I had fallen so deeply in love with.

A Surprising Answer To Prayer

When Darrell at last revealed that he cared for me too, I was extremely happy and I believed he was too. It was not possible for us to hide our secret from our children, our church family, our Bible study group, or the single's club and we didn't try. We were so happy, we wanted the whole world to know.

Our days and hours were filled with activity. Darrell was a busy state traffic officer and I was working full-time at the Auburn radio station, which was not very far from where he lived.

On his way to work every morning, Darrell would stop by to see me. I thought he was really handsome in his neat uniform and I admired him so much in every way. I was proud to have my co-workers know that I had such a special friend.

His little visit each morning was a perfect break for me. I was getting up at 4:30 a.m. to get school lunches ready for my two teenagers and to get to work by 6 o'clock. Knowing I was going to see my sweetheart when he stopped by on his way to work made it all a little easier. I was thankful that I could go to work that early so that I could get off at 2 p.m. and be home by the time the boys got home from school.

It all worked out well for me and for the station. My first duty that early in the morning, was to gather, edit and type local news stories from three counties, Placer, Nevada and El Dorado, and get them ready to go on the air at 7 a.m. It was a real rush hour for me.

I had to call the various law enforcement agencies and the fire department, then write the stories and have them ready for the newscaster. Some news came in from other sources too, such as the wire service, which I also had to edit and write up.

I had a scanner just above my desk which kept me alerted to late-breaking stories. When an emergency vehicle was dispatched to the scene of an accident or fire, I was usually able to follow up and get the story, often before the newspaper did. Even though I was acting as news director my official title was "traffic manager", which meant that I was responsible for coordinating the contracts and the commercials that went on the air. [Darrell and I were both managers of "traffic". We thought that was sort of neat.]

I had to see that everyone's radio advertisements got on the air at the proper time. As it turned out, I also worked as the receptionist and did just about everything except bookkeeping. After I left they hired several people to do all the work that I had done.

The work was rigorous and tiring and I was not paid what I should have been for the many responsibilities, but I was thankful for the job and I enjoyed the work. It had opened up to me in answer to prayer and it had enabled us to survive. It also spared us from losing our property at Lake of the Pines.

I will never forget how hard I prayed when our taxes were coming due and the only way I knew to look was up. In blind faith I trusted the Lord. I couldn't imagine how He would answer.

At that time my only contact with the radio station was through my radio programs. One September morning I stopped by the radio station to leave off my broadcasts, as I did each week. I had several hours of on-the-air time every Sunday morning and on that particular day the manager seemed to be waiting for me.

"How would you like to go to work for us full-time?" I was asked.

I thought he was kidding me, but he wasn't. He began asking questions about my experience. He knew I had been producing radio programs for many years and that I had been around a lot of radio stations and knew something about the way they operated. He also knew that I was a Christian, and probably reasoned that I would be dependable.

He also asked if I could type, since I would have to type the news and business letters. I could, I told him, but not at a high rate of speed. [I had learned on my own.]

Had I had any journalistic experience? Fortunately, I had worked for the Petaluma Argus Courier for a year before moving out of the area.

The radio station hired me, I'm sure, more for their sake than mine. But God had it all worked out beyond their knowledge, so that my prayers would be answered, and our taxes paid—on time.

The traffic manager I would replace wanted to resign because her husband was ill with cancer. She agreed to give me a few hours of training.

I went to work at the radio station with fear and trembling, not knowing if I was capable of doing such a complicated job, especially with so many responsibilities. It was easy to see that a lot was going to be piled on me. I knew God would have to give me strength, ability, and grace. He would also have to help me deal with the unfairness of some of the work load.

Of course He DID help me, just as He always had in every other situation. With my family obligations, radio broadcasts, Bible study group, the singles's club, our publication and church involvement, and now a full time job, it was a miracle that I was able to keep going. Somehow I managed to juggle everything and keep it all under control. To my surprise I found that being in love gave me surges of super strength.

Two Become One

In spite of our numerous activities, Darrell and I found time to get acquainted with each other's children. The only ones who lived nearby were my two youngest, both still at home. His youngest son, and my other five children all lived in California, within a few hours from us. Only his oldest lived far away, in Virginia. My children all loved Darrell from the outset and I hoped that I would be accepted by his children.

We both found it interesting that Darrell had been born and raised in Walnut Creek, where we had moved from. His elderly mother, his only sister, and a couple brothers still lived there. When we began considering marriage he took me down to meet each of them.

You can be sure we did a lot of praying in those days, because we both wanted to be sure of God's approval of our union. We scheduled several premarital discussion sessions with our pastor.

When we were convinced it was God's will that we spend the rest of our lives together, we set our wedding date for the following June 18th.

A simple ceremony was held in the church where we had met. We invited our family and friends to witness our vows and enjoy the occasion with us. Darrell's youngest son, and my only daughter stood up with us, as our pastor read and we repeated the marriage vows that transformed us into man and wife. It was a memorable day. I awoke early that morning. Actually, I had hardly slept, I was so excited. I was extremely very happy, but I was also secretly a little uneasy that Darrell might be wishing he hadn't gone that far. Then, the phone rang. My heart almost stopped beating. It was Darrell. What if he had decided not to go through with the ceremony?

"Do you still want to get married?"

"Don't you?" I asked, practically holding my breath.

"You bet!" he replied triumphantly. "I'm rarin' to go."

In my heart I silently prayed, "Thank you Lord!" In a matter of hours we were at the church, happily saying "I do" and "I will".

The reception was held in the kitchen of our old church. Our loved ones and friends expressed their best wishes, as we enjoyed cake and punch together. Then we drove to Grass Valley and had dinner at a historic old restaurant. From Grass Valley we went to Donner Lake, where we had made reservations at a hotel.

When we arrived, the proprietors greeted us with special congratulations and offered us a bottle of champagne. We graciously accepted the congratulations but declined the champagne.

It had been quite a day. We were tired but supremely happy. We didn't need champagne to bolster us in any way. It was almost too wonderful to believe it could be true—we were man and wife. Darrell was MY husband. I loved him so much. And I did not doubt that he loved me also.

When we awoke the next morning, which was Sunday, it was daylight and we saw a door in our room which we hadn't noticed the night before. When Darrell opened it, we discovered a small deck right over Donner Lake. It was a gorgeous Lord's day morning, but we knew we wouldn't be attending church that day. We might as well enjoy the lovely lake we decided. Just as we were both wishing we had our fishing poles, the proprietor appeared and asked if he could loan us some fishing gear.

"Fishing is pretty good from this spot," he said with a smile.

[We have pictures of your new grandpa and me fishing in Donner Lake on Sunday morning, the first day of our married life together. And we caught several fish too.]

We both thoroughly enjoyed the quiet beauty and restful atmosphere. Since we both had to be back to work the following day, we tried to take advantage of the opportunity to relax and rest.

When it was time to head for home that afternoon, we decided to take some back roads through the Sierras, so as to extend our little getaway, before returning to our busy schedules.

We saw the back side of the beautiful forested mountain country and felt rewarded that we had discovered an alternate route to the busy interstate highway. We also saw some areas which your grandpa Darrell pointed out to me would be great deer hunting country. We both enjoyed the drive through the woods, as we made our way back to our home and a new life together.

An Unexpected Development

We had planned a honeymoon trip in October or November so we didn't really mind getting back to our busy routine so soon.

Before we were married we had agreed to live in the house I had built in Lake of the Pines, to sell his home in rural Auburn, and to look for property on which to build OUR home.

That summer we were busy with our projects and Darrell's work. I was no longer working at the radio station. We were also looking at property and planning a belated honeymoon. Then an unexpected problem arose. Despite the fact that Darrell was keeping his diabetes under control and experiencing no interference with it on the job, the state of California decided anyone requiring insulin would not be permitted to drive a patrol car.

He was informed very suddenly that his job was in jeopardy. Although he was an outstanding officer and his performance was not at all affected by his being on insulin, the state was firm in their decision.

He was allowed to work at a desk job for one year. After that, he was told that unless he could get completely off insulin he should plan for early retirement.

This all came as a complete shock to us. We had counted on his retirement. The sudden development sent us to our knees in prayer. At one point the state agreed that if he could control his diabetes with one of the new oral medications on the market, they would allow him to remain on the force. His doctor agreed to let him try the alternative medication. For three weeks it seemed to be working well, except that he lost seventeen pounds and strangely resembled a ghost as he drove down the road in a CHP vehicle. Then suddenly the insulin substitute ceased having any effect on his pancreas and he was forced to go back to his regular insulin shots.

It was a crisis time for us. We knew it was unfair for him to have to retire with a limited pension when he had worked so hard and so faithfully for over twenty-six years and wanted to work another two years.

Adopting Our Terry

We decided to proceed with our plans to take a honeymoon trip across the United States. We would go first to the Chicago area where I had lived and where my brother and one of my sisters still lived. Then we would move on to Pennsylvania to see another sister and her family who were home on furlough from missionary service in Bolivia. From there we would go on to the East Coast to see Grandpa Darrell's oldest son, and finally drive through the southland to visit my numerous relatives there. Our last stop would be in Houston, Texas to visit my oldest brother who was suffering from cancer, possibly brought on by exposure to "Agent Orange".

I didn't feel up to, and I wasn't willing to travel by car and stay in a different motel every night for a month, struggling with the inconvenience of dragging suitcases in and out, from car to room and back again. And just thinking about sleeping in a different bed every night, never sure if it was clean, made me very uncomfortable. Besides that, Grandpa Darrell's diet restrictions would have made it difficult to eat all of our meals in restaurants. And there was his blood-sugar testing and insulin shots to deal with twice a day.

I suggested we consider getting a travel trailer. That way we would have our own bed, I could cook most of our meals, and traveling for a month would be a lot cheaper too. At first your grandpa Darrell was not the least bit interested. But after a while, when he realized I was firm in my convictions regarding accommodations, he agreed to at least look at some used travel trailers. He didn't even know what they were like. We went to some local lots, checked out various styles and determined about how much we could expect to pay for one. Then we decided to watch the newspaper ads for a good buy. Since it was the end of a recreation season we hoped to get a good deal. Sure enough, we soon read about one that appeared to suit our needs for a reasonable price. It was an older model, but it hadn't been used very much and seemed to be in good condition. It was a nineteen foot Terry trailer. After looking at several trailers we became more and more excited about having our own bathroom facilities, kitchen, bed and linens, and closets—all trailing behind us as we drove across the country in our '67 Thunderbird.

We bought our little travel "house" a few weeks before the date we had decided to leave and began getting it ready for the trip.

Rancho In The Pines

While we were planning our belated honeymoon, your grandpa's house in Auburn sold. We intensified our search for property to build on. I took a day from my busy trip preparation and had a real estate agent show me around the area we were interested in. We had agreed to try and find some acreage in the Lake of the Pines Ranchos. They were five-plus acreage parcels adjoining the enclosed Lake of the Pines community where we were living. We had both decided we wanted property on a hill with lots of trees. And we wanted a view, not just any view, but a view of a mountain range. I knew what we both wanted, so to save time, I would pick out some parcels for your grandpa Darrell and I to consider together.

At the end of the day, I still hadn't seen anything worth pointing out to your grandpa or taking the time to investigate. Just as we were ready to head home we came to a pretty area, with lots of beautiful pine trees.

"Now, this is what we're looking for," I told the realtor.

Around the corner, we saw a "for sale" sign on the lot I was especially attracted to.

"We'd be interested in looking into this one!" I spoke up, suddenly alive with renewed interest.

The young realtor who had seemed rather bored on our tour replied that he would look into it and get back to us. I thought to myself, "Right now, he's probably getting hungry for his dinner. I don't think he is really anxious to help us find the right property."

I couldn't wait to tell your grandpa Darrell about the spot I had discovered. That evening we drove by so he could see it also. We jotted down the name of the realtor whose sign was posted on the property, just for our own reference. It was a good thing we did, because we never again heard from the young man who had shown me around.

We called the number posted on the property and to our surprise, we discovered the realtor was Mr. Willard Schollerman, the man who had helped the boys and me with our questions and decision to exchange our Lake Wildwood property for a lot in Lake of the Pines. He and his wife Jean had started the Christian school which happened to be near this new property I had found.

Mr. Schollerman took us to see the acreage right away. We loved it. While we were walking it over, we observed another couple who was also there with their realtor.

It was a beautiful piece of property with many wonderful trees and it had a nice northwest view. We were hoping for a view of the Sierra Nevada Mountains in the opposite direction, but we were trusting the Lord for the right place for our retirement home. We knew God was aware of what we needed and desired. He knew what the future held for us.

We liked the property so much we decided to make an offer on it. Later we learned that the other couple liked it also, and had made an almost identical offer, at the same time. We realized there was only a chance we would get it. To our surprise, the owner refused both offers. He may have decided that if it was that much in demand he had better hold on to it.

We were really disappointed. [I actually saw tears in your grandpa Darrell's eyes. I felt the pain too, but I had seen disappointment turn into something better many times, so I had less reason to doubt God's hand in the matter.]

Mr. Schollerman felt bad that he had not been able to help us get the property we liked so much.

"There's another rancho, just up the road, that is for sale, even though there isn't a sign on it," he told us. He intimated that he thought it was as nice, maybe even nicer, than the one we didn't get, and it was on the eastern side of the hill. "It doesn't look that great from the road," he explained, "because it needs to be cleaned up down near the road where you would put your entrance."

"But", he added, "when you walk on it, you will be really surprised."

When we didn't respond, he smiled and suggested, "There are a lot of pine trees on it, and it has a gorgeous view." We told him we'd think about it and get back to him, then we headed home. We were still feeling the effects of disappointment.

A few days later we were ready to take a look at Rancho Number 137.

We walked across the property and up to the top of the hill. Mr. Schollerman stood by patiently, ready to answer any questions.

When we reached a certain point, we turned around to catch the view of the mountain range beyond the imposing pine trees. We caught our breath. The view was overwhelming. The whole property suddenly took on a different appearance to us.

We could picture a nice home where we were standing, with a view from both the living and dining rooms. Maybe even a bedroom. By this time the unattractiveness of the undeveloped frontage area was no problem at all.

It was easy to see, there were more beautiful, healthy pine trees on this exciting lot than the other rancho that we had liked so much, as well as some large oak trees which would mean welcome shade in the summertime.

"Let's make an offer on this one," we both said in unison. And we did.

The following day Mr. Schollerman called to tell us that the owner had accepted our offer. We were ecstatic.

"You'll be surprised to hear that the owner of the first property, that you liked so much, has changed his mind," Mr. Schollerman said with a funny smile, as he started to draw up the papers. "You can have the other one if you prefer."

"There is no way we would choose that one now," we stated firmly. "Let the other man keep his property. He had his chance. Let him be the one disappointed this time."

The more we thought about it, the easier it was to see that God had intervened. He had closed the door on the first possibility because He had something better for us. That's just the way the Lord works. We can be so much happier when we accept that concept and leave the choice to Him.

We're Off, And Away We Go

So much had happened those first few months that wonderful year that we were married. By mid-October we were ready to leave on our belated honeymoon.

Our newly acquired, miniature "house", that was going to be our home away from home for the next month was ready for the little kitchen to be stocked with our choice of groceries. The closet and storage drawers were clean and awaiting our clothing and linens in preparation for our long journey across and around the United States. The new way of traveling was going to be an adventure for us and we looked forward to the prospect of an exciting trip.

On one crisp October morning, your new grandpa and I, a little anxiously I'm afraid, settled into our old 1967 Thunderbird and drove off. We looked back to see if the trailer was actually coming along too, then we braced ourselves for the stop sign at the end of Singing Hills Court. I think we felt unsure that our funny little house and our car would stop at the same time. By the time we got out onto the main highway we were more comfortable, and a little more brave.

We left on a Sunday, in time to stop and attend the morning worship service at our church, and then to head out onto the interstate. It seemed to us that attending church was a good send-off, especially since we were going to be gone for a whole month. Our church family waved us off and wished us well.

Soon after we left church we pulled into a fast-food restaurant for a quick, hot sandwich. [I will never forget the funny expression on Grandpa Darrell's face as we sat down to eat our first meal at the table in our new little home. It reminded me of when my brothers and I used to play house when we were kids. Your grandpa had that same I'm-not-so-sure-I-want-to- play look that my brothers had way back then.]

In a very short time we were on our way, highly anticipating a great vacation.

Chicago Bound

We planned to first visit my brother, and my sister and their families in the Chicago area and to attend services at my "home church" in Illinois the following Sunday if we were there at the right time. I was anxious to see what the Barrington area was like after thirty years. I had lived there before moving to Hawaii. I even wondered if I would recognize people or places. I knew it would be different after so many years, but I was not prepared for the shock that awaited me. Nothing looked the same as I had remembered it.

I wanted to see the dairy farm were we had lived. When we finally got there, we found a gate across the road leading to the place and a sign that read KEEP OUT—GAME RESERVE.

I had really wanted to see the farm again after so long and I wanted to show your grandpa Darrell the place I had told him so much about.

There were two lakes on the farm and the areas around them were bird sanctuaries, even when I lived there.

The farm had been a natural habitat for wildlife such as quail and pheasant. I remembered how much our family had enjoyed the various small animals that frequented the farm, most of them native to the area.

I went away from that spot which had carved such deep memories with a sense of gratitude that a monument and barrier had been set up to preserve the place. My disappointment was balanced with appreciation.

[We drove out to the church that had meant so much to me. The old structure, which had been a recruiting station during the civil war, was still holding up quite well. I remembered how hard we had all worked to preserve the building when your grandpa Brown and I had been a part of the church.] As we drove up, I saw that the building had been remodeled so that it hardly resembled its former design. I was saddened to see it so different, but happy to know it was still being used for worship.

Since we could see we were not going to be in the area at the right time for Sunday services, we were glad to find the caretaker there when we dropped by. He invited us to come inside and was happy to show us around.

We explored the old cemetery in back of the church where my little daughter who died so long ago was buried. My brother's twin babies were also buried there.

While in Illinois, we parked at my brother's home north of Chicago. He and his family were the first of my family to meet my new husband.

I had not seen my youngest brother for over twenty years, the last time being at my mother's funeral in another state. He had changed so much that I was rather shocked. I guess I had expected him to still look the same even though none of us escape the process of change that comes with aging.

My brother's hair was white. I learned that he had grayed abnormally fast after he had been severely injured in an automobile accident.

My sister Sue and her husband, lived in a Chicago suburb. They both worked, so the only time we could visit them was on Sunday. We went to church with them, and after sharing the noon meal at their home, they gave us a grand tour of Chicago and the Lake Michigan waterfront.

Since it was Sunday there was less traffic downtown than I had ever seen there. Your grandpa Darrell had never been to Chicago and it had been many years since I had been there, so we both enjoyed the tour tremendously. They even took us to the top of the Sears building, which at that time was the tallest building in the world. That was quite an experience. What a view of the great city of Chicago, and the Lake! We also enjoyed visiting their church that day. We were surprised to learn that they also attended a church of the same denomination that we belonged to.

The next morning when we left my brother Ken's place for the next stretch of our journey east, a cold fog hugged the ground in the late autumn atmosphere. [I don't know if we were brave or stupid to be there at that time of year with a travel trailer.]

Missionary Reunion

From Illinois we headed for Pennsylvania, where my youngest sister Dorothy lived. A chilly light rain, the first we had encountered on our trip, began to fall that afternoon. We started looking for a place to park our trailer for the night. We soon discovered, as we had in Illinois, that campgrounds for the convenience of travelers were not nearly as plentiful as they are in the western part of the United States.

To our dismay, darkness began to descend quickly. We began to pray for a place to stay. Then almost as if miraculously, we discovered a sign indicating a campground on a lake. We spent the night there.

Travel conditions were improved the following morning, for which we thanked the Lord, as we made our way to my sister's place in Lancaster, Pennsylvania.

Dorothy and her family were home on furlough, having spent several terms as missionaries in the South American country of Bolivia. I had not seen her for quite a few years. I was looking forward to our visit and to introducing them to my new husband.

We enjoyed remembering old times and talking about the Lord and how He had blessed us. We had a lot of missionary experiences to share. I particularly enjoyed getting acquainted with her two sons and their little Bolivian girl they had adopted while on the mission field.

While in the Lancaster area we observed the unusual lifestyle of some of the Amish people who lived in that part of the country. I had learned about them in school and found their way of life quite interesting. Their old fashion dress, lifestyle, and mode of travel gave us the feeling of being transported backwards in time, perhaps a hundred years. It was like living in history.

After leaving my youngest sister's home, our next stopover was in Wheeling, West Virginia, where we spent the night with my beloved cousin, Moleva, whom I had not seen for many years. It was a precious time for both of us. We never dreamed that it was the last time we would see each other in this world. Less than five years later, the Lord, whom she loved so dearly, took her home to be with Himself.

[Up to that point, your grandpa Darrell was being initiated into my family; now it was my time to visit some of his family. The next stop was Alexandria, Virginia, to visit his oldest son Bob and his family. They had a brand new baby, Darrell's second grandchild.]

I had met both of his children when they were in Auburn for their mother's funeral. Our brief visit there gave me an opportunity to get to know my stepson and his family better, and we enjoyed the new baby.

While in Alexandria, we drove across the Potomac River and got our first glimpse of the White House and Washington, D.C. We would have liked to have seen so much more but had to settle for a view of Washington's Monument and a quick tour of the Smithsonian Museum. Ever since I was a child I had dreamed of someday going to the nation's capitol. I finally got to, even though the tour was terribly short.

We were thrilled to have the opportunity to drive into Maryland to witness the autumn colors that we had heard so much about. Unfortunately, we were a week too late for the best variety of colors, but it was still breathtakingly beautiful.

On The Road Again

We were glad to get on the road again toward the beautiful Blue Ridge Mountains and hopefully some relief from the miserable humidity. It was now early November. We were fortunate to get by with some morning fog and at times light rain. We prayed that it wouldn't get cold enough to freeze the water pipes in our trailer. Our prayers were honored; God was merciful to us. The biggest problem we encountered was finding a place to park for the night. As in the other states we went through in that part of the country, trailer parks as we know them in California, were few and far between.

One evening after finally finding a large travel park described in our travel guide, we discovered it was closed. We were terribly disappointed, until we spotted a sign that read: SORRY, WE ARE CLOSED FOR THE SEASON. JUST MAKE YOURSELF AT HOME. With a sigh of relief, we parked for the night and rested in a park that showed evidence of plenty of activity during the summer months. We realized that in season, and busier times, we might have encountered a NO VACANCY sign.

We were excited about visiting our friends Jim and Emy Howell in Memphis, Tennessee. They had visited us earlier that year when they had vacationed on the West Coast. [Mr. Howell was your grandpa Darrell's navigator when he piloted a B-17, while on duty in Europe during World War II.] The Howell's were a wonderful Southern couple. We had a great time together when they came to California. After having toured San Francisco, they had traveled by bus to Auburn. When we picked them up at the bus station, they had a ready question.

"Where are the beautiful mountains everyone told us about?" they wanted to know.

"Oh, we'll show you," we promised. And we did. After a one day grand tour of the Sierra Nevada range they agreed that the description they had heard about the magnificent mountains in Northern California was not exaggerated.

Now, we were visiting them in Memphis and they were determined to make our visit as memorable as we had made theirs.

Just visiting in their home was a delightful experience. Jim is an exceptionally skilled craftsman. He has made almost all of their furniture, including the dining room pieces, and their beds.

When we were ushered into the guest bedroom for the night, we were in for a real experience, especially your grandpa Darrell. The lovely bed we were to sleep in was so high your grandpa suggested to me in a subdued whisper, "We'll need a ladder to get up onto it." Neither of us had ever seen a bed that high. However, being from the South myself, I was familiar with beds that were higher than those he was used to.

When I moved to California I was surprised at how close to the floor many beds were. It was almost like sleeping on a pallet, as we had sometimes done when I was a child. Wherever we had lived after I moved out of the South, we had somehow managed to always have a bed that was higher than most so that I could feel comfortable sleeping on it.

Once in bed that night, I was afraid to go to sleep for fear I would fall off the side. You can be sure we slept close together in the middle of that bed. In the morning, Grandpa jumped down, then lifted me down. We were happy to be safe at floor level again.

We were soon intrigued with other equally exciting revelations around their house. For instance, exploring the living room furnishings. One unusual couch reminded me of pictures I had seen of those thought to be the type Jesus and His disciples reclined on in New Testament days. It was a true antique; beautifully preserved and restored. Their home was filled with fascinating pieces of furniture, but none more interesting than that unusual couch.

The Howell's enjoyed sharing their true "southern hospitality". And they insisted on showing us some of the attractions in their beloved state of Tennessee.

First, they took us to see the home of Elvis Presley, which is what most people visiting Memphis want to see. While we were not among his fans, it was interesting to see what so many people are so fascinated with. They also took us up to Pickwick Lake and Shiloah Park, a one day tour. Loving history as I do, I found the relics and mementos of earlier days in Tennessee most interesting. More than all the attractions, we enjoyed just being with this lovely couple. [Your grandpa Darrell was able to renew a friendship of many years and I became better acquainted with new friends.]

I don't know how we were able to get so much in such a short visit. All too soon, it was time for us to move on to our next scheduled stop.

Going Home Again

When we left the state of Tennessee, we were only a matter of hours from the beautiful Crowley's Ridge area in northeast Arkansas, where I was born and raised. My sister Louise, who had moved to Illinois with us but now lived in Arkansas, and I had aunts and uncles and many cousins still living there. It would be quite a reunion.

It had been more than twenty years since I had been there, and then only briefly to attend my mother's funeral. She had not been living there when she died, but had been visiting while on vacation from her home in Northern Illinois. She had become suddenly ill, and died while hospitalized. I flew back for the funeral, and only got to see relatives and friends who attended the service. I left immediately and went with my brother Ken and my sister Sue back to their home in Northern Illinois. I was now anxiously looking forward to seeing everyone, including some former schoolmates with whom I still corresponded. Some of them I had not seen for over thirty five years.

The first person we saw when we arrived was my sister Louise. I was so happy to introduce her to my new husband.

I hardly knew my way around after all those years. Even the places that probably hadn't changed that much were strange to me because I had forgotten what they were actually like. Memory has a way of altering things but I was not disappointed. What a blessing to have my precious sister take us around in her car to all the places I wanted to see and to be able to show them to your grandpa. She knew just where to go, and at the same time we enjoyed the pure pleasure of being with her.

One day we went out to the town of Bono to see my dear Aunt Lola, the aunt that I had been so close to when I was growing up and the only one of my dad's sisters and brothers still living. I was saddened to see how feeble she was, but her sweet face was still beautiful to me. Her husband, my beloved Uncle Beecher, was not very well and only lived a few years after we saw them that day.

I was so happy to find that this aunt was now a Christian. Oh, how she enjoyed talking to me about the Lord. She wanted us to spend more time with her but we were far from home and had so many people we wanted to see. We had to visit quickly and do a lot of remembering in a short time. My precious auntie was impressed with my new husband and so happy that God had given me someone so kind and loving.

While we were at Aunt Lola's home, two of my girl friends that I had been close to when we were young came to see me. Aunt Lola had called them and invited them. What a lovely surprise to see Helen and Pearlie. I also had the pleasure of introducing them to the one I was so much in love with.

I was glad he could meet my friends of yesteryears.

More Memories

Our next reunion was at the home of my mother's two sisters who had never married; Aunt Leton and Aunt Vauntee, the two who went to Hawaii with me. They, like Aunt Lola, were much older and showing it. Strangely, I did not feel that much older myself. However I knew I too was coming along, not far behind them.

With their typical thoughtfulness, they had invited relatives from far and near to come to see us. They knew our time was too limited for us to get around and see everyone. Many of those who came I had not seen for over forty years. It was a strange feeling; a mixture of unspeakable thrill along with a tinge of indescribable pain, realizing how time was passing away, and how we had all changed. We all did a lot of remembering, sometimes through laughter and sometimes with tears.

The following day we went out into the country again, this time to see my Aunt Leton's twin sister, and her family. Aunt Letha had married many years before and was living in a nearby rural community with her husband, Uncle Alva. Their children lived nearby.

Uncle Alva had graduated from college as an agricultural engineer and rather enjoyed being called by that prestigious title, rather than simply a farmer. He was well respected in the community where he served as

County Farm Agent.

I drank in all the pleasure of looking at old photos and recalling many delightful memories, and wept tears of gratitude as I thanked the Lord for allowing me the privilege and blessing of going back at least one more time to see those I love so dearly, most of whom I would probably never see again. Parting with each one was painful.

My sister Louise took us still another direction another day to see my children's step-grandmother, Mrs. Ethel Brown. [Your great grandpa had been dead for many years.] Grandma Brown was touched that we would come to see her. She enjoyed hearing about all the grandchildren back in California.

I had remembered to take an album of recent pictures for all of our families to see. It proved to be the next best thing to seeing them in person. Before we left she took me aside and whispered, "Ardelle, how did you manage to find someone so much like your children's father?"

A Strange Lapse In Time

While in the vicinity we also visited Virginia. [She was one of my closest girl friends when I was growing up and now lived near your great-grandma Brown.] We had kept in contact over the years, but I hadn't even seen a picture of her since our early days together. Now, when I saw her after such a long time, she looked exactly like her dear mother did back when Virginia and I were in school together. It was like seeing Mrs. Tyner alive again; like a strange lapse in time.

How precious the experience of being reunited with a friend of my younger days again. Memories of happy times and sad ones flooded around us. I shall always treasure the short time we got to visit together that day.

We finally had to say goodbye, but while in the area Louise drove us by Walcott High School, where Virginia and I had spent so many happy times together. Sad memories, as well as happy ones, were revived there. Virginia and my other close girlfriends had graduated there. [Due to health problems, I did not get to finish even the tenth grade. I relived that great regret again that day.]

What a nostalgic feeling, standing in front of the old high school building, remembering back over the years. So much had happened in my own life. I wondered about each fellow student who marched by in my thoughts. Tears stung my eyes as I remembered those I knew who had died in the war, those who had died in accidents, and others who had succumbed to illnesses.

My sister Louise gently brought me back to reality as she hurried us along. She wanted me to have time to recall some of the wonderful times we had all enjoyed in the magnificent state park near the school. My heart swelled with rapid recollections as she slowly drove through the once so familiar park roads.

I had forgotten how really spectacular the stately trees were.

"Thank you, Lord for preserving them," I silently prayed.

Because the day was getting away from us and there were still so many things we wanted to see and do, we had to hurry on.

Several miles down the road we approached the area where Louise and I had been raised.

"There's our forest, remember? Sure looks different, doesn't it?" Louise commented, watching my reaction.

To my dismay, our wonderful forest had almost dwindled away. Seeing the sparsely growing trees brought a touch of pain to my heart.

As we turned onto our old familiar road, I could see that beloved spot where we had lived. The house that had been our home for so many years had burned down after our parents had leased it out and moved to Illinois. The spot was still just as beautiful as I had remembered it. [Now I was seeing it through your grandpa Darrell's eyes and I realized I had not been exaggerating when I tried to describe it to him.]

When we arrived at the cemetery just a half mile or so up the road, I was pleased to see how well it had been kept up. Many who were buried in that old hillside cemetery had been very dear to me. Both my parents, my brother who had drowned at age fifteen, my maternal grandparents, and numerous aunts, uncles and cousins were buried there.

Grandpa tenderly held my hand as we went from headstone to headstone and I described departed loved ones who had been so precious to me. He was kind and sympathetic, even though he had not known any of them. [I have often wished my parents and your grandpa Darrell could have known each other, as I've also wished I could have known his father.]

It was comforting to me and it seemed appropriate to spend that time in the old Pleasant Hill Cemetery, flanked by two people I loved so dearly, my sister Louise and my loving husband. Those few minutes, I knew, would probably have to suffice—until the resurrection day.

Back To Where It All Began

Before leaving to go back to my sister's home in Jonesboro, she suggested we drive by the old Baptist church, and the neighborhood where I had been born. We had moved away when I was seven years old, but I could still see it all clearly in my mind.

The old house was gone, as would be expected. It was old even when we had lived there. I was surprised to find that one of my aunts lived in a fairly new house nearby. The beautiful hillside was every bit as lush and vibrant as it had been that memorable day when I fell into the bubbling little stream and was duly punished.

By that time it was getting late and time for us to get back to my sister's home. As we drove through familiar areas, I was pleased that many were even nicer than I had remembered.

Many times as a child I had traveled that road from Loredo to Jonesboro in a wagon, long before anyone had heard of automobiles. In those days, houses were very few and far between. Considerable development had occurred during the intervening years.

Louise stopped once more briefly to show us a beautiful manmade lake, which had been built on property that had belonged to one of my aunts, land that we had farmed when I was growing up.

"I wish we could go fishing together while you're here," Louise said. We agreed, especially Grandpa Darrell, but it was getting late so we had to move along.

Heading For Houston

Early the following morning, we said goodbye to Louise and set out on the next leg of our journey. We were headed for Houston to visit my brother C.N. whom I had not seen for twenty-one years. A few years earlier he had been diagnosed with cancer and I desperately wanted to see him again.

It was a long way from where we were to Houston, and it seemed even further pulling our miniature home every mile of the way. But we did enjoy seeing a lot of new country every day and watching God answer our prayers for a place to stay each night.

It was now Sunday morning and as we drove along, our minds were on which church we might find to stop at for the morning service. We certainly didn't anticipate the next development that was in store for us.

Our thoughts were suddenly interrupted by a strange noise coming from underneath the Thunderbird. Something was definitely wrong. Your grandpa pulled the car and trailer off the narrow road. We had broken down.

At that point it would have been easy to panic. We had no idea what was wrong or how far we were from possible help. The fact that it was Sunday morning and probably nothing would be open scared us. We were already in tune with the Lord, praying and watching for a place to worship with other Christians. Why, we wondered, should this happen to us on a Sunday morning?

A verse that had meant a lot to me many times in the past came to mind. *"And we know that all things work together for good to those who love God, to those who are the called according to His purpose.* Romans 8:28

It was hard to understand why, but we knew it wasn't necessary for us to know why. It was our duty, as God's children, to trust Him, no matter what happened.

Your grandpa Darrell got out of the car to investigate. He knew I would continue to pray as he looked for the trouble spot. After a while he reported back to me.

"It looks like the universal joint has gone out," he said.

I didn't know what that meant, but God did.

"What do we do next, Lord?" we prayed.

We were parked a short distance from an old farm house. Your grandpa Darrell decided to go inquire how far we were from a town or service station.

A pleasant black lady answered the door. She told him her husband was very old and unable to communicate, but that she would do anything she could to help us. The poor woman appeared to be starved for someone to talk to and after a stream of conversation, she finally told your grandpa the junk yard was just over the hill. She offered him her car. He thanked her, but said that since it was so close, he would walk. When he came back to the car to tell me what he had found out, he suggested I go talk to the nice lady who had volunteered her help, while he was gone.

It took only a few minutes for me to learn that the woman's name was Lucinda, that she was a Christian and desperately needed to be refreshed and encouraged. I talked to Lucinda for quite a while and learned that one of her sons was in Bible school, preparing for the ministry. She almost burst with pride as she told me about him and the rest of her family. She was radiating with praise to the Lord for her blessings.

We didn't get to attend a regular church service that Sunday morning, but the Bible says that where two or three are gathered together in His name, He is there in their midst.

With great difficulty, I was finally able to pull away from my new friend, explaining that I had to get back to the car by the time my husband did, and try to help him.

Your grandpa Darrell finally returned—with visible evidence of answer to prayer. He had found a used universal joint for the Thunderbird and for a very low price. The next step was to get it installed. He went to work under the car while I prayed.

A passing motorist stopped to see if we needed help. When he learned the nature of our problem, he just smiled.

"I'm a mechanic," he announced. "Let me help you."

[Now, I ask you, do you believe God answers prayer?]

After about six hours of work, including the help of the kind mechanic, and nine dollars for the used part, we were on our way again, wondering if it was possible for us to make it to Houston that day, where my brother's family was expecting us.

A Timely Reunion

After many hours of driving and considerable confusion after getting lost in Houston, (what a city!) we finally drove up to their place that evening about 8:30.

It was so wonderful to be able to see my brother and his family again. Twenty-one years had changed us all. I honestly wondered secretly if I would have recognized my brother if I had met him unexpectedly on the street.

C.N. did not look as much older as I had expected him to, and to my surprise, he really looked quite healthy. Since he had been battling cancer for several years, I thought he would be thin and emaciated. Instead, he looked like a typical, healthy Texan. I was so thankful to see him that way.

My brother seemed so happy, enjoying his wife and children and his little granddaughter. His daughter Debbie was a beautiful blonde, as pretty as any we had seen in the state known for its pretty girls.

Our reunion in Houston was almost like a dream, tying the past and present together, in one grand stage production. The Lord is so good to give us such meaningful moments at times during our fleeting life upon this earth.

After our brief but blessed visit, we bade my brother's family goodbye. It was to be our final farewell. C.N.'s health began to deteriorate rapidly, and he died the following year.

After we left their place I felt a tremendous burden to pray for my brother and his family, for his physical needs, and for the entire family's spiritual welfare.

Not long after we were there, Debbie wrote that she had become a Christian. In the following months she wrote us many letters, sharing her insight into God's Word. And she kept us abreast of her dad's constant downward progress. We all prayed that C.N. would accept Christ as his personal Savior before he died. I rejoiced with Debbie when she called to tell me she was convinced that her pastor had been able to lead him into that relationship. Knowing she had the assurance that her dad had indeed made the most important decision in his life was very comforting to me.

I shall always be grateful for the opportunity of seeing him once more in this life, before his time was up. I look forward to being with him in heaven.

* * *   * * *   * * *

"I don't know about you Joanna, but I'm getting a little tired. Just remembering that really long trip makes me feel weary. Let's go to bed."

CHAPTER 22

Life Goes On - In California

"Grandma, when did you move to this nice place in the country?" Kathye questioned, as we finished clearing the kitchen after dinner.

"Oh Kathye," Karl broke in, "Grandpa and Grandma moved in when they got their house finished. They built it themselves, you know. Didn't you, Grandma?"

"Yes, we did!" I answered with pride. "Would you like to hear about that?"

"Oh yes!" they both responded.

"And Grandma, could you also tell us about when you were a pink lady?" Kathye suggested.

"Very well," I agreed. "Find yourself a comfortable seat in the living room. I'll be right there."

* * *   * * *   * * *

We Build Our New House

We finally returned home from our long trip, after encircling almost the entire United States, including four days just getting across Texas alone. Thanksgiving Day was coming soon and we had a lot to be thankful for. God had been merciful to us.

We had traveled thousands of miles, very late in the season, through parts of the country where winter and sometimes heavy snow have been known to arrive much earlier. Fortunately, we had not encountered weather cold enough to freeze the water pipes in our little home on wheels.

Ironically, the night we arrived home the temperature dropped into the teens at our home in Lake of the Pines. It was a good thing we had drained the water system in the trailer before we went to bed.

The past year had been a critical one. We had gotten married in June, Grandpa Darrell was forced to retire due to his diabetes, we had bought property on which to build our new house, and we had taken a month-long belated honeymoon. Now our thoughts turned to building our retirement home on our "hill with a view."

We made arrangements to have a well dug to make sure we had

water before starting to build. If none turned up, we had the option of getting our money back from the property.

When the drilling rig arrived, your grandpa was working, so I stood by praying while the men worked at getting a well that would deliver our water supply. I asked the Lord for as much water as we would need. I didn't know how much that should be—but God did and I was right there on the spot, reminding Him that I was trusting Him for a good well. When the well drillers had to go deeper and deeper, I prayed harder and harder. When at last they hit water, I began to cry, thankfully at first. But when I realized the amount was less than we were hoping for, I began to cry and pray some more.

We were disappointed but we realized we should trust the Lord as we always had. He certainly was in control of our water supply.

Before your Grandpa Darrell installed our new pump, we hired a reputable pump dealer to double check and determine for sure how much water we really did have. To our surprise and delight, they reported that our new well could be depended upon to produce twice as much water as the well drillers had estimated.

We thanked the Lord for answer to prayer. [Do you know that we have never needed more water than our well provided? I will always remember how I labored in prayer for that well.] When the water system was established, we began to work excitedly on house plans. Then it was time to get our long driveway cut in. Choosing a path and watching it turn into a road that would lead to our new home was a thrilling experience. We tried to choose a route that would spare as many trees as possible, but unfortunately some had to be removed. As soon as the road was blazed in and was dry enough, we moved our travel trailer from the Lake of the Pines campground to our new home site. It provided a place to eat our noon meals and take rest breaks while building our new house.

Grandpa Darrell had built several houses so he knew what he was doing. And I was by his side for every step. We were so industrious we even decided to dig our own footings. [We would never do that again, I assure you.] We quickly discovered the numerous poison oak plants that were growing everywhere. It seemed like every foot was plagued with the stubborn plant. The whole Lake of the Pines area seemed to be overrun with it.

Our problem was not unique but I seemed to be more susceptible to the pesky nuisance plant than most. Your grandpa also fought the problem. When we tried to eradicate the poison oak plants and roots, we discovered it was easier desired than carried out. When we tried to cut the plant out by the roots, it only reacted by growing more profusely. The soil was full of the stubborn roots. We were subjected to "cut roots" constantly during the early stages of building our house, and we both suffered almost constant rash. What a relief, to finally get the footings in and the foundation poured, so that we could work on wood above the soil.

Our good neighbor agreed to allow the power company to put an above-the-ground pole, right in the middle of his superb view of the Sierra Mountain range, so that we could avoid taking out a number of large trees. Few people I know would have been so congenial. We were fortunate.

We both worked patiently and tirelessly on our personal project, which took almost a year for us to complete.

As much as we wanted to say we built it all with our four hands, we finally gave in and got some subcontractors to do the plumbing, electrical, cabinets, and roof. Grandpa Darrell could have done any or all of them, but for the sake of time, we were willing to hire others. What an exciting experience to finally be able to move into our brand new home on the spot that God had so definitely led us to.

My Personal Postman

During the year when we were building our house, your grandpa had not retired officially. He had accumulated about a year of sick leave after more than twenty-six years as a highway patrolman, so continued to receive his regular pay check for more than a year. This helped us tremendously.

The time came when he was forced to retire. It seemed unfair but we tried to accept it gracefully. His fellow workers honored him with a retirement dinner along with a program highlighting his faithful, competent service in law enforcement.

Our income was reduced considerably, so the following year your Grandpa Darrell decided to apply for an opening to deliver mail on a rural route as a substitute carrier. He took a civil service exam, along with twenty-four other applicants and finished with the highest score. He and one of the women applicants were hired.

Most often he got to work the route that included our house. It was neat to have my own personal postman—someone to deliver the mail straight from the post office.

We both learned a lot about the U.S. mail system during those years. It was not as romantic as I had always imagined, delivering mail from a faraway place to people anxiously awaiting it.

[After working in the structured discipline of the Highway Patrol, your Grandpa Darrell found his job as a mail carrier very stressful. The pay was good, but lax methods and management finally became too much for him. He stayed with it for six years, until we were eligible to begin receiving a small Social Security check to supplement our income.]

Sharing God's Word

During the busy days when my personal postman was working, I was busily involved with a number of projects.

Living in the quiet woods was conducive to praying and reading, especially the Scriptures. The first year we were in our new home, your grandpa read the entire New Testament aloud to me. And every night, just before we went to sleep, he read from our devotional booklet, *"Our Daily Bread"*, a Radio Bible Class publication. He still does. In fact, we have missed very few days reading that little sermon all the years since we've been married.

Every place I've ever lived, I have endeavored to host an ongoing Bible study in my home, either taught by me or someone else. Our new home in the woods fairly begged for that same privilege, so I began to pray about it. One night I approached a couple we had gotten to know at church, who lived near us.

"Would you like to study the Bible with us?" I asked them.

To my surprise, the husband quickly responded, "Yes, I think we would."

[Your grandpa Darrell had expressed a desire to know the Bible better too. Together, the four of us, and sometimes our friend's granddaughter, began a concentrated study of the Scriptures that eventually would take us through the entire Bible, book by book. Martin, Marcella, Jennifer, and your grandpa Darrell and I became so involved in these enriching sessions, no one wanted to even take time out for refreshments.]

We continued that fulfilling Bible study for over five years. We were on our way through the Bible the second time, when our precious friends decided to move out of the area.

On Becoming A Pink Lady

We had only been studying the Bible with our friends a short time when I also undertook another interesting project.

A friend of mine who had worked as a volunteer at Auburn Faith Hospital for several years, invited our new pastor's wife and me to a salad luncheon and fashion show benefiting the hospital.

While we were enjoying our lunch together, my friend abruptly questioned, "Ardelle, wouldn't you like to become a Pink Lady at Auburn Faith? You would be good at it and besides, we need you." (Pink Ladies were volunteers, who wore pink uniform tops to distinguish them from the regular nurses.)

She explained what would be involved and I liked the idea. I admired the ladies for their noble efforts, and you know how I love working with people. I told her I would talk to your grandpa about it and get back to her. It was not that I needed something more to do to help me pass the time away, or keep me from becoming bored. I was simply challenged by the opportunity to serve people. I hoped to be able to help patients and their families with their spiritual needs.

The more I thought about working as a volunteer at the hospital, the more it seemed like something I should do. When I asked your grandpa's opinion and advice, he agreed. It was my choice, he said. I had to drive to Auburn once a week anyway to deliver my taped radio broadcasts, why not do a shift at the hospital while I was there, I reasoned.

My friend Floread was thrilled when I volunteered to be trained for different services at the hospital, so that I could help out where I was needed most, at any given time.

For a long time I worked at the information desk, directing visitors, assisting staff, selling meal tickets and flowers, and handling patient mail. [We thought it was neat that your grandpa and I were now both handling mail.]

I especially enjoyed taking a break to deliver the mail to patients. I always took with me some lovely little booklets and tracts. I would especially greet those who had not received mail, saying, "I'm sorry, I don't have mail for you today, but here is something you might enjoy reading."

Sometimes those who did get mail would ask if they could have a booklet also. Patients always received the literature gladly. These little booklets which I had purchased from the Christian Women's Club were so beautiful, so well written, and so true to the Bible, I never needed to apologize to anyone for them. My biggest problem was keeping enough of them on hand so as not to disappoint anyone.

I thoroughly enjoyed patient contact, and I felt I was a blessing to those whose lives I was permitted to touch, even in this small way.

One day I mentioned to a social worker who stopped by the information desk, that I wished there could be a service that would allow me to spend my entire shift going from patient to patient.

"We're working on that right now," she said, surprised that I would mention it at that particular time. "When the program is approved, I'll let you know."

Eventually the Patient's Representative Service was organized. I was among the first group to be trained for the work. You can imagine how much I enjoyed working with individual patients. During our entire four hour shift, we talked with patients, listening to their questions and concerns. Patients of all ages, male or female, would feel free to open up and discuss their feelings with us. I worked in that capacity until a sudden turn of events ended my career of almost four years as a Pink Lady.

I Experienced A Miracle

It was an ordinary day, with no hint of what the next few hours would bring. I was on my way home from Auburn Faith Hospital where I had worked my usual Tuesday morning shift. As I made my way home through the busy highway traffic, I meditated and prayed as I always do when I am traveling alone. In my thoughts I reviewed the contacts I had made that day with patients. I had soothed the anxiety a newly admitted patient was experiencing, listening closely for the real source of her fears. I was able to alleviate a great deal of her unnecessary worry. All she needed was the reassurance that her needs would be met and that her concerns would be addressed. As I left her she said, ever so sincerely, "You'll never know how much you have helped me."

As I drove home, I breathed a prayer for this lady as I had promised.

I also prayed for the man who told me it was his twenty-first day in the hospital. He was thinking of his wife at home alone. He was remembering the snow that had left his wife marooned in their mountain location the previous weekend. Just to have someone willing to listen attentively as he verbally expressed his concerns, meant a lot to him. He could tell that I really cared. More importantly, I assured him that God cared. When I promised to pray for him and his wife, he showed genuine relief. There was the anxious family in the surgery waiting room who had been there for hours, waiting to hear how their loved one had come through a long operation. As often as possible, between visits with patients, I stopped to comfort them. When I completed my shift, they still had not heard. I couldn't help being uneasy about the situation. I continued to ask the Lord to be with that family in a special way.

"Dear Lord," I interceded audibly, while driving home, "I know you can help all these dear people who need you so much. Please do." As I turned onto the road leading to our home, I glanced at my watch. It was getting late, and I knew your grandpa Darrell with his diabetes would need his lunch soon. I always hurried straight home from the hospital so that I could prepare his meal.

Before turning up our long driveway, I stopped to pick up our mail. Seeing it was too far back in the box for me to reach, I pulled the car up, set the brake, and leaving the engine running and the door open, I got out to retrieve that day's mail.

As I turned back toward the car, I heard a strange noise which I soon realized was the brake being released. The transmission had vibrated enough to release the automatic emergency brake.

I saw the car start to move, coming towards me. Since it was on a slope, I thought the door might slam shut and miss me; instead, it caught me and threw me onto the road surface. When I saw the car was going to hit me, I thought, "This is it!" I watched helplessly, fully aware of all that was happening. The car started to turn so that the back wheel missed me, but the left front wheel and the weight of that heavy Thunderbird rolled over my body diagonally. It made its first contact on my left thigh, as I lay there on my right side where I had been thrown, then it rolled right over me.

I noticed that my uniform was soiled with road grime mixed with blood, which was oozing from my arm.

I started to pray. God was not far away. I had just been talking to Him.

"Oh, Lord," I cried in desperation. "Let Darrell hear me call."

Then I yelled for help with all the volume I could muster, "DARRELL, PLEASE COME HELP ME!"

Normally, you would not be able to hear a person calling from that distance, unless you were outside, but Grandpa Darrell had seen me and thought it was strange that I had not come up the driveway yet. He came outside to see what had happened at just the right moment to hear me call. I believe it was the Lord looking after me.

When he saw the car, backed into a dirt bank across from the mailbox, he jumped into our truck and was by my side in minutes. God had heard my prayer! I shall always thank Him for that.

Your grandpa could not leave me to go for help because I was lying on the roadway, in great danger of being run over if a car should come over the hill from the opposite direction. The driver would not have been able to see me in time to stop. Very shortly, a neighbor we had never met came along and offered to help. Your grandpa asked her to call the Highway Patrol office, explaining that they would dispatch an ambulance.

A traffic officer, rescue vehicles, a fire truck, and an ambulance were all on the scene within minutes. Paramedics carefully lifted me into the ambulance and tried to make me comfortable for the sixteen mile trip to Sierra Nevada Memorial Hospital in Grass Valley. Enroute, one of them asked me, "What day is today?"

"It's February second," I replied, managing a smile. "It's Groundhog Day."

Their eyes met knowingly, but I was unable to interpret their silent communication.

I had no idea what the extent of my injuries were. As the ambulance raced toward the hospital, I kept telling myself, "At least I'm alive!" My greatest fear was that I might become an invalid, totally dependent on your grandpa. That really troubled me, but I had the feeling that somehow God was in complete control. That was comforting.

In the emergency room, my doctor checked me over and over again and looked at the x-rays several times. Shaking his head he said, "It's a miracle! You have no broken bones. That sometimes happens when children are run over by a car, but rarely with older people."

As much as I hated to admit my age (I was almost 62), I soon realized the newspaper report would spill it anyway.

I was fortunate that my bones were still intact, but I was severely bruised around the hips. And I suffered a huge hematoma, about six inches in diameter, from the leakage of blood into the tissue.

The huge blood clot and the terrible pain really concerned me, especially when I found that I was unable to stand up. At first the doctor thought I might be able to go home without being hospitalized. Then it became evident that I was more seriously injured than they realized. Loved ones and friends shared my anxiety and many rallied in prayer. As much as I wanted to go home, there was no way I could. I finally conceded, there must be a reason why I must stay.

During those long days and nights, I received the best of care. Doctors and nurses were all receptive to my insistence that God had spared my life. They all agreed that I had indeed experienced a miracle. Your grandpa Darrell spent hours at my bedside and kept things under control at home. My children, though busy with their work and families, gave me a lot of attention in my crisis hour.

Lovely flower arrangements brightened my room. I had numerous visitors, many phone calls, and lots of mail. My pastor and his wife drove the thirty miles from Auburn to Grass Valley several times to see me. Physical therapists worked with me until I could finally stand, and then walk for a few minutes with a walker. After what seemed like a month, though it was only a little over a week, I was allowed to go home. During that time of crisis, my church overwhelmed me with their love and thoughtfulness. In one day I received twenty-seven encouragement notes from our church congregation. Of course I was church secretary at the time and was well known to all. The cards continued to arrive every day. I was always aware of the prayers of those who cared.

After several weeks, I was finally able to get around pretty well in the safety of a walker. By Mother's Day, I had improved considerably. Your Grandpa Darrell took me to church that morning and in the afternoon, between the calls and visits of my children, I fell asleep in the recliner in the living room. Suddenly, the phone rang. Only half awake, I forgot my limitations. In my attempt to get to the phone I stumbled and fell, hitting my chin and arm, first on the piano bench, then the corner of the television. Your Grandpa, who was outside, heard my distress call and soon found me, bleeding and swelling. My right arm felt like it was broken. He remarked that I appeared to be in worse condition than after the accident I was recovering from.

In spite of all my injuries, I managed to continue my broadcasts. I also kept doing the church secretarial work, which I took care of at home, since the time the church did not have an office. In November of that year, I resigned from the church secretary position, after serving for three years. I felt compelled to get started on a project which I had known for some time I had to do, but just kept putting off.

Writing My Book

I realized that God had spared my life for a purpose. I believe I had a close brush with death the day my car ran over me. I was fully aware that if that heavy vehicle had hit me a little higher up, my upper body and chest would have been crushed, and possibly my life snuffed out. But God had more for me to do, including an assignment I had been putting off, though many times was overwhelmingly convinced that I must do it.

When one of my precious daughter-in-laws reminded me again, as she had several times before, that I ought to write a book about the way God had worked in my life, that did it. On that very day I promised the Lord—and myself, that I would do it. I would write my story, to the very best of my ability.

High Tech Grandma

Soon after I began outlining and making notes for my book, I started attending a writing class, which proved to be both informative and inspiring. The discipline helped me keep on track.

During one of the sessions, a fellow student brought a newfangled computer to class, to demonstrate word processing for writers.

Computers were becoming quite popular, and we were all anxious to see one operate. Being a self-taught typist, and a very poor one—and slow as well, I immediately saw that I would benefit from the advantages of the new technology.

This classmate took us through the various steps, showing us the almost magical feats the computer could perform. He also told us they were quite expensive. For most of us present, the new marvel was pretty much out of reach. However, at that point I began to pray for a computer.

I believed strongly that I needed one to help me write my book, and I also believed that God could, and would provide one. Then I began to pray that He would help me find the right one. The following year I switched to writing with a word processor—on my own computer.

After years of use I had no doubt that God led me to the right computer, and "letter quality" printer, in order that I might accomplish His purpose.

The first thing I typed on my new computer, then printed out, was a prayer. It read: "Dear Lord, you'll have to help me conquer this apparatus. I can't do it by myself. I will do my best, but you will have to help me. I know you will. I am asking this in Jesus' name, and for His glory. Amen."

I will admit, when I first got the computer, it was so frustrating I even wondered if I had made the right decision. There was so much to learn and it was so technical. A few times I threw up my hands and declared, "It's just impossible for me to learn WordStar." Then I remembered my reason for getting the new device was to help expedite my book. I determined to make it work for me. I knew it was worth the pressure and the time it took for me to learn the procedures and commands, and to become comfortable with them.

In time, after much practice, I finally conquered my computer. It was very "user friendly" and easy to use. I found I could type much faster than I ever dreamed possible, and I could perform technical functions like a professional. It no longer seemed intimidating to me.

When I made mistakes, correcting them was quick and easy. My spelling checker proved to be a tremendous help as I worked on my enormous project. I am not sure I could have ever completed my book manuscript without the help of my miraculous, modern computer.

Lessons From My Computer

In paying respect to my faithful computer I must say it has taught me some valuable lessons in life—with almost biblical significance. For instance, mistakes are inexcusable. Commands must be exact. It is kind, however, and makes provisions for me to cancel any misdirected command, and start over, just as if I had never "sinned" or "erred". I can eliminate incorrect errors and "reform" my output simply by obeying a prescribed command. It will not obey a command it does not understand. I have to be perfectly specific. It is far too precise to allow me to fool around with thoughtless applications.

I'm sure my knowledge and observations concerning computers seem elementary to you, Karl, and to all my grandchildren. I know you all learn about them at an early age in school, and most of you have one in your own bedroom at home.

I realize that while many good things can be accomplished when computers are used to perpetrate purposes, projects, and programs that are designed for the good of mankind, there is no doubt that this modern, futuristic technology is used to promote much evil, and we haven't seen anything yet. It will certainly be instrumental in helping carry out the fulfillment of prophecy in the end-times scenario. It will help bring in the new world order and then manage global government under the wicked reign of the Antichrist. All of this is clearly spelled out in the Bible.

I am determined to use my computer for the sole purpose of carrying out God's will for my life, through the ministries which He has entrusted to me. I pray I will never use it myself, or allow it to be used in any way that will not bring honor and glory to my Lord and Savior.

Epilogue

Writing my story turned out to be a long, challenging project, but also a rewarding and fulfilling experience. It took me more than five years to complete the first draft. Because of my continuing heavy schedule, which has not let up significantly as I've grown older, I had to work out a specific writing plan, then stick with it for a long period of time.

As you know, I happen to be an early riser so it was not difficult for me to get up early and write consistently—every day, including most weekends, from 5 to 8 a.m. It was actually a pleasurable as well as a productive time. I thank the Lord for helping me carry the project through to completion.

I am truly grateful that God has granted me a long, rich life. He has answered my prayers and delivered me from numerous situations which could have ended much differently. He has brought me through serious illnesses such as asthma and arthritis, and I have given Him all the glory.

He has graciously granted me the privilege and pleasure of traveling in more than forty of the fifty United States, including Alaska and Hawaii. And I have enjoyed a number of trips to Canada, seeing much of beautiful British Columbia, and the province of Alberta, as well as some of central Canada. I love Canada!

I would love to tell you more about my traveling experiences but time will not allow.

* * *   * * *   * * *

I have enjoyed our time together. There is so much more to tell but this will have to do for now.

Some of you grandchildren will know about many of the changes that will come. I hope you will be thoughtful and faithful to share with the younger ones. God bless you!"

A Special Message:

Beloved, It's Up To You

My beloved grandchildren, I challenge you to read the Bible for yourself so that you will KNOW what God Himself says and wants you to know. If you have not yet accepted Jesus as your Savior and Lord, I pray that you will be convicted, even as I was in my early years, and won't be able to eat or sleep until you get the matter between you and God settled. There is nothing more important to you.

I am not asking you to embrace my ideas, only pleading with you to research the Bible and accept God's plan of salvation. You can have the assurance that only God can give, or you can live in limbo, not knowing where you stand. You can also foolishly rest in a false hope. You must decide for yourself. You know I will be praying for you as long as I have breath.

Some of you don't know, or even suspect, that there is a great war on at this very moment and YOU are involved, whether you realize it or not. It's being fought for the souls of mankind. But the war itself has already been won. We know who the victor is. The Bible tells us. The only question that remains is the result of the battle for individual souls; including yours and mine

Yes, the victory was achieved at Calvary, and the penalty for sin was paid. The blight that first came over the world was staged in Eden. It was the result of the defeat of the first woman and man. It was Eve who lost first, if you remember, and Adam was close behind. (It took the devil himself to deceive Eve, but Adam was deceived by a woman.)

The Bible is the account of a long list of succeeding battles; Satan trying for the souls of individuals; men, women, youth, boys and girls—of all time. God's love is reaching down in an unrelenting effort to rescue and save them.

The Scriptures tell us that Satan even tried to kill Jesus, God's Son, before He could accomplish His mission on earth, to set mankind free from the clutches of the evil one. Thank the Lord he didn't win that one. Oh yes, the devil is a powerful, deceitful personage, but God is all-powerful.

Every individual must choose his or her own destiny; whether to spend eternity with God in the wonderful place He has prepared for those who love and follow Him, or with the devil in that awful place prepared for him and his angels. The Bible calls that place hell.

Our loving Heavenly Father has provided a way of escape from the penalty of sin and hell, and He has created us with the power of choice. It is completely up to us. Every person before and since Calvary, who has believed in and accepted Jesus as their personal Savior, will be saved from Hell. If you don't know Him personally, please come to Him soon. I PRAY that you will.

Don't let anyone deceive you. There is nothing that can save you, apart from the work of Jesus on the cross. As the old song says, and as the Bible clearly states, nothing can wash away our sins; nothing but the blood of Jesus. The two lies that Satan wants you to believe are that you can save yourself, and that there is no such place as hell. This is the major thrust of the devil's time-proven strategy in his attempt to win the battle for your soul. Because of the lateness of the hour, these warnings and admonitions are all the more urgent. Be alert. Be aware. BEWARE!

*** *** ***

I have appreciated the opportunity to share my heart with you. God has given me an unceasing concern for each of you; especially for your spiritual welfare. You are in my constant prayers.

You know how much I love the Lord and His Word. Most of you know that I have failed Him in many ways, but just as those we read about in the Scriptures, He has been merciful and forgiven me. He will do the same for you and for anyone who comes to Him in true repentance.

I am looking forward to spending eternity with Jesus, and with all of my loved ones, including YOU. Please don't disappoint me, and please don't disappoint Jesus who has made every provision for you and me.

The End